FOREWORD

When, back in the early 1960s, having left local journalism, I started out into the world that was to become known as 'Public Relations', famous people were comparatively few and far between. They came predominantly from the world of music, entertainment, sport, politics and society.

Then, in my experience, the great majority were obviously talented in one way or another. The Beatles, Frank Sinatra and Muhammad Ali were some of those who dominated the media for obvious reasons.

Promoting and protecting clients was much simpler and easier then than today. The media world was but a small village compared to the vast global world of 2010 and dealing with the media on the private lives of the rich and famous was generally simple, straightforward and easily controlled.

Nowadays vast numbers of people are famous of whom many clearly have no talent whatsoever, but possess an all consuming desire to be famous.

Celebrity culture is very much alive and growing in Britain today. However, handling the increasingly complex relationship between the journalists and celebrities and/or stars is now a media minefield.

For me, therefore, this book is at the right time and the right place and is certainly much needed.

It is a comprehensive guide to all of the many, often complex legal issues regarding famous people's relationship and dealings with the media.

The book essentially concerns the law relating to privacy, reputation, image and creative endeavour. These areas of law particularly affect celebrities, and celebrities have usually featured in most of the major cases which have been responsible for developing the law. The law is broadly concerned with protecting individuals from intrusion (eg, the so-called privacy law, defamation and harassment) and with enabling individuals to exploit their image and talents, for example through way of endorsement, sponsorships and publishing deals.

The aim of the book is to provide a fairly comprehensive guide to navigating these various areas of law so it will be of particular relevance to celebrities and those advising them. Most celebrities at some stage are subjected to unwanted media intrusion. Many will enter contracts exploiting their celebrity status.

Loss of privacy, harassment and media intrusion are particularly dealt with in the book and are recurring themes for those dealing with celebrities.

To my knowledge this is the first book of its kind that deals specifically with this growing area of law and it will be a real help to many of us dealing and involved with the ever-increasing world of celebrity culture.

Max Clifford
December 2009

PREFACE

We wish to thank Lindsay Gale and Mary Kenny of Jordans and Cheryl Prophett for their editorial advice and guidance. Particular thanks are also due to Max Clifford for finding time in his busy schedule to contribute the Foreword and to Michael Couling (Chambers Director of 11 Stone Buildings) for helping to initiate the project. Thanks are also due to the Hon Mr Justice Tugendhat for his timely observations on super injunctions in *LNS v Persons Unknown* [2010] EWHC 119 (QB). Writing this book was a team enterprise and our shared enthusiasm at our regular meetings at 11 Stone Buildings made it a rewarding experience for each of us. The following individuals are mentioned for the help and support they gave in various ways.

Tim Toulmin, Stephen Abell and William Gore at the PCC gave helpful commentaries on the early drafts of the PCC chapters and their advice on the selection and editing of the case study adjudications was especially helpful.

Ian Beales' authoritative *Editors' Codebook* is now firmly established as the first text that editors consult when deciding whether the publication of a story is likely to breach the Code of Practice. It is also the first port of call for those writing about the principles and practice of press self-regulation.

Cyril Glasser served for many years as the PCC's legal adviser and the cogent in-house commentaries he wrote for the PCC in that capacity have lost none of their relevance with the passage of time.

Keith Ames and David Fenton at the Musicians' Union and Nick Stein at Clintons advised on points in the recording agreement, Susan Smith at MBA Literary Agents Limited advised on points in the publishing chapter and Trevor Tayleur, Associate Professor at The College of Law, Moorgate, London advised on EU law points.

On a personal note Nigel Lipton would also like to thank Elaine Dyer and Dick Lewzey, Nathan Hennah at Hornby Baker Jones and Wood Solicitors and Trevor, Gill, Sarah and John Tayleur. Special thanks are due to Andrew, Rhian, Angharad, Llywelyn and Sioned Collingbourne and David, Lucy, Chantal and Shaun Woolf for being there when times were difficult. Above all

Nigel would like to thank his late father and best friend Leonard Lipton (1930–2008) whose love, total support and constant encouragement is and will continue to be so greatly missed.

Robert Deacon
Barrister
11 Stone Buildings, Lincoln's Inn

Nigel Lipton
Solicitor
Proprietor, London Legal Training

Robert Pinker
Emeritus Professor of Social Administration,
London School of Economics, and
International Consultant at the Press Complaints Commission
London, January 2010

CONTENTS

Part IV
Bringing Proceedings

Chapter 16

Chapter 17

TABLE OF CASES

References are to paragraph numbers.

TABLE OF STATUTES

References are to paragraph numbers.

TABLE OF STATUTORY INSTRUMENTS

References are to paragraph numbers.

Introduction – Celebrities and the Media

FROM DIGNITARIES TO CELEBRITIES

All celebrities are public figures but not all public figures are celebrities. When the first edition of *Who's Who* was published in 1849, the list of entries was confined to peers, members of the House of Commons, archbishops, bishops, judges, diplomats and a few leading figures in the worlds of banking and insurance.

Most of the names listed in *Who's Who* and other biographical gazetteers of the time belonged to what Walter Bagehot once described as 'the Dignified and the Efficient parts of the Constitution'.[1] Members of the Royal Family, the House of Lords and eminent Anglican churchmen were numbered amongst the 'Dignified'. Although they were not celebrities in the current meaning of the term, they were to be celebrated and deferred to from a distance by 'the masses'. They were to be respected, not for what they *did*, but for what they *were* and what they symbolised, as figureheads of tradition and established authority.

The appearance of dignity, however, is best maintained at a distance from those it is intended to impress. Since even holders of high public office cannot reasonably be expected to conduct their private lives with unremitting dignity, revealing as little as possible about their private lives has always been the most sensible way of keeping up appearances. The establishment figures of mid-Victorian Britain were well aware of the significance of social distance in maintaining deference and due respect for authority. The private lives of dignitaries and other public figures may have been subjects of gossip and speculation but material of this kind seldom appeared in published form. For the greater part, editors of newspapers and magazines were content to live under a self-denying ordinance not to publish such material.

Members of the Cabinet, the Commons and the judiciary made up the 'Efficient' part of the Constitution. They were there to attend to the serious business of governing, policy making, legislating and implementing the law. Their private lives were also treated as sacrosanct – provided they did not behave in reckless ways that exposed them to public scrutiny. A politician's clandestine infidelities went unreported in the press: being cited in a divorce action could end his political career.

Nearly 50 years later, the number of names listed in the 1897 edition of *Who's Who* had grown to roughly five-and-a-half thousand. The selection criteria had been extended to include a great diversity of previously unlisted people who had, in one way or another, affected 'the political, economic, scientific and artistic life of the country'. They were chosen because their lives and achievements were deemed to be particularly interesting, either because 'they decide our destinies, spend our money, influence our taste or because they are especially prominent in their fields – the arts, education, medicine, sport, the trade unions …'. The list was left open-ended and has been growing ever since.

---

[1]   Walter Bagehot (1867) and RHS Crossman (ed) *The English Constitution* (Fontana, 1963).

Two other changes in the coverage of the 1897 edition should be noted. Editors of 'significant newspapers and magazines' who 'lead public opinion' appeared for the first time and all contributors were invited to include 'family and other individual details' such as their recreational activities in their entries. It was now taken for granted that some basic information about the private lives of public figures might be of interest to the general public. It is doubtful whether, at that time, anyone could have foreseen how the interest of the editors of newspapers and magazines in such information would burgeon thereafter.[2]

The current edition of *Who's Who* lists over 32,000 names and brief biographies of people who agreed to have their record of public achievements formally recognised in this way. We have no means of discovering the invisible number of those who declined the invitation to be listed, or the reasons why they refused. Modesty and a desire to protect their privacy are two likely explanations. Such refusals remind us that some people are strongly averse to publicity of any kind. The fact that they have been invited, however, means that they have already been identified as public figures.

Gazetteers of biographical information do not *confer* distinction or celebrity status. They simply note and *confirm* records of personal achievement and influence that are already established in the public domain. Once people achieve the status of being a public figure they become actual or potential subjects of sustained public interest and media attention and are, thereafter, on the way to becoming celebrities.

BECOMING A CELEBRITY

The key feature that distinguishes celebrities from other high-profile public figures is the degree and intensity of the general interest and media attention that they attract with regard to *both* their public and their private lives. For all practical purposes, a celebrity can be defined as anybody who is able to convince the public that they are one, and anybody on whom the public – of its own volition – confers the status of celebrity. The media play a crucially important role in bringing about the convergence of these two processes. They are the midwives and, sometimes, the undertakers in the world of celebrity. Just as some people become celebrity hunters so others yearn to be their celebrated quarries. People are motivated to become celebrities for a variety of reasons – a belief in their own intrinsic talents and a conviction that they have something distinctive to offer the world, an overriding desire for fame and to be noticed and the prospect of becoming very rich.

A similarly complex mix of motives triggers and sustains the public's interest in celebrities – appreciation and enjoyment of what they do in public, intense curiosity about what they do in their private lives and the search for role models whom they can admire and emulate. Others are drawn by the prospect of witnessing pride come before a fall and fame turn to ignominy. *Schadenfreude* is a vicarious pleasure and watching the world of celebrity gives ample scope for indulging it.

In order to succeed, celebrities must respond effectively to the diversity of needs and motives that give momentum to the public's interest in their activities. Part of their appeal derives from the fact that the worlds that celebrities inhabit are remote and very different from those of ordinary people. At the same time, however, many of their

---

[2]   *Who's Who, An Annual Biographical Dictionary* (A & C Black, 1987).

admirers want to identify with them and discover what they have in common with the celebrities they most admire. Stories about the private lives of celebrities meet that need. They satisfy peoples' curiosity. They give reassurance that, in some respects at least, celebrities share the same hopes and fears, and experience the same pleasures and problems as everyone else.

Drawing on his years of experience in show business, Mark Borkowski makes a similar point in his recent study of Hollywood celebrities. All show business celebrities, he contends, are brand names and have a sell-by date. Their average shelf life is about 15 months and if they want to stay longer in the public eye they 'must be prepared to pay for it'.

Every celebrity brand name 'needs a story' and 'story telling is a key element of fame'. Without continuous publicity, 'fame follows an exponential slide to obscurity'. Under the guidance of a skilful professional publicist, however, 'the repeated, carefully altered telling of stories can prolong the brand's period of fame'. The media play a crucially important role in telling the stories and the growth of new media outlets creates new opportunities for prolonging the shelf life of celebrities.[3]

Celebrities, however, are not simply brand names with a limited shelf life. Even those who revel in their fame and strive to prolong it have private lives which, from time to time, they feel bound to protect from intruders. Others have fame thrust upon them and remain deeply averse to any kind of publicity that jeopardises their privacy. They are still celebrities, albeit reluctant ones.

Enthusiastic and reluctant celebrities alike are bound to be subjects of sustained public interest and media attention once the status is achieved or thrust upon them. They must, therefore, be prepared to deal, in one way or another, with requests for information about their public and professional activities, inquiries about their personal lives and intrusions into their privacy. Refusals to divulge personal information will not deter the media from obtaining it through other sources and may well increase the likelihood of inaccurate information being published. Celebrities are at some degree of risk, whether they say too much, too little or nothing at all.

Editors may also resort to subterfuge and the use of clandestine devices in cases where they have reasonable grounds for believing that the information they seek will prove to be of genuine public interest and that it could not be obtained by any other means. Evidence of a refusal to co-operate in the first instance may add credibility to an editor's claim that there were no other means available.

Relatively low-profile celebrities, like their high-profile counterparts, can swiftly become subjects of intense and widespread media attention because of adverse changes in their personal circumstances. When, for example, personal relationships break down in acrimony and recrimination, the partner who is averse to publicity is left at the mercy of the one who readily accepts a newspaper's invitation to 'tell their side of the story'. The newsworthiness of 'human interest' and 'kiss and tell' stories is always enhanced when one or more of the people involved are celebrities.

---

[3]   Mark Borkowski *The Fame Formula* (Sidgwick and Jackson, 2008a), pp 370–380; see also Mark Borkowski (2008b) 'The Fame Formula' *The Guardian*, 28 July 2008, 52.10.

Whatever their degree of prominence, most celebrities have families and close friends, and their rights to privacy are always mutually contingent on how each of them conducts their private lives and responds to media attention once it is aroused. Whilst the Press Complaints Commission (PCC) has always made it clear that celebrities and their close relatives and friends will be accorded the same rights to privacy and protection under its Code of Practice as other members of the public, it also recognises that they stand at greater risk of press intrusions into their private lives than the relatives and friends of ordinary people.

CHOOSING BETWEEN THE COURTS AND THE PCC

Celebrities of one kind or another figure significantly amongst the clientele of media, entertainment and intellectual property lawyers. Most of them are seeking redress for invasions of their privacy, inaccurate reporting and violations of their image rights. Since there has always been a substantial degree of overlap between the jurisdiction of the courts and the remit of the PCC, notably with regard to claims and complaints involving privacy intrusion and inaccurate reporting, celebrities also seek redress for their grievances from the PCC.

In all cases where prospective complainants can choose between going to the PCC or taking legal action, they are told that they can complain to the PCC either *before* or *after* they have sought legal redress. The PCC does not deal simultaneously with such complaints because of the risk that its involvement might prejudice the conduct of ongoing legal proceedings.

Unlike the great majority of complainants, most of the celebrities who use the PCC's services choose to be legally represented, either by their own solicitors or those of their agencies or employers. All complaints received by the PCC are dealt with in exactly the same way, irrespective of the complainant's status and whether or not they are legally represented.

Given the choice, most people – including celebrities – choose the PCC because they know that their case will be dealt with *in private* and settled one way or another in a matter of weeks. They will not be awarded damages but neither will they incur any costs beyond the price of a phone call. By contrast, people who complain to the courts about privacy intrusion face the daunting prospect of stressful cross-examination in public and a lengthy wait for justice. Conditional fee arrangements have reduced the financial risks that were once associated with bringing privacy actions. Nevertheless, many celebrities still choose the self-regulatory option, possibly for two main reasons.

First, celebrities and the press are locked into a relationship from which, in the long run, there is no escape. Celebrities must promote themselves through the media if they are to remain in the public eye. The press, for its part, needs a constant flow of stories about celebrities because the public wants to read about them. From time to time, however, newspapers and periodicals overstep the mark and what was once a mutually advantageous relationship breaks down in conflict and rancour.

Bringing an action for privacy intrusion may offer the prospect of a decisive outcome and an award of compensatory damages but going to law is an adversarial and combative experience for all concerned. It is not generally conducive to restoring good working relationships. By contrast, bringing a complaint to the PCC offers the possibility of resolving the grievance *and* repairing the relationship. It is essentially a damage limitation exercise.

The PCC today sees itself primarily as a dispute resolution service. Over the past 15 years, editors have become much more willing to offer voluntary apologies and corrections for breaches of the Code of Practice. The great majority of investigated complaints are resolved to the satisfaction of those concerned by means of informal conciliation. Only a very small number are taken to formal adjudication, either because the breach is potentially so serious that an apology, a published letter or a correction would not be sufficient remedy, or because the editors concerned are convinced that a formal adjudication will vindicate them.

Secondly, the PCC's proceedings are conducted in private from start to finish. Newspapers do not reveal any material made available to them either during or after the investigative process. Complainants do not have to give evidence in public and their privacy is protected throughout the proceedings. The PCC's final rulings can also be anonymised at the complainant's request.

It was widely assumed at the time of the incorporation of the European Convention on Human Rights into the Human Rights Act 1998 that many more people with grievances against the press would, henceforward, seek redress from the courts rather than the PCC. This has not happened, as Cyril Glasser notes in a recent consultative paper he wrote for the PCC in his capacity as its legal adviser over many years.[4]

Glasser believes that 'a healthy choice had been created by the decision to incorporate'. In his view:[5]

> 'Clients and their legal advisers are the best judges of their own best interest and they will decide in any particular case whether to make a complaint to the PCC or bring proceedings in the courts having considered which route was likely to achieve the result they desired. Some had predicted that a two-tier system would develop, with the well-off taking the court route while those with limited financial resources would be confined to using the PCC. This has not happened. The Commission's caseload remains very mixed with the so-called 'celebrity' complainants often choosing to approach the PCC in order to assist in negotiations with the newspaper or magazine concerned.'

He notes that the PCC offers a service that is fast, free and fair, and the prospect that the complaint will be resolved or formally adjudicated in a matter of weeks. (The average length of time it currently takes for the PCC to make a ruling on a privacy complaint is 35 days.)

In Glasser's opinion, the legal option may be preferred in privacy cases where there is 'a need to obtain an immediate injunction to prevent material getting into the public domain where the privacy issue is secondary to matters involving defamation where complicated issues of law and fact arise; where disclosure of documents either from the parties or the third parties and cross-examination of witnesses under oath are necessary; and where a specific remedy such as damages is required'.

---

[4]   C Glasser *Recent Developments in Privacy Law*: PCC Paper No 3896 (2007).
[5]   Ibid, at pp 22–23.

TREATING COMPLAINANTS EQUALLY

In its commitment to the principle of equal treatment the PCC takes account of the special needs and circumstances of all vulnerable people who complain to it about privacy intrusion. To do otherwise would be tantamount to treating some people *unequally*. Some categories of people are defined as being vulnerable under the Code of Practice because of their age, ill health or infirmity or because they stand at special risk of being subjected to unwarranted forms of discriminatory reporting.

Celebrities and other public figures undoubtedly stand at special risk of having their privacy invaded by the media, although this degree of potential vulnerability does not exempt them from accepting responsibility for protecting their own privacy where they are able to do so. Over the years, the PCC has developed its own distinctive procedures and 'case-law' in dealing with complaints involving celebrities. These procedures take account of the extent to which celebrities have sought publicity in the past, the kinds of personal and even intimate information they have voluntarily revealed to the press or otherwise placed in the public domain and whether the substance of their complaint has more to do with issues of image control and copyright protection than genuine privacy.

The PCC's commitment to the principle of equal treatment has been demonstrated in numerous adjudications involving famous people, including members of the Royal Family, the aristocracy and their close friends. It may seem paradoxical that a special case for equal treatment has to be made on behalf of a highly privileged group of people. It is, however, the case that those members of the Royal Family who stand closest in line to accession to the Throne are inescapably seen as celebrated public figures and are therefore the subjects of constant and intense media attention. Editors have more than ample scope for claiming that intrusions into their private lives are justified on grounds of legitimate public interest.

Twelve years before the Court of Appeal delivered its judgment in the case of *HRH Prince of Wales v Associated Newspapers Limited*,[6] the PCC had to take special measures in order to protect the privacy of Prince William when he started school at Eton. In doing so, the PCC pointed out that these measures were necessary in order to ensure that the prince could enjoy the *same* rights to protection under the Code of Practice as any other child or young person.

As recently as 60 years ago, royalty were not thought of as celebrities in the current meaning of the term. Details about their private lives were not regularly reported in the popular press. With the gradual democratisation of our social institutions, those days of self-denial on the part of press and public have long since passed away. And there is some evidence to suggest that the views of the general public regarding the privacy rights of famous people and their entitlement to equal treatment are at odds with those of the PCC.

These issues were explored in a focus group survey of 1,500 people, commissioned by the BBC in 2002.[7] Only 16% of the participants thought that members of the Royal Family should have full rights to privacy and 18% thought they should have none or almost none. As few as 6% believed that politicians should have equal rights and as

---

6   [2006] EWCA Civ 1776, [2006] 2 All ER 139.
7   D Morrison and M Svennevig *The Public Interest, The Media and Privacy* (BBC, BSC, ICSTIS, ITC, IPPR and the Radio Authority, 2002).

many as 40% thought they should have none or almost none. The investigators concluded that these views were 'mirrored' throughout all the subgroups within the overall sample. There was a widely shared consensus over what rights different people and different roles have in respect of privacy from the media.

At the other end of the celebrity spectrum the PCC also recognises that infamous people – no matter how horrendous their crimes – have rights to privacy. Although criminals cannot be described as celebrities in any positive meaning of the term, they are perennial subjects of intense public curiosity and media attention. Just as every Madame Tussauds has its Chamber of Horrors, so does every hall of fame have its cellars of infamy.

Notorious criminals may never appear in public during their years of incarceration but their notoriety often outlives the fame of many show business celebrities. There is a huge public appetite for stories about infamous people and, in this respect, it is worth noting that an overwhelming 77% of the respondents in the survey previously cited thought that very serious offenders should have no rights to privacy at all. Nevertheless, from time to time, some criminals do complain to the PCC about unwanted media attention and there have been occasions when it has had to remind newspapers that the Human Rights Act 1998 confers rights to privacy on everyone, no matter how horrendous their crimes.

It should be noted, however, that offenders who seek publicity in order to profit from their crimes receive short shrift from the PCC. Clause 16 of the Code of Practice prohibits the 'payment or offers of payment for stories, pictures, or information which seek to exploit a particular crime or to glorify or glamorise crime in general'. Such payments 'must not be made directly or via agents to convicted or confessed criminals or to their associates – who may include family, friends and colleagues'. When editors invoke the public interest to justify payments or offers of payment they must 'demonstrate that there was good reason to believe the public interest would be served if, despite payment, no public interest emerged, then the material should not be published'. The PCC receives very few complaints under the provisions of this clause.

Notably in the fields of entertainment and sport, some celebrities attract additional media interest in their private lives by acquiring a reputation for outrageous behaviour as hell-raisers, binge drinkers, drug takers and fornicators. They live on the edge of the darker side of celebrity – a world which also encompasses the darker side of privacy and the haunts of the truly infamous. There is a huge market for stories about their public and private exploits.

Celebrities as litigants

No matter where celebrities are ranked in the social hierarchies of eminence and newsworthiness, they are all exposed to a far greater risk of media intrusion and exploitation than so-called ordinary people. The greater their aversion to media attention the greater the care they must take in protecting their privacy. The more assiduously they seek publicity, the greater the care they must take in protecting what little is left of their privacy. Even the most recklessly indiscreet of celebrities may eventually discover that they also have a breaking-point when a particularly intrusive photograph or story about them is published and they turn to seek redress for their grievances as litigants to the courts or as complainants to the PCC.

It is therefore not surprising that celebrities account for a substantial proportion of the claimants who bring actions for privacy intrusion and seek injunctions from the courts in order to prevent the publication of stories to which they object. They possess the means to do so and access to no-win, no-fee conditional fee arrangements has substantially reduced the financial risks involved in bringing a legal action.

The original intention of the Government's 'Access to Justice' scheme was to make it easier for people of limited means to sue for redress of their grievances. The most notably successful users of the scheme, however, have proved to be wealthy celebrities like Naomi Campbell, Ashley Cole, Craig Bellamy and Cherie Blair.

The burden of financial risk now falls most heavily on the poorest publishers of newspapers and magazines, who face the prospect of having to pay substantial legal costs if they decide to defend their actions in court and subsequently lose. Even the wealthiest publishers confront the possibility of having to pay legal costs in excess of £500,000 with considerable trepidation. Under such circumstances, the likeliest outcome today is that the publisher will settle out of court and the right to privacy will take precedence over the right to freedom of expression through force majeure and not through the due processes of law in open court.

In cases where privacy actions brought by celebrities *are* defended, the significance of the judgments handed down by the courts derives not from their number, but from the disproportional influence they are having on the pace and direction of developments in UK privacy law jurisprudence. There is a public interest to be served in protecting both the right to privacy and the right to freedom of expression. When, however, the pace and direction of change is being overly driven by a small minority of people who stand at far greater risk of privacy intrusion than other members of the public it becomes more likely that privacy rights will be accorded precedence over the rights to freedom of expression and the general public's rights to know. The threshold of privacy entitlement will be set at a level that meets the exceptional needs of celebrities but above that which is necessary to protect the great majority of citizens and serve wider public interest in the context of a democratic society.

CONCLUSION

If the first edition of *Who's Who* had been published 100 years earlier in 1749, most of its entries would have been members of the landed aristocracy and gentry. Since they *were* the legislators of the time they could confidently rely on the law to protect both their property and their privacy against the clandestine intrusion of poachers and trespassers. And whenever they appeared in public places, the deference shown to them by their law-abiding social inferiors would have added the protection of social distance to that which the courts provided.

Today's celebrities are not legislators but they have easy access to the courts and the services of highly experienced legal representatives. They also have the same ease of access to the services of the PCC, whether or not they choose to be legally represented. Far from enjoying the benefits that deference and social distance confer, they seek the benefits that accrue from publicising themselves whilst protecting themselves from a media and public who want to know more about their private lives than they are willing to disclose.

Today's celebrities are seldom troubled by intruders in the form of poachers laying traps for their game-birds and rabbits. They are far more concerned about intruders in the form of journalists and photographers because they, themselves, happen to be the quarries.

Paradoxically, whenever celebrities bring actions for privacy intrusion they are catapulted back into the public domain for days and weeks as details of the disclosures to which they originally objected are repeated in open court and republished in the press.

For this reason alone, the privacy actions that celebrities bring to the courts have become the thunder and lightning *motifs* in the stormy debates currently echoing about the shifting frontiers that demarcate the public and private domains of all our daily lives. It is the landmark judgments handed down in these cases that are shifting the frontiers. It is the litigant celebrities – whether they happen to be 'figures of contemporary society par excellence' like Ms Naomi Campbell or 'relatively public figures' like Princess Caroline von Hannover – who are setting the pace and direction of change in the development of privacy law in the UK and other member states throughout the EU.

The PCC, for its part, has played a pioneering role as an adjudicator of complaints about privacy intrusion and the Editors' Code of Practice is recognised as a 'relevant Privacy Code' under s 12 of the Human Rights Act 1998.

Part I

THE PRESS COMPLAINTS COMMISSION

Chapter 1

THE PRESS COMPLAINTS COMMISSION – WHAT IT IS AND WHAT IT DOES

1.1   The Press Complaints Commission (PCC) is an independent, self-regulatory body which deals with complaints from individuals and organisations about the editorial content of UK newspapers and magazines. It administers and enforces a 16-clause Code of Practice which sets out the principles and rules that the PCC applies and interprets in dealing with complaints and that editors and journalists are required to uphold.

1.2   The PCC provides a service to the public that is fast, free and fair. The average time taken in dealing with complaints that raise a possible breach of the Code of Practice is 35 days. Complainants incur no costs beyond the price of a postage stamp. The PCC is completely independent in its procedures from the industry it regulates.

MEMBERSHIP, FUNDING AND REMIT

1.3   The PCC currently consists of 17 members. Ten of them, including the Chairman, are lay or public members and seven are working editors. Lay members are appointed through open advertisement and competition. Editorial members are appointed through consultation with the industry. All appointments to the PCC and the Code Committee are subject to ratification by an independent Appointments Commission, which has a majority of lay members.

1.4   The PCC is funded by a Press Standards Board of Finance which, as an independent third party body, is responsible for collecting registration fees from across the entire industry. This arrangement ensures that, in the conduct of its business, the PCC is as constitutionally independent from the industry that funds its activities as it is from government.

1.5   Both printed and online versions of publications come within the Code's remit. As Ian Beales explains in *The Editors' Codebook*:[1]

> 'The rules apply to online versions of the newspapers and magazines – as opposed to free standing online publications – and, as with the print versions, embrace *editorial material only.*'

1.6   When the remit of the Code was extended in 2007 to include audio-visual material a distinction was drawn between material for which editors could reasonably be held responsible under the terms of the Code and user-generated content for which they

---

[1]   I Beales *The Editors' CodeBook* (Press Standards Board of Finance, revised 2nd edn, 2009) ('*The Editors' CodeBook*'), at p 10.

could not reasonably be held responsible. As Beales explains, 'User-generated content such as blogs and chatrooms' remain outside the Code's remit:[2]

'... as does audio visual material that has been produced to conform to the standards of another regulator – such as live or syndicated TV or radio programmes. This reflects the traditional approach applied to print versions, where for example, Letters to the Editor are covered by the code, but advertising and marketing material is not.'

1.7   The preamble to the Code states that it must be:

'... honoured not only to the letter but in the full spirit. It should not be interpreted so narrowly as to compromise its commitment to respect the rights of the individual, nor so broadly that it constitutes an unnecessary interference with freedom of expression or prevents publication in the public interest.'

1.8   Editors are also held responsible for checking the provenance of all material, including photographs, bought in from outside agencies and freelance journalists and ensuring that the circumstances under which they were obtained were 'compliant' with the Code's requirements.[3] As Beales points out, the Code 'places on publishes and editors the ultimate duty of care to ensure that the rules are implemented'.[4]

THE DIVISION OF RESPONSIBILITIES

1.9   The British system of press self-regulation is based on a clear-cut but complementary division of responsibilities between the PCC and the industry which it regulates. One of the preconditions that must be met in appointing new lay Commissioners is that they should have had no previous connections with the newspaper and magazine industry. The same precondition holds with regard to the PCC's staff.

1.10   Whilst the PCC is responsible for administrating the Code of Practice, the Code itself belongs to the industry. An Editors' Code of Practice Committee is responsible for keeping the Code up to date in response to changes in the law, new developments in media technology and any deficiencies exposed in the process of investigating and adjudicating complaints.

1.11   The PCC and the Code Committee maintain a close and continuous working relationship in keeping these issues under review. The Committee conducts an annual audit of the Code's remit and requirements but, most importantly, the close working relationship it maintains with the PCC ensures that the British system of self-regulation is able to respond swiftly and effectively to new challenges and changes whenever they arise. Whatever needs to be done can be implemented in a matter of weeks. In the past, there have been occasions when – after consultation with the government of the day – changes have been made to the Code in order to obviate the need for new legislation.

---

2   Ibid, at p 11.
3   Code of Practice 2009.
4   See footnote 1 above.

1.12 In September 2009, the UK Editors' Code of Practice Committee made three revisions to the Code. These changes were ratified by the PCC and took effect as from 19 October 2009. They cover:

'• **Privacy** – Clause 3 has been amended to make clear that the PCC will take into account relevant previous disclosures made by the complainant.

• **Harassment** – Clause 4 will require journalists in situations where harassment could become an issue to identify themselves if requested to do so.

• **The Public Interest** exceptions will include journalistic activity where editors can demonstrate a *reasonable belief* that they were acting in the public interest at the time.'

1.13 In announcing these changes, the Code Committee Secretary Ian Beales said:

'These amendments are intended to strengthen and clarify the Code, for the benefit of both complainants and the press, by incorporating elements that largely reflect embedded PCC jurisprudence or existing industry best practice.

For example, when considering complaints of alleged intrusions into privacy, the PCC has traditionally had regard for any relevant previous disclosures by the complainant. That has now been codified.

Also, it would be unusual for journalists in pursuit of a story not to identify themselves to the person they wanted to interview or photograph – unless there was some public interest reason for not doing so. The Code now reflects that.

Similarly with the public interest exceptions: currently, editors must demonstrate how their action actually served the public interest. But that doesn't allow for publication of investigative activity that genuinely appeared to be in the public interest, even where none actually emerged. Increasingly in the courts – and especially under Data Protection law – the test is whether there was *reasonable belief* that the action was in the public interest.

In reality the PCC would also be likely to take into consideration, under the spirit of the Code, whether the action would have seemed reasonable. So now, having taken legal advice, we have modified the Code to reflect that. It means editors must convince the PCC that they have good reasons to believe their action was in the public interest. It is a stiff test – shallow or spurious reasons won't do – but a fair one.'

1.14 The full text of the Code of Practice which is published as Appendix 1 in this book includes these revisions as do all references to Clause 3 (Privacy), Clause 4 (Harassment) and the Public Interest statement.

THE PCC, THE CODE AND THE COURTS

1.15 There has always been a substantial degree of overlap between the jurisdiction of the courts and the remit of the PCC, notably with regard to the complaints that the PCC receives about inaccurate reporting and privacy intrusion. The ground rules governing this relationship were agreed between the PCC and the industry in 1991 and they have remained unchanged since then. They are summarised in *The Editors' Codebook*, which states that 'the Code of Practice does not attempt to duplicate the law'. Consequently, 'the golden rule ... when applying any of the key tests under the Code is to ask: is it safe legally? The Code may require more than the law, but never less'.[5]

1.16   Although defamation, as such, is not mentioned in the Code of Practice, some of the complaints received about inaccurate reporting have potentially defamatory connotations. Almost three-quarters of all the complaints received in 2008 which raised possible breaches of the Code were about inaccurate reporting.

1.17   Approximately a quarter of all rulings made by the PCC in the same year were concerned with press intrusions into personal privacy and other related matters such as harassment, the protection of children, hospital patients, victims of sexual assault and other vulnerable people. It would have been open to some of these complainants to seek redress in the courts. They could, for example, have brought actions for breach of confidence or under the provisions of the Data Protection Acts, the Protection from Harassment Act 1997, the Human Rights Act 1998 or a combination of these statutes. Very few of them chose to do so.

1.18   In all cases where a complainant can choose between going to the PCC or taking legal action, they are told that they can complain to the PCC either *before* or *after* they have sought legal redress. The PCC does not deal simultaneously with such complaints because of the risk that its involvement might prejudice the conduct of legal proceedings.

1.19   It remains open to debate whether or not the PCC is a public authority but, for all practical purposes, it is treated as if it is one. The courts, for example, are required under the Human Rights Act 1998 to 'have particular regard to the importance' of the European Convention for the Protection of Human Rights and Fundamental Freedoms (ECHR) right to freedom of expression when proceedings relate to 'journalistic, literary or artistic matters' and also to the provisions of 'any relevant Privacy Code' which includes 'the Code operated by the PCC'.[6]

1.20   Under the provisions of the Data Protection Acts, editors are allowed to advance a public interest defence when faced with an action by the Data Protection Commissioner on the grounds that what they have published complies with a Code of Practice 'designated' by Parliament for the purposes of the Act. In doing so, they must also demonstrate that the information has been obtained by fair and lawful means.

1.21   All of the PCC's adjudications are open to challenge by dissatisfied complainants, who can apply to the High Court for a judicial review of the PCC's rulings. So far, only a handful of such applications have been made, none of which were successful.

1.22   Demand for the services of the PCC has remained buoyant since the incorporation of the ECHR into the Human Rights Act 1998 and the introduction of conditional fee arrangements. There has been no noticeable change in the mix of celebrity and non-celebrity complaints and the total number of complaints received and investigated goes on rising year by year.

---

5   Ibid, at p 13.
6   Human Rights Act 1998, Ch 42, s 12(4).

1.23   The PCC offers a service that is fast, free and fair. The law offers a service that is slower, potentially costly – but not necessarily so since the introduction of conditional fee arrangements – and fair. People seeking damages will litigate, if they can afford to do so, whilst those who would be content with non-financial remedies will complain to the PCC.

1.24   As Glasser points out,[7] the legal option may be preferred in privacy cases where there is 'a need to obtain an immediate injunction'. It may also be preferred in cases 'involving defamation where complicated issues of law and fact arise; (and) where disclosure of documents … and cross examination of witnesses under oath are necessary …'.

1.25   Since the PCC does not conduct oral hearings, complainants are never publicly or privately cross-examined. All of its proceedings are conducted in private and complainants' privacy is protected throughout. By contrast, litigants who bring actions for privacy intrusion face the daunting prospect that disclosure of sensitive personal information to which they originally objected will be repeated in open court and reported again in the media.

1.26   The expectation that conditional fee arrangements would be of greatest help to people of limited means has not been realised. Wealthy celebrities, with easy access to the services of the best media lawyers, have been the most successful beneficiaries.

1.27   Nevertheless, a steady flow of celebrities and other public figures continue making use of the PCC's services. Celebrities need media publicity in the furtherance of their careers. The press needs good stories about them in order to sell its newspapers. Complaining to the PCC opens up the possibility of resolving the complaint *and* repairing the relationship.

1.28   Going to law is a confrontational event that takes place in public and it seldom, if ever, results in good working relationships being restored between the contestants – especially when substantial costs and damages are awarded against the losing parties.

1.29   These are some of the issues that legal advisers will discuss with their clients before they decide whether to complain to the PCC or bring proceedings in the courts.

The Code of Practice and the distribution of complaints received and investigated

1.30   The Code of Practice consists of a preamble that summarises the general principles underpinning the philosophy and spirit of press self-regulation; 16 clauses which set out the practical rules of professional conduct that editors are required to uphold in gathering and reporting the news; and a public interest statement.

1.31   Ten of the 16 clauses are marked (in whole or part) with an asterisk which denotes that, in exceptional cases, editors may advance a public interest defence when they have published information or resorted to methods of newsgathering that would otherwise have breached the Code.[8] In all such cases, the onus of proof that the public interest was served rests with the editor.

---

[7]   C Glasser *Recent Developments in Privacy Law*: PCC Paper No 3896 (2007).

[8]   Clauses 3 (Privacy), 4 (Harassment), 5(ii) (Intrusion into grief or shock), 6 (Children), 7 (Children in sex

1.32   For administrative and publication purposes the 16 clauses are grouped under four main headings. The first of these headings includes clauses 1 (Accuracy) and 2 (Opportunity to reply) which, taken together, have always accounted for the majority of the complaints received, investigated and ruled on by the PCC. In 2008, they accounted for 71.9% of all the rulings made.

1.33   The second group of clauses covers privacy and intrusion related issues. It includes clauses 3 (Privacy), 4 (Harassment), 5 (Intrusion into grief or shock), 6 (Children), 7 (Children in sex cases), 8 (Hospitals) and 9 (Reporting crime). For the purposes of this study, clause 10 (Clandestine devices and subterfuge), which the PCC categorises as a 'newsgathering' clause, has been added to the 'privacy and intrusion' group. In 2008, complaints about privacy and intrusion related issues accounted for 25.1% of all the rulings made, including those under clause 10 (1.3%).

1.34   Complaints made under clause 12 (Discrimination) make up the third group. The number of complaints received under this clause has fluctuated markedly over the past 12 years. In 1997, they accounted for just over 6% of all rulings made by the PCC. In 2000, this figure rose to just over 10%, largely as a result of extensive press reporting on immigration and asylum issues. Thereafter, in the wake of the 2001 terrorist attack on the New York Trade Centre, the proportion of complaints about discriminatory reporting rose to nearly 18% in 2003. They currently account for 1.9% of all rulings made by the PCC.

1.35   The fourth group of clauses covers issues relating to methods of newsgathering, which includes clauses 10 (Clandestine devices and subterfuge), 11 (Victims of sexual assault), 13 (Financial journalism), 14 (Confidential sources), 15 (Witness payments in criminal trials) and 16 (Payment of criminals). Taken together, complaints about methods of newsgathering (excluding those made under clause 10) accounted for 1.1% of all rulings made in 2008.

THE PUBLIC INTEREST

1.36   The Code of Practice recognises that there will be exceptional cases in which an editor may decide to breach its requirements and advance a public interest justification for doing so. All of the privacy-related clauses (in whole or part) make provision for a public interest defence.

1.37   The grounds on which such a defence may be advanced are set out in the Code as follows.

1.38   There may be exceptions to the clauses marked * (see fn 8 above) where they can be demonstrated to be in the public interest.

(1)   The public interest includes, but is not confined to:
    (i)   detecting or exposing crime or serious impropriety;
    (ii)   protecting public health and safety; and
    (iii)   preventing the public from being misled by an action or statement of an individual or organisation.

---

cases), 8 (Hospitals), 9 (Reporting of crime), 10 (Clandestine devices and subterfuge), 15(ii) and (iii) (Witness payments in criminal trials) and 16 (Payments to criminals).

(2)   There is a public interest in freedom of expression itself.

(3)   Whenever the public interest is invoked, the PCC will require editors to demonstrate fully that they reasonably believed that publication, or journalistic activity undertaken with a view to publication, would be in the public interest.

(4)   The PCC will consider the extent to which material is already in the public domain, or will become so.

(5)   In cases involving children under 16, editors must demonstrate an exceptional public interest to override the normally paramount interest of the child.

1.39   Politicians who publicly support policies that have implications for the ways in which ordinary people arrange their private lives and personal relationships always stand at risk of having their own private activities investigated by the press. Under clause I(iii) of the Public Interest Statement,[9] they may be accused of 'misleading' the public by making such pronouncements. Ministers and Members of Parliament and other UK legislative bodies have as much right as anyone else to comment on such matters, but when they do so their statements carry a special significance because they are in a position to recommend and introduce changes in the boundaries between those aspects of personal conduct which are subject to legal sanction and those that are not.

1.40   Some politicians use their spouses and families to advance their public careers. It helps in electoral campaigning to cultivate an impression of marital harmony and commitment to 'family values'. If newspapers can show that this impression is a false one by revealing evidence of infidelity in such a politician's private life, they may advance a public interest defence when doing so. Politicians also put themselves at risk when they advocate public policies with which they themselves do not conform in the conduct of their private lives. If, for example, they publicly support the principle of equal educational opportunities whilst sending their own children to private schools they are bound to attract media attention and comment.

1.41   The Code's Public Interest Statement conforms with the requirements of the ECHR under which the provisions of Arts 8 and 10 are subject to a number of public interest qualifications, including the protection of national security and public safety, the prevention of disorder and crime, the protection of public health and morals and the protection of the rights and freedoms of other people.

1.42   How the Code's requirements are applied and interpreted by the PCC in dealing with complaints about privacy intrusion and other related matters is discussed in greater detail in Chapters 5–9. The full text of the Code is reproduced at Appendix A.

The PCC's procedures for dealing with complaints

1.43   In 2008, the PCC received a total of 4,698 complaints, including 584 complaints about a comment piece in *The Times* on which only one ruling had to be made.[10] The PCC ruled that in this case there had been no breach of the Code. The PCC issued 1,420 rulings on those complaints which fell properly within its remit. These were all cases in

---

9   PCC Editors' Code of Practice 2009.

10   M Parris 'What's smug and deserves to be decapitated?' at www.timesonline.co.uk/tol/comment/columnists/matthew_parris/article309746 (27/10/2009).

which a formal conclusion was reached by the PCC either resolving the complaints, issuing a decision or publishing an adjudication.

1.44   A more detailed breakdown of these rulings shows that 721 raised no prima facie breach of the Code and 552 were resolved through mediation to the satisfaction of the complainants. In 102 cases the newspaper undertook or offered remedial action that the PCC considered sufficient but was not accepted by the complainants. Of the 45 complaints that went to formal adjudication, 24 were upheld.

1.45   The average time taken in reaching these rulings in 2008, including those that were taken to a formal adjudication, was 36 days. If the majority of complaints investigated had gone to formal adjudication, the process of resolution would have been far more confrontational and taken much longer to complete.[11]

1.46   The success of the PCC and the industry in creating a new climate of conciliation, conflict resolution and voluntary compliance has never been accorded the recognition that it merits. The misunderstanding that persists regarding the PCC's procedures was exemplified in the erroneous claims made by Nick Davies in his recent book, *Flat Earth News*.[12] He alleged that, over an unspecified period of 10 years, 'just over 90%' of the complaints received were 'rejected on technical grounds without the PCC ever investigating their content'.[13]

1.47   If Davies had asked the right questions when he visited the PCC he would have discovered that it has issued in excess of 1,000 rulings every year over the past decade. And, in hundreds more cases, the PCC's 'advice and intervention meant that there was no need for a formal complaint at all'.[14]

1.48   It is certainly the case that many complaints are disallowed, but this happens for very good reasons. In 2008, 667 complaints were disallowed because they fell outside the remit of the PCC. In every such case, the PCC wrote to the relevant body on the complainant's behalf. One hundred and twenty-one complaints fell outside the PCC's remit because they were concerned with issues of taste and decency, on which it does not adjudicate. A further 82 complaints were disallowed because they were submitted by third parties not directly involved in the complaint. In some of these cases, the first party was asked if they wished to complain on their own behalf. In others, the PCC considered carefully whether it would be possible to proceed without the first party being involved. Thirteen complaints were ruled out because they were out of time (complaints must be submitted within 2 months of the date on which the offending material was published). If there were good reasons for the delay, the PCC proceeded with the complaint.[15]

The PCC's procedures for making a complaint

1.49   The procedures that the PCC follows in dealing with complaints are clearly set out in its guidance note on 'Making a Complaint' which is reproduced in Appendix B. All the PCC's guidance literature is published in a range of languages to assist

---

[11]   Press Complaints Commission 08 The Review.
[12]   N Davies *Flat Earth News* (Chatto and Windus, 2008).
[13]   Ibid, at p 364.
[14]   T Toulmin 'PCC Does Not Refuse to Consider Ruling', *Press Gazette*, 7 September 2008, at p 12.
[15]   Press Complaints Commission 08 The Review.

complainants whose first language is not English. A Textphone service is provided for those who are deaf or have hearing difficulties and literature on audio-cassette is available for the visually impaired.

1.50   Most importantly, members of staff are always on hand to assist people throughout the process of preparing their complaint. Once a complaint has been taken up, a named complaints officer is assigned to the complainant and remains in contact throughout the investigative process. The same services are available to the legal representatives of the complainants.

SANCTIONS AND OTHER REMEDIES

1.51   The PCC does not impose fines on publications that breach the Code of Practice. In all cases where an adjudication is made, it relies exclusively on moral censure. When a complaint is upheld, the offending newspaper or magazine is required to publish the PCC's critical adjudication 'in full and with due prominence, including headline reference to the PCC'.[16]

1.52   No publication has, so far, refused to do so – even in those cases where the editors in question remained convinced that they had not breached the Code.

1.53   In cases where a breach of the Code is deemed to be exceptionally serious, the PCC may formally draw it to the attention of the publisher. Since an obligation to uphold the requirements of the Code is written into many editors' and journalists' contracts of employment such referrals can result in dismissal.

1.54   Over the years, the PCC has developed two complementary procedures for the resolution of complaints. Some are resolved by means of informal conciliation and others go all the way to formal adjudication. Cases that go all the way to adjudication do so either because there are prima facie grounds for believing that the breach is potentially so serious that an informal apology in a published letter or a voluntary correction would not be sufficient remedy or because the editors concerned are convinced that they have not breached the Code and that a formal adjudication will vindicate them. Only a very small number of investigated complaints are currently taken to a formal adjudication.

1.55   When the PCC started work in 1991, its relations with many editors were highly confrontational. Every complaint was the subject of prolonged negotiation and dispute. With the passage of time, editors have become much more willing to make voluntary corrections and apologies for breaches of the Code. This change in editorial attitudes provides a crucially important measure of the extent to which the PCC and the industry has created a new climate of conciliation and voluntary compliance in the resolution of complaints.

1.56   The PCC today sees itself primarily as a dispute resolution service, and the introduction of fines would have serious consequences with regard to the quality and range of services that the PCC currently provides. Editors would become less willing to volunteer remedies to complaints and it would not be long before the worst features of a

---

[16]   Code of Practice 2009.

compensation culture would be imported into the system, with all the delays that would inevitably follow. The PCC may be treated under the law as if it were a public authority, but it is not a statutory authority and without legal powers to enforce payments its credibility would be seriously undermined if a publication refused to pay. Once endowed with legal powers, the system would cease to be self-regulatory and would have to be replaced by a statutory body.

1.57   The PCC's conciliation service, which is very popular with complainants, would be seriously undermined if editors refused to offer corrections or apologies for fear of admitting liability and exposing themselves to a fine later on.

1.58   It also happens to be the case that fines are not particularly popular as a remedy with either complainants or the general public. A survey conducted by Ipsos MORI in 2006 showed that the most popular forms of resolution for a possible breach of the Code were a published apology, followed by a private apology. Less than one-third of the respondents supported the idea of fines.[17]

1.59   The majority of complainants want a satisfactory resolution to their grievances that is fast, free and fair. The PCC offers a whole range of remedies to complaints about privacy intrusion which would be lost under a formal, fines-based system of regulation. As matters stand, it is able to:

- negotiate the removal of intrusive material from websites quickly so that it does not get picked up elsewhere;

- organise legal warnings to be tagged to publications' archives to ensure private information is not accidentally republished;

- encourage the destruction or removal of intrusive information from databases or libraries;

- obtain personal apologies from editors, and undertakings about future conduct;

- secure prominent public apologies;

- help negotiate agreed, positive follow-up articles;

- use the power of negative publicity by 'naming and shaming' a publication's conduct in a critical ruling (which must be published in full and with due prominence by the editor); and

- organise a combination of the above, or, depending on the circumstances, the purchase of specific items in order to make amends (eg a wheelchair), ex gratia payments or donations to charity.

1.60   Celebrities – and their legal representatives – are discovering that their complaints can be resolved to their express satisfaction in a matter of days or weeks through mediation by one of the PCC's complaint officers and that they can obtain remedial action by the editor without having to wait for a formal adjudication.

---

[17]   Ipsos MORI, 2006, Perceptions of the Press Complaints Commission.

Sometimes the PCC is able to respond so quickly to a request for help that there is no need for the person involved to lodge a complaint.

1.61 In 2008, the PCC dealt with the privacy concerns of nearly a thousand people, either informally or formally. It made 329 formal rulings, resolved 131 through successful mediation, issued 55 advisory notes to the UK press on behalf of individuals and helped hundreds of people with pre-publication advice on preventive intervention at an early stage, thereby removing the need to make a formal complaint.

1.62 For example, Ms Katie Price and Mr Peter Andre complained, through their solicitors, that *Heat Magazine* had published a sticker which showed Katie's young son Harvey with the imposed speech bubble, 'Harvey wants to meet me!'. In the complainants' view, this sticker was intrusive in breach of clause 6 (Children) of the Code. It also constituted a prejudicial and pejorative reference to Harvey's disability, as Harvey was – unfortunately – a sufferer of the condition known as septo-optic dysplasia, one of the effects of which was to make him overweight.

1.63 The complaint was resolved when the magazine apologised privately to the complainants, published an apology online and the following text in the hard copy:[18]

> 'Last week, we included 50 free stickers with the magazine. One of these was a head shot of Harvey Price, son of Katie Price (aka Jordan), with the words 'Harvey wants to meet me!'. It was never our intention to cause offence to Harvey's family and friends nor to you, our readers. In particular, it was never our aim to make fun of Harvey's disabilities. We now accept that the decision to include this sticker was a mistake and we recognise that it has caused offence, not only to Katie and Peter Andre, but to a number of readers. Immediately following publication, we apologised unreservedly to Katie and Peter. We wish to apologise publicly to Harvey, Katie and Peter for any embarrassment and distress caused. Heat has voluntarily decided to make a donation to The Vision Charity, an organisation that Katie and her family have worked with over a number of years, as a mark of its regret.'

1.64 When Natasha Kaplinsky, the Channel 5 newscaster, told the PCC in 2008 that she was being harassed by photographers it was able to respond swiftly and effectively to her request for help. As she subsequently told the PCC:

> 'When I had my baby last year, I didn't want to be followed around by photographers every time I left the house, as happened when I was pregnant. We asked the PCC to issue a private request to photographers to stop following us, and to newspapers and magazines not to use pictures of me taken when I was with my family in private time. The degree of compliance was very impressive, and I would recommend this service to anyone is a similar position.'

1.65 In June 2009, Ms Susan Boyle was catapulted from obscurity into the media spotlight when she reached the final of a popular ITV talent contest. Widely tipped to emerge as the winner, she broke down after coming second to a dance group and was admitted to a private medical clinic suffering from exhaustion.

1.66 Against a background of escalating media attention, Ms Boyle's representatives asked the PCC to intervene. The PCC immediately e-mailed all editors warning them not to invade Ms Boyle's privacy by reporting details of her health and treatment in breach of clause 3 (Privacy) of the Code of Practice. No further complaints were received on her behalf.

---

[18]   T Toulmin *The Irish Times*, 26 September 2006.

1.67   A self-regulatory body like the PCC, working in a developing culture of voluntary Code compliance, is uniquely well placed and qualified to provide these kinds of proactive and preventive services. As the PCC's Director, Tim Toulmin, wrote in 2006, it is difficult to 'convince some people that media Codes of Practice work in relation to privacy because so much of the PCC's work is preventive in character. Since these activities are never reported, the evidence of their success remains invisible'.

Monitoring and maintaining service quality

1.68   The PCC's work in dealing with complaints is subject to the independent scrutiny of a Charter Commissioner and a Charter Compliance Panel. After 6 years of distinguished service as Charter Commissioner, Sir Brian Cubbon was succeeded in 2009 by Lieutenant General Sir Michael Willcocks.

1.69   The Charter Commissioner provides dissatisfied complainants with an opportunity to have their grievances reviewed by an independent assessor. The Charter Compliance Panel fulfils an audit role and every year identifies an area of the PCC's work that it wants to review. It then chooses a sample of case files to examine. Neither the PCC nor its staff have any say over which cases are investigated.

1.70   The Charter Commissioner and the Compliance Panel publish separate annual reports and make their recommendations about standards of service and any deficiencies in the handling of individual complaints directly to the PCC.

1.71   The PCC also conducts annual surveys of the people who use its services. In the 2008 survey, 357 complainants answered their questionnaire. Of the respondents, 81% thought that their complaint had been dealt with 'thoroughly' or 'very thoroughly'; 75% considered that their complaint had been handled 'satisfactorily' or 'very satisfactorily'; 79% thought that the time taken in dealing with their complaint was 'about right'; and 70% rated the helpfulness of the PCC's staff either 8, 9 or 10 out of 10.[19] These surveys, in company with the work of the Charter Commissioner and Compliance Panel, are integral elements in the PCC's commitment to maintaining the high standards set out in its own Complainants Charter.

1.72   The PCC is also in the process (August 2009) of reviewing its organisational and procedural effectiveness. Shortly after taking over as Chairman of the PCC, Baroness Buscombe announced plans for an independent review of its governance. The review group:[20]

> '... will examine the operations of the PCC's board, sub-committees and secretariat; how the transparency of the system can be enhanced; whether the independent systems of accountability – the Charter Commissioner and the Charter Compliance Panel – can be improved; and the PCC's Articles of Association.'

The review group will be chaired by a former Commissioner, Ms Vivien Hepworth and will report back later in 2010.

---

[19]   See www.pcc.org.uk/makingacomplaint/feedback.html.
[20]   PCC Press release, 6 August 2009.

Chapter 2

PRESS SELF-REGULATION AND THE LAW SINCE 2000

SOME KEY JUDGMENTS

2.1 As we have noted, self-regulatory councils like the Press Complaints Commission (PCC) must ensure that the requirements of their codes of practice remain consistent with those of the law. Since 2000, the PCC has had to be especially mindful of developments in European law, the judgments of the European Court and how UK judges apply these judgments and interpret the requirements of the Human Rights Act 1998 (HRA 1998).

2.2 After HRA 1998 became operative in 2000, it remained to be seen how the UK courts would interpret and apply the European Convention for the Protection of Human Rights and Fundamental Freedoms (ECHR), Arts 8 and 10 in privacy actions. Under HRA 1998, s 12, the courts were required to have 'particular regard' for the right to freedom of expression and 'any relevant Privacy Code' when considering whether to grant applications for injunctions preventing publication.

2.3 When the Human Rights Bill was being debated in Parliament in 1998 the then Chairman of the PCC, Lord Wakeham, drew attention to the possibility that the new law might, with the passage of time, become 'a back door privacy law accessible only to the rich and famous'. At best, this would result in a two-tier system for the redress of grievances. At worst, it would undermine the work of the PCC to such an extent that it would cease to be effective. It would leave the great majority of prospective claimants who could least afford to litigate with no redress at all.

2.4 The Government accepted these arguments and moved an amendment to the Bill which became s 12 of HRA 1998. This section was to apply 'if a court is considering whether to grant any relief which, if granted, might affect the exercise of the Convention right to freedom of expression'. The court was required to 'have particular regard to the importance' of this right when the proceedings related to 'journalistic, literary or artistic material' and also to the provisions of 'any relevant Privacy Code'.

2.5 In the course of the debate, the then Home Secretary Jack Straw gave the following reassurance:[1]

> '... the new clause [in the Bill] provides an important safeguard by emphasizing the right to freedom of expression. Our intention is that this should underline the consequent need to preserve self-regulation. That effect is reinforced by highlighting in the amendment the significance of any relevant privacy code, which plainly includes the code operated by the PCC.'

---

[1] *Hansard*, HC Deb, ser 6, col 541, 2 July 1998.

2.6   The Home Secretary went on to say that:[2]

> 'I am glad that we have been able to frame an amendment that reflects the Government's stated commitment to the maintenance of a free, responsible press, and the consequent need for self-regulation, while maintaining the protection of the Convention that all our citizens should and do enjoy.
>
> I have explained the effect that we want to achieve with our new clause. If, for any reason, it does not work as we envisage, and press freedom appears at risk. We shall certainly want to look again at the issue.'

2.7   A similar amendment was made to the Data Protection Bill in its passage through Parliament. In its original form the Bill would have classified as private information large amounts of data that were not intrinsically private in nature. As such, the Act would have posed a substantial threat to press freedom. After some months of negotiation the Government agreed to an amendment which struck a more equitable balance between reconciling the rights of newspapers and magazines to report on matters of public interest with the privacy rights of individual citizens. The amendment allowed editors to advance a public interest defence when faced with an action by the Data Protection Commissioner on the grounds that what they had published complied with a Code of Practice 'designated' by Parliament for the purposes of the Act and that the information had been obtained by 'fair and lawful means'. This was the first time that the PCC's Code had been 'designated' in this way.

2.8   Despite these additional safeguards and the assurances of the Home Secretary, many editors and journalists remained deeply concerned that the courts would give undue precedence to the right to privacy over the right to freedom of expression and the people's right to know. They feared that some judges would use the Data Protection Act to introduce a law of privacy 'by the back door'.

2.9   Two years after HRA 1998 became operative there were some grounds for believing that these concerns on the part of the press were without foundation. The UK courts had delivered three important rulings which suggested that a reasonable balance was being held between the rights to privacy and freedom of expression.

2.10   When, in 2000, the newscaster Anna Ford's complaint against the *Daily Mail* and *OK!* magazine was not upheld by the PCC she applied for a judicial review against its decision. She maintained that the two publications had invaded her privacy in breach of clause 3 of the PCC Code of Practice. Her application was refused and in his ruling Mr Justice Silber said that:[3]

> '... the type of balancing operation [between privacy and freedom of expression] conducted by a specialist body, such as the PCC, is still regarded as a field of activity to which the courts should and will defer. The Commission is a body whose membership and expertise makes it much better equipped than the courts to resolve the difficult exercise of balancing the conflicting rights [of] privacy and of the newspapers to publish.'

2.11   A second important ruling was made in 2002 by the Court of Appeal, under the Lord Chief Justice Lord Woolf, in the case of *A v B & C*[4] – or, as was subsequently

---

[2]   Ibid, col 541.
[3]   *R (on the application of Ford) v The Press Complaints Commission* [2001] EWHC Admin 683 QBD.
[4]   [2002] EWCA Civ 337.

revealed, the footballer, Gary Flitcroft, and the *Sunday People*. In overturning an injunction which had been granted to the footballer by Mr Justice Jack restraining publication of an article about his extra-marital affairs, the Court of Appeal ruled that publication should go ahead. The ruling – repeating, in effect, PCC 'case-law' – stated that:[5]

> 'Whether you have courted publicity or not you may be a legitimate subject of public attention. If you have courted public attention then you may have less ground to object to the intrusions which follow.'

The ruling also stated that:[6]

> 'Once it is accepted that freedom of the press should prevail, then the form of reporting in the press is not a matter for the courts but for the Press Complaints Commission and the customers of the newspaper concerned.'

2.12   The third ruling concerned the international model, Ms Naomi Campbell who sued Mirror Group Newspapers for the distress and injury caused to her feelings by a story and photograph published in the *Daily Mirror*.

2.13   In February 2001 Ms Campbell was photographed by the *Daily Mirror* in a public place whilst leaving a Narcotics Anonymous clinic. The newspaper published a front page story with the headline 'Naomi – I am a Drug Addict' and an accompanying photograph. The newspaper defended its action on the grounds that she had, in the past, repeatedly claimed that she did not take drugs and that there was a public interest to be served in setting the record straight.

2.14   In 2002, Ms Campbell's action was heard in court. She objected to the unauthorised publication of intimate and personal details about her health and the treatment she was receiving in the context of a confidential relationship with her therapists. Initially, she had also claimed that her privacy rights under the provisions of HRA 1998 had been invaded but subsequently withdrew that part of her action. She also subsequently admitted that she had lied about her drug addiction which was, arguably, a matter of public interest. The court did not make a finding with regard to Ms Campbell's privacy after she withdrew this part of her action. It did, however, award her damages of £3,500 against the *Daily Mirror* for breach of confidence and infringement of the Data Protection Act 1998. The court also found that the newspaper had acted lawfully in revealing that she had not told the truth about her drug problems and the fact that she was receiving therapy.

2.15   A number of conclusions were drawn (prematurely by the PCC) and some sectors of the press from the substance of these three judgments. First, that as matters then stood, the courts were not interpreting the requirements of HRA 1998 in ways likely to create a privacy law 'by the back door'. Secondly, the safeguards built in to s 12 of the Act were both fit for purpose and fulfilling their purpose. Thirdly, the courts were generally satisfied that press self-regulation was working effectively.[7]

---

[5]   Ibid, at [11].
[6]   Ibid, at [48].
[7]   *Submission to the Culture, Media and Sport Select Committee* (PCC, February 2003) at pp 129–130.

2.16   Shortly after the *Campbell* judgment was delivered a further note of reassurance was sounded in the Government's response[8] to the House of Commons Committee's report on *Privacy and Media Intrusion*.[9] The Government rejected the Committee's suggestion that there were grounds for considering the introduction of a privacy law. It took the view that more legislation of this kind 'is not only unnecessary but undesirable'. It went on to state that: 'the weighing of competing rights in individual cases is the quintessential task of the courts ... Parliament should only intervene if there were signs that the courts are systematically striking the wrong balance; we believe that there are no such signs.' Resolving disputes on a case-by-case basis was preferable to legislation that attempted to 'cover all events'. It also noted with approval that the PCC gave careful consideration to the claims of the public interest in 'weighing up the right to privacy against the freedom of the press' when making its adjudications.

2.17   There were, however, to be further developments in the *Campbell* case and they would culminate in a benchmark judgment that would shift the direction and quicken the pace of change in UK privacy law jurisprudence and the PCC's privacy 'case-law'.

2.18   *The Daily Mirror* appealed against the *Campbell* judgment. In October 2002, the Court of Appeal overturned the trial judge's decision and ruled that the information disclosed about Campbell's therapy did not amount to a disclosure of confidence and that the article had served the public interest. Ms Campbell took her case to the House of Lords, which delivered their ruling in May 2004. The Lords reached a majority decision of three to two in her favour. They ruled that disclosures of this kind constituted a potential threat to the claimant's health and that there was insufficient public interest in them to override her fundamental privacy rights as defined in Art 8 of the ECHR as incorporated in HRA 1998. The dissenting Law Lords took a contrary view. Nevertheless, as Mr Justice Sedley pointed out, 'they were unanimous that, whilst invasion of privacy was still not a freestanding tort, breach of confidence now had to include unjustified invasions of privacy'. He went on to conclude that 'the common law (had) now developed to a point where it could protect personal privacy without having to construct an artificial relationship of confidence between parties'.[10]

2.19   It should also be noted that the requirements of the Data Protection Act 1998 regarding the misuse of sensitive personal data were engaged in determining the eventual outcome of Ms Campbell's action against the *Daily Mirror*. In its judgment, the House of Lords agreed that there was a public interest in reporting that she had a drug problem. It went on to rule, however, that it was not 'fair and lawful' to disclose that she was receiving treatment or to publish details of her treatment or to resort to subterfuge in taking pictures of her leaving the clinic.

2.20   When Princess Caroline von Hannover's case went before the European Court of Human Rights in October 2004, shortly after the *Campbell* judgment, the court unanimously upheld her application. It ruled that the publication of the photographs on which her complaint was based, taken by paparazzi, violated her rights under Art 8 of the ECHR. The right to freedom of expression under Art 10 did not extend to these

---

8   Government's Response 2003, Department for Culture, Media and Sport Committee, *Privacy and Media Intrusion, The Government's Response to the Fifth Report of the Culture, Media and Sport Select Committee on 'Privacy and Media Intrusion'* HC 458-1, Session 2002–2003, Cm 5985 London, Stationery Office), paras 2.3–2.6, pp 2–3.
9   Ibid.
10   S Sedley 'Towards a Right to Privacy', *London Review of Books*, 8 June 2006, at pp 20–21.

photographs because they 'did not concern the dissemination of "ideas"' but only 'images containing very personal or even intimate information about an individual'.

2.21 In the court's view, however, the 'decisive factor in balancing the protection of private life against the right to freedom of expression' was whether the published material contributed to 'a debate of public interest'. The court ruled that it did not do so. It also ruled that the distinction that the German courts had drawn between a figure of contemporary society 'par excellence' and a 'relatively public figure' was 'not sufficient to ensure the effective protection of the applicant's private life'. Everyone, including public figures 'par excellence', had a 'legitimate expectation' that their private lives would be respected. This expectation extended to public places like restaurants and shopping precincts when they were engaged in activities of 'a purely personal nature' that make 'no contribution to a debate of public interest' in a democratic society.

2.22 The key paragraphs in the ruling said that in balancing Art 8 and Art 10 rights against each other:[11]

> '... a fundamental distinction needs to be made between reporting facts – even controversial ones – capable of contributing to a debate in a democratic society relating to politicians in the exercise of their functions, for example, and reporting details of the private life of an individual who, moreover, as in this case, does not exercise official functions ... The situation here does not come within the sphere of any political or public debate because the published photos and accompanying commentaries relate exclusively to details of the applicant's private life.'

2.23 In reaching their decision, the judges noted that the photographs were taken without Princess Caroline's knowledge or consent by means of subterfuge, that they contained images of a 'very personal and intimate nature', and that her distress was compounded by 'the climate of continual harassment' in which the photographs were taken.[12]

2.24 In reviewing the significance of the European Court's judgment and its implications for UK privacy law jurisprudence, Mr Justice Sedley concluded that, henceforward: 'Individuals ... had a legitimate expectation that their private life, whether in a secluded or a private place, would be respected, because it was something in which the public had no legitimate interest unless genuine public debate required it.'[13]

2.25 Opinions differ regarding the extent to which these two judgments have given a new momentum to the development of a free-standing law of privacy in the UK. In 2007, Cyril Glasser, who served for many years as the PCC's legal adviser, said that, in the *Campbell* case:[14]

> 'The House of Lords rejected the opportunity to create a new freestanding law of privacy, preferring instead to absorb the values enshrined in Article 8 (Privacy) and Article 10 (Free Expression) of the European Convention into a reinvigorated law relating to breach of confidence, which can be categorized as now covering all aspects of the misuse of private information.'

---

11 *Von Hannover v Germany*, at paras 63–64.
12 Ibid, at paras 59–74.
13 Sedley (2006), n 10 above, at 20–21.
14 C Glasser *Recent Developments in Privacy Law*: PCC Paper No 3896 (2007), at p 3.

2.26   Glasser went on to say that this development had been accompanied by the adoption of one form of:[15]

'... "the horizontal effect" which has imposed a positive obligation on United Kingdom Courts (notwithstanding the express terms of Articles 8 and 10 limiting their scope to acts by public authorities) to render s.6, Human Rights Act effective by applying Convention rights to all cases, including actions by and against individuals and corporate bodies.'

2.27   Glasser says that four key principles were established in UK law by *Campbell v MGN*. First, that 'the law of breach of confidence has been developed into one relating to the misuse of private information'. Secondly, 'the touchstone of private life is whether, in respect of the disclosed facts, the person in question has a reasonable expectation of privacy'. Thirdly, private information is identified as something worth protecting which focuses on the protection of human autonomy and dignity'. Fourthly, 'the right to privacy must be balanced against the right of the media to impart information to the public' and that right 'has to be balanced in its turn against the respect that must be given to private life'.[16]

2.28   In the commentary on *Campbell v MGN*, later in this book, it is said that:[17]

'Private information is now protected without having to show that it has been discussed in violation of a pre-existing confidential relationship or of an obligation of confidence. Information which is by its nature private will be protected from disclosure; how it is obtained is of secondary importance. The protection afforded to private information is under the umbrella of the cause of action for breach of confidence. This cause of action (still referred to as "breach of confidence") in consequence now has two distinct limbs:

- The original limb encompassing old-fashioned breach of confidence and
- The new limb affording protection to personal information because it is private.'

2.29   The cause of action 'has now dispensed with the need for an initial confidential relationship. The law now imposes a "duty of confidence" whenever a person receives information he knows or ought to know is fairly and reasonably to be regarded as confidential'.[18] For these reasons, it has been suggested that 'the verbal difficulty of how to describe the new cause of action (for privacy intrusion) can be avoided by calling the action: "misuse of private information" rather than "breach of confidence"'.[19]

2.30   Misuse of private information violates a person's reasonable expectation of privacy and thereby his autonomy and dignity as a human being, which Glasser describes as the 'touchstone(s) of private life'.

2.31   On the question of balancing the right to freedom of expression and the right to privacy, the 'underlying test' is 'whether the restriction on freedom of expression is necessary in a democratic society' and whether 'there is a *stronger* public interest in publication than in upholding the obligation of confidence involved'.[20] The focus, however, has shifted from confidential relationships, as such, to the confidential nature of the information under consideration.

---

[15]   Ibid.
[16]   Glasser (2007), n 14 above, at 28–29.
[17]   See **11.14**.
[18]   See **11.51**.
[19]   See **11.51**.
[20]   See **11.21**.

2.32 In *Von Hannover v Germany*, the European Court ruled that:[21]

> '... private life ... includes a person's physical and psychological integrity; the guarantee afforded by article 8 of the convention is primarily intended to ensure the development, without outside interference of the personality of each individual in his relations with other human beings ... There is therefore a zone of interaction of a person with others, even in a public context, which may fall within the scope of a private life.'

In balancing ECHR, Art 8 and Art 10 rights against each other, a 'fundamental distinction' must be drawn between material that contributes to a debate in a democratic society and material that is essentially private in nature.

2.33 In his commentary, written in January 2007, Glasser noted that:[22]

> '... in recent months there have been a number of important court decisions involving privacy and freedom of expression issues which have adopted the formula laid down by the House of Lords in the *Campbell* case. These (decisions) demonstrate the support for the wide discretion which judges have been given to develop privacy rights, using a balancing test and the concept of proportionality.'

2.34 In Glasser's view, these decisions 'have concentrated on extending the concept of privacy, and explicitly downgrading the greater importance which has traditionally been accorded to freedom of expression in this country'. The key decisions he cites as indicators of these trends include *Theakston v MGN*,[23] *McKennitt v Ash*,[24] *HRH Prince of Wales v Associated Newspapers Ltd*[25] and *CC v AB*.[26] He concludes that, taken together, these decisions may now be regarded as 'settled law' which must also be taken into account by the PCC when applying the requirements of its Code of Practice to privacy-related complaints. Although Glasser does not mention *Von Hannover* in this context, that judgment has had a similarly significant impact on the development of UK privacy law jurisprudence and the PCC's 'case-law'.[27]

AFTER *CAMPBELL*[28] AND *VON HANNOVER*[29]

2.35 As it happened, the PCC had to be very quick off the mark in taking account of the *Campbell* judgment. A few weeks later it rejected a complaint from the publisher Ms Kimberly Fortier, that the *Sunday Mirror* had photographed her without consent whilst she was entering a library in Los Angeles, in breach of clauses 3 (Privacy) and 4 (Harassment) of the Code of Practice. Since it found that in this case there had been no harassment, the PCC saw no reason to divert from its general principle that the taking and publication of photographs of people in public places did not breach clause 3.

2.36 With the *Campbell* judgment in mind, however, the PCC went on to say that 'exceptions might have to be made ... in rare circumstances when a photograph reveals

---

21 At para 50.
22 Glasser (2007), n 14 above, at p 3.
23 [2002] EMLR 398.
24 [2006] EMLR 178.
25 [2006] EWCA Civ 1776.
26 [2007] EMLR 11.
27 Glasser (2007), n 14 above, at pp 28-30.
28 *Campbell v MGN* [2004] UKHL 22.
29 (2004) 40 EHRR 1.

something about an individual's health that is not in the public interest'.[30] Soon after this ruling a very similar complaint was made by Ms Allegra Versace Beck in which the published article did include speculative remarks about the state of her health. On receipt of the complaint, *Now!* magazine published an immediate and prominent apology to the complainant's satisfaction. The complaint was thereby resolved and not taken to formal adjudication.[31]

2.37   Glasser cited *Theakston v MGN Ltd*[32] in his list of key court decisions, possibly because the judge's ruling anticipated the significance that would be attached to the publication of unauthorised photographs revealing sensitive personal information after the *Campbell* judgment was delivered. In *Theakston*, Ousely J refused to grant an injunction in favour of a well-known television and radio presenter who wanted to restrain a newspaper from publishing a story about his sexual activities in a brothel. Ousely J allowed the story to be published but granted an injunction restraining publication of the accompanying photographs.

2.38   In his ruling Mr Justice Ousely said that:[33]

> 'Whilst [Theakston] may not be presented as a role model, nonetheless the very nature of his job as a TV presenter of programmes for the younger viewer means that he will be seen as somebody whose lifestyle, publicized as it is, is one which does not attract moral opprobrium and would at least be generally harmless if followed ... It is insufficient to say that the newspaper could take this information to the BBC. The free press is not confined to the role of a confidential police force; it is entitled to communicate directly with the public for the public to reach its own conclusion.'

2.39   In the case of *McKennitt v Ash*,[34] Loreena McKennitt, a Canadian folk singer, applied for an injunction to prevent the author Niema Ash from publishing certain passages in her forthcoming book, *Travels with Loreena McKennitt: My Life as a Friend*. The passages in question described aspects of Ms McKennitt's personal, sexual and family life in some detail, including a dispute over a property transaction, how many bunk beds she provided for visitors and the impact that the death of McKennitt's fiancé had on her personal health and well-being. She was awarded £5,000 damages and granted an injunction.

2.40   Mr Justice Eady applied the *Campbell* test with great thoroughness in deciding which parts of Ms Ash's book should be struck out as personal and confidential material and which could be left in as 'anodyne' or already in the public domain. He dismissed the claim that 'once a person has revealed or discussed some information falling within a particular "zone" of their lives they had a greatly reduced expectation of privacy in relation to any other information that fell within that "zone"'. He said that 'there is in this context a significant difference between choosing to reveal aspects of private life with which an individual feels "comfortable" and allowing disclosure to the public every detail of personal life, feelings, thoughts and foibles of character'.[35]

2.41   Eady J also dismissed the claim that there was a public interest in exposing instances where a public figure had presented a false image of herself. He said that 'a

---

[30]   PCC Report No 68–69, October 2004–March 2005.
[31]   PCC *Annual Review 2004*; PCC Report No 68–69, October 2004–March 2005.
[32]   [2002] EMLR 398.
[33]   Ibid, at [69].
[34]   [2005] EWHC 3003 Eady J and in the Court of Appeal [2006] EWCA Civ 1714.
[35]   See **11.45**.

very high degree of misbehaviour must be demonstrated' in the context of this particular case to justify a public interest defence.[36] In 2006, Ms Ash took her case to the Court of Appeal where she claimed that she had a right to tell her own side of the story. This argument was dismissed on the grounds that the book was largely about Ms McKennitt. Ms Ash also claimed that there could not have been any breach of confidence or invasion of Ms McKennitt's privacy because Eady J had found some parts of the book to be untrue. This claim was dismissed on the grounds that the truth of falsity or such revelations was irrelevant when they touched on matters of a highly personal and confidential nature.

2.42 In reaching its judgment, the Court of Appeal noted that McKennitt had, in the past, taken great care to protect her personal privacy. The appeal judges also agreed with Eady J's ruling that publishing even trivial but personal details about a person's home without consent constituted an 'unauthorized use of private information' and, as such, a breach of confidence. In the aftermath of these two judgments it was widely construed that in future 'Kiss and tell' actions, litigants would not have to prove that the disclosures were untrue but only that they constituted an unwarranted invasion of privacy.

2.43 In the case of *CC v AB*,[37] Eady J applied the *Campbell* test when granting an injunction in favour of a married sports celebrity who wanted to prevent the husband of the woman with whom he was having an affair from selling 'his side of the story' to a newspaper. The husband was also threatening to name the celebrity as correspondent in his action for divorce. The injunction was granted on the grounds that the celebrity's wife had already suffered considerable mental distress as a result of her husband's adultery. Publishing the story was likely to exacerbate her condition and adversely affect the well-being of the couple's children.

2.44 Both *Campbell* and *Von Hannover* were engaged in the case of *HRH Prince of Wales v Associated Newspapers Limited*,[38] which concerned the unauthorised publication of Prince Charles's private diaries recording his thoughts about the ceremonial handing over of Hong Kong to the People's Republic of China where he had been in attendance. The diaries had been circulated to a number of his friends and a former secretary in the Prince's household had given a copy to the newspaper without authorisation.

2.45 The case was heard by a single judge, Mr Justice Blackburne. The *Mail on Sunday* said that the diaries were not personal documents but records of public events in which the Prince had taken part in his duties as a public servant. Blackburne J rejected this claim on the grounds that the contents of the diaries made 'at best' a 'minimal' contribution to any debate of public interest that was 'necessary in a democratic society'.[39]

2.46 The case went to the Court of Appeal, which ruled that:[40]

---

[36]   At [97].
[37]   [2007] EMLR 11.
[38]   [2006] EWCA Civ 1776.
[39]   T Welsh, W Greenwood and D Banks *McNae's Essential Law for Journalists* (Oxford University Press, 2007), at p 328.
[40]   See **11.62**.

'... the action was not concerned solely with a claim for breach of privacy but that, in the action, were all the elements of a claim for old-fashioned breach of confidence ... and the disclosure was in breach of an express contractual duty of confidence ... of which the publisher of the information was aware. The information was disclosed in breach of the well-recognised relationship of confidence which exists between employer and employee and the disclosure was in breach of an express contractual duty of confidentiality.'

2.47   The Court of Appeal acknowledged that the public was interested in even relatively trivial information about Prince Charles. Nevertheless, the public disclosure of such information could still be particularly intrusive and the trial judge was 'right to have regard to this' when he said:[41]

'Not the least of the considerations that must be weighed in the scales to the claimant's counter veiling claim to what was described in argument as "his private space" was the right to be able to commit his private thoughts to writing and keep them private, the more so as he is inescapably a public figure who is subject to constant and intense media interest ... The claimant is as much entitled to enjoy confidentiality for his private thoughts as an aspect of his own "human autonomy and dignity" as is any other.'

2.48   The Court of Appeal upheld the judge's decision and ruled that when private information was revealed in breach of an obligation of confidence it was not sufficient to show that the publication was in the public interest. In a democratic society it was also necessary to show that it was in the public interest that the duty of confidence should be breached.[42]

2.49   More recently, Dr Neil Murray and his wife, the celebrated author JK Rowling, won a landmark ruling in the Court of Appeal. Their action began in 2004 when an agency photographer took a long lens photograph of Ms Rowling and her husband whilst they were walking their 18-month-old son in his pushchair on a street near their Edinburgh home. The pictures were taken covertly, without consent and published in the *Sunday Express*.

2.50   The Murrays decided to bring an action for invasion of privacy against *Express Newspapers* and the *Big Picture Agency*. The newspaper settled out of court. The agency successfully applied to a High Court judge and the Murrays' claim was struck out. In his ruling, Mr Justice Patten stated that 'the law does not in my judgement (as it stands) allow them to carve out a press free zone for their children in respect of absolutely everything'.[43]

2.51   In 2008, the Murrays went on to win a ruling in the Court of Appeal. In overturning the High Court judgment, Sir Anthony Clarke stated that: 'If a child of parents who are not in the public eye could reasonably expect not to have photographs of him published in the media, so too should the child of a famous parent.'[44]

2.52   As noted later in this book, 'The Court of Appeal in *Murray v Big Pictures Limited* highlighted the fact that Lord Hoffman in *Campbell v MGN* had drawn an important distinction between the mere taking of a photograph and its publication' and

---

41   See **12.13**.
42   Welsh, Greenwood and Banks (2007), n 39 above, at p 328.
43   *Murray v Big Picture Agency* [2008] EWCA Civ 446.
44   Ibid.

that the question to be asked is 'what a reasonable person of ordinary sensibilities would feel if she was placed in the same position as the claimant and faced with the same publicity'.[45]

2.53 The Court of Appeal agreed with Lord Hope's opinion that in such cases it was necessary to take account of all the circumstances of the case including:[46]

> '... the attributes of the claimant, the nature of the activity in which the claimant was engaged, the place at which it was happening, the nature and purpose of the intrusion, the absence of consent and whether it was known or could be inferred, the effect on the claimant and the circumstances in which and the purposes for which the information came into the hands of the publisher.'

2.54 The Court of Appeal 'emphasized the child's distinct right to privacy and the fact that ... it was not the taking of the photographs that was the problem so much as their subsequent publication'. In the *Murray* case a series of photographs were taken clandestinely without consent and with the intention of selling them for publication.[47]

2.55 On the general issue of covert photography in public places, it is noted later in this book that clause 3(i) of the PCC's Code of Practice states that: 'a person may have a reasonable expectation of privacy in a public place. Public places can plainly be part of a celebrity's "private space" or "zone of interaction" with others.'[48]

2.56 In summary, the Court of Appeal said that 'it was at least arguable that the child had a reasonable expectation of privacy and the fact that he was a child had greater significance than the judge thought'. As noted later in this book, clause 6(v) of the PCC's Code of Practice states that: 'Editors must not use the fame, notoriety or position as sole justification for publishing details of a child's private life.' In addition, the PCC is on record as stating that 'the acid test to be applied by newspapers in writing about the children of public figures who are not famous in their own right (unlike the Royal Princes) is whether a newspaper would write such a story if it was about an ordinary person'.[49]

2.57 The Court of Appeal in *Murray* concluded that 'subject to the facts of the particular case, the law should protect children from intrusive media attention' but that:[50]

> '... a reasonable expectation of privacy is only the first step. There must still be a balance between the child's right to privacy under Article 8 and the publisher's right to freedom of expression under Article 10. This approach is consistent with the approach in Von Hannover, to which it is permissible to have regard.'

2.58 In Professor Helen Fenwick's opinion, the Court of Appeal's decision brought UK law closer to the findings of *Von Hannover* by indicating that 'even photos of innocuous activities, such as walking in the streets, might potentially be covered as private information if the photo is published without consent'.[51] Amber Melville-Brown

---

[45] See **12.40**.
[46] See **10.19**.
[47] See **12.61** and **12.62**.
[48] See **12.45**.
[49] See **12.65**.
[50] See **12.69**.
[51] H Fenwick 'Developments in "Privacy" Law', *Student Law Review*, 1 October 2008.

noted that although the decision made it clear that this action 'was not brought to protect the privacy of the parents', it raised the possibility that some celebrities 'might use their children to protect themselves from media attention in future'.[52]

2.59   Clare Dyer cited Hugh Tomlinson's concern that the decision marked 'another stage in establishing a law of privacy for children',[53] and Jonathan Rozenberg pointed out that it was 'founded firmly' on the European Court's ruling in *Von Hannover* which 'of course, applies to adults'.[54]

2.60   In *Mosley v MGN Ltd*,[55] Mr Mosley brought an action against the *News of the World* alleging breach of privacy and claiming unlimited damages. The newspaper had published a story with accompanying photographs in which it was alleged that he had taken part in a 'depraved NAZI-STYLE orgy' with a number of women, one of whom had secretly videoed the activities and passed on the footage to the newspaper. Mosley's action was based on a claim for breach of confidence and/or the unauthorised disclosure of personal information in violation of his rights under Art 8 of the ECHR.[56]

2.61   In his judgment, Mr Justice Eady said that the defendant: 'had committed an "old fashioned breach of confidence" as well as a violation of the Article 8 rights of all those involved'. The issue was whether one of the women taking part also owed a duty of confidence to the other participants in the orgy, including the claimant.[57] He awarded Mr Mosley £60,000 in privacy damages.

2.62   With regard to the issue of 'where the public interest really lies – in suppression or disclosure' of the material in question, Eady J said that everything depended on the 'careful application of proportionality to the facts'. The balancing test was 'whether the intrusion, or the degree of intrusion which actually took place into the claimant's privacy was proportionate to the public interest which is supposed to justify it'.[58]

2.63   Eady J noted Lord Bingham's observation that 'what engages the interest of the public may not be material which engages the public interest'.[59] He also said that: 'it is sometimes legitimate to infringe an individual's privacy for the greater good of exposing or detecting crime and that this was expressly recognized in the PCC Code in a manner originally derived from the draft attached as a schedule to the Calcutt Report.'[60]

2.64   Where, however, 'there has been no breach of the law, the private conduct of adults is to be seen as essentially no-one else's business' and the public interest is not therefore engaged. There would have to be strong public policy reasons, such as 'a contribution to debate on matters of general public interest as opposed to satisfying public curiosity ... before publication of details of a sexual relationship could be justified'.[61]

---

[52]   A Mellville-Brown 'Media Law', *Gazette* (*Weekly Journal of the Law Society*), 5 June 2008, at pp 23–24.
[53]   C Dyer 'J. K. Rowling Wins Ban on Photos of Her Son', *The Guardian*, 8 May 2008, at p 5.
[54]   J Rozenberg 'J. K. Rowling's Son Wins Privacy Battle in Court', *Daily Telegraph*, 8 May 2008.
[55]   [2008] EWHC 1777 (QB).
[56]   See **11.65**.
[57]   See **11.65**.
[58]   See **11.70**.
[59]   See **11.103**.
[60]   *Mosley v NGN* [2008] EWHC 1777 (QB), at [110].
[61]   See **12.22** and **12.25**.

2.65 Eady J referred to *Campbell* when he said that with regard to the use of photographs, privacy will usually be infringed if their content causes humiliation or severe embarrassment to the subject even when taken in a public place. When they are taken in a private place by resort to subterfuge and/or the use of clandestine devices, they constitute an infringement of privacy whether or not they cause humiliation and embarrassment.

2.66 Eady J also said that there was nothing 'landmark' about his judgment. It was 'simply the application to rather unusual facts of recently developed but established principles'.[62] One such principle related to the uniquely intrusive nature of covertly taken photographs of people engaged in activities of a highly personal nature, including their sexual activities, in places where they have a reasonable expectation of privacy. In reviewing the development of this principle, Eady J cited the Court of Appeal's ruling in the case of *Douglas v Hello!*[63] that 'special considerations attach to photographs in the field of privacy ... As a means of invading privacy, a photograph is particularly intrusive'. He also referred to the injunction obtained by Jamie Theakston in 2002 preventing photographs of him in a brothel from being published, even though descriptions of what Theakston did in the brothel were not restrained. Eady J also noted 'that a number of comments made about intrusion by photography or video recording have been made in the context of images recorded in more or less public spaces. This was so in *Von Hannover v Germany*[64] itself and in *Peck v United Kingdom*'.[65]

2.67 Eady J's comments on the issue of photographs leads to the conclusion that whilst a story may be legitimately published in the public interest, a stronger public interest would need to be demonstrated in order to justify an intrusive photograph that illustrates it than to justify the publication of the story itself. This was an important principle that the PCC would also have to bear in mind in dealing with privacy complaints.

AFTER *MOSLEY V NGN*

2.68 The *Mosley v NGN*[66] judgment triggered a wide-ranging and, at times, acrimonious debate about its implications for press freedom and developments in UK privacy law. In a speech to the Society of Editors' Annual Conference in Bristol in 2008, Paul Dacre, Editor in Chief of Associated Newspapers launched a swingeing critique of the 'wretched' HRA 1998 in general and Mr Justice Eady's judgment in particular. The essence of his critique was that, because of the requirements of the Act the British press was having a privacy law 'inexorably and insidiously' imposed on it. In a democratic society, such a significant development should be subject to the 'will of Parliament rather than the judges and, in particular, the succession of rulings delivered by Eady J'.[67]

2.69 Dacre also described Mr Mosley's conduct as the 'very abrogation of civilized behaviour of which the law is supposed to be the safeguard' and Eady J's judgment as being 'indicative of a subjective and highly relative moral sense' with regard to such behaviour.

---

[62] *Mosley v NGN Ltd* [2008] EWHC 1777 (QB), at [234].
[63] [2007] 4 All ER 545.
[64] [2004] 40 EHRR 1.
[65] (2003) 36 EHRR 41.
[66] *Mosley v NGN Ltd* [2008] EWHC 1777 (QB), at [234].
[67] The full version of Paul Dacre's speech is available at www.pressgazette.co.uk/story.asp?storycode=42394.

2.70   *The Guardian* thought that Dacre 'was right to question whether a single judge should have such a disproportionate influence over the development of law relating to freedom of expression'. It suggested, however, that 'it was more debatable whether "Mr Eady deserved to be singled out for such a personalized attack" since "any judge would have been obliged to perform the same balancing act between the relevant articles of the Human Rights Act"'.[68]

2.71   In a letter to *The Times*, four leading QCs wrote in to say that Eady J was 'doing no more than applying the law, as he was bound to do, developed by the House of Lords in the Naomi Campbell case and in the European Court of Human Rights in the case of Princess Caroline'. In their view, the suggestion 'that Mr Justice Eady is conducting a one-man mission to create a law of privacy, thereby circumventing the function of Parliament, does not bear examination'. He was doing no more than 'applying the law as Parliament intended and Parliament made it unlawful for a court to act in a way which is incompatible with a Convention Right'.[69]

2.72   Early in 2009, Sir Christopher Meyer looked back on the debate and suggested that 'The problem was not Justice Eady' – it was HRA 1998 and the European Court of Human Rights which posed the greatest threat to press freedom and press self-regulation in the UK. Many of the European Court judges were drawn from countries which had 'very different traditions of press freedom from the UK'.[70]

2.73   Sir Christopher went on to say that under HRA 1998, s 12, UK judges are required to take account of the PCC's Code of Practice but they are increasingly disposed to interpret and apply it in ways that were undermining rather than underpinning the right to freedom of expression.

2.74   Meanwhile, Mr Mosley has decided to take his case to the European Court of Human Rights, where his lawyers will argue that UK law, as it now stands, provides insufficient protection for people's privacy rights. Mr Mosley wants the law to be changed so that editors are required to contact the subjects of their stories before publishing any photographs or articles that might intrude on their privacy – a proposal that has much in common with the recommendation set out in Sir David Calcutt's second Report[71] when it was published 16 years ago.

2.75   In November 2008, the House of Commons Culture, Media and Sport Committee announced that it would be undertaking an inquiry into recent developments in UK privacy law and other related matters. The remit of this inquiry and the events leading up to it are reviewed in the following chapter.

---

[68]   Editorial, *The Guardian* 'Lashing Out at the Law' 11 November 2008, at p 32.
[69]   D Browne, A Caldecott, A Page and R Rampton 'Privacy Law and Press Freedom' *The Times*, 11 November 2008.
[70]   M Brown 'PCC Chairman warns of European threat to press freedom' www.guardian.co.uk, Tuesday 13 January 2009, 14.53 GMT.
[71]   Sir David Calcutt *Review of Press Self-Regulation*, Cm 2135 (1993) (Calcutt Review).

Chapter 3

THE DEVELOPMENT OF PRESS SELF-REGULATION IN THE UNITED KINGDOM

3.1   This chapter reviews the succession of events that marked a critical turning point in the history of British press self-regulation – the confrontations that gave rise to the publication of the first Calcutt Report[1] in 1990, the establishment of the Press Complaints Commission (PCC) in 1991 and the critical review of its subsequent performance by the second Calcutt Report[2] in 1993. These were the years in which the future of British press self-regulation hung in the balance and in this chapter they are taken as the point of reference for reviewing the progress made since then, in establishing the PCC as an independent self-regulatory body that administers a Code of Practice recognised as a 'relevant privacy code' under the Human Rights Act 1998 (HRA 1998) and which deals swiftly, fairly and efficiently with over 4,600 complaints a year.

3.2   Three key issues dominated the British debate about press self-regulation throughout those early crisis-ridden years – whether we should have statutory or self-regulation, whether we should have a privacy law and whether there should be more stringent forms of prior restraint on publications deemed likely to constitute unjustifiable intrusions into people's privacy. The debate continues today, albeit in less confrontational terms and, as is the case in all democratic societies, how such issues are eventually resolved largely determines the kind of balance that is struck between the need to protect press freedoms and the need to protect the public from abuses of those freedoms by the press.

THE ORIGINS OF THE PRESS COMPLAINTS COMMISSION

3.3   From the very beginning, celebrities – as high-profile litigants and victims of unethical press conduct – were key players in the dramatic events that culminated in the establishment of the PCC in 1991.

3.4   The origins of press self-regulation in the UK date from 1947 when the first post-war Labour Government appointed a Royal Commission under the Chairmanship of Sir David Ross. Its brief was to undertake a review of the finance, control, management and ownership of the press and to advise Parliament on how these arrangements could be improved. When the Commission reported in 1949 it recommended that a self-regulatory General Council of the Press should be established

---

[1]   David Calcutt *Report of the Committee on Privacy and Related Matters*, Cm 1102 (1990).
[2]   Sir David Calcutt *Review of Press Self-Regulation*, Cm 2135 (1993).

as soon as possible. The Council's tasks were to include safeguarding press freedom and raising standards 'of public responsibility and public service' throughout the industry.[3]

3.5 The newspaper industry responded to this proposal with great scepticism and did nothing about it until 1953, when it was confronted by the alarming prospect of a Private Members' Bill proposing the establishment of a quasi-statutory press council. Only then did the industry agree with great reluctance to establish its own General Council of the Press charged with the responsibility of safeguarding the freedom of the press and combating abuses of that freedom. These tasks were to be undertaken without benefit of a Code of Practice or any enforceable sanctions.

3.6 Unsurprisingly, throughout the following 8 years the new Council received and dealt with an annual average 'of a mere sixty-odd complaints'.[4] A second Royal Commission, reporting in 1962 and chaired by Lord Shawcross,[5] criticised the General Council on several counts and recommended that it appoint a lay chairman and some lay members. The Council duly appointed Lord Justice Devlin to the Chair, added a few lay members, established a complaints subcommittee and agreed to receive third party complaints. It also changed its name to the Press Council.

3.7 Throughout the 1960s and early 1970s new kinds of conglomerate media ownership began to emerge as the competition war between the tabloids grew fiercer. The number of complaints about press intrusions into peoples' privacy increased as more aggressive kinds of investigative journalism became common practice.

3.8 In response to mounting parliamentary and public concern, a third Royal Commission under the chairmanship of Sir Morris Finer was appointed in 1974. When Sir Morris died the following year, Professor OR McGregor succeeded him as Chairman and the Commission's Report appeared in 1977.[6] It was highly critical of the escalating incidence of press misconduct, notably with regard to the growing number of flagrant intrusions into peoples' privacy, the irresponsible use of cheque-book journalism and the prevalence of inaccurate reporting.

3.9 McGregor's Commission also urged the Press Council to adopt a Code of Practice and appoint a majority of lay members. The Council agreed to create a lay majority but it refused to draft a Code of Practice. Thereafter, as the circulation war between the tabloids intensified, standards of press conduct went on declining and the exhortations of the Council were ignored. Levels of political and public concern escalated and the pressures for reform intensified.

3.10 In 1989 Dr Louis Blom-Cooper was appointed as the new Chairman with a brief from the industry to reform the workings of the Council. His efforts were overtaken by a new spate of press scandals including the irresponsible reporting of the Hillsborough football stadium tragedy in 1989 and the Strangeways Prison riots in 1990, a gross libel of the popular singer Elton John and repeated intrusions into the private life of the television celebrity Russell Harty through what proved to be the last stages of his terminal illness. The Press Council initiated five investigations into these scandals to no effect whatsoever.

---

[3]   R Shannon *A Press Free and Responsible Self-regulation and the Press Complaints Commission 1991–2001* (John Murray, 2001); Royal Commission *Royal Commission on the Press, 1947–1949*, Cmd 7700 (1949).
[4]   Shannon (2001), n 3 above, at p 13.
[5]   Royal Commission *Royal Commission on the Press 1962, Report*, Cmnd 1811 (1962).
[6]   Royal Commission (*Royal Commission on the Press, 1997, Final Report*, Cmnd 6801-1-6 (1977).

3.11   Public confidence in the integrity and goodwill of the British popular press had reached an all-time low. In Parliament, there was growing cross-party support for a new law of privacy and a statutory council invested with legal sanctions.

3.12   In early 1989, the patience of the Conservative Government ran out and the then Home Secretary, Douglas Hurd, appointed a Home Office Committee, under the chairmanship of David Calcutt, to review the whole situation and advise him on what should be done to stop the escalating number of press intrusions into the private lives of individuals. Calcutt was given 12 months in which to do the job. The Newspaper Publishers Association and the Press Council belatedly set about drafting Codes of Practice and plans for reforming the self-regulatory system. On 21 December 1989, David Mellor, who was then a Minister of State at the Home Office, told viewers in a television programme that, in his opinion, 'the popular press is drinking in the last chance saloon'.

3.13   Nevertheless, the Press Council went ahead and published its proposals for a Code of Practice and a new set of disciplinary sanctions. Short of funds and now bereft of credibility with Parliament, press and the general public, Blom-Cooper and the Council still hoped to survive and stay in business after Calcutt's report was published. Then, in the last few weeks of the Calcutt Committee's deliberations the industry scored what Shannon describes as a 'spectacular own goal'.[7] A well-known and very popular stage and television actor, Gorden Kaye, was rushed to hospital after sustaining severe head and brain injures in a car accident. After 3 days on a life-support machine he was transferred to a private room where notices were pinned prohibiting admission to unauthorised persons. A journalist and a photographer from the *Sunday Sport* gained access by subterfuge, took pictures and started to interview him. They refused to leave when asked to do so and had to be ejected from the premises. Mr Kaye was deemed to be in no condition to give informed consent to an interview.

3.14   This incident was 'held to be a scandal too far' and 'instantly became a landmark in atrocious intrusiveness'.[8] It did not prove to be, as was widely expected, the death-knock of self-regulation, but it was the last nail in the coffin of the old Press Council.

3.15   Whilst Mr Kaye was in hospital, his legal representative sued the editor of the newspaper for malicious falsehood because it was about to publish an article claiming that he had consented to be interviewed and photographed.[9] The Court of Appeal ruled that any such claim was bound to be malicious because at that time Mr Kaye was too ill to give informed consent. The court, therefore, granted an order preventing the newspaper from publishing any material claiming that he had done so. The court, however, was unable to prevent publication of the story itself.

3.16   In making its ruling, the court expressed regret that no further action could be brought against the newspaper for gross intrusion into Mr Kaye's privacy. It also noted that, since Mr Kaye was a hospital patient, and not the legal occupier of the property on which the intrusion took place, he was unable to sue for trespass.

---

[7]   Shannon (2001), n 3 above, at p 26.

[8]   Ibid.

[9]   *Kaye v Robertson & Sport Newspapers Ltd* (1990) The Times, 21 March, CA.

The first Calcutt Report[10]

3.17   The Calcutt Report was published in June 1990. It recommended that the press should be given one last chance to make self-regulation work. To that end, the old Press Council should be disbanded and replaced by a Press Complaints Commission (PCC). The new PCC should be given a year in which to establish itself. If it subsequently failed to deliver, it should be closed down. The Government accepted these proposals. In doing so, it gave the new PCC an additional 18 months in which to demonstrate its effectiveness. Calcutt would then undertake a second review and if the PCC failed this test, it would be replaced by a statutory tribunal.

3.18   Self-regulation had survived, but only on a probationary basis, and the industry had been warned that if 'maverick publications persistently declined to respect the authority' of the new PCC it would be closed down. As far as Calcutt was concerned, the case of a 'single maverick newspaper ignoring the proposed new code of conduct' would be sufficient grounds for doing so.[11]

3.19   In Richard Shannon's view, 'the evidence, then and later suggests that Calcutt thought of the Commission as an interim transitory body, half way to his ultimate objective of a statutory press tribunal'.[12] The constitutional model that the Report proposed was certainly tailor-made for instant conversion into such a body. All appointments were to be made by another independent authority whose members would also be independently appointed, possibly by the Lord Chancellor. The Chairman was to be a judge or a senior lawyer.

3.20   Although the Report did not propose the introduction of a tort of privacy, it did recommend that, in privacy cases, the new PCC 'should be able to restrain publication of material in breach of the code of practice by means of injunctions. No injunction should be granted if the publisher could show that he had a good arguable defense'. Complainants would thereby be able 'to obtain a legally-enforceable redress' before the PCC. In order to do so they would have to waive their rights to sue in the courts. The PCC would also have the power to award compensation in privacy and inaccuracy cases – subject to certain statutory limitations.[13] Calcutt clearly intended that the new PCC should be invested with statutory powers.

3.21   The Committee described the attributes of privacy in terms of 'personal information' and went on to propose 'a possible definition' of such information 'in terms of an individual's personal life, that is to say, those aspects of life which reasonable members of society would respect as being such that an individual is ordinarily entitled to keep to himself, whether or not they relate to his mind or body, to his home, to his family, to other personal relationships, or to his correspondence or documents'. On the question of what might constitute 'a good arguable defense' for invading a person's privacy, the Committee expressed a 'serious reservation about a general defence merely labelled "public interest"'. It suggested instead that its own definition of personal information 'already provides for flexible interpretation by the courts' and that 'we would see difficulty in introducing a further variable which would be likely to mean different things to different people'.[14]

---

[10]   David Calcutt *Report of the Committee on Privacy and Related Matters*, Cm 1102 (1990) ('Calcutt Report').
[11]   Calcutt Report (1990), n 10 above, at para 16.7, p 74.
[12]   Shannon (2001), n 3 above, at p 29.
[13]   Calcutt Report (1990), n 10 above, at p xii and paras 16–17, p 75.
[14]   Ibid, at paras 12, 17, p 49.

3.22   The Committee, however, went on to recommend that:[15]

'... the additional defense would have to be limited to any infringement where the defendant had reasonable grounds for believing that:

a)   publication of the personal information would contribute to the prevention, detection or exposure of any crime or other seriously anti-social conduct; or
b)   it would be necessary for the protection of public health and safety; or
c)   there would, but for the publication, be a real risk that the public, or some section of the public, would be seriously misled by a statement previously made public by or on behalf of any individual whose privacy would otherwise be infringed (whether the plaintiff or otherwise).'

3.23   These were the three grounds on which the Calcutt Committee thought that 'a good arguable defense' for intruding into a person's privacy might be based. Although they were not included in the Committee's own draft Code of Practice they were subsequently modified and included as addenda to four of the privacy-related clauses in the Editors' Code of Practice for the new PCC to administer.

3.24   With the case of Gorden Kaye clearly in mind, the Committee also proposed that the following three forms of physical intrusion should be made criminal offences: entering private property, placing surveillance devices and taking photographs without consent of the lawful occupant with intent to obtain and publish personal information – subject to 'a good arguable defense'. Neither this proposal, nor those relating to prior restraint, were taken up by the Government.

3.25   Calcutt's constitutional proposals were also set to one side. In order to get things moving the Government allowed the industry to appoint an independent lay Chairman. The industry, for its part, acted swiftly in establishing a Press Standards Board of Finance (Pressbof) which was made responsible for raising the necessary budget through a pro rata levy across the industry.

3.26   Rather than waiting for the Lord Chancellor to constitute an Appointments Committee, the Government also agreed that, in the first instance, the Chairman and Commissioners should be appointed through the agencies of Pressbof. Within a matter of weeks, Lord McGregor was appointed as the PCC's first Chairman and by the end of the year all 16 of the first Commissioners were in post. Contrary to Calcutt's wishes, the new PCC did not have a lay majority as it does today.

3.27   An Editors' Code Committee was appointed and set to work soon after McGregor took office. From the start McGregor insisted that the editors should write the Code, the industry should publicly endorse it and the PCC should administer it. Thereafter, he argued, it would be impossible for disgruntled publishers and editors to complain that the Code had been imposed on them by people outside the industry who were unfamiliar with the realities of day-to-day newspaper practice. Against all expectations, the new PCC was ready to start work 6 months in advance of the agreed deadline when it met for its first meeting on 30 January 1991.

3.28   The Calcutt Committee had recommended that the PCC 'should concentrate on providing, on a non-statutory basis, an effective means of redress for complaints against

---

[15]   Ibid, at para 3.20, p 8 and paras 12.22 and 12.33, p 50.

the press'. It thought that 'if it performed this task effectively, the Press Complaints Commission would in fact be serving press freedom better that it would by acting as an overtly campaigning body'.[16]

3.29   The PCC agreed with this recommendation whilst seeking, in accordance with its articles of association to promote 'generally established freedoms, including freedom of expression, and the public's right to know, and the defence of the Press against improper pressure from the Government or elsewhere'.[17]

3.30   It may be questioned whether so much could have been achieved so quickly if Calcutt's constitutional proposals had been imposed on the industry. The arrangements that were put in place had the industry's full support from the start and, it can be argued, they were of a kind that positively encouraged the subsequent growth of a new culture of voluntary Code compliance on the part of the industry.

The first 5 years

3.31   The PCC – and the industry – now had 18 months in which to persuade a still sceptical Government and general public that it was up to the job. Unlike the old Press Council, it had the backing of an industry-endorsed Code of Practice. The question in everyone's mind, however, was whether or not the publishers and editors would go on supporting the Code when they were put to the test – and most notably with regard to complaints about press intrusion into people's privacy. In 1992, the House of Commons National Heritage Committee began its own inquiry into privacy intrusion on the part of the press.

3.32   Meanwhile, the future of the PCC hung in the balance as it got down to the task of handling complaints whilst preparing for the second Calcutt review. From the start, the PCC worked under the spotlight of public scrutiny as it dealt with a succession of high-profile complaints about intrusions into the private lives of members of the Royal Family, politicians and other public figures. Its work on behalf of less well-known members of the general public went largely unnoticed.

3.33   The second Calcutt review was completed and published in early 1993.[18] As was widely expected, it recommended that the PCC should be replaced by a statutory Press Complaints Tribunal invested with draconian powers. In the same year the House of Commons Select Committee also proposed the creation of a statutory Commission which would be overseen by an ombudsman with enforceable legal sanctions.[19] Nearly 2 years were to pass before the Government responded to these proposals.

3.34   Calcutt's second report was highly critical of the PCC's performance and constitution. It was not, in his view, 'an effective regulator of the press'. It was, 'in essence', a body set up, financed and dominated by the industry. It operated a Code 'devised by the industry and which is over favourable to the industry'.[20]

3.35   Calcutt now wanted a statutory tribunal chaired by a judge or senior lawyer appointed by the Lord Chancellor with two lay members appointed by a Secretary of

---

[16]   Ibid, at para 15.3, p 66.
[17]   PCC *Submission to the Review of Press Self-Regulation* (October), at p 12.
[18]   Sir David Calcutt *Review of Press Self-Regulation*, Cm 2135 (1993) ('Calcutt Review').
[19]   National Heritage Committee *Privacy and the Media*, HC 294-1 (HMSO, 1990)).
[20]   Calcutt Review (1993), n 18 above, at pxi.

State. It would draft a new Code, keep it under review and, as before, be invested with the power to restrain publications. It could be proactive in starting investigations into reports of unethical conduct if it believed there were prima facie grounds for doing so. It would also be empowered to award compensation and costs and to impose fines.

3.36   Calcutt again proposed that the same three forms of physical intrusion should be made criminal offences. He went on, however, to recommend that the High Court should also be given powers to grant injunctions restraining the publication of material obtained by such means. Individuals affected by such publications should have a right of action for any losses suffered. The same civil remedy should be made available if the intrusion took place in another country with the intention of publishing in England and Wales.[21] Having decided that self-regulation had failed, Calcutt concluded that there was now an urgent need for a new tort of privacy which, in conjunction with a new statutory tribunal, would give complainants access to two legally enforceable means of redress for their grievances.[22]

3.37   Whilst the industry waited for the Government's response to these proposals, and those of the Heritage Committee, concern about continuing press intrusions into the private lives of public figures intensified. One such intrusive story was based on an intercepted telephone conversation that allegedly took place between the Prince of Wales and Mrs Camilla Parker Bowles (as she was then known). Shortly afterwards, pictures were published of the Princess of Wales which were taken with a clandestine camera in her gymnasium. In neither of these cases did the PCC receive a complaint.

3.38   In 1994, the Government launched a new 'Back to Basics' campaign advocating a return to traditional values, including those of trust and fidelity. This initiative predictably triggered a spate of newspaper investigations into the private lives of ministers and MPs who had spoken out in support of these 'basic values' but failed to uphold them in their private lives. Some of the victims of these stories complained to the PCC. In those cases where the editors were able to demonstrate that there was a public interest to be served in exposing inconsistencies between what the complainants said in public and what they did in their private life, the complaints were not upheld.

3.39   In January 1995, Lord Wakeham succeeded Lord McGregor as Chairman of the PCC. Another high-profile complaint involving four newspapers was received from Earl Spencer, the brother of Princess Diana, about intrusions into the privacy of his wife, Lady Spencer. Two of the complaints were upheld. In the case of one of the newspapers involved, the PCC considered the breach to be so serious that it drew the attention of the publisher to the actions of his editor. A third complaint was resolved and a fourth was rejected.

3.40   In July 1995, the Government announced that it would not be implementing the proposals of either the second Calcutt Review or those of the House of Commons Select Committee. It was not persuaded that self-regulation had failed. It was, however, persuaded that self-regulation was preferable to any of the alternatives such as a statutory council, an ombudsman or a law of privacy.

3.41   Why, then, had neither of these critical reviews carried the day and in what ways can the PCC be said to have succeeded? Considerable progress had been made in raising

---

[21]   Ibid, at paras 7.1–7.17, pp 56–57.
[22]   Ibid, at paras 7.33–7.42, pp 56–57.

standards of service to the general public and standards of conduct across the industry. Neither Calcutt nor the Heritage Committee, in their preoccupation with complaints from public figures, had given due credit for what the PCC had achieved on behalf of so-called ordinary people. Of the 2,500 complaints received in 1995, the great majority came from ordinary people. Internal procedures for handling complaints had been radically reviewed and improved. The backlog of unresolved complaints left behind by the Press Council had been cleared. New complaints were being resolved more quickly than ever before. New information literature in eight languages and an office-manned helpline were raising the PCC's public profile and making it more easily accessible to members of the public.

3.42   The PCC had also established an excellent working relationship with the Editors' Code Committee. The Committee had been quick to respond whenever a crisis or a complaint exposed a serious weakness or oversight in the Code's provisions. Tougher rules had been applied regarding the use of long lens photography in private places and new guidelines had been introduced to ensure that the children of public figures, including the Royal Princes, could enjoy the same rights to privacy as all other children. Soon after the publication of Princess Diana's gymnasium pictures, the PCC had established a new post of Privacy Commissioner, with special responsibility for handling complaints about alleged intrusions into privacy. The PCC was already responding quickly and effectively to changing circumstances and new challenges.

3.43   At the end of its first 5 turbulent years, the PCC had survived as a beleaguered institution in a largely hostile political environment. There were to be more times of crisis in the years ahead. Nevertheless, from 1995 onwards, the PCC was able to look forward to a future that was no longer overshadowed by the imminent prospect of its own demise.

DEVELOPMENTS FROM 1995 TO 2009

3.44   The following sections review the record of the PCC's activities since 1995 and the extent to which it has succeeded in restoring public trust in the institutions of press self-regulation. They focus on three aspects of the PCC's work which bear directly on the issue – the progress it has made in helping to create a new climate of voluntary compliance in the resolution of complaints, the continuing evolution of the Code of Practice in response to new challenges and opportunities, and the impact of new legislation and key legal judgments on self-regulatory principles and practice.

The growth of voluntary Code compliance

3.45   Over the past 15 years, the PCC has developed two complementary procedures for the resolution of complaints. Some are resolved by means of informal conciliation and others go all the way to a formal adjudication. Cases that go all the way to adjudication do so either because there are prima facie grounds for believing that the breach is potentially so serious than an informal apology, published letter or voluntary correction would not be a sufficient remedy or because the editors concerned are convinced that they have not breached the Code and that a formal adjudication will vindicate them.

3.46   When the PCC started work in 1991, its relations with many editors were highly confrontational. Every complaint was the subject of prolonged negotiation and dispute. With the passage of time, editors have become much more willing to make voluntary corrections and apologies for breaches of the Code. The great majority of all complaints investigated are now resolved in this way to the satisfaction of the complainants.

3.47   In cases of complaint where editors are convinced that they have *not* breached the Code, they will always put up a vigorous defence of their position and invest much time and effort in doing so. They would not respond in this way if they did not care about having to publish a critical adjudication against themselves. All the evidence suggests that they care very much. Similarly, editors are prepared to offer prompt corrections when shown to be necessary because they are firmly committed to upholding the provisions of their Code.

3.48   Very few complainants want financial compensation or financial sanctions imposed on offending newspapers. Few, if any, successful complainants go on to seek further redress in the courts, if only because they know that the legal option can be expensive and take months or years to be concluded. What most complainants want is a prompt apology, a correction or an opportunity to reply. Conciliation and voluntary compliance on the part of editors makes it much easier to provide a service that is free, fair and swift in its conduct of business. The growth of a culture of voluntary compliance on the part of editors has made it possible to provide such a service. In 2008, the average time taken in dealing with all complaints on which formal rulings were made under the Code was 36 days.

3.49   Freedom of expression has been protected and the press has come to exercise that freedom with greater responsibility. Most importantly, serious breaches of the Code occur far less frequently than they did in the early years of the PCC.

Responding to change and updating the Code

3.50   The Code of Practice has been kept under continuous review by the Code Committee in close consultation with the PCC. Some revisions have been made in response to deficiencies and gaps exposed in the process of adjudicating complaints. Others were made in response to new legislation or in order to obviate the need for further legislation. The annual reviews are widely publicised by the Editors' Code Committee and members of the public as well as special interest groups are invited to submit comments and recommendations.

3.51   The first comprehensive review of the Code was undertaken in 1997, shortly after the death of Diana, Princess of Wales. Some of the changes in the Code requirements were made in anticipation of the imminent incorporation of the European Convention for the Protection of Human Rights and Fundamental Freedoms (ECHR) into UK law.

3.52   The clause on harassment was rewritten in order to ban the obtaining of information or pictures by means of persistent pursuit. Digital manipulations of photographs with intent to mislead were also banned. The definitions of privacy and private places were clarified and broadened. The protection of children's privacy rights was extended beyond the age of 16 to cover the whole period during which they were at school. Payments to children, their parents or guardians for any information relating to their own welfare or that of any other children were prohibited unless they could be shown to be in the child's interests. Editors were required to provide a justification for any information they published about the private lives of children other than the fame, notoriety or position of their parents or guardians.

3.53   The decision to incorporate the provisions of the ECHR and other EU directives into UK law made it all the more necessary for the PCC to develop a closer working relationship with the Government. At the time when the Human Rights Bill came before Parliament, the PCC and the industry were greatly concerned about its potentially damaging impact on the right to freedom of expression. The Government listened to these concerns and agreed to amend the legislation by introducing a new s 12, which required the courts to show 'particular regard' to the right to freedom of expression in proceedings that related to 'journalistic, literary or artistic material'. The courts were also required to take account of the extent to which such material was already in the public domain, whether its publication would be in the public interest as well as the provisions of 'any relevant privacy code'. The PCC's Code of Practice would be designated as such a code for the purposes of the Act.

3.54   A similar amendment was made to the Data Protection Bill in its passage through Parliament. In its original form the Bill would have classified as private information such large amounts of data that were not intrinsically private in nature. As such, the Act would have posed a substantial threat to press freedom. After some months of negotiation the Government agreed to an amendment which struck a more equitable balance between reconciling the rights and obligations of newspapers and magazines to report on matters of public interest with the privacy rights of individual citizens. The amendment allowed editors to advance a public interest defence when faced with an action by the Data Protection Commission on the grounds that what they had published complied with a Code of Practice 'designated' by Parliament for the purposes of the Data Protection Act 1998 and that the information had been obtained by 'fair and lawful means'. This was the first time that the PCC's Code had been 'designated' in this way.

3.55   In 1999, a new subclause was added to the Code's public interest statement which recognised that there was 'a public interest in freedom of expression itself', in order to keep the requirements of the Code in line with those of the HRA 1998.

3.56   The PCC also successfully negotiated a change in the provisions of the Financial Services and Markets Act 2000 during its passage through Parliament when the Government agreed to exclude financial journalists from the provisions of the Act if they were subject to and conformed with the requirements of the Code of Practice. The PCC subsequently published a Best Practice Note of Guidance on financial journalism after consultations with the industry. In this respect, it is worth noting that the Code's requirements on financial journalism have remained unchanged since 1991. The only serious breach occurred in 1999 when the PCC launched its own investigation into a share-tipping scandal.[23]

3.57   The PCC's success in negotiating amendments to the provisions of these three statutes during their passage through Parliament demonstrated the growth of the British Government's confidence in the effectiveness of the voluntary Code of Practice and of the PCC in its administration of the Code. Two years later, the PCC was similarly successful in persuading the Committee of European Securities Regulators (CESR) to

---

[23]   Report No 53, January–March 2001, at p 5; Report No 50, April–June 2000.

amend the provisions of the EU Directive on Market Abuse[24] so that no changes to the Code would be required when it was implemented in the UK.

The House of Commons Culture, Media and Sport Committee Review 2003

3.58   Sir Christopher Meyer was appointed Chairman of the PCC in 2003, shortly after the launch of a major inquiry into privacy and media intrusion by the Culture, Media and Sport Committee of the House of Commons. This was the first such inquiry since the second Calcutt review and the Report of the National Heritage Committee in 1993.

3.59   The Committee had started its inquiry in December 2002. The PCC was prepared for a hostile reception. It was well aware that some members of the Committee believed, like the late Sir David Calcutt, that the PCC was, in essence, a body 'devised by the industry and which was over favourable to the industry'. They wanted a new law of privacy and a new kind of PCC invested with powers to impose fines on publications that breached the Code and to be vigorously proactive in starting its own investigations into reports of unethical press conduct.

3.60   The PCC was faced with the task of convincing the Committee that, over the previous decade, it had succeeded in raising standards of press conduct, that the Code of Practice was being upheld by the industry and that the great majority of complaints were being swiftly and effectively resolved to the satisfaction of ordinary people as well as celebrities and other high-profile public figures.

3.61   When the Committee reported early in 2003,[25] it made a number of proposals for enhancing the effectiveness of the PCC's work, but its overall conclusions were that standards of press behaviour and the performance of the PCC had improved over the preceding decade. It went on to acknowledge that the PCC had the confidence of the industry and its jurisprudence on privacy was more developed than that of any other regulator. It also noted that most of the investigated complaints were resolved swiftly without having to resort to formal adjudication The Committee did, however, set out a case for considering the introduction of a privacy law.[26]

3.62   The Government's response to the idea of privacy law was that more legislation of this kind 'is not only unnecessary but undesirable'. It noted that the provisions of the HRA 1998, and in particular those of s 12, were designed to ensure that the right balance was struck between freedom of expression and the right to privacy. It went on to state that 'the weighing of competing rights in individual cases is the quintessential task of the courts ... Parliament should only intervene if there were signs that the courts are systematically striking the wrong balance; we believe there are no such signs'. Resolving disputes on a case-by-case basis was preferable to legislation that attempted

---

[24]   Council Directive 2003/6/EC
[25]   Department for Culture, Culture, Media and Sport Committee *Privacy and Media intrusion. Fifth Report of Session 2002–2003. Vol 1*, HC 458-1 (TSO, 2003).
[26]   Ibid, at para 111 and pp 10, 20–21 and 39.

to 'cover all events'. It also noted with approval that the PCC took careful account of the claims of the public interest in 'weighing the right to privacy against the freedom of the press' in its adjudications.[27]

3.63   The Committee did not favour a system of prior restraint but it did recommend that the PCC should set up 'a dedicated pre-publication team to handle enquiries from the public and liaison with the relevant editor on matters raised'. The Government thought that the advice already on offer to editors was sufficient to meet the need.[28] The Committee made numerous other procedural recommendations. Those which were endorsed by the Government were swiftly implemented by the PCC.

The PCC's response – 'permanent evolution'

3.64   In response to these recommendations Sir Christopher Meyer outlined the components of a forward looking policy of permanent evolution directed towards maintaining and enhancing still further the quality of the PCC's services to the public and its national profile as a regulatory body.

3.65   In order to reinforce the PCC's manifest independence as a regulatory body, the majority of lay members over press members was raised to a ratio of 10:7 and their appointment made open to public competition. The PCC's handling of complaints was made subject to the scrutiny of an external Charter Compliance Panel and an independent Charter Commissioner. The Panel now scrutinises all aspects of the PCC's handling of complaints, reviews as many complaints files as it deems necessary and publishes an annual report with advice on how customer service might be improved. The Charter Commissioner provides dissatisfied complainants with an opportunity to have the PCC's handling of their complaints reviewed by an independent assessor.

3.66   New procedures were introduced in order to keep the Code of Practice up to date and effective as an evolving document. The Code Committee now undertakes an annual 'audit' of the Code's provisions and publishes a handbook designed to assist editors in their interpretation of the Code. *The Editors' Codebook*, written by Ian Beales, the Code Committee's Secretary, was published in 2005 and was followed by a revised, updated edition in 2009.[29]

3.67   The PCC launched a new ongoing programme of Open Day meetings throughout the UK. Members of the public, local politicians and editors were invited to meet a panel of Commissioners and staff members in question and answer sessions focused on their local circumstances and interests. The first such meeting took place in Manchester in November 2003 and since then the programme has proved to be highly successful in raising public awareness of the PCC's services.

3.68   In 2004, the Code Committee completed and published another review of the Code's remit and requirements. It incorporated the term 'gender' into the categories covered by the discrimination clause in order to make its requirements consistent with those of a new Gender Recognition Act 2004. The clauses on harassment, intrusion into grief and shock, the protection of children and access to hospitals were clarified and

---

[27]   Department for Culture, Media and Sport, *Privacy and Media Intrusion: The Government's Response to the Fifth Report of the Culture, Media and Sport Select Committee on 'Privacy and Media Intrusion'*, HC 458-1, Cm 5985 (2003), at paras 2.3–2.6, pp 2–3.

[28]   Ibid, at para 4.5, p 5.

[29]   I Beales *The Editors' Codebook* (Press Standards Board of Finance, revised 2nd edn, 2009).

made stricter. The newly revised Code also stipulated that editors must include a headline reference to the PCC when publishing its critical adjudications.

3.69 By 2005, all the recommendations of the Select Committee that had been endorsed by the Government had been fully implemented. Meanwhile, the PCC was reviewing its procedures for dealing with complaints about privacy intrusion and the use of intrusive photography following the successful actions brought by Princess Caroline von Hannover and Ms Naomi Campbell in 2004.[30]

3.70 In 2006, Sir Christopher Meyer started his second term as Chairman by setting out the PCC's Policy agenda for the next 3 years. He began by noting that 'the campaign in some quarters to replace self-regulation with something else has, for the most part, gone quiet'. He went on to add that 'this cannot be taken for granted … One really contentious, high profile case is all it takes to ignite new fires of controversy and breathe new life into those who, for example, would like to replace us with a statutory body'. The need to be continuously watchful in such matters also meant 'keeping an eye on the European Commission in Brussels in case the regulating reflex should start to threaten press self-regulation through the backdoor'.

3.71 As for the policy agenda, the core mission would continue to be the delivery of 'effective, speedy and cost-free solutions to complaints with a minimum of fuss' and to 'convince people that this is happening'. At the same time the PCC had to anticipate and respond to the 'phenomenon of media convergence … the challenge of podcasting, the transmission of audio-visual material on publications' websites and so on'.[31]

3.72 In the event, 2006 turned out to be a year of signs and portents and highly significant developments in European and UK privacy jurisprudence. The pace of change had been set by the House of Lords judgment in the case of *Campbell v MGN* and that of the European Court in the case of *Von Hannover v Germany* in 2004. It gathered moment through a succession of rulings handed down in actions brought by Michael Douglas and Catherine Zeta Jones, Loreena McKennitt and an unnamed sports celebrity. Prince Charles brought a successful action for breach of confidence and copyright against Associated Newspapers Limited following its unauthorised publication of extracts taken from his private diaries.

3.73 In January 2007, the royal editor for the *News of the World*, Clive Goodman, and his freelance investigator, Glenn Mulcaire, were tried and received custodial sentences for conspiracy to intercept communications without legal authority. In 2006 and 2007, the Information Commissioner published two reports based on the findings of Operation Motorman, an investigation undertaken by his office into apparent offences committed under the data protection laws involving 32 publications and 305 journalists.[32] In January 2007, the media's harassment of Ms Kate Middleton, the girlfriend of HRH Prince William, gave rise to widespread public indignation and concern.

---

[30]   *Von Hannover v Germany*, App No 59320/00 (2005) 40 EHRR 1; *Campbell v MGN Limited* [2004] UKHL 22.

[31]   PCC *Annual Review 2005* at pp 1–2.

[32]   *What price privacy?*, HC 1056 (TSO, 2006); *What price privacy now?*, HC 36 (TSO, 2007).

The House of Commons Culture, Media and Sport Committee Review 2007

3.74 A few weeks later, the House of Commons Select Committee decided to undertake a third review of the effectiveness of press self-regulation in the aftermath of these events. As the PCC prepared its memorandum for submission to the Committee, there was much speculation that either the Goodman scandal or the harassment of Ms Middleton would prove to be the kind of 'really contentious high profile case' that would 'ignite new fire of controversy' about the future of self-regulation.

3.75 In his evidence to the Committee, the Information Commissioner drew attention to his claim that over 30 publications had allowed their journalists to pay sums of money to a private investigator, Stephen Whittamore, in return for illegally obtained personal information about members of the Royal family and other public figures. He called on the PCC and the industry to 'take a much stronger line to tackle any involvement by the press' in this illegal trade. To this end, he recommended that the Data Protection Act 1998 rules on paying for confidential information should be incorporated into the Editors' Code of Practice. He also proposed that the penalty for breaching the Act should be increased to 2 years' imprisonment, with no exemptions for journalists.

3.76 During the course of the Committee's hearings, Les Hinton, who was then the Executive Chairman of News International, was asked: 'You carried out a full, rigorous internal inquiry, and you are absolutely convinced that Clive Goodman was the only person who knew what was going on?'. Mr Hinton replied: 'Yes, we have and I believe he was the only person, but that investigation [at the *News of the World*], under the new editor, continues.'[33]

3.77 In its submission to the Committee, the PCC reiterated its condemnation of telephone tapping and went on to reaffirm its position that 'offering money for confidential information, directly or indirectly through third parties may be illegal and that journalists must have regard to the terms of the Data Protection Act'.[34]

3.78 The PCC, however, also thought that it was vitally important to maintain a clear distinction between its own responsibilities and those of the law enforcement authorities. If this distinction became blurred the PCC would not be able to 'investigate overlapping matters satisfactorily' because publications would be very reluctant 'to volunteer information if there was a danger of further investigation by a legal authority which might put one of their journalists in prison'.[35]

3.79 Increasing the penalties would have a 'chilling effect' on legitimate investigative journalism and send out a reassuring signal to those repressive regimes throughout the world that 'make a regular practice of jailing journalists who ask uncomfortable questions'.[36]

3.80 The PCC was not convinced that greater penalties were called for. Since the Information Commissioner's evidence was several years old it was not possible to test

---

[33] Department of Culture, Media and Sport Committee ('HC Committee') *Self-Regulation of the Press, Seventh Report of Session 2006–07*, HC 375 (TSO, 2007), EF 40 Q 96.

[34] Ibid, EV 61, at para 121.

[35] Ibid, EV 61-2, at para 125.

[36] Ibid, EV 62, at para 128.

whether the existing penalties were a sufficient deterrent – or to establish whether the behaviour of the journalists cited in his second report was illegal or might have been justified on grounds of public interest.

3.81　The Editors' Code Committee, for its part, pointed out that incorporating the Data Protection rules into the Code could not possibly work because the PCC 'has no vested legal standing or empowerment'. The Code and the law were 'complementary' and 'the systems work whilst the two cultures remain distinct. Problems arise if they become enmeshed'. If this were to happen, the ethos of voluntary Code compliance 'would be threatened and its benefits lost'. Incorporating the language of the law into the Code would mean that 'a breach of the Code would automatically be a breach of the law' and expose journalists to the risk of 'subsequent prosecution in the Criminal courts, a form of double jeopardy'.[37] As for the possibility of imposing prison sentences, the Society of Editors pointed out that this could have a dramatic limiting effect on legitimate journalistic investigation and that, in itself, would not be in the public interest.[38]

3.82　Ms Middleton's harassment started on 9 January 2007 after a wave of media speculation that an announcement of her engagement to Prince William was imminent. A scrum of journalists, paparazzi and amateur photographers camped outside her flat and pursued her down the street whenever she went out.

3.83　The Committee asked the PCC why it had been so slow in acting to protect Ms Middleton. The PCC explained it could not issue 'desist notices' or intervene in any other way without the prior consent of the people affected. Throughout Ms Middleton's ordeal, it had been in continuous contact with her solicitors. At the start of the harassment, News International had announced that it would not buy any photographs taken by paparazzi. Some, but not all, publishers followed this lead. On 12 January, at the request of Ms Middleton's solicitors, the PCC sent a letter to all editors warning them that if they persisted in using pictures supplied by the paparazzi a formal complaint would be submitted to the PCC. Shortly afterwards, the media scrum dispersed and the harassment ceased.

3.84　In March 2007, Ms Middleton's solicitors lodged a formal complaint against the *Daily Mirror* after it had published a photograph of her walking along the street. The next day, the editor published a formal apology, explaining that the picture was taken by a freelance photographer 'in circumstances where we were later told she felt harassed. We got it wrong and we sincerely regret that'.[39]

3.85　The publication of the Culture, Media and Sport Committee's Report in July 2007 marked a significant turning point in the history of the PCC. In the case of Clive Goodman, the Committee concluded that the events leading to this conviction 'amounted to one of the most serious breaches of the Code uncovered in recent times'. It was left in:

> '… no doubt that the Editor of the *News of the World* was right that he had no choice but to resign. By doing so, a clear message has been sent that breaches of this kind cannot be tolerated and that editors must accept final responsibility for what happens on their watch.'

---

[37]　Ibid, Evidence, at p 26, paras 3.1–3.7.
[38]　Ibid, Evidence, at p 31, para 3.
[39]　PCC Report No 75, April–September 2007 at p 35.

3.86   The Committee welcomed the subsequent remedial actions taken by the *News of the World* in response to the recommendations on newsgathering methods issued in May 2007 by the PCC. It expected that these recommendations would be 'adopted as a matter of course by all newspapers and magazines publishers'.[40]

3.87   In the aftermath of the Goodman trial, the PCC carried out its own inquiry into the circumstances that gave rise to such a very serious breach of the Code. It also undertook a comprehensive review of current practices throughout the industry. All publishers were asked to review their training programmes, with special reference to their 'subterfuge protocols'. They also agreed to review their audit controls on all cash payments and to ensure that they were rigorously enforced.

3.88   The list of requirements in the PCC's guidance circular on the use of subterfuge and newsgathering methods included the following:

- contracts between newspapers and magazines and external contributors should contain an explicit requirement to abide by the Code of Practice;

- a similar reference to abide by the Data Protection Act 1998 should be included in contracts of employment for staff members and external contributors;

- although contractual compliance with the Code for staff journalists was widespread, it should without delay become universal throughout the industry;

- publications should review internal practice to ensure that they have an effective and fully understood 'subterfuge protocol' for staff journalists. This should include who should be consulted for advice about whether the public interest is sufficient to justify subterfuge;

- there should be regular training and briefing on developments in privacy cases and compliance with the law; and

- there should be rigorous audit controls for cash payments where such payments are unavoidable.

3.89   The Committee noted that the PCC and the Code Committee had rejected the Information Commissioner's proposal that the Code 'should be amended so that it would specify that it was unacceptable either to obtain information about an individual's private life without their consent by payment to a third party or by impersonation or subterfuge, or to pay an intermediary to supply any information which was, or which might have been, obtained by such means'. The Committee, nevertheless, accepted an alternative form of wording in clause 10 of the Code which made it explicit that 'illegal trading in confidential information and engaging in misrepresentation or subterfuge via agents on intermediaries' was prohibited under the Code.[41]

---

[40]   HC Committee (2007), fn 34 above, at pp 13–14.
[41]   HC Committee (2007), fn 34 above, at pp 17–18.

3.90   The PCC has always made it clear that journalists must act within the law when they resort to subterfuge and 'cannot use undercover means for speculative "fishing expeditions" to look for information when there are no prima facie grounds for doing so'.[42]

3.91   In the past, the PCC has received very few complaints involving the use of clandestine devices and resort to subterfuge. In the case of the Goodman scandal, the Code was overtaken not by a change in the law, but by a singular event that neither a statutory nor a self-regulatory system could have anticipated. Whether or not it was symptomatic of a more widespread problem throughout the industry remained open to debate, but one such scandal was one too many. The necessary steps had been taken to ensure that it did not happen again.

3.92   The remit of the Code was extended to include 'both printed and on-line versions of publications'. Clause 10 was amended and now explicitly precludes the 'accessing' of 'digitally-held private information without consent' unless it be justified in the public interest. The subclause which stated that 'engaging in misrepresentation or subterfuge can generally be justified only in the public interest, and then only when the material cannot be obtained by other means' was amended to include 'agents or intermediaries' in its remit.

3.93   On the issue of sanctions, the Committee took the view that 'sufficient safeguards (existed) to protect legitimate investigative journalism and (did) not believe that the introduction of custodial sentences for offences under section 55 of the Data Protection Act 1998 would have the chilling effect claimed by the press'. It therefore supported 'the decision of the DCA, and subsequently the Ministry of Justice to introduce the necessary legislation'.[43] (After consultations with the industry, the Government decided that it would keep custodial sentences in the new legislation but not to implement this provision, unless the Minister of Justice identified a need to do so at some future time – and then only after further consultations.)

3.94   In the case of Ms Middleton, the Committee concluded that 'the PCC appeared to have waited for a complaint to materialise. It could and should have intervened sooner'. It went on, however, to 'recognise the force of the argument that an individual who seeks the protection of the PCC should make a formal complaint'.[44]

3.95   Although the issues raised following the case of Clive Goodman and that of Kate Middleton undoubtedly added up to 'really contentious, high profile' examples of serious press misconduct, they were not deemed sufficient for the Committee to call the future of the PCC into question or to reopen the debate about the need for a new law of privacy.

3.96   The Committee concluded that:[45]

'... to draft a law defining a right to privacy which is both specific in its guidance but also flexible enough to apply fairly to each case which would be tested against it could be almost

---

[42]   House of Commons (2006–2007) fn 34 above, at para 130.
[43]   HC Committee (2007), n 34 above, at p 20.
[44]   Ibid, at pp 23–24.
[45]   Ibid, at p 26.

impossible. Many people would not want to seek redress through the law, for reasons of cost and risk. In any case, we are not persuaded that there is significant support for a privacy law'.

3.97   On the question as to whether press regulation should be put on a statutory footing, the Committee stated that this would:[46]

> '... represent a very dangerous interference with the freedom of the press. We continue to believe that statutory regulation of the press is a hallmark of authoritarianism and risks undermining democracy. We recommend that self-regulation should be retained for the press, while recognizing that it must be seen to be effective if calls for statutory intervention are to be resisted.'

3.98   The Committee did not find 'all the PCC's arguments against the introduction of fines convincing', but it accepted that 'giving the PCC powers to impose fines would risk changing the nature of the organization and might need statutory backing to make the power enforceable'. And it went on to say that 'this would be a major step which we would not recommend without a broader examination of the subject'.[47]

3.99   The Committee recognised the advantages of resolving complaints through conciliation rather than proceeding to formal adjudications in the great majority of cases. It went on, however, to say that 'it would be helpful to publish details of the resolution if the complainant so wishes. We believe that such a practice would enhance the public's view of the effectiveness of the PCC and would strengthen the understanding by the press and by the public of the principles which underline the Commissions' work'. In this respect the Committee cogently noted that when Ms Middleton's complaint against the *Daily Mirror* was settled through conciliation, 'the Commission published no adjudication and the fact that there was a breach of the Code has not, therefore, received the exposure which we believe it deserves'.[48]

3.100   The Committee noted, with approval, the wide range of pre-publication and preventive activities that the PCC was undertaking. Offers of assistance to individuals and organisations at the centre of high-profile stories, 'liaising before publication between newspapers and those in the news, with the result that stories may be altered for publication or even not appear' were cited as examples of 'some of the most valuable work undertaken by the Commission'.[49]

3.101   The key roles played by the Charter Commissioner and the Charter Compliance Panel in reviewing complaints about the PCC's procedures and rulings were identified as one of the 'strengths' of the self-regulatory system.

3.102   The Committee also said that 'it was right for the PCC to extend its remit to cover editorial audio and visual contents on newspaper websites and' noted with approval the improvements it had made to its own website.[50]

3.103   Finally, the Committee acknowledged the progress the PCC had made in gaining 'the trust and respect of the industry', as well as the 'high level of satisfaction amongst

---

46   Ibid, at p 26.
47   Ibid, at p 33.
48   Ibid, at p 32.
49   Ibid, at p 29.
50   Ibid, at pp 28–29.

complaints with the PCC's handling of their complaints …'. It also took note of 'criticisms that the PCC applies the Code of Practice with far too light a touch … that it should do more to enforce the Code and take editors to task for breaches of the Code …' and be 'more willing to accept third-party complaints'.[51]

Some 'contentious' cases and other recent developments

3.104 In 2006, Sir Christopher Meyer warned that 'the campaign in some quarters to replace self-regulation with something else has, for the most part gone quiet'. Under normal circumstances, the Culture, Media and Sport Committee's recommendation that 'self-regulation should be retained for the press' might have marked a near total, if temporary, suspension of that campaign.

3.105 Sir Christopher, however, had also warned the newspaper industry that 'one really contentious high profile case is all it takes to ignite new fires of controversy and breathe new life into those who, for example, would like to replace us with a statutory body'.[52]

3.106 As it happened, the first in what was to become a succession of 'really contentious high profile' cases made headline news in May 2007, a few weeks before the Committee published its Report. It concerned the disappearance of the 6-year old daughter of Gerry and Kate McCann from their holiday home in Portugal whilst they were dining with friends in a nearby villa.

3.107 Shortly after the local police began their search, the distraught couple appealed to the media for help in finding their daughter, Madeleine. Although the McCanns had never previously been in the public eye, they now found themselves facing the same dilemma that all celebrities confront in dealing with the media – they needed publicity but the media wanted a steady flow of newsworthy stories in return. Since the police were making no progress whatever in their search for Madeleine, the McCanns had no newsworthy stories about her disappearance to offer the media.

3.108 After the McCanns were named by the Portuguese police as 'arguidos', or 'official suspects', they themselves became the focus of a continuous flow of highly speculative and distressing stories about their possible role in their daughter's disappearance. A local British resident, Robert Murat, also became a focus of intensive media speculation after he was named as an 'arguido', as were two of his acquaintances after a number of British newspapers named them as suspects.

3.109 As the incidence of speculative and potentially libellous stories gathered momentum over the following weeks, the McCanns made repeated requests to the media to be left alone so that they could concentrate on searching for their daughter. Their appeals went largely unheeded. The Express Newspaper titles were singularly unremitting in the frequency with which they published their scurrilous articles. In desperation, the McCanns, Mr Murat and his two acquaintances, Mr Serge Malinka and Ms Michaela Walczuch, decided to seek redress in the courts.

3.110 In March 2008, the McCanns were awarded £550,000 in damages plus costs against the Express Newspaper titles for publishing over 100 'seriously damaging' stories

---

[51]   Ibid, at pp 29–30.
[52]   PCC (2005), n 31 above, at pp 1–2.

about them. The stories included totally unfounded allegations that they were responsible for their daughter's death, engaged in wife-swapping and had sold their daughter to child traffickers.

3.111 After the settlements, an unnamed *Express* reporter told *The Guardian* that it had become 'received wisdom' in their newspapers that 'there would be a story about Madeleine on the front page, whether or not there had been any development'. As he put it: 'To suggest there was no story would be seen as absolute heresy.'[53] Express Newspapers was also required to publish an unqualified apology.

3.112 In July 2008, Mr Murat and his two co-complainants were awarded £800,000 damages plus costs against 11 British newspapers, including three *Express* titles, for publishing nearly 100 'seriously defamatory stories', some of which had wrongly implicated them in Madeleine's disappearance. The newspapers were also ordered to publish unqualified apologies.

3.113 After the trial, Max Clifford – who had acted throughout as the Murat family's unpaid adviser – suggested that Mr Murat should have received a more substantial settlement because the 11 newspapers had been 'far more vicious to him than they were to the McCanns'.[54]

3.114 The PCC received only one complaint on behalf of the McCanns, which was subsequently withdrawn, and there were surprisingly few complaints from third parties urging it to intervene. Roy Greenslade pressed the PCC to agree 'that enough is enough on this matter and decide to take it up. For once it might be justified to entertain a third party complaint. And here it is'.[55]

3.115 The PCC had been proactive in other ways from the start by establishing contact with the British Embassy in Lisbon 2 days after Madeleine's disappearance. In January 2008, Sir Christopher met the McCanns in London and explained how the PCC could help if asked to do so. This offer was renewed when they met for a second time in February. By then, the McCanns were already in the process of bringing their action for defamation against Express Newspapers.

3.116 Towards the end of his term as chairman, Sir Christopher was asked whether he thought that 'the widespread reporting of unproven allegations that the parents of Madeleine McCann were involved in her disappearance' constituted 'a failure for the PCC'. His reply was that 'the McCanns had to make a decision over whether to go to us or the courts, and in the end they did both. There's a time for the courts and a time for the PCC. We protected the family and the children from the media circus on their return to the UK – defamation and libel are matters for the courts'.[56]

3.117 The PCC stayed in touch with the McCanns throughout their ordeal. Launching an investigation on the basis of a third party complaint would have served no useful purpose and, given the circumstances of this tragic case, it is not surprising that the McCanns decided to bring an action for libel in order to remedy a surfeit of libels.

---

53   Owen Gibson 'Newspapers apologise to McCanns', *The Guardian*, 20 March 2008, at p 9.
54   Patrick Smith 'Furious lawyer attacks tabloids pack-dog mentality over stories', *Press Gazette*, 25 July 2008, at p 7.
55   *Guardian Unlimited Blogs* (2008), http://blogs.guardian.co.uk/greensalde.
56   'Exit interview. So long to: Sir Christopher Meyer, chairman of the PCC', *Press Gazette*, May 2009, at p 7.

3.118 Whilst the McCann and Murat families were contending with the press and preparing to seek redress in the courts, another chapter was opening in the story of the phone-tapping scandal.[57] One of its victims – Gordon Taylor, the Chief Executive of the Professional Footballers' Association – decided to sue the *News of the World* for its involvement in the unlawful interception of messages left on his mobile phone.

3.119 Mr Taylor's lawyers made a successful application for a court order requiring the Information Commissioner to disclose details of the number of journalists who had been involved in the newsgathering methods that breached the data protection laws. The dossier handed over listed 27 *News of the World* and four *Sun* journalists.

3.120 Mr Taylor's action was settled out of court on a confidential basis in July 2008 – the same month in which Mr Max Mosley won his action against the *News of the World* for breach of confidence and/or the unauthorised disclosure of personal information in violation of his rights under Art 8 of the ECHR.[58]

3.121 At the time, *Mosley v NGN Ltd* was the latest in a succession of successful privacy actions brought by celebrities and other public figures after the incorporation of the ECHR into UK law and in the wake of the judgments delivered in *Von Hannover v Germany*[59] and *Campbell v MGN Ltd*.[60]

3.122 The debate continues about the significance of these judgments and those delivered in *McKennitt v Ash*,[61] *CC v AB*,[62] *HRH Prince of Wales v Associated Newspapers Ltd*[63] and *Murray v Big Pictures Limited*.[64] Some legal and media commentators welcomed them as indicators that the courts were, at last, beginning to strike a more equitable balance in protecting the right to privacy under Art 8 against the right to freedom of expression under Art 10.

3.123 Others were in no doubt that the UK courts in general were interpreting and applying the HRA 1998 in ways that posed a serious threat to freedom of expression, the conduct of responsible investigative journalism and the work of the self-regulatory system. The courts, in effect, were incrementally introducing a law of privacy 'through the backdoor' through a succession of piecemeal judgments, mostly in cases where the public interest was not strongly engaged. In addition, these developments were taking place at a time when conditional fee arrangements were raising the costs of defending privacy (and libel) actions to prohibitive levels.

3.124 By the summer of 2008, it had become clear that this succession of 'contentions high profile cases' was raising issues of such importance that they would have to be reviewed by the Culture, Media and Sport Committee. In November 2008, the Committee announced that it would be undertaking a wide-ranging inquiry into 'press standards, privacy and libel'. It would also examine any other 'areas of interest' that were raised during the course of its inquiry.[65]

---

[57]   See **3.73** above.
[58]   *Mosley v NGN Ltd* [2008] EWHC 1777 (QB).
[59]   (2004) 40 EHRR 1.
[60]   [2004] UKHL 22.
[61]   2005] EWHC 3003 (QB).
[62]   [2007] EMLR 11.
[63]   [2006] EWCA Civ 1776.
[64]   [2008] EWCA Civ 446.
[65]   Culture, Media and Sport Committee *Committee Announcement* No 67 (2008).

3.125 One such matter of considerable interest was raised in July 2009 when articles by Nick Davies appeared in *The Guardian* alleging that, in its confidential settlement of the action brought against it by Gordon Taylor, the *News of the World* had paid him £700,000 in damages and costs on the condition that he agreed not to speak about the case in future. Davies also claimed that the *News of the World* had 'persuaded the court to seal the file on Taylor's case to prevent all public access, even though it contained prima facie evidence of criminal activity'. A further £300,000 had been paid to 'at least two other football figures', subject to the same confidentiality clauses.[66]

3.126 In a second article, Davies claimed that the full police files showed that 'several thousand public figures were targeted' by the News Corp investigators 'during one month in 2006'.[67]

3.127 As this book went to press at the end of July 2009, Davies had already appeared before the Culture, Media and Sport Committee and defended his allegations. The PCC had started its own inquiry into the issues that they raised.

3.128 The *News of the World* had published a rebuttal in which it said that 'we can state with confidence' that it had found no evidence that any of its journalists had accessed voice-mails or used the services of third parties for such purposes. It went on to claim that *The Guardian*'s reporting in this matter had been 'inaccurate, selective and misleading'.

3.129 In their evidence to the Committee, the editor and former editor of the *News of the World*, Colin Meyer and Andy Coulson, its former managing editor, Stuart Kuttner, and the head of News Corp's legal department, Tom Crone, 'all testified that, to the best of their knowledge, Goodman and Muclaire were the only people connected to the *News of the World* involved in phone-hacking'.[68]

CONCLUSION

3.130 As one contentious issue after another comes helter-skelter onto the agenda of the Culture, Media and Sport Committee it becomes more difficult to second-guess how its inquiry will develop and what its conclusions will be. The first and second Calcutt Committees focused their attention on three key issues – whether the self-regulatory system should be retained or replaced by a statutory body, whether we should have a privacy law and whether more stringent forms of prior restraint should be imposed on methods of newsgathering material likely to constitute unjustifiable intrusions into peoples' privacy.

3.131 What has changed since then is the broader political and legal context in which the courts and the PCC balance the rights to privacy and freedom of expression against each other, as well as the claims of the public interest, when making their rulings in cases where these rights and claims are engaged. Since the incorporation of the ECHR into the HRA 1998, the courts and the PCC have had to take careful account of ongoing developments in the jurisprudence of Arts 8 and 10 of the ECHR.

---

[66] Nick Davies 'Revealed: Murdoch's $1m bill for hiding dirty tricks', *The Guardian*, 9 July 2009, at pp 1–2.
[67] Nick Davies 'Trial of hacking and deceit under host of Tory PR Chief', *The Guardian*, 9 July 2009, at pp 6–7.
[68] 'Fighting in the Street', *Press Gazette*, August 2009, at pp 8–9.

3.132 The list of issues that the Committee will review in its inquiry is not set out in any particular order of priority, but a useful distinction can be drawn between those which raise questions of compatibility between the development of European and UK jurisprudence and those which are primarily matters of domestic concern and discretion.

3.133 Such distinctions can seldom be drawn along clear-cut institutional lines. The PCC's rulings, and the Code of Practice, for example, must be compatible with the requirement of both European and UK law. The PCC, itself, however, is formally accountable for its operational effectiveness only to the UK Parliament, its Charter Commissioner and the industry it regulates. The ultimate decision as to whether the British press should be subject to statutory or self-regulation rests exclusively with the UK Parliament.

3.134 Two issues of European provenance stand out from the others listed in the Committee's review programme. It invites submissions from interested parties on 'what effect the European Convention on Human Rights has had on the courts' views on the right to privacy as against press freedom' and 'whether, in the light of recent court rulings, the balance between press freedom and personal privacy is the right one'.

3.135 Some legal and media commentators agree with Glasser that the overall effect of these recent court rulings has been towards 'extending the concept of privacy, and explicitly downgrading the greater importance which has traditionally been accorded to freedom of expression in this country'.[69] Other commentators agree about the direction of the trend but welcome it as a sign that the courts are belatedly reaching what they see as more equitable outcomes in balancing the right to privacy under Art 8 against the right of freedom of expression under Art 10.

3.136 Opinions also differ regarding the extent to which these recent court rulings have created a new, free-standing law of privacy in all but name, and whether such a law is (or would be) a good or a bad law. Many of the commentators who believe that a general law of privacy is needed take strong exception to the way in which it is being developed incrementally on a case-by-case basis in the courts. Most of these privacy actions are brought by celebrities and other public figures, who are at far greater risk of privacy intrusion than other members of the public.

3.137 A succession of court rulings in such cases over time is likely to establish a level of privacy entitlement that meets the exceptional needs of people who are constantly in the public eye, but exceeds the level required to protect the great majority of citizens and serve the wider public interest.

3.138 Whatever the pros and cons of a privacy law may be, there is also much substance in the argument that the proper place in which they should be debated and resolved is Parliament and not the courts.

3.139 Ideally, the range of that debate – should it ever take place – ought to extend beyond the activities of the media to include those of the state and Parliament itself. In Britain today, it may be argued that government itself poses a greater threat to people's privacy rights than the press.

---

[69]   C Glasser *Recent Developments in Privacy Law*: PCC Paper No 3896 (2007), at p 4.

3.140 As Simon Jenkins recently reminded us, the present Government has 'passed some 14 measures intruding on the privacy of British citizens in the past decade', not only for reasons of national security but for more questionable purposes like health and well-being.[70] Exactly the same point is made by Henry Porter when he writes that, 'what we should understand is that in this vast, bossy, communitarian project, a theft is taking place of a prized possession – privacy, the thing that once defined us'.[71]

3.141 With regard to press standards and the effectiveness of press self-regulation, the Committee invited views on:

> '... why the self-regulatory regime was not use in the McCann case; why the Press Complaints PCC has not invoked its own inquiry, what changes news organizations themselves have made in the light of the case, and whether the successful action against the Daily Express and others for libel in the McCann case indicates a serious weakness with the self-regulatory regimes.'

3.142 The Committee also invited views on 'the interaction between the operation and effect of UK libel laws and press reporting'; whether 'financial penalties for libel or invasion of privacy, applied either by the courts or by a self-regulatory body might be exemplary rather than compensatory'; the 'impact of conditional fee agreements on press freedom; and whether self-regulation needs to be toughened to make it more attractive to those seeking redress'.

3.143 Toughening up the Commissioner's procedures would probably mean requiring the PCC to be more proactive in taking up third-party complaints and launching complaints of its own volition.

3.144 In a recent House of Lords debate on a related matter, Lord Wakeham pointed out that:[72]

> 'First, if a person does not want to complain there is no basis on which the Press Complaints Commission should investigate a complaint, many people would much prefer that the complaint is not gone into. Secondly, if a person decides to go to law over the case, there is also no role for the Press Complaint Commission to intervene.'

3.145 Tougher sanctions would clearly mean investing the PCC with powers to impose and enforce financial penalties. As the Committee itself acknowledged in its 2007 Report, 'giving the PCC powers to enforce fines would risk changing the nature of the organization and might need statutory backing to make the power enforceable'.[73] It would also undermine the whole framework of voluntary Code compliance on the part of editors and publishers that has been developed over many years. As that framework of support was weakened, a wide range of other effective remedies to grievances against the press would be lost.

3.146 The Committee is currently investigating the extent to which the *News of the World* and some other publications were involved in the unlawful interception of voicemail messages and other offences under the data protection laws. It remains to be

---

[70]   Simon Jenkins 'Ministers who justify state snooping might now learn that biters can be bit', *The Guardian*, 10 July 2009, at p 31.
[71]   Henry Porter 'Max Mosley's victory has a hollow ring for the rest of us', *The Observer*, 27 July 2009, at p 31.
[72]   *Hansard*, HL Deb, ser 5, col 1267, 2009.
[73]   HC Committee (2007), n 34 above, at p 33.

seen whether it finds that these practices were widespread and systematic or whether it was a unique event involving a few journalists who were acting without the knowledge and consent of those to whom they were accountable.

3.147 During the course of the Committee's inquiry there may be another opportunity to assess the effects of the ECHR on the development of UK privacy law from a different vantage point. In the wake of his successful action against NGN Ltd,[74] Max Mosley is seeking further redress in the European Court. He believes that UK law provides insufficient protection for people's privacy rights. He wants a new law that will require editors to contact the subjects of their stories before they publish articles or photographs that might intrude on their privacy.

3.148 The first Calcutt Report had something similar in mind when it proposed that the new PCC – once established – 'should be able to restrain publication of material in breach of the code of practice by means of injunctions. No injunction should be granted if the publishers could show that he had a good arguable defence'.[75] The second Calcutt Review proposed that the PCC should be replaced by a statutory tribunal empowered to restrain publications and impose fines.[76]

3.149 Nearly all of Europe's democratic nation-states have two complementary systems of press regulation. People with grievances against the press can seek redress through the courts or through the agencies of self-regulatory press councils. Although voluntary Codes of Practice may never ask less of editors than the law requires they may, in some cases, offer more protection to complainants than the law provides.

3.150 Lord Justice Devlin, a former Lord of Appeal and Chairman of the old Press Council, once wrote that 'the last and the biggest thing to be remembered is that the law is concerned with the minimum and not with the maximum'. He went on to say that:[77]

> '… we all recognise the gap between the moral law and the law of the land. No man is worth much who regulates his conduct with the sole object of escaping punishment, and every worthy society sets for its members standards which are above those of the law'.

3.151 The members of the Editors' Code Committee may have been thinking along the same lines when they included in their Code of Practice the requirement that it must be 'honoured not only to the letter but in the full spirit'.

---

[74]   *Mosley v NGN Ltd* [2008] EWHC 1777 (QB).
[75]   See **3.20**.
[76]   See **3.33** and **3.35**.
[77]   Patrick Devlin *The Enforcement of Morals* (Oxford University Press, 1965), at p 19.

Chapter 4

THE DEVELOPMENT OF PRESS SELF-REGULATION IN EUROPE

PRESS SELF-REGULATION AND THE EUROPEAN CONVENTION

4.1   In recent years the expanding membership of the EU has been complemented by a steady growth in the number of member states with well-established self-regulatory Press Councils. Twenty-one of the 27 member states currently have fully operative Councils or are in the process of establishing one. Ten non-member European states also have self-regulatory Councils.

4.2   Most of these Councils are active members of the Alliance of Independent Press Councils of Europe (AIPCE) which was formed in 1999. AIPCE promotes the growth of press self-regulation throughout Europe and provides a forum for the exchange of views and information on such matters as developments in European media law and procedures for dealing with complaints. Councils must, at all times, ensure that the requirements of their Codes of Practice remain consistent with developments in the jurisprudence of both the European Court of Human Rights (ECtHR) and their own domestic courts.

4.3   The expanding membership of the EU accounts, in large part, for the growth in the number of self-regulatory Councils both within and beyond its frontiers. When countries apply for accession to the Union they are required to provide evidence that they meet three essential preconditions before the negotiations leading up to an accession treaty can begin. They must satisfy the European Commission that they are stable and well-established democracies, governed by the rule of law and with free market economies.

4.4   The standard test that the Commission applies in evaluating the democratic credentials of applicant states is whether, in practice as well as in principle, their political, legal and civic institutions match up to the requirements of the European Convention for the Protection of Human Rights and Fundamental Freedoms (ECHR).

4.5   Articles 8 and 10 of the ECHR have salient significance regarding the rights and responsibilities of a free press and the role of regulatory bodies in ensuring that these responsibilities are fulfilled.

4.6   Article 8 states that:

> '1. Everyone has the right to respect for his private and family life, his home and his correspondence.

2. There shall be no interference by a public authority with the exercise of this right except such as is in accordance with the law and is necessary in a democratic society in the interests of national security, public safety or the economic well-being of the country, for the prevention of disorder or crime, for the protection of health or morals, or for the protection of the rights and freedoms of others.'

4.7   Article 10 states that:

'1. Everyone has the right to freedom of expression. This right shall include freedom to hold opinions and to receive and impart information and ideas without interference by public authority and regardless of frontiers.

2. The exercise of these freedoms, since it carries with it duties and responsibilities, may be subject to such formalities, conditions, restrictions or penalties as are prescribed by law and are necessary in a democratic society, in the interests of national security, territorial integrity or public safety, for the prevention of disorder or crime, for the protection of health or morals, for the protection of rights of others, for the prevention of disclosure of information received in confidence, or for maintaining the authority and impartiality of the judiciary.'

4.8   Neither Article, it should be noted, refers specifically to the media, apart from a passing reference to licensing matters. At the time when the ECHR was being drafted, its authors were primarily concerned with protecting peoples' rights to privacy and freedom of expression from 'interference' by the state through the agencies of its 'public authorities'.

4.9   Both Articles, however, recognise that such 'interferences' should be permitted if and when they are carried out 'in accordance with the law' and are 'necessary in a democratic society'. Most of the Convention rights are qualified in this way and the contingencies covered all relate to considerations of genuine public interest.

4.10   As we have noted, Art 8 makes no specific provisions for protecting the private lives of individuals from the media. Article 10 recognises that the right to freedom of expression 'carries with it duties and responsibilities' including obligations to respect people's right to privacy and their reputations. The enforcement of these responsibilities, however, is left exclusively to the due processes of the law.

4.11   All stable and well-established democracies accept the need to place some limits on the exercise of freedom of expression. Media freedom has always been subject to many legal restraints which, in the UK, include laws of defamation, data protection, copyright, confidence and the Human Rights Act 1998, which incorporated the provisions of the ECHR.

4.12   The challenge that all democratic states confront is how to regulate the freedom of the press in ways that are compatible with the core values of democracy itself and that do not rely exclusively on the agencies of the state.

4.13   A free press is one of the fundamental institutional characteristics of a free and democratic society. You cannot have one without the other. Newspapers and periodicals are public watchdogs. They scrutinise those who hold power in every walk of life. They help voters make informed choices and reach considered opinions. They frequently criticise government policies and the conduct of political office-holders. Left to their own devices and without any form of effective regulation, however, some sectors of the press would undoubtedly abuse their freedom to the detriment of other people's democratic rights, including their right to privacy.

4.14   These are the obvious reasons why some legal restraints on press freedom are necessary in democratic societies. The law, however, works best when it serves as a last rather than a first resort for people seeking redress for grievances against the press. Self-regulatory Press Councils are able to provide an alternative but complementary way of resolving such issues that is easily accessible, swift in the conduct of its business and provided at no cost whatever to the complainants.

4.15   The state itself could become directly involved in regulating the day-to-day activities of news-gathering and publishing, or it could do so indirectly through the agency of a statutory Press Council. All totalitarian societies resort to such stratagems and, invariably, the end result is synonymous with statutory censorship of the printed word or prudential self-censorship on the part of publishers and editors.

4.16   The problem with statutory Press Councils is that they are inevitably seen by press and public alike as agencies of the state, beholden to the government that appoints their members and drafts or oversees their regulatory Codes of Practice. Since newspapers and periodicals are public watchdogs they are often the subject of complaints by government ministers, Members of Parliament and public authorities. In such cases it is difficult for statutory Councils to be perceived as anything other than judges and juries in their own cause.

4.17   For all these reasons: most of the EU member states have opted for the self-regulatory way of dealing with complaints about unethical journalism. The institutional independence of such councils from their governments ensures that their status is compatible with the democratic values and rights embodied in the ECHR. As their self-regulatory 'case-law' develops they are proving to be particularly effective in dealing with complaints about privacy intrusion in which the rights under the provisions of Art 8 conflict with those under Art 10.

The growth of press freedom and press self-regulation in Europe

4.18   The principles and practices of press self-regulation were not invented by the EU. They were pioneered by Sweden and Norway – both stable and very well-established democracies – nearly half a century before the establishment of the European Economic Community.

4.19   By the mid-1990s only six member states, including the UK, had fully operative self-regulatory Councils but the Commission was already receiving an increasing number of requests for advice on how to establish a council from other member states and prospective applicants for accession.

4.20   In 1998, the parliamentary Assembly of the Council of Europe debated the subjects of press regulation, privacy intrusion and harassment a few months after the accident which cost Diana, Princess of Wales, her life. The Assembly passed a resolution reaffirming 'the importance of every person's right to privacy, and of the right to freedom of expression as fundamental to a democratic society'. And the Assembly went on to draw attention to the dilemma that all member states and their regulatory authorities must live with, namely that: 'These rights are neither absolute nor in any hierarchical order since they are of equal value.'

4.21   The Assembly also called on the governments of member states to encourage their media 'to create their own guidelines for publication and to set up an institute with which an individual can lodge complaints for invasion of privacy and demand that a rectification be published'. At the same time, the Assembly urged the governments of member states 'to pass legislation, if no such legislation yet exists, guaranteeing the right to privacy' and to 'facilitate access to the Courts and simplify the legal procedures relating to press offences'.[1]

4.22   These resolutions were followed shortly afterwards by a new round of applications for accession to the EU, mostly from central and east European countries. Membership of AIPCE increased, as did the number of requests for advice from the Commission on how to establish and fund self-regulatory Councils. Although there are no universally applicable blue-prints for successful self-regulation that other countries can adopt ready made for their particular purposes, there are now over 20 fully operative Councils and Codes of Practice available for study and comparison. Students will discover that they are characterised as much by their differences as their similarities.

4.23   All self-regulatory Press Councils serve the same two purposes in dealing with complaints about unethical press conduct. They protect press freedoms and they protect the public from abuses of those freedoms by the press. In dealing with complaints, they all have to reconcile both of these claims to consideration with those of the public interest. Europe's self-regulatory Press Councils resemble one another in some respects and differ in others. Their similarities relate mainly to the political and legal preconditions that must be met in *any* society before self-regulation can work effectively. Their differences relate to other preconditions that are culturally specific to *particular* societies and notably with regard to the distinctive ways in which each Council interprets and applies the general principles embodied in its Code of Practice in the practical business of mediating and adjudicating complaints.

4.24   The findings of the latest Global Press Freedom Survey provide useful comparative data on the varying degrees of press freedom that currently prevail across Europe and the member states that have established Press Councils.[2]

4.25   This Survey takes the requirements of Art 19 of the Universal Declaration of Human Rights as the benchmark against which these degrees of freedom should be measured, namely that:

> 'Everyone has the right to freedom of opinion and expression; this right includes freedom to hold opinions without interference and to seek, receive, and impart information through any media regardless of frontiers.'[3]

4.26   The questions asked in the Survey cover three broad institutional categories – the political environment and the extent to which the press is subject to governmental control; the legal environment and the extent to which the law protects freedoms; and the economic environment, including the extent to which the media is controlled by government and private ownership is highly concentrated.

---

[1]   Resolution 1165 (1998) of the Parliamentary Assembly of the Council of Europe on the right to privacy, 26 June 1998.

[2]   *Freedom of the Press 2008: A Global Survey of Media Independence* (Freedom House, Washington DC and New York, 2008).

[3]   The wording of Art 10 of the ECHR is almost identical.

4.27   In the process of ranking each country:

'... a lower number of points is allotted for a more free situation, while a higher number of points is allotted for a less free environment. A country's final score is based on the total of the three categories. A score of 0 to 30 places the country in the Free press group; 31 to 60 in the Partly Free press group; and 61 to 100 in the Not Free press group.'

4.28   In Tables 4.1 and 4.2 these scores have been matched with the useful data on European Councils that Manuel Puppis collated in his forthcoming paper on the subject.[4]

Table 4.1   Freedom ranking scores of EU member states with self-regulatory Press Councils

Austria*	21	Italy	19
Belgium – Flanders – Wallonia	11	Lithuania	18
Bulgaria	33	Luxembourg	12
Cyprus	22	Malta	20
Denmark	10	Netherlands	13
Estonia	16	Romania*	44
Finland	9	Spain – National – Catalonia – ...	23
France*	22	Slovakia	22
Germany	16	Sweden	11
Hungary*	21	United Kingdom	18
Ireland	15		

*In the process of establishing Councils

4.29   All but two of the EU member states included in Table 4.1 are listed as Free press countries in the Global rankings. The Czech Republic, Greece, Latvia, Poland and Slovenia are left out because they do not have Councils. The table also excludes Portugal, which has the only fully operative statutory Council in the Union.

4.30   Comparing the scores of the EU member and non-member states reveals some interesting differences in their range and distribution.

Table 4.2   Freedom ranking scores of other European states with self-regulatory Press Councils

Albania*	50	Macedonia*	47
Armenia	66	Montenegro	38
Azerbaijan	77	Norway	10
Bosnia-Herzegovina	45	Russia	78

---

4   M Puppis 'Regulatory Organizations in Media Regulation: The Example of European Press Council' (2008) available at www.mediapolicy.uzh.ch.

| Iceland | 9 | Switzerland | 13 |
| Kosova | ? | Ukraine | 53 |

4.31   In Table 4.2 only three states – Iceland, Norway and Switzerland – are listed as Free press societies and they are all placed at, or very near, the top of the ranking order. Belarus, Croatia, Georgia, Moldova and Serbia are not included in the table because they do not have Councils. Their respective scores are 91, 36, 60, 66 and 39. Turkey, with a score of 51, is not listed because it is generally considered to have a statutory Council.

4.32   At the time of their accession to the EU, the countries with self-regulatory Councils and Free press rankings were deemed to be stable democracies governed by the rule of law and with free market economies. The other three member states without self-regulatory Councils, in company with Portugal, were also listed as having a Free press. The three non-member states with self-regulatory Councils and Free press rankings would easily meet the EU accession criteria were they ever to apply for membership. They are all democracies of very long standing.

4.33   The remaining ten non-member states with Councils, along with the three without Councils, are ranked as having either a Partly Free or a not Free press. Some of them are in the process of becoming stable democracies and others are standing still or moving in the opposite direction.

4.34   On the basis of these findings, it seems reasonable to conclude that the majority of European countries which have self-regulatory Councils and a free press are stable democracies, governed by the rule of law, with free market economies.

4.35   The positive association between these institutional factors is strong but not invariable. In the case of two democratic member states with self-regulatory Councils, the press is ranked as being only Partly Free, whilst the four democracies without Councils are ranked as having a Free press. In those countries where democratic institutions are relatively unstable and the rule of law cannot be relied on to protect press freedoms, self-regulatory Councils are difficult to establish and – where they exist – they struggle to survive in hostile political and legal environments.

4.36   It would seem, therefore, that democratic governance and the rule of law are two of the institutional preconditions that must be met before a free press can flourish. Conversely, it may be argued that without a free press, democracy itself cannot flourish.

4.37   A commitment to democracy and doing what is 'necessary in a democratic society' flows like a political *leitmotif* through the Articles of the ECHR and the judgments of the ECtHR. At the same time, many voters remain convinced that the Union's political institutions suffer from a serious 'democratic deficit'. Nevertheless, since self-regulatory institutions only flourish in democratic societies we need to ask why this happens to be the case.

Self-regulatory Press Councils and democracy

4.38   The principles that underpin the idea of democracy include the separation of executive, legislative and judicial powers, the rule of law and accountable forms of government. In practice, democracy means that people are free to express their views, to form interest groups and political parties and to contest elections without fear of intimidation. As public watchdogs, newspapers and magazines play a vitally important role in all these activities. This *plurality* of interest groups and political parties constitutes 'the defining essence of what a viable democracy is all about'.[5]

4.39   The ethos of pluralist democratic values extends beyond the statutory systems of governance and political activities to encompass the institutions of civil society. These institutions include the family and its kinship networks, large sectors of the economy with its markets, industries and occupational associations, religious and charitable affiliations and the media.

4.40   In pluralist democracies, we will always find places where governments do not intervene and seek to regulate the private lives and social activities of citizens. Most of these places are to be found in the institutions of civil society which is where people learn to regulate their own lives, to co-operate with their fellow citizens in the pursuit of commonly shared objectives and to reconcile their sectional interests with those of the wider society to which they belong.

4.41   The boundaries drawn between the regulatory responsibilities of the state and civil society vary from one democracy to another. They are seldom clear-cut and are subject to change over time. As has been noted, nearly all of Europe's stable democracies have two different but complementary systems of statutory regulation through the courts and non-statutory regulation through Press Councils.

4.42   Unlike democracies, totalitarian states seek to regulate every institutional aspect of the civil societies they govern – and to keep under continuous surveillance as much of the private lives of their citizens as they are able to do.

4.43   Totalitarian governments do not tolerate a diversity of political objectives and beliefs. Since they always know what is best for their citizens, there is nothing that needs to be questioned and, therefore, no need for freedom of expression and public debate. Consequently, the press and broadcasting media are always the first institutions of civil society that totalitarian governments seek to control and regulate for their own purposes on taking power.

4.44   It is one of the paradoxes of political life that the more power governments accrue to themselves the less competently they exercise it. The more they regulate the institutions of civil society, the less effectively they perform. In pluralist democracies, there are always places where government does not intervene. In the words of Michael Oakeshott: 'The silence of the law will brood over large tracts of the subject's life, and where there is silence there is liberty, the liberty of not being subject to unnecessary laws'.[6]

4.45   Democratic societies foster institutional diversity but, if they are to survive *as societies*, this diversity must be held together by a cultural framework of values with which people can identify as members of the same nation. This idea of a national culture encompasses the traditions, values and informal rules of conduct that underpin a nation's way of life and give a sense of shared meaning and purpose to the lives of its citizens. For the greater part, they will take these values and rules for granted and voluntarily comply with them.

---

[5]   J Dearlove and P Saunders *Introduction to British Politics* (Polity, 2000), at p 773.
[6]   M Oakeshott 'Introduction' in T Hobbes *Leviathan* (Basic Blackwell, 1946), at p xliii.

4.46   Some of these values relate to fundamental rights and duties that are generally agreed to be so central to a nation's way of life that they are incorporated into its laws. The rule of law works best when its sanctions only have to be invoked in exceptional cases. Voluntary compliance on this scale is most likely to be found in democratic societies where the law's requirements are broadly compatible with the customary values and rules by which the majority of people are content to live.

4.47   In practice, however, this degree of voluntary consensus is difficult to achieve and it can never be taken for granted. Very few pluralist democracies have national cultures that are completely unitary in character. Most of them also have a multicultural dimension made up of various regional, ethnic and religious minority groups. Each of these has their own distinctive cultural traditions that co-exist more or less easily with those of the national culture. When co-existence breaks down and compromises cannot be reached, the disagreements that have arisen can turn into open conflicts that put the rule of law in jeopardy and tear apart the institutions of both state and civil society – as happened in Northern Ireland and the former state of Yugoslavia.

Self–regulatory Press Councils

4.48   There are a number of reasons why the constitutions and Codes of Practice that Councils adopt must be compatible with the requirements of the law if self-regulation is to work effectively.

4.49   First, in democratic societies, self-regulatory Councils are legally accountable for what they do. In the UK, all of the Press Complaints Commission's (PCC's) adjudications are open to challenge by dissatisfied complainants, who can apply to the High Court for a judicial review of the PCC's rulings. Similar provisions are made in other European countries for appeals against their Council's adjudications. The incidence and outcomes of such reviews are useful measures of a Council's effectiveness.

4.50   Secondly, in democratic societies, there is a considerable degree of overlap between the jurisprudence of the courts and the remit of self-regulatory Councils, notably with regard to complaints about inaccurate reporting that might also have defamatory connotations and privacy intrusion. It should also be noted that s 12(4) of the UK Human Rights Act 1998 requires the courts to take account of the PCC's Code of Practice in their proceedings in privacy cases and recognises it as a 'relevant privacy code' for the purposes of the Act.

4.51   Thirdly, the rule of law both limits and protects the right to freedom of expression. In democratic societies, most of these limitations are imposed in order to ensure that this right is not exercised in ways that abuse or infringe on other people's legal rights. Nevertheless, in countries where the requirements of self-regulatory Codes of Practice are consistent with those of the law, voluntary compliance on the part of editors and journalists greatly reduces the risk that they will find themselves in breach of the law.

4.52   Respect for the rule of law and consistency with its requirements are absolute preconditions for effective self-regulation. In countries where publishers are able to flout the rule of law with impunity, they will feel no obligation to uphold the requirements of their Codes of Practice. Conversely, in countries where the rule of law prevails and Councils fail, for one reason or another, in the discharge of their duties, governments will intervene and replace them with statutory authorities.

Self-regulatory Press Councils in their cultural contexts

4.53 The requirements of self-regulatory Codes of Practice must also be compatible with the cultural values and expectations of the industries and people they serve. Since Councils are not legal authorities, voluntary compliance on the part of publishers, editors and journalists becomes the sine qua non of self-regulation. In making their rulings and adjudications, Councils for their part must take account of the realities of digital age journalism in which the flow of information is increasing and swift decisions must often be made in the face of inflexible deadlines.

4.54 Self-regulatory Councils are also dependent on the voluntary participation of potential complainants. Newly established Councils have to raise public awareness and convince people that their complaints will be dealt with promptly and fairly. Complainants have choices in such matters. Some will be able to seek redress in the courts. Others may decide to do nothing. They will be more likely to choose the self-regulatory option if they trust their Council and feel able to identify, in terms of cultural familiarity and affinity, with the principles and values embodied in its Code of Practice.

4.55 Some Councils, like the PCC, see themselves primarily as providers of a dispute resolution service. Only a very small number of complaints are taken to formal adjudication, either because the breach is thought to be so serious that an apology, a published letter or a correction would not be a sufficient remedy, or because the editors are convinced that a formal adjudication will vindicate them. The great majority of complaints are resolved by means of informal conciliation and the voluntary compliance of editors. Other Councils take most of their complaints to formal adjudication but their credibility, as regulators, is still dependent on the force of moral authority and voluntary compliance.

4.56 Self-regulatory Councils must also be funded on terms which guarantee their independence from external control by their governments or the industries they regulate. Puppis lists seven EU member states where governments provide a proportion of their Councils' budgets or are involved to some degree in the process of regulation itself. In the early years of AIPCE, concerns were frequently expressed that such arrangements would jeopardise the independence of these 'hybrid' or 'co-regulatory' Councils.

4.57 Puppis, however, lists Denmark, Ireland, Lithuania and Luxembourg as countries with 'co-regulatory' Councils and Belgium, Finland and Germany with 'hybrid' Councils that are partially funded by the state. In the Global Press Freedom rankings, all seven are listed as having a free press and five of them are placed at, or very near, the top of the ranking order.

4.58 These findings suggest that a limited degree of statutory involvement is not necessarily at odds with the principles of press freedom and self-regulatory independence. It should, however, be noted that all but one of these countries are long-established democracies.

4.59 Puppis focuses on the structural similarities and differences that characterise Press Councils.[7] The present author's primary concern is with their Codes of Practice

---

[7]   Puppis, n 4 above.

and, in particular, the cultural differences that become evident in the process of interpreting and applying Code requirements to similar kinds of complaint in particular societies.

4.60 All European self-regulatory Codes of Practice are based on similar frameworks of general principles and values which, in turn, are consistent with those embodied in the ECHR. They are also similar, if not identical, with regard to the kinds of complaint that they accept and the grounds on which editors may advance a public interest defence in cases where they have breached the requirements of their Codes.

4.61 They differ in the following respects. Some Codes of Practice include a requirement that complainants should be given a fair opportunity for reply to inaccuracies when reasonably called for whilst others allow them an unqualified right to reply.

4.62 Some Councils accept complaints that raise issues of taste and decency whilst others do not. They also differ with regard to the kinds of complaint about discriminatory reporting that they will accept. Some Codes of Practice only protect individuals from discriminatory remarks made about them in published material whilst others extend this protection to collectivities like nation states and religious and ethnic minority groups.

4.63 Councils like the PCC take the view that such extensions would seriously infringe the right to freedom of expression and inhibit robust debates on a wide range of controversial topics – as would be the case if they were to accept complaints about taste and decency. Other Councils give greater priority to what they believe are considerations of public interest in deciding where such lines should be drawn.

4.64 Councils are bound to differ on such matters if the requirements of their Codes of Practice are to remain consistent with those of their national laws and the cultural values and expectations of the industries and people they serve. Their Codes may uphold similar ethical principles or rights but, in practice, Councils interpret and apply these principles in ways that mirror the diversity of their national cultures and legal systems.

4.65 In dealing with complaints, self-regulatory Councils have to resolve conflicts of interest that arise between 'the legitimate rights of a free press and the legitimate rights of people who attract media attention'.[8] Complaints about privacy intrusion exemplify the different ways in which Councils interpret and apply these rights and balance their claims to consideration against each other and those of the public interest.

4.66 The direction in which they tip the balance depends on the importance they attach to the claims of the public interest – and how they define these claims. Most Codes of Practice state that editors may advance a public interest defence in cases where it was necessary to breach the Code in order to detect or expose crime or serious impropriety, to protect public health and safety or to prevent the public from being misled by an action or statement by an individual or organisation.

---

[8] W Gore 'Self-regulatory bodies: Ensuring respect for a code of ethics' in M Haraszti (ed) *The Media Self-regulation Guidebook* (Organisation for Security and Cooperation in Europe (OSCE), Vienna, 2008), at p 34.

4.67 The UK's Code of Practice states that 'there is a public interest in freedom of expression itself' and it does so for a very good reason. The right to freedom of expression and the public's right to know can never be taken for granted – even in democratic societies. Editors and journalists believe that the public interest is best served by extending the scope of these freedoms. More and more governments are acting today as if they believed that the public interest is best served by restricting them. As for the right to privacy, it is this author's belief that the state remains a greater threat to people's privacy than the press has ever been.

Press regulation in its European context

4.68 The ECtHR's judgment in the case of Princess Caroline von Hannover[9] added a new dimension to the debate on what counts as a matter of public interest and where the balance should be struck between the claims of privacy and freedom of expression. The court ruled that the right to freedom of expression did not extend to photographs taken by paparazzi because they 'did not concern the dissemination of "ideas"' but only 'images containing very personal or even intimate information about an individual'. The 'decisive factor in balancing the protection of private life against freedom of expression' was, in the court's view, whether the published material contributed to 'a debate of public interest'.

4.69 The ECtHR went on to state that:[10]

> '… a fundamental distinction needs to be made between reporting facts – even controversial ones – capable of contributing to a debate in a democratic society relating to politicians in the exercise of their functions, for example, and reporting details of an individual, who, moreover, in this case, does not exercise official functions.'

Although the press exercises a 'vital role of "watchdog" in a democracy' and the public's right to be informed 'is an essential right in a democracy', the situation in this case 'does not come within the sphere of any political or public debate because the published photos and accompanying commentaries relate exclusively to details of the applicant's private life'.

4.70 The courts and Press Councils of EU member states must take account of the requirements of European law but, in the case of the UK it remains open to debate as to how binding those requirements are meant to be. Glasser points out that under s 2 of the Human Rights Act 1998 (HRA 1998), 'British Courts only need to have "regard" to decisions of the European Court rather than be bound by them'.[11]

4.71 He goes on to note that under s 6 of the Act it is unlawful for a public body (which term includes a court or a tribunal) to act in a way which is incompatible with a Convention right 'and since a court is a public authority, its duty to act compatibly with the Convention means that it has to apply Convention values to all civil disputes, including those between private parties'.[12]

4.72 Glasser also draws attention to the:[13]

---

[9]   *Von Hannover v Germany*, App No 59320/00 (2005) 40 EHRR 1.
[10] At paras 63–64.
[11] C Glasser *Recent Developments in Privacy Law*, PCC Paper No 3896 (2007) at p 18.
[12] Ibid.
[13] Ibid.

'... ongoing debate between a number of judges on this subject in which some take the view that "the court has an absolute duty under Section 6 to interpret and apply existing law to make it compatible with the Convention." Other judges take a contrary view, believing that "the court should take account of Convention principles when making common law adjudications (while) giving them an appropriate weight in deciding the matter".'

4.73   There is currently a growing concern throughout the UK newspaper industry that some judges in the UK are taking disproportionate account of the need to ensure that their judgments in privacy cases are fully compatible with those of the ECtHR and ECHR principles. Many publishers, editors and journalists are detecting a significant trend in these judgments towards the development of a freestanding UK law of privacy in line with what the Council of Europe was recommending to member states in 1998.

4.74   The PCC also views these developments with trepidation because the requirements of its Code of Practice must remain compatible with those of the law. It is also concerned that, although s 12 of the HRA 1998 requires the courts to take account of its Code of Practice as a 'relevant privacy code' for the purposes of the Act, most judges are currently making their own interpretations of the Code without reference to those of the PCC.

4.75   The courts and Councils of the 27 European member states are still in the process of incorporating the requirements of the *Von Hannover* judgment into their own national laws and procedures for dealing with privacy actions and complaints. Given the diversity of their national cultures, it may prove difficult to reach a European-wide consensus on what counts as 'a debate of public interest' and what kinds of published material are 'capable of contributing to a debate in a democratic society' or are 'necessary' in such a society.

4.76   It is difficult enough to reach a working consensus on what these terms and phrases mean in practice at the level of individual nation states but these difficulties multiply when we try to derive common legal denominators from the distinctive cultural traditions of 27 democratic societies.

4.77   Democratic societies are pluralist societies, which means that they are characterised as much by their cultural differences as by their similarities and that their citizens value the differences as much as the similarities because, as free people, they played their part in making them in their own collective image.

4.78   In pluralist democracies, all working definitions of the 'public interest' are essentially uneasy compromises between expert and popular opinion. It is the experts, drawn from a variety of professions and walks of life, who draw patronising distinctions between what counts as 'public interest' and 'what happens to interest the public'. In all such matters it is 'necessary' to ask how democratic are the processes by which the public interest is defined.

4.79   The EU encompasses a plurality of national cultures and the *Von Hannover* judgment raises many new questions regarding the extent to which their cultural differences, as well as their similarities, are receiving sufficient consideration by the ECtHR.

CONCLUSION

4.80   Self-regulation only works effectively in countries where governments uphold the right to freedom of expression and allow their citizens a generous degree of freedom in regulating their own lives and associational activities within the institutional contexts of their civil societies. These are the contexts in which their culturally distinctive traditions of voluntary co-operation and compliance take root and grow.

4.81   Making self-regulation work is an integral part of the same processes. There are no political or legal short-cuts to success. Making democracy work *in practice* takes a good deal longer than drafting democratic constitutions and the same is true of Press Councils and their Codes of Practice.

4.82   The Press Councils of democratic nation states share an attachment to the same general principles in upholding the rights to freedom of expression, the public's right to know, individual rights to privacy and the claims of the public interest. They differ most significantly with regard to the ways in which they interpret, apply and balance these rights and claims against each other in the practical business of mediating and adjudicating complaints.

Chapter 5

COMPLAINTS UNDER CLAUSE 3(I) AND (II) (PRIVACY)

INTRODUCTION – THE CODE OF PRACTICE AND THE PUBLIC INTEREST

5.1   The Press Complaints Commission's (PCC's) Code of Practice can be described as the moral compass by which the editors navigate and the Commissioners adjudicate their ethical seamanship.

5.2   The Code has 16 clauses which are grouped under the following four headings in the PCC's *Annual Reviews*:

(i)   Accuracy and opportunity to reply;

(ii)   Privacy and other related issues such as harassment and the protection of vulnerable people like children etc;

(iii)   Methods of newsgathering; and

(iv)   Discrimination.

5.3   The Code recognises that there will always be exceptional cases in which an editor may breach its requirements and advance a public interest defence for doing so. The grounds on which a public interest defence may be advanced are set out in the following statement:

'**The public interest**

There may be exceptions to the clauses marked * where they can be demonstrated to be in the public interest.

1.   The public interest includes, but is not confined to:
       (i)   Detecting or exposing crime or serious impropriety.
       (ii)   Protecting public health and safety.
       (iii)   Preventing the public from being misled by an action or statement of an individual or organization.
2.   There is a public interest in freedom of expression itself.
3.   Whenever the public interest is invoked, the PCC will require editors to demonstrate fully that they reasonably believed that publication, or journalistic activity undertaken with a view to publication, would be in the public interest.
4.   The PCC will consider the extent to which material is already in the public domain, or will become so.

5.   In cases involving children under 16, editors must demonstrate an exceptional public interest to over-ride the normally paramount interest of the child.'

5.4   In *The Editors' Codebook*,[1] Ian Beales, who currently serves as secretary to the Editors' Code Committee sets out a number of key questions that editors should ask themselves when deciding whether the material they intend publishing and the methods of newsgathering by which the material will be obtained are likely to constitute a possible breach of the Code. These questions are substantially the same as those which the PCC asks when dealing with complaints and deciding whether the Code has been breached and whether the public interest has been successfully engaged as a defence. Since the *Codebook's* wordings of these questions are fully endorsed by both the PCC and the Editors' Code Committee, they are used throughout these chapters as required. They are also the kinds of questions that legal representatives might find helpful to bear in mind when advising prospective complainants to the PCC on how best to proceed. It should be noted, however, that these questions are indicative rather than exclusive in character. It is for the PCC to interpret and apply the requirements of the public interest statement and the relevant clause(s) to the particular circumstances of each complaint under consideration.

5.5   The key questions asked when deciding whether a public interest defence is justified are:[2]

'*How would publication serve the public interest?*'

The PCC would require a full explanation.

'*If clandestine methods, harassment or payments to criminals or witnesses are involved, could the information have been obtained by other means?*'

'*Is the information (already) in the public domain, or likely to become so?*'

'*If children are involved, is the public interest in publication exceptional?*'

5.6   Seven of the 16 clauses in the Code address privacy related issues. Six of these clauses are marked with an asterisk denoting that editors are allowed to advance a public interest defence under their provisions.

5.7   The seven privacy-related clauses are:

- Clause 3* Privacy;

- Clause 4* Harassment;

- Clause 5 Intrusion into grief or shock (* subclause (ii) only);

- Clause 6* Children;

- Clause 7* Children in sex cases;

---

1   I Beales *The Editors' Codebook* (Press Standards Board of Finance, revised 2nd edn, 2009).
2   Ibid, at p 77.

- Clause 8* Hospitals; and

- Clause 9* Reporting of crime

5.8 Under clause 5 editors are only allowed to advance a public interest defence with regard to the provisions of subclause (ii), which states that 'when reporting suicide, care should be taken to avoid excessive detail about the methods used.'

5.9 These are the clauses that the PCC lists as 'privacy and intrusion' related for its statistical record keeping and publication purposes. For the purposes of this book, clause 10 (Clandestine devices and subterfuge) has been taken from the list of 'newsgathering' clauses and included in the 'privacy and intrusion' list.

5.10 This has been done on the grounds that it is difficult to imagine how 'news gatherers' can resort to the use of 'hidden cameras or clandestine listening devices' or remove peoples' 'documents or photographs' without intruding into their privacy. The Code allows a public interest defence under clause 10. Although complaints made under clause 10 account for only a small number of those which the PCC investigates and makes rulings on in a given year, they figure rather more significantly in those involving celebrities.

5.11 There are two other kinds of complaint, apart from those involving privacy related issues, against which editors can advance a public interest defence. The Code recognises that there may be occasions when payments by newspapers and magazines to witnesses in criminal trials and to criminals can be justified as being in the public interest. These contingencies are respectively covered under subclauses (ii) and (iii) of clause 15 (Witness payments in criminal trials) and clause 16 (Payment to criminals).

5.12 We are left with six clauses covering complaints against which editors *cannot* advance a public interest defence[3] for the following reasons. There cannot be a public interest in refusing to correct inaccuracies or in denying a reasonable request to provide an opportunity to reply. Similarly, there cannot be a public defence against failing to show due sensitivity in cases involving people suffering grief or shock or the victims of sexual assault. The clause on discrimination prohibits 'prejudicial or pejorative references to an individual's race, colour, religion, sexual orientation or to any other physical or mental illness or disability'.[4] Discriminatory reporting of this kind can never be in the public interest. The clauses on financial journalism and the protection of confidential sources are specifically intended to *uphold* the public interest. Payments to witnesses in criminal trials can be defended on public interest grounds under certain circumstances but they cannot be defended on such grounds once criminal proceedings become active.

---

3   Clauses 1 (Accuracy), 2 (Opportunity to reply), 11 (Victims of sexual assault), 12 (Discrimination), 13 (Financial journalism) and 14 (Confidential sources).
4   Editors' Code of Practice 2009.

RESOLVING CONFLICTS OF INTEREST AND RIGHTS UNDER THE CODE

5.13   The Code of Practice provides the framework within which the PCC has to resolve the conflicts of interest that arise between 'the legitimate rights of a free press and the legitimate rights of people who attract media attention'.[5]

5.14   Complaints about privacy intrusion exemplify the key ethical issues that arise in balancing these claims against each other. Press self-regulation serves two main purposes: it protects press freedoms and it protects citizens from abuses of those freedoms by the press. Freedom of expression and privacy are both fundamental human rights but they can seldom, if ever, be treated as absolute rights because they so frequently come into conflict with each other. In seeking to reconcile these conflicts, regulatory bodies must also give due consideration to the claims of the public interest.

5.15   The same balancing test has to be applied in the courts, as is noted later in this book:[6]

> 'Ultimately, the central question to be addressed is where the public interest lies, or move precisely, whether the public interest justifies the intrusion. It is a question of balance between protecting private life and freedom of expression.
>
> •   The justifications for interfering with or restricting each right must be taken into account, and
> •   the proportionality test must be applied to each. This is sometimes called the ultimate balancing test.'

And as is noted further:

> '•   In all such cases there must be an intense focus on the facts before appropriate conclusions can be received.'

5.16   When dealing with privacy complaints the PCC asks whether the disclosures complained about are already in the public domain, whether they raise issues of genuine public interest and whether the past behaviour of the complainant has, in any way, compromised his right to privacy. In all such cases, the PCC seeks to establish whether or not the disclosures in the article complained about are proportionate to the information already in the public domain. With regard to stories about children or other relatives of public figures, the PCC asks whether or not they would have been published at all if the familial links had not existed. Complainants who have previously revealed details of their personal lives do not necessarily forfeit their future rights to privacy.

CELEBRITIES AND THE CODE OF PRACTICE

5.17   The PCC recognises that show business and sports celebrities must promote themselves through the media if they are to fulfil their contractual obligations and remain in the public eye. They may, however, jeopardise their privacy rights if they

---

5   W Gore 'Self-regulatory Bodies: Ensuring Respect for a Code of Ethics' in M Haraszti (ed) *The Media Self-Regulation Guidebook* (OSCE, 2008), at p 35.
6   See **10.46** and **10.48**.

voluntarily disclose intimate details about their private – as distinct from their professional – lives, and especially so if they accept payments for such stories. The PCC has made it clear in a previous landmark ruling that privacy is 'not a commodity which can be sold on one person's terms'.[7]

5.18 Celebrities must, therefore, take particular care not to act in ways that compromise their privacy rights or those of their partners, children and other close relatives and friends. Their close relatives and friends need to be equally careful in such matters.

5.19 The Code of Practice recognises that the claims of the public interest may be engaged to justify invasions of privacy as well as restrictions on the right to freedom of expression. The resolution of these conflicts of interest is a central concern of the courts, self-regulatory councils and members of the public whose privacy is invaded. Paradoxically, people can only learn to value and protect their privacy by growing up in a society and becoming sociable. Since neither the right to privacy nor the right to invade it are absolutes, this is a dilemma with which all members of the public have to live – and this is one of the facts of life that many celebrities learn to their personal and financial cost.

Clause 3 (Privacy)

5.20 Clause 3 of the Code of Practice, which covers the general attributes of privacy, reads as follows:

'3* Privacy

(i) Everyone is entitled to respect for his or her private and family life, home, health and correspondence, including digital communications. Editors will be expected to justify intrusions into any individual's private life without consent.
(ii) Editors will be expected to justify intrusions into any individual's private life without consent. Account will be taken of the complainant's own public disclosures of information.
(iii) It is unacceptable to photograph individuals in a private place without their consent. *Note – Private places are public or private property where there is a reasonable expectation of privacy.'*

5.21 In 2008, the 125 rulings issued by the PCC on complaints made under clause 3(i) and (ii) accounted for nearly 9% of all rulings issued in that year. The key questions asked when dealing with such complaints are as follows:[8]

- *Was consent given for publication* – formally or by implication?

- *Has the entitlement to privacy been compromised* – for example, by the subject courting publicity or setting it on their own terms?

- *Is the individual a public figure, or role model* – and does the material reveal conduct reflecting on their public or professional status or image?

---

7 *Attard v Manchester Evening News*, PCC Report No 55, July–September 2001.
8 *The Editors' Codebook*, n 1 above, at p 31.

- *Was the information already in the public domain* – would it be reasonable for it to be retrieved and made private?

- *Did individuals photographed without consent have a reasonable expectation of privacy* – were they out of public view and engaged in private activity?

- *Was the publication in the public interest?*

- *Was the breach proportionate to the public interest served?*

5.22 In the following case studies, complaints under subclauses (i) and (ii) are discussed in that order. It should be noted that some of these complaints were made under both subclauses, or more than one clause.

Privacy intrusion complaints under clause 3(i) involving the disclosure of sensitive personal data

5.23 The following case studies illustrate the kinds of complaint that celebrities and their close relatives and friends have brought to the PCC under clause 3(i) of the Code of Practice over the past 18 years.

5.24 It should be noted that when the Code of Practice was reviewed by the Editors' Code Committee in January 1998 following the tragic death of Princess Diana, what was then clause 4 was renumbered as clause 3. The old wording in subclause (i) that referred only in general terms to 'an individual's private life' was changed to read 'his or her private and family life, home, health and correspondence'.

5.25 The new wording was taken largely from the European Convention for the Protection of Human Rights and Fundamental Freedoms shortly before its provisions were incorporated into UK law. This revision ensured that the Code's requirements would conform with those of the Human Rights Act 1998 and Data Protection Acts 1984 and 1998 regarding the misuse of private and personal information (or the disclosure of sensitive personal data).

Greer v The Mail on Sunday[9]

5.26 In 1994, the PCC delivered one of its earliest benchmark adjudications involving such disclosures when Dr Germaine Greer complained through her solicitors that information in an article published by *The Mail on Sunday* was obtained through an unjustified use of subterfuge which resulted in a gross intrusion into her privacy. The complaint was raised under clause 4 (Privacy) and what was then clause 7 (Misrepresentation) which stated that 'subterfuge can be justified only in the public interest and only when material cannot be obtained by any other means'.

5.27 Dr Greer had written an article for *The Big Issue* in which she discussed the difficulties of owning and sharing a home with other people. She offered to share her home with any genuinely homeless person who was not put off by the circumstances she had described.

---

[9]   PCC Report No 23, January–February 1994.

5.28 Shortly afterwards, the newspaper sent an undercover reporter to her home. He pretended to be a homeless person and she took him in as a lodger. He lived as a member of the household for several weeks after which he disappeared, leaving a letter of apology in which he explained that he had been 'trying to investigate' the world of modern-day homeless people and gain an insight into their problems. The article that followed gave a very detailed description of Dr Greer's home and its contents, including the items stored in her kitchen and bathroom cupboards.

5.29 In its adjudication, the PCC rejected the editor's claims that resort to subterfuge was 'the only way in which the article could have been written and there can be no doubt that when an outspoken and famous person makes a genuine offer to help the homeless, this is a matter of public interest'. In the PCC's view, the article was 'not about the life of a genuinely homeless person' but 'about the experience of a guest in Dr Greer's home who gained entry by subterfuge'.

5.30 The PCC upheld the complaint on the grounds that no conceivable public interest was served that could justify the use of subterfuge and the disclosure of information obtained by such methods. It went on to state that: 'In view of the degree of intrusion in this case and the space accorded in the article about Dr Greer, the PCC would expect this adjudication to be published with significant prominence in the newspaper.'

5.31 Although this adjudication dates back to 1994, its tenor and sentiment invite comparison with those expressed by Eady J in his judgment in the case of *McKennitt v Ash*, where he stated that:[10] 'To describe a person's home, the décor, the layout, the state of cleanliness, or how the occupiers behave inside it … is almost as objectionable as spying into the home with a long distance lens and publishing the resulting photographs.'

5.32 The following five case studies illustrate how the PCC's 'case-law' in dealing with 'kiss and tell' stories has developed over time, notably with regard to issues of proportionality and the extent to which complainants may have previously compromised their own rights to privacy.[11]

Julia Carling v The Sun[12]

5.33 In 1995, Ms Julia Carling complained that a story published in *The Sun* had invaded her privacy in breach of clause 3 of the Code of Practice. The article included highly personal details about her past relationships – and that of her husband, Will Carling, the ex-England rugby captain, and Princess Diana. The PCC noted that Mrs Carling had previously placed similarly personal details of her past and current relationships in the public domain when promoting her own career.

5.34 As we have noted, complainants who have previously sought publicity and received payment for interviews and articles do not automatically disentitle themselves to protection under the Code. In this case, however, the details complained about were not sufficiently different from those that the complainant herself had already placed in the public domain. The complaint was, therefore, rejected.

---

10   [2006] EWCA Civ 1714.
11   PCC Report No 24, March–April 1994.
12   PCC Report No 33, January–March 1996.

Selina Scott v News of the World[13]

5.35   In 1995, Ms Selina Scott complained that an article published in the *News of the World* had invaded her privacy in breach of clauses 4 (Privacy) and 1 (Accuracy). The article concerned the allegations of a man about his alleged affair with her that had occurred 15 years earlier.

5.36   In its adjudication, the PCC noted that the matter was neither current nor currently in the public eye and that the allegations focused on events that pre-dated Ms Scott's celebrity. It concluded that her subsequent exposure to publicity did not disentitle her to respect for privacy in a matter that she, herself, had never placed in the public domain. It also noted that Ms Scott had never revealed information of a similar or a proportionate nature in interviews that she had previously given to the press in the furtherance of her career.

5.37   The PCC also considered the complaint about privacy intrusion in conjunction with the complaints about inaccuracy. It ruled that since the newspaper had failed to substantiate its allegations, the article was in itself misleading. It therefore followed that, as Ms Scott was entitled in any event to be protected from unsubstantiated allegations, her privacy had been unjustifiably invaded. The complaint was upheld.

5.38   The following complaints were all adjudicated after the implementation of the Human Rights Act 1998 in 2000. From 2004 onwards, the PCC had to be particularly mindful of the principles established in *Campbell v MGN Ltd*[14] and *Von Hannover v Germany*[15] and the subsequent rulings of the European and the UK courts in its privacy-related adjudications.

Pirie v News of the World[16]

5.39   In 2000, Granada Television complained on behalf of Coronation Street actress Jacqueline Pirie that an article published in the *News of the World* invaded her privacy in breach of clause 3 of the Code of Practice. The article included deeply personal details about her relationship with her former fiancé, who was extensively quoted in the piece.

5.40   The PCC noted that the newspaper had not sought to justify the article on grounds of public interest or of consent. Neither had it denied that the article was intrusive. It contended, instead, that Ms Pirie had, in the past, actively sought publicity for herself, openly discussed aspects of her private life and, thereby, disentitled herself to the protection of the Code.

5.41   The PCC found that although Ms Pirie had previously given a number of press interviews, she had not spoken about such highly intimate matters as those revealed in the article. It also noted the absence of any proportionality between the subject matter of the article – which was extremely personal and devoid of public interest – and the material about the relationship that was already in the public domain. Ms Pirie's complaint was upheld.

---

[13]   PCC Report No 33, January–March 1996.
[14]   [2004] UKHL 22.
[15]   (2005) 40 EHRR 1.
[16]   PCC Report No 49, January–March 2000.

Bing v The Mirror[17]

5.42 In 2001, Steve Bing complained to the PCC through his solicitors that an article published in *The Mirror* included material in breach of clause 3 (Privacy) of the Code of Practice. The article followed a public disagreement between the actress Elizabeth Hurley and her former lover, Steve Bing, over the paternity of her child. The newspaper criticised him for 'turning his back' on Ms Hurley and published the main switchboard number of his Los Angeles film company. It also invited readers to call this number if they thought Mr Bing was a 'bigger cad than James Hewitt'.

5.43 Mr Bing's solicitors argued that he was not a public figure and that he had been subjected to threatening phone calls. The newspaper claimed that the phone number was in the public domain and that Mr Bing had publicly suggested that he might not be the father of Ms Hurley's child.

5.44 The PCC noted that the material published was already in the public domain, and that since the phone number was for the general switchboard of his company there had been no invasion of Mr Bing's privacy. It recognised that some people might have had misgivings about the decision to encourage people to telephone the number but, in circumstances where there have been no breach of the Code, this was deemed to be a matter for editorial discretion.

5.45 Since there was no intrusion into privacy, the newspaper did not have to justify itself in terms of the public interest. For the same reason, it was not relevant whether or not the complainant could be described as a 'public figure' in his own right. He had, however, been involved in a high profile relationship with a famous actress and had subsequently publicly argued with her about the paternity of her child. In the PCC's view, scrutiny by the press in these circumstances was inevitable and the complaint was, therefore, rejected.

Primrose Shipman v The Mirror[18]

5.46 In July 2001, Mrs Primrose Shipman complained to the PCC through her solicitors that material contained in an article headlined 'Shipman wife begs him: tell me truth' published in *The Mirror* was obtained in breach of clause II (Misrepresentation) and was intrusive in breach of clause 3 (Privacy) of the Code of Practice. (In 2004, clause II was combined with what was then clause 8 (Listening devices) to make up what is now clause 10 (Clandestine devices and subterfuge.)

5.47 The article included extracts from a letter the complainant had sent to her husband, the convicted murderer Dr Harold Shipman, in which she expressed a 'lingering doubt' as to whether he had told the truth. She claimed that the letter had been stolen from her husband by his cell-mate, Tony Fleming, a convicted thief, in breach of clause II. Her solicitors also claimed that publication of the extract constituted a breach of her copyright. The newspaper insisted that the letter had been given by Dr Shipman to Mr Fleming and it sent the PCC a copy of an article published in the *Manchester Evening News* in February 2000. The article was based on an interview with Mr Fleming in which he stated that Dr Shipman had given him a number of letters. It also included a letter sent by Mrs Shipman to her husband and no

---

[17] PCC Report No 54, April–June 2001.
[18] PCC Report No 56–57, October 2001–March 2002.

complaint had been lodged about its publication at that time. The newspaper sent the PCC a full copy of this letter, which it had quoted in its own article. The complainant maintained that the *Manchester Evening News* cutting was irrelevant and that the newspaper's source was not to be trusted.

5.48   In its adjudication, the PCC pointed out that the publication of private correspondence would usually constitute a breach of the Code unless it could be shown that consent had been given, that there was a public interest in such publication or that the contents were otherwise legitimately about to be made public. In this case, having read the entire letter, the PCC 'was clear that the contents were personal and that their publication therefore constituted a breach of clause 3'.

5.49   In upholding this part of the complaint, however, the PCC decided not to censure the newspaper for the following reasons. First, although there was disagreement about how the letters were obtained, it noted that Mr Fleming's claims that he had been given the letters by Dr Shipman had not been challenged when they were last made public. If these claims had been correct, which it was not possible to ascertain, 'there would have been implied consent for their publication from the recipient of these letters'.

5.50   Secondly, the PCC acknowledged that, given the complainant's uniquely intimate relationship to Dr Shipman and the fact that 'she had stated hardly anything in public about his crimes', there was bound to be considerable public interest in any statement that she did make and for the editor to believe that there was a public interest in publishing an except from the letter. In the event, he had not published much more from it, even though he could have done so.

5.51   Thirdly, the editor may have had regard to the fact that another letter had previously been published elsewhere without complaint.

5.52   The PCC made no finding under clause II. There was no way in which it could be expected 'to make a reasoned judgment about the relative probity of these two convicted criminals' and it concluded that 'the exact circumstances of the transfer of the correspondence would be impossible to establish'. If the complainant's allegations about how the material was obtained were shown to be true then 'they would clearly be matters for the police to consider'. As for the complaint about an alleged breach of copyright, this was 'clearly a legal matter which was not for the Commission to consider'.

A woman v Daily Mail[19]

5.53   In September 2006, 'a woman' complained to the PCC that an article published in the *Daily Mail* had intruded into her daughter's privacy, in breach of clause 3 (Privacy) of the Code of Practice. The article was headlined 'The aristocrat's wife, the jobless jailbird and the "Lady Chatterley" affair that put her marriage under threat'. It reported that 'the complainant's daughter – who had married into an aristocratic family had had an affair'. The man's girlfriend was quoted extensively in the piece. Her comments included remarks about the complainant's daughter which the complainant maintained were intrusive and were devoid of any public interest.

---

[19]   PCC Report No 74, October 2006–April 2007.

5.54   The newspaper expressed sincere regret for the distress caused to the daughter and said that it had already removed the article from its website and marked its cuttings for future reference. It maintained, however, that it did not believe the Code had been breached and that the girlfriend, as one of the wronged parties in the affair, had a right to tell her side of the story.

5.55   In its adjudication, the PCC agreed that the girlfriend did have a right to tell her story. In balancing her right to freedom of expression against the complainant's daughter's right to privacy, it concluded that a reasonable balance had been struck. The newspaper had taken sufficient care in allowing the girlfriend to tell her story 'without including gratuitously intrusive details about the complainant's daughter'. The complaint was not upheld.

A woman v News of the World[20]

5.56   The same woman also complained to the PCC on behalf of her daughter that an article published in the *News of the World* intruded into her daughter's privacy, in breach of clause 3 of the Code of Practice. The article, which was headlined 'Lady Mucky wanted me rough and ready', gave an account of the same affair. It was, however, written from the man's point of view and included intimate details of their sexual activities. The mother claimed that her daughter was not a celebrity and had not sought to publicise the affair.

5.57   In its adjudication, the PCC accepted that the man concerned was entitled to speak about the relationship. It concluded, however, that in this account, 'the information contained in the article was out of proportion to that already in the public domain'. Some of the information, 'particularly the description of sexual activity – was of an intimate nature'. The complainant's daughter had not courted publicity, 'and any limited public interest inherent in exposing adultery committed by someone who was married into an aristocratic family was insufficient to justify the level of detail in the piece'. The complaint was upheld.

5.58   Although celebrities and their close relatives are entitled to the same protection of their privacy rights under the Code of Practice as ordinary people, they are at risk of compromising these rights whenever they seek publicity for either professional or personal reasons or when they accept payments for stories and interviews. The PCC still takes these matters into account, but its general approach has changed over time in response to recent court decisions in similar cases. Its key consideration today is whether the degree of intrusion is proportionate to the degree of public interest revealed in the published material and any countervailing freedom of expression arguments. Whether the complainant has previously sought publicity still has some bearing on the degree of public interest inherent in the story.

5.59   The complaints received from Julia Carling, Selina Scott and an unnamed woman were all concerned with the unauthorised disclosure of sensitive personal data in the form of 'kiss and tell' stories told from one person's point of view. Mr Bing had already placed personal information in the public domain in the course of a publicly aired disagreement with his former lover.

---

[20]   PCC Report No 74, October 2006–April 2007.

5.60   In adjudicating such cases, the PCC asks whether the details disclosed were similar and proportionate to those previously placed in the public domain by the complainant. On the question of the public interest, the Code recognises that 'there is a public interest in freedom of expression itself'. Consequently, people have a right under the Code to 'tell their own side of the story', provided that the references to 'kisses' and other intimate matters meet the test of proportionality. In the case of the two complaints made on behalf of the 'unknown woman' about the same story, one version met the test and the other did not.

5.61   The requirements of the Data Protection Act 1998 regarding sensitive personal data played a key role in determining the eventual outcome of Ms Campbell's action against the *Daily Mirror*. In its 2004 judgment,[21] the House of Lords agreed that there was a public interest in reporting that she had a drug problem. It went on to rule, however, that it was not 'fair and lawful' to disclose that she was receiving treatment or to publish details of her treatment or to resort to subterfuge in taking pictures of her leaving the clinic.

5.62   In *Campbell*, Lord Hoffman said 'if Ms Campbell had been an ordinary citizen. I think that the publication of her attendance at (NA) would have been actionable ...'.[22] Lord Hope also thought that 'unjustified intrusion on such an obviously private area of an individual's life can adversely affect treatment' and 'that the fact that publication had the potential to harm the subject of intrusion was of great weight'.[23]

5.63   The PCC, mindful that it administered a relevant Code of Practice under the Human Rights Act 1998, took immediate note of the implications of the *Campbell* judgment when it adjudicated a complaint from the publisher, Ms Kimberly Fortier, which it received shortly after it was delivered.

Fortier v Sunday Mirror[24]

5.64   In 2004, Ms Kimberly Fortier complained through her solicitors to the PCC that an article published on 29 August in the *Sunday Mirror* headlined 'Blunkett lover: It's all over' included a photograph that had been taken in a manner that breached clause 4(ii) (Harassment) of the Code of Practice. She also complained that publication of the image intruded into her privacy in breach of clause 3 (Privacy) of the Code and breached clause 4(iii) (Harassment) because the photograph constituted 'non-compliant material'.

5.65   This complaint is discussed in greater detail in Chapter 6 (clause 4 (Harassment) cases) at **6.48** et seq. The PCC's ruling on that part of the complaint made under clause 3 (Privacy) is mentioned here because, in rejecting it, a rider – the first of its kind – was added which took due note of the *Campbell* judgment.

5.66   The complaint under clause 3 was rejected on the grounds that:

---

21   *Campbell v MGN Ltd* [2004] UKHL 22.
22   Ibid; and see **12.49**.
23   See **12.50**.
24   PCC Report No 68–69, October 2004–March 2005.

'... the PCC does not generally consider that the publication of photographs of people in public places breach the Code. In this case – in circumstances where there had been no harassment – the PCC did not consider that there was any particular reason to divert from this general principle.'

5.67   The PCC, however, went on to add that: 'Exceptions might be made if there are any particular security concerns, for instance, or in rare circumstances when a photograph reveals something about an individual's health that is not in the public interest.'

Beck v Now! Magazine[25]

5.68   Shortly after the *Fortier* adjudication, Ms Allegra Versace Beck complained through her solicitors that *Now! Magazine* had published photographs of her whilst she was out shopping in London in breach of clause 3 (Privacy) of the Code. The photographs were accompanied by an article that included speculative remarks about her health and well-being. At a very early stage in the process of mediation – and in response to the clear indicative guidelines that had just been set out in the Fortier adjudication – the magazine agreed to publish an immediate and prominent apology for its intrusion into Ms Versace Beck's private life.

5.69   The magazine also accepted that it had breached the Code and undertook 'not to republish the article under complaint, or any further material concerning Ms Versace Beck's private life (including photographs taken without consent whilst engaged in private life activities and not at any public event) except where those matters have been put in the public domain by Ms Versace Beck on her representatives'. The complaint was resolved to the full satisfaction of the complainant and not taken forward to adjudication.

5.70   This sequence of events demonstrates the speed and effectiveness with which a self-regulatory council is able to respond to changes in what the law requires. The PCC maintains a close and continuous working relationship with the industry, partly through the agency of the Editors' Code Committee and partly through its other informal day-to-day consultations with newspapers and magazines. These arrangements ensure that a high degree of voluntary compliance is maintained throughout the industry and that the PCC is able to respond quickly to changing needs and circumstances.

5.71   The next four complaints illustrate how the PCC currently takes account of the requirements of the *Campbell* judgment when dealing with cases in which the complainants allege that highly personal details about their health and well-being have been published without their consent and without serving the public interest.

Grantham v Daily Star, The Sun, Daily Record, Daily Mirror and the Sunday Mirror[26]

5.72   In May 2004, the actor Leslie Grantham complained to the PCC through his solicitors that a number of published articles contained material that intruded into his

---

25   PCC Report No 66–67, April–September 2004.
26   PCC Report No 66–67, April–September 2004.

private life, in breach of clause 3 (Privacy) of the Code of Practice. The articles under complaint were published in the *Daily Star, The Sun,* the *Daily Record,* the *Daily Mirror* and the *Sunday Mirror*.

5.73   The articles reported that 'he had a specific medical condition in the form of an addiction and that he was undergoing, or was to undergo, treatment for that condition'. The condition took the form of an addiction to conducting 'internet sex sessions' with strangers. The BBC, Mr Grantham's employer, had ordered him to seek treatment for his addiction.

5.74   The complainant's solicitors maintained that there was no public interest in the material's publication and the stories would still have been intrusive even if the newspapers had only reported the outcome of a confidential meeting between the complainant and his employers. The solicitors also drew attention to the decisions reached a few weeks earlier in the action brought by Naomi Campbell against the *Daily Mirror*.

5.75   The five newspapers defended their actions on very similar grounds. They pointed out that the complainant's problems had already been the subject of extensive media coverage and that he, himself, had revealed that he was suffering from an addiction by his own conduct. All they had done was to report that the complainant had been ordered by his employer to seek professional help and advice. They had not revealed any details of medical treatment or even claimed that he had decided to seek treatment.

5.76   The PCC rejected the solicitors' claim that the information contained in these articles 'concerned a medical condition suffered by [their] client and treatment for which [their client was] undergoing for his mental health'. In the PCC's view:

> '... the articles in fact reported that the complainant had been ordered by his bosses at the BBC to undergo treatment for a "sex addiction". They did not say that such an addiction had been diagnosed by a health care professional, or even hint that the complainant had complied with any such order made by the BBC. Neither did they say where any such treatment was taking place, nor [give] any details about what the treatment did – or even might – involve. The information complained about ... related to a requirement that had allegedly been made by the complainant's employer following a disciplinary hearing.'

5.77   In reaching its decision, the PCC also considered the extent to which the complainant's behaviour had already become a subject of public debate following the alleged incident that gave rise to the disciplinary hearing. The incident involved 'an explicit act carried out by the complainant and broadcast by him to a stranger over the Internet using a webcam'. The complainant had apologised publicly for this incident and he had not complained after this was reported in another newspaper. It, therefore, followed that 'the public had a right to know what the outcome of the disciplinary hearing was'.

5.78   This was a complex case in which the PCC had to balance the complainant's right to privacy against the newspapers' right to freedom of expression. In the PCC's view, the information concerning the disciplinary hearing was 'less private than the complainant had suggested – and certainly far less so than material obtained from a medical record ...'. The events leading up to the disciplinary hearing had been 'firmly established in the public domain without complaint' and the public had a right to be kept informed of subsequent developments in the story. The complaints were, therefore, rejected.

Riding v The Independent[27]

5.79   In March 2006, the actress Ms Joanna Riding complained through her agents that an article published in *The Independent* intruded into her privacy, in breach of clause 3 (Privacy). The article reported that the complainant had withdrawn from a theatre role because she had fallen pregnant. It also said she had pulled out from a previous role 'at the last minute' because of a pregnancy and suggested that her 'efforts to start a family are getting in the way of her career'.

5.80   The complainant said the article intruded into her privacy by announcing her pregnancy before she had even told her family. The only people she had informed were her agent and the producer of the show. A press release explaining her withdrawal referred only to 'unforeseen personal circumstances'. The complainant subsequently suffered a miscarriage.

5.81   Initially, the newspaper responded to Ms Riding's agent by saying that whilst it regretted the distress she had suffered, its columnist had no reason to believe that the pregnancy was not public information. It offered to consider a letter for publication in response to the article and said that the item had been removed from its website. During the PCC's investigation, the newspaper apologised privately for revealing the pregnancy and also offered to publish an apology. The complainant rejected this offer and said she wanted the matter adjudicated.

5.82   In its adjudication, the PCC stated that, 'as a matter of commonsense, newspapers and magazines should not reveal news of an individual's pregnancy without consent before the twelve week scan, unless the information is known to such an extent that it would be perverse not to refer to it'. It went on to say that: 'This is because of the risk of complications or miscarriages, and because it should be down to the mother to share the news with her family and friends at an early stage.' In this case, the newspaper had revealed the information before the complainant had told her family. The action taken and offered by the newspaper in response to the complaint was welcomed but was not considered to be a sufficient remedy for what was a 'serious intrusion' into the complainant's private life and a 'significant breach' of clause 3 (Privacy) of the Code. The complaint was upheld.

Church v The Sun[28]

5.83   In February 2007, the singer, Ms Charlotte Church, complained to the PCC through a representative that an article published by *The Sun*, headlined 'Baby rumours for sober Church', intruded into her privacy in breach of clause 3 (Privacy) of the Code of Practice.

5.84   The newspaper had published an article referring to rumours that Ms Church was pregnant after her PR agent had requested it to treat this information as private until after the 12-week scan or a doctor had confirmed that it would be safe to tell her

---

[27]   PCC Report No 73, April–September 2006.
[28]   PCC Report No 75, April–September 2007.

family and friends. The newspaper defended its action on the grounds that it had merely reported rumours that the complainant was pregnant because of recent changes in her drinking behaviour.

5.85   In its adjudication, the PCC referred to its recent ruling in the case of Ms Riding, namely that the facts of someone's pregnancy should not be revealed before the 12-week scan without consent. In this case, the newspaper had failed to provide any evidence in support of the alleged rumours and 'had not denied that it had known for a fact' that Ms Church was pregnant. The newspaper had 'simply tried to circumvent the privacy provisions of the Code by presenting the story as speculation'. Such an action was 'not acceptable within the spirit of the Code'. The complaint was upheld.

HRH The Duke of Edinburgh v Evening Standard[29]

5.86   In August 2008, HRH The Duke of Edinburgh complained through his solicitors that the *Evening Standard* had published a front page story claiming that he was suffering from prostate cancer. The complaint was swiftly resolved through mediation when the newspaper accepted that the allegation was untrue and apologised unreservedly for intruding into the complainant's private life.

5.87   The front page of the newspaper carried a statement that 'The Evening Standard apologises to the Duke of Edinburgh', and the full text of the apology was published in an agreed position on p 5. The article was removed from the newspaper's website and replaced with the full text of the apology which appeared on the home page and was archived permanently.

5.88   From start to finish, the resolution of this complaint, to the satisfaction of the complainant, took less than 48 hours.

Privacy intrusion complaints under clause 3(ii) involving the photographing of people in places where they claimed they had a reasonable expectation of privacy

5.89   In the past, the PCC has applied a simple geographical test when dealing with complaints about the taking and publication of photographs. In the absence of any harassment, the chief consideration is whether the complainant had a reasonable expectation of privacy in the place where they were photographed.

5.90   Some publicly accessible places, such as restaurants, churches, offices – even the jungle or the foothills of the Andes – have been defined as places where someone would have such an expectation. In other adjudications, it has been made clear that 'public highways, petrol station forecourts, public beaches, car parks and so on are not such places'.[30]

---

[29]   PCC Report No 77, April–September 2008.
[30]   PCC *Annual Review 2004*, at p 6.

McCartney v Hello![31]

5.91   In 1998, Sir Paul McCartney complained that the publication of photographs of him with his family in Paris in *Hello!* magazine constituted an invasion of privacy and intruded into his grief, in breach of clause 3 (Privacy) and clause 5 (Intrusion into grief a shock), of the Code of Practice.

5.92   The photographs, under the headline 'A month after losing wife Linda – Sir Paul McCartney – Getting by with a little help from his children', showed Sir Paul, his son and his daughters walking in Paris, seated by the Seine and eating lunch outside a café. One photograph showed the family inside Notre Dame Cathedral in which the magazine described how they 'lit a candle for Linda and took some time to meditate in peace'.

5.93   Sir Paul said that these 'highly intrusive photographs of us in our most private moments at this very difficult time in our lives' had been taken without his knowledge or consent.

5.94   The editor replied that the photographs had been obtained from news agencies. She said that they were obviously not taken secretly since one of them showed Sir Paul and his son walking towards the camera. She conceded that the photograph taken in the cathedral should not have appeared: it had been added without her knowledge by the magazine's office in Madrid. She had written directly to Sir Paul to apologise for any distress caused and added: 'They were such loving pictures of you all that we were touched to see your wonderfully close relationship – which is, I am certain, what readers also felt when they saw them.'

5.95   In its adjudication, the PCC pointed out that the Code makes absolutely clear that *editors* are responsible for the content of their publications. The fact that the photographs had been obtained from news agencies was irrelevant. It was similarly unimpressed with the editor's statement that the photograph of the family inside Notre Dame Cathedral had been added without her knowledge.

5.96   The PCC agreed with Sir Paul that the photographs were deeply intrusive. It did not believe that the public interest was served by showing how 'wonderfully close' his relationship with his children was. In particular, the PCC deplored the publication of the photograph of the family inside the cathedral. The PCC pointed out that it had previously stated that it 'expects journalists to respect the sanctity of individual's acts of worship' and believed that a cathedral is a clear example of a place 'where there is a reasonable expectation of privacy, as defined in the Code of Practice'. Both complaints were upheld.

John v Daily Sport[32]

5.97   In January 1999, Sir Elton John complained through his solicitors that the taking and publication of photographs of guests relaxing in the privacy of his home in the south of France by the *Daily Sport* constituted a breach of privacy contrary to clause 3 (Privacy) of the Code of Practice.

---

[31]   PCC Report No 43, July–September 1998.
[32]   PCC Report No 45, January–March 1999.

5.98   The guests in question were David Beckham, the footballer, and his future wife, Victoria Adams of the *Spice Girls*. The newspaper claimed that, before it decided to publish the picture, their consent had been obtained. Sir Elton John, who had not been with them at the time, pointed out that he had *not* been consulted and – through his solicitors 'forcefully reminded' the PCC that 'the Code had been modified just under a year before when new provisions were introduced including "a reference to the privacy of one's *home*"'.

5.99   The newspaper said that the photographs had been obtained from a picture agency and were taken from a public footpath near to Sir Elton's properly. Sir Elton's solicitors maintained that they had been taken secretly, possibly from the top of a ladder placed against the wall of his house.

5.100   In its adjudication, the PCC noted that clause 3(i) of the Code protected an individual's right to respect for his home life. In this case, the taking of photographs and their subsequent publication had intruded into the complainant's home life, and the privacy to which he and his guests were entitled. No consent was given and there was no public interest justification. The complaint was therefore upheld.

Sir Elton John v The Daily Sport[33]

5.101   There was a most unfortunate sequel to this adjudication when, in April 2001, Sir Elton John complained a second time through his solicitors that the *Daily Sport* had republished a photograph of a guest relaxing at his home in the south of France in breach of clause 3 (Privacy) of the Code of Practice.

5.102   On this occasion the editor gave a written undertaking that the photograph would never appear in the newspaper again and that the newspaper had destroyed any copies in its possession.

5.103   In its adjudication, the PCC ruled that the re-publication of the photograph was unacceptable and represented a serious breach of the Code. Nothing had changed between the PCC's first adjudication and April 2001 to justify the printing of the picture, which should in any case have been tagged after the initial complaint to ensure that it was not printed again. The PCC did not expect to have to adjudicate twice on the same matter and trusted that the editor's undertaking and belated destruction of his copies of the photograph would ensure that it is not published again.

Ford and Scott v Daily Mail and OK! Magazine[34]

5.104   In 2000, Ms Anna Ford, the TV newscaster, and Mr David Scott complained to the PCC through their solicitors that photographs of them published in the *Daily Mail* and in *OK! Magazine* intruded into their privacy in breach of clause 3 (Privacy) of the Code of Practice.

5.105   This was a case in which the dissatisfied complainants went on to apply for a judicial review of the PCC's ruling. The full adjudication reads as follows:

---

[33]   PCC Report No 54, April–June 2001.
[34]   PCC Report No 52, October–December 2000.

'The photographs were taken while the complainants were on holiday in Majorca and showed them on a beach while they were wearing their swimwear. They said that the hotel had been booked privately and that they understood that the beach in front of the hotel, where they were photographed, was private. They maintained that the area in which they were photographed was one where they could have a reasonable expectation of privacy.'

5.106 *OK! Magazine* said that whilst the hotel backed on to a stretch of the beach, the beach itself was not private property or reserved exclusively for the use of the hotel guests. The magazine provided the name of a hotel employee who confirmed that the beach was a public area and not restricted to hotel guests only. The beach also stretched for some distance away from the hotel and was overlooked by a number of apartments and the area could in no way be described as private. The *Daily Mail* added that the photographs were taken at the height of the holiday season and submitted a number of newspaper articles from May 2000 which had put the fact of the complainant's friendship clearly into the public domain. Among these articles was one by Ms Ford herself.

5.107 In its adjudication, the PCC considered the manner in which the photographs were taken and whether their publication showed a lack of the respect for private and family life to which everyone is entitled under clause 3.

5.108 Clause 3 (ii) says that 'the use of long lens photography to take pictures of people in private places without their consent is unacceptable'. It was clear to the PCC both that long lens photography had been used and that consent had not been given: the issue for the PCC to decide in the first instance was therefore whether the couple were in a place where they had a reasonable expectation of privacy. Although the hotel where the complainants were staying may have owned the seats directly outside the hotel, there did not appear to be any evidence that the beach itself was private and not generally accessible to members of the public. Neither had the assertion that the beach was overlooked by a number of properties unconnected with the hotel been challenged. Although the PCC could understand why the complainants were uncomfortable at having been photographed in this way it could do nothing more than apply strictly the terms of the Code. It could not conclude that a publicly accessible Majorcan beach was a place where the complainants could have had a reasonable expectation of privacy. There was therefore no breach of the clause 3(ii) of the Code.

5.109 Regarding the publication of the photographs, the PCC looked to the terms of clause 3(i), which entitles everyone to respect for his or her private and family life and mirrors the terms of the Human Rights Act 1998 (HRA 1998). Having already concluded that the complainants were not in a place where they could reasonably expect privacy, the remaining issue for the PCC to consider was whether publication of the photographs of the complainants in their swimwear showed a lack of respect for their private lives. The PCC had a degree of sympathy with the complainants because the attention that they had attracted was clearly unwanted. However, it had to bear in mind the nature of the photographs – which were, in the PCC's opinion, innocuous and the sort taken regularly of well-known people in public places. The pictures neither intruded into any intimacy nor left the complainants open to ridicule and the PCC did not consider that by their nature they had shown the complainants a lack of respect for their private lives. Furthermore, as the *Daily Mail* had demonstrated in submitting numerous newspaper cuttings, the photographs had not illustrated anything about the complainants' relationship that was not already in the public domain. The complaints were, therefore, not upheld.

5.110 When Ms Ford and Mr Scott applied for a judicial review the PCC's adjudication was upheld by the Divisional Court. In his ruling, Mr Justice Silber said that:[35]

> '... the type of balancing operation [between rights to privacy and freedom of expression] conducted by a specialist body, such as the PCC, is still regarded as a field of activity to which the courts should and will defer. The PCC is a body whose membership and expertise makes it much better equipped than the courts to resolve the difficult exercise of balancing the conflicting rights ... [of] privacy and of the newspapers to publish.'

Renate John v Sunday Mirror[36]

5.111 In 2000, Sir Elton John's ex-wife, Renate, complained through her solicitors that photographs of her in a car park and on a petrol station forecourt were taken by the *Sunday Mirror* in places where she had a reasonable expectation of privacy in breach of clause 3 of the Code of Practice. She also complained that the reporters had harassed her in breach of clause 4 and resorted to subterfuge by not revealing their identities in breach of clause 10.

5.112 The PCC noted that Mrs John was out of doors in places where any number of people were entitled to be without any restriction. At the time 'she was not engaged in any private activity' and the content of the article did not contain any material that concerned 'details of her private life – for example, details of her state of health, current relationships, private conversations or photographs of her in private places'.

5.113 Mrs John herself had pointed out that 'she was not a celebrity in her own right and that since her divorce fourteen years previously she had endeavoured to stay out of the public spotlight rejecting offers of money from the media – including the *Sunday Mirror* – for interviews'.

5.114 The PCC accepted 'that a free press will from time to time write about people who have formerly been in the public eye' but it went on to say that:

> ' . . . it is not the Commission's job either to restrict this right or to afford individuals a veto over future publicity; provided, of course, that newspapers abide by the terms of the Code in such reporting. In this case, they had done so – because the article did not contain any material that on any reasonable criteria could be described as private.'

5.115 Nevertheless, the PCC ruled that the newspaper had breached the Code in one instance: by including details of the complainant's address. The complaint was upheld under clause 3 on this count. The complaints about harassment and misrepresentation were not upheld.[37]

5.116 Mrs Renate John made a second complaint under clause 3 that *Hello!* magazine had also photographed her in the car park at the same time. In this instance, the reporters did not resort to subterfuge or harassment. The article did not reveal details of her address or any other information about her that could be described as private. The complaint was not upheld.

---

[35]   High Court of Justice, Queen's Bench Division, 31 July 2001.
[36]   PCC Report No 53, January–March 2001.
[37]   PCC Report No 53, January–March 2001.

Stewart-Brady v Liverpool Echo, The Mirror and the Daily Record[38]

5.117 In 2000, Ian Stewart-Brady complained through his solicitors that photographs published in the *Liverpool Echo*, *The Mirror* and the *Daily Record* represented an unjustified intrusion into his privacy, in breach of clause 3 (Privacy) of the Code of Practice. The photographs were taken when Brady was on hunger strike and being driven, under police guard, from Ashworth Hospital to Fazakerley Hospital for tests.

5.118 Two of the newspapers claimed that Brady had forfeited his rights to privacy when he committed the crimes for which he was convicted. He had already sought publicity for his condition in his campaign for the right to starve himself to death. He had also failed to complain about a number of previously published articles which related to his health and his campaign to be allowed to die. The publication of these stories and photographs was therefore justified on grounds of public interest.

5.119 In its adjudication, the PCC noted that the picture had been taken in an area of the hospital grounds which was open to the public and that Mr Stewart-Brady was visible to anyone outside through the window of the van. There was no evidence that he had been harassed. It also noted that Mr Stewart-Brady had been conducting a public campaign about his current position and that this was clearly a matter of public interest. The publication of the pictures did no more than illustrate the statements that he had been issuing to the media. They were comparable 'to those considered by the Court of Appeal when, on a previous occasion, Mr Stewart-Brady unsuccessfully took the Commission to judicial review on a complaint he had made'.

5.120 The PCC also noted that Mr Stewart-Brady had failed to complain to the PCC about a number of previous articles which related to his health and his then current campaign to starve himself to death.

5.121 The PCC rejected the complaint but it also rejected the claim made by two of the newspapers that Mr Brady had forfeited any right to privacy. It went on to state that, 'there are no circumstances in which the PCC would adopt such a line. The Code – in line with the Human Rights Act – confers rights to privacy on everyone, no matter how horrendous their crimes'.

Goodyear v The People[39]

5.122 In 2002, Ms Julie Goodyear complained that *The People* had intruded into her privacy in breach of clause 3 of the Code of Practice when it published long lens photographs of her sitting in her back garden where she had a reasonable expectation of privacy. The editor claimed that her garden was visible from public places bordering her garden and that she had previously been paid by *The People* for features and stories about her home.

5.123 The complaint was upheld on the grounds that since it was necessary to use long lens photographs, it was unlikely that any passers-by would have been able to identify her. Although people might limit their rights to future protection by selling information

---

[38] PCC Report No 49, January–March 2000.
[39] PCC Report No 60, October 2002–March 2003.

and pictures of a personal nature, they did not necessarily forfeit them and the Code's provisions regarding the use of long lens photography without prior consent were extremely strict.

Ms Dynamite v Islington Gazette[40]

5.124 In 2003, the singer Ms Dynamite complained to the PCC through her record company Polydor that an article (and accompanying photograph) headlined 'Chart star's dream house is right next door to mum' published in the *Islington Gazette* intruded into her privacy in breach of clause 3 (Privacy) of the Code of Practice.

5.125 The article gave the name of the street in which the house was purchased, accompanied by a photograph of the specific property. The complainant's representatives said that the inclusion of such detail made identification of Ms Dynamite's new home possible and could put her at risk from obsessive fans.

5.126 The editor wrote directly to Ms Dynamite and expressed sincere regret for any problems that the article had caused and promised that in future the newspaper would not publish photographs of her home in conjunction with the road name.

5.127 In its adjudication, the PCC was pleased to note that the editor had made efforts to resolve the complaint. It had, however, previously made clear that when publishing details about a celebrity's home without consent, care must be taken to ensure that editors do not publish the precise address or material that would enable people to find the whereabouts of the home. When making this point the PCC had been mindful of the particular security problems that some celebrities have encountered. The complaint was upheld.

Cox v The People[41]

5.128 In 2003, the Radio 1 DJ star, Sarah Cox complained to the PCC through her solicitors that *The People* had published naked pictures of her on honeymoon in the Seychelles with her husband, in breach of clause 3 of the Code of Practice. The pictures were taken with a telephoto lens by an agency photographer. The couple were on a private beach accessible only to paying guests. The editor claimed that he did not know that the island was private property. He was reminded that it was his responsibility to find out and also to ascertain from the photographic agency the provenance under which the pictures were taken.

5.129 The PCC quickly negotiated a voluntary settlement in which the newspaper offered to publish an unqualified apology which was published on p 3 on the following Sunday. Ms Cox's solicitors had previously been advised that if they preferred the complaint to go to formal adjudication, this would be done. She decided, however, to bring an action under the HRA 1998 but, in the event, a settlement was reached in the High Court before a judge. No ruling was made. Damages of £50,000 were agreed with £30,000 awarded to Ms Cox and £20,000 to her husband. The legal costs incurred under a conditional fee arrangement were in the order of £200,000.

---

[40]   PCC Report No 62–63, April–September 2003.
[41]   Not PCC listed (complaint withdrawn).

Rowling v Daily Mirror[42]

5.130 In 2005, the author, Ms JK Rowling complained through her solicitors to the PCC that an article in the *Daily Mirror* headlined 'The J.K. Rowling story: Day Three' intruded into her privacy in breach of clause 3 (Privacy) of the Code of Practice.

5.131 The article contained a photograph of the complainant's London property with the name of the road on which it was located. Her solicitors said that there was sufficient information to identify its exact location in breach of the Code. This was in circumstances where the complainants had previously been subject to security threats at their various homes.

5.132 The newspaper argued that the address was in the public domain, the name of the road had already been published in another newspaper and the electoral register identified her as the owner.

5.133 In its adjudication, the PCC was satisfied that the photograph and its caption identified the exact location of the property. The newspaper had failed to demonstrate that the information was in the public domain to such an extent as to justify publishing it in this way. There was, therefore, a breach of clause 3 on this point.

5.134 The solicitors also complained that the publication of photographs and other information about Ms Rowling's other two houses breached clause 3. The newspaper claimed that other newspapers had published details of the Edinburgh property.

5.135 In its adjudication of this part of the complaint the PCC found that the information published about these properties was not sufficient to identify them. In addition, the PCC did not believe that the very general reference to the security systems of the two properties and a statement that the complainant and her family spent time at weekends in their country house were intrinsically private. Publication of these details did not therefore constitute a failure to respect the complainant's private and family life in breach of clause 3 of the Code. On this point the complaint was not upheld.

Sheridan v The Scottish Sun[43]

5.136 In October 2006, Mrs Gail Sheridan, the wife of a high-profile Scottish politician, complained to the PCC through her solicitors that an article in *The Scottish Sun* headlined 'Gail's pain' was accompanied by a photograph of her taken in a private place in breach of clause 3 (Privacy) of the Code of Practice.

5.137 The complainant said that the photograph showed her in her back garden, a place where she had a reasonable expectation of privacy, and was taken with a long lens camera. There was no public interest in its publication, particularly as she had appeared at a press conference the previous day.

5.138 The newspaper claimed that the photographer was on a public road when he took the picture and that the complainant was visible to the public at the time. She was not engaged in any private activity as she was merely standing in the driveway with her keys in her hand. She was a public figure with a high media profile and had previously

---

[42]   PCC Report No 72, October 2005–April 2006.
[43]   PCC Report No 75, April–September 2007.

posed for photos in her garden. It agreed, however, to annotate its records to reflect the complainant's concerns 'as a gesture of goodwill'.

5.139 In its adjudication, the PCC stated that it applied 'a common sense test' in such cases. It pointed out that 'there are publicly accessible places such as cafes, churches or offices where there is a reasonable expectation of privacy, whilst ground which is privately owned but completely visible to passers-by may be considered less private'.

5.140 In this case the complainant was visible and identifiable from the street and not engaging in any particularly private activity. The photograph was innocuous in content. The PCC also pointed out that 'the Code does not distinguish between long lens and other types of photography. It is the location of the individual – in this case, whether the complainant was visible and identifiable from the street – that is important, not the means by which a photograph is taken'. The complaint was not upheld.

Rowling v Daily Mirror, Daily Record and Mail on Sunday[44]

5.141 In June 2008, Ms JK Rowling complained through her solicitors about articles in the *Daily Mirror*, *Daily Record* and *Mail on Sunday*. They reported that she had bought a property close to the estate that she already owned in Perthshire. Ms Rowling said that the articles identified the whereabouts of her Perthshire home and thereby invaded her privacy in breach of clause 3 (Privacy) of the Code of Practice.

5.142 The PCC had previously ruled that identifying the whereabouts of the homes of high-profile people who may attract stalkers or unwanted attention from obsessed fans may breach the Code. Indeed, in 2005, the PCC upheld a complaint from Ms Rowling after the *Daily Mirror* published sufficient information to identify the address of her London home.

5.143 Similarly, in this case, the PCC had to consider whether the newspapers had themselves been responsible for putting new material into the public domain. The PCC found that Ms Rowling's ownership of her Perthshire home, the name of the property, the country in which it was situated and the town it was near were all in the public domain to a considerable extent – far more so than simply appearing on land registry documents and the electoral roll. Restraint upon further publication of the information would, in the PCC's view, serve no purpose. Moreover, the PCC noted that the articles under complaint had not given the precise whereabouts of Ms Rowling's Perthshire home. They had not named the road on which the property was situated and had not specified precisely where it was in relation to the nearest town.

5.144 In these circumstances, the complaints were not upheld.

---

[44]   PCC Report No 77, April–September 2008.

Chapter 6

COMPLAINTS UNDER CLAUSE 4
(HARASSMENT)

6.1   Clause 4 (Harassment) of the Press Complaints PCC's (PCC's) Code of Practice reads as follows:

'4 * Harassment

(i)   Journalists must not engage in intimidation, harassment or persistent pursuit.

(ii)   They must not persist in questioning, telephoning, pursuing or photographing individuals once asked to desist; nor remain on their property when asked to leave and must not follow them. If requested, they must identify themselves and whom they represent.

(iii) Editors must ensure these principles are observed by those working for them and take care not to use non-compliant material from other sources.'

6.2   As in the case of complaints about privacy intrusion, editors are allowed to advance a public interest defence of their actions when responding to complaints about harassment. In the context of the Code requirements, harassment is treated as a more or less continuous form of privacy intrusion and, as we shall see, it is this 'more or less' factor that often makes it difficult to draw a clear-cut distinction between the two kinds of complaint. As Beales points out:[1]

> '... while formal complaints are, therefore, rare, adjudications are even less common. And they are often difficult as there tends to be wide discrepancy between the accounts of complainants and journalists of the contact between them.'

6.3   The requirements of clause 4 are very similar to those of the Protection from Harassment Act 1997, which states that 'a person must not pursue a course of conduct (defined as at least two events or occasions) which amounts to harassment of another and which he or she knows, or ought to know, would amount to harassment of the other'.[2] The Act does not define harassment, as such, beyond stating that it includes conduct that causes a person alarm or distress. Responsible investigative journalism, amongst other activities, is excluded from the provisions of the Act.

6.4   Since January 2003 the PCC has operated a 24-hour emergency help-line for people who feel that they are being harassed by journalists and want them removed from their doorsteps. PCC staff advise callers what to say and do and also immediately alert the editors involved, warning them that a complaint has been received. The helpline has been extended to include broadcasters. As such, it acts as a clearing house that passes on 'desist' requests as soon as they are received to print and broadcast media organisations alike. This service has been particularly effective in preventing the kinds of unintentional

---

[1]   I Beales *The Editors' Codebook* (Press Standards Board of Finance, revised 2nd edn, 2009), at p 33.

[2]   Section 1(1) and (2).

Privacy and Personality Rights

media 'scrums' that used to occur in the wake of tragedies such as rail disasters or acts of terrorism. Since 2003, the PCC has issued hundreds of desist notices. The PCC does so only when help is requested but, in cases of harassment that are already in the public domain or are drawn to its attention, it gets in touch with the people affected and offers its services. The PCC's note on what to do in cases of harassment is reproduced at Appendix C.

6.5 In dealing with harassment complaints, simply totting up the number of 'desist' requests that have to be made over a period of time does not always produce the right answers. As *The Editors' Codebook* points out:[3]

> 'A *desist* request does not last forever. The passage of time may lessen the risk of harassment. Circumstances can alter, sometimes rapidly, and a fresh approach may then be legitimate. There can be no set formula for deciding this ... the PCC assesses each case on its merits. But it would normally require editors to show reasonable grounds, such as a material change in circumstances, for a renewed approach.'

6.6 The PCC holds editors responsible for checking the provenance of stories and photographs which they buy in from agencies, freelance journalists and photographers. It is the editors' job to ascertain that any material supplied by them has been obtained by means that conform with the requirements of the Code. The PCC cannot stop agencies or paparazzi from harassing members of the public. It can and does sanction editors who publish stories and photographs obtained in non-compliant ways that breach the Code.

6.7 The key questions asked when dealing with complaints under clause 4 are as follows:[4]

'•   *Was there a request to desist?* Subsequent pursuit, etc, would need to be justified in the public interest or by changed circumstances.
•   *Did non-staff contributors comply?*
•   *Was there a public interest?'*

6.8 In 2008, the 48 rulings issued by the PCC under clause 4 accounted for 3.4% of all the rulings issued in that year.

CASE STUDIES

6.9 The following case studies illustrate the kinds of issues that arise in dealing with complaints about harassment.

Szurma v The People[5]

6.10 In September 1993, Ms Sonia Szurma complained to the PCC that *The People* had published a photograph of her that was taken without permission in circumstances

---

[3]   *The Editors' Codebook*, n 1 above, at p 33.
[4]   *The Editors' Codebook*, n 1 above, at p 35.
[5]   PCC Report No 21, October–November 1993.

which breached what was then clause 8 (Harassment) of the Code of Practice. The photograph was published with an article headlined 'Revealed at last ... it's the changing face of Mrs Ripper'.

6.11   Mrs Szurma said that, having gone into the garden at the rear of the house to relax in the sunshine, the sound of a camera attracted her attention and she saw a man up a tree in the field adjoining her house taking photographs.

6.12   The complaint was put to the editor, who was asked to reply within 7 days. She replied after 2 weeks following a reminder, saying the picture was not commissioned by her but was taken by a freelance. She could not, therefore, be held responsible for the circumstances under which it was taken. She justified the publication of the photograph in the public interest as it showed the strain on Mrs Szurma following the imprisonment of her husband for the so-called Yorkshire Ripper crimes.

6.13   The PCC was 'unimpressed by the editor's attempt to justify the publication of the photograph in circumstances in which no public interest was served'. It found her failure to accept responsibility for the manner in which the photograph was taken to be 'lamentable'. This was a clear breach of the Code and the complaint was upheld.

6.14   This complaint illustrates just how confrontational a minority of editors could be in their dealings with the PCC during the early 1990s. In this instance, the editor's response was indifferent with regard to her responsibilities under the Code and lackadaisical in her failure to reply in the first instance.

Prince William and Prince Harry

6.15   Two years later, in 1995, the PCC upheld a complaint from Ms Mary Livesley that her 15-year-old son had been approached by a reporter from the *Accrington Observer and Times* as he was leaving school. The reporter was seeking information concerning other pupils, in breach of what was then clause 12 (Interviewing or photographing children) of the Code. This adjudication coincided with the impending arrival of Prince William at Eton College and mounting concern at Buckingham Palace that pupils at Eton and local residents were already being 'lined up by some newspapers to supply stories about the Prince when he began his schooling in September'.[6]

6.16   The then Chairman of the PCC, Lord Wakeham, took this opportunity to deliver a speech at St Bride's Institute in which he linked the adjudication in the case of the Accrington boy with the prospect of media harassment facing the young Prince William. He insisted that the Prince 'was entitled to the same protection under the Code as any other child, and that what goes for a child in Accrington goes for a child in Eton'.[7]

6.17   An agreement was subsequently reached between the Palace, the PCC and the press that the Princes William and Harry would enjoy, not *extra* protection or *less* protection, but simply the *same* respect for their privacy as any other children.

---

[6]   R Shannon *A Press Free and Responsible Self-regulation and the Press Complaints Commission 1991–2001* (John Murray, 2001), at pp 202–203.
[7]   PCC *Moving Ahead* (1995), at pp 5–8.

6.18   The Palace, for its part, recognising the legitimate public interest in the children, agreed to ensure that photographs and information about them would from time to time be made available to the press and broadcasters. This agreement was to be 'a balancing act – legitimate privacy and legitimate access: in other words, a common sense solution based on the terms of a commonsense Code of Practice'.[8]

6.19   For the next 2 years the agreement worked well. Prince Harry started school at Eton in 1998 and 'virtually no photographs of them taken without parental consent' were printed in British newspapers. Indeed, the Code had been so successful and the agreement honoured so widely that the paparazzi, who were once very much in evidence in and around Eton, [had] ... virtually disappeared from the school – aware that there was no market for their pictures in the British press'.[9]

6.20   Then, in November 1998, the Palace complained informally about a number of apparently harmless stories recounting trivial events in the daily lives of Prince William and Prince Harry – that one or other had scored a goal, had had his hair cut differently or had sustained a minor injury. None of the stories on their own constituted a serious breach, if any, of the Code. Over a period of weeks and months, however, they were beginning to amount to cumulative intrusion of a kind likely to have an incrementally negative effect on the Princes' privacy and quality of life. Their cumulative effect would eventually add up to harassment.

6.21   After further consultations with the Palace and the industry the PCC reviewed the original agreement and published three additional 'rule of thumb' guidelines in April 1999. In summary form they said that:[10]

- While individual stories in themselves may be harmless, it could not be right for boys such as Prince William and Prince Harry to be exposed to weekly headlines and splashes about them:
  - there could not be a total blackout on stories about the Princes at school; and
  - editors should consider the proportionality of any story – assessing both the potential damage to the children's education, as well as the prominence given to a particular article and the cumulative build up of similar stories across the media.

6.22   These guidelines for reporting on the Royal Princes were designed to protect them from both privacy intrusion and harassment. Where the line should be drawn between these two kinds of breach would always depend on the specific circumstances of the complaint under consideration. They provided a clarification regarding the requirements of clause 4 and a warning that if the guidelines were not observed and a complaint was received then it was very likely to be upheld. In the unlikely event that the children of parents not in the public eye were also subjected to this kind of 'cumulative intrusion' by the press, they would receive exactly the same degree of protection as the Royal Princes.

6.23   The protection of the Royal Princes' privacy became an issue once more when, in the summer of 2000, Prince William left school to continue his studies at St Andrews.

---

8   PCC Report No 51, July–September 2000, at p 21.
9   PCC Report No 46, April–June 1999, at p 6.
10 PCC Report No 46, April–June 1999, at p 7.

Rumours were already circulating in some quarters that once he was 18 he would be beyond the protection of the Code and 'fair game' for sustained and continuous media attention.

6.24 On 28 June 2000, Lord Wakeham addressed this issue in a second speech given at the St Bride's institute. He announced that after extensive consultations with editors he was reassured that 'they want to continue to make things work', to ensure that Prince William got as much privacy as possible and their readers could 'read about him and see pictures of him ... all of them acknowledge that he has a right to a private life'.

6.25 Lord Wakeham went on to emphasise that 'no one is asking for special treatment for Prince William. The principles on which I am expanding here, apply to everyone else as much as to him ...'. The principles in question related to issues concerning photographs, facts, privacy and physical intrusion.

6.26 First, with regard to the photographs, now that Prince William was 18 he could expect to be photographed in public places like any other young adult. It would not, however, be justifiable to publish pictures of him obtained as a result of intimidation or harassment, or to publish 'snatched' pictures of him taken when he was in a private place where there was a reasonable expectation of privacy.

6.27 Secondly, with regard to the facts, more stories would be written about Prince William. As both a public figure and 'also a very young man' editors had a special obligation to check the accuracy of their stories before publishing them. In particular, inaccurate stories about alleged relationships could be potentially damaging to both him and the girls concerned. This obligation, in turn put 'an onus on St James's Palace to ensure that they respond constructively to legitimate enquiries about stories relating to Prince William'.

6.28 Thirdly, clause 3 of the Code gave everyone the same entitlement to privacy. At this point in his speech, Lord Wakeham drew attention to a recent adjudication on a complaint from Ian Brady in which it was reiterated that 'even serial killers are entitled to their privacy' under the European Convention for the Protection of Human Rights and Fundamental Freedoms (ECHR). It was, therefore, 'unthinkable that the second in line to the throne should not be treated to the same respect'.

6.29 After listing the relevant requirements of the Code, Lord Wakeham said:

> 'I do not believe it possible or desirable to prohibit newspapers entirely from speculation and reports about young ladies. But ... endless intrusion of the sort we have not seen for five years ... would make his life a misery, make his friends' life a misery and make it much more difficult for him to forge proper and meaningful relationships.'

6.30 Fourthly, with regard to physical intrusion, the Code was very clear on the issue of harassment. It would, therefore, be 'quite unacceptable for paparazzi photographers to pursue Prince William around whichever University he attends – and quite unacceptable for newspapers to publish photographs which have been obtained in this manner'. The absence of paparazzi at Eton over the previous 5 years had been a significant success, and 'Prince William's eighteenth birthday [was] not an invitation for them to return'.[11]

---

[11] PCC Report No 51, July–September 2000, at pp 21–26.

6.31   Throughout these negotiations, the PCC had held fast to the principle that everyone had the same entitlement to privacy under the Code – as it was bound to do. At the same time, it recognised the fact that the Royal Princes – as high-profile public figures in their own right – were uniquely exposed to the risks of sustained media attention and intrusions into their private lives.

6.32   If the PCC had allowed Prince William to become 'fair game' for the paparazzi at university it would have exposed his fellow students to exactly the same risks. The right to privacy includes the right to be left alone in the company of other people. The privacy rights of the young Prince and his peers were therefore indivisible because they were mutually interdependent. You could not protect the one without protecting the others.

6.33   As a consequence, the protective remit of the Code had been incrementally extended over a 10-year period from children to 'young persons' completing their 'time at school', and thence onwards to include their time at university. The whole exercise provides an illuminating case study in how to find 'a commonsense solution based on the terms of a commonsense Code of Practice' to the problem of balancing and reconciling the rights embodied in Arts 8 and 10 of the ECHR.

6.34   The terms of this new agreement between the Palace, the press and the PCC were generally upheld and Prince William was able to complete his time at university free from media harassment. As in all such arrangements, there were a few isolated occasions when the Code was breached. One such incident occurred off campus.

St James' Palace v OK! Magazine[12]

6.35   In October 2000, St James' Palace complained on behalf of HRH Prince William that photographs of the Prince published in *OK! Magazine* were taken in breach of clause 4 (Harassment) and published in breach of clause 3 (Privacy) of the Code of Practice.

6.36   The photographs were taken in southern Chile in the foothills of the Andes where the Prince was travelling during his gap year between school and university. They showed him involved in a number of activities including hiking and crossing a river. The complainants said that the photographs had clearly been taken as a result of persistent pursuit in breach of clause 4 and that their publication would only inflate the market for paparazzi pictures of the Prince.

6.37   The editor claimed that their publication was in the public interest because they showed the young Prince in preparation for his future role as monarch. He went on to apologise for any distress that had been caused but argued that the pictures were taken in a public place. The complainants counterclaimed that the Prince was in a distant and isolated place where he could reasonably have expected to be left alone. The media had already been given an opportunity for photo calls in order to obviate the need for the press to buy paparazzi photographs.

6.38   Both complaints were upheld on the grounds that Prince William was in a place where he had a reasonable expectation of privacy. Other British publications had been offered these photographs and declined them. On the issue of harassment, the PCC

---

[12]   PCC Report No 52, October–December 2000.

ruled that all young people had the same right to protection from persistent pursuit under the Code 'so that they could go about their normal lives without physical intimidation' and unwanted publicity. *OK! Magazine* was seriously at fault in not checking the circumstances under which the photographs were taken.

6.39   In its adjudication, the PCC also drew attention to the new guidelines which stated that it was difficult to foresee any circumstances in which it would be justifiable to publish pictures of Prince William that have been obtained 'as a result of intimidation or persistent pursuit'. The complaints were upheld.

6.40   In 2001, the agreement was unexpectedly broken once again when a television company owned by HRH Prince Edward tried to take unauthorised photographs of his nephew, Prince William, on the campus of St Andrew's University. The matter was swiftly resolved on an informal basis within Palace circles and the PCC did not receive a formal complaint. The incident served as a reminder that close relatives can sometimes pose a greater threat to a person's privacy than editors. Apart from these incidents, the British press honoured the terms of the agreement and the paparazzi were unable to sell their photographs to British publications.

6.41   As has been noted, difficulties frequently arise in dealing with complaints about harassment because complainants and journalists often disagree about what actually happened between them. Celebrity events like Christmas and birthday parties attract a very high level of media interest and, as such, are likely targets for overly intrusive journalists and photographers.

6.42   The next complaint illustrates how the protection afforded by a 'desist notice' can be overtaken by substantial new developments in the story being covered.

Fortier v Sunday Mirror[13]

6.43   A few weeks after the *Campbell* judgment,[14] the PCC received a complaint from the publisher, Kimberly Fortier, through her solicitors that an article published in the *Sunday Mirror* on 29 August 2004 headlined 'Blunkett lover: It's all over', included a photograph that had been taken in a manner that breached clause 4(ii) (Harassment) of the Code of Practice. Ms Fortier also complained that publication of the image intruded into her privacy in breach of clause 3 (Privacy) and breached clause 4(iii) (Harassment) because the photographs constituted 'non-compliant' material.

6.44   This incident followed the publication of an article in another newspaper alleging that Ms Fortier had been having an affair with the then Home Secretary, David Blunkett. Her solicitors had contacted the PCC, claiming that she was being harassed. The PCC immediately sent desist notices to several newspapers, including the *Sunday Mirror*, which were followed by letters from the solicitors sent on 16 August.

6.45   Ten days later, after the complainant was photographed with her son entering the grounds of a library in Los Angeles, her solicitors warned several newspapers that the publication of these pictures would constitute publication of 'non-compliant' material in breach of clause 4(iii) (Harassment). This happened after the *Sunday Mirror* published its picture that Ms Fortier's solicitors submitted their complaint to the PCC.

---

[13]   PCC Report No 68–69, October 2004–March 2005.
[14]   *Campbell v MGN Limited* [2004] UKHL 22.

6.46   That part of the complaint made under clause 3 is discussed in Chapter 5 at **5.64** et seq. In its adjudication of the complaint under clause 4, the PCC noted that 'it did not appear that the photographer had "persisted" in taking her photograph after having been asked to desist'. At some point '– either before he spoke to her or afterwards – he took the photograph'. Ms Fortier had not agreed to be photographed, 'but this did mean the complainant had been harassed because there had been, as both sides agreed, only one approach'.

6.47   The solicitors, however, maintained that the desist notice of 16 August warning photographers to stop approaching Ms Fortier was still in force on 26 August. Any approach made after 16 August would, therefore, constitute a breach of the Code.

6.48   The PCC, however, concluded that 'it did not consider it appropriate – or within the meaning of clause 4 – to assume that a request for journalists and photographers to desist from approaching a complainant lasts in perpetuity'.

6.49   In this case, the PCC noted that the approach had taken place 10 days after the request to desist, during which time there had been substantial developments in the story. These developments had been reported in the article accompanying the photograph in the *Sunday Mirror* – namely that Ms Fortier had contacted the House Secretary in order to bring to an end their alleged relationship. Given this change in circumstances 'it followed that there was also no breach of Clause 4(iii) regarding the use of non-compliant material'.

6.50   Finally, the PCC noted that the complainant's solicitors and the newspaper disagreed about whether Ms Fortier was a public figure and whether publication of the material was in the public interest. The PCC ruled that:

> '... whether or not this was the case, it had been alleged publicly that she was having a relationship with a senior politician. No complaints had been received from the politician or the complainant concerning the content of the numerous articles about their alleged relationship. The Commission could not agree that, in this context the publication of a photograph – which contributed to the debate and which was taken in accordance with the Code at a time when the story was developing – was intrusive. For all these reasons, the complaint was upheld.'

Kate Middleton

6.51   Ms Middleton's harassment started on 9 January 2007 after a wave of media speculation that an announcement of her engagement to Prince William was imminent. A scrum of journalists, photographers and amateurs with mobile phone cameras camped outside her flat and pursued her down the street whenever she went out.

6.52   Throughout these events, the PCC maintained regular contact with her solicitors. News International announced that it would not buy any photographs taken by paparazzi and some other publishers followed this lead. On 12 January, at the request of Ms Middleton's solicitors, the PCC circulated a letter to all editors warning them that if they persisted in using pictures supplied by the paparazzi a formal complaint would be submitted to the PCC. Shortly afterwards, the media scrum dispersed and the harassment ceased.

6.53 In March 2007, Ms Middleton's solicitors lodged a formal complaint against the *Daily Mirror* after it had published a photograph of her walking along the street. The next day, the editor published a formal apology, explaining that the picture was taken by a freelance photographer 'in circumstances where we were later told she felt harassed. We got it wrong and we sincerely regret that'.[15]

6.54 In its seventh Report, the House of Commons Culture, Media and Sport Committee questioned whether the 'media circus should have gone on as long as it did'. It thought that the PCC was too slow in acting to protect Ms Middleton whilst recognising 'the force of the argument that an individual who seeks the protection of the PCC should make a formal complaint'.[16]

6.55 There are, however, a number of good reasons why the PCC does not issue desist notices without the prior consent of the people affected. It can, and does, discreetly advise people who are being harassed of the kinds of protection it is able to provide *when* such cases are drawn to its attention. If, however, the PCC issued a notice without prior consent and the harassment continued it would be possible for the PCC to act on the basis of a third-party complaint or launch an investigation of its own volition. It would, however, be difficult to conduct a fair and even-handed investigation without the consent and co-operation of the individual involved.

6.56 People who are experiencing media harassment should be left free to decide whether or not they wish to make a formal complaint. Throughout Ms Middleton's ordeal, the PCC remained in continuous contact with her solicitors and promptly circulated their warning letter to all editors 3 days after the harassment started. The PCC works proactively and discreetly in many other ways to prevent harassment. In the case of the sequence of murders near Ipswich in 2006, for example, it alerted the local constabulary liaison officers that it was on hand to advise and assist relatives and friends of the deceased should they be approached by the press or feel harassed by their inquiries.[17]

6.57 Harassment can be contained and its incidence can be reduced but neither the courts nor the PCC can put an end to it. The paparazzi will not stop harassing celebrities because they are unable to sell their 'non-compliant' pictures to British newspapers and magazines: there is a vast and buoyant international market for such material that is largely unregulated.

6.58 The problems that arise in regulating this market are currently being compounded by the growing number of amateur or 'citizen' photographers in search of jackpot payments from overseas publishers. We may be reaching the point where it is becoming as easy for ordinary citizens to transform themselves into paparazzi as it is for celebrities to reinvent themselves as single-issue politicians and Third-World poverty lobbyists.

6.59 It is well known that many celebrities reach understandings on an individual basis with the media on lines very similar the agreement that was reached between the Palace, the press and the PCC regarding the Royal Princes. Nevertheless, as Emine Saner

15   PCC Report No 75, April–September 2007, at p 35.
16   Department of Culture, Media and Sport Committee ('HC Committee') *Self-Regulation of the Press, Seventh Report of Session 2006–2007*, HC 375 (TSO, 2007), para 40, p 21 and para 46, p 24.
17   Press Complaints Commission, 2006 Annual Review, at 7.

suggests, the days when 'there was usually an informal agreement' in which 'the star would pose for a picture, and in return the pack would largely then leave them alone' may be drawing to an end.[18]

6.60   Saner goes on to say that this is one of the main reasons why more celebrities are seeking protection and redress for their grievances in the courts. The new generation of amateur paparazzi are complete opportunists who have no need to enter into informal agreements with anyone. Saner mentions, as indicators of this trend, the recently successful applications for injunctions made on behalf of pop stars like Amy Winehouse and Lily Allen, and the actor Sienna Miller.

6.61   In 2008, Ms Miller won an action against the *Daily Star* after the newspaper ignored a PCC desist notice warning the UK press not to publish photographs of her obtained by non-complaint means. In the same year she successfully sued *News Group Newspapers* for publishing pictures that invaded her privacy. She was awarded £35,000 in damages. Shortly afterwards, Ms Miller brought a third successful action for privacy intrusion and harassment against the *Big Picture Agency* and was awarded £53,000 in damages with her legal costs. The agency had to agree that it would not, henceforward, photograph her at her home or in other places where she would have a reasonable expectation of privacy.[19]

6.62   It remains to be seen whether more high-profile celebrities will turn to the courts rather than to the PCC for protection against privacy intrusion and harassment. Most show business celebrities are well aware that they are ultimately dependent on media publicity in the furtherance of their careers. For this reason alone, bringing their complaints to the PCC – with the possibility of resolving their grievances and repairing their relationships with the press – may still prove to be a more attractive option than going to law.

---

[18]   E Saner 'Have Celebrities Finally Snapped?' *Media Guardian*, 4 May 2009, at pp 3–4.
[19]   D Brown 'Sienna Miller Victory May Clip Paparazzi's Wings', *The Times*, 22 November 2008.

Chapter 7

COMPLAINTS UNDER CLAUSE 5
(INTRUSION INTO GRIEF OR SHOCK)

7.1   Clause 5 (Intrusion into grief or shock) of the Press Complaints Commission's (PCC's) Code of Practice reads as follows:

> **'5 Intrusion into grief or shock**
>
> (i)   In cases involving personal grief or shock, enquiries and approaches must be made with sympathy and discretion and publication handled sensitively. This should not restrict the right to report legal proceedings, such as inquests.
>
> *(ii)   When reporting suicide, care should be taken to avoid excessive detail about the method used.'

7.2   The requirements of clause 5(i) apply both to the descriptive content of what is published and to the manner and means by which the information is obtained. No asterisk is appended to this subclause because there cannot be a public interest justification for failing to show due sensitivity when gathering information from people in a state of grief or shock, or when reporting on the events in question.

7.3   In the early years of the PCC, there were frequent complaints from bereaved relatives about the lurid details included in reports of coroners' inquests. There were also occasional complaints about reporters who had been the first people to inform close relatives or friends of the death of a loved one. Conduct of this kind constitutes a breach of clause 5(i), but these kinds of insensitive reporting are rarely the subject of complaints today.

7.4   Subclause 5(ii) was added to the Code in 2006. It recognises that there may be a public interest in reporting details about the methods used in suicide cases but that care should always be taken to avoid excessive detail.

7.5   The 98 rulings issued by the PCC under clause 5 in 2008 accounted for 6.9% of all rulings issued in that year. The key questions asked when dealing with such complaints are as follows:[1]

- *Did journalists break the news of the death* to close relatives?

- *Were insensitive and unnecessary details* published about the death?

- *Were photographs taken at a private funeral* without consent?

- *Were humorous or insensitive obituaries* or reports of death published?

---

[1]   I Beales *The Editors' Codebook* (Press Standards Board of Finance, revised 2nd edn, 2009), at p 40.

- *Were the details* of the method used to commit suicide excessive?

- *Was the coverage likely to glamorise suicide?*

CASE STUDIES

7.6   It should be noted that although in law, the dead cannot be libelled the Code of Practice provides a degree of posthumous redress for their grieving relatives under clause 1 (Accuracy) and clause 5 (Intrusion into grief or shock) as the following case study shows.

Kelliher v British Medical Journal[2]

7.7   In 2003, Mr Adam Kelliher complained to the PCC on behalf of the family of the late Dr Horrobin that an obituary published in the *British Medical Journal* was inaccurate in breach of clause 1 (Accuracy) and intrusive at a time of grief in breach of clause 5 (Intrusion into grief or shock) of the Code of Practice.

7.8   Following an immediate offer of remedial action from the editor, the PCC considered that no further action would be necessary. It decided, nevertheless, to proceed to a formal adjudication because the complainant was not satisfied with the editor's remedial action. He made it clear that his complaint was not about the publication of legitimate criticism but of unjustified 'slander' and 'character assassination' which had caused 'genuine hurt' to Dr Horrobin's family and friends.

7.9   Among other pejorative remarks, the obituarist described Dr Horrobin as a 'rotter' who might 'prove to be the greatest snake-oil salesman of his age'.

7.10   The journal had offered to publish corrections of factual inaccuracies and an apology for the inaccuracies but not for the nature of the article. The editor had already published three responses himself, explaining the rationale behind the obituary and his 'philosophy of obituaries' in general. However, he made it clear that obituaries should contain critical material and not be mere eulogies for the deceased. He was, nevertheless, prepared to offer an apology to the complainants on the grounds that the obituary 'may have lacked sensitivity'.

7.11   The complainant did not consider that the apology was genuine or that it responded to their contention that the article was substantially inaccurate. He suggested a wording covering both issues which the journal declined to publish.

7.12   In its adjudication, the PCC stated that it was not in a position to make a reasoned or fully informed judgment on the substance of the complaint under clause 1. It noted, however, that the journal had been prepared to correct a number of factual inaccuracies and to publish a large number of responses to the obituary. These actions were 'within the spirit of the Code'.

7.13   Under clause 5, the PCC concluded that:

---

2   PCC Report No 62–63, April–September 2003.

'... the tenor of the article – and some of the comments made by the journal – had certainly, and with some reason, been construed as insensitive by Dr Horrobin's family and friends at a time of grief. It was not unacceptable for newspapers and journals to publish critical obituaries but in doing so they must show due regard for the position of families at such times.'

7.14   The PCC was pleased that the editor offered to publish an apology for the distress caused by the obituary. It was now satisfied that no further action was required under the Code.

7.15   Dr Horrobin was not a celebrity or even well known outside his specialist field of expertise. Nevertheless, scholarly conventions are changing in this field of reportage and it is possible that in future some celebrities will also become the subject of highly critical or defamatory obituaries. Since their legal representatives cannot seek redress in the courts on behalf of their distressed relatives and friends, they may, in future, decide to make a complaint to the PCC. The case of Dr Horrobin illustrates how the PCC applies the Code under clause 5 in such matters.

Smillie v Sunday Mail[3]

7.16   Funerals are also occasions when people are especially susceptible to intrusions into their privacy that compound their feelings of grief and shock – as the following case study demonstrates.

7.17   In January 2000, the TV star Ms Carol Smillie complained to the PCC through her solicitors that an article published in the *Sunday Mail* headlined 'TV Star Carol's grief over mum' was an intrusion into her grief in breach of clause 4 (Intrusion into grief and shock) of the Code of Practice.

7.18   The article, on the front page and two inside pages, was accompanied by pictures taken outside the crematorium. Ms Smillie's solicitors claimed that the article was an unjustified intrusion into her grief, which had been compounded by its prominence. The photographers at the church had been asked to leave, but the mourners had not seen the ones at the crematorium who were located at some distance, using long lens cameras.

7.19   The newspaper said that it was not uncommon for the funerals of prominent individuals or their relatives to be reported and, in this case, the funeral had been publicly announced. The prominence of the article was a matter for editorial discretion. The papers' own photographer had left the church when asked to do so and the pictures had been supplied by a freelance. Since this photographer had not been detected by anyone there could not have been any intrusion at this time. A short statement had subsequently been published explaining that it was not the newspaper's intention to cause any further distress to Ms Smillie or her family.

7.20   In its adjudication the PCC ruled that the editor would have known that the family did not appreciate the presence of photographers when he decided to publish the pictures. It was not persuaded by the claim that the funeral involved a celebrity and had previously been announced in a newspaper. The funeral was not of a celebrity but of the relative of one. Ms Smillie had not sought to exploit it for publicity reasons and the article itself had noted that it was 'a private service'.

---

[3]   PCC Report No 50, April–June 2002.

7.21   In normal circumstances the PCC would have agreed that the question of prominence was a matter for editorial discretion. In this instance, however, the article itself acknowledged that this was a time of grief and, as such, the reporting should have been handled with sensitivity in accordance with the Code. The prominence of the article had a direct impact on the sensitivity with which the matter was reported and the result was a breach of the Code. The subsequent publication of a short statement was not a sufficient remedy and the complaint was therefore upheld.

7.22   The following complaints made under clause 5 involved, amongst other matters, the levelling of defamatory allegations against the recently deceased son of an internationally renowned author and scholar.

Tolkein family v Sunday Mercury[4]

7.23   In 2003, the Tolkein family complained through their solicitors that articles published in the *Sunday Mercury*, headlined 'Tolkein son's child abuse shame', 'Tolkein, the archbishop and the lie' and 'Church must come clean on perverts', were inaccurate in breach of clause 1 (Accuracy) and intrusive in breach of clauses 3 (Privacy) and 5 (Intrusion into grief and shock) of the Code of Practice.

7.24   The family also complained that the taking and publication of photographs for the articles were in breach of clause 4 (Harassment) and that their clients had not been given a sufficient opportunity to reply to the specific allegations, in breach of clause 2 (Opportunity to reply). A further article headlined 'Excommunicated' had repeated the inaccuracies and compounded the intrusion.

7.25   The main article concerned the alleged paedophilic history of Father John Tolkein, who had recently died. It was based primarily upon the allegations of one man, Christopher Carrie, who had accused Father Tolkein of abusing him as a child and 'hundreds of other children' as well. The solicitors considered that the newspaper had breached clause 1 in two ways: by failing to take care that material on which the articles were based was accurate; and failing to distinguish between comment, conjecture and fact concerning offences that had never been proven in court. The newspaper had also breached clause 2 by denying the complainant an opportunity to reply in detail to the points raised in the articles.

7.26   The solicitors went on to claim that the taking and publication of a picture of Father Tolkein standing in the corridors of a building outside his sheltered accommodation constituted an intrusion into his privacy in breach of clauses 3 and 4 of the Code. As regards the family itself, the publication of such sensational and insensitive articles (including a follow-up piece) intruded upon their lives at a time of particular grief, in breach of clauses 3 and 5 of the Code.

7.27   The newspaper maintained that it had acted professionally and that there was sufficient evidence to suggest that they had 'got the right man'. An initial investigation by police regarding four alleged victims had passed the Crown Prosecution Service's evidential test – which indicated a professional assessment that there was a 70–75% chance of obtaining a conviction and that the case would have gone to trial had it not been for Father Tolkein's ill health. Subsequent to publication, a man from Canada had contacted the newspaper recounting his similar experiences with Father Tolkein.

---

4   PCC Report No 62–63, April–September 2003.

7.28   On the other issues raised by the complaint, the newspaper did not consider that a dead person could be said to have a private life into which a newspaper might intrude. In any event, the photograph had itself been taken in 2000 and no official complaint had been lodged at the time. The newspaper went on to contend that it was impossible to report the death of Father Tolkein sensitively, given his background and previous activities – the nature of which would inevitably upset his family.

7.29   The complainants maintained that the articles were not factually sound. Their central complaint was not that the allegations were inaccurate – which could not now be proven – but that the newspaper had failed to present them accurately or taken care that there was sufficient evidential support for them. Its reliance on one unreliable witness and unnamed police sources did not indicate a high level of care. In response to this part of the complaint the newspaper offered to publish a clarification acknowledging that the allegations had never been proven in court and that they had always been denied by Father Tolkein. It insisted, however, that there was a clear public interest in publishing the story.

7.30   In its adjudication, the PCC ruled that the newspaper had not presented its allegations with sufficient care and accuracy. It drew attention to the requirements of clause 1 of the Code which states that newspapers 'must distinguish clearly between comment, conjecture and fact'. In this case:

> '... while it was clear that the newspaper believed that Father Tolkein was guilty of abuse – based on the evidence of an alleged victim and other sources – it had misleadingly presented its belief as an explicit statement of fact. By publishing such extremely serious allegations without sufficient qualification, the newspaper had, therefore, breached the terms of Clause 1 of the Code.'

7.31   The newspaper's offer to provide a short correction on this point 'did not constitute sufficient remedial action in light of the nature of the breach or thereby represent a sufficient opportunity to reply to the article. There was also, therefore, a breach of Clause 2 of the Code'.

7.32   The PCC went on to acknowledge that the newspaper:

> '... had a right to publish the serious allegations levelled against Father Tolkein – particularly as it was now clear that they would never be heard in a court – but it also had an obligation to do so fairly. Its failure to do this demonstrated, additionally, a lack of sensitivity towards the grieving family and a breach of Clause 5 thereby resulted from the breach of Clause 1 of the Code.'

7.33   The PCC also noted that the family's solicitors had raised concerns over the accuracy of the newspaper's claim that it had been 'gagged', or legally prevented from the publication of the allegations. On this part of the complaint, the PCC ruled that since it was not disputed that the solicitors had tried to ensure non-publication, any inaccuracy in the newspaper's accounts of this matter was not sufficiently significant to raise a breach of clause 1.

7.34   In conclusion, the PCC ruled that there was not a case to pursue under the terms of clauses 3 and 4. It could not make a judgment concerning something that had occurred nearly 3 years ago and about which it had not received a complaint at that time. The PCC did not consider that questions of privacy and intrusion could be related to the deceased or that, as publication had been subsequent to the death of Father

Tolkein, it could consider this aspect of the case any further. It ruled that the articles had not intruded specifically into the private lives of other members of the family, in breach of clause 5 (Intrusion into grief or shock) of the Code of Practice. The complaints under clause 1 (Accuracy) and 2 (Opportunity to reply) were both upheld.

Jade Goody and OK! Magazine

7.35   In 2009, *OK! Magazine* breached all conventional standards of propriety when it published a 28-page 'official tribute issue' commemorating the life of reality TV star and Big Brother contestant Jade Goody a few days before her death from cancer. The issue was written in the past tense and included photographs of her children. The front page carried a black border and the sub-headlines 'in loving memory Issue 666' and '1981–2009'. It was, in all but name, an obituary.

7.36   The PCC received over 100 complaints from outraged readers none of whom, it transpired, had any connection with Ms Goody or her family. The complaints were made under clauses 1 (Accuracy), 3 (Privacy), 5 (Intrusion into grief or shock) and 6 (Children).

7.37   Ms Goody had previously entered into commercial agreements with a number of media outlets, including *OK! Magazine*, in order to ensure the future financial security of her two young children. The PCC contacted with the office of the family's public relations representative, Max Clifford, and with Jade and her family and it was made clear that the family did not wish to raise a formal complaint.

7.38   The PCC had to respect their wishes and, on that basis, concluded that it would not take forward the complaints under clauses 3, 5 and 6 of the Code. It pointed out that 'these clauses clearly relate to the personal experience of given individuals. It would not be possible to investigate them properly, or to resolve them satisfactorily, without the strong input of those individuals themselves'. The PCC went on to recognise that the complaints under clause 1 (Accuracy) 'raised a slightly different issue'. The misleading aspects of the coverage may have impacted negatively on the family and misinformed the readers. There was, however, 'no question of readers being misled, to any significant or longstanding degree, about the position surrounding Jade's health'.

7.39   Given the particular circumstances of the case, the PCC decided that it would not, therefore, be 'appropriate to pursue an investigation (the outcome of which would be likely to be public) that would prolong attention on the final moments of Jade's life. It felt that it would require the consent of the family before doing so'. That consent had not been given and, as Sir Christopher Meyer pointed out at a subsequent press briefing: 'We have never said "No" to third party complaints. What we have always said is that you can't have a third party trumping the rights and wishes of a first party'.

Michael Jackson and OK! Magazine

7.40   Three months later, *OK! Magazine* published another 'Official Tribute Issue', this time 'In loving memory' of the singer Michael Jackson. The cover page showed a picture of him receiving treatment in an ambulance on his way to hospital. The PCC received seven complaints under clauses 1 (Accuracy), 3 (Privacy), 5 (Intrusion into grief or shock) and 6 (Children). None of the complainants had connections with Mr Jackson or his family, who had not lodged a complaint.

7.41   The PCC ruled that it could not take forward the complaints made under clauses 3, 5 and 6 of the Code independently of the bereaved family. One of the complainants claimed that the article was in breach of clause 1 (Accuracy) because it implied that Mr Jackson was still alive in the front page photograph, when he had been dead 'for over half an hour'. The PCC noted that the image showed paramedics trying to resuscitate the star on the way to hospital. Against that background, the PCC was satisfied that the magazine's description of the images as 'the last pictures' was not misleading in breach of clause 1 (Accuracy).

7.42   Clearly, conventions are changing in the obituary columns of publications and, since the dead cannot be libelled, the PCC is the only regulatory agency to which bereaved relatives and friends can turn for redress of their grievances. It cannot, however, respond to the complaints of shocked and outraged third parties. Relatives and friends are not third parties because they themselves have been the victims of intrusion into their lives at a time of grief and shock.

Chapter 8

COMPLAINTS UNDER CLAUSES 6 (CHILDREN) AND 7 (CHILDREN IN SEX CASES)

CLAUSE 6 (CHILDREN)

8.1   Clause 6 (Children) of the Press Complaints Commission's (PCC's) Code of Practice reads as follows:

'6 * Children

(i)   Young people should be free to complete their time at school without unnecessary intrusion.

(ii)   A child under 16 must not be interviewed or photographed on issues involving their own or another child's welfare unless a custodial parent or similarly responsible adult consents.

(iii)   Pupils must not be approached or photographed at school without the permission of the school authorities.

(iv)   Minors must not be paid for material involving children's welfare, nor parents or guardians for material about their children or wards, unless it is clearly in the child's interest.

(v)   Editors must not use the fame, notoriety or position of a parent or guardian as sole justification for publishing details of a child's private life.'

8.2   In its original form, the Code of Practice did not allow editors to advance a public interest defence under what was then clause II (Interviewing or photographing children). At that time, the Code did not have a free-standing public interest statement as such. Each of the four clauses under which a public interest defence was allowed simply replicated the grounds on which it could be advanced.

8.3   A free-standing Public Interest clause was added to the Code and clause 11 was renumbered clause 12 in 1993. In December 1997, this clause became a free-standing statement. The clauses under which a public interest defence could be advanced were clearly marked with an asterisk and, for the first time, editors were allowed to advance such a defence in cases involving children. Most significantly, the new Public Interest statement made it absolutely clear that 'in cases involving children editors must demonstrate an exceptional public interest to over-ride the normally paramount interests of the child'.

8.4   The current wording of clause 6(i) gives added protection to children as they grow up by extending its remit to 'young people', who 'should be free to complete their time at school without unnecessary intrusion'. This extension also dates from 1997 when the old clause 12 was redrafted and renumbered as clause 6.

8.5   Through a combination of landmark adjudications and changes in the Code, the manner in which journalists and photographers approach and write about children has changed dramatically – and for the better – over the past 18 years. Complaints under clause 6 currently account for a very small proportion of all rulings made by the PCC.

8.6   Journalists and photographers today rarely, if ever, approach children for interviews or photograph them without parental consent, offer them money for information about the welfare of other children, approach them at school or write stories about them simply because of the position, fame or notoriety of their parents. Editors, for their part, have assiduously interpreted and upheld the requirements of clause 6 'not only to the letter but in the full spirit of the Code'.

8.7   Parents, for their part, must take care not to compromise the privacy rights of their children by placing them in the public eye or revealing personal information about them for payment or in order to advance their own careers.

8.8   The key questions asked when dealing with complaints under clause 6 are as follows:[1]

- *Is the child under 16 or still at school?* If so, clause 6 applies.

- *Could the interview or photograph involve or affect a child's welfare?* If so, consent will be needed.

- *Has consent been given by the appropriate responsible adult or school?*

- *Is a payment to either a child or parents/guardian in the child's interests?*

- *Is there a justification for publication other than the fame etc of parents or guardians?*

- *Is there an exceptional public interest in publication?* No such defence has yet succeeded.

8.9   The 48 rulings issued by the PCC on complaints made under clause 6 accounted for 3.4% of all rulings issued in that year.

8.10   The following case studies illustrate how the PCC's 'case-law' in dealing with complaints involving children and young persons has developed since 1991.

Buckingham Palace Press Office v The People[2]

8.11   The PCC received its first complaint on behalf of the child of a celebrity in July 1991 when the Buckingham Palace Press Office complained on behalf of the Duke and Duchess of York's baby daughter, Princess Eugenie. *The People* had published two photographs of the Princess running naked in the high-walled garden of her house in breach of what were then clause 4 (Privacy) and clause II (Interviewing or photographing children) of the Code of Practice. The pictures were taken without the knowledge or consent of her parents.

---

[1]   I Beales *The Editors' Codebook* (Press Standards Board of Finance, revised 2nd edn, 2009), at p 45.
[2]   PCC Report No 2, July–September 1991.

8.12 The PCC immediately informed the editor that a complaint had been made on behalf of Princess Eugenie. The newspaper responded by republishing the main photograph along with one of the Duke obtained from a French magazine that had already appeared in another English newspaper.

8.13 Readers were also invited to phone in and say whether they thought any of these pictures were 'offensive'. The newspaper defended its actions on the grounds that the photographs were both 'charming' and 'natural' and that under English law 'anybody is free to take a photograph of anybody else'.

8.14 The PCC ruled that the pictures were taken 'in flagrant contempt' of the industry's Code of Practice and constituted a deliberate attempt to undermine the complaints procedure. The complaint was upheld on both counts. This complaint serves as a useful benchmark for measuring the progress that has been made since then towards developing a new culture of voluntary Code compliance in protecting children from invasions of their privacy by the press.

8.15 The watershed point was passed in this development, when, in 1995, the PCC received a complaint from an ordinary member of the public which coincided with mounting public concern about the future privacy rights of the young Prince William.

Livesley v Accrington Observer and Times[3]

8.16 Early in 1995, the PCC received a complaint from Ms Mary Livesley that her 15-year-old son was approached as he was leaving his school by a reporter from the *Accrington Observer and Times* who was seeking information concerning other pupils in breach of what was then clause 12 (Interviewing or photographing children) of the Code of Practice.

8.17 The editor explained that on the morning of 4 July the newspaper had received 'a strong tip-off' that a party of school pupils had been sent home early from an adventure weekend because of bad behaviour and it was thought that some of those responsible might have been expelled. In seeking to justify this approach to the pupils the editor said:

> 'As we clearly did not have sufficient information at that stage to contact the school directly about the allegations, it was decided that a reporter should speak to pupils leaving the school at the end of the day with the sole intention of asking them to point us in the right direction, ie, by giving us names of people who were actually on the trip. Our reporter spoke to a few of the oldest-looking pupils, one of whom was Mrs Livesey's son. She did not realize that all 16-year-olds had already left the school after their exams.'

8.18 In its adjudication, the PCC ruled that there had been a clear breach of the terms of clause 12, which provided that children under 16 should not be interviewed or photographed on subjects involving their personal welfare in the absence of or without the consent of a parent or other adult who was responsible for them. Further, and more specifically, children should not be approached or photographed whilst at school without the permission of the school authorities.

---

3   PCC Report, No 30, May–July 1995.

8.19   In this case, the complainant's son was approached leaving school premises and asked about matters which plainly involved the personal welfare of children at the school. The editor may have wanted more facts before approaching the authorities about the rumour of expulsions from the school – but the questioning of minors was not an acceptable method of gathering such information. The complaint was upheld.

8.20   This adjudication coincided with the impending arrival of Prince William at Eton college and mounting concern at Buckingham Palace that pupils at Eton and local residents were already being 'lined up by some newspapers to supply stories about the Prince when he began his schooling in September'.[4]

8.21   In a speech delivered at St Bride's Institute Fleet Street on 23 August, the then Chairman of the PCC, Lord Wakeham, forcefully reminded the press that 'Next month Prince William starts at a new school. Prince William is not an institution: nor a soap star: nor a football hero. He is a child' and, as such, he was entitled to exactly the same protection with the Code of Practice as any other child.[5]

8.22   Lord Wakeham was to return these issues in 2000 when Prince William was preparing to leave Eton for university. Since the issues in question had as much to do with harassment as privacy intrusion they are discussed in greater detail in Chapter 6 on complaints made under clause 4 (Harassment), at **6.15** etc seq.

8.23   The next complaint was made under clause 6 but it could also have been made under clause 3(i) because so much of its substance is concerned with the disclosure of sensitive personal data about the parents.

Lisa Carling v Daily Mail[6]

8.24   In 2000, Mrs Lisa Carling complained to the PCC that an article headlined. 'Carling stole my family' published in the *Daily Mail* intruded into the privacy of her son and daughter in breach of clause 6 (Children) of the Code of Practice.

8.25   The article took the form of an interview with the complainant's ex-husband. Amongst other matters, it detailed his attempt to gain greater access to his two children, who were living with the complainant and her new husband, the ex-England rugby captain Will Carling.

8.26   The complainant regarded the article as a 'salacious and crude exploitation of her children as a weapon to attack her new husband with no public interest'. The two children had been thrust into the 'glare of publicity' simply because of the fame of their stepfather.

8.27   Since publication of the article, the complainant had gained an injunction handed down from the Family Division of the High Court which restrained her ex-husband from discussing publicly any matters relating to the lives, well-being or custody arrangements of her children.

---

[4]   R Shannon *A Press Free and Responsible* (John Murray, 2001), at pp 202–203.
[5]   PCC *Moving Ahead* (1995), at pp 5–8.
[6]   PCC Report No 50, April–June 2000.

8.28 The newspaper vigorously defended the publication of the article. The complainant and her new husband had both sought publicity and placed the children in the public domain by speaking to the *Daily Mail* about them. They were not therefore 'in a position where they can turn publicity on and off or dictate that they are the only ones who have a right to speak about their children. Their father had an equal right to tell his side of the story'.

8.29 The PCC, in considering this case, had two fundamental principles to bear in mind. First, the PCC had previously made clear that even when individuals do put matters concerning the private lives of their families in the public domain the press cannot reasonably justify thereafter publishing articles on any subject concerning them. The PCC therefore considered whether the material concerning the children in the article was proportional to that already placed in the public domain. The PCC reviewed the material submitted by the newspaper, and in particular the interview given by the complainant to the *Daily Mail* in July 1999. Specifically, the PCC noted that the complainant had spoken about her son's emotional character, quoted his reaction to her sleeping arrangements with her then boyfriend, detailed the custody arrangements as they then stood and detailed both children's concerns following the break-up of their parents' marriage. The PCC recognised that these could be viewed as matters of an intensely personal and private nature for the children. The PCC further noted that the complainant had supplied a photograph of the children which had been published by the newspaper.

8.30 Secondly, the PCC was also required to have regard to freedom of expression and the public's right to be informed of matters of public interest. This may include cases where one side in a relationship, whether extant or terminated, details their own account of events or matters related to them, including their families. The PCC noted that the complainant had freely given her own account of the marriage break-up and its resultant effect on the children and therefore considered that, under the terms of the Code, her ex-husband was free to express his views on the matter. It was clear that the complainant herself had put matters relating to her children into the public domain and in the PCC's view the interview with her former husband was in proportion to the previously published material. The injunction sought by the complainant was subsequent to the publication of the article and any breaches of it would not be a matter for the PCC. The complaint was not upheld.

8.31 The next two case studies raised issues concerning the taking and publishing of photographs of children in public places without prior consent.

Donald v Hello![7]

8.32 In 2000, Mr and Mrs Donald complained that photographs taken of their son and published in *Hello!* magazine intruded into his privacy in breach of clause 6 (Children) of the Code of Practice. Mrs Donald's sister, a well-known fashion designer, was photographed in the street along with her boyfriend and the complainant's son, who was sitting in a pushchair.

8.33 In its adjudication, the PCC noted that the Code did not require editors to seek consent from a responsible person before publishing *any* pictures of a child under the age of 16, as this would mean that no pictures of children, however innocuous, could be

---

[7] PCC Report No 52, October–December 2000.

published without such consent. Instead, the Code requires editors to seek consent before interviewing or photographing children 'on subjects involving the welfare of the child'. In this case, the photographs were clearly taken in a public place and in no way influenced or affected the child's welfare or intruded into his privacy. The complaint was not upheld.

Rowling v OK![8]

8.34   In 2001, Ms Rowling complained through her solicitors that *OK!* magazine had intruded into her 8-year-old daughter's privacy whilst she was sitting on a Mauritian beach in her swimsuit in contravention of clause 3 (Privacy) and clause 6 (Children) of the Code of Practice. Long lens photographs had been taken without consent when she was in a place where she had a reasonable expectation of privacy. The pictures had caused her considerable embarrassment and were taken only because of her mother's fame. It was also pointed out that Ms Rowling had never courted publicity, either for herself or her daughter.

8.35   The editor cited the *Donald* adjudication in defence of her decision to publish the pictures. On the basis of the evidence submitted, however, the PCC concluded that the circumstances relating to Ms Rowling's case differed significantly from those of the Donalds' complaint. The photographs of Ms Rowling's daughter had been taken with a long lens in a place where she had a reasonable expectation of privacy. Her mother had gone to considerable trouble in seeking out a beach that was not overlooked in a secluded resort and had gone there in the low season to avoid unwanted attention. The photographs had adversely affected the child's welfare by depicting her in her swimwear and they had been taken without consent. In these circumstances, Ms Rowling's child was entitled to the full protection of the Code and both complaints were therefore upheld.

8.36   As celebrity parents, the Murrays have always been assiduous in protecting the privacy of their children. In 'Hannoverian' terms, they are reluctant celebrities 'par excellence'. In 2004, however, an agency photographer took long lens photographs of Ms Rowling and her husband, Dr Neil Murray, whilst they were walking their 18-month-old son in his pushchair on a street near their Edinburgh home. The pictures were taken covertly, without consent, and published in the *Sunday Express*. The circumstances under which the photographs were taken seem to have been very similar to those that pertained in the *Donald* case.

8.37   The Murrays decided to bring an action for invasion of privacy against Express Newspapers and the Big Picture Agency. The newspaper settled out of court. The agency successfully applied to the High Court and the Murrays' claim was struck out. In his ruling, Mr Justice Patten stated that 'the law does not in my judgement (as it stands) allow them to carve out a press free zone for their children in respect of absolutely everything'.[9] In 2008, the Murrays went on to win a ruling in the Court of Appeal. In overturning the High Court judgment, Sir Anthony Clarke stated that:[10] 'If a child of parents who are not in the public eye could reasonably expect not to have photographs of him published in the media, so too should the child of a famous parent.'

---

8   PCC Report No 56–57, October 2001–March 2002.
9   [2007] EWHC 1908 (Ch).
10   [2008] EWCA Civ 446.

8.38   As matters now stand, it remains to be seen whether the law will now protect children from being photographed in public places under any circumstances, unless their parents have already previously exposed them to publicity. Clearly, as Lord Hope said in *Campbell*,[11] in a 'free community' a distinction must be drawn between 'a person who just happens to be in the street when the photograph is taken' and photographing 'one or more persons' in a public place 'who constitute the true subject of the photograph'.[12]

8.39   The following three case studies of complaints made under clause 6 (Children) were all concerned with the children of high–profile politicians. The Code recognises that it is manifestly the role and responsibility of the press to scrutinise and comment on Government policies and the conduct of those who are responsible for them. These complaints raised key issues about the extent to which, and the manner in which the press is entitled to relate such scrutiny to the children of politicians in cases where their conduct in matters relating to their *own* children might have an impact on policy or give rise to reasonable charges of hypocrisy.

The Blairs v The Mail on Sunday[13]

8.40   In January 1999, the then Prime Minister Tony Blair and his wife, Cherie Blair, complained that articles and a leader in *The Mail on Sunday* were misleading in breach of clause 1 (Accuracy) of the Code of Practice, and intruded into their daughter's privacy in breach of clause 6 (Children).

8.41   This was the first occasion on which the PCC considered a complaint about the child of a public figure under the provisions of clause 6 of the Code since their revision in December 1997 (see **8.3**).

8.42   The article, including one on the front page headlined 'Parents' fury over Blairs in School Place Row' and the accompanying leader comment, reported the decision of a local Catholic high school to admit Kathryn Blair whilst rejecting other local children. The leader said that the decision gave rise to suspicion that the school was operating an 'under-the-counter' selection policy. The Blairs were not poor and could have paid for the private education of their daughter.

8.43   The complainants said that their daughter was being raised as a Roman Catholic, Sacred Heart was their first choice of school and Kathryn was accepted entirely in line with standard procedures. The newspaper had failed to produce any evidence in support of its allegations. It was perfectly possible to scrutinise the Government's educational policies without infringing the privacy of their children.

8.44   The newspaper said that the thrust of the story was not special treatment, but a group of parents' justifiable complaint that their daughters had been denied promised places at a school which accepted Mr Blair's daughter, even though she appeared to be no better qualified. The newspaper was reporting their anger and the alleged hypocrisy of the Prime Minister. His conduct in making choices which Government policy was preventing others from making was an issue of genuine public interest. The article had not intruded into Kathryn's private life and had not carried a picture of her.

---

[11]   *Campbell v MGN Limited* [2004] UKHL 22.
[12]   *The Editors' Codebook*, n 1 above, at p 14, para 31.
[13]   PCC Report No 47, July–September 1999.

8.45   The complainants' response was that a newspaper should not be able to justify a story about children by repeating a false allegation when there was no evidence to support it. For a child to start a new school amid allegations that she got in as a result of special treatment was a grotesque attack on her right to a private life. The Headmistress supported the complaint in a lengthy submission.

8.46   In its adjudication, the PCC concluded that there was no evidence to support the allegation that Kathryn was unfairly admitted or had received special treatment. The newspaper simply repeated the unsubstantiated allegations made by other parents. The PCC also believed that an article could have been written about the school's selection procedures without making Kathryn the focus of the story. It, therefore, concluded that 'to focus on Kathryn Blair in circumstances where there was a breach of clause 1 of the Code was clearly not within the terms of clause 6 of the Code and appeared to arise solely because of the position of her father'.

8.47   The PCC went on to consider whether there was any 'exceptional public interest' which justified the references to Kathryn Blair – in a manner proportionate to the issues and facts involved and in circumstances where there might be reasonable substance to the allegations made and it was necessary to identify the child, and that child alone, as the centre of the story.

8.48   On these matters, the PCC could find no justification for naming Kathryn alone since there was no evidence of special treatment in her favour. Allegations of 'hypocrisy' on Mr Blair's part were also based on inaccurate evidence. It also noted that the Prime Minister and Mrs Blair had gone to great lengths in seeking to protect their children's privacy.

8.49   The PCC, therefore, concluded that:

> '... if every story about the Prime Minister's children which relates to their education, is to be justified on the basis that he has made statements about education, then clause 6 provides no protection for his children or others in a similar position. The PCC intends the industry's Code – drawn up by editors themselves – to be effective and to provide real protection for all children.'

The complaint was upheld.

The Blairs v The Daily Telegraph and Daily Mail[14]

8.50   In December 2001, the then Prime Minister Tony Blair and his wife, Cherie Blair, complained that *The Daily Telegraph* and the *Daily Mail* had published articles containing information about the private life of their son, Euan, in breach of clause 6 (Children) of the Code of Practice. The articles gave details of Euan's application for admission to an Oxbridge college.

8.51   *The Daily Telegraph* explained that it had learned of Euan's application through the list of names posted up in the college to which he had applied. The story was not about Euan himself but about the choices that his parents were making with regard to their son's education. This was a matter of legitimate public interest in the context of a recent public debate about the admission policies of Oxbridge colleges.

---

[14]   PCC Report No 56–57, October 2001–March 2002.

8.52   The *Daily Mail* advanced a similar defence. It also pointed out that the Downing Street press office had made no comment when invited to do so prior to the publication of its follow-up to a story that had been put into the public domain elsewhere.

8.53   In its adjudication, the PCC dealt first with the complaint against *The Daily Telegraph*. It drew attention to the specific purpose of clause 6(i) of the Code which states that 'young people should be free to complete their time at school without unnecessary intrusion'. Clause 6(v) 'added further protection for the children of famous people – ensuring that nothing is written about young people simply because of the position of their parents'.

8.54   The PCC went on to point out that although this part of the Code relates to children under the age of 16, it was clear that its spirit could be applied in this instance and the newspaper had in any event argued its case under this part of the complaints.

8.55   Applying to university from school was 'a time of anxiety for young people' and 'the effect of this piece had been to thrust Euan Blair's university entrance procedures into the public eye in a way which could damage both his education and welfare'. The newspaper had failed to make a case that this article was 'necessary' as it was required to do under the terms of the Code.

8.56   The PCC rejected the public interest defence advanced by the newspaper. It found that no reference had been made in the story to the public debate about the admissions policies of the Oxbridge colleges. It disagreed with the newspaper's contention that 'the story was essentially about the choices that the Prime Minister and his wife make about their children's education – principally because such a choice would have been the private choice of Euan and his school'. In any event, the Code clearly stated 'that in cases of public interest involving children a newspaper must demonstrate that such public interest is so exceptional that it over-rides the normally paramount interests of the child' and this the newspaper had failed to do.

8.57   The PCC also rejected the newspaper's claim that information about Euan's application had already been placed in the public domain 'by virtue of it being posted in the College Porter's Lodge'. The fact that the college had pinned a list of applicants on its own property 'did not give *carte blanche* to newspapers to write intrusive stories about the applicants'. The complaint was therefore upheld.

8.58   In dealing with the complaint about the *Daily Mail*, the PCC noted that it had not caused the original breach of the Code. It had merely published a follow-up piece. It also noted that the newspaper had contacted the Downing Street press office prior to publication and been told that it had no comment to make. Had the newspaper been advised of any objections it would have reconsidered whether or not to run the story. Given the similarities in the two stories, however, it was clear to the PCC that the newspaper had also breached the Code. Nevertheless, the PCC decided to take these mitigating circumstances into account and gave the newspaper an opportunity to resolve the complaint against it through voluntary conciliation. The matter was subsequently resolved to the satisfaction of the complainants.

8.59   The PCC ruled that:

> ' . . . the acid test that any newspaper should apply in writing about the children of public figures who – like the Prime Minister and Mrs Blair's children, and unlike the Royal Princes

– are not famous in their own right is whether a newspaper would write such a story if it was about an ordinary person. Academic achievement or successful entry to a university might well fall into such a category; private details about the nature of such an application, or indeed private details about an individual's time at university would not.'

8.60   Public figures, for their part, should note that 'it is much more difficult to protect any individual where he or she begins to acquire a public profile in their own right, for instance by making public appearances. Privacy is best maintained when not compromised in any way'.

Kelly v Daily Mirror[15]

8.61   In January 2007, Mrs Ruth Kelly MP complained that the *Daily Mirror* had published an article reporting that she had decided to send one of her children, who had learning difficulties, to a private school in breach of clause 6 of the Code of Practice. The article followed a report of her decision in the previous day's *Mail on Sunday*, which had not named the complainant. By naming her, the *Daily Mirror* had identified her child, disclosed details of his private life and particular condition and negatively affected his welfare. The story had only been published because of the position of the parent and no 'exceptional public interest' had been served in doing so.

8.62   The newspaper claimed that readers:

> '... had a right to know when those who run crucial public services – and repeatedly tell us how much they are improving – conclude they are actually failing their own families and can then afford to opt out. This was a matter of profound public interest. During her time at the Education department, the complainant had presided over the closure of more state special school places annually than any other Labour education secretary since 1997.'

Minimal details about the child had been published. In the first edition of the newspaper there was a reference to a particular kind of learning difficulty but this had been removed in later editions.

8.63   Mrs Kelly claimed that government policy had never been opposed to parents making use of the private sector and that the debate about fee-paying schools could have been held without the complainant – and therefore her child being identified. The consequence of the *Daily Mirror* naming her was that all the other media had followed suit.

8.64   In its adjudication, the PCC ruled that:

> '... the subject highlighted in the article was a matter of considerable public interest. The fact that a Cabinet Minister – who had previously been Secretary of State for Education and Skills ... did not feel that the current state system could meet her child's requirements raised questions about the nature of publicly funded schooling and its ability to cater for children with special needs (including those whose families would not be able to pay for private schooling).'

8.65   The PCC still had to decide whether the newspaper had acted within the requirements of clause 6 of the Code in striking 'an appropriate balance between taking care to avoid unnecessary intrusion into the privacy – and schooling – of the child, and

---

[15]   PCC Report No 74, October 2006–April 2007.

publishing a story that served the public interest'. The relevant parts of clause 6 were that: 'young people should be free to complete their time at school without unnecessary intrusion' and 'editors must not use the fame, notoriety or position of a parent or guardian as sole justification for publishing details of a child private life'. The Code also required that 'in cases involving children under 16, editors must demonstrate an exceptional public interest to override the normally paramount interests of the child'.

8.66   On the issue of 'unnecessary intrusion' the PCC noted that the newspaper had omitted any references to the name of the child, his school and precise details of his condition. It judged that 'the naming of the complainant herself – even though it carried with it an implicit identification of her child – was necessary in the context of the story and enabled a fuller, legitimate discussion of the issues at stake'. As had already been noted, these issues were deemed to be of 'considerable public interest'.

8.67   On the issue of the public standing of the complainant, the PCC concluded that 'the story was about the decision of the parents – one of whom was a Minister and MP who had been responsible for the national policy on education – rather than the private life of the child'. The PCC 'did not consider that the Code was designed to prevent scrutiny of this sort'.

8.68   Whilst there was unquestionably an intrusion felt by the complainant and her child, the PCC 'was satisfied that the newspaper had acted within the requirements of Clause 6 on this occasion. The complaint was not upheld on that basis'.

CLAUSE 7 (CHILDREN IN SEX CASES)

8.69   Clause 7 (Children in sex cases) of the Code of Practice reads as follows:

'7 * Children in sex cases

1.   The press must not, even if legally free to do so, identify children under 16 who are victims or witnesses in cases involving sex offences.
2.   In any press report of a case involving a sexual offence against a child –
      (i)   The child must not be identified.
      (ii)   The adult may be identified.
      (iii) The word "incest" must not be used where a child victim might be identified.
      (iv)   Care must be taken that nothing in the report implies the relationship between the accused and the child.'

8.70   Breaches of the Code relating to child victims (and perpetrators) of sexual assault have very seldom been the subject of complaints since the requirements of this clause were made more stringent in 1995. New procedures for pre-publication checking were also agreed with other media regulators in order to ensure that the names of victims – and of victims and perpetrators in incest cases – were not inadvertently revealed through 'jigsaw identification'.

8.71   The key question asked when dealing with complaints under clause 7 is:[16]

•   *Could the report lead to the identification of a child in the case, including a defendant?*

8.72   The PCC issued two rulings on complaints made under clause 7 in 2008. Neither complaint was adjudicated. It is not known whether any complaints involving celebrities or their children have been made under this clause. The following complaints illustrate how such cases are adjudicated.

A man v News of the World[17]

8.73   In 1995, the father of a 15-year-old boy complained, that an article in the *News of the World* identified his son as the accused in a sexual assault case, in breach of what was then clause 13 (Children in sex cases) of the Code of Practice.

8.74   The article reported the allegation of a serious sexual offence and the police investigation. It did not name the complainant's son but included other identifying information.

8.75   The complainant said that as his son was under the age of 16 and was involved in a case concerning a sexual offence, he should not have been identified by the newspaper. He said that, in the circumstances, the information given would have been sufficient to identify the boy to readers.

8.76   The newspaper said that it had not named the complainant's son and that the information given would only have been sufficient to identify him to friends already acquainted with the incident.

8.77   In its adjudication, the PCC considered that clause 13 applied in this case as the complainant's son was under the age of 16 and was accused of committing a sexual offence. In reaching this decision the PCC took into account the purpose of this clause of the Code which is to protect minors in cases concerning sexual offences. It noted that the police decided not to prosecute the boy and that the reports concerned the allegations that had been made and the police decision. However, the PCC took the view that the term 'cases concerning sexual offences' in clause 13 must refer not only to those cases where legal proceedings are underway but also to those where allegations are made which could lead to such proceedings, even where, in the event, there is a decision not to prosecute.

8.78   The PCC noted that the *News of the World* did not name the complainant's son. However, it considered that, in the circumstances, the information given by the newspaper was sufficient to identify the boy to readers. The complaint was upheld.

A woman v Strathspey and Badenoch Herald[18]

8.79   In 2007, a woman complained to the PCC that an article published in the *Strathspey and Badenoch Herald* could have identified her daughter as a victim of sexual

---

16   *The Editors' Codebook*, n 1 above, at p 47.
17   PCC Report No 34, April–June 1996.
18   PCC Report No 75, April–September 2007.

assault in breach of clause 11 (Victims of sexual assault), intruded into her shock in breach of clause 5 (Intrusion into grief or shock) and breached clause 6 (Children) of the Code.

8.80   The article reported the conviction of a man for sexual offences against underage girls. The complainant is the mother of one of the victims. She said the level of detail – in particular the reference to a visible injury previously suffered by her daughter, coupled with the location and time in which she and the man in question had first met – would have assisted those in her small community in identifying her daughter. This being the case, there were also breaches of clauses 5 and 6.

8.81   The newspaper did not believe that any detail in the article would have led to the identification of the girl. The article did not disclose her name, address or school. The town in which the incidents took place was a busy holiday resort with hundreds of thousands of visitors every year, and the family did not live there. The article was a fair and accurate account of court proceedings. The paper noted that the complainant had indicated that no third party had identified her daughter as a result of the article.

8.82   In this adjudication it was noted that the terms of clause 11 of the Code are tightly drawn in order to protect victims of sexual assault – one of the most vulnerable groups of people – and rigorously enforced by the PCC. While the information about the girl's injury may have seemed to some to be insignificant, it was a superfluous but specific detail which the PCC was persuaded could have been sufficient to identify her, or confirm the suspicions of those who already knew something about the case. While the editor arguably had a difficult job to do in striking the balance between what was legitimate detail and what was likely to contribute to the girl's identification, the PCC considered that he could have taken greater care in this case by omitting the reference to the injury. As the PCC found that the material was likely to have contributed to the girl's identification in this way, it followed that the content of the article would have had a considerable impact on the girl in breach of clauses 5 and 6. The complaint was upheld on that basis.

8.83   The breach of the Code in this case arose from the possible identification of the victim. While the PCC acknowledged the complainant's additional concerns that the article had included sensationalised and gratuitous detail about the case, it emphasised that newspapers were entitled to report fully on information revealed in open court, provided the identity of the victim was properly protected.

Chapter 9

COMPLAINTS UNDER CLAUSES 8 (HOSPITALS), 9 (REPORTING CRIME) AND 10 (CLANDESTINE DEVICES AND SUBTERFUGE)

CLAUSE 8 (HOSPITALS)

9.1   Clause 8 (Hospitals) of the Press Complaints Commission's (PCC's) Code of Practice reads as follows:

'8 * Hospitals

(i)   Journalists must identify themselves and obtain permission from a responsible executive before entering non-public areas of hospitals or similar institutions to pursue enquiries.

(ii)   The restrictions on intruding into privacy are particularly relevant to enquiries about individuals in hospitals or similar institutions.'

9.2   The wording of this clause has remained virtually unchanged since it was originally drafted by the Editors' Code Committee in December 1990, a few months after the actor Gorden Kaye's privacy was scandalously invaded by a journalist and a photographer whilst he was being cared for in an off-limits hospital room. The numbering of this clause was changed from 9 to 8 in 2004.

9.3   Editors are expected to be especially mindful that they observe the requirements of this clause 'not only to the letter but in the full spirit'. In a landmark adjudication issued in 1995, the PCC ruled that any institution in which people are receiving treatment or care for health-related needs falls within the remit of clause 8.[1]

9.4   In a second landmark ruling in 2002, it was made clear that the term 'similar institutions' includes residential care homes for the elderly. In this case, a journalist had interviewed an elderly lady without first identifying himself to a responsible executive. It was subsequently established that publicity literature of the home made no reference to the fact that some of its residents were receiving medical and nursing care. Once appraised of this fact, the editor decided not to publish the story. The PCC did not, therefore, censure the newspaper or uphold the complaint although there was a technical breach of the Code. Residential homes for the elderly were, however, clearly recognised as coming within the terms of clause 8.[2]

---

[1]   *Spencer v News of the World et al*, PCC Report No 29, March–April 1995.
[2]   *A man v Daily Mail*, PCC Report No 58–59, April–September 2002.

9.5   The key questions asked when dealing with complaints under clause 8 are as follows:[3]

•   *Were editorial staff in a non-public area?*

•   *Did they identify themselves to a responsible executive?* The term executive was introduced to ensure appropriate seniority.

•   *Was there a public interest in publication?*

9.6   Very few complaints are received under clause 8. The PCC issued two rulings under this clause in 2008.

9.7   Three years before the incorporation of the European Convention for the Protection of Human Rights and Fundamental Freedoms (ECHR) into UK law, Earl Spencer complained to the PCC, on behalf of his wife, the Countess Spencer, and with her consent, that four newspapers had unjustifiably intruded into her privacy by taking photographs of her whilst she was walking in the grounds of a private addiction clinic where she was receiving treatment for bulimia. The complaints were separately but simultaneously adjudicated.

Spencer v News of the World[4]

9.8   In April 1995, the *News of the World* published a three-page story containing material and photographs in breach of what were then clauses 4 (Privacy), 6 (Hospitals) and 8 (Harassment) of the Code of Practice.

9.9   The articles described Countess Spencer's alleged health problems in considerable detail and were accompanied by a front-page photograph of her walking in the grounds of the clinic where she was receiving treatment, taken by using a telephoto lens without permission.

9.10   The newspaper claimed that Earl Spencer was a public figure who had previously courted publicity and told stories to the press about his family and home. Countess Spencer had also spoken publicly about her illness. It went on to claim that the clinic was not a hospital but a health centre and that it had no doctors on its staff.

9.11   The newspaper admitted that it may have breached the Code. It did so because Earl Spencer had admitted to planting false information on such matters and it wanted 'to prove our story was true'.

9.12   In its adjudication, the PCC ruled that although Earl Spencer may have sought publicity and misled the press in the past, this did not leave the press free to report on matters affecting the health or psychological well-being of the Countess. There could be no public interest justification for publishing the articles and photographs. The clinic in which the Countess was receiving treatment clearly came within the category of 'similar institutions' under clause 6. The apology offered to the Countess was an insufficient remedy for the distress that had been caused.

---

3   I Beales *The Editors' Codebook* (Press Standards Board of Finance, revised 2nd edn, 2009), at p 50.
4   PCC Report No 29, March–April 1995.

9.13   The PCC ruled that the conduct of the newspaper constituted such a serious and calculated breach of the Code that it should be formally drawn to the attention of the publisher. All of the complaints were upheld.

9.14   Shortly after the adjudications were published, Mr Rupert Murdoch, Chairman of News International plc, issued a statement in which he said that: 'I have reminded Mr Morgan forcefully of his responsibility to the Code to which he, as an editor – and all our journalists – subscribe in their terms of employment.' He went on to add that his company 'will not tolerate its papers bringing into disrepute the best practices of popular journalism which we seek to follow'.

9.15   Mr Piers Morgan, the editor, also issued a statement in which he accepted full responsibility for the decision to publish and offered his 'sincere apologies to the Countess Spencer for any distress that our actions may have caused ...'.

Spencer v The People[5]

9.16   The complaints against *The People* were made under what were then clauses 4 (Privacy) and 6 (Hospitals). In its adjudication, the PCC noted that although the newspaper had invaded the Countess's privacy by taking photographs of her in a private place, the editor had decided not to publish them because she thought that, in doing so, she would have been in clear breach of the Code. Nevertheless, the complaints were upheld.

Spencer v The Mail on Sunday[6]

9.17   The complaints against the *Mail on Sunday* were made under what were then clauses 4 (Privacy), 6 (Hospitals) and 7 (Misrepresentation).

9.18   The newspaper said that it had received information that the Countess was receiving treatment at the clinic. It sent a medical reporter and a photographer to the clinic to make inquiries. Their approach to a responsible executive was rebuffed. They then faxed a letter to Earl Spencer asking for confirmation or otherwise of the information they had received.

9.19   The PCC noted that the journalist and photographer had acted professionally and in accordance within the Code. It also noted that the editors decided not to publish any information about the Countess's medical condition or treatment. The complaints were rejected.

Spencer v Daily Mirror[7]

9.20   The complaints against the *Daily Mirror* were made under the then clauses 4 (Privacy) and 8(ii) (Harassment) of the Code of Practice.

9.21   An article was published headlined 'Vicky's Bravest Battle' with an accompanying photograph. The editor said that the photograph has been provided by a usually reliable agency. He subsequently noted that the statement made by Earl Spencer

---

5   PCC Report No 29, March–April 1995.
6   PCC Report No 29, March–April 1995.
7   PCC Report No 29, March–April 1995.

on 2 April 1995 complaining of that day's press reporting of his wife's illness contained no reference to the photographs, even though it had appeared in another paper.

9.22 Nevertheless, a prominent and unreserved apology to the Earl and Countess was immediately published in the *Daily Mirror*. The editor accepted at once and without reservation that the photograph was published in breach of the Code and should not have appeared.

9.23 In its adjudication, the PCC accepted that the photograph was published inadvertently and said that it was impressed by the speed and direct manner in which the editor dealt with the complaint. In these circumstances, and given the full and immediate apology that was published and which the Earl accepted, the PCC was pleased to conclude that the complaint was resolved.

9.24 When Gorden Kaye sought legal redress for his grievances in 1990 his representatives were unable to sue for trespass because he was a hospital patient and not therefore a legal occupier. After the *Spencer* adjudications, editors were left in no doubt that the Code of Practice provided the same degree of protection to sick and vulnerable people whether they were resident in hospitals, similar institutions or their own homes.

9.25 Earl Spencer, however, was not satisfied that justice had been entirely done or that it could be done in the domestic courts because there was no tort of privacy under UK law. He therefore instructed his solicitors to apply to the European Commission for permission to bring an action before the European Court of Human Rights (ECtHR) on the grounds that UK law provided insufficient protection from intrusions into peoples' privacy.

9.26 The European Commission refused Earl Spencer's application on the ground that before making his application, he had not exhausted all of his possible domestic remedies in accordance with the principle of subsidiarity.

9.27 Nearly 10 years on since Earl Spencer's application was rejected, Mr Max Mosley's lawyers are in the process of taking a rather different kind of case to the ECtHR where they will argue that UK law still provides insufficient protection for people's privacy rights.

9.28 Shortly after the *Spencer* adjudications the PCC received its first complaint from a special hospital patient, Ian Brady.

Brady v The Sun[8]

9.29 In July 1995, the Chief Executive of the Special Hospital Services Authority complained to the PCC that a report headlined 'Well-fed face of evil child murderer Ian Brady' published in *The Sun* was illustrated by photographs of Brady inside a hospital building which constituted an invasion of his privacy, in breach of the then clauses 4 (Privacy), 6 (Hospitals) and 8(ii) (Harassment) of the Code of Practice.

9.30 The photographs showed Brady standing in front of a window in Ashworth Hospital, which had been taken with a long range telephoto camera from outside the perimeter of the hospital.

---

8   PCC Report No 31, August–October 1995.

9.31 In its adjudication, the PCC noted that clause 6 was designed to protect the privacy of patients in hospitals or similar institutions and to prevent distress and unwanted publicity for those who, because of their illness, may be in a vulnerable position. It went on, however, to say that, 'as well as being a patient at Ashworth, Ian Brady is also a notorious child murderer – a matter, in itself, which justifies scrutiny of him in the public interest'. The PCC also noted that the indistinct photograph of him published by *The Sun* was only able to be taken because he was in a position from which he could be photographed.

9.32 In the particular circumstances of this case, the PCC took the view that the publication of the photograph of Ian Brady was not a matter which warranted censure under the Code.

9.33 Brady was subsequently granted legal aid to apply for a judicial review of the PCC's ruling. His application was rejected, as was a later plea on his behalf before Jowitt J in the High Court. His appeal was also disallowed by Lord Justice Woolf.[9]

9.34 The only recently adjudicated complaint under clause 8(i) was made on behalf of a man who was not a public figure. It is included because it illustrates how strictly the Code is enforced in such cases by editors as well as the PCC.

Jennings v Eastbourne Gazette[10]

9.35 In 2003, Ms Emily Jennings of Crawley complained that a reporter from the *Eastbourne Gazette* approached both her and members of her family in breach of clauses 4 (Harassment) and 9 (Hospitals) of the Code of Practice.

9.36 The complainant's father had suffered a motorcycle accident that left him in a coma. On Sunday 4 August, during his first visit home after regaining consciousness, a journalist approached the house and was told that the family would call him at a more appropriate time if they wished to speak about the accident. The journalist left an answerphone message later in the week, and telephoned again on Friday 9 August asking for permission to visit the complainant's father despite the fact that his injuries were such that 'he barely knew his own name'.

9.37 The newspaper agreed to the 'basic facts of the case', although the complainant's father had been happy to talk to the journalist on his first visit to the house, when it was agreed that the time was inappropriate, and then in hospital, a full 3 weeks after the accident. When the complainant telephoned the newspaper it apologised verbally and promised not to publish any material, an undertaking it had honoured. It subsequently apologised to the complainant in writing, and explained that the journalist had been dismissed following a disciplinary hearing.

9.38 The complainant insisted that it had been made clear when the journalist visited the house that her father did not want to talk, and the assumption that he was fit to be interviewed 3 weeks after the accident when he had spent one of those weeks on a life support machine was ill-founded.

---

9   R Shannon, *A Press Free and Responsible* (John Murray, 2001), at p 217.
10   PCC Report No 60/61, October 2002–March 2003.

9.39   In its adjudication, the PCC reminded editors that clause 9(i) of the Code – which is one of the central provisions relating to the protecting of the vulnerable clearly states that 'journalists or photographers making enquiries at hospitals or similar institutions must identify themselves to a responsible executive and obtain permission before entering non-public areas'. The newspaper had rightly conceded a clear breach of this clause as, while there was some dispute about the response to the journalist's initial approach, the request to desist should have been heeded prior to the hospital visit.

9.40   The PCC noted with approval that the newspaper had apologised in writing, undertaken not to publish the material, and taken disciplinary action against the journalist, but it emphasised that the responsibility to ensure that material is gathered in accordance with the requirements of the Code lies with editors. In this instance the PCC believed that this was a serious breach of the Code which no action could effectively remedy and therefore upheld the complaint under clauses 4 and 9.

CLAUSE 9 (REPORTING OF CRIME)

9.41   Clause 9 of the Code of Practice reads as follows:

'9 * Reporting of Crime

(i)   Relatives or friends of persons convicted or accused of crime should not generally be indentified without their consent, unless they are genuinely relevant to the story.

(ii)   Particular regard should be paid to the potentially vulnerable position of children who witness, or are victims of, crime. This should not restrict the right to report legal proceedings.'

9.42   Prior to 1999, complaints under clause 9 were dealt with under what was then clause 10 (Innocent relatives and friends). The following four case studies illustrate the kinds of complaint which are received under this section of the Code. Neither of the first two complainants could be described as 'figures of contemporary society par excellence' or 'celebrities'. Both, however, were 'relatively public figures' who were well known in their local communities. The last two are case studies of complaints received from celebrities under clause 9 (or clause 10) since the PCC was established in 1991.

9.43   The key questions asked in dealing with complaints under clause 9 are as follows:[11]

•   *Did relatives or friends consent to identification?* Consent might be implied by being publicly involved or pictured with the defendant.

•   *Are they genuinely relevant to the story?* Do they have a role, either in the case, or through a close involvement with the defendant? Could they be personally or professionally affected by the case or its outcome?

•   *Is mention in the public interest?* Is this relationship in the public domain; could the case affect the public life of the relative or friend?

•   *Is the focus proportionate to the involvement of the relative or friend?*

---

[11]   *The Editors' Codebook*, n 3 above, at p 52.

- *Has sufficient care been taken to protect vulnerable children?*

9.44   In 2008 the 16 rulings issued by the PCC under clause 9 accounted for 1.1% of all rulings issued in that year.

Lacey v Eastbourne Gazette[12]

9.45   Councillor Bob Lacey OBE of Eastbourne Borough Council complained on behalf of Councillor Mrs Ann Murray that an article headlined 'Tory son's drink-drive disgrace' published in the *Eastbourne Gazette* on 8 July 1998 identified her in breach of clause 10 (Innocent relatives and friends) of the Code of Practice.

9.46   The front-page article was accompanied by a photograph of Mrs Murray. The complainant said that the article identified Mrs Murray in breach of clause 10 and he complained that the photograph further made her the focus of the story.

9.47   The editor said that Mrs Murray was a prominent figure in the local community who had also spoken out about family values. He suggested that he could have been accused of political bias had the newspaper concealed Mrs Murray's identity.

9.48   In its adjudication the PCC ruled that the prominence that had been accorded to Mrs Murray was unnecessary and regretted the resulting distress that had been caused to her. Whilst the PCC considered that there would indeed have been a public interest in mentioning Mrs Murray in the article – given her local standing and the fact that she had appeared in court with her son – it did not see how the public interest was served by making her so obviously the focus of the story. The complaint was upheld.

Gloag v The Scottish Sun[13]

9.49   In 2007, Mrs Ann Gloag complained to the PCC through her solicitors that an article headlined 'Stay away' published in *The Scottish Sun*, identified her as the relative of someone accused of crime in breach of clause 9 (Reporting of crime) of the Code of Practice.

9.50   The article reported that the complainant's son-in-law had been arrested for assaulting his wife – the complainant's daughter – and that his bail conditions included a ban on him going to the complainant's home, Kinfauns Castle.

9.51   The complainant's solicitors said that Mrs Gloag was not in any way involved in the assault and was not 'genuinely relevant to the story' and should not, therefore, have been identified. They also said that the paper had breached an undertaking given in 2003 following a previous complaint that there would be no repetition of stories about the complainant and her family that breached clause 9 of the Code.

9.52   The newspaper claimed that the complainant was relevant to the story as her house was named in relation to the bail's conditions. Her ownership of Kinfauns Castle was well established in the public domain after her involvement in a high-profile

---

[12]   PCC Report No 44, October–December 1998.
[13]   PCC Report No 75, April–September 2007.

challenge to the Land Reform (Scotland) Act 2003 concerning the access rights of ramblers to part of the estate. The relationship between the accused and the complainant was also public knowledge.

9.53 In its adjudication, the PCC ruled that since the complainant's home was specifically named in the court papers, she was genuinely relevant to the story. Being related to the accused did not give her rights of anonymity that would otherwise not exist. It concluded that it would in fact have been perverse for the article not to have referred to the complainant in circumstances where the newspaper was entitled to publish details of the court order – including the name of Kinfauns Castle – and where the ownership of the castle had previously been well established in the public domain. The complaint was not upheld.

Welch and Healy v Press Association[14]

9.54 In 2000, the actors Ms Denise Welch and Mr Tim Healy complained that a news item issued by the Press Association breached clause 10 (Innocent relatives and friends) of the Code of Practice. The complaint was upheld.

9.55 The news item reported that the couple were related to an individual who was to be tried for alleged crimes which he had denied. The managing editor of the Press Association accepted that the Code had been 'inadvertently' breached and apologised both to the PCC and personally to the complainants. He said that those involved had been reminded of their responsibilities with regard to the Code and of the Association's own stringent guidelines.

9.56 In its adjudication the PCC agreed with the complainants and the Press Association that the report had breached clause 10 of the Code and was pleased that the Association had swiftly acknowledged the error and sought to remedy it as soon as possible. However, as there was no public interest in mentioning the complainants – who had no connection with the alleged crimes and whose names had not previously been placed in the public domain – the complaint was upheld. The PCC noted that the trial was yet to take place and took this opportunity to remind all editors of their responsibilities under the Code, which should be strictly adhered to in any future reporting of the case.

Terry v The Sun[15]

9.57 In April 2009, Mr John Terry complained to the PCC through his solicitors that three articles headlined 'John Terry's mum arrested for shoplifting', 'Girls' flip flops, kiddies' sweets, men's and ladies' watches, tight black leggings, casual shirts, groceries, pet food … and a green tracksuit' and 'JT mums' shop haul was £1,450' published in *The Sun* identified him in breach of clause 9 (Reporting of crime) of the Code of Practice.

9.58 The articles reported that England football captain John Terry's mother, Sue Terry, and his mother-in-law, Sue Poole, had received formal cautions for shoplifting. The complainant's solicitors argued that the coverage, the tone of which sought to mock the complainant, was almost entirely focused on him – referring to his past, professional position and reaction to the matter – when he was not genuinely relevant to the story. He

---

14 PCC Report No 49, January–March 2000.
15 PCC Report No 79, April–September 2009.

had not been involved in the incidents and the fact of his relationship to those at the centre of the story was irrelevant. Neither Mrs Terry nor Mrs Poole had sought publicity for themselves or sought to exploit their connection to the complainant. No public interest was served by the naming of the complainant.

9.59   The newspaper said that the complainant's mother and mother-in-law had accepted cautions for shoplifting from Tesco, one of the England team's corporate sponsors, and Marks & Spencer, which supplied suits to the England football team. The crime was therefore genuinely relevant to the complainant's high-profile position as England captain, and in the public interest. Both Mrs Terry and Mrs Poole – who had featured heavily in the exclusive media coverage of the complainant's wedding for a national magazine – had benefited from his personal wealth, living in properties he had bought for them. They had apparently stolen property from stores which helped to contribute to the complainant's wealth.

9.60   The complainant's solicitors said that the link between the stores concerned and the England football team was tenuous, and did not make the naming of the complainant genuinely relevant to the story.

9.61   The PCC has previously made clear when dealing with complaints under this clause that it will have regard for the extent to which the relationship between the parties has been established in the public domain. In this instance, it was not in dispute that the complainant's relationship to both his mother and Mrs Poole had been placed in the public domain, not least as part of the high-profile coverage of the complainant's wedding. It was not the case that the newspaper had revealed a hitherto unknown connection between the parties.

9.62   The PCC was also convinced by the argument that the complainant was genuinely relevant to the coverage and could legitimately be made its focus. Mrs Terry and Mrs Poole had accepted cautions for stealing items from stores which directly sponsored the England football team. The complainant, as captain, could reasonably be said to be the public face of the team. He was also one of the highest-earning footballers in the world who, it was said, provided for his family financially. The fact that – despite such wealth – his mother and mother-in-law had been involved in claims of shoplifting was clearly relevant to the matter. The complaint was not upheld.

CLAUSE 10 (CLANDESTINE DEVICES AND SUBTERFUGE)

9.63   Clause 10 of the Code of Practice reads as follows:

'10 * Clandestine devices and subterfuge

(i)   The press must not seek to obtain or publish material acquired by using hidden cameras or clandestine listening devices; or by intercepting private or mobile telephone calls, messages or email; or by the unauthorized removal of documents or photographs; or by accessing digitally-held private information without consent.

(ii)   Engaging in misrepresentation or subterfuge can generally be justified only in the public interest and then only when the material cannot be obtained by other means.'

9.64 The origins of this clause date back to 2004 when what was then clause 8 (Listening devices) and clause 11 (Misrepresentation) were combined to make up clause 10 as it reads today.

9.65 The clause allows editors to advance a public interest justification for allowing their journalists to resort to subterfuge and the use of clandestine devices. They must provide evidence that they had prior and reasonable grounds for believing that a legitimate public interest would be served and that the material could not have been obtained by any other means. Clandestine 'fishing expeditions' undertaken in the hope that something of public interest will turn up will always constitute a breach of the Code.

9.66 Nevertheless, as Ian Beales points out, the Code allows resort to subterfuge 'for harmless journalistic spoofs – such as April Fool Stories – intended to amuse rather than mislead'.[16]

9.67 The Editors' Code Committee keeps this clause under continuous review so that it remains up to date with new developments in information technology and changes in the law. The accessing of digitally-held private information without consent was explicitly prohibited in 2007, following the Clive Goodman scandal. The PCC must at all times apply the requirements of clause 10 in ways that are consistent with those of the Data Protection Act 1998 and the Regulation of Investigatory Powers Act 2000. It sets a very high threshold for editors to cross when they seek to justify recourse to clandestine devices and subterfuge on grounds of public interest.

9.68 The key questions asked when dealing with complaints under clause 10 are as follows:[17]

- *Did the publication seek to obtain or publish the material?* Genuinely unsolicited material may not be affected.

- *If the publication used undercover methods was there reason to believe it was in the public interest?* Fishing expeditions don't count.

- *Was the clandestine activity related directly to the public interest?*

- *Could the material have been obtained by other means?*

- *Were agents or intermediaries used to acquire confidential information not in the public interest, without consent?* If so it would breach both the Code and the law.

9.69 The 19 rulings issued by the PCC under clause 10 in 2008 accounted for 1.3% of all rulings issued in that year.

---

[16]   *The Editors' Codebook*, n 3 above, at p 55.
[17]   Ibid, n 3 above, at p 56.

Foster v The Sun[18]

9.70   In 2002, Mr Peter Foster complained to the PCC that private telephone conversations between him and his mother had been intercepted and published in *The Sun* in breach of what was then clause 8 (Listening devices) of the Code of Practice.

9.71   In late 2002, a number of newspapers reported that the complainant had been involved in negotiating the purchase of property in Bristol by the Prime Minister and his wife. As part of its investigations into the affair, *The Sun* obtained and published details of phone conversations between the complainant and his mother.

9.72   The newspaper, then under a former editor, did not deny that private conversations had been intercepted and then published. It argued, however, that their publication was in the public interest because they helped to ensure that the public was not misled further by those involved in the saga and because they established a clearer picture of events surrounding what subsequently became known as 'Cheriegate'.

9.73   The complainant said that publication of the conversations was not in the public interest since they did not contradict anything he had said which might have misled the public. Indeed, he had made no public statements of any kind. The simple fact that the story was high profile did not justify the newspaper's intrusion into his privacy.

9.74   In its adjudication, the PCC started from the premise that eavesdropping into private telephone conversations – and then publishing transcripts of them – is one of the most serious forms of physical intrusion into privacy. It recognised that publication can be justified under the Code of Practice where the public interest is clearly served. Nevertheless, in view of the serious nature of such an intrusion the PCC had to set the public interest hurdle 'at a demonstrably high level'. Having considered the text of the telephone conversations it concluded that they generally served only to illustrate the story in a manner which was already well known.

9.75   The PCC noted that some new information had been added to the story but it was not of the significance required to justify breaching the strict terms of the Code. 'Eavesdropping into private telephone conversations – and then publishing transcripts of them – [was] one of the most serious forms of physical intrusion into privacy' and, consequently the PCC expected 'a very strong public interest defense for breaching this clause – and the newspaper's defense did not meet it'. The complaint was upheld.

9.76   Mr Foster also complained that the Sun articles were inaccurate in breach of clause 1 (Accuracy) of the Code, as was a subsequent article. These complaints were rejected.

Caplin v News of the World[19]

9.77   In 2005, Ms Carole Caplin complained through her solicitors to the PCC that articles in the *News of the World* and headlined 'Yeah, Prime Minister', 'Caplin's right off her trolley' and 'Time to dump Caplin, Cherie', were intrusive in breach of clause 3 (Privacy) and followed harassment and subterfuge in breach of clauses 4 (Harassment) and 10 (Clandestine devices and subterfuge) of the Code.

---

[18]   PCC Report, No 62–63, April–September 2003.
[19]   PCC Report No 72, October 2005–April 2006.

9.78   Two journalists had joined one of Ms Caplin's lifestyle classes under false names and used hidden cameras and listening devices in order to record conversations with other clients in which she discussed aspects of her special relationship with the Blairs.

9.79   The complainant's solicitors claimed that the journalist had used hidden cameras and clandestine listening devices, and was engaged in subterfuge in a way that could not be justified in the public interest. They noted that clause 10 says that subterfuge can generally be justified 'only when the material cannot be obtained by other means'. The solicitors said that there was no evidence that any other means had been pursued.

9.80   The solicitors also claimed that such sustained underhand activity constituted 'persistent pursuit' in breach of clause 4 of the Code and a failure to respect the complainant's private life in breach of clause 3. In addition the photographs of the complainant in a London hotel and at the gym where she worked were taken and published in breach of clause 3, as she had a reasonable expectation of privacy when the pictures were taken.

9.81   The newspaper said that there was an overwhelming public interest in the published article. Ms Caplin was known to have an extraordinary relationship with the Blairs. Its journalists had received information that she was willing to exploit that relationship and betray the family's trust in order to promote her business. Subterfuge was necessary as a direct approach would obviously not have yielded the information. The newspaper insisted that the investigation showed that the claims were true.

9.82   Since the newspaper had admitted that it had resorted to subterfuge under clause 10 the PCC's task was to decide whether there was sufficient public interest in the articles to justify its use. It found that the published material did not relate to the complainant's personal life but only to her professional opinions and work. There was a clear public interest in testing the claim that she was exploiting her relationship with the Blairs in order to promote her business and the published material showed that she was doing so.

9.83   The articles showed that the complainant had made repeated references to the Prime Minister and his family in conversation with the journalists. They included comments about the Prime Minister's health and claims that she had spoken to him in order to influence the Government's position in respect of a European directive. The complainant had not disputed these facts and there was clearly a public interest in publishing such information.

9.84   There was also no breach of clause 3. The subject matters of Ms Caplin's comments on 'lifestyle issues' related to her work rather than her private and family life, home, health and correspondence. Although the photographs were taken in places where she had a reasonable expectation of privacy, they showed her engaging in professional negotiations and there was a public interest in taking and publishing them. There was nothing gratuitously humiliating or demeaning in their content.

9.85   Finally, clause 4 had not been engaged by this complaint. Its terms were designed to protect people from 'persistent pursuit' and did not generally apply to the kinds of undercover operation involved in this particular case. The complaints were not upheld.

Coonan (Sutcliffe) v News of the World[20]

9.86   In August 2006, Mr Peter Coonan (formerly Peter Sutcliffe) complained to the PCC through his solicitors that an article headlined 'The Ripper Tapes' published in the *News of the World* on 23 July 2006, and on the newspaper's website, intruded into his privacy in breach of clause 3 (Privacy) of the Code of Practice. He also complained that information had been obtained by use of a clandestine listening device, in breach of clause 10 (Clandestine devices and subterfuge) of the Code.

9.87   The article included the transcript of a telephone conversation between the complainant – who was a patient in Broadmoor Special Hospital – and another individual. The complainant's solicitors pointed out that 'the transcript included reference to their client's mental health, medical treatment and relationships, all of which was private information deserving of the highest level of protection'. Consent had not been given for either its recording or publication.

9.88   The fact that the complainant had been convicted of the commission of serious crimes did 'not strip him of his right to conduct a private conversation'. Contrary to the PCC's original ruling in this matter, the details of their client's medical condition and treatment were not widely known – and this was also the case with regard to the relationship he maintained with his ex-wife. In addition, the solicitors claimed that the PCC had illogically described some of the information as 'anodyne' whilst also regarding the story as a matter of public interest.

9.89   The newspaper argued that, since there was no duty of confidence between the complainant and the other individual involved, there was no reason why this individual should not pass on the information. The complainant was a notorious murderer who had blamed his crimes – at least in part – on his mental state. He was now claiming that the medication had worked and that an appeal was mandatory. All this information was 'of the highest order of public interest'.

9.90   In its adjudication, the PCC reiterated that 'individuals do not forfeit their right to privacy under the Code or the European Convention if they have committed serious crimes'. It also recognised that the complainant 'had committed some extremely grave crimes which had bestowed on him a considerable notoriety and earned him the enduring scrutiny and interest of the press and the public'. It was well known that since his incarceration, the complainant had been diagnosed and received treatment for schizophrenia.

9.91   At the start of its investigation, the PCC had to decide whether or not a confidential relationship – either contractual or presumed – had ever been established between the complainant and the other person. It found no evidence of such a relationship. They had corresponded, spoken on four occasions and never met. Since the complainant had been in Broadmoor, he had also conducted a considerable correspondence with many members of the public.

9.92   The complainant's solicitors agreed that he had corresponded with many people, but had never consented to the publication of information which he considered private. In this instance, they claimed, the article included details of his drug treatment, the duration of his treatment and his response to medication.

---

[20]   PCC Report No 74, October 2006–April 2007.

9.93 The PCC, however, found that there was only one reference to the complainant's treatment, which referred to the use of 'anti-psychotic' drugs which is 'simply a generic term for medication used in the treatment of schizophrenia'. Since it was always well known that he had suffered from this condition, this information was not 'particularly intrusive in its detail or disproportionate to what was already in the public domain'.

9.94 The solicitors also objected to the fact that the article included references to an improvement in their client's mental health and a possible appeal against the sentence and conviction. They did not believe that any such appeal was being pursued. The PCC found that this claim had already been established in the public domain for some time without any official complaint. Its re-publication did not, therefore, constitute a breach of the Code. It also found that other references to the complainant's relationships were so 'anodyne' that they did not reveal anything of a personal nature.

9.95 Finally, the complainant's solicitors claimed that clause 3 of the Code included a public interest exception which was at variance with its counterpart, Art 8 of the ECHR. They noted that 'derogation from Article 8 is allowed only where the public authority can show that the breach of the right is necessary to protect another right (here the newspaper's Article 10 right to freedom of expression)'. The PCC, however, took the view that:

> '... the principle of derogation has nothing to do with the content of either Articles 8 or 10 but arises under Article 15, and refers to the right of a contracting state to withdraw from its obligations arising from the European Convention in times of war or other public emergency.'

9.96 In summary, the PCC's conclusions under clause 3 were that 'the information in the article was either anodyne and did not therefore have the qualities that would require the protection of the privacy provisions of the Code – or in the public domain to such a significant degree that it could not be regarded as private'.

9.97 As for the complaint under clause 10 (Clandestine devices and subterfuge), the PCC noted that the individual concerned had done no more than take a recording of the conversations. The information was freely given, no confidential relationship had arisen between Mr Coonan and the other person. Given that 'there was a legitimate and enduring public interest in scrutiny of the complainant, the Commission took the view that the complaint under Clause 10 was not upheld either'. The complaints were not upheld.

Details of all PCC adjudicated and resolved complaints published from 1996 onwards can be visited at www.pcc.org.uk/cases.

Part II

PRIVACY LAW

Chapter 10

PRIVACY LAW: AN INTRODUCTORY SUMMARY

10.1   Celebrity status inevitably carries with it a serious loss of privacy and the protection given to what privacy remains is by no means absolute. This is because the right to privacy has always to be balanced against the right to freedom of expression, a right which is vigorously protected by the media. The following summary of the legal principles applicable to privacy cases has been extracted from recent important case-law.[1] It is intended to impart a general understanding of the law's development and help identify and clarify the main issues which need to be examined. For the sake of simplicity citation of authority has been dispensed with.

10.2   The law's development started with the Human Rights Act 1998 (HRA 1998) which requires the values enshrined in the European Convention for the Protection of Human Rights and Fundamental Freedoms (ECHR) to be taken into account in our law. The foundation of the jurisdiction to restrain publicity is now derived from Convention rights under the ECHR.

10.3   The cause of action in privacy cases is primarily breach of confidence or, more precisely, misuse of private information. There is no tort of invasion of privacy as such – something which is often overlooked. The focus of the cause of action is the *misuse* of private *information.* Photographs and text are conveyers of information and it is their misuse (usually by publication in the media) that gives rise to the cause of action. Thus it is not the taking of a photograph of a celebrity that is objectionable but the *publication* of the *information* it conveys. Equally, mere reading of a private diary is not objectionable as such whereas the publication of the information conveyed by the contents of the diary is. Primarily, therefore, misuse of private information is concerned with protecting celebrities from having information about their private lives *published* in the media. The cause of action is based on the values enshrined in Arts 8 and 10 of the ECHR, that is to say, the right to a private life and freedom of expression. The underlying inquiry is to determine how these values interact and are applied to the facts of any particular case. In other words the issue is usually about how much information about their private lives celebrities can legitimately keep out of the media versus how much information about them the media can legitimately publish.

10.4   Article 8, the 'Right to respect for private and family life', provides:

> '1.   Everyone has the right to respect for his private and family life, his home and his correspondence.

---

[1]   Reference should be made to the following central authorities: *Campbell v MGN Limited* [2004] UKHL 22; *McKennitt v Ash* [2006] EWCA Civ 1714; *Lord Browne of Madingley v Associated Newspapers* [2007] EWCA Civ 295; *Murray v Big Pictures Limited* [2008] EWCA Civ 446. In particular see the judgment of the Court of Appeal handed down by Sir Anthony Clarke MR in the *Lord Browne of Madingley* appeal.

2.   There shall be no interference by a public authority with the exercise of this right except such as is in accordance with the law and is necessary in a democratic society in the interests of national security, public safety or the economic well-being of the country, for the prevention of disorder or crime, for the protection of health or morals, or for the protection of the rights and freedoms of others.'

10.5   Article 10, 'Freedom of expression', provides, so far as relevant:

'1.   Everyone has the right to freedom of expression. This right shall include freedom to hold opinions and to receive and impart information and ideas without interference by public authority and regardless of frontiers ...

2.   The exercise of these freedoms, since it carries with it duties and responsibilities, may be subject to such formalities, conditions, restrictions or penalties as are prescribed by law and are necessary in a democratic society, ... for the protection of the reputation or rights of others, for preventing the disclosure of information received in confidence, or for maintaining the authority and impartiality of the judiciary.'

10.6   The word 'confidence' in the phrase 'breach of confidence' is the confidence arising out of a confidential relationship. The cause of action, however, has now dispensed with the need for an initial confidential relationship. The law now imposes a 'duty of confidence' whenever a person receives information he knows or ought to know is fairly and reasonably to be regarded as confidential.

10.7   The continuing use of the phrase 'duty of confidence' and the description of the information as 'confidential' is not altogether apt when dealing with information about an individual's private life because this would not normally be called 'confidential' and would more naturally be called 'private'.

10.8   The values enshrined in Arts 8 and 10 have become part of the cause of action for breach of confidence and are as much applicable in disputes between individuals or between an individual and a non-governmental body such as a newspaper as they are in disputes between individuals and a public authority.

10.9   In developing a right to protect private information, including the implementation in the English courts of Arts 8 and 10 of the ECHR, the English courts have had to proceed through the tort of breach of confidence, into which the jurisprudence of Arts 8 and 10 has to be 'shoehorned'.

10.10   This is not an entirely comfortable fit because the action for breach of confidence is employed where no pre-existing relationship of confidence between the parties exists. However, the 'confidence' arises from the defendant having acquired by unlawful or surreptitious means information he should have known he was not free to use.

10.11   The law now affords protection to information in respect of which there is a reasonable expectation of privacy, even in circumstances where there is no pre-existing relationship giving rise of itself to an enforceable duty of confidence.

10.12   The verbal difficulty of how to describe the new cause of action can be avoided by calling the cause of action 'misuse of private information'. There is no English domestic law tort of invasion of privacy (although the cause of action is sometimes referred to as a tort). Articles 8 and 10 of the ECHR are now the very content of the domestic tort that the English court has to enforce.

10.13 Where there is a claim for an interlocutory injunction to restrain the publication of information the court must consider 'whether to grant any relief which, if granted, might affect the exercise of the Convention right to freedom of expression' because this is a requirement of HRA 1998, s 12(1).

10.14 HRA 1998, s 12(3) and (4) provides:

> '(3)   No such relief is to be granted so as to restrain publication before trial unless the court is satisfied that the Applicant is likely to establish that publication should not be allowed.

> (4)   The court must have particular regard to the importance of the Convention right to freedom of expression and, where the proceedings relate to material which the Respondent claims, or which appears to the court, to be journalistic, literary or artistic material (or to conduct connected with such material), to –

> (a)   the extent to which –
>   (i)   the material has, or is about to, become available to the public; or
>   (ii)   it is, or would be, in the public interest for the material to be published;
> (b)   any relevant privacy code.'

10.15 Section 12 should be approached first by considering whether Art 8 is engaged and then by considering whether Art 10 is engaged and, critically, whether the applicant has shown he is likely to establish at a trial that publication should not be allowed within the meaning of HRA 1998, s 12(3).

10.16 Privacy denotes personal 'space' which should be free from intrusion. An infringement of privacy is an affront to the personality, which is damaged both by the violation and by the demonstration that the personal space is not inviolate.

10.17 The first question under Art 8 (and the touchstone of a private life) is whether in respect of the disclosed facts the claimant has a reasonable expectation of privacy in the particular circumstances of the case. There is probably no need for such a test where 'the information is obviously private'.

10.18 Whether the information is public or private will sometimes be obvious. Where it is not, it has been suggested that the broad test is whether disclosure of the information about an individual would give substantial offence to that individual, assuming that that particular individual was placed in similar circumstances and was a person of ordinary sensibilities.

10.19 The question whether there is a reasonable expectation of privacy is a broad one, which takes account of all the circumstances of the case. These include the attributes of the claimant, the nature of the activity in which the claimant was engaged, the place at which it was happening, the nature and purpose of the intrusion, the absence of consent and whether it was known or could be inferred, the effect on the claimant and the circumstances in which and the purposes for which the information came into the hands of the publisher.

10.20 Information will be confidential if it is available to one person (or a group of people) and not generally available to others, provided that the person (or group) who possesses the information does not intend that it should be available to others.

10.21 'Private information' includes information that is personal to the person who possesses it and is not intended that it should be imparted to the general public. The nature of the information, or the form in which it is kept, may suffice to make it plain that the information satisfies these criteria.

10.22 The courts have wrestled with the problem of identifying the basis for claiming privacy or confidence in respect of unauthorised or purloined information, ie where there is no pre-existing relationship of confidence.

10.23 Where there is no pre-existing relationship of confidence the primary focus is on the nature of the information. The primary focus has to be on the nature of the information, because it is the recipient's perception of its confidential nature that imposes the obligation on him.

10.24 When concluding that information is private it is not always easy to identify the extent to which this is because of the nature of the information, the form in which it is conveyed and the fact that the person disclosing it was in a confidential relationship with the person to whom it relates. Usually these factors form an interdependent amalgam of circumstances.

10.25 Although the mere fact information is imparted in the course of a relationship of confidence does not necessarily satisfy the 'expectation of privacy' test, the nature of the relationship is usually of great importance in determining whether there was an expectation of privacy. Where the parties had a pre-existing relationship, such as marriage or a relationship of friendship, or an intimate and sexual relationship, it is likely that there will be a reasonable expectation of privacy in relation to information learned or activities witnessed during the relationship. This is not always so, however, and it is still necessary to look carefully at the information to see if it is of the type which an individual normally would expect to be kept private.

10.26 Thus the relationship between the relevant parties is of considerable importance in determining whether there was a reasonable expectation of privacy. There are a number of potentially relevant questions, depending upon the circumstances, which include whether the recipient received information he knew or ought reasonably to have known was fairly and reasonably to be regarded as confidential or private.

10.27 The mere fact that a piece of information is trivial is not, without more, decisive although it may prove to be so.

10.28 Whether or not any particular piece of information qualifies as private and the claimant has a reasonable expectation of privacy in respect of it, requires a detailed examination of all the circumstances on a case-by-case basis. The circumstances include the nature of the information itself and the circumstances in which it has been imparted or obtained.

10.29 Information relating to business activities will not be characterised as private merely because it is communicated or learned in a domestic environment, or in the course of a personal relationship. Whether it is so all depends upon the circumstances of the particular case.

10.30 The courts determine issues as they arise on a case-by-case basis and the question is whether there was a reasonable expectation of privacy. If, in respect of particular information, there is a reasonable expectation of privacy, Art 8 is engaged and the question is then whether interference with those rights should be permitted under Art 8(2).

10.31 The underlying question in all cases where it is alleged that there has been a breach of the duty of confidence is whether the information that was disclosed was private and not public. There must be some interest of a private nature that the claimant wishes to protect.

10.32 If, on the facts, there is no breach of a confidential relationship the form and content of the particular information in question might clearly constitute it private information entitled to the protection of Art 8(1) as qualified by Art 8(2) irrespective of how the information might have been obtained (for example, a copy of a celebrity's intimate personal diary brought to a newspaper having been found in the street).

10.33 The home is expressly entitled to 'respect' under Art 8 and correspondingly is likely to import an obligation of confidence so that even relatively trivial details would be protected from disclosure because of the traditional sanctity accorded to hearth and home.

10.34 Most complaints in privacy cases are still what might be called old-fashioned breach of confidence by way of conduct inconsistent with a pre-existing relationship, rather than simply of the purloining of private information. In cases where there is a pre-existing relationship the duty of confidence arises from the transaction or relationship between the parties. In such cases:

- there must first be conducted the more elemental inquiry into breach of confidence in the traditional understanding of that expression (ie 'old-fashioned breach of confidence'); and

- only then should attention be turned to whether the material obtained during such a relationship is indeed confidential.

10.35 Thus where there is a previous relationship of confidence, the focus is different and the nature of any relationship between the relevant persons or parties becomes of considerable potential importance.

10.36 Where the Art 8 right is based on the protection of private information, the basis for interference with that right to protection will usually, though not in every case, be found in the rights and freedoms created by Art 10.

10.37 The right to freedom of expression is exercised under Art 10(1) of the ECHR. Article 10(2) provides that the right to freedom of expression includes the freedom to receive information. That right must be balanced against any Art 8 rights of privacy.

10.38 The balance to be struck is between the claimant's rights under Art 8 and the right to freedom of expression under Art 10.

10.39 In respect of each piece of information in dispute it must be considered whether the justification in Art 10(2) is established.

10.40 Article 10(2) expressly provides that the freedom of expression may be subject to such restrictions (and the like) as are prescribed by law and necessary in a democratic society for the protection of the reputation or rights of others and for preventing the disclosure of information received in confidence.

10.41 The balancing exercise comes into play if the first hurdle can be overcome, by demonstrating a reasonable expectation of privacy. The balancing exercise requires weighing the competing Convention rights in the light of an intense focus upon the individual facts of each case.

10.42 The balancing exercise is essentially a question of fact with the weight to be attached to the various considerations being of degree and essentially a matter for the trial judge. In carrying out the balancing exercise of weighing the competing Convention rights no one Convention right takes automatic precedence over another.

10.43 In order to determine which should take precedence, *in the particular circumstances*, it is necessary to examine the facts closely as revealed in the evidence at the trial and to decide whether (assuming a reasonable expectation of privacy to have been established) some countervailing consideration of public interest may be said to justify any intrusion which has taken place.

10.44 In carrying out the balancing exercise the justifications for interfering or restricting rights under Arts 8 and 10 must be taken into account. Finally proportionality must be applied to each, which is called the ultimate balancing test. The judge will have to ask whether the intrusion, or perhaps the degree of intrusion, into the claimant's privacy was proportionate to the public interest supposedly being served by it.

10.45 In weighing up the relative worth of one person's rights against those of another the use to which a person has put or intends to put his rights is to be taken into account.

10.46 Ultimately the central question to be addressed is where the public interest lies or, more precisely, whether the public interest justifies the intrusion. It is a question of balance between protecting private life and freedom of expression. In summary:

- neither article has as such precedence over the other;

- where the values under the two Articles are in conflict, an intense focus on the comparative importance of the specific rights being claimed in the individual case is necessary;

- the justifications for interfering with or restricting each right must be taken into account; and

- the proportionality test must be applied to each which is the ultimate balancing test.

10.47 The requirement in s 12(4) of HRA 1998 to pay particular regard to Art 10 of the ECHR requires the court to pay particular regard to the rights of others in accordance with Art 10(2). The balance does not start tilted in favour of Art 10.

10.48 With regard to photographs, when carrying out the balancing exercise and the intense focus on the facts in the individual case, if the case involves competing rights under Art 10 to publish a photograph and Art 8 to restrain publication a court should be alive to the potential, depending on the particular facts of each individual case, that as a means of invading privacy a photograph is particularly intrusive. Consideration should be given to whether it really is necessary that the information should be imparted by means of a photograph at all.

10.49 Although freedom of expression extends to the publication of photographs, the protection of the rights and reputation of others in the case of photographs takes on particular importance because the issue is not about the freedom to disseminate ideas but about images containing very personal or even intimate 'information' concerning an individual.

10.50 Photographs appearing in the tabloid press are often taken in a climate of continual harassment which induces in the person concerned a very strong sense of intrusion into their private life or even of persecution.

Chapter 11

PROTECTING CONFIDENTIAL AND PRIVATE INFORMATION FROM UNAUTHORISED DISCLOSURE

INFORMATIONAL PRIVACY

11.1   The protection of privacy is a serious issue in celebrity culture. This chapter is about the law relating to what is loosely termed informational privacy. This covers the sort of damaging and distressing information celebrities often want kept out of the papers. Underlying this developing area of law is the recognition of the fundamental human right to privacy and in particular the individual right to protection against unwarranted intrusion into personal space or interference with emotional well-being. It is these areas of protection, rather than protection of reputation[1] or image as such, that are the concern of this chapter.

11.2   The unauthorised publication of private information is controlled by rules developed to reflect the right to privacy and the competing right to freedom of speech. The rules have been strongly influenced by Arts 8 and 10 of the European Convention for the Protection of Human Rights and Fundamental Freedoms (ECHR); by decisions of the European Court of Human Rights (ECtHR); and by the explanations and pronouncements of our own judges. Because the law is developing and changing it is necessary to focus on what judges have said in recent privacy cases particularly since the House of Lords decision in *Campbell v MGN Limited*.[2]

THE CELEBRITY PERSONA

11.3   Celebrities thrive on publicity and, for that reason, largely enjoy a different relationship with the media from that of the general public. Newspapers sell copy by publishing (sometimes exposing) intimate details of the lives of well-known celebrities. Statements made about Ms Naomi Campbell in the House of Lords revealed the current attitude to celebrity culture. Lord Hoffman in *Campbell* described her as:[3]

> '... a famous fashion model who lives by publicity. What she has to sell is herself: her personal appearance and her personality. She employs public relations agents to present her personal life to the media in the best possible light just as she employs professionals to advise her on dress and make-up. That is no criticism of her. It is a trade like any other. But it does mean that her relationship with the media is different from that of people who expose less of their private life to the public.'

---

[1]   Although some European cases suggest that Art 8 protects 'reputation' broadly understood: see Buxton LJ in *McKennitt v Ash* [2006[EWCA Civ 1714, at [80].

[2]   [2004] UKHL 22.

[3]   *Campbell v MGN Limited* [2004] UKHL 22, at [37].

11.4   The importance of a good reputation to the celebrity image was emphasised by Lord Hope in *Campbell* who said that the business of fashion modelling:[4]

> '... in which ... Naomi Campbell has built up such a powerful reputation internationally, is conducted under the constant gaze of the media. It is also highly competitive. It is a context where public reputation as a forceful and colourful personality adds value to the physical appearance of the individual. Much good can come of this, if the process is carefully and correctly handled ...'

11.5   Two reputations are likely to be put at stake when there is unauthorised publication of personal information – that of the celebrity wishing to restrain publication and uphold his privacy and image, on the one hand, and that of the publisher wishing to increase circulation, on the other. A sense of reality and perspective is necessary when endeavouring to evaluate and strike a balance between the two interests at stake. Lady Hale said in *Campbell* that it was:[5]

> '... a prima donna celebrity against a celebrity-exploiting tabloid newspaper. Each in their time has profited from the other. Both are assumed to be grown-ups who know the score. On the one hand is the interest of a woman who wants to give up her dependence on illegal and harmful drugs and wants the peace and space in which to pursue the help which she finds useful. On the other hand is a newspaper which wants to keep its readers informed of the activities of celebrity figures, and to expose their weaknesses, lies, evasions and hypocrisies. This sort of story, especially if it has photographs attached, is just the sort of thing that fills, sells and enhances the reputation of the newspaper which gets it first.'

ARTICLES 8 AND 10 OF THE ECHR

11.6   Articles 8 and 10 of the ECHR, as set out in the Human Rights Act 1998 (HRA 1998), Sch 1, Pt 1, are the foundation of the law's development of protection for private information. The interaction of those rights and the qualifications made to them were central to the decision in *Campbell*.[6] The right of privacy and the right of freedom of speech are enshrined in Arts 8 and 10 respectively and these Articles are the starting point for any discussion on privacy law.

11.7   Article 8 provides:

> '1. Everyone has the right to respect for his private and family life, his home and his correspondence.
>
> 2. There shall be no interference by a public authority with the exercise of this right except such as is in accordance with the law and is necessary in a democratic society in the interests of national security, public safety or the economic well-being of the country, for the prevention of disorder or crime, for the protection of health or morals, or for the protection of the rights and freedoms of others.'

11.8   Article 10 provides:

---

[4]   At [80].
[5]   At [143].
[6]   *Campbell v MGN Limited* [2004] UKHL 22.

'1. Everyone has the right to freedom of expression. This right shall include freedom to hold opinions and to receive and impart information and ideas without interference by public authority and regardless of frontiers.

2. The exercise of these freedoms, since it carries with it duties and responsibilities, may be subject to such formalities, conditions, restrictions or penalties as are prescribed by law and are necessary in a democratic society, in the interests of national security, territorial integrity or public safety, for the prevention of disorder or crime, for the protection of health or morals, for the protection of rights of others, for the prevention of disclosure of information received in confidence, or for maintaining the authority and impartiality of the judiciary.'

THE INCORPORATION OF ARTS 8 AND 10 OF THE ECHR INTO ENGLISH LAW

11.9 Private information has been identified in human rights law as worthy of protection; the equivalent of Art 8 has been enacted as part of English law and the values underlying Arts 8 and 10 are now applied equally to disputes between individuals as between individuals and the state.[7] Even now that the equivalent of Art 8 has been enacted as part of English law, it is not directly concerned with the protection of privacy against private persons or corporations but is, by virtue of s 6 of HRA 1998, a guarantee of privacy only against public authorities. Since human rights law has identified private information as something worth protecting as an aspect of human autonomy and dignity, it was not logical for a person to have less protection against a private individual than against the state in respect of the unauthorised publication of personal information.[8]

11.10 The positive obligations imposed on the state by Art 8 to promote the interests of private life and the right of the individual to complain if that right is interfered with were considered by Buxton LJ in *McKennitt v Ash*,[9] who said the individual is entitled to complain against the state if his private life is interfered with. Article 8 imposes not merely negative but also positive obligations on the state: to respect, and therefore to promote, the interests of private and family life. This means a citizen can complain against the state about breaches of his private and family life committed by other individuals. That, as Buxton LJ noted, has been Convention law at least since *Marckx v Belgium*.[10] Buxton LJ referred to a particularly strong statement of the obligation to be found in *X and Y v Netherlands*.[11]

11.11 Although there has been difficulty explaining how that state obligation is articulated and enforced in actions between private individuals, Buxton LJ thought[12] that judges of the highest authority have concluded that that follows from s 6(1) and (3) of HRA 1998 which placed on the courts the obligations appropriate to a public authority. Buxton LJ continued[13] that in order to find the rules of the English law of breach of confidence the courts have to look in the jurisprudence of Arts 8 and 10 which are now not merely of persuasive or parallel effect but, as Lord Woolf said in *A v*

---

[7] Lord Nicholls in *Campbell v MGN Limited* [2004] UKHL 22, at [17] and [18].
[8] Lord Hoffman in *Campbell*, at [49] and [50].
[9] See *McKennitt v Ash* [2006] EWCA Civ 1714, at [9].
[10] (1979) 2 EHRR 330.
[11] (1985) 8 EHRR 235.
[12] See *McKennitt v Ash*, at [10].
[13] At [11].

B plc,[14] are the very content of the domestic tort that the English court has to enforce. Buxton LJ referred to Lady Hale in *Campbell*;[15] Lord Phillips of Worth Matravers in *Douglas v Hello!*;[16] and in particular the following statement of Lord Woolf in *A v B plc*:[17]

> 'Under section 6 of the 1998 Act the court, as a public authority, is required not to act "in a way which is incompatible with a Convention right". The court is able to achieve this by absorbing the rights which articles 8 and 10 protect into the long-established action for breach of confidence. This involves giving a new strength and breadth to the action so that it accommodates the requirements of those articles.'

CAMPBELL V MGN (HL) AND *VON HANNOVER V GERMANY* (ECTHR)

11.12 Shortly after *Campbell v MGN*[18] the ECtHR delivered its decision in *Von Hannover v Germany*[19] and issues arose about the relationship between these two important decisions. The Court of Appeal in *Murray v Big Pictures (UK) Limited*[20] confirmed[21] it was bound by *Campbell*, the House of Lords having made it clear in *Kay v Lambeth LBC*,[22] that in the event of conflict between a decision of the House and a later decision of the ECtHR, lower courts, including the Court of Appeal, must follow the former.[23] The primary focus of the Court of Appeal in *Murray* was, therefore, upon the speeches in *Campbell*. In a penetrating analysis of where the law had reached after *Campbell* Lord Steyn in the House of Lords in *Re S (a child)* said:[24]

> '[17] The interplay between articles 8 and 10 has been illuminated by the opinions in the House of Lords in *Campbell v MGN Ltd* [2004] 2 WLR 1232. For present purposes the decision of the House on the facts of *Campbell* and the differences between the majority and the minority are not material. What does, however, emerge clearly from the opinions are four propositions. First, neither article has *as such* precedence over the other. Secondly, where the values under the two articles are in conflict, an intense focus on the comparative importance of the specific rights being claimed in the individual case is necessary. Thirdly, the justifications for interfering with or restricting each right must be taken into account. Finally, the proportionality test must be applied to each. For convenience I will call this the ultimate balancing test. This is how I will approach the present case.'

'OLD-FASHIONED BREACH OF CONFIDENCE'

11.13 It has long been the case that, in certain circumstances, types of private information have received protection from disclosure by the courts. This protection was primarily based on the claim for breach of confidence (often now referred to as

---

14   [2002] EWCA Civ 337, [2003] QB 195, at [4], [2002] 2 All ER 545.
15   At [132].
16   At [53]; *Douglas v Hello!* [2005] EWCA Civ 595.
17   [2002] EWCA Civ 337, [2003] QB 195, at [4], [2002] 2 All ER 545.
18   [2004] UKHL 22.
19   *Von Hannover v Germany* (2004) 40 EHRR 1.
20   [2008] EWCA Civ 446, at [3], per Buxton LJ.
21   At [35].
22   [2006] UKHL 10, [2006] 2 AC 465.
23   See per Lord Bingham at [43]–[44] in a passage quoted by the judge at [61].
24   [2005] 1 AC 593.

'old-fashioned breach of confidence' in order to distinguish it from the newer extended form of breach of confidence which embraces purely private information). Previously, private information was protected from disclosure only if it could be categorised as 'confidential information', that is to say, information which had been disclosed in circumstances importing an obligation of confidence. Under old-fashioned breach of confidence information was initially protected if it had been disclosed in violation of a confidential relationship rather than because it was, by its very nature, private.

11.14 Private information is now protected without having to show that it has been disclosed in violation of a pre-existing confidential relationship or of an obligation of confidence. Information which is by its nature private will be protected from disclosure; how it was obtained is of secondary importance. The protection afforded to private information is under the umbrella of the cause of action for breach of confidence. This cause of action (still referred to as 'breach of confidence') in consequence now has two distinct limbs:

- the original limb encompassing old-fashioned breach of confidence; and

- the new law limb affording protection to personal information because it is private.

11.15 It has been said that 'shoehorning' private information into breach of confidence has been difficult because the concept of confidential information and the concept of private information are quite different. Lord Hoffman in *Campbell* explained the transformation of the cause of action for breach of confidence in order to extend protection to purely private information:[25]

> '... the equitable action for breach of confidence ... has long been recognised as capable of being used to protect privacy. Thus in the seminal case of *Prince Albert v Strange* (1849) 2 De G & Sm 293, 1 Mac & G 25 the defendant was a publisher who had obtained copies of private etchings made by the Prince Consort of members of the royal family at home. The publisher had got them from an employee of a printer to whom the Prince had entrusted the plates. Vice-Chancellor Knight-Bruce, in granting an injunction restraining the publication of a catalogue containing descriptions of etchings, said (2 De G & SM 293, 313) that it was
> –
>
> > "an intrusion – an unbecoming and unseemly intrusion ... offensive to that inbred sense of propriety natural to every man – if, intrusion, indeed, fitly describes a sordid spying into the privacy of domestic life – into the home (a word hitherto sacred among us) ..."
>
> ... although the action for breach of confidence could be used to protect privacy in the sense of preserving the confidentiality of personal information, it was not founded on the notion that such information was in itself entitled to protection ... equity traditionally fastens on the conscience of one party to enforce equitable duties which arise out of his relationship with the other. So the action did not depend upon the personal nature of the information ... but upon whether a confidential relationship existed between the person who imparted the information and the person who received it. Equity imposed an obligation of confidentiality upon the latter and (by a familiar process of extension) upon anyone who received the information with actual or constructive knowledge of the duty of confidence.'

---

[25] [2004] UKHL 22, at [43] and [44].

The three 'limiting principles' which apply to breach of confidence

11.16 Whether an 'old-fashioned' breach of confidence should have the effect of restraining publication will depend upon whether any of the three 'limiting principles' apply:

- first, that breach of confidence only protects information which is truly confidential and has not entered the public domain;

- secondly, that breach of confidence does not apply to trivial or useless information; and

- thirdly, that the public interest in maintaining the confidence may be outweighed by an opposing public interest in publication.

11.17 The third, often referred to as the iniquity defence, is probably the most important limiting principle. The classic exposition of how the limiting principles come into play was given by Lord Goff in the *Spycatcher* litigation:[26]

> '• The first limiting principle (which is rather an expression of the scope of the duty) ... is that the principle of confidentiality only applies to information to the extent that it is confidential. In particular, once it has entered what is usually called the public domain (which means no more than that the information in question is so generally accessible that, in all the circumstances, it cannot be regarded as confidential) then, as a general rule, the principle of confidentiality can have no application to it. ...
> • The second limiting principle is that the duty of confidence applies neither to useless information, nor to trivia.
> • The third limiting principle is of far greater importance. It is that, although the basis of the law's protection of confidence is that there is a public interest that confidences should be preserved and protected by the law, nevertheless that public interest may be outweighed by some other countervailing public interest which favours disclosure. This limitation may apply ... to all types of confidential information. It is this limiting principle which may require a court to carry out a balancing operation, weighing the public interest in maintaining confidence against a countervailing public interest favouring disclosure.
>
> Embraced within this limiting principle is, of course, the so called defence of iniquity. In origin, this principle was narrowly stated, on the basis that a man cannot be made "the confidant of a crime or a fraud": see *Gartside v Outram* (1857) 26 LJ Charity 113, 114, per Sir William Page Wood V-C. But it is now clear that the principle extends to matters of which disclosure is required in the public interest: see *Beloff v Pressdram Ltd* [1973] 1 All ER 241, 260, per Ungoed-Thomas J, and *Lion Laboratories Ltd v Evans* [1985] QB 526, 550, per Griffiths LJ. It does not however follow that the public interest will in such cases require disclosure to the media, or to the public by the media. There are cases in which a more limited disclosure is all that is required: see *Francome v Mirror Group Newspapers Ltd* [1984] 1 WLR 892.'

11.18 The general ECtHR view, which tended against the suppression of publication of information which is of genuine public interest, was referred to in *HRH Prince of Wales v Associated Newspapers Limited*,[27] where the Court of Appeal said that where the information relates to a matter of major public concern, even medical confidentiality

---

26   *A-G v Guardian Newspapers (No 2)* [1990] 1 AC 109, at 282B–282F.
27   [2006] EWCA Civ 1776, at [50]–[55].

may not prevail: *Editions Plon v France*.[28] However, it was pointed out that this did not assist in determining what weight should be given to the fact that the publication under consideration involves 'the disclosure of information received in confidence' and that no ECtHR decision had been cited where this question received express consideration, other than that given to medical confidentiality in *Editions Plon v France*.

11.19 Before HRA 1998 came into force, the publication of information could be justified on public interest grounds in English law even if it had been disclosed in breach of confidence in the following circumstances:

- initially under the so-called 'iniquity rule' meaning that confidentiality could not be relied upon to conceal wrongdoing; and

- later, in *Lion Laboratories Ltd v Evans*,[29] when a more general test of public interest was upheld.

11.20 In the *Lion* case Griffiths LJ held[30] that the defence of public interest was well established in actions for breach of confidence and referred to circumstances in which it might be 'vital in the public interest' to publish confidential information. Confidentiality thus will not be used to suppress disclosure of wrong doing or criminality (the so-called 'iniquity rule') nor, under the less stringent rule, if the circumstances show that publication is 'vital in the public interest'. Before HRA 1998 came into force publication of information might be suppressed if it was received in confidence regardless of whether any right to privacy under Art 8 could be invoked.

The public interest and contractual obligations of confidence

11.21 The underlying test when determining whether publication of information arising from such relationships should be suppressed is whether the restriction on freedom of expression is necessary in a democratic society. It is important to note that the test is not whether the information is of public interest but whether, in all the circumstances, it is in the public interest that the duty of confidence should be breached. It must be shown that there is a *stronger* public interest in publication than in upholding the obligation of confidence involved. It is in the public interest that obligations of confidence arising from contractual relationships should be rigorously upheld, particularly where someone has expressly agreed to maintain privacy in respect of specified information. Since the test is one of proportionality significant, often decisive, weight is given to the fact that confidential relationships are normally sacrosanct. An obligation of confidence based on a contractual relationship will be particularly strong and, if the information is private as well, even stronger. The outcome of the balancing exercise, as usual, will depend on the facts of the case.

BREACH OF CONFIDENCE AND THE PROTECTION OF PRIVATE INFORMATION: TWO MAJOR DEVELOPMENTS

11.22 The two major developments which transformed the cause of action for breach of confidence so that it came to embrace private, in addition to confidential,

---

[28] (2004) 42 EHRR 705.
[29] [1985] QB 526.
[30] At p 550.

information were described by Lord Hoffman in *Campbell*[31] as typical examples of the capacity of the common law to adapt itself to the needs of contemporary life:

- one has been an acknowledgement of the artificiality of distinguishing between confidential information obtained through the violation of a confidential relationship and similar information obtained in some other way; and

- the second has been the acceptance, under the influence of human rights instruments such as Art 8 of the ECHR, of the privacy of personal information as something worthy of protection in its own right.

First: violation of a confidential relationship is no longer required

11.23 To establish a claim for breach of confidence it used to be necessary to show, first that the information in question was confidential and, secondly, that it had been disclosed in circumstances which imported an obligation of confidence – usually by showing that the information had been obtained in violation of a confidential relationship. The requirement to establish a violation of a confidential relationship was eventually dropped and information was protected if it could be shown that it was obviously confidential. The focus had thus shifted from the confidential relationship to the confidential nature of the information under consideration. This development was described by Lord Nicholls in *Campbell v MGN Limited*:[32]

> '[13] ... The breach of confidence label harks back to the time when the cause of action was based on improper use of information disclosed by one person to another in confidence. To attract protection the information had to be of a confidential nature. But the gist of the cause of action was that information of this character had been disclosed by one person to another in circumstances "importing an obligation of confidence" even though no contract of non-disclosure existed: see the classic exposition by Megarry J in *Coco v A N Clark (Engineers) Ltd* [1969] RPC 41, [1968] FSR 415, 47–48. The confidence referred to in the phrase "breach of confidence" was the confidence arising out of a confidential relationship.'

11.24 Lord Goff of Chieveley in *A-G v Guardian Newspapers Ltd (No 2)*[33] gave, as illustrations of cases in which it would be illogical to insist upon violation of a confidential relationship, the 'obviously confidential document ... wafted by an electric fan out of a window into a crowded street' and the 'private diary ... dropped in a public place' and formulated the principle as being that 'a duty of confidence arises when confidential information comes to the knowledge of a person ... in circumstances where he has notice, or is held to have agreed, that the information is confidential, with the effect that it would be just in all the circumstances that he should be precluded from disclosing the information to others'.

11.25 This statement of principle, which omits the requirement of a prior confidential relationship, was accepted as representing current English law by the ECtHR in *Earl Spencer v United Kingdom*[34] and was applied by the Court of Appeal in *A v B plc*[35] and is now firmly established.

---

[31] [2004] UKHL 22, at [46].
[32] At [13].
[33] [1990] 1 AC 109, at 281, described by Lord Hoffman in *Campbell v MGN* [2004] UKHL 22, at [47].
[34] (1998) 25 EHRR CD 105.
[35] [2003] QB 195, at 207.

Secondly: personal private information protectable in its own right

11.26 Once breach of confidence came to protect information solely because it was confidential it became possible to include purely private information within the ambit of protection irrespective of whether it was confidential.[36] The courts, under pressure from Europe not to act incompatibly with convention rights, developed the claim for breach of confidence so that it extended protection to purely private information. Lady Hale explained this development in *Campbell* as follows:

> '[132] ... [t]he [Human Rights Act 1998] does not create any new cause of action between private persons. But if there is a relevant cause of action applicable, the court as a public authority must act compatibly with both parties' Convention rights. In a case such as this, the relevant vehicle will usually be the action for breach of confidence, as Lord Woolf CJ held in *A v B plc* [2002] EWCA Civ 337, [2003] QB 195, 202, para 4:
>
> > "[Articles 8 and 10] have provided new parameters within which the court will decide, in an action for breach of confidence, whether a person is entitled to have his privacy protected by the court or whether the restriction of freedom of expression which such protection involves cannot be justified. The court's approach to the issues which the applications raise has been modified because, under section 6 of the 1998 Act, the court, as a public authority, is required not to 'act in a way which is incompatible with a Convention right'. The court is able to achieve this by absorbing the rights which articles 8 and 10 protect into the long-established action for breach of confidence. This involves giving a new strength and breadth to the action so that it accommodates the requirements of these articles."
>
> [133] The action for breach of confidence is not the only relevant cause of action: the inherent jurisdiction of the High Court to protect the children for whom it is responsible is another example: see In *Re S (a child) (identification: restrictions on publication)* [2003] EWCA Civ 963, [2003] 3 WLR 1425. But the courts will not invent a new cause of action to cover types of activity which were not previously covered: see *Wainwright v Home Office* [2003] 3 WLR 1137 ... That case indicates that our law cannot, even if it wanted to, develop a general tort of invasion of privacy. But where existing remedies are available, the court not only can but must balance the competing Convention rights of the parties.'

11.27 The absorption or 'shoehorning' of the right to privacy into the ambit of protection afforded by breach of confidence was not an easy fit. This was because breach of confidence was extended to cover situations where there was no pre-existing relationship of confidence and where the information in question was not confidential as traditionally understood. This uneasiness was described by Buxton LJ in *McKennitt v Ash*:[37]

> 'ii) ... in developing a right to protect private information ... the English courts have to proceed through the tort of breach of confidence, into which the jurisprudence of arts 8 and 10 has to be 'shoehorned': *Douglas v Hello! (No 3)* [2005] EWCA Civ 595, [2006] QB 125, 53, [2005] 4 All ER 128.
>
> iii) That feeling of discomfort arises from the action for breach of confidence being employed where there was no pre-existing relationship of confidence between the parties, but the "confidence" arose from the Defendant having acquired by unlawful or surreptitious

---

[36]   This is because it was no longer necessary to show violation of a pre-existing relationship of confidence.
[37]   [2006] EWCA Civ 595, at [8].

means information that he should have known he was not free to use: as was the case in *Douglas*, and also in *Campbell v MGN* [2004] UKHL 22, [2004] 2 AC 457, [2004] 2 All ER 995 ...'

11.28 Breach of confidence was expanded to cover situations where purely private information was 'purloined', for example, a telephoto lens shot of a celebrity at home by the pool. Despite the absence of a confidential relationship or an obligation of confidence, a claim in respect of the publication of such a photograph could now be made.

11.29 An important distinction, however, remains between the situation where there has been purloining of private information where no confidential relationship is involved on the one hand and the situation where there has been a violation of a pre-existent confidential relationship on the other. The latter case (as indicated above) is often referred to as 'old-fashioned breach of confidence'. In *McKennitt v Ash*, Buxton LJ specifically pointed out that the nature of the claim in that case involved old-fashioned breach of confidence and distinguished it from the new form of complaint where no confidential relationship was involved:[38]

'v) ... the complaint here is of what might be called old-fashioned breach of confidence by way of conduct inconsistent with a pre-existing relationship, rather than simply of the purloining of private information.'

11.30 For the new form of complaint – purloining of private information – what matters is that the information disclosed is private and not public. Lord Hope made this clear in *Campbell v MGN Ltd*:

'[92] The underlying question in all cases where it is alleged that there has been a breach of the duty of confidence is whether the information that was disclosed was private and not public. There must be some interest of a private nature that the claimant wishes to protect: *A v B Ltd* [2003] QB 195,206, para 11(vii).'

The relevance of establishing that information was disclosed in the course of a relationship of confidence

11.31 Sir Anthony Clarke MR stated in *Lord Browne of Madingley v Associated Newspapers*[39] that the mere fact that information was imparted in the course of a relationship of confidence would not automatically mean that it satisfied Lord Nicholls' test of 'expectation of privacy'. The example given was of a husband telling his wife that Oxford or Cambridge won the boat race in a particular year. The important point remains, however, that a confidential relationship is likely to be of decisive importance in considering whether there was an expectation of privacy. Reference was made to Buxton LJ in *McKennitt*[40] and the point he made – that to inquire into whether information was private without paying any regard to the nature of the pre-existing relationship between the parties is unlikely to produce anything but a distorted outcome – was expressly approved. In summary, the Court of Appeal in the *Lord Browne of Madingley* case[41] was firmly of the view that the authorities supported the conclusion that the relationship between the relevant persons or parties is of considerable

[38] At [8] and see [15] et seq.
[39] [2007] EWCA Civ 295, at [29].
[40] At [15].
[41] At [31].

importance in determining whether there was a reasonable expectation of privacy. The court said that in answering that question there are a number of potentially relevant questions, depending upon the circumstances, which include whether the person concerned received information which he knew or ought reasonably to have known was fairly and reasonably to be regarded as confidential or private.

IS ART 8 ENGAGED?

11.32 Every case must be decided on its own facts and the single question to ask in every case is whether there was a reasonable expectation of privacy in respect of the information under consideration.[42]

A private life

11.33 The ECtHR in *Von Hannover v Germany* defined a private life in the following terms making useful reference to a 'private zone' of interaction in one's life and to the proper development of one's personality:[43]

'… private life, in the court's view, includes a person's physical and psychological integrity; the guarantee afforded by article 8 of the Convention is primarily intended to ensure the development, without outside interference, of the personality of each individual in his relations with other human beings … There is therefore a zone of interaction of a person with others, even in a public context, which may fall within the scope of "private life".'

The right to privacy

11.34 The right to maintain and protect privacy is a human right of fundamental importance to an individual's enjoyment of life and personal development. Lord Nicholls explained in *Campbell v MGN Ltd* that:[44]

'A proper degree of privacy is essential for the well-being and development of an individual. And restraints imposed on government to pry into the lives of the citizen go to the essence of a democratic state: see La Forest J in *R v Dymont* [1988] 2 SCR 417, 426.'

11.35 Lord Mustill referred to the damaging effects of any infringement of the right to privacy in *R (on the application of BBC) v Broadcasting Standards Commission* in the following terms:[45]

'An infringement of privacy is an affront to the personality, which is damaged both by the violation and by the demonstration that the personal space is not inviolate.'

Privacy as underlying value not a cause of action

11.36 Lord Hoffman in *Campbell* said that the right to privacy is an important underlying value in various causes of action including privacy although it is not of itself

---

[42]   See e g Sir Anthony Clarke in *Lord Brown of Madingley*, ibid, at [36].
[43]   (2005) 40 EHRR 1.
[44]   At [12].
[45]   [2001] QB 885, at 900, [2000] 3 All ER 989.

the tort or cause of action.[46] It was, he said, decided in *Wainwright v Home Office*[47] that there is no general tort of invasion of privacy. He emphasised that the right to privacy is in a general sense one of the values, and sometimes the most important value, which underlies a number of more specific causes of action, both at common law and under various statutes. Significantly Lord Hoffman said[48] human rights law identified private information as something worth protecting as an aspect of human autonomy and dignity. As an underlying value (enshrined in Art 8), privacy has influenced the tort of breach of confidence in developing protection in respect of private information.

The invasion of privacy

11.37 The law of privacy (or 'privacy') is concerned with the unauthorised disclosure and *publication* of private information not, directly, with the means which might have been used to obtain the information in the first place. For example, long lens photography or surveillance might result in violation or invasion of an individual's privacy but it is not that but the subsequent *publication* of the private information contained in the photographs or tapes with which the law of privacy is concerned.

11.38 In *Campbell* Lord Nicholls said[49] that, unlike the US, there is no overarching, all-embracing cause of action for 'invasion of privacy' here and referred to the decision of the House of Lords in *Wainwright v Home Office*.[50] Although he referred to privacy as a tort, however labelled, he said it afforded, in the case of individuals, respect for one aspect of an individual's privacy and that:[51]

> 'That is the value underlying this cause of action. An individual's privacy can be invaded in ways not involving publication of information. Strip-searches are an example ... Miss Campbell's common law claim was throughout presented in court exclusively on the basis of breach of confidence, that is, the wrongful *publication* by the "Mirror" of private *information*.'

11.39 Lord Nicholls noted[52] that photographs taken covertly of Ms Campbell in the road outside the building where she attended Narcotics Anonymous could be deeply distressing, even damaging, to a person whose health was fragile. But he emphasised she did not complain that the taking of the photographs infringed her privacy. Her complaint was that the information in the photographs was private so the fact they were taken surreptitiously added nothing to her complaint.

The touchstone of a private life: is Art 8 engaged?

11.40 In *Australian Broadcasting Corpn v Lenah Game Meats Pty Ltd* Gleason CJ observed that there was a large area in between what was necessarily public and what was necessarily private:[53]

---

[46]   It was established in *Douglas v Hello! (No 3)* [2006] QB 125 that misuse of private information is an equitable cause of action and is not a tort.
[47]   [2003] UKHL 53, at [43], [2003] 4 All ER 969, [2003] 3 WLR 1137.
[48]   At [50].
[49]   [2004] UKHL 22, at [11].
[50]   [2003] UKHL 53, [2003] 3 WLR 1137, [2003] 4 All ER 969.
[51]   At [15].
[52]   At [30].
[53]   (2001) 185 ALR 1, at 13, para 41.

'An activity is not private simply because it is not done in public. It does not suffice to make an act private that, because it occurs on private property, it has such measure of protection from the public gaze as the characteristics of the property, the nature of the activity, the locality, and the disposition of the property owner combine to afford. Certain kinds of information about a person, such as information relating to health, personal relationships, or finances, may be easy to identify as private, as may certain kinds of activity which a reasonable person, applying contemporary standards of morals and behaviour, would understand to be meant to be unobserved ...'

11.41 As stated above, Art 8 is engaged when an individual has a reasonable expectation of privacy in respect of specified information. This is an objective reasonable expectation test. The alternative test – whether the individual concerned would find publication of the information 'highly offensive' – has not found favour as a threshold test. The 'highly offensive' test (propounded by Gleeson CJ in the High Court of Australia in *Australian Broadcasting Corpn v Lenah Game Meats Pty Ltd*[54] – that 'disclosure or observation would be highly offensive to a reasonable person of ordinary sensibilities') should more properly be considered at the later stage when considering proportionality for two reasons.[55] First, the 'highly offensive' phrase suggests a stricter test of private information than a reasonable expectation of privacy and, secondly, the 'highly offensive' formulation tends to bring into account – when deciding whether information is private – considerations more properly the concern of proportionality and this can cause confusion.[56]

11.42 Lady Hale explained in *Campbell*[57] that once information is identified as 'private' the court must balance the claimant's interest in keeping the information private against the countervailing interest of the recipient in publishing it. In cases of breach of the duty of confidence the question is whether the information in issue is private and not public. In many cases the answer to this is obvious – although the law of privacy is not intended for the protection of the unduly sensitive.[58]

Obviously private information

11.43 Where it is obvious that information is private (which is often the case) the inquiry can stop there because the individual involved can expect privacy to be respected. Lord Hope said in *Campbell*[59] if the information is obviously private the person to whom it relates can reasonably expect their privacy to be respected.

---

[54] Ibid, at 13, para 42.

[55] The second Restatement of Torts in the United States (1977), art 652D, p 394, uses the formulation of disclosure of matter which 'would be highly offensive to a reasonable person'. In *Australian Broadcasting Corpn v Lenah Game Meats Pty Ltd* (2001) 185 ALR 1, at 13, para 42, Gleeson CJ used words, widely quoted, having a similar meaning.

[56] Lord Nicholls in *Campbell*, at [21] and [22]; Lord Carswell at [166].

[57] At [135] and [137].

[58] *Campbell*, at [94]. In *Murray v Big Pictures (UK) Limited* [2008] EWCA Civ 446 the Court of Appeal said it was clear Lord Nicholls in *Campbell* regarded the 'highly offensive test' as stricter than his own formulation of 'reasonable expectation of privacy'. The Court of Appeal also thought that, insofar as it was relevant to consider whether publication of information was 'highly offensive', it was relevant not to whether Art 8 was engaged but to issues of proportionality and the balance between Art 8 and Art 10.

[59] At [96].

11.44 Information about events in the home cannot lightly be intruded upon and even relatively minor details will usually be considered to be obviously private. This is because the disclosure of such details is plainly intrusive and likely to be distressing. Buxton LJ amplified on this in *McKennitt v Ash*:[60]

> '[12] The judge listed a large number of parts of the book that were said by Ms McKennitt to consist of private information. He refused protection for many of them because he regarded their content as "anodyne", imprecise or already known to the public. In ... *M v Secretary of State for Work and Pensions* [2006] UKHL 11, [2006] 2 AC 91, 83, [2006] 4 All ER 929 Lord Walker of Gestingthorpe pointed out that interference with private life had to be of some seriousness before art 8 was engaged ... the general nature of the information sought to be restrained was indicated by the Judge in his para 11:
>
> > "Ms McKennitt's personal and sexual relationships.
> >
> > Her personal feelings and, in particular, in relation to her deceased fiancé and the circumstances of his death.
> >
> > Matters relating to her health and diet.
> >
> > Matters relating to her emotional vulnerability.
> >
> > The detail of an unhappy dispute between Ms McKennitt, on the one hand, and Ms Ash and Mr Fowkes on the other, concerning monies advanced to them by Ms McKennitt to assist in the purchase of a property in 1997 and the subsequent litigation in the Chancery Division (which was settled on the basis of a Tomlin order without ever coming to a public hearing) ..."
>
> [22] ... art 8 cases have tended to be concerned with the security or stability of residence, rather than with privacy within the home. But the Judge ... [pointed] out that it should have been and was obvious that events in a person's home cannot be lightly intruded upon; and ... *"it is intrusive and distressing for Ms McKennitt's household minutiae to be exposed to curious eyes"*. And I would also respectfully agree with his comparison with long distance photography ... publication of the fruits of [the defendant's] inspection of the cottage and of what happened there was unacceptable.'

The public domain and the 'zone' of a private life

11.45 It remains a general principle that information in the public domain (ie already known by the public) cannot claim the protection of a private life. Buxton LJ in *McKennitt v Ash* referred to the fact that although the inquiry is now conducted under Art 10, the inquiry is still largely conducted in the traditional terms of the English law of confidence. It was argued in *McKennitt* that once a person had revealed or discussed some information falling within a particular 'zone' of their lives they had a greatly reduced expectation of privacy in relation to any other information that fell within that zone. This is still an open question which depends on the particular facts of each case. Eady J at first instance in *McKennitt*[61] explained that the defendant had relied on the fact that the claimant had, in a number of articles in the past, revealed certain aspects of her personal life and beliefs to the general public and submitted that those aspects could no longer be protected by the law of privacy. Eady J dismissed this argument on the facts on the basis that details of conversations with, or behaviour in the presence of,

---

60   [2006] EWCA Civ 1714.
61   [2005] EWHC 3003 per Eady J at [79]–[80].

close personal friends is significantly different from the sort of material the claimant had revealed in the past. Eady J said that there is in this context a significant difference between choosing to reveal aspects of private life with which an individual feels 'comfortable' and allowing disclosure to the public every detail of personal life, feelings, thoughts and foibles of character.

11.46 The context in which the claimant in *McKennitt v Ash* had chosen to reveal information about herself was her attempts to promote water safety and to support the Cook-Rees Memorial Fund. Eady J thought that revelations in this context would not give the defendant the right to reveal the claimant's 'pitifully grief-stricken reaction to the death of [her fiancé], his brother and a friend'. The judge thought that an individual's reactions and communications to a friend in the immediate aftermath of personal bereavement are a classic example of material in respect of which there would a reasonable expectation of privacy.

11.47 Buxton LJ agreed with Eady J's approach.[62] He said that if 'information is my private property, it is for me to decide how much of it should be published' and that the 'zone' argument completely undermines that reasonable expectation of privacy. Buxton LJ rejected the argument that it would be possible for public figures to censor or control what was published about them. This is a different argument and ultimately is resolved by competing public interest considerations.

11.48 Not all disclosures will put the material in the public domain. In the *Lord Browne of Madingly v Associated Newspapers*[63] information about the fact of the relationship in that case was already in the public domain and the question arose whether it would be unrealistic to restrain publication and (closely related to that question) whether information had become 'so generally accessible that, in all the circumstances, it cannot be regarded as confidential'. The Court of Appeal considered that there was potentially an important distinction between information made available to a person's circle of friends or work colleagues and information which is widely published in a newspaper. If there has been limited disclosure it may well be possible to restrain further, wider disclosure.

Article 8 and the PCC Code of Practice

11.49 The court is obliged by HRA 1998, s 12(4)(b) not only to have particular regard to the importance of the ECHR right to freedom of expression, but also to any relevant privacy code.[64] The Press Complaints Commission (PCC) Editors' Code of Practice (October 2009 revision) provides as follows:

'3. Privacy

i)   Everyone is entitled to respect for his or her private and family life, home, health and correspondence including digital communications.

ii)   Editors will be expected to justify intrusions into any individual's private life without consent. Account will be taken of the complainant's own public disclosures of information.

iii)   It is unacceptable to photograph individuals in private places without their consent.

---

62   *McKennitt v Ash* [2005] EWHC 3003 , at [54] and [55].
63   [2007] EWCA Civ 295, at [61].
64   Lady Hale in *Campbell*, at [159].

Note – Private places are public or private property where there is a reasonable expectation of privacy.

The public interest

There may be exceptions to the clauses marked * where they can be demonstrated to be in the public interest.

1. The public interest includes:

i)   Detecting or exposing crime or a serious impropriety.
ii)   Protecting public health and safety.
iii)   Preventing the public from being misled by an action or statement of an individual or organisation …'

THE ABSORPTION OF PRIVATE INFORMATION INTO BREACH OF CONFIDENCE

11.50   Lord Nicholls said[65] that the values enshrined in Arts 8 and 10 are now part of the cause of action for breach of confidence and, echoing Lord Woolf CJ, said that the courts have achieved this by absorbing the rights protected by Arts 8 and 10 into this cause of action.[66]

11.51   The absorption of privacy into breach of confidence transformed the nature of the cause of action for breach of confidence. It continues to provide a remedy where a pre-existing confidential relationship is violated or if confidential information is misused but has been extended to provide a remedy where *private* information has been misused regardless of any prior confidential relationship or traditional element of confidentiality. The new cause of action – in its extended form – is sometimes more accurately called 'misuse of private information'. Lord Nicholls said in *Campbell* that:

> '[14]   This cause of action has now firmly shaken off the limiting constraint of the need for an initial confidential relationship. In doing so it has changed its nature … Now the law imposes a "duty of confidence" whenever a person receives information he knows or ought to know is fairly and reasonably to be regarded as confidential. Even this formulation is awkward … Information about an individual's private life would not, in ordinary usage, be called "confidential". The more natural description today is that such information is private. The essence of the tort is better encapsulated now as misuse of private information.'

Breach of confidence and misuse of private information: one cause of action

11.52   In its present form breach of confidence thus embraces two differing forms of protection:

- old-fashioned breach of confidence which upholds confidential relationships and the duty of good faith; and

---

65   *Campbell v MGN Limited* [2004] UKHL 22, at [17].
66   See *A v B plc* [2002] EWCA Civ 337, [2003] QB 195, at [4].

- misuse of private information (the new element to this cause of action) which upholds human autonomy and dignity in respect of private information regardless of whether a breach of a confidence is involved.

11.53 The right to object to the unauthorised publication of private information is a new form of protection previously unknown in our law. It derives from the right to privacy enshrined in the ECHR which is now enforced directly by our courts. Lord Hoffman said in *Campbell v MGN Ltd* that:[67]

> '[49] ... Until the Human Rights Act 1998 came into force, there was no equivalent in English domestic law of art 8 the European Convention or the equivalent articles in other international human rights instruments which guarantee rights of privacy. So the courts of the United Kingdom did not have to decide what such guarantees meant ...

> [50] ... The incremental changes to breach of confidence do not merely extend the duties arising traditionally from a relationship of trust and confidence but there is a new approach to the underlying value which the law protects. Instead of the cause of action being based upon the duty of good faith applicable to confidential personal information and trade secrets alike, it focuses upon the protection of human autonomy and dignity – the right to control the dissemination of information about one's private life and the right to the esteem and respect of other people.'

11.54 Frequently the information in question is both confidential and private and in such cases the two forms of protection are in play. Lord Hoffman observed that the cause of action in *Campbell*[68] fitted:[69]

> '... squarely within both the old and the new law. The judge found that the information about Ms Campbell's attendance at NA had been communicated to the *Mirror* in breach of confidence and that the *Mirror* must have known that the information was confidential ...'

11.55 Sometimes the information in question is purely private, not having resulted from breach of a confidential relationship. This applies to so-called 'purloined' information, for example, a photograph taken with a long lens of a celebrity lounging by his garden pool. The photograph contains private information but, since no breach of a confidential relationship would have occurred, the focus is on protecting the *information*, which is private, rather than on enforcing a confidential *relationship*.

11.56 Where the information in question is derived from both a violation of a confidential relationship and a violation of the right to privacy the court first applies old-fashioned breach of confidence principles before considering Art 8. The issue is whether there is a sufficiently strong public interest to displace an obligation of confidence. Contractual obligations of confidence (express or implied) are particularly strong and will usually bind a celebrity's agent and employees. The importance attached to the need to focus initially on enforcing obligations of confidence, in all cases, was highlighted by Buxton LJ in *McKennitt v Ash*:[70]

---

[67] Lord Hoffman in *Campbell* referring to Sedley LJ in *Douglas v Hello! Ltd* [2001] QB 967, at 1001, [2001] 2 All ER 289.

[68] [2004] UKHL 22. See also Lord Carswell at [163]: 'It was not in dispute that the information was imparted in confidence to the respondents ...'

[69] At [53].

[70] [2006] EWCA Civ 1714.

'[15] ... *Campbell, Douglas* and ... *Von Hannover v Germany* (2005) 40 EHRR 1, have wrestled with the problem of identifying the basis for claiming privacy or confidence in respect of unauthorised or purloined information ... the primary focus has to be on the nature of the information, because it is the recipient's perception of its confidential nature that imposes the obligation on him ... But ... in the vast majority of cases the duty of confidence will arise from a transaction or relationship between the parties [where the inquiry] reverts to a more elemental enquiry into breach of confidence in the traditional understanding of that expression. That does not of course exempt the court from considering whether the material obtained during such a relationship is indeed confidential; but to enquire into that latter question without paying any regard to the nature of the pre-existing relationship between the parties, as the argument for the Appellant in this court largely did, is unlikely to produce anything but a distorted outcome.

[24] ... If the contractual documents had fallen off the back of a lorry and been picked up by a third party there might be some question as to whether they were of such a nature that he was bound to hold them in confidence. The documents might not come within the category of self-evident privacy that was in the mind of Laws J in his famous example in *Hellewell v Chief Constable of Derbyshire* [1995] 4 All ER 473, [1995] 1 WLR 804 at 807. But there is no such issue in the case of a person who finds out details of contractual terms because she is in a relationship of confidence with the contracting party. As the Judge said in his para 144:

> "... Ms McKennitt is entitled to a reasonable expectation of privacy as to her contractual terms. They are certainly not for Ms Ash to reveal".'

11.57 Those who engage employees, or who enter into other relationships that carry with them a duty of confidence, ought to be able to be confident that they can disclose, without risk of wider publication, information that it is legitimate for them to wish to keep confidential. Contractual obligations of confidence should always be specified clearly in all celebrity contracts, and will usually be enforced even in favour of those who have courted publicity because of the strong public interest in upholding contracts. Previous authority suggesting otherwise, such *Woodward v Hutchins*,[71] is likely to be confined to its own facts. *Woodward* concerned the dismissed publicity agent of a well-known group of singers (including Tom Jones) who wished to write a series of articles dealing with their private lives and conduct. The group failed to obtain an interlocutory injunction to prevent publication. Bridge LJ said:[72]

> 'It seems to me that those who seek and welcome publicity of every kind bearing upon their private lives so long as it shows them in a favourable light are in no position to complain of the invasion of their privacy by publicity that shows them in an unfavourable light.'

11.58 Buxton LJ in *McKennitt v Ash*[73] pointed out that *Woodward* had come in for a good deal of criticism particularly the fact the court was not reminded of the relevance of the contractual relationship between the agent and his former employers. He said that that largely deprived the decision of any direct authority in or relevance to the facts of *McKennitt v Ash*.

11.59 In *McKennitt v Ash* the written contract set out significant obligations of confidentiality but Ms Ash was found to be bound, in any event, by obligations of confidentiality. The provisions of the written contract were held not to add much to the obligations Ms Ash owed in equity by reason of the closeness of her personal

---

[71]   [1977] 1 WLR 760.
[72]   At 765D.
[73]   At [32] and [34].

relationship with Ms McKennitt. Where personal relationships such as this are involved the contractual provisions and independent equitable obligations should primarily be relied on.[74]

11.60 In *HRH Prince of Wales v Associated Newspapers Ltd*,[75] which concerned the unauthorised publication of the Prince Charles's private diaries, the Court of Appeal said that the judge had commenced his analysis of the claim for breach of confidence with the statement: 'The modern starting point in a claim of this kind is the decision of the House of Lords in *Campbell v MGN Ltd* [2004] 2 AC 457' as though there were only two significant issues:

- whether the subject matter of the journal 'private' so that the newspaper's publication of it interfered with Prince Charles's rights under Art 8(1) of the ECHR; and if so

- whether the newspaper's publication was none the less justifiable under Art 8(2) as being necessary for the protection of the Art 10 rights of the newspaper and of the public.

11.61 The Court of Appeal said it was an oversimplification to deal with the matter as if it was a simple conflict between the rights under Arts 8 and 10 of the ECHR. The case raised the question whether the principles permitting publication of information disclosed in breach of an obligation of confidence required to be revised in order to give full effect to Art 10 rights. The Court of Appeal[76] said there was a distinction between whether a claimant can reasonably expect those in a confidential relationship to keep information confidential and whether a claimant can reasonably expect the media not to publish such information if the duty of confidence is breached. As to the latter it had been argued that if the circumstances are such that Art 8 rights of privacy in relation to particular information are likely to be trumped by Art 10 rights of freedom of expression, it cannot be reasonable to expect the information to remain confidential. But the Court of Appeal said that this approach blurred the question of whether Art 8 is engaged with the question of how the balance should be struck between Art 8 and Art 10 rights. The court said that the better approach is to consider the points made in relation to the subject matter in question in the context of the *competition* between Art 8 and Art 10 rights and that the fact that information has been disclosed in breach of the duties of good faith that arise in a relationship of trust and confidence is relevant when considering the balance between the requirements of Arts 8 and 10.

11.62 The Court of Appeal in *HRH Prince of Wales* emphasised that the action was not concerned solely with a claim for breach of privacy but that in the action were all the elements of a claim for old-fashioned breach of confidence. The information was disclosed in breach of the well-recognised relationship of confidence which exists between employer and employee and the disclosure was in breach of an express contractual duty of confidentiality.

11.63 Article 10(2) provides that the freedom to receive and impart information 'may be subject to such formalities, conditions, restrictions or penalties as are prescribed by law ... for preventing the disclosure of information received in confidence'. The ECHR

---

[74]   Buxton LJ, at [43].
[75]   [2006] EWCA Civ 1776.
[76]   At [45] and [48].

recognises that it may be necessary, in a democratic society, to give effect to an old-fashioned duty of confidence at the expense of freedom of expression. This is quite independent of any privacy issues.

11.64 Express weight should always be given to the fact that information was received in confidence – particularly under a contractual duty of confidence – and that the publisher of the information *was aware* of the breach of confidence.

11.65 Old-fashioned breach of confidence will apply to all relationships where an obligation of confidence can reasonably be expected. Sexual relationships – from long-standing relationships to one-night stands – are particularly important. In *Mosley v NGN*[77] the claimant, with a number of women, took part in what was described as an orgy as part of the 'scene'. Eady J found that 'old-fashioned breach of confidence' was involved as well as a violation of the Art 8 rights of those involved. The issue was whether one of the women owed a duty of confidence to the other participants in the orgy, including the claimant. The judge said that those who participate in sexual or personal relationships may be expected not to reveal private conversations or activities. There was a recognised code of discretion on 'the scene' and the judge concluded that the defendant had committed an 'old-fashioned breach of confidence' *as well as* a violation of the Art 8 rights of all those involved. The argument that the claimant forfeited any expectation of privacy partly because of the numbers involved, coupled with the fact that he liked to record the gatherings on video, was firmly rejected in the light of the ECtHR decision in *ADT v UK*.[78]

11.66 The Court of Appeal summarised the position in *HRH Prince of Wales v Associated Newspapers Limited*[79] by saying that whether the publication in question involved a breach of a relationship of confidence, an interference with privacy or both, it is necessary to consider whether these matters justify the interference with Art 10 rights that will be involved if publication is restrained. A balance has to be struck and the following rules were laid down:

- where the disclosure relates to 'information received in confidence' this itself is a factor that Art 10(2) recognises is capable of justifying restrictions on freedom of expression; and

- where no breach of a confidential relationship is involved, that balance will be between Art 8 and Art 10 rights and will usually involve weighing the nature and consequences of the breach of privacy against the public interest, if any, in the disclosure of private information.

11.67 Today the test is whether a fetter of the right of freedom of expression is, in the particular circumstances, 'necessary in a democratic society'. This was said by the Court of Appeal to be a test of proportionality, albeit that a significant element to be weighed in the balance was the importance in a democratic society of upholding duties of confidence that are created between individuals. It is not enough to justify publication that the information in question is a matter of public interest. The test to be applied when restriction on freedom of expression was under consideration in order to prevent disclosure of information received in confidence is whether, in all the circumstances, it is

---

[77]   [2008] EWHC 1777 (QB), at [105]–[109].
[78]   (2000) 31 EHRR 33.
[79]   At [65]–[68].

in the public interest that the duty of confidence should be breached. The court will need to consider whether it is legitimate for the owner of the information to seek to keep it confidential or whether it is in the public interest that the information should be made public.

11.68 In applying the test of proportionality, the Court of Appeal in *HRH Prince of Wales* said[80] that the nature of the relationship that gives rise to the duty of confidentiality may be important and approved the statement made by the Court of Appeal in *Campbell v Frisbee* that:[81]

> '... it is arguable that a duty of confidentiality that has been expressly assumed under contract carries more weight, when balanced against the restriction of the right of freedom of expression, than a duty of confidentiality that is not buttressed by express agreement ...'

11.69 The extent to which a contract adds to the weight of duty of confidence arising out of a confidential relationship depends upon the facts of the individual case. The importance of the public interest in employees respecting the obligations of confidence that they have assumed was recognised. Both the nature of the information and of the relationship of confidence under which it was received might in particular cases weigh heavily in the scales favouring upholding the duty of confidence.

11.70 Eady J in *Mosley*[82] said that the third limiting principle is about finding where the overall public interest really lies – in suppression or disclosure. It is an issue that depends upon the careful application of proportionality to the facts. He said[83] that the 'ultimate balancing test' turns largely upon proportionality and referred, by way of example, to Sedley LJ in *Douglas v Hello! Ltd*.[84] What has to be weighed in the balance is whether the intrusion, or the degree of the intrusion which actually took place into the claimant's privacy, was proportionate to the public interest which is supposed to justify it.

CELEBRITY EVENTS AND COMMERCIALLY VALUABLE PERSONAL INFORMATION

11.71 The developing protection given to private information is concerned with protecting an individual's *privacy*; it is not concerned with protecting personal information because it happens to be commercially valuable to a celebrity. This important distinction must be borne in mind in relation to the protection given to personal information (such as that derived from clandestine photography) at restricted admission celebrity events. A celebrity may wish to restrict the publication of personal information either because publication would infringe the celebrity's right to privacy or because the celebrity wishes to maintain the commercial value of the information. In the latter situation the primary protection is given by old-fashioned breach of confidence.

---

[80] At [69]–[74]
[81] [2003] ICR 141, at [22].
[82] At [13].
[83] At [14].
[84] [2001] QB 967, at [137].

Privacy and Personality Rights

11.72 The rules applicable to commercially valuable personal information (such as photographs of an exclusive celebrity wedding as in *Douglas v Hello!*[85]) were explained by Lord Hoffman in *OGB v Allen*[86] in the context of *OK!* magazine's claim over the disclosure of photographs of the Douglases' wedding by the rival publication *Hello!*. *OK!*'s claim was brought to protect exclusive rights over *all* photographs taken of the wedding, authorised or not. The claim was for 'old-fashioned' breach of confidence and had nothing to do with protecting personal or private information as such. The fact that the rights to exclusivity in respect of all photographs of the wedding had been sold meant the rival's unauthorised photographs of the wedding were nonetheless treated as confidential and, as Lord Hoffman explained, it was not in point that the information in them happened to be personal and private. Lord Hoffman said:[87]

> 'In recent years, English law has adapted the action for breach of confidence to provide a remedy for the unauthorised disclosure of personal information: see *Campbell v MGN Ltd* [2004] 2 AC 457. This development has been mediated by the analogy of the right to privacy conferred by article 8 of the European Convention on Human Rights and has required a balancing of that right against the right to freedom of expression conferred by article 10. But this appeal is not concerned with the protection of privacy. Whatever may have been the position of the Douglases, who, as I mentioned, recovered damages for an invasion of their privacy, "OK!'s" claim is to protect commercially confidential information and nothing more. So your Lordships need not be concerned with Convention rights. "OK!" has no claim to privacy under article 8 nor can it make a claim which is parasitic upon the Douglases' right to privacy. The fact that the information happens to have been about the personal life of the Douglases is irrelevant. It could have been information about anything that a newspaper was willing to pay for. What matters is that the Douglases, by the way they arranged their wedding, were in a position to impose an obligation of confidence. They were in control of the information.'

11.73 Personal information might (for the purposes of ascertaining the basis on which it might be protected) be categorised as confidential information or as purely private information. The distinction between confidential information and private information was drawn in general terms by the Court of Appeal in *Douglas v Hello! Ltd (No 3)*[88] who said that information would be treated as confidential:[89]

> '... if it is available to one person (or a group of people) and not generally available to others, provided that the person (or group) who possesses the information does not intend that it should become available to others.'

11.74 The Court of Appeal in that case said, in relation to the nature of private information, that it:[90]

> '... must include information that is personal to the person who possesses it and that he does not intend shall be imparted to the general public. The nature of the information, or the form in which it is kept, may suffice to make it plain that the information satisfies these criteria.'

---

[85] *Douglas v Hello!* [2005] EWCA Civ 595.
[86] [2007] 4 All ER 545, HL.
[87] At [118].
[88] [2006] QB 125.
[89] At [55].
[90] At [83].

FREEDOM OF EXPRESSION

11.75 The right protected by Art 10 to express and publish a wide range of ideas and views is not restricted to those which might be favourably received. It extends to shocking, offensive and distasteful ideas and views. Freedom of expression is a democratic right and value which fosters individual development and in a democratic society it is curtailed only on grounds of *necessity*. It is not for the courts or media to stipulate what should be protected. The right is not absolute and must be balanced with other rights such as privacy.[91] Weight is given to whether, in any particular case, the press is exercising an important 'watchdog' role in public affairs so certain types of speech receive greater protection in a democratic society than others. Political speech tops the list of types of speech receiving most protection but weight is accorded to information to do with the political and social life of the community or the intellectual, artistic or personal development of individuals. Tabloid tittle-tattle is lower down the scale but does sell copy. The extent to which it is in the public interest to encourage the press to enjoy healthy circulation figures so that a variety of newspapers can be enjoyed might be debateable.[92] Lady Hale in *Campbell* said that:[93]

> 'One reason why press freedom is so important is that we need newspapers to sell in order to ensure that we still have newspapers at all. It may be said that newspapers should be allowed considerable latitude in their intrusions into private grief so that they can maintain circulation and the rest of us can then continue to enjoy the variety of newspapers and other mass media which are available in this country. It may also be said that newspaper editors often have to make their decisions at great speed and in difficult circumstances, so that to expect too minute an analysis of the position is in itself a restriction on their freedom of expression.'

11.76 Lady Hale in *Campbell*[94] described the attributes of different types of speech:[95]

- Political speech is most deserving of protection because the free exchange of information and ideas on matters relevant to the organisation of the economic, social and political life of the country is crucial to any democracy. This includes revealing information about public figures, especially those in elective office, which would otherwise be private but is *relevant to their participation in public life*.

- Intellectual and educational speech and expression are also important in a democracy, not least because they enable the development of individuals' potential to play a full part in society and in democratic life.

- Artistic speech and expression is important for similar reasons, in fostering both individual originality and creativity and the free-thinking and dynamic society we so much value.

---

[91] See e g the ECtHR judgment in *Times Newspapers Ltd (Nos 1 and 2) v United Kingdom* (App Nos 3002/03 and 23676/03), 10 March 2009.

[92] The fact that the public is interested in particular information does not mean that it is in the public interest that the information should be published.

[93] *Campbell v MGN Limited* [2004] UKHL 22, at [143].

[94] At [148] and [149].

[95] In R Clayton and H Tomlinson *The Law of Human Rights* (Oxford University Press, 2000), at para 15.162, it is pointed out that the court has distinguished three kinds of expression: (1) political expression (to which the court consistently attaches great importance than it does to artistic or commercial expression); (2) artistic expression; and (3) commercial expression.

11.77 It was thought difficult to make such claims on behalf of a tabloid because the publication of intimate details of celebrities' private lives does little to assist the political and social life of the community or the intellectual, artistic or personal development of individuals.

11.78 In *Jersild v Denmark*[96] the ECtHR declared that freedom of expression constituted one of the essential foundations of a democratic society and that the safeguards to be afforded to the press are of particular importance. The court added these comments:[97]

> 'Whilst the press must not overstep the bounds set, inter alia, in the interest of "the protection of the reputation and rights of others", it is nevertheless incumbent on it to impart information and ideas of public interest. Not only does the press have the task of imparting such information and ideas: the public also has a right to receive them. Were it otherwise, the press would be unable to play its vital role of "public watchdog".'

11.79 The ECtHR also said in *Jersild*:[98]

> '... the methods of objective and balanced reporting may vary considerably, depending among other things on the media in question. It is not for this court, nor for the national courts for that matter, to substitute their own views for those of the press as to what technique of reporting should be adopted by journalists. In this context the court recalls that article 10 protects not only the substance of the ideas and information expressed, but also the form in which they are conveyed.'

11.80 In *Fressoz v France*[99] the ECtHR said, in essence, that Art 10 leaves it for journalists to decide whether or not it is necessary to reproduce material to ensure credibility, adding:[100]

> 'It protects journalists' rights to divulge information on issues of general interest provided that they are acting in good faith and on an accurate factual basis and provide "reliable and precise" information in accordance with the ethics of journalism.'

11.81 The Court of Appeal in *HRH Prince of Wales v Associated Newspapers Limited*[101] said that decisions of the Strasbourg court identify, as a common theme, the importance of the role of the press in a democratic society and cited a recent formulation of the relevant principles to be found in *Fressoz v France*:[102]

> '(i)   Freedom of expression constitutes one of the essential foundations of a democratic society. Subject to paragraph 2 of article 10, it is applicable not only to "information" or "ideas" that are favourably received or regarded as inoffensive or as a matter of indifference,

---

96   (1994) 19 EHRR 1, at para 31.
97   At para 31.
98   At p 26, para 31.
99   (2001) 31 EHRR 28, at para 54 (also at (1999) 5 BHRC 654).
100   Lord Hope also referred at [117] to R Clayton and H Tomlinson *The Law of Human Rights* (Oxford University Press, 2000), at para 15.162, which pointed out that the court has distinguished three kinds of expression: political expression, artistic expression and commercial expression, and that it consistently attaches great importance to political expression and applies rather less rigorous principles to expression which is artistic and commercial. He said that according to the court's well-established case-law, freedom of expression constitutes one of the essential foundations of a democratic society and one of the basic conditions for its progress and the self-fulfilment of each individual: *Tammer v Estonia* (2001) 37 EHRR 857, at para 59.
101   [2006] EWCA Civ 1776, at [49].
102   (2001) 31 EHRR 28, at para 45 (also at (1999) 5 BHRC 654).

but also to those that offend, shock or disturb. Such are the demands of pluralism, tolerance and broadmindedness without which there is no "democratic society".

(ii)   The press plays an essential role in a democratic society. Although it must not overstep certain bounds, in particular in respect of the reputation and rights of others and the need to prevent the disclosure of confidential information, its duty is nevertheless to impart – in a manner consistent with its obligations and responsibilities – information and ideas on all matters of public interest. In addition, the court is mindful of the fact that journalistic freedom also covers possible recourse to a degree of exaggeration, or even provocation.

(iii)   As a matter of general principle, the "necessity" for any restriction on freedom of expression must be convincingly established. Admittedly, it is in the first place for the national authorities to assess whether there is a "pressing social need" for the restriction and, in making their assessment, they enjoy a certain margin of appreciation. In cases, such as the present one, concerning the press, the national margin of appreciation is circumscribed by the interest of democratic society in ensuring and maintaining a free press. Similarly, that interest will weigh heavily in the balance in determining, as must be done under paragraph 2 of article 10, whether the restriction was proportionate to the legitimate aim pursued.'

BALANCING THE RIGHT TO PRIVACY AGAINST FREEDOM OF EXPRESSION

11.82   Once a reasonable expectation of privacy has been established the following questions must be addressed:[103]

- whether the objective of the restriction on the right guaranteed by Art 10 is sufficiently important to justify limiting the fundamental right to freedom of expression which the press assert on behalf of the public; and

- whether the means chosen to limit the Art 10 right are rational, fair and not arbitrary and impair the right as minimally as is reasonably possible.

11.83   The factors that need to be weighed when balancing freedom of expression against the right to privacy are:[104]

- First, the duty recognised in *Jersild v Denmark*[105] to impart information and ideas of public interest which the public has a right to receive, and the need, recognised in *Fressoz v France*,[106] for the court to leave it to journalists to decide what material needs to be reproduced to ensure credibility.

- Secondly, against that, the degree of privacy to which the claimant was entitled under the law. Keene LJ said in *Douglas v Hello! Ltd*[107] that any consideration of Art 8 rights must reflect the fact that there are different degrees of privacy. The potential for disclosure of the information to cause harm is an important factor to be taken into account in the assessment of the extent of the restriction that was needed to protect an individual's right to privacy. The more intimate the aspects of

---

[103]   Lord Hope in *Campbell*, at [115].
[104]   Lord Hope, ibid, at [116]–[118].
[105]   (1994) 19 EHRR 1, at para 3.
[106]   (2001) 31 EHRR 28, at para 54.
[107]   [2001] QB 967, at [168].

private life which are being interfered with, the more serious must be the reasons for doing so before the interference can be legitimate.[108]

11.84 The rights embodied in Arts 8 and 10 are not absolute. Article 8 expressly recognises that intrusions into private life will be justified in certain circumstances, such as where the intrusion is necessary for the protection of the freedoms and rights of others, and Art 10 expressly recognises that freedom of expression may, likewise, have to accommodate other rights. Difficult issues of proportionality arise because the Articles are accorded equal weight and neither is paramount. The central issue is whether there is sufficient public interest in publication to justify overriding the competing right to privacy.

11.85 Lord Nicholls said in *Campbell*[109] that the importance of privacy has been stressed less often than that of freedom of expression but the right to privacy nonetheless lay at the heart of liberty in a modern state. Lord Hoffman[110] said the question was the extent to which it was necessary to qualify one right in order to protect the underlying value protected by the other and that the extent of the qualification must be proportionate to the need.[111] He said[112] that where there is no contrary public interest recognised and protected by the law, the press is free to publish anything it likes and, subject to the law of defamation, it does not matter how trivial, spiteful or offensive the publication may be. But when press freedom comes into conflict with another interest protected by the law a balance has to be struck.

11.86 Privacy must be balanced against freedom to impart information which in turn must be balanced against respect for private life.[113] This type of balancing exercise was well known in English law (see Lord Goff in *A-G v Guardian Newspapers (No 2)*[114]) but account is now taken of the guidance given by the ECtHR on the application of Arts 8 and 10. Sedley LJ pointed out in *Douglas v Hello! Ltd*:[115]

> 'The European Court of Human Rights has always recognised the high importance of free media of communication in a democracy, but its jurisprudence does not – and could not consistently with the Convention itself – give article 10(1) the presumptive priority which is given, for example, to the First Amendment in the jurisprudence of the United States' courts. Everything will ultimately depend on the proper balance between privacy and publicity in the situation facing the court.'

11.87 Article 10 confers a conditional right and is balanced against other rights as was explained in *Bladet Tromsand Stensaas v Norway*:[116]

> 'Article 10 of the Convention does not, however, guarantee wholly freedom of expression ... Under the terms of paragraph 2 of the Article the exercise of this freedom carries with it "duties and responsibilities" which ... are liable to assume significance when ... there is question of attacking the reputation of private individuals and examining the "rights of others" ... the safeguard afforded by article 10 to journalists in relation to reporting on issues

---

[108] See the decision of the ECtHR in *Dudgeon v United Kingdom* (1981) 4 EHRR 149, at para 52.
[109] *Campbell v MGN Limited* [2004] UKHL 22, at [12] and [20].
[110] At [55].
[111] Sedley LJ in *Douglas v Hello! Ltd* [2001] QB 967, at 1001, [2001] 2 All ER 289.
[112] At [56].
[113] Lord Hope, at [105] and [106].
[114] [1990] 1 AC 109.
[115] [2001] 1 QB 967, at 1004, [135].
[116] (2000) 29 EHRR 125, at para 65.

of general interest is subject to the proviso that they are acting in good faith to provide accurate and reliable information in accordance with the ethics of journalism.'

11.88 Clause 3(i) of the PCC Code of Practice recognises that the right to privacy is not absolute. For example, before it was recently revised the code stated that a person may have a *reasonable* expectation of privacy in a public place. The Revised Code (as at October 2009) at 3 iii) states that it 'is unacceptable to photograph individuals in private places without their consent' and notes that 'Private places are public or private property where there is a reasonable expectation of privacy'. Sedley LJ explained the inevitability of the proportionality test in the contest between press freedom and privacy in *Douglas v Hello! Ltd*:[117]

> 'The case being one which affects the Convention right of freedom of expression, section 12 of the Human Rights Act 1998 requires the court to have regard to article 10 … This, however, cannot … give the article 10(1) right of free expression a presumptive priority over other rights. What it does is require the court … to bring into the frame the conflicting right to respect for privacy. This right, contained in article 8 and reflected in English law, is in turn qualified in both contexts by the right of others to free expression. The outcome, which self-evidently has to be the same under both articles, is determined principally by considerations of proportionality.'

11.89 The weighing of relevant competing Convention rights[118] requires an 'intense focus' on the individual facts of the case. The balancing exercise is undertaken against the background of Arts 8 and 10 of the ECHR. Articles 8(2) and 10(2) each separately recognise that the rights and freedoms of others are entitled to protection. Neither Art 8 nor Art 10 is pre-eminent over the other and they are neither absolute nor in any hierarchical order, since they are of equal value in a democratic society.[119] Resolution 1165 (2008) of the Parliamentary Assembly of the Council of Europe, para 10 states that:

> 'The Assembly reaffirms the importance of everyone's right to privacy, and of the right to freedom of expression, as fundamental to a democratic society. These rights are neither absolute nor in any hierarchical order, since they are of equal value.'

11.90 No one Convention right takes automatic precedence over another and our law no longer demands that virtually unqualified weight be given to the concept that it is in 'public interest that the truth should out'.[120] Rights of free expression protected by Art 10 do not simply 'trump' any privacy rights that may be established.

11.91 The Art 10 right 'carries with it duties and responsibilities'. The rights in both Arts 8 and 10 are qualified.[121] The following are important in the balancing exercise:

- whether the publication of the material in question pursues a legitimate aim set out in each Article;

---

[117] [2001] QB 967, at [137].

[118] See eg *Campbell v MGN* [2004] UKHL 22 and *Re S (A Child)* [2005] 1 AC 593, cited by Eady J in *Mosley v NGN* [2008] EWHC 1777 (QB).

[119] Resolution 1165 of the Parliamentary Assembly of the Council of Europe (1998), para 11.

[120] See Lord Denning MR in *Fraser v Evans* [1969] 1 QB 349, at 360F–360G.

[121] Article 8(2) provides for 'the protection of the rights and freedoms of others'. Article 10(2) provides for 'the protection of the reputation or rights of others' and for 'preventing the disclosure of information received in confidence'. The rights referred to may either be rights protected under the national law or, as in this case, other Convention rights.

- whether the benefits that will be achieved by publication are proportionate to the harm that may be done by the interference with the right to privacy;

- whether the interference with or restriction on the right is 'necessary in a democratic society', meets a 'pressing social need' and is no greater than is proportionate to the legitimate aim pursued;

- whether the restriction is 'in accordance with the law' and has a basis in national law which conforms to the ECHR standards of legality; and

- whether the reasons given for any restriction are both 'relevant' and 'sufficient' for this purpose.

11.92 The ECtHR has developed jurisprudence which explains how these principles are to be understood and applied in the context of the facts of each case.[122]

The curtailment of media intrusion into the lives of celebrities

11.93 It is not enough to deprive an individual of their right to privacy because they are a celebrity and that their private life is newsworthy. Normally when an infringement of an individual's right to privacy under Art 8 rights is identified it is only right that the individual is afforded a remedy and that the right is vindicated. There is only one permitted exception and that is where there is a countervailing public interest which in the particular circumstances is strong enough to outweigh the right to privacy. This is where it must be established that at least one of the established 'limiting principles' has come into play.[123]

11.94 The question which arises in such a case is whether it was necessary and proportionate for the infringement of privacy to have occurred. The sort of situation which might justify the infringement might be, for example, in order to expose illegal activity or to reveal the lies and hypocrisy of those in public life. Another instance where it might be necessary to infringe a right to privacy is where the information in question would make a contribution to 'a debate of general interest'.[124] This is a very high test.

11.95 It is not possible to state clearly how far these tests will be applied to situations where a right to privacy has been established in respect of photographs taken in public places. It would appear to be very difficult to justify such photographs by the application of any of the established limiting principles and, if this is right, celebrity photography and, indeed, the whole of celebrity culture along with it will have to be greatly curtailed and reviewed. There is little, if any, public interest in satisfying the public curiosity about details of the private lives of celebrities or those in the public eye.

11.96 These principles were affirmed in Strasbourg in the case of *Leempoel v Belgium*:[125]

---

[122] Lord Hope in *Campbell*, at [112].
[123] See generally Eady J in *Mosley v NGN* [2008] EWHC 1777 (QB).
[124] The words of the Strasbourg court in *Von Hannover*, at [60] and [76].
[125] App No 64772/01, 9 November 2006. The above principles were set out by Eady J in *Mosley v NGN*, at [131]–[133], as was this reference.

'In matters relating to striking a balance between protecting private life and the freedom of expression that the Court had had to rule upon, it has always emphasised ... the requirement that the publication of information, documents or photographs in the press should serve the public interest and make a contribution to the debate of general interest ... Whilst the right for the public to be informed, a fundamental right in a democratic society that under particular circumstances may even relate to aspects of the private life of public persons, particularly where political personalities are involved ... publications whose sole aim is to satisfy the curiosity of a certain public as to the details of the private life of a person, whatever their fame, should not be regarded as contributing to any debate of general interest to society.'

Allowing the press a degree of latitude

11.97 A margin of appreciation will be given to the journalist and it will sometimes be the case that an individual's right to privacy may be limited by the public's interest in knowing about certain traits of their personality and certain aspects of their private life.[126]

11.98 How material that it is legitimate to convey to the public is presented without breaching a duty of confidence is a matter for the journalists. The choice of language and editorial decisions over whether or not to use photographs are matters the courts do not like to interfere with. The media is entitled to a reasonable margin of appreciation in taking decisions as to what details needed to be included in an article to give it credibility as part of the journalistic process.[127] This is illustrated by two statements made in *Campbell*, as follows.

11.99 The Court of Appeal in *Campbell* said:[128]

'Provided that publication of particular confidential information is justifiable in the public interest, the journalist must be given reasonable latitude as to the manner in which that information is conveyed to the public or his article 10 right to freedom of expression will be unnecessarily inhibited.'

11.100 Lord Hoffman in *Campbell* said:

'[59] ... judges are not newspaper editors ... I agree with the observation of the Court of Appeal, at p 660, para 52, that it is harsh to criticise the editor for "painting a somewhat fuller picture in order to show [Ms Campbell] in a sympathetic light."'

11.101 If the substance of a story is justified questions, therefore, arise over how far newspapers are allowed some margin of choice in the way they present stories and whether they are to be strictly liable if matter is printed which does not satisfy the high test set out above. It has been said that the practical exigencies of journalism demand some latitude must be given; that editorial decisions have to be made quickly and with less information than is available to a court, which reviews the matter at leisure, and that it is unreasonable to expect that in matters of judgment, any more than in accuracy of reporting, newspapers will always get it absolutely right.[129]

---

[126] Lord Hope in *Campbell*, at [120].
[127] Lord Hope in *Campbell*, at [113].
[128] [2003] QB 633 at [64] (referred to with approval by Lord Hoffman on appeal at [2004] UKHL 22, at [65]).
[129] *Campbell* [2004] UKHL 22, at [62].

11.102   A parallel was drawn by Lord Hoffman in *Campbell*[130] with the decision of the House of Lords in *Reynolds v Times Newspapers Ltd*[131] and he suggested that to require editors to get it absolutely right every time would tend to inhibit the publication of facts which should in the public interest be made known. He thought that the *Reynolds* principle was equally applicable to the publication of private personal information in the cases in which the essential part of that information can legitimately be published. Lord Carswell in *Campbell* was in agreement with Lord Nicholls and Lord Hoffmann in allowing a proper degree of journalistic margin to the press to deal with a legitimate story in its own way, without imposing unnecessary shackles on its freedom to publish detail and photographs which add colour and conviction. He did not minimise these factors and thought them part of the legitimate function of a free press which required to be given proper weight.[132]

11.103   Eady J in *Mosley v NGN*[133] emphasised that it is for the court to decide whether a particular publication was in the public interest. He referred to the fact that some authorities placed emphasis on the need to make due allowance for editorial judgment and also for a wide discretion so far as taste and modes of expression are concerned. He also referred by way of example to *Jameel (Mohammed) v Wall Street Journal Sprl*[134] in the context of privilege in the law of defamation, where Lord Bingham made these observations:

> '[31]   The necessary precondition of reliance on qualified privilege is that the matter published should be one of public interest ... what engages the interest of the public may not be material which engages the public interest.

> [32]   ... assuming the matter to be one of public interest ... Lord Nicholls proposed [in *Reynolds v Times Newspapers Ltd*], at p 202, a test of responsible journalism, a test repeated in *Bonnick v Morris* [2003] 1 AC 300, 309 ... that there is no duty to publish and the public have no interest to read material which the publisher has not taken reasonable steps to verify. As Lord Hobhouse observed ... at p 238, "No public interest is served by publishing or communicating misinformation."... the publisher is protected if he has taken such steps as a responsible journalist would take to try and ensure that what is published is accurate and fit for publication.

> [33]   Lord Nicholls, at p 205, listed certain ... pointers which might be more or less indicative, depending on the circumstances ... not ... a series of hurdles to be negotiated by a publisher before he could successfully rely on qualified privilege. Lord Nicholls recognised, at pp 202–203 ... it had to be ... the court, which decided whether a publication was protected by qualified privilege. But this does not mean that the editorial decisions and judgments ... are irrelevant. Weight should ordinarily be given to the professional judgment of an editor or journalist in the absence of some indication that it was made in a casual, cavalier, slipshod or careless manner.'

11.104   It was considered that a decision on public interest must be capable of being tested by objectively recognised criteria by Eady J in *Mosley*.[135] He referred to the observation of Sir John Donaldson MR in *Francome v Mirror Group Newspapers Ltd*,[136] that: 'The media ... are peculiarly vulnerable to the error of confusing the public interest

---

[130]   At [63].
[131]   [2001] 2 AC 127.
[132]   At [169].
[133]   At [135].
[134]   [2007] 1 AC 359, at [31]–[33].
[135]   At [138] and [139].
[136]   [1984] 1 WLR 892, at 898.

with their own interest.' Eady J thought that there might be a case for saying, when 'public interest' has to be considered in the field of privacy, that a judge should inquire whether the relevant journalist's decision prior to publication was reached as a result of carrying out inquiries and checks consistent with 'responsible journalism' and said he must not disregard the remarks of Lord Phillips MR in *Campbell*[137] to the effect that the same test of public interest should *not* be applied in the 'two very different torts'.

Privacy and defamation

11.105 In *McKennitt v Ash*[138] Buxton LJ said that if it could be shown that a claim in breach of confidence was brought where the nub of the case was a complaint of the falsity of the allegations in order to avoid the rules of the tort of defamation objections could be raised in terms of abuse of process. However, he said[139] that provided the matter complained of is by its nature such as to attract the law of breach of confidence the defendant cannot deprive the claimant of his Art 8 protection simply by showing that the matter is untrue. He said that some support is given to that approach by the European cases that indicate that Art 8 protects 'reputation', broadly understood. This approach might raise issues on applications for interim injunctions because the threshold test for the grant of an interim injunction in a privacy case differs from a defamation case. Latham LJ[140] identified the question in a case of misuse of private information as being whether the information is private not whether it is true or false. He said that the truth or falsity of the information is an irrelevant inquiry in deciding whether the information is entitled to be protected and judges should be chary of becoming side-tracked into that irrelevant inquiry.

Privacy and photographs and films

11.106 Where a person who for private or domestic purposes commissions the taking of a photograph or the making of a film (eg for a private celebrity wedding) the copyright in the resulting photographs or films will usually belong to the photographer. However, the person who commissions the photographer (ie the celebrity in the example) has the moral right not to have copies of the photographs and film issued to the public or exhibited or communicated to the public. This right is given by s 85 of the Copyright, Designs and Patents Act 1988. The right is not infringed in various circumstances, the most important of which is where the images are incidentally included in an artistic work, film or broadcast. By s 103(1) an infringement of a moral right is actionable as a breach of statutory duty owed to the person entitled to the right.

DAMAGES FOR INVASION OF PRIVACY

The nature of compensatory damages in privacy cases

11.107 Privacy cases are not primarily concerned with reputation. Eady J in *Mosley*[141] underlined that infringement of privacy cases are not, therefore, directly concerned with compensating for, or vindicating, injury to reputation. The purpose of damages in

---

[137] [2003] QB 633, at [61].
[138] [2006] EWCA Civ 1714, at [78] and [79].
[139] At [80].
[140] In *McKennitt v Ash*, at [86].
[141] *Mosley v NGN* [2008] EWHC 1777 (QB): see at [214]–[231].

privacy cases is to address the specific public policy factors in play when there has been 'an old-fashioned breach of confidence' and/or an unauthorised revelation of personal information:

- the law is concerned to protect such matters as personal dignity, autonomy and integrity;

- the inquiry should not be distracted by considerations which relate purely to taste or moral disapproval;

- matters going to personal dignity should not be dismissed because a particular sexual activity or inclination itself may seem undignified;

- damages may include distress, hurt feelings and loss of dignity;

- damages might also include vindication to mark the infringement of a right,[142] although this is different from vindication of reputation (which is a factor in libel damages);

- '... there is no reason why an award of compensatory damages should not also fulfil a vindicatory purpose';[143]

- damages must be proportionate, not open to the criticism of arbitrariness and accord with a readily identifiable scale;

- in awarding such damages it is legitimate to have some regard to current personal injury awards to maintain a sense of proportion;

- aggravating conduct may be taken into account in privacy cases where it increases the hurt to the claimant's feelings or 'rubs salt in the wound';

- persisting in unpleasant allegations at trial publicly and without success is a legitimate element to take into account and to reflect in any award;

- the claimant's conduct may be relevant to take into account;

- contributory negligence is not a distinct issue in privacy claims but the extent to which the claimant's conduct contributed to the nature and scale of the distress *might* be a relevant factor on causation;

- injury to reputation is not a directly relevant factor. Whereas reputation can be vindicated by an award of damages, that is not possible where embarrassing personal information has been released for general publication because once privacy has been infringed, the damage is done;

---

[142] See e g *Ashley v Chief Constable of Sussex* [2008] 2 WLR 975, at [21]–[22]; and *Chester v Afshar* [2005] 1 AC 134, at [87].
[143] Lord Scott observed in *Ashley*, ibid.

- an infringement of privacy cannot ever be effectively compensated by a monetary award so the only realistic course is to select a figure which marks the fact that an unlawful intrusion has taken place whilst affording some degree of solatium to the injured party; and

- where the traditional object of restitution is not available the figure selected should not be such that it could be interpreted as minimising the scale of the wrong done or the damage it has caused.

Exemplary damages and compensatory damages

11.108 An award of exemplary damages may only be made where an element of punishment is thought appropriate *and* the amount to be awarded by way of compensation (including aggravated damages) is not sufficient to serve a punitive as well as a compensatory function.[144] Exemplary damages are appropriate in two categories of case:

- those concerned with examples of arbitrary or unconstitutional conduct by public officials; and

- where there has been a deliberate and knowing commission of a tort *and* a calculation that more is to be gained by the wrongful act than is likely to be suffered by paying compensatory damages on the basis that the underlying public policy is that 'tort does not pay'.

11.109 Eady J considered[145] that breach of privacy which involved balancing competing Convention rights evolved from the equitable doctrines that traditionally governed the protection of confidential information and that although there is some judicial support for its recognition as a tort in *Wainwright v Home Office*,[146] their Lordships expressly refused to declare the existence of 'a previously unknown tort of invasion of privacy'. Punitive damages were considered anomalous because:

- they brought in the notion of punishment when damages are about compensation;

- the defendant's means can be taken into account;

- the sum awarded represents a windfall; and

- where a jury is still available, it is the jury rather than the judge which determines the amount.

11.110 It was considered that exemplary damages could not be awarded in an infringement of privacy claim because apart from the lack of existing authority such an award would fail the tests of necessity and proportionality. Damages for infringement of privacy are confined to a compensatory award which can include an element of aggravation, if appropriate.

---

[144] See Eady J in *Mosley v NGN*, at [176]–[211].
[145] *Mosley*, at [181].
[146] [2004] 2 AC 406, at [31]–[35].

The Data Protection Act 1998

11.111 The Data Protection Act 1998 (DPA 1998) is primarily concerned with protecting individual privacy. Large amounts of personal information about individuals is routinely processed and published and the Act is concerned with such activity. DPA 1998 defines the information subject to protection, the subjects of protection and the activities which give rise to liability. 'Personal data' are defined in the Act as data relating to a living individual identifiable from those data, or from those data and other information in the possession of, or likely to come into the control of, the data controller. The 'data subject' is the subject of personal data and includes any expression of opinion about an individual and any indication of the intentions of the data controller or any other person in respect of the individual. 'Processing' is widely defined and, in relation to information or data, means obtaining, recording or holding the information or data or carrying out a variety of operations on the information or data. 'Using' or 'disclosing', in relation to personal data, includes using or disclosing the information contained in the data. This would include publication of personal data in newspapers and magazines and similar.[147]

11.112 Relevant personal data might include written material, records and photographs. The publisher of such material will be a data controller and the obtaining, holding, preparation for publication and publication of such material is likely to amount to processing of the data for the purposes of DPA 1998. If this is done without the consent of the subject of the material, it is likely to constitute a breach of statutory duty if it was processed in breach of the data protection principles, for example, to process the data fairly and lawfully. It would not be lawful, for example, if it was done by misusing the subject's personal information and in breach of confidence. The issue would then be whether or not the processing could be shown to be justified under the Act. If the processing is not justified the claimant must show that he has suffered damage or distress and is entitled to compensation under the Act.

11.113 'Personal data' was considered by the Court of Appeal in *Durant v Financial Services Authority*,[148] where it was made clear that it by no means included all information about someone held on file. Simply mentioning the data subject in a document held by a data controller did not create personal data within DPA 1998. Whether or not it did so would depend on how relevant or proximate the information was to the data subject and the degree of the data subject's involvement in the situation or transaction with which the information was concerned. The biographical nature and focus on the data subject in relation to the information were of relevance. The main point was whether or not the information affected the data subject's privacy in his personal or family life, or business or professional capacity.

11.114 Sensitive personal data includes information as to the racial or ethnic origin of the data subject; his political opinions; his religious beliefs or other beliefs of a similar nature; his physical or mental health or condition; his sexual life; the commission or alleged commission by him of any offence, or any proceedings for any offence committed or alleged to have been committed by him and the disposal of such proceedings or the sentence of any court in such proceedings.

---

[147] A useful summary of the position appears in *Campbell v MGN Ltd* [2002] EWCA Civ 1373, at [72] et seq, esp at [102]–[106].

[148] [2003] EWCA Civ 1746.

11.115   Part 1 of Sch 1 to DPA 1998 sets out the eight 'data protection principles'. These provide that:

- personal data shall be processed fairly and lawfully and, in particular, shall not be processed unless: (1) at least one of the conditions set out in Sch 2 is met, and (2) in the case of personal sensitive data, at least one of the conditions in Sch 3 is met;

- personal data shall be obtained only for one or more specified and lawful purposes, and shall not be further processed in any manner incompatible with that purpose or those purposes;

- personal data shall be adequate, relevant and not excessive in relation to the purpose or purposes for which they are processed;

- personal data shall be accurate and, where necessary, kept up to date;

- personal data processed for any purpose or purposes shall not be kept for longer than is necessary for that purpose or those purposes;

- personal data shall be processed in accordance with the rights of data subjects under DPA 1998;

- appropriate technical and organisational measures shall be taken against unauthorised or unlawful processing of personal data and against accidental loss or destruction of, or damage to, personal data; and

- personal data shall not be transferred to a country or territory outside the European Economic Area unless that country or territory ensures an adequate level of protection for the rights and freedoms of data subjects in relation to the processing of personal data.

11.116   Where there is no public interest justifying unauthorised publication of personal data comprising private information DPA 1998 may well provide a remedy. The protection the Act affords in respect of a photograph containing what was alleged to be private information was considered by Patten J in *Murray v Express Newspapers and others*[149] and reviewed on appeal in the Court of Appeal.[150] At first instance it was held that Art 8 was not engaged and the photograph of the claimant could not, therefore, be confidential information for the purposes of DPA 1998. There was an issue over whether the photograph contained personal sensitive information, for example, about race and ethnicity, but it was held that being public it fell within the exemption. The judge held that for the photograph to comprise sensitive personal data under DPA 1998, s 2(e) it would have to be of someone with some clearly identifiable physical condition which was exposed by the photograph. It was said that a photograph of an apparently healthy individual in fact tells nothing about his actual state of health. The judge said that when dealing with sensitive personal data conveyed by an image alone exposing the image by appearing in a public place satisfies condition 5.

11.117   With regard to compensation, DPA 1998, s 13 provides that an individual who suffers damage by reason of any contravention by a data controller of any of the

---

[149]   [2007] EWHC 1908 (Ch), [2008] 1 FLR 704, at [69]–[92].
[150]   *Murray v Big Pictures (UK) Limited* [2008] EWCA Civ 446, at [62].

requirements of DPA 1998 is entitled to compensation from the data controller for that damage. An individual who suffers distress by reason of any contravention of any of the requirements of DPA 1998 is entitled to compensation for that distress if (a) the individual also suffers damage by reason of the contravention or (b) the contravention relates to the processing of personal data for the special purposes. Provision is made that it is a defence to prove that such care had been taken as in all the circumstances was reasonably required to comply with the requirement concerned.

11.118 In *Douglas v Hello!*[151] Brooke LJ made general comments about the application of DPA 1998 to photographs and the right to compensation arising from contravention of the requirements of the Act:

> '[55] ... In the present case "Hello!" wished to publish in this country over half a million copies of its issue 639 which it had imported from its printers in Spain. In another case, however, a newspaper might wish to publish a photograph, taken on a private occasion, which it possessed in this country in digital form. In such a case it might run into serious difficulties.

> [56] These difficulties would arise out of the provisions of the Data Protection Act 1998. This statute was enacted, in part, to implement Council Directive 95/46/EC, which was self-avowedly concerned with the protection of an individual's Convention rights to privacy: see paragraphs (2), (10), (11) and (17) of the preamble to the Directive and article 9 of the Directive itself. It follows that unless the newspaper asserted a section 32(1)(b) justification (viz that it reasonably believed that, having regard in particular to the special importance of the public interest in freedom of expression, publication would be in the public interest), a claimant who could show that the photograph had been taken of him on some private occasion without his consent would be able to satisfy a court that it was highly probable that an article 10(2) justification would succeed at trial: see the Data Protection Act 1998, section 4 and Schedule 1, Part I, paragraph 1(a) and Schedule 2. Section 13 of this Act, incidentally, grants an individual a statutory right to compensation for damage (including distress, in certain specified circumstances) against a "data controller" who contravenes any of the requirements of the Act. This entitlement is subject to any of the defences the Act may provide.'

11.119 The right to compensation in respect of the publication of a photograph was considered by the judge at first instance in *Murray*. The taking of the photograph and its subsequent publication in the *Murray* case did not cause distress, nor did it cause damage which, under DPA 1998, s 13(1), meant ordinary pecuniary loss.[152] The claimant sought compensation for general rather than special damage and it was held that the claim was not made out. The judge refused to award compensation referable to the market value of the data which had been misused. Sometimes such awards are made as a restitutionary remedy or where the proper remedy is a form of equitable compensation or accounting designed to require the defendant to disgorge profits derived from use of the claimant's property. In either case it is compensation for loss of bargaining opportunity or the compulsory acquisition by the defendant of his rights. Since such principles of compensation depended on an analogy with property rights and the court's power to enforce contracts the judge thought they were not applicable to compensation under DPA 1998. The Act did not give the data subject property in his personal data but merely regulated the way in which it could be processed. In summary,

---

[151]   [2001] QB 967.
[152]   See *Johnson v Medical Defence Union* [2007] EWCA Civ 262, [2007] 3 CMLR 181, at [74], per Buxton LJ.

it was held that the Act did not give a cause of action based upon misuse of data where the subject did not suffer damage or distress even though the data controller profited from the material

11.120 The Court of Appeal in *Murray* said that had the judge at first instance held that Art 8 was engaged and that the balance between Arts 8 and 10 was in the claimant's favour, the defendant's admitted processing of the claimant's personal data would have been unlawful and unfair in that none of the conditions of Sch 2 to DPA 1998 (including the only condition relied upon, namely that in para 6(1)) would have applied. The Court of Appeal said that the issues raised below under the Act would need revisiting after the facts had been determined. They included those relating to causation and damage which the Court of Appeal thought raised a number of important questions including the meaning of 'damage' in DPA 1998, s 13(1). It was also thought at least arguable that 'damage' had been construed too narrowly, having regard to the fact that the purpose of the Act was to enact the provisions of the relevant Directive.[153]

---

[153] Council Directive 95/46/EC.

Chapter 12

PARTICULAR INSTANCES OF PROTECTION GIVEN TO CONFIDENTIAL AND PRIVATE INFORMATION

INTRODUCTION

12.1 The most difficult (and most practically useful) task is applying the developing law relating to the misuse of private information to the facts in particular cases. Every case is different and each requires an intense focus on the facts in order to determine the outcome. There is often fierce disagreement about what should and should not be protected, for example, the extent to which politicians or others in the public eye ought to be able to keep their sex lives private. Precedents are only guides to the court's likely approach but recent cases constitute solid practical examples of how the law is applied and is developing. For this reason, recent cases are dealt with in some detail below. The following general topics are covered (some of which inevitably overlap):

- shared experiences;

- the right to tell one's own story;

- public figures and role models;

- celebrity status/public figures/seeking publicity;

- false statements/hypocrisy/selective publicity/setting the record straight;

- criminality;

- sexual relationships and activity;

- clandestine surveillance;

- photographs;

- covert photographs in public places;

- medical treatment/health;

- drugs;

- children of celebrities/child celebrities; and

- children of celebrities in divorce proceedings.

SHARED EXPERIENCES

12.2   It has been suggested that there can be no confidentiality where experiences are shared and one party does not want to maintain confidentiality. This is not the case. Confidentiality will be maintained in respect of a relationship if, on the facts, that is what the parties to the relationship would be taken to have agreed. Difficult issues arise as to the sort of relationships which are likely to be protected. The suggestion that relationships of casual sex will not normally be protected is now open to debate. Details of sexual relationships in all their various forms have a strong claim to protection even though several individuals might be involved (eg an orgy as in *Mosley*[1]). It depends on the facts. If the parties involved have expressly agreed the details will be kept confidential this should be decisive. Buxton LJ in *McKennitt v Ash* said:[2]

> '[28]   Ms Ash argued that all of the matters ... were not merely Ms McKennitt's experience, but her own experience as well. That gave her a property in the information that should not be ... readily subordinated, to that of Ms McKennitt. This argument ... is ... relied on to say that the information was not confidential in the first place.
>
> [29]   ... *A v B plc* [2002] EWCA Civ 337, [2003] QB 195, [2002] 2 All ER 545 ... concerned a married professional footballer [A] who sought to prevent publication by a newspaper [B] of his casual sexual relations with two women [C and D] ... this court said that the right of protection of one party to a bilateral relationship might be affected by the attitude of the other party, and ...:
>
>> "Although we would not go so far as to say there can be no confidentiality where one party to a relationship does not want confidentiality, the fact that C and D chose to disclose their relationships to B does affect A's right to protection of the information. For the position to be otherwise would not acknowledge C and D's own right to freedom of expression."
>
> [30]   ... the relationship between Ms McKennitt and Ms Ash ... was miles away from the relationship between A and C and D ... a relationship of casual sex. A could not have thought, and did not say, that when he picked the women up they realised that they were entering into a relationship of confidence with him. Small wonder that Lord Woolf said, *A v B* at para 45:
>
>> "Relationships of the sort which A had with C and D are not the categories of relationships which the court should be astute to protect when the other parties to the relationships do not want them to remain confidential."
>
> Lord Woolf would have been unlikely to say the same about the relationship between Ms McKennitt and Ms Ash.
>
> [31]   Second ... the book is not in any real sense about [the defendant] at all ...

---

[1]   *Mosley v NGN* [2008] EWHC 1777 (QB).
[2]   [2006] EWCA Civ 1714.

[32] ... the matters related in the book were specifically experiences of and the property of [the claimant]. [The defendant] cannot undermine their confidential nature by the paradox of calling in aid the confidential relationship that gave her access to the information in the first place.'

12.3   The numbers involved and the fact that the claimant liked to video proceedings did not deter Eady J from deciding in *Mosley* that privacy was maintained. He said[3] an argument that the claimant forfeited any expectation of privacy partly because of the numbers involved, coupled with reliance upon the fact that he liked to record the gatherings on video, could be safely rejected in the light of the European Court of Human Rights (ECtHR) decision in *ADT v UK*.[4]

THE RIGHT TO TELL ONE'S OWN STORY

12.4   It was argued in *McKennitt v Ash*[5] that Ms Ash had been deprived of her Art 10 of the European Convention for the Protection of Human Rights and Fundamental Freedoms (ECHR) right to tell her own story and that Ms McKennitt's Art 8 rights, if any, were to be subordinated to Ms Ash's Art 10 rights. Buxton LJ dismissed this argument on the grounds that it completely ignored the judge's findings of fact; that – importantly – Ms Ash had no story to tell that was her own as opposed to being Ms McKennitt's and that even if that were not so, it needs no intense focus to conclude that on the facts Ms Ash's rights of freedom of expression must inevitably yield to Ms McKennitt's right to privacy.[6]

PUBLIC FIGURES AND ROLE MODELS

12.5   It is often argued that there is a public interest in publishing private information about public figures, particularly if they misbehave or are guilty of hypocrisy. The media's argument is that the public have a right in such cases to have the record put straight.[7] There is no clear principle to that effect. It depends on whether publication of the facts is truly in the public interest and capable of contributing to debate in a democratic society. It also depends on whether the press is exercising its watchdog role in publishing. Plainly there is less public interest in the publication of private details about individuals who, although well known, do not hold a public position. This will tend to cut out the usual tabloid kiss-and-tell type stories, which tend to be about show business or sporting celebrities rather than holders of public office. In *McKennitt v Ash* the Court of Appeal referred to the distinction drawn in *Von Hannover*[8] between the media's watchdog role in the democratic process and the reporting of private information about individuals who, although of interest to the public, were not public figures. The ECtHR in *Von Hannover* explained the position in the following way:

'[63] The court considers that a fundamental distinction needs to be made between reporting facts – even controversial ones – capable of contributing to a debate in a democratic society relating to politicians in the exercise of their functions, for example, and

---

3   At [109].
4   (2000) 31 EHRR 33.
5   [2006] EWCA Civ 1714.
6   Buxton LJ in *McKennitt v Ash* at [52] and [54].
7   Buxton LJ in *McKennitt v Ash* [2006] EWCA Civ 1714, at [56].
8   *Von Hannover v Germany* (2005) 40 EHRR 1.

reporting details of the private life of an individual who, moreover, as in this case, does not exercise official functions. While in the former case the press exercises its vital role of "watchdog" in a democracy by contributing to imparting information and ideas on matters of public interest it does not do so in the latter case.'

[64] Similarly, although the public has a right to be informed, which is an essential right in a democratic society that, in certain special circumstances, can even extend to aspects of the private life of public figures, particularly where politicians are concerned, this is not the case here. The situation here does not come within the sphere of any political or public debate because the published photos and accompanying commentaries relate exclusively to details of the Applicant's private life.'

12.6   In *McKennitt v Ash* Buxton LJ thought that even assuming that Ms McKennitt was a public figure in the relevant sense (which he suspected the ECtHR would find a surprising proposition), there were no 'special circumstances' apart from the allegation of hypocrisy to justify or require the exposure of the claimant's private life. Buxton LJ referred[9] to the decision in *A v B* and in particular to the defendant's reliance on the following paragraphs of that decision:

'[11]   ... (xi) Where an individual is a public figure he is entitled to have his privacy respected in the appropriate circumstances. A public figure is entitled to a private life. The individual, however, should recognise that because of his public position he must expect and accept that his actions will be more closely scrutinised by the media. Even trivial facts relating to a public figure can be of great interest to readers and other observers of the media. Conduct which in the case of a private individual would not be the appropriate subject of comment can be the proper subject of comment in the case of a public figure. The public figure may hold a position where higher standards of conduct can rightly be expected by the public. The public figure may be a role model whose conduct could well be emulated by others. He may set the fashion. The higher the profile of the individual concerned the more likely that this will be the position. Whether you have courted publicity or not you may be a legitimate subject of public attention. If you have courted public attention then you have less ground to object to the intrusion which follows. In many of these situations it would be overstating the position to say that there is a public interest in the information being published. It would be more accurate to say that the public have an understandable and legitimate interest in being told the information. If this is the situation then it can appropriately be taken into account by a court in deciding on which side of the line a case falls. The courts must not ignore the fact that if newspapers do not publish information that the public are interested in, there will be fewer newspapers published, which will not be in the public interest. The same is true in relation to other parts of the media.'

'[43]   ... (vi) Footballers are role models for young people and undesirable behaviour on their part can set an unfortunate example. While [the trial judge] was right to say on the evidence that was before him that A had not courted publicity, the fact is that someone holding his position was inevitably a figure in whom a section of the public and the media would be interested.'

12.7   Reference was made to the issues surrounding 'role models' in *McKennitt v Ash*. Buxton LJ considered that the argument that 'role models', voluntary or not, have less expectation of privacy may well have to be adjusted and that the width of the rights given to the media by *A v B* cannot be reconciled with *Von Hannover*. It was pointed out that no Convention authority of any sort was even mentioned in *A v B* and it was

---

postulated that it was that aspect of the case that caused a later division of the Court of Appeal to comment (per Lord Phillips of Worth Matravers MR in *Campbell v MGN*[10]):[11]

> 'When Lord Woolf spoke of the public having "an understandable and so a legitimate interest in being told" information, even including trivial facts, about a public figure, he was not speaking of private facts that a fair-minded person would consider it offensive to disclose. That is clear from his subsequent commendation of the guidance on striking a balance between art 8 and art 10 rights provided by the Council of Europe Resolution 1165 of 1998. For our part we would observe that the fact that an individual has achieved prominence on the public stage does not mean that his private life can be laid bare by the media. We do not see why it should necessarily be in the public interest that an individual who has been adopted as a role model, without seeking this distinction, should be demonstrated to have feet of clay.'

12.8   The conclusion reached in *McKennitt v Ash*[12] was that *A v B* was not binding authority on the content of Arts 8 and 10; that content is to be found in *Von Hannover* where, unlike in *A v B*, the judgment did not place automatic limits on the privacy rights of public figures. Ms McKennitt was clearly considered not to fall within Lord Woolf's first category and 'hold a position where higher standards of conduct can be rightly expected by the public'. The sort of figures that would apply to would be the headmasters and clergymen category, which might include politicians, senior civil servants, surgeons and journalists. Doubt was placed on whether Lord Woolf's second category, of involuntary role models, actually existed as a valid concept. This doubt echoed Lord Phillips in *Campbell* in the Court of Appeal. Ms McKennitt, who made efforts not to open up her life, would not fall within such a category even if it existed.

12.9   Doubt was also cast in *McKennitt v Ash* on Lord Woolf's second general point that weight must be given to the commercial interest of newspapers in reporting matters that interest the public, ie that it is somehow in the public interest that newspapers should have large circulation figures. This is of considerable importance to the reporting of tabloid kiss-and-tell type stories, in particular the seemingly insatiable demand for information about the sex lives of sports and show business celebrities. It was thought that giving any weight to the media's desire to sell lots of copy was difficult to reconcile with the long-standing view that what interests the public is not necessarily in the public interest. This was a view expressed by Baroness Hale of Richmond in *Jameel v Wall Street Journal*:[13]

> 'The public only have a right to be told if two conditions are fulfilled. First, there must be a real public interest in communicating and receiving the information. This is, as we all know, very different from saying that it is information that interests the public – the most vapid tittle-tattle about the activities of footballers' wives and girlfriends interests large sections of the public but no-one could claim any real public interest in our being told all about it.'

CELEBRITY STATUS/PUBLIC FIGURES/SEEKING PUBLICITY

12.10   Even celebrities who seek out publicity have a residual area of privacy in their lives which they are entitled to protect from exposure. The argument that celebrities who

---

[10]   [2002] EWCA Civ 1373, [2003] QB 633, at [40]–[41], [2003] 1 All ER 224.
[11]   *McKennitt v Ash*, at [61]–[63].
[12]   At [64]–[66].
[13]   [2006] UKHL 10, [2006] 2 AC 465, at [147], [2006] 4 All ER 128.

thrive on publicity cannot really complain if they do not like some of the exposure they are getting is not sound. Public figures and celebrities are entitled to protection along with the rest of us in respect of core areas of their private lives.[14] The issue is what the core area of private life comprises in a particular case. Lord Hoffman, in *Campbell*[15] said one must consider why it is being said there is a public interest justifying publication of information about a public figure or celebrity which would not be justified about someone else. Ms Campbell's relationship with the media was relevant but not, without more, decisive in her case and the fact she was a public figure with a long and symbiotic relationship with the media did not justify publication of matters which fell into her residual area of privacy. The trial judge in *Campbell* identified[16] the 'essential question' as being whether public figures (including international celebrities) who court publicity are nonetheless left with a residual area of privacy which the court should protect if its revelation would amount to a breach of confidentiality. Lord Hoffman[17] said Ms Campbell had a 'residual area of privacy', so the question was whether it was infringed. To answer that it was necessary to assess the disclosures said to be objectionable in the light of the disclosures conceded to be legitimate and then ask whether the journalists exceeded the latitude allowed to them in presenting their story.

12.11 Lord Hope put this simply in *Campbell* when he said that publicity about the private life of a celebrity does not, of itself, deprive the celebrity of a private life. He said[18] that a person's right to privacy may be limited by the public's interest in knowing about certain traits of their personality and certain aspects of their private life, as L'Heureux-Dubé and Bastarache JJ in the Supreme Court of Canada recognised in *Aubry v Les Éditions Vice-versa Inc.*[19] But it was not enough to deprive Ms Campbell of her right to privacy that she is a celebrity and that her private life is newsworthy.

12.12 *McKennitt v Ash*[20] was an extreme case of celebrity known to guard her private life closely notwithstanding the occasional release of bits of information about herself. Buxton LJ said[21] that the nub of her claim was that a substantial part of the offending book revealed personal and private detail she was entitled to keep private against the background that she carefully guarded her personal privacy. The celebrity was able to control what was on and what was off limits. Reference was made to the fact that the judge at first instance rightly saw it as a matter of great importance that:

> '[6]   Ms McKennitt has vehemently asserted in these proceedings that she has always sought to keep matters connected with her personal and business life private and confidential ... whenever a press conference or interview takes place, it is impressed upon those concerned that enquiries about her personal life are very much off limits ...

> [7]   In so far as there have been exceptions to her primary rule of protecting her privacy, Ms McKennitt ... occasionally released some information which "she felt comfortable with", and in respect of which she was able to control the boundaries herself ...

---

14   Sometimes referred to as a 'zone of privacy' – an especially sensitive topic in relation to celebrities out in public places.
15   *Campbell v MGN Ltd* [2004] UKHL 22, at [57].
16   At [35].
17   At [68].
18   At [120].
19   [1998] 1 SCR 591, at [57]–[58].
20   [2006] EWCA Civ 1714.
21   At [6].

[8] Ms McKennitt, therefore, places at the centre of her present claim the proposition that her private life and indeed her business affairs are entitled to protection on the basis of a duty of confidence, and are not in the public domain by reason either of her fame in itself or of the limited revelations to which I have referred.'

12.13 The 'private space' of the heir to the throne was considered by the Court of Appeal in *HRH Prince of Wales v Associated Newspapers Limited*.[22] The Court of Appeal said that as heir, Prince Charles was an important public figure and the public takes an interest in information about such persons that is relatively trivial.[23] For that reason it was thought that public disclosure of such information can be particularly intrusive and the Court of Appeal affirmed the following view expressed by the judge at first instance:

'[133] Not the least of the considerations that must be weighed in the scales is the claimant's countervailing claim to what was described in argument as "his private space": the right to be able to commit his private thoughts to writing and keep them private, the more so as he is inescapably a public figure who is subject to constant and intense media interest. The fact that the contents of the Hong Kong journal are not at the most intimate end of the privacy spectrum does not, to my mind, lessen the force of this countervailing claim. The claimant is as much entitled to enjoy confidentiality for his private thoughts as an aspect of his own "human autonomy and dignity" as is any other.'

12.14 Eady J in *Mosley*[24] confronted the suggestion that public figures, particularly role models, somehow enjoyed less right to complain if disclosure of private matters put them in a bad light. The point was well made that generalisations are best avoided even as guidelines. Eady J said[25] that the modern approach of applying an 'intense focus' is incompatible with making broad generalisations about whether public figures and role models have a right to privacy. Sometimes generalisations have a role to play in the 'ultimate balancing exercise', but can never be determinative. In every case it all depends upon what is revealed by the intense focus on the individual circumstances.

HYPOCRISY (FALSE IMAGE)/SELECTIVE PUBLICITY/SETTING THE RECORD STRAIGHT

12.15 It debateable how far the media are entitled to disclose private information in order to deal with hypocrisy and, as they say, put the record straight. Eady J in *McKennitt v Ash*[26] said that 'a very high degree of misbehaviour must be demonstrated' to trigger a public interest defence. The Court of Appeal in *McKennitt v Ash*[27] emphasised that it depends on the facts and that as general statement, divorced from context, Eady J's statement may go too far. It was noted that in *Campbell*[28] Ms Campbell said not merely that she did not take drugs but emphasised in that regard she was unlike other fashion models. She was trying to get some advantage for herself from the lie and so deprived otherwise private material of protection.

---

[22]   [2006] EWCA Civ 1776.
[23]   At [70].
[24]   *Mosley v NGN* [2008] EWHC 1777 (QB).
[25]   At [12].
[26]   At [97].
[27]   [2006] EWCA Civ 1714.
[28]   [2004] UKHL 22.

12.16 As the Court of Appeal noted in *Campbell v MGN*,[29] where public figures present a false image and make untrue pronouncements about their life the press are normally entitled to step in to put the record straight even in respect of matters normally considered private, such as use of (or at least addiction to) drugs. Particular attention will be given to whether the celebrity has been manipulative and selective by trying to benefit from a false comparison with other celebrities.

12.17 In the House of Lords in *Campbell*,[30] Lord Hoffman described Ms Campbell as a public figure who had made very public false statements about a matter in respect of which even a public figure would ordinarily be entitled to privacy, namely her use of drugs. It was conceded that these falsehoods made it justifiable for a newspaper to report the fact that Ms Campbell was addicted. Their Lordships were divided only on the question of whether the newspaper went too far in publishing associated facts about her private life. It was emphasised that Ms Campbell had given wide publicity, in interviews with journalists and on television, to a claim which was false, namely that (unlike many of her colleagues in the fashion business) she had not succumbed to the temptation to take drugs. Lord Hoffman accepted[31] that the fact that she had specifically given publicity to the very question of whether she took drugs and had falsely said that she did not created sufficient public interest in the correction of the impression she had previously given.

12.18 Lord Hope pointed out[32] that Ms Campbell had sought to benefit from making comparison with others in the fashion industry and it was the misleading of the public that was important rather than any right the public might have to be given details of her addiction or treatment. He said there were aspects of her exploitation of her status as a celebrity that attracted criticism and that she had been manipulative and selective in what she has revealed about herself. In short, she had engaged in a deliberately false presentation of herself as someone who, in contrast to many models, kept clear of illegal drugs whereas in truth she had made a practice of abusing drugs. In the circumstances she cannot complain when publicity was given to the fact that she was a drug addict. Lord Hope referred the Court of Appeal's observation[33] that where a public figure chooses to make untrue pronouncements about his private life, the press will normally be entitled to put the record straight. But Lord Hope emphasised[34] that it was to be recognised that the right of the public to receive information about the details of her treatment was of a much lower order than the undoubted right to know that she was misleading the public when she said that she did not take drugs.

12.19 In summary, any public interest in seeing role models extol the virtues of avoiding drugs is outweighed by the public interest in having their false statements set straight. The claimant's hypocrisy in *Campbell* made any claim to complete privacy hopeless but the press was, nevertheless, entitled to publish only the minimum necessary to put the record straight.

12.20 Ms Campbell was still undergoing treatment and it was considered that there is a public interest in seeing this is not unduly affected by press intrusion. This part of the

---

[29]   [2003] QB 633, at 658.
[30]   [2004] UKHL 22, at [36] and [38].
[31]   At [58].
[32]   [2004] UKHL 22, at [80] and [82].
[33]   [2003] QB 633, at 658, [43].
[34]   At [117].

balancing exercise was explained by Lady Hale in *Campbell*[35] who questioned why, if a role model adopted a stance which is beneficial rather than detrimental to society, it should be revealed that she has feet of clay. Lady Hale said the possession and use of illegal drugs is a criminal offence and a matter of serious public concern and the press must be free to expose the truth and put the record straight and[36] it was that consideration which justified the publication of the fact that, contrary to her previous statements, Ms Campbell had been involved with illegal drugs. Lady Hale said it also justified publication of the fact that she was trying to do something about it by seeking treatment but that it was not necessary for those purposes to publish any further information, especially if this might jeopardise the continued success of that treatment.

CRIMINALITY

12.21 Where serious criminality is involved it is unlikely a right of privacy will be engaged or confidentiality maintained in respect of such conduct. But there are limits and even in serious cases of criminality any intrusion must be proportionate to be justified. Even serious criminals do not forfeit all their rights to privacy; yet again it depends on the facts. The exercise must be proportionate. For example, *Campbell*[37] involved a claimant who had regularly been in possession of prohibited drugs but that did not automatically undermine her Art 8 rights.[38] This was explained by Eady J in *Mosley v NGN* who said[39] that it is legitimate sometimes to infringe an individual's privacy for the greater good of exposing or detecting crime and that this was expressly recognised in the Press Complaints Commission (PCC) Code in a manner originally derived from the draft attached as a schedule to the Calcutt Report.[40] Eady J said[41] that there must be some limits and, even in more serious cases, any such intrusion should be no more than is proportionate. In *Mosley* itself he said there was no question of a sexual offence being committed, since everything was consensual[42] and[43] even those who have committed serious crimes do not thereby become 'outlaws' so far as their own rights, including rights of personal privacy, are concerned.[44] He said[45] that it was recognised in *Campbell*[46] that drug dependency was a matter which ordinarily a person might expect to keep private (as in the case of other problems affecting health) notwithstanding that it is implicit that the person concerned has regularly been in possession of prohibited drugs. This emphasises that illegal behaviour does not automatically undermine a person's Art 8 rights.

---

[35] At [151].
[36] At [152].
[37] *Campbell v MGN Limited* [2004] UKHL 22.
[38] Lord Hoffman in *Campbell*, at [36], said that 'even a public figure would ordinarily be entitled to privacy ... [about] ... her use of drugs'.
[39] [2008] EWHC 1777 (QB), at [110].
[40] *Report of the Committee on Privacy and Related Matters*, Cm 1102 (1990).
[41] At [111].
[42] At [112].
[43] At [118].
[44] Reference was made eg to *Silver v UK* (1983) 5 EHRR 347 and *Polanski v Condé Nast Publications Ltd* [2005] 1 WLR 637.
[45] At [119].
[46] At [56].

SEXUAL RELATIONSHIPS AND ACTIVITY

12.22 We live in changing times and moral attitudes and religious beliefs can no longer be said to conform to a single recognised standard. Judges and journalists must strive to adopt a neutral moral stance when assessing whether information should be considered private and protected from disclosure. Sexual morality and opinions vary widely over what is and what is not acceptable behaviour. Moral judgments should be avoided when assessing the relative moral value of competing rights and personal distaste put to the side. Competing public interest considerations are what matter not personal preferences. It is not simply a matter of personal privacy versus the public interest. The modern perception is that there is a public interest in respecting personal privacy. It is thus a question of taking account of conflicting public interest considerations and evaluating them according to increasingly well recognised criteria. Eady J said[47] that it is important, in the new rights-based jurisprudence, to ensure that remedies are not refused because journalists or judges find particular conduct distasteful or contrary to moral or religious outlook. Where there has been no breach of the law the private conduct of adults is to be seen as essentially no one else's business. Adulterous relationships and unconventional or even 'perverted' tastes do not give the media *carte blanche*. Eady J explained this in *Mosley*[48] by reference to an extract from the first instance decision in *CC v AB*[49] where it was said that:

> '[25] Judges need to be wary about giving the impression that they are ventilating, while affording or refusing legal redress, some personal moral or social views, and especially at a time when society is far less homogeneous than in the past. At one time, when there was, or was perceived to be, a commonly accepted standard in such matters as sexual morality, it may have been acceptable for the courts to give effect to that standard in exercising discretion or in interpreting legal rights and obligations. Now, however, there is a strong argument for not holding forth about adultery, or attaching greater inherent worth to a relationship which has been formalised by marriage than to any other relationship.
>
> [26] A judge, like anyone else, is obviously entitled to hold personal moral views about the issues of the day, but it is important not to let them intrude when interpreting and applying the law. Such issues are best avoided – at least without some statutory sanction. No doubt many people, especially those with a strong religious faith, will disapprove of adultery. Many others, on the other hand, will not give it a second thought, while moving easily through a series of medium or short-term relationships as they feel it appropriate.
>
> [27] With such a wide range of differing views in society, perhaps more than for many generations, one must guard against allowing legal judgments to be coloured by personal attitudes. Even among judges, there is no doubt a wide range of opinion ...'

12.23 In *Douglas v Hello! Ltd* Keene LJ made reference to the fact that:[50]

> 'The European Court of Human Rights ruled in *Dudgeon v UK* (1981) 4 EHRR 149 that the more intimate the aspect of private life which is being interfered with, the more serious must be the reasons for interference before the latter can be legitimate: see p 165, [52]. Personal sexuality, as in that case, is an extremely intimate aspect of a person's private life.'

---

[47] *Mosley v NGN* [2008] EWHC 1777 (QB), at [128].
[48] At [129].
[49] [2007] EMLR 11 – a decision at first instance which did not go to appeal because permission was refused (in January 2007).
[50] [2001] QB 967 at 168, [2001] 2 WLR 992, [2001] 2 All ER 289.

12.24 In *Stephens v Avery*[51] Sir Nicholas Browne-Wilkinson VC held that information relating to the sex lives of lesbian partners was confidential. He said that:[52]

'In principle, therefore, I can see no reason why information relating to that most private sector of everybody's life, namely sexual conduct, cannot be the subject matter of a legally enforceable duty of confidentiality.'

12.25 Thus sexual relationships and activity are usually treated as confidential and the right to privacy will be engaged in respect of them regardless of whether those involved are public figures or celebrities. It depends on the facts, but good reasons will usually be needed to justify the disclosure of intimate details about a relationship. Casual or even fetishist sex between consenting adults normally will be protected. Strong public policy reasons – such as a contribution to debate on matters of general public interest as opposed to satisfying public curiosity – would be needed before publication of details of a sexual relationship could be justified. Those involved in sexual relationships should normally not reveal private details of the relationship and disclosure of photographs or visual recordings will rarely, if ever, be justified.

12.26 Eady J explained in *Mosley v NGN*[53] that in deciding whether there was a reasonable expectation of privacy the question must be addressed in the light of all the circumstances of the particular case.[54] He said anyone indulging in sexual activity is entitled to a degree of privacy – especially if it is on private property and between consenting adults (paid or unpaid). He referred to the considerable body of jurisprudence in the ECtHR and elsewhere which recognises that sexual activity engages the rights protected by Art 8. Particular reference was made to *Dudgeon v UK*,[55] where it was said there must exist particularly serious reasons before interferences on the part of public authorities can be legitimate for the purposes of Art 8(2) because sexual behaviour 'concerns a most intimate aspect of private life' and[56] that Art 8 rights protect in this respect an essentially private materialisation of the human personality. Eady J made the following points:

- People's sex lives are essentially their own business – provided at least the participants are genuinely consenting adults and there is no question of exploiting the young or vulnerable.

- 'Public figures' are entitled to a private personal life and that the notion of privacy covers not only sexual activities but personal relationships more generally.

- The clandestine recording of sexual activity on private property must be taken to engage Art 8 and those who participate in sexual or personal relationships may be expected not to reveal private conversations or activities.

- Although 'there is no confidence in iniquity' it is highly questionable whether in modern society that is a concept that can be applied to sexual activity, fetishist or otherwise, conducted between consenting adults in private.

---

[51] [1988] Ch 449, [1988] 2 WLR 1280, [1988] 2 All ER 477.
[52] [1988] Ch 449 at 455.
[53] At [99]–[108].
[54] He referred e g to *Murray v Big Pictures* [2008] EWCA Civ 446, at [35]–[39].
[55] (1981) 4 EHRR 149.
[56] See at [60].

- The fact that the claimant paid the women participants would not preclude an obligation of confidence but in the *Mosley* case there was a large element of friendship involved.

- Irrespective of payment, woman E committed an 'old-fashioned breach of confidence' as well as a violation of the Art 8 rights of all those involved.

- When the courts identify an infringement of a person's Art 8 rights, and in particular in the context of their freedom to conduct their sex life and personal relationships as they wish, it is right to afford a remedy and to vindicate that right. The only permitted exception is where there is a countervailing public interest which in the particular circumstances is strong enough to outweigh it; that is to say, because one at least of the established 'limiting principles' comes into play.[57]

- Intimate photographs or recording of private sexual activity, however unconventional, would be extremely difficult to justify at all by ECtHR standards: see, for example, *Dudgeon v UK*,[58] 'titillation for its own sake could never be justified'.[59]

- More recently the principles have been affirmed in the ECtHR in the case of *Leempoel v Belgium*:[60]

    'In matters relating to striking a balance between protecting private life and the freedom of expression ... publication of information, documents or photographs in the press should serve the public interest and make a contribution to the debate of general interest ... the right for the public to be informed ... under particular circumstances may even relate to aspects of the private life of public persons, particularly where political personalities are involved ... publications whose sole aim is to satisfy ... curiosity ... as to the details of the private life of a person, whatever their fame, should not be regarded as contributing to any debate of general interest to society.'

- In the modern climate none of the visual images could be justified in the public interest. Nor could the information conveyed in the verbal descriptions.[61]

CLANDESTINE SURVEILLANCE

12.27 There has, as yet, been no authority in this country where it has been held that the mere fact that a photograph has been taken covertly is sufficient to make the information contained in the photograph confidential. It is necessary for the activity photographed to be private. In most cases, however, the fruit of clandestine or covert activity will be subject to a right of privacy. Eady J referred to the line of authority addressing surveillance and clandestine recording in *Mosley v NGN*.[62] He referred to *PG and JH v UK*,[63] where the Government conceded that secret recording at a flat interfered

---

[57] See at [131].
[58] (1981) 4 EHRR 149, at [49]–[53].
[59] See at [132].
[60] See at [133] and the citations at App No 64772/01, 9 November 2006.
[61] See at [134].
[62] At [103] and [104].
[63] App No 44787/98, BAILII: [2001] ECHR 550.

with rights under Art 8 but unsuccessfully contested the issue in relation to the recordings at the police station. Eady J also referred to *Craxi (No 2) v Italy*,[64] where, in a case concerning the former Prime Minister of Italy, the court held that it was a violation of Art 8 rights to play, even in court in the course of a prosecution for corruption, covertly recorded private telephone conversations. Eady J said that the clandestine recording of sexual activity on private property must be taken to engage Art 8 and that what required closer examination was the extent to which such intrusive behaviour could be justified by reference to a countervailing public interest.

PHOTOGRAPHS

12.28 Photographs are classed as a form of information but they are generally regarded as capable of conveying more information of events and people than narrative description. The Court of Appeal in *Douglas v Hello!*[65] said that special considerations attach to photographs in the field of privacy. It was said that they are not merely a method of conveying information that is an alternative to verbal description but that:[66]

'... they enable the person viewing the photograph to act as a spectator, in some circumstances voyeur would be the more appropriate noun, of whatever it is that the photograph depicts. As a means of invading privacy, a photograph is particularly intrusive. This is quite apart from the fact that the camera, and the telephoto lens, can give access to the viewer of the photograph to scenes where those photographed could reasonably expect that their appearances or actions would not be brought to the notice of the public.'

12.29 The Court of Appeal said that the intrusive nature of photography was reflected by the various media codes of practice and was recognised by the authorities. Reference was made to Ouseley J's judgment in *Theakston v MGN Ltd*:[67]

'The authorities cited to me showed that the courts have consistently recognised that photographs can be particularly intrusive and have showed a high degree of willingness to prevent the publication of photographs, taken without the consent of the person photographed but which the photographer or someone else sought to exploit and publish. This protection extended to photographs, taken without their consent, of people who exploited the commercial value of their own image in similar photographs, and to photographs taken with the consent of people but who had not consented to that particular form of commercial exploitation, as well as to photographs taken in public or from a public place of what could be seen if not with a naked eye, then at least with the aid of powerful binoculars. I concluded that this part of the injunction involved no particular extension of the law of confidentiality and that the publication of such photographs would be particularly intrusive into the claimant's own individual personality. I considered that even though the fact that the claimant went to the brothel and the details as to what he did there were not to be restrained from publication, the publication of photographs taken there without his consent could still constitute an intrusion into his private and personal life and would do so in a peculiarly humiliating and damaging way. It did not seem to be remotely inherent in going to a brothel that what was done inside would be photographed, let alone that any photographs would be published.'

---

64 (2004) 38 EHRR 47.
65 [2005] EWCA Civ 595. See Lord Phillips at [84]–[87].
66 At [84].
67 [2002] EMLR 398, at [78].

12.30 In *D v L* Waller LJ said that:[68]

> 'A court may restrain the publication of an improperly obtained photograph even if the taker is free to describe the information which the photographer provides or even if the information revealed by the photograph is in the public domain. It is no answer to the claim to restrain the publication of an improperly obtained photograph that the information portrayed by the photograph is already available in the public domain.'

12.31 In *Von Hannover v Germany*, the ECtHR remarked that:[69]

> 'Although freedom of expression also extends to the publication of photos, this is an area in which the protection of the rights and reputation of others takes on particular importance. The present case does not concern the dissemination of "ideas", but of images containing very personal or even intimate "information" about an individual. Furthermore, photos appearing in the tabloid press are often taken in a climate of continual harassment which induces in the person concerned a very strong sense of intrusion into their private life or even of persecution.'

12.32 Consideration must always be given to whether it is necessary that the use of photographs to illustrate an article is justified if the privacy of the subject is in issue. Lord Nicholls in *Campbell*[70] that the photographs used did not intrude on the claimant's privacy beyond what was written about her. He said[71] that in general photographs of people contain more information than textual description and that is why they 'are worth a thousand words'.

12.33 Lord Hoffman, when considering the practicalities of journalism in *Campbell*, considered photographs an essential part of a story from a journalistic point of view and would give a fair degree of latitude over where to draw the line in respect of publication of photographs. He thought[72] that it would have been possible for the *Mirror* to have published the article without pictures but that ignored the realities of journalism. Complete precision of judgment about what should be published, whether text or photographs, is impossible. In *Campbell* he thought the pictures were, allowing appropriate latitude, within the margin of editorial judgment.

12.34 The important point was made by Lord Hoffman that sometimes the publication of photographs is not justified even though verbal description of the same matter might be justified. This is because the normal tests must be applied separately to photographs and applying those tests photographs might amount to an unjustified invasion of privacy. Photographs taken without the subject's consent are not, without more, a wrongful invasion of privacy although since *Von Hannover* lack of consent will be of considerable importance. Celebrities must put up with a degree of intrusive photography when out in public and it is not always easy to discern precisely where the line will be drawn. Privacy will probably be found to have been infringed if the published photographs:

- reveal a situation of humiliation or severe embarrassment for the subject even if in a public place; or

[68] [2004] EMLR 1, at [23].
[69] (2004) 40 EHRR 1, at para 59.
[70] *Campbell v MGN Limited* [2004] UKHL 22.
[71] At [31].
[72] At [77].

- result from intrusion into a private place such as with a long distance lens regardless of whether the images are embarrassing.

12.35 Lord Hoffman explained these issues in *Campbell* as follows:

'[72] ... a photograph is in principle information no different from any other information. It may be a more vivid form of information than the written word ("a picture is worth a thousand words"). That has to be taken into account in deciding whether its publication infringes the right to privacy of personal information. The publication of a photograph cannot necessarily be justified by saying that one would be entitled to publish a verbal description of the scene: see *Douglas v Hello! Ltd* [2001] QB 967. But the principles by which one decides whether or not the publication of a photograph is an unjustified invasion of the privacy of personal information are in my opinion the same as those which I have already discussed.

[73] ... the pictures were taken without Ms Campbell's consent. That in my opinion is not enough to amount to a wrongful invasion of privacy. The famous and even the not so famous who go out in public must accept that they may be photographed without their consent, just as they may be observed by others without their consent. As Gleeson CJ said in *Australian Broadcasting Corpn v Lenah Game Meats Pty Ltd* (2001) 185 ALR 1, 13, para 41:

"Part of the price we pay for living in an organised society is that we are exposed to observation in a variety of ways by other people."

[74] ... the fact that we cannot avoid being photographed does not mean that anyone who takes or obtains such photographs can publish them to the world at large. In the recent case of *Peck v United Kingdom* (2003) 36 EHRR 41 Mr Peck was filmed on a public street in an embarrassing moment by a CCTV camera. Subsequently, the film was broadcast several times on the television. The Strasbourg court said (at p 739) that this was an invasion of his privacy contrary to art 8:

"the relevant moment was viewed to an extent which far exceeded any exposure to a passer-by or to security observation and to a degree surpassing that which the applicant could possibly have foreseen when he walked in Brentwood on August 20, 1995."

[75] ... the widespread publication of a photograph of someone which reveals him to be in a situation of humiliation or severe embarrassment, even if taken in a public place, may be an infringement of the privacy of his personal information. Likewise, the publication of a photograph taken by intrusion into a private place (for example, by a long distance lens) may in itself be such an infringement, even if there is nothing embarrassing about the picture itself: *Hellewell v Chief Constable of Derbyshire* [1985] 1 WLR 804, 807. As Lord Mustill said in *R (on the application of BBC) v Broadcasting Standards Commission* [2001] QB 885, [2000] 3 All ER 989, 900:

"An infringement of privacy is an affront to the personality, which is damaged both by the violation and by the demonstration that the personal space is not inviolate."'

12.36 Lord Hope in *Campbell* drew the important distinction in respect of photographs taken in public between where an individual appears incidentally in a photograph of, say, a public scene and where the individual is the deliberate subject of the photograph, albeit taken in public. He thought that celebrities cannot complain if the photographs are taken to show a street scene and later published to show a street scene even if a celebrity happens to be in the photographs. The position is different, however, if the celebrity is the deliberate subject of the photograph. Lord Hope identified the issue as being whether the public's right to information can justify the dissemination of a photograph without authorisation. He said that:

'[122] ... The taking of photographs in a public street must ... be taken to be one of the ordinary incidents of living in a free community ... A person who just happens to be in the street when the photograph was taken and appears in it only incidentally cannot as a general rule object to the publication of the photograph ... But the situation is different if the public nature of the place where a photograph is taken was simply used as background for one or more persons who constitute the true subject of the photograph. The question then arises [whether] the public's right to information can justify dissemination of a photograph taken without authorisation ... a person who walks down a public street will inevitably be visible to any member of the public who is also present and, in the same way, to a security guard viewing the scene through closed circuit television ... But ... private life considerations may arise once any systematic or permanent record comes into existence of such material from the public domain. In *Peck v United Kingdom* [2003] 36 EHRR 719, para 62 the court held that the release and publication of CCTV footage which showed the applicant in the process of attempting to commit suicide resulted in the moment being viewed to an extent that far exceeded any exposure to a passer-by or to security observation that he could have foreseen when he was in that street.

[123] ... Miss Campbell could not have complained if the photographs had been taken to show the scene in the street by a passer-by and later published simply as street scenes. But these were ... taken deliberately, in secret and with a view to their publication in conjunction with the article. The zoom lens was directed at the doorway of the place where the meeting had been taking place ... the photographs were published and her privacy was invaded ...

[124] Any person ... assuming her to be of ordinary sensibilities but assuming also that she had been photographed surreptitiously outside the place where she been receiving therapy for drug addiction ... would have been distressed on seeing the photographs. She would have seen their publication, in conjunction with ... details about her engagement in the therapy, as a gross interference with her right to respect for her private life ...'

12.37 The fact that in this country we have not developed an image right was highlighted by Lady Hale in *Campbell*.[73] Celebrities have no control over the publication of photographs of their image save to the extent of existing causes of action such as the developing law of privacy. The views expressed in *Campbell* about the inability of celebrities to complain about photographs of them going about their business in a public street may need to be adjusted in view of *Von Hannover*. Lady Hale referred to the impact of photographs and their potentially damaging effects:

'[154] Publishing the photographs contributed both to the revelation and to the harm that it might do. By themselves, they are not objectionable. Unlike France and Quebec, in this country we do not recognise a right to one's own image: cf *Aubry v Les Éditions Vice-versa Inc* [1998] 1 SCR 591. We have not so far held that the mere fact of covert photography is sufficient to make the information contained in the photograph confidential. The activity photographed must be private. If this had been, and had been presented as, a picture of Naomi Campbell going about her business in a public street, there could have been no complaint ... Readers will obviously be interested to see how she looks if and when she pops out to the shops for a bottle of milk. There is nothing essentially private about that information nor can it be expected to damage her private life ... there is nothing to justify interfering with it. (This was the view of Randerson J in *Hosking v Runting* [2003] 3 NZLR 385, which concerned a similarly innocuous outing; see now the decision of the Court of Appeal, 25 March 2004.)

---

73   At [154] and [155].

[155] ... A picture is "worth a thousand words" because it adds to the impact of what the words convey; but it also adds to the information given in those words ...'

12.38 Lord Carswell in *Campbell*[74] emphasised the power of the photographic image in *Campbell*. He said that photographs are a powerful prop to a written article and a much-valued part of newspaper reporting, especially in the tabloid or popular press and thought the Court of Appeal dismissed them too readily as adding little to the reports already published. He said the Court of Appeal was not justified in rejecting the judge's conclusions on this.

12.39 Photographs can be considered private (and their publication actionable) even though the celebrity subjects of the photographs are perfectly content for them to be published provided that publication is on the celebrities' terms. In referring to *Douglas v Hello!*, Buxton LJ in *McKennitt v Ash*,[75] said that in *Douglas* it was concluded that:

'[14] ... unauthorised photographs of a wedding were private even though the couple were perfectly content, indeed contractually bound, to allow authorised photographs of the same event to be published ...

[22] ... But the Judge [pointed] out that it should have been and was obvious that events in a person's home cannot be lightly intruded upon ... And I would also respectfully agree with his comparison with long distance photography, an exercise generally considered to raise privacy issues ...'

12.40 The Court of Appeal in *Murray v Big Pictures Limited*[76] referred to the important distinction drawn by Lord Hoffmann in *Campbell* between the mere taking of a photograph and its publication. The Court of Appeal provided a useful summary of the principles when considering the approach to be taken to the publication of photographs. This is essentially whether there is a reasonable expectation of privacy in respect of the publication of the photograph(s) in question:

'[35] ... so far as the relevant principles to be derived from *Campbell* are concerned, they can we think be summarised in this way. The first question is whether there is a reasonable expectation of privacy. This is of course an objective question. The nature of the question was discussed in *Campbell*. Lord Hope emphasised that the reasonable expectation was that of the person who is affected by the publicity. He said at [99]:

"The question is what a reasonable person of ordinary sensibilities would feel if she was placed in the same position as the claimant and faced with the same publicity."

We do not detect any difference between Lord Hope's opinion in this regard and the opinions expressed by the other members of the appellate committee.

[36] As we see it, the question whether there is a reasonable expectation of privacy is a broad one, which takes account of all the circumstances of the case. They include the attributes of the claimant, the nature of the activity in which the claimant was engaged, the place at which it was happening, the nature and purpose of the intrusion, the absence of consent and whether it was known or could be inferred, the effect on the claimant and the circumstances in which and the purposes for which the information came into the hands of the publisher.'

---

[74] At [165].
[75] [2006] EWCA Civ 1714 at [14] and [22].
[76] [2008] EWCA Civ 446.

12.41 Not 'every gory detail' need be made public even in cases where privacy cannot otherwise be enforced. Photographs are especially intrusive because they enable the viewer to act as a spectator or voyeur of what is depicted. Long lens photography intrudes into spaces those photographed would reasonably believe were entirely private. The publication of photographs (particularly with salacious detail) may be considered disproportionate and unreasonable even where a story of the same events might not be. The public interest test needs to be applied to each *separate* piece of information to determine whether or not publication is justified. Both the means by which photographs are obtained and the fact of their proposed publication should be tested against the public interest. The publication of improperly obtained photographs might be restrained even where the subject matter of the photographs is in the public domain and might be freely reported on. The central issue is whether or not visual images are a reasonable method of conveying the information concerned; in effect, it is a question of proportionality. The publication of visual images of sexual activity on private property will rarely, if ever, be justified. Eady J explained the significance of visual images in *Mosley*. He made reference to the PCC Editors' Code[77] and said that sometimes there may be a good case for revealing the fact of wrongdoing to the general public; it will not necessarily follow that photographs of 'every gory detail' also need to be published to achieve the public interest objective. Nor will it automatically justify clandestine recording, whether visual or audio. So much is acknowledged in the relevant section of the PCC Editors' Code at clause 10:

'i)   The press must not seek to obtain or publish material acquired by using hidden cameras or clandestine listening devices; or by intercepting private or mobile telephone calls, messages or emails; or by the unauthorised removal of documents or photographs or by accessing digitally-held private information without consent.

ii)   Engaging in misrepresentation or subterfuge, including by agents or intermediaries, can generally be justified only in the public interest and then only when the material cannot be obtained by other means.'

12.42 Eady J in *Mosley*[78] said although the very fact of clandestine recording was an intrusion and an unacceptable infringement of Art 8 rights, a separate issue needed to be considered as to the appropriateness of publication of such photographs either on a limited basis or generally to the world at large. He pointed out that the intrusive nature of photography was fully discussed in the ECtHR in *Von Hannover v Germany*[79] and also in domestic jurisprudence, the point having been articulated by Waller LJ in *D v L*:[80]

'A court may restrain the publication of an improperly obtained photograph even if the taker is free to describe the information which the photographer provides or even if the information revealed by the photograph is in the public domain. It is no answer to the claim to restrain the publication of an improperly obtained photograph that the information portrayed by the photograph is already available in the public domain.'

12.43 Normally, the addition of salacious details or intimate photographs will be considered disproportionate and unacceptable, even if they accompany a legitimate disclosure of the sexual relationship, because they would be too intrusive and

77   At [16].
78   At [17] and [18].
79   (2005) 40 EHRR 1.
80   [2004] EMLR 1, at [23].

demeaning. Thus, Eady J said[81] that even if the subject-matter is a matter of public interest showing a film or photographs is not always a reasonable method of conveying that information – it is a question of proportionality. He pointed out[82] that an injunction was granted by Ouseley J in *Theakston v MGN Ltd*[83] to restrain publication of photographs taken inside a brothel, even though it was recognised that it was not appropriate to restrain verbal descriptions of what occurred there.[84]

12.44 The provisions contained in s 85 of the Copyright, Designs and Patents Act 1988 give a right to privacy in certain photographs and films which have been commissioned. It provides that where a person commissions the taking of a photograph or the making of a film for private and domestic purposes, and where copyright subsists in the resulting work, that person has the moral right not to have copies of the work issued to the public, the work exhibited or shown in public or the work communicated to the public. Section 103 provides that an infringement of a moral right is actionable as a breach of statutory duty owed to the person entitled to the right.

COVERT PHOTOGRAPHY IN PUBLIC PLACES

12.45 Clause 3(i) of the Code of Practice of the PCC states that a person may have a reasonable expectation of privacy in a public place. Public places can plainly be part of a celebrity's 'private space' or 'zone of interaction with others' deserving of protection. *Von Hannover*[85] was of considerable assistance in clarifying the law in this area and statements made in *Campbell*[86] need to be considered carefully in the light of the more recent ECtHR decision. The fact that protection from publication might be given in respect of photographs of celebrities in public places was argued to amount to recognition of a form of 'image right' under our law. This notion was rejected by Lady Hale in *Campbell* – there is no image right. Celebrities have a right to protect their privacy not their image as such. Statements were made in *Campbell* about what activities a celebrity might undertake in public which might or might not be protectable. Lady Hale[87] contrasted the position here with France and Quebec. In this country we do not recognise a right to one's own image.[88] Lady Hale said that if the picture had been of Ms Campbell going about non-private business in a public street, there could have been no complaint. It was thought there was nothing essentially private or damaging to her private life about how Ms Campbell might look when out at the shops for a bottle of milk. Although it might not be of a high order of freedom of speech it was thought there was nothing to justify interfering with it.[89] This view might need to be adjusted in the light of subsequent decisions.

12.46 In *McKennitt v Ash*[90] Buxton LJ made reference to the tension existing between *Campbell* and *Von Hannover* in relation to the extent of privacy a celebrity might expect

---

81 At [21].
82 At [23].
83 [2002] EMLR 22.
84 The passage in Ousley J's judgment giving reasons for restraining publication of the photographs was cited and endorsed by the Court of Appeal in *Douglas v Hello! Ltd (No 3)* [2005] EWCA Civ 595, at [85].
85 *Von Hannover v Germany* (2005) 40 EHRR 1.
86 *Campbell v MGN* [2002] EWCA Civ 1373, [2003] QB 633, [2003] 1 All ER 224.
87 At [154].
88 Lady Hale referred to *Aubry v Les Éditions Vice-versa Inc* [1998] 1 SCR 591.
89 This followed the view of Randerson J in *Hosking v Runting* [2003] 3 NZLR 385, which concerned a similarly innocuous outing; see now the decision of the Court of Appeal, 25 March 2004.
90 [2006] EWCA Civ 1714.

when out in public on routine, even mundane, activities. It was said in *Von Hannover* that there was a zone of interaction a person may have with others, even in a public context, which may fall within the scope of 'private life' and that the publication of photographs of Princess Caroline in her daily life either alone or with others fell within the scope of her private life. *Von Hannover* cannot be explained away simply as a case involving a campaign of media intrusion. Buxton LJ said:

'[38] Princess Caroline of Monaco sought to prevent the publication in two German magazines of photographs of her indulging in ... fairly banal activities in public or effectively public places. The ... most general statement was in [the ECtHR's] para 50, cited by Eady J ...:

"... private life, in the court's view, includes a person's physical and psychological integrity; the guarantee afforded by article 8 of the Convention is primarily intended to ensure the development, without outside interference, of the personality of each individual in his relations with other human beings ... There is therefore a zone of interaction of a person with others, even in a public context, which may fall within the scope of 'private life'."'

12.47 Buxton LJ said that based on that general principle, the ECtHR held, in its para 53, that:

'... in the present case there is no doubt that the publication by various German magazines of photos of the Applicant in her daily life either on her own or with other people falls within the scope of her private life.'

12.48 Buxton LJ thought[91] that it was far from clear that the House of Lords which decided *Campbell* would have handled the facts of *Von Hannover* in the same way as did the ECtHR. The House of Lords needed great persuasion before allowing Ms Campbell to enjoin the publication of photographs of her in the public street, and then only because of their connection with her medical condition. Buxton LJ thought that had the House had the benefit of *Von Hannover* a shorter course might have been taken. He said[92] that the English courts should give respectful attention to *Von Hannover* and that it remains for the national courts to apply Art 8 case-law, as it currently stands, to the facts before it. He continued[93] by rejecting the argument that the ECtHR went no further in *Von Hannover* than to hold that the Princess's privacy had been invaded by a campaign of media intrusion into her life, of which the enjoined photographs were the fruit. He referred to authority from the ECtHR decided since *Von Hannover* that applies those statements in situations that were not ones of media intrusion, in particular *Sciacca v Italy*[94] which applied *Von Hannover* to a case that was not one of press harassment and cited *Von Hannover* in entirely general terms.

---

[91]   At [39].
[92]   At [40].
[93]   At [41].
[94]   App No 50774/99, at paras 27 and 29 of the judgment of the ECtHR.

MEDICAL TREATMENT/HEALTH

Drugs

12.49 Information about medical treatment is usually considered both obviously confidential and private as being intimately bound in with human autonomy and dignity. In *Campbell*[95] Lord Hoffman said he considered details of a non-celebrity's drug treatment to be plainly private:

> '[53] …The judge found that the information about Ms Campbell's attendance at NA had been communicated to the *Mirror* in breach of confidence and that the *Mirror* must have known that the information was confidential. As for human autonomy and dignity, I should have thought that the extent to which information about one's state of health, including drug dependency, should be communicated to other people was plainly something which an individual was entitled to decide for herself … If Ms Campbell had been an ordinary citizen, I think that the publication of information about her attendance at NA would have been actionable …

> [71] As for the Court of Appeal's own approach … [i]t was saying only that the support provided by NA for large numbers of drug addicts is so well known that it cannot be compared with the details of individual clinical treatment. This seems to me no more than common sense.'

12.50 The public interest in protecting details of treatment for addiction was highlighted in *Campbell* by Lord Hope who pointed to the adverse affect of unjustified intrusion on medical treatment and the likelihood it would be particularly distressful. He thought publication of intrusive details of group therapy will be justified only in extreme case such as *Campbell* itself and thought[96] few areas needed privacy more than combating addiction to drugs or alcohol because intrusion may cause treatment to be delayed or curtailed. Ms Campbell's attendance at Narcotics Anonymous was plainly considered to be private because an assurance of privacy is essential to the treatment and Lord Hope thought[97] great weight attached to the fact that publication of details of her treatment coupled with covertly taken photographs had potential to cause harm.

12.51 Lord Hope said[98] that where a person is undergoing treatment, in order to assess whether disclosure would be objectionable, one must put oneself into the shoes of a reasonable person in need of that treatment. Otherwise, he thought, the exercise is divorced from its context: that of a drug addict receiving treatment.

12.52 The sensibilities of a reasonable person in the position of the addict needed to be taken into account and it is critical whether disclosure might disrupt treatment. The question is what a reasonable person of ordinary sensibilities would feel if placed in the same position as the claimant and faced with the same publicity. Lord Hope[99] referred to *P v D*[100] where the claimant, a public figure, was told that the fact he had been treated at a psychiatric hospital was about to go public. Lord Hope considered that the objective test was correctly described and applied by Nicholson J in that case[101] when he said:

---

95   [2004] UKHL 22.
96   See at [81].
97   See at [119].
98   See at [98] and [99].
99   At [100].
100   [2000] 2 NZLR 591.
101   At [39].

'The factor that the matter must be one which would be highly offensive and objectionable to a reasonable person of ordinary sensibilities prescribes an objective test. But this is on the basis of what a reasonable person of ordinary sensibilities would feel if they were in the same position, that is, in the context of the particular circumstances. I accept that P has the stated feelings and consider that a reasonable person of ordinary sensibilities would in the circumstances also find publication of information that they had been a patient in a psychiatric hospital highly offensive and objectionable.'

Other medical treatment (non-drugs)

12.53 Confidentiality in respect of medical treatment arises both from the confidential nature of the doctor-patient relationship and from the nature of the information itself. Such information has dual protection:

- breach of confidence (arising from the nature of the doctor-patient relationship and from the confidential nature of the information itself); and

- misuse of private information (arising from the fact that the information is such that a reasonable expectation of privacy is likely in respect of it).

12.54 As a matter of public policy patients must feel that medical confidences (often involving intimate personal details) are strictly protected from disclosure otherwise medical treatment and the profession generally will be undermined. The public interest demands that medical confidences are strictly enforced.

12.55 Lady Hale in *Campbell* thought it was a matter of balancing competing public interest considerations on the facts of any particular case. She said[102] that that it had always been accepted that information about a person's health and treatment for ill health is both private and confidential and this stems not only from the confidentiality of the doctor-patient relationship but also from the nature of the information itself. As the European Court of Human Rights put it in *Z v Finland*:[103]

'Respecting the confidentiality of health data is a vital principle in the legal systems of all the Contracting Parties to the Convention. It is crucial not only to respect the sense of privacy of a patient but also to preserve his or her confidence in the medical profession and in the health services in general. Without such protection, those in need of medical assistance may be deterred from revealing such information of a personal and intimate nature as may be necessary in order to receive appropriate treatment and, even, from seeking such assistance, thereby endangering their own health and, in the case of transmissible diseases, that of the community.'

12.56 Lady Hale in *Campbell*[104] said that *all* of the information about Ms Campbell's addiction and attendance at Narcotics Anonymous was both private and confidential because:

- it related to an important aspect of her physical and mental health and the treatment she was receiving for it; and

- it had been received from an insider in breach of confidence.

---

[102]   At [145].
[103]   (1997) 25 EHRR 371, at para 95.
[104]   At [147].

She said the starting point must be that it was all private and its publication required specific justification.

12.57 Lord Carswell in *Campbell* considered that information about therapy from Narcotics Anonymous and details of a medical condition were both private and he did not accept that a distinction could be drawn between the two.[105] He considered that the information was all private and that the publication of the details of the course of treatment at Narcotics Anonymous and of the photographs taken surreptitiously in the street of her emerging from a meeting went significantly beyond the publication of the fact that she was receiving therapy or that she was engaged in a course of therapy with Narcotics Anonymous. Lord Carswell said it intruded into what had some of the characteristics of medical treatment and it tended to deter her from continuing the treatment which was in her interest.

12.58 The fact that medical information is both confidential and private and, in consequence, subject to a high degree of protection from disclosure was emphasised by Buxton LJ in *McKennitt v Ash*[106] who said[107] that a person's health is in any event a private matter, as the *Campbell* case demonstrated and is doubly private when information about it is imparted in the context of a relationship of confidence.

12.59 Not every statement about a person's health will be considered confidential or risk harming that person's physical or moral integrity. Lady Hale pointed out[108] that it is not always easy to discern from the authorities precisely what information is protected, for example, are mundane or routine details such as a cold or broken leg likely to be categorised as private information? Lady Hale thought that the privacy interest in the fact that a public figure has a cold or a broken leg is unlikely to be strong enough to justify restricting the press's freedom to report it. This view may need to be adjusted in view of later pronouncements in *Von Hannover*[109] and *McKennitt v Ash*. For Lady Hale it was the risk of harm that was what mattered at this stage rather than the proof that actual harm has occurred.

CHILDREN OF CELEBRITIES/CHILD CELEBRITIES

12.60 Children of celebrities have an independent right to have their privacy respected irrespective of their parents' own right to privacy. In some situations celebrity parents might be unable to object to press intrusion but this does not mean their children cannot complain. It is not artificial for celebrity parents to bring proceedings on behalf of their children to protect their children's privacy. The substance of complaint is the unauthorised publication of private information about the children of celebrities and the matter should be viewed from the perspective of both the parents and the child.

12.61 In the case involving the well-known author JK Rowling (*Murray v Big Pictures Limited*[110]) the Court of Appeal said that in that case it was not the taking of the photographs that was the problem so much as their subsequent publication. It was

---

[105] See at [164] and [165].
[106] [2005] EWCA Civ 595.
[107] At [23].
[108] *Campbell*, at [157].
[109] *Von Hannover v Germany* (2005) 40 EHRR 1.
[110] [2008] EWCA Civ 446.

emphasised[111] that children have their own right to respect for their privacy distinct from that of their parents. Although a small child is probably oblivious of photographs being taken and therefore neither distressed nor harassed as a result of the taking (or indeed publication) of photographs the Court of Appeal disagreed that the issue of principle was as described by the judge:

> '... whether the Claimant who is not a public figure in his own right but is the child of one, is entitled to protection from being photographed in a public place even where a photograph shows nothing embarrassing or untoward but in which he is shown depicted with his parents.'

12.62 The Court of Appeal said[112] that it depends on all the circumstances whether taking a photograph of a child in a public place would engage Art 8 of the ECHR. In *Murray* it was not a case of a single photograph taken in the street but clandestine taking and subsequent publication of a series of photographs taken for sale for publication, in circumstances in which it reasonable to infer consent would have been refused.

12.63 Young children generally would not be too concerned about being photographed in the street when out with their parents or that photographs of them were in the papers. Parents can still protect their children's private lives looking at the situation objectively taking into account the reasonable expectations of both the children and their celebrity parents. Whether a child has a reasonable expectation of privacy must be considered in the light of what the child's celebrity parents would reasonably expect in any given set of circumstances. Celebrities who thrust their children into the limelight can reasonably expect less in the way of a private life for their children than those who jealously guard their children's privacy. This was made clear by the Patten J, the judge at first instance in *Murray v Big Pictures*, whose views, in that regard, were approved by the Court of Appeal:[113]

> '[23] This test cannot, of course, be applied to a child of the Claimant's age who has no obvious sensitivity to any invasion of his privacy which does not involve some direct physical intrusion into his personal space. A literal application of Lord Hope's words would lead to a rejection of any claim by an infant unless it related to harassment of an extreme kind. A proper consideration of the degree of protection to which a child is entitled under Art. 8 has, I think, for the reasons which I gave earlier to be considered in a wider context by taking into account not only the circumstances in which the photograph was taken and its actual impact on the child, but also the position of the child's parents and the way in which the child's life as part of that family has been conducted. This merely reinforces my view about the artificiality of bringing the claim in the name of the child. The question whether a child in any particular circumstances has a reasonable expectation for privacy must be determined by the Court taking an objective view of the matter including the reasonable expectations of his parents in those same circumstances as to whether their children's lives in a public place should remain private. Ultimately it will be a matter of judgment for the Court with every case depending upon its own facts. The point that needs to be emphasized is that the assessment of the impact of the taking and the subsequent publication of the photograph on the child cannot be limited by whether the child was physically aware of the photograph being taken or published or personally affected by it. The Court can attribute to the child reasonable expectations about his private life based on matters such as how it has in fact been conducted by those responsible for his welfare and upbringing.'

---

[111] At [16].
[112] At [17].
[113] See [2008] EWCA Civ 446, at [37], referring to the judgment at first instance, [2007] EWHC 1908 (Ch), at [23].

12.64 Parents who courted publicity by procuring the publication of photographs of their child to promote their own interests might be treated quite differently parents who have taken care to keep their children out of the public gaze. The Court of Appeal in *Murray*[114] emphasised that at each stage the questions to be determined are essentially questions of fact. The courts will always be astute generally to protect children.[115] Such protection will extend to their private lives and that all things being equal children of celebrity parents should be able to expect the same protection for their private lives as children of non-celebrity parents. One acid test is whether or not material would be published irrespective of whether the child had a celebrity parent. The publication of photographs taken surreptitiously and not authorised by the parent or child is difficult to justify.

12.65 The Court of Appeal, in relation to JK Rowling's son in *Murray v Big Pictures*,[116] said that it was at least arguable the child had a reasonable expectation of privacy and the fact that he was a child had greater significance than the judge thought. Children have rights in many different contexts and this is recognised by the international community.[117] Clause 6 of the PCC Editors' Code of Practice contains this sentence under the heading Children:

> 'v) Editors must not use the fame, notoriety or position of the parent or guardian as sole justification for publishing details of a child's private life.'

12.66 Reference was made by the Court of Appeal to a publication called *The Editors' Codebook*, which refers to the Code and to the above statement. The Court of Appeal thought that it all depended on the facts although it did point to the Codebook which states[118] in a section headed 'Intrusion' that the PCC has ruled that the mere publication of a child's image cannot breach the Code when it is taken in a public place and is unaccompanied by any private details or materials which might embarrass or inconvenience the child. The Court of Appeal[119] made reference to *Tugendhat and Christie* on *The Law of Privacy and the Media*[120] and to the fact that the PCC has stated that:

> '... the acid test to be applied by newspapers in writing about the children of public figures who are not famous in their own right (unlike the Royal Princes) is whether a newspaper would write such a story if it was about an ordinary person.'

12.67 The following general statements, made by the Court of Appeal in relation to privacy and children, particularly photographs,[121] are a useful guide in this area:

- it is at least arguable that photographs of children should be approached in a similar way to writing about them;

---

[114] At [41].
[115] Baroness Hale in *Campbell* at [157].
[116] At [45].
[117] See eg *R v Central Independent Television Plc* [1994] Fam 192, at 204–205, per Hoffmann LJ; and the UN Convention on the Rights of the Child, to which the UK is a party.
[118] At p 51.
[119] At [46].
[120] At para 13.128 (in connection with a complaint made by Mr and Mrs Blair).
[121] See at [47], [50] and [54].

- if a child of parents who are not in the public eye could reasonably expect not to have photographs of himself published in the media, so too should the child of a famous parent;

- it is at least arguable that children of 'ordinary' parents could reasonably expect that the press would not target them and publish photographs of them;

- Connell J in *MGN Ltd v Attard*[122] expressed doubts as to whether Art 8 was engaged in respect of the publication of a photograph taken in a Malta street of the survivor of conjoined twins (but the facts were very different because the parents would have permitted publication if they could have agreed a price with the newspaper);

- parents' wishes, on behalf of their children, to protect their freedom to live normal lives without the constant fear of media intrusion are (at least arguably) entirely reasonable and, other things being equal, should be protected by the law;

- photographs once published would be disseminated to a potentially large number of people on the basis that they were children of well-known parents, leading to the possibility of further intrusion in the future;

- if the photographs had been taken to show the scene in a street by a passer-by and later published as street scenes, that would be one thing, but photographs taken deliberately, in secret and with a view to their subsequent publication, is different particularly where it is known or can be inferred that the parents would have objected to them;

- the focus should not be on the taking of a photograph in the street, but on its publication;

- in the absence of distress or the like caused when the photograph is taken, the mere taking of a photograph in the street may well be entirely unobjectionable; and

- the application of these principles will not have created an image right.

12.68 It is not possible to be prescriptive about what circumstances would give rise to a child having a reasonable expectation of privacy; the underlying point is that children can reasonably expect to be protected from undue media intrusion and, in particular, from being targeted by the press. The Court of Appeal, in *Murray v Big Pictures*,[123] said that a clear distinction cannot be drawn, in principle, between a child (or an adult) engaged in family and sporting activities and something as simple as a walk down a street or a visit to the grocers to buy the milk. An expedition to a café, at least arguably, was considered to be recreation time which might be adversely affected by intrusive publicity by disrupting such trips in the future. It depends on the circumstances whether routine acts such as a visit to a shop or a ride on a bus should attract a reasonable expectation of privacy.

---

[122] Unreported, 9 October 2001.
[123] At [55].

12.69 Subject to the facts of the particular case, the Court of Appeal in *Murray*[124] considered that the law should protect children from intrusive media attention, at any rate to the extent of holding that children have a reasonable expectation that they will not be targeted in order to obtain photographs in a public place for publication which the person taking the photographs knew would be objected to on behalf of the child. This would not mean children are guaranteed privacy – a reasonable expectation of privacy is only the first step. There must still be a balance between the child's right to privacy under Art 8 and the publisher's rights to freedom of expression under Art 10. This approach is consistent to the approach in *Von Hannover*, to which it is permissible to have regard. In that case the campaign of harassment conducted by the German media was part of the context in which the decision was made. Some of the published photographs held to infringe Princess Caroline's Art 8 rights showed her doing no more than walking in public.

CHILDREN OF CELEBRITIES IN DIVORCE PROCEEDINGS

12.70 A particular problem arises when the children of celebrities become embroiled in divorce proceedings between their parents. The appetite for 'human interest' stories in relation to celebrity parents means the press will want to attend hearings and may be entitled to by virtue of a recent amendment to the Family Proceedings Rules 1991. The issues involved in such cases were dealt with by Sir Mark Potter P in *Re X (a child) (residence and contact: rights of media attendance)*.[125] In that case the court heard an application that the media be excluded altogether from their presumptive right under r 10.28 to be present at proceedings for the purpose of exercising a watchdog role, albeit with limited reporting rights. The court ultimately made a direction excluding the media from attending the proceedings, or any part of them, on the basis that it was necessary in the interests of the child concerned in the proceedings and because justice would otherwise be impeded.

12.71 It was emphasised by the President that private law family cases concerning the children of celebrities are no different in principle from those involving the children of anyone else. Applications by celebrities who cannot agree over appropriate arrangements for their children have no more right to request privacy than other parents caught up in the court process. It is the interests of the child not the parents that matter. Press interest is, of course, more intense in the case of children of celebrities and there is greater danger that information will be leaked to the public so there is often more need to protect them from intrusion or publicity.

12.72 *Re X (a child)* concerned residence and contact in relation to the young daughter of 'celebrity' parents. A county court judge had made an order prohibiting the publication of information about the child until she reached her 18th birthday but this was in breach of the President's Direction dated 18 March 2005[126] and went beyond the scope of s 12(1) of the Administration of Justice Act 1960 (AJA 1960) and s 97(2) of the Children Act 1989. Such orders can only be made in the High Court and the application for the order should have been founded on Convention rights and was subject to s 12(2) of the Human Rights Act 1998 (HRA 1998) (ie injunctions restricting the exercise of the right to freedom of expression must not be granted where the person against whom

---

[124]   See at [57], [58] and [59].
[125]   [2009] EWHC 1728 (Fam).
[126]   [2005] 2 FLR 120.

the application is made is neither present nor represented unless the court is satisfied (a) that the applicant has taken all practical steps to notify the respondent or (b) that there are compelling reasons why the respondent should not be notified).

12.73 Paragraph 2 of the President's Direction sets out provisions for service of the application on the National News Media via the Press Association's CopyDirect Service. The Family Proceedings (Amendment No 2) Rules 2009 (SI 2009/857) inserted into the FPR a new r 10.28, which provides that during a hearing held in private duly accredited media representatives (previously excluded) are permitted to be present, subject to the power for the court to direct their exclusion during all or part of the proceedings for one of a number of reasons specified in para 4 of the new rule.

12.74 The ECtHR in *B v United Kingdom*[127] said that residence and contact proceedings are prime examples of cases where the exclusion of the press and public may be justified in order to protect the privacy of the child and/or the parties and to avoid prejudicing the interests of justice. The ECtHR said[128] that it is essential that the parents and other witnesses feel able to express themselves candidly on highly personal issues without fear of public curiosity or comment. The court also said[129] that while Art 6(1) states a general rule that civil proceedings should take place in public it was not inconsistent with this provision for a state to designate juveniles as an exception to the general rule where their interests require it for the protection of the private life of the parties.

12.75 Rule 10.28 confers upon the media in the form of 'duly accredited representatives of news gathering and reporting organisations' the right to be present at private hearings of children proceedings, subject to the court directing that they may not attend on grounds set out in r 10.28(4)(a) and (b).

12.76 If media representatives attend the proceedings the press are entitled to report on the nature of the dispute and to identify the issues and the identity of the participating witnesses (unless that would reveal the child's identity) but not to set out the evidence or details of matters investigated by the court. The media thus exercises a role of 'watchdog' for the purpose of informed comment upon the court's workings and the behaviour of its judges.

12.77 The President thought it was incumbent upon an applicant who wished to exclude the media from a substantive hearing *ab initio* to raise the matter with the court prior to the hearing for the court to consider whether the media should be notified in advance of the proposed application and whether notification should be via the CopyDirect service in accordance with the procedure provided for in the CAFCASS Practice Note.

12.78 In deciding whether or not to exclude the press in the welfare or privacy interests of a party or third party the court must conduct a balancing exercise in accordance with the principles enunciated in *Campbell*[130] and in *Re S (A Child)*[131] regarding the

---

[127]   (2001) 34 EHRR 529.
[128]   At para 38.
[129]   At para 39.
[130]   [2004] UKHL 22, [2004] 2 AC 457, [2004] 2 All ER 995.
[131]   [2004] UKHL 47, [2005] 1 AC 593, [2004] 4 All ER 683.

interplay between Arts 8 and 10 of the ECHR. The specific points the court will take into account when considering whether or not to exclude the press under r 10.28(4)(a)(i) are as follows:

(1)   The focus is upon the interests of the child and not the parents.

(2)   The court must be satisfied that it is *necessary* to do so.

(3)   The media's clear prima facie right to be present during the proceedings, subject only to exclusion on limited grounds, is plainly Convention compliant from the point of view of the media's Art 10 rights.

(4)   The court strictly does not have a *discretion* to exclude media representatives from all or part of the proceedings so much as a duty to apply a test of necessity in relation to a series of questions as to legitimacy and proportionality through the balancing exercise making a value judgment as to the conflicts which arise.

(5)   The burden is upon the party or parties who seek exclusion, or the court itself in a case where it takes steps of its own motion, to exclude the press.

(6)   Regard must be had to the nature and sensitivities of the evidence and the degree to which the watchdog function of the media may be engaged but this does not place on the media any burden of proof which remains with the Applicant.

Part III

RELATED FORMS OF PROTECTION

Chapter 13

DEFAMATION

INTRODUCTION

13.1 Celebrities know the value of reputation because it forms part of their stock in trade. Once damaged, reputation is difficult to salvage, so damaging statements require quick, decisive action. Those subjected to damaging statements in the media are entitled to sue those responsible provided they do so within one year from the date of publication of the defamatory material.[1] Various causes of action may be available. We are concerned here with defamation, i e libel and slander. Defamation is concerned with vindication of reputation. Defamation claims must not be brought to pursue a vendetta or harass the defendant. If this is done the claim is liable to be struck out on the grounds of abuse of process.[2] To bring a defamation claim it is necessary to establish that defamatory material was published which referred to the claimant. It is not necessary to prove the information published is false,[3] but if it is proved to be true the claim will fail. In libel, damage is presumed whereas in slander in many cases it must be proved. It is not always easy to *prove* that a slander has caused special damage.

13.2 It was recently said that the long-term effect of a libel has commonly been expressed in metaphorical terms, such as 'the propensity to percolate through underground passages and contaminate hidden springs'.[4] The flow of information has massively increased with the advent and development of the internet. Search engines enable information about individuals on the web to be turned up easily and quickly. Postings on the web are difficult to remove and the press maintain large (and, some would argue, historically important) web archives of material published conventionally. There is a tendency to resist attempts to interfere with the integrity of such archives by removal or alteration of their content.[5] It has recently been held by the European Court of Human Rights (ECtHR) that the requirement to publish an appropriate qualification to an article contained in an internet archive, where it had been brought to the notice of a newspaper that a libel action had been initiated in respect of that same article published in the written press, did not constitute a disproportionate interference with the right to freedom of expression.[6]

---

[1] Limitation Act 1980, s 4A, as substituted by the Defamation Act 1996, s 5(2) – subject to the court's discretion to extend the period (Limitation Act 1980, s 32A, as substituted by Defamation Act 1996, s 5(4)).

[2] *Wallis v Valentine* [2003] EMLR 8 and see *Jameel (Yousef) v Dow Jones and Co Inc* [2005] QB 946, at [56], [58] and *Noorani v Richard Calver (No 1)* [2009] EWHC 561, where Coulson J struck out as an abuse of process a slander action in respect of comments made to the wife and daughter of the complainant where there was no evidence of substantial publication or damage to reputation and it was considered wholly disproportionate to involve a judge and the court in respect of such an allegation when the costs would far outweigh any result and there was no question of any need to vindicate reputation. Costs on an indemnity basis were eventually awarded against the claimant (see [2009] EWHC 592 (QB)).

[3] The falsity of words is presumed in the claimant's favour.

[4] Tugendhat J in *Clarke v Bain* [2008] EWHC 2636, citing e g *Slipper v BBC* [1991] 1 QB 283, at 300.

[5] See the article by Siobhain Butterworth in *The Guardian*, 20 October 2008 dealing with this issue.

[6] *Times Newspapers Ltd (Nos 1 and 2) v United Kingdom* (App No 3002/03 and 23676/03).

13.3   Celebrities are usually claimants in defamation actions but claims against them are not unknown, particularly in the realm of the celebrity autobiography when offence is taken and a writ ensues. Recently parents have sued children who have published biographies about childhood abuse. It has been suggested that it might be advisable to wait until the death of the subject because the right to sue for libel does not survive death.[7]

THE DISTINCTION BETWEEN LIBEL AND SLANDER

13.4   Apart from the need to prove damage in the case of slander the distinction between libel and slander is that libel is concerned with publications in permanent form[8] and slander is concerned with publication by speech or other non-permanent (or transient) form. Libel, therefore, consists of the written word or matter broadcast for general reception such as television and radio,[9] or in the public performance of a play[10] or the on the soundtrack of a film.[11] Words published on the internet are actionable in libel.

13.5   Slander is actionable without proof of actual injury (special damage) in the following classes of case:

- where it alleged that the claimant has committed a crime punishable with death or imprisonment.[12] Words which carry mere suspicion that the claimant has been guilty of a crime will not support an action without proof of special damage;[13]

- where it is alleged that the claimant was suffering from a contagious disease at the time of publication;[14]

- where the words complained of are calculated[15] to disparage the claimant in any office, profession, calling, trade or business held or carried on by him at the time of publication, whether or not the words are spoken of the claimant in the way of his office, profession, calling, trade or business;[16] and

- where the words impute unchastity or adultery to any woman or girl.[17]

---

[7]   Article by Rod Dadak (2009) 153(3) *Solicitors Journal* 6.

[8]   *Monson v Tussauds Ltd* [1894] 1 QB 671, at 692, per Lopes LJ, who said: 'Libels are generally in writing or printing, but this is not necessary; the defamatory matter may be conveyed in some other permanent form. For instance, a statue, a caricature, an effigy, chalk marks on a wall, signs, or pictures may constitute a libel.'

[9]   Broadcasting Act 1990, s 166.

[10]   Theatres Act 1968, s 4(1).

[11]   *Youssoupoff v MGM* (1934) 50 TLR 581, where it was suggested that it was necessary to show not only that the communication was permanent but that it was visible – a permanent matter to be seen by the eye. The better view is probably that the correct test is whether the communication is in permanent form.

[12]   *Hellwig v Mitchell* [1910] 1 KB 609: it is not enough if the crime is punishable by a fine. See also *Gray v Jones* [1939] 1 All ER 798 where the defendant stated that the claimant was 'a convicted person' and 'I will not have you here'.

[13]   *Simmons v Mitchell* (1880) 6 App Cas 156, PC.

[14]   Words imputing serious contagious or infectious diseases are required e g STDs or AIDS.

[15]   'Calculated to' is generally interpreted as 'likely to'.

[16]   Defamation Act 1952, s 2.

[17]   Slander of Women Act 1891, s 1. See *Kerr v Kennedy* [1942] 1 KB 409, at 411, per Asquith LJ.

13.6   If these classes of case do not apply it is necessary to prove that the slander has caused actual injury and mere loss of reputation is not sufficient, nor is losing friends. Losing the hospitality of friends might be enough if that amounts to a material loss.[18] It is a matter of historical accident that this distinction between libel and slander remains, but it is firmly entrenched.

WHAT MUST BE PROVED FOR LIBEL AND SLANDER?

Reference to the claimant

13.7   It must be established that the words complained of refer to the claimant.[19] This means that an ordinary reasonable reader would identify the claimant as the person referred to, if necessary, from the special facts known at the time of publication.[20] Identification of the claimant may be by name, description, pun or any reasonable inference. The special facts from which the claimant might be identified must be pleaded, together with particulars of the persons or classes of persons who both read the words complained of and knew the facts relied on. Where the facts from which the claimant could be identified are well known the court will sometimes infer that a number of unidentifiable persons would have known them and understood that the words complained of referred to the claimant. The issue is not who was meant to be referred to but who was hit.[21]

13.8   Sometimes the words complained of refer to a group of people – in such cases it is often difficult to prove that any particular individual is identified by the words. In *Knuppfer v London Express Newspapers*,[22] where it was claimed in an article that a political party comprising émigrés from the Soviet Union consisted of 'quislings', the plaintiff, who was head of the British branch, sued for libel and the issue arose whether the words were reasonably capable of being understood as referring to him. It was held in the House of Lords that there was nothing in the words which referred to any one member of the group rather than another and the dismissal of the claim was upheld.[23]

What is the meaning of defamatory matter?

13.9   The test of what is defamatory is objective, which means that the defendant's intentions are irrelevant.[24] It is the words (or other matter) used that are important – they must be such that they injure a person's reputation.[25] Whether words or matter are defamatory is a matter of fact.[26] It is the reaction of the ordinary reader of the

---

[18]   *Moore v Meagher* (1807) 1 Taunt 39 and *Davies v Solomon* (1871) LR 7 QB 112.
[19]   *Knuppfer v London Express Newspapers Ltd* [1944] AC 116, at 120, per Viscount Simon LC.
[20]   *Morgan v Odhams Press* [1971] 1 WLR 1239, HL, where it was held that before an article could be said to be defamatory of someone, it was not the case that the article had to have to be within it some 'key or pointer' indicating that the article referred to that person. It was also held that, where necessary, extrinsic evidence could be admitted to prove that apparently innocent words in fact bore a defamatory meaning.
[21]   *E Hulton & Co v Jones* [1910] AC 20, per Lord Loreburn LC.
[22]   [1944] AC 116.
[23]   In *Aspro Travel Ltd v Owners Abroad Group* [1996] 1 WLR 132 it was held that a defamatory statement concerning a family company might be seen as referring to each director.
[24]   *Slim v Daily Telegraph* [1968] 2 QB 157, at 172–173: 'the argument between lawyers as to the meaning of words starts with the unexpressed major premise that any particular combination of words has one meaning which is not necessarily the same as that intended by him who published them or understood by any of those who read them'.
[25]   Words that do not injure reputation may still be actionable under malicious falsehood.
[26]   It is a jury question (and will be determined by a jury if one is empanelled).

publication that is important.[27] There have been various formulations of what is defamatory. Lord Atkin's classic formulation is that defamatory matter is such as would 'tend to lower the claimant in the estimation of right-thinking members of society generally',[28] which includes matter which tends to make the claimant shunned or avoided by right-thinking members of the public or exposes the claimant to ridicule.[29] Another, older, formulation is that the words complained of were 'calculated to injure the reputation of another by exposing him to hatred, contempt, or ridicule'.[30] The law is concerned with the *tendency* of the words so it is not relevant whether the words are actually believed.[31] The essential point is that the words or other matter must impugn the claimant's reputation, so insults and jokes will not be defamatory unless they undermine reputation. Matter, for example, which renders someone ridiculous might undermine reputation. It is a question of fact whether insults, jokes, banter and the like go over the line to the extent that the attitude of others to the individual concerned is adversely affected. In *Charleston v NGN*[32] computer-generated pictures of popular soap stars were superimposed on the bodies of porn models on a front page spread. The House of Lords held that although the images were 'deeply offensive and insulting' they were not defamatory if read with the publication as a whole, which made it clear the stars were unwitting stars of a computer game.

13.10 In *Berkoff v Burchill*[33] Miss Burchill, a well-known journalist, suggested in reviews that Stephen Berkoff (the actor/director) was 'hideous-looking' and 'hideously ugly' and the question before the Court of Appeal was whether this in law was capable of being defamatory. It was held that 'reputation' was to be interpreted in a broad sense as comprehending all aspects of a person's standing in the community. It was thought a jury might conclude that to say this of someone in the public eye who makes a living from acting gave the impression they were actually repulsive and this could lower them in the estimation of the public. The question whether words have damaged a claimant by exposing him to ridicule cannot be answered simply by considering the natural and ordinary meaning of the words used. The circumstances in which the words are used must be looked at.[34]

13.11 There are other examples of defamatory statements such as imputing criminal conduct or even, possibly, a civil wrong.[35] Calling someone dishonest or a liar is capable of being defamatory. In sexual matters it has been held that calling a married man 'gay' is capable of being defamatory.[36] Attitudes in sexual matters have changed considerably so older authorities in this area might not apply now. To allege that a woman has been raped, although not reflecting on her moral credit, may be capable of being defamatory.[37]

---

27   Neill J in *Berkoff v Burchill* [1996] 4 All ER 1008.
28   *Sim v Stretch* [1936] 2 All ER 1237, at 1240.
29   As in *Berkoff v Burchill* [1996] 4 All ER 1008, at 1018.
30   *Parmiter v Coupland* (1840) 6 M&W 105, at 198, per Parke B. An older still formulation is that the words tend to make right-thinking people shun or avoid the claimant (*Villiers v Monsley* (1769) 2 Wils 403).
31   Unless the words are such that no reasonable person would believe them: see *Loukas v Young* [1968] 2 NSWR 549 (witchcraft).
32   [1995] 2 AC 65.
33   [1996] 4 All ER 1008.
34   Millett LJ dissenting had no doubt that the words were intended to ridicule Mr Berkoff but did not think they made him look ridiculous or lowered his reputation in the eyes of ordinary people.
35   If civil liability entails fault (*Groom v Crocker* [1939] 1 KB 194).
36   *Cruise v Express Newspapers plc* [1999] QB 931.
37   *Youssoupoff v MGM* (1934) 50 TLR 581.

13.12 In *Jameel v Wall Street Europe*[38] the House of Lords by a majority declined to alter the rule that a company can sue for libel and claim damages without having to prove special damage (identifiable financial loss). A company can sue 'in respect of defamatory matters which damage its business'.

13.13 The meaning of the words (or other material) used must be focused on, but it is not always the literal meaning of words that matters; sometimes what is important is the inference that can be drawn from the words used. Words must be read in their context within the publication as a whole to get to the meaning. One of the claimant's most important tasks is stating what the words complained of mean. This leads to much controversy because the court must determine whether the words complained of are capable of bearing the defamatory meaning pleaded in the claim or any meaning defamatory of the claimant.[39]

13.14 The court is concerned to determine what the public as a whole *should* think about the offending material not what the public actually does think about it. The court is concerned with the public as a whole not a section of it.[40] The court looks to determine the beliefs of average 'right-thinking members of society' – the question being whether the right-thinking person would construe the words in their ordinary meaning as lowering the reputation of the claimant. Words suggesting that the claimant has given information about the commission of a crime to the police will not be considered capable of being defamatory,[41] and it is irrelevant that the words might damage the claimant's reputation in the minds of some criminally minded section of the public. The court will not have regard to what a limited class of people would or should think. There might be a question mark these days over whether it is always possible to identify a clear consensus of moral opinion on some issues. In such cases the court looks to see whether a considerable body would hold a particular opinion.

Publication

13.15 All those responsible for the publication are liable to be sued. The defamatory matter must have been published to a third party (ie someone other than the person making the statement and the person of whom it is made) for a defamation claim to lie. Publication occurs at the place where the defamatory material is received (read or heard). Liability will arise if the defamatory matter is proved to have been read in the ordinary course of business by persons other than the addressee.[42] The accepted practice in the case of books and newspapers is that where there is publication to the world at large the claimant does not have to prove publication to individual publishees. In the case of publication on the internet a claimant is not entitled to rely on a presumption of law that there had been substantial publication within the jurisdiction but must prove that the material had been accessed and downloaded.[43]

---

[38]   [2006] UKHL 44, [2007] 1 AC 359.
[39]   See *Mapp v NGN* [1998] QB 520.
[40]   *Tolley v Fry* [1930] 1 KB 467, at 479.
[41]   *Byrne v Deane* [1937] 1 KB 818.
[42]   *Pullman v Hill* [1891] 1 QB 524.
[43]   *Al Amoudi v Brisard* [2006] EWHC 1062, [2006] 2 All ER 294. Some facts, of course, can be proved by inference and it was held that publication to a particular individual could be proved by calling the individual to say he had accessed the material and downloaded them within the jurisdiction and wider publication might be proved by establishing a platform of facts from which it could be inferred that substantial publication had occurred.

13.16 Each republication of defamatory material constitutes a separate cause of action and either each republication can be separately pleaded or alternatively the claimant can seek damages as part of the original claim in respect of the repetition of the libel provided that it is not too remote.[44] The person responsible for the original defamatory statement may thus be responsible for its publication; for its republication with his authorisation (which constitutes a separate cause of action) and for its foreseeable repetition by third parties (which is not a separate cause of action but goes to the award of damages for the original publication). There must be evidence that the defendant had authorised the subsequent publication or the claim will be struck out.[45]

13.17 If a defamatory statement is made to one's spouse about a third party the statement is not actionable by the third party. This is on the basis that 'according to a well recognised principle, husband and wife are in the same position, and therefore that the uttering of a libel by a husband to his wife is no publication'.[46] But if a third party makes a defamatory statement about someone to their spouse the third party can be sued.[47]

13.18 Publication on the internet occurs each time the material is accessed and each fresh publication gives rise to a new cause of action.[48] The author is the publisher of the material. Internet service providers (ISPs) and moderators of chat rooms or bulletin boards may be considered publishers and responsible for defamatory words if they had knowing (as opposed to passive) involvement in the publication of the relevant words.[49] If the material simply passes through the ISP's server the ISP is not liable because it does not participate in the process of publication but acts as mere facilitator, ie as a means of transmission. The position is different if the ISP is put on notice of the defamatory posting. If defamatory material appears on the net it is, therefore, important to put the ISP on notice. The Electronic Commerce (EC Directive) Regulations 2002[50] provide a defence to an ISP where it is the mere conduit of the transmission of the defamatory material, that the material resulted from automatic caching and that it was merely hosting the material that it did not know and had no reason to know was unlawful.

13.19 A libel action may be struck out as an abuse of the process where the evidence is that the extent of publication within the jurisdiction is very small.[51] In *Carrie v Tolkien*[52] the claimant discovered comments on a blog within hours of the posting but failed to remove them and it was held that a properly directed jury would inevitably conclude that the claimant had consented to and acquiesced in the publications subsequent to their discovery. It was confirmed that there was no presumption in law to the effect that placing material on the internet led automatically to a substantial publication and the court emphasised that it was necessary to plead and establish any publication relied upon. Pleading that the posting had been accessed 'by a large but unquantifiable number of readers' was no more than bare assertion and some solid basis for the inference had to be pleaded. The minimal level of publication meant that the claim would be classified as an abuse of process, although the court accepted that sometimes it

---

44   *Slipper v BBC* [1991] 1 QB 283.
45   *Campbell v Safra* [2006] EWHC 819 (QB).
46   *Wennhak v Morgan* (1888) 20 QBD 635.
47   *Wenman v Ash* (1853) 13 CB 836.
48   See *Godfrey v Demon Internet Ltd* [2001] QB 201 and *Loutchansky v Times Newspapers Ltd (No 2)* [2001] EWCA 1805, [2002] QB 783; and see Chapter 15 on libel and the internet.
49   See Eady J in *Bunt v Tilley* [2007] 1 WLR 1243.
50   SI 2002/2013.
51   *Jameel v Dow Jones* [2005] EWCA Civ 75.
52   [2009] EWHC 29, Eady J.

was necessary to pursue a claim, notwithstanding the sparse evidence of substantial publication, in order to obtain an injunction and silence the defendant from continuing to defame the claimant if it was likely the defendant would publish similar allegations in the future.

Jurisdiction

13.20 Normally, a claim can only be brought in these courts against those who can be served with a claim form in England and Wales. Leave may be granted to serve a claim form outside the jurisdiction in cases where the damage is suffered or results from an act committed within the jurisdiction. In libel cases the damage is suffered and the act is committed where the libel is published.

13.21 Where a libel is published in more than one country it is possible that it could give rise to a cause of action in each country in which the claimant had a reputation and suffered injury. It has been argued that in such cases (ie multi-jurisdictional libel cases) the entire publication should be treated as giving rise to one cause of action and the court should determine whether or not it has clearly been proved that the action was best tried in England. The global theory has been rejected as contrary to well-established principles of libel law that each publication constitutes a separate tort. Where the constituent elements of the tort had occurred in England (ie significant distribution and reputations which could be damaged) the foreign publisher can normally be sued in England.[53]

13.22 A person libelled by a statement in a foreign publication distributed in several contracting states[54] but with a circulation within this jurisdiction may sue either in the courts of the contracting state where the publisher is established (which would have jurisdiction to award damages in respect of all the harm caused) or in the English courts (where damages will be limited to those warranted by the extent of publication within this jurisdiction).[55]

13.23 An action for libel and slander can be maintained against a defendant domiciled in this jurisdiction in respect of publication outside the jurisdiction.[56] Section 13 of the Private International Law (Miscellaneous Provisions) Act 1995 makes recovery for defamatory statements published abroad dependent on whether the claims were actionable by the laws of the foreign country.

13.24 Particular problems arise in relation to internet publications. Eady J said in *Mardas v New York Times*[57] that it may be in due course that an international agreement will be reached as to the appropriate way of resolving claims arising out of internet publication but for the time being the courts must apply the law as it stands. In *Mardas* it was held that if the claimant established that he had been libelled here, and a real and substantial tort thus committed within the jurisdiction, he was entitled to bring proceedings.[58] The claimant in *Mardas* had a reputation in and connection with this

---

[53] *Berezovsky v Michaels* [2002] 2 All ER 986. This has given rise to complaints of 'libel tourism'.
[54] The Brussels Convention on Jurisdiction and the Enforcement of Judgments in Civil and Commercial Matters 1968.
[55] *Shevill v Presse Alliance SA* [1995] 2 AC 18.
[56] Although there may well be issues as to which is the appropriate forum.
[57] [2008] EWHC 3135 (QB).
[58] See eg *Berezovsky v Michaels* [2000] 2 All ER 986, [2000] 1 WLR 1004, [2000] IP & T 1136 and *Shevill v Presse Alliance SA* [1995] 2 AC 18.

jurisdiction and it was considered that there was no artificiality about seeking to protect his reputation within this country. The claim was not an example of 'libel tourism' or forum shopping and it was held that there was no reason in law why the courts of England and Wales should decline jurisdiction. English law permitted the claimant to claim whatever was appropriate compensation and vindication in respect of the smaller local publication here. The approach has long been to recognise that where a tort has been committed the appropriate forum will usually be that of the jurisdiction where the tort took place. What a claimant cannot do is to claim damages in this jurisdiction in respect of, for example, publications in the US.

The defamatory meaning

13.25 The judge and jury have differing functions when dealing with the meaning of words:[59]

- the role of the judge is to decide whether the words used were capable of bearing the meaning contended for and, if so, whether any of those meanings was legally capable of being defamatory, determined in the temporal context in which the words have been used;[60] and

- it is first and foremost a matter for the jury to determine the meaning of the words used, namely what they would convey to the ordinary reader.

13.26 It is necessary to specify in the particulars of claim the defamatory meaning which it is alleged the words or matters convey. There are two types of meaning:

- the defamatory meaning the words or matter complained of convey in their *natural and ordinary* meaning (this encompasses the literal meaning of the words and any implication or inference from the words themselves – as to which see further below); and

- the defamatory meaning the words or matter complained of convey in their *innuendo* meaning (that is, something alleged to be conveyed to some person by reason of knowing facts extraneous to the words complained of[61]). Note that other passages in the same publication are not extrinsic facts but form part of the context in which the words are used.

13.27 It follows that in all cases the claimant must first identify and clearly state what defamatory meaning is alleged. Even if the words complained are clear and concise and bear only one literal meaning the modern practice is to plead the meaning which the claimant contends that the words bear, however obvious that may be. No particulars will be ordered in respect of natural and ordinary meanings. Where the meaning is not obvious caution must be exercised over pleading wide and extravagant meanings because they increase the scope for defending on the ground of justification (truth). A claimant cannot contend for a higher meaning at trial than that pleaded or for an entirely different meaning.[62] Meanings can be pleaded in the alternative. For example, where an offending article is about an individual under investigation for a crime it is

---

[59]   See Keene LJ in *Burstein v Associated Newspapers* [2007] EWCA Civ 600, at [10].
[60]   The principles to be applied in ascertaining whether the words in question are capable of bearing a defamatory meaning were summarised by Neill LJ in *Gillick v BBC* [1996] EMLR 267, at 272–273.
[61]   Civil Procedure Rules 1998, SI 1998/3132 (CPR), PD 53, para 2.3(1).
[62]   *Slim v Daily Telegraph* [1968] 2 QB 157.

permissible to plead 'that there were strong grounds to believe, or alternatively that there were reasonable grounds to suspect' that the individual was guilty in respect of the matter under investigation.[63]

13.28 There is tension over how wide and extravagant a meaning should be pleaded because if it is too wide and extravagant there is increased scope to justify. Conversely, a narrow and restricted meaning will diminish the claim.

13.29 *The natural and ordinary meaning of the words.* The jury is required to consider first the meaning of the words in their 'natural and ordinary meaning'. If the claimant alleges that the words bear a meaning that is not their literal meaning but an inference or implication from the words themselves (a false or popular 'innuendo') the question for the jury will be whether a reasonable reader might 'read between the lines'[64] in order to reach that meaning. In such a case the natural and ordinary meaning of the words is not their literal, but their inferential meaning.

13.30 The court should give the words the natural and ordinary meaning they would have conveyed to the ordinary reader of the publication in question reading the article once. The ordinary, reasonable reader is not naive and he can read between the lines. But he is not unduly suspicious and not avid for scandal. He would not select one bad meaning where other non-defamatory meanings are available. The court must read the article as a whole and not indulge in over-elaborate analysis and, also, too literal an approach. The intention of the publisher is not relevant.[65]

13.31 *The innuendo meaning of the words.* Where the words complained of bear a special defamatory meaning arising from facts and circumstances extrinsic to the words themselves and known to some or all of those who read them (the true innuendo) the claimant must give particulars of the relevant extraneous facts – because without them the innuendo cannot be proved.[66] The matters pleaded must be outside the libel.[67] The claimant must also give particulars of the publishees or classes of publishee who knew the extrinsic facts and, therefore, understood that the words bore the true innuendo alleged. Sometimes the court might infer that a substantial number of unidentified persons would have known the facts, read the words complained of and understood them to refer to the claimant.

13.32 In pleading the claim the claimant should set out the following in separate numbered paragraphs:

- the actual words used;

- what is contended to be the natural and ordinary meaning of the words (ie the literal or (if appropriate) inferential meaning of the words derived from the words themselves); and

- the innuendo meaning of the words (ie the meaning of the words in the light of the special facts not apparent from the words themselves). Particulars of the special facts need to be pleaded under this paragraph.

---

[63] See e g *Flood v Times Newspapers Ltd* Tugendhat J 16 October 2009.
[64] *Lewis v Daily Telegraph* [1964] AC 234.
[65] These guiding principles are taken from Lord Hoffman's opinion in *Bonnick v Morris* [2002] UKPC, at [9].
[66] CPR Part 53 PD 5, para 2.3 (2) and see Lord Devlin in *Lewis v Daily Telegraph Ltd* [1964] AC 234, at 281.
[67] *Grubb v Bristol United Press* [1963] 1 QB 309.

13.33 The legal principles relevant to meaning were in summarised in *Jeynes v News Magazines Limited*:[68]

- the governing principle is reasonableness;

- the hypothetical reasonable reader is not naive but he is not unduly suspicious. He can read between the lines. He can read in an implication more readily than a lawyer and may indulge in a certain amount of loose thinking but he must be treated as being a person who is not avid for scandal and someone who does not, and should not, select one bad meaning where other non-defamatory meanings are available;

- over-elaborate analysis is best avoided;

- the intention of the publisher is irrelevant;

- the article must be read as a whole, and any 'bane and antidote' taken together;

- the hypothetical reader is taken to be representative of those who would read the publication in question;

- in delimiting the range of permissible defamatory meanings, the court should rule out any meaning which, 'can only emerge as the produce of some strained, or forced, or utterly unreasonable interpretation ...';[69] and

- it follows that 'it is not enough to say that by some person or another the words *might* be understood in a defamatory sense'.[70]

13.34 If the judge decides that any pleaded meaning falls outside the permissible range, then it will be the judge's duty to rule accordingly.[71] Rulings on meaning should not be too restrictive of possible meanings the words might bear. The test is:[72]

> '... not what the words mean but what a jury could sensibly think that they meant. Such an exercise is an exercise in generosity, not in parsimony ... if ... it appears that the judge has erred on the side of unnecessary restriction of meaning, [the Court of Appeal] may be readier to take another look.'

13.35 A court should only exclude a pleaded meaning if satisfied that a jury would actually be perverse to uphold it.[73] The jury's function is to decide what a reasonable reader of the publication in question would make of the article.

13.36 Chaff and banter are not the proper subject of defamation proceedings:[74]

---

68 [2008] EWCA Civ 130, per Sir Anthony Clarke MR, referring to *Skuse v Granada Television Ltd* [1996] EMLR 278, at 285–287, per Sir Thomas Bingham MR.
69 See Eady J in *Gillick v Brook Advisory Centres* [2002] EWHC 829 QBD, approved by the Court of Appeal [2001] EWCA Civ 1263, at [7]; and see P Milmo QC, W V H Rogers, G Busuttil, Richard Parkes QC et al *Gatley on Libel and Slander* (Sweet & Maxwell, 11th edn, 2008), at para 32.5.
70 See *Neville v Fine Arts Co* [1897] AC 68, at 73, per Lord Halsbury LC.
71 *Gillick v Brook Advisory Centres* [2001] EWCA Civ 1263, at [7].
72 *Berezovsky v Michaels* [2002] 2 All ER 986, at [16].
73 See Eady J in *Glen Johnson v MGN Ltd* [2009] EWHC 1481, applying *Jameel v Wall Street Journal Europe SPRL (No 1)* [2003] EWCA Civ 1694, (2004) EMLR 6.
74 *Berkoff v Burchill* [1996] 4 All ER 1008, at 1018j, per Millett LJ.

'Many a true word is spoken in jest. Many false ones too. But chaff and banter are not defamatory, and even serious imputations are not actionable if no-one would take them seriously. The question, however, is how the words would be understood, not how they were meant, and that is pre-eminently for the jury.'

13.37 When lengthy pieces are under consideration it is important not to miss the wood for the trees and it must be borne in mind that assessing meaning is largely a matter of impression. The test is objective and it always has to be borne in mind that the task is to determine how a reasonable reader or viewer would interpret what was written or said. Often it is the overall flavour that is important so an over-analytical approach in the sense of subjecting the offending article to a leisurely or legalistic breakdown should be avoided.[75]

13.38 In *Cassidy v Daily Mirror Newspapers*[76] a wife sued over a photograph of her husband with another woman, with words suggesting her husband was going to marry the lady. The wife sued not because the words were directly about her but because it could be inferred she lived in immoral cohabitation with her husband. It was held in the Court of Appeal that (1) words published about A (the husband) could be indirectly defamatory of B (the wife) and (2) the words used were capable of meaning the husband was a single man and were published to people who knew the wife professed to be married to him and might think she lived in immoral cohabitation with him. It was held the judge must decide if the words are capable of two meanings; if he does so decide the jury must determine which meaning was intended.[77] By 'intended' is meant that a man is liable for the reasonable inferences to be drawn from the words he used by persons who know the facts from which the inferences might be drawn. It was for the jury to say whether those who knew the wife professed to be married to the husband could reasonably draw the inference that she was living in immoral cohabitation with him. The defendant's knowledge of the facts is irrelevant because the defendant must take the consequences of defamatory inferences reasonably drawn from the words used.[78]

13.39 In *Lewis v Daily Telegraph*[79] it was alleged in the newspapers that a company and its subsidiaries were subject to investigation by the fraud squad. The chairman and the companies sued on the basis that the words meant and were understood to mean that the companies' affairs were conducted fraudulently or in such a way that the police suspected fraud. The papers argued that they were doing no more than conveying accurate information about a police inquiry. The essential question was whether these words were capable of meaning the companies were guilty of fraud. The question was to be answered by looking at what the words would convey to the ordinary man who reads between the lines in the light of his general knowledge and experience. What the ordinary man would infer without special knowledge is the natural and ordinary meaning of words. The sting was held to be in the fact that the fraud squad was making the inquiry. What inferences should be drawn from this was a matter for the jury. It was held that as a matter of law the words were not capable of meaning that the companies were guilty of fraud and it could not be left to the jury to infer that. Lord Reid said:

---

[75]   See Eady J in *Bond v BBC* [2009] EWHC 539.
[76]   [1929] 2 KB 331.
[77]   Scrutton LJ agreeing with a view expressed arguendo in *Simmons v Mitchell* (1880) 6 App Cas 156, at 158.
[78]   This finding, which held the defendants liable regardless of whether they took reasonable care in checking the facts, lead to the new statutory defence of unintentional defamation where the defendant can show reasonable care was taken not to defame the claimant – the most recent version of which is s 2 of the Defamation Act 1996.
[79]   [1964] AC 234.

'I do think that [the ordinary man] would infer guilt of fraud merely because an inquiry is on foot. And if that is so then it is the duty of the trial judge to direct the jury that it is for them to determine the meaning of the paragraph but that they must not hold it to impute guilt of fraud because as a matter of law the paragraph is not capable of having that meaning.'

13.40 What have come to be known as the Chase levels of meaning[80] have been adopted by the courts as a means of categorising the seriousness of the allegation within a statement about investigations by the authorities such as the police:

- Chase level one – positive conclusion of guilt;

- Chase level two – strong grounds to suspect; and

- Chase level three – reasonable grounds to suspect.

13.41 The meaning of slang, technical or foreign words not generally known to the public should be pleaded as a true innuendo.[81] The special or extraneous facts might be the explanation of a slang word or a technical term understood by the publishee but of no sense to the general public. Reliance cannot be placed on special facts occurring or discovered after the offending words have been published because the cause of action is complete on publication.[82] It is permissible for counsel at trial to ask publishees what they understood the words to mean in the case of legal innuendo (which is not permissible where only a natural and ordinary meaning is relied on because meaning in such cases is an objective test).

13.42 It is usually best to plead the meaning as the natural and ordinary meaning and in the alternative as a true innuendo if there is doubt whether the word or expression is in general usage. Where the defendant wishes to argue that the words bear a different meaning from that contended for by the claimant it is best practice for the defendant to set out the different meaning regardless of whether a substantive defence of justification or fair comment is raised.[83]

13.43 Where the defamatory statement is in a foreign language the original must be set out in any pleading and translated into English. It is necessary to plead that the persons reading the words would have understood them.

DEFENCES TO LIBEL AND SLANDER

13.44 The following can be raised by way of defence to a defamation claim:

- that the action has been brought after the expiration of one year from the date on which the cause of action accrued (limitation);

- that the defendant was not responsible for publishing the defamatory material;

- that the words complained of are not capable of bearing a defamatory meaning;

---

[80]   See *Chase v NGN* [2002] EWCA Civ 1772.
[81]   *Dakhyl v Labouchere* [1908] 2 KB 325, HL.
[82]   *Grapelli v Block* [1981] 1 WLR 822.
[83]   *Armstrong v Times Newspapers* [2006] EWHC 1614 (QB).

- that the words complained of do not bear and are not capable of bearing the meaning relied on by the claimant;

- that there are extrinsic facts known to the publishees which make what appear to be defamatory words innocent or which make what appear to be references to the claimant references to some other person;[84]

- that the words complained of bear a different meaning from that relied on by the claimant;[85]

- that the words complained of are true (justification);

- that the words complained of are fair comment on a matter of public interest;

- that the words were published on an occasion of absolute privilege;

- that the words complained of were published on an occasion of qualified privilege;

- that the claimant consented to the particular publication complained of;

- that the words complained of were innocently disseminated; and

- that the defendant has made an offer of amends pursuant to the Defamation Act 1996, s 2.

Limitation

13.45 Section 4A of the Limitation Act 1980 provides that in actions for libel or slander (or slander of title, slander of goods or other malicious falsehood) no action shall be brought after the expiration of one year from the date on which the cause of action accrued. The cause of action for defamation accrues on publication which is an objective question irrespective of the claimant's knowledge.[86] Section 32A of the Limitation Act 1980 provides that if it appears equitable to allow an action to proceed having regard to prejudice to the claimant and the defendant the court may direct that the section shall not apply to the action. The court has regard to all the circumstances, in particular (a) the length of and reasons for the claimant's delay, (b) the date when the claimant became aware of the facts[87] and the extent to which he acted promptly and reasonably once he knew he might have a cause of action and (c) the extent to which relevant evidence is likely to be unavailable or less cogent than it would have been had the action been brought within one year of publication.

Justification

13.46 It is a defence to show that the words published are true in substance and fact (minor inaccuracies do not, therefore, preclude a defence). This is the defence of

---

[84] Where the person the words in fact refer to has the same name as the claimant.
[85] Per Mustill LJ in *De L'Isle v Times Newspapers* [1988] 1 WLR 49, at 60.
[86] *Edwards v Golding* [2007] EWCA Civ 416.
[87] Ie those facts which it is necessary to plead and prove to establish a prima facie case not those capable of rebutting possible defences (*C v MGN* [1996] EMLR 518, CA).

justification. It is important to identify the sting of the defamatory publication that is its real thrust or gravamen. In *Grobbelaar v NGN*[88] (a case concerning a well-known professional goalkeeper), by the end of the trial the claimant was arguing that the sting lay in the allegation that he had deliberately fixed or 'thrown' matches and the defendant was arguing that that the sting lay simply in the statement that he had taken bribes. The jury took the view that the sting of the accusation was match fixing, which the defendants were unable to justify.

13.47 Justification as a defence is only available if the defendant believes the words are true and intends to support the defence at trial with reasonable evidence or has reasonable grounds to believe evidence will be available at trial to prove what was alleged. Enough must be justified as meets the sting of the charge and if anything in the charge does not add to the sting it need not be justified.

13.48 Where the defamatory publication puts a false slant on events it is often problematical to determine whether what was published created an impression of a greater degree of misconduct on the part of the claimant than could by justified by the facts. Each case must depend on its own facts, but if what is published puts the claimant in a worse light than the facts would justify there is no defence. Similarly, it is not possible to justify allegations of general misconduct by pointing to a specific instance of misconduct and an allegation of a specific instance of misconduct cannot be justified by evidence of other general misconduct.[89]

13.49 Where a number of defamatory allegations are made it is necessary to determine whether there is one defamatory sting or several. If one common sting is involved there is a complete defence if this is justified even if other allegations in the publication are not. Where there are two or more distinct charges for the defence of justification to succeed it must address each of the meanings attributed to the words by the jury.

13.50 As stated earlier, where the case concerns the publication of matter about investigations by the police or other authorities the courts often set levels of defamatory meaning of descending gravity in relation to the misconduct which is the subject of the investigation.[90] In *Armstrong v Times Newspapers* the judge,[91] who was required to sit without a jury to determine the single meaning of an article as a preliminary issue, rejected the defendant's submissions that it could justify the article with a level two meaning (that there were reasonable grounds for suspecting that the claimant had taken performance enhancing drugs). The judge held that the defence of justification would only succeed if it was proved true or substantially true that the claimant did in fact take performance enhancing drugs and denied having done so.

13.51 *The repetition rule.* It is no defence for a defendant to contend he was only repeating what he had been told.[92] The central issue is what the defendant's words mean.

---

[88]   [2002] 1 WLR 3024.
[89]   See *Bookbinder v Tebbit* [1989] 1 WLR 640 (where a specific allegation of squandering public funds could not be justified by pointing to other instances of squandering public funds) and *Williams v Reason* [1988] 1 WLR 96 (where it was held that a specific allegation that an amateur rugby player wrote a book for gain imported a sting of 'shamateurism' which could be justified by other acts of such a nature).
[90]   (1) level one (that the claimant is guilty of the misconduct); (2) level two (that the claimant is reasonably suspected of being guilty); and (3) level three (that there are reasonable grounds to inquire or investigate whether the claimant is guilty of the misconduct).
[91]   Eady J, upheld on appeal [2006] EWCA Civ 519.
[92]   *Stern v Piper* [1997] QB 123 at 128. In *Aspro Travel Ltd v Owners Abroad Group* [1996] 1 WLR 132 it was considered that there might be circumstances where existence of a rumour entitles a person to repeat the

If the defendant says a person is under suspicion it is not necessarily an allegation that the person is guilty, but usually it is implied that there are reasonable grounds for the suspicion[93] and the defendant can justify only if he can prove that the claimant acted in such a way as to cause a reasonable observer to be suspicious.[94] This can only be done by pleading and proving *objective facts* tending to give rise to suspicion of guilt; merely relying on the fact that accusations have been made is not sufficient because that is just repeating what others have said.[95]

13.52 CPR Part 53 PD 11, para 2.5 provides that where a defendant alleges that the words complained of are true he must (1) specify the *defamatory* meanings he seeks to justify and (2) give details of the matters on which he relies in support of that allegation. (Note the meanings the defendant seeks to justify must be *defamatory* meanings.) The defendant must set out in the 'particulars of justification' plainly and unambiguously the material he relies on to prove that the words (in the meaning for which he contends) are true.[96] CPR Part 53 PD 19, para 2.8 provides that where a defendant alleges that the words complained of are true the claimant must serve a reply specifically admitting or denying the allegation and giving the facts on which he relies.

13.53 Although the defendant must state precisely what defamatory meaning is alleged to be true or it is intended to justify, this does not mean the defendant has to state that this is the meaning which the words actually bear.[97] The important point is that the defendant must inform the claimant and the court precisely what meaning he will seek to justify.[98] In summary, the defendant is obliged to plead the meaning he intends to justify but he is not obliged to plead the meaning that he says the words bear.[99] It has been recommended that where the defendant seeks to argue that the words bear a different meaning from that contended for by the claimant he should set out the meaning he contends for in the defence regardless of whether a defence of justification is pleaded.[100]

13.54 Section 5 of the Defamation Act 1952 provides that in an action for libel and slander 'in respect of words containing *two or more distinct charges* against the claimant, a defence of justification shall not fail by reason only that the truth of every charge is not proved if the words proved to be true do not materially injure the claimant's reputation having regard to the truth of the remaining charges' (emphasis added). This does not apply if there is only one charge or the charges are not distinct or the charged proved to be true is materially less serious than the other charges not proved to be true.

13.55 It should be noted with regard to justification:

- that the defendant is not required to justify the meaning pleaded by the claimant. The defendant can justify any meaning the words in their proper context within

rumour even before he satisfies himself that the rumour is true and in such circumstances it is possible to plead in justification that there were in truth such rumours.
[93] *Lewis v Daily Telegraph* [1964] AC 234, at 275.
[94] *Shah v Standard Chartered Bank* [1998] 4 All ER 155.
[95] See *Musa King v Telegraph Group Ltd* [2004] EWCA Civ 613 and *Shah v Standard Chartered Bank* [1999] QB 240.
[96] CPR Part 53 PD 13.
[97] *De L'Isle v Times Newspapers Ltd* [1988] 1 WLR 49.
[98] See *Lucas-Box v NGN* [1986] 1 WLR 147 and Mustill LJ in *Viscount De L'Isle v Times Newspapers* [1987] 3 All ER 499.
[99] See Nicholls LJ in *Prager v Times Newspapers* [1988] 1 WLR 77, at 91.
[100] *Armstrong v Times Newspapers Ltd* [2006] EWCA Civ 519, [2006] 1 WLR 2462.

the whole publication are capable of bearing.[101] Obviously, if the defendant fails to justify the claimant's meaning and that meaning is found to be the correct meaning the plea of justification will fail; and

- if there are several defamatory statements in a publication which refer to the claimant it is necessary to determine whether or not they constitute one overall defamatory sting or whether they are separate and distinct defamatory statements.[102] If they are separate and distinct the claimant is entitled to complain of only one of them even though the publication contains more. The defendant must deal with and seek to justify only this one defamatory statement relied on by the claimant and cannot attempt to justify the others.

13.56 In seeking to justify the words complained of the defendant is not restricted to matters which occurred at or prior to the time of publication, but those facts must be relevant to prove the truth of what was published at the time of publication.[103] Where it is alleged that there were reasonable grounds for *believing* the claimant had been guilty of wrongdoing, events occurring after publication will not be relevant because they could not have affected the defendant's belief.

13.57 If a spent conviction under the Rehabilitation of Offenders Act 1974 is relied on by way of justification that part of the defence which relies on the conviction will be defeated if the claimant is able to prove malice in respect of the reference to the conviction.[104]

Fair comment on a matter of public interest

13.58 A defamation claim can be defended on the basis that the words complained of were fair comment on a matter of public interest. The defence applies to expressions of opinion not statements of fact. If made out this provides a complete defence to an action.[105] The defence is not limited to those who have a duty to publish but is available to anyone. All are free to comment on matters of public interest. It is necessary for the defendant to plead and prove that the words are indeed comment and not fact. If the words are fact not comment the defence is not available. Keene LJ stated in *Burstein v Associated Newspapers*[106] in respect of an offending review which, it was suggested, commented on the claimant personally:

> 'No reasonable person could read it as a statement about the claimant in respect of any matter not contained in that review. There is no suggestion that the reviewer was otherwise acquainted with the claimant. That is important for the reasons set out in *Carr v. Hood* (ante), which was cited with approval by Somervell LJ in the Court of Appeal in *Kemsley v. Foot* [1951] 2 KB 34 at 41. The final sentence in the review was patently drawing an inference from the facts which had been set out earlier in the review, and on the principles approved by the House of Lords in *Kemsley v. Foot* [1952] AC 345 it was unmistakably comment. The

---

[101] CPR Part 53 PD 12; and see *Waters v Sunday Pictorial Newspapers Ltd* [1961] 1 WLR 967; *Prager v Times Newspapers* [1988] 1 WLR 77, at 86; *Polly Peck v Trelford* [1986] QB 1000; and *Williams v Reason* [1988] 1 WLR 96.
[102] *Polly Peck Plc v Trelford* [1986] QB 1000, at 1032, per O'Connor LJ.
[103] *Pamplin v Express Newspapers Ltd* [1988] 1 WLR 116, at 121.
[104] Rehabilitation of Offenders Act 1974, s 8(5).
[105] In *Burstein v Associated Newspapers Ltd* [2007] EWCA Civ 600 it was held by the CA that the words (a review of an opera) were unarguably fair comment and the claim was struck out.
[106] Ibid.

point was vividly put by Lord Ackner in *Telnikoff v. Matusevitch* [1992] 2 AC 343 at 358 B, adopting a passage from *Winfield and Jolowicz on Tort*, 11th edition:

> "To say that 'A is a disgrace to human nature' is an allegation of fact, but if the words were 'A murdered his father and is therefore a disgrace to human nature' the latter words are plainly a comment on the former.'"

13.59 Fair comment plainly must be based on facts that are true. The defendant is not confined to the facts stated in the words complained of. It is important that the reader is able to distinguish fact from comment. What is 'fair' comment is an objective test and depends upon whether an honest person could have made it having knowledge of those facts which are proved at trial.[107] These facts need not be the words the claimant complains of or even those set out in the publication itself provided they existed at the time of publication[108] and were known in general terms to the person who made the comment upon them which is alleged to be fair.[109] If the facts are not set out in the publication the defendant is entitled to rely on extrinsic facts if there was a general public awareness of the subject matter of the comment and the subject matter is clearly identified.

13.60 The following general principles apply to the defence:

- a matter is a matter of public interest if it is such as to affect people at large so that they might be legitimately interested in, or concerned at, what is going on;[110]

- the defendant's allegations must be comment not fact – a distinction which depends not just upon the content of the allegation but also the context and manner of expression;

- whether or not the comment has a basis in truth the substratum of truth must be clearly referred to in the publication (this does not mean that the facts have to be set out fully in the publication[111]); and

- to be considered 'fair' the comment must be such as might have been written by 'any honest man, however prejudiced he might be, or however exaggerated or obstinate his views'.[112]

13.61 CPR Part 53 PD 14, para 2.6 provides that where a defendant alleges that the words complained of are fair comment on a matter of public interest he must: (1) specify the defamatory meaning he seeks to defend as fair comment on a matter of public interest; and (2) give details of the matters on which he relies in support of that allegation. (The comment relied on must be pleaded with sufficient precision to enable the claimant to know the precise case he must meet.[113] The 'single meaning' doctrine applies, ie the first thing is to identify the meaning of the words and then decide if the

---

[107] *Merivale v Carson* (1887) 20 QBD 275, at 280.

[108] *Lowe v Associated Newspapers* [2006] EWHC 320 (QB), [2007] 1 QB 580 and *Cohen v Daily Telegraph* [1968] 1 WLR 916.

[109] *Lowe v Associated Newspapers* [2006] EWHC 320 (QB), [2007] 1 QB 580.

[110] *London Artists v Littler* [1969] 2 QB 375.

[111] See *Kemsley v Foot* [1952] AC 345.

[112] *Burstein v Associated Newspapers Ltd* [2007] EWCA Civ 600 (where the CA found it was not open to a jury to find that the opinions contained in a review of an opera could not have been held by a person who had seen the opera); and see *Turner v MGM* [1950] 1 All ER 449, at 461.

[113] *Control Risks v New Library Ltd* [1990] 1 WLR 183.

defence of fair comment is established.[114]) As with justification the defendant must plead the meaning he seeks to defend as fair comment. Although not stated in para 2.6 the defendant should specify the matter of public interest relied on.[115]

13.62 Since the comment must be founded on facts which are true the defence of fair comment will fail if it can be shown that the facts relied on to support the comment were untrue.[116] It is essential, therefore, to ensure that the facts relied on to support a plea of fair comment are true and that there is evidence to prove them or reasonable grounds for supposing that such evidence will be available at trial.[117]

13.63 As is the case with regard to justification:

- the defendant is not required to plead fair comment in respect of the meaning pleaded by the claimant. The defendant can plead fair comment in respect of any meaning the words in their proper context within the whole publication are capable of bearing. Obviously if the defendant fails to plead fair comment in relation to the claimant's meaning and that meaning is found to be the correct meaning the plea of fair comment will fail; and

- if there are several defamatory statements in a publication which refer to the claimant it is necessary to determine whether or not they constitute one overall defamatory sting or whether they are separate and distinct defamatory statements. If they are separate and distinct the claimant is entitled to complain of only one of them even though the publication contains more. The defendant must deal with and plead fair comment only in relation to the one defamatory statement relied on by the claimant and cannot attempt to plead fair comment in relation to the others.

13.64 The defence of fair comment will be defeated if it is proved that the defendant published the words maliciously.

13.65 The principles governing the legal requirements as to the commentator's state of knowledge at the time of publication were summarised by Eady J in *Lowe v Associated Newspapers* as follows:[118]

'(1) Any fact pleaded to support fair comment must have existed at the time of publication. (2) Any such facts must have been known, at least in general terms, at the time the comment was made, although it is not necessary that they should all have been in the forefront of the commentator's mind. (3) A general fact within the commentator's knowledge (as opposed to the comment itself) may be supported by specific examples even if the commentator had not been aware of them (rather as examples of previously published material from Lord Kemsley's newspapers were allowed). (4) Facts may not be pleaded of which the commentator was unaware (even in general terms) on the basis that the defamatory comment is one he *would have* made *if* he had known them. (5) A commentator may rely upon a specific or a general fact (and, it follows, provide examples to illustrate it) even if he has forgotten it, because it may have contributed to the formation of his opinion. (6) The purpose of the defence of fair comment is to protect honest expressions of opinion upon, or inferences honestly drawn from, specific facts. (7) The ultimate test is the objective one of

---

114   *Lowe v Times Newspapers Ltd* [2006] EWHC 320.
115   CPR Part 53 PD 16.
116   *Branson v Bower (No 2)* [2001] EMLR 33.
117   *McDonald's Corpn v Steel* [1995] 3 All ER 615, at 621.
118   [2006] EWHC 320 (QB).

whether someone could have expressed the commentator's defamatory opinion (or drawn the inference) *upon* the facts known to the commentator, at least in general terms, and upon which he was purporting to comment. (8) A defendant who is responsible for publishing the defamatory opinions or inferences of an identified commentator (such as in a newspaper column or letters page) does not have to show that he, she or it also knew the facts relied upon – provided they were known to the commentator. (9) It is not permitted to plead fair comment if the commentator was doing no more than regurgitating the opinions of others without any knowledge of the underlying facts – still less if he was simply echoing rumours.'

13.66 CPR Part 53 PD 19, para 2.8 provides that where a defendant alleges that the words complained of are fair comment on a matter of public interest the claimant must serve a reply specifically admitting or denying the allegation and giving the facts on which he relies. Paragraph 2.9 provides that if the defendant contends that any of the words or matters are fair comment on a matter of public interest and the claimant intends to allege that the defendant acted with malice, the claimant must serve a reply giving details of the facts and matters relied on.

13.67 Malice is treated differently in defamation cases depending on context. In contrast to malice required to defeat a defence of qualified privilege (as to which see below), a defence of fair comment will be defeated only if there is proof that the defendant genuinely did not hold the view he expressed and spite and ill will on its own will not be sufficient to defeat the defence.[119] It is the state of mind of the individual responsible for the defamatory statement that matters.[120]

ABSOLUTE PRIVILEGE

13.68 Section 14(1) of the Defamation Act 1996 provides that a fair and accurate report of proceedings before a court to which the section applies, if published contemporaneously with the proceedings, is absolutely privileged. The courts covered are any court in the UK, the European Court of Justice or any court attached to it, the European Court of Human Rights and any international criminal tribunal established by the Security Council of the UN or by an international agreement to which the UK is a party.

13.69 CPR Part 53 PD 17, para 2.7 provides that where a defendant alleges that the words complained of were published on a privileged occasion he must specify the circumstances he relies on in support of that contention. This applies to both absolute and qualified privilege.

13.70 Words published on an occasion of absolute privilege cannot give rise to an action even if published maliciously. The defence is based on the public interest and in summary applies to:

- proceedings in Parliament;

- statements made in the course of judicial or quasi-judicial proceedings;

---

[119] Lord Nicholls in *Tse Wai Chun Paul v Albert Cheng* [2001] EMLR 777.
[120] *Broadway v Odhams Press* [1965] 1 WLR 805, at 813.

- reports published contemporaneously with judicial proceedings;[121]

- communications between informants and the police;[122]

- communications between officers of state in the course of their duties;

- the internal documents of a foreign embassy;

- fair and accurate report of proceedings in public before a national court and certain foreign courts[123] which are published contemporaneously;

- various communications to or from the Parliamentary Commissioner;[124] and

- reports by the Monopolies Commission or the Director of Fair Trading.[125]

Qualified privilege

13.71 The defence of qualified privilege is of much broader scope than absolute privilege and covers those occasions when defamatory material is published in pursuance of some pressing duty such as a legal, social or moral duty, or so as to protect or further a legitimate interest, to a person *with a like duty or interest*[126] to receive the material. There is, therefore, a degree of reciprocity. It is solely for the judge to determine whether or not a moral or social duty to communicate exists on the basis that the duty would be such that it would be 'recognised by English people of ordinary intelligence and moral principle'.[127] A person has a right to defend himself reasonably from attack in the press and elsewhere and an interest in communicating may arise which is sufficient to raise the privilege.

13.72 If communication goes beyond the class with the corresponding interest or duty in receiving it the communication to that extent will not be protected.[128] Complaints of wrongdoing should normally be made to the appropriate authorities and should normally be investigated before being disclosed any further. As with absolute privilege this defence is based on public policy on the footing that sometimes policy dictates that defamatory material should be allowed to be published even if it turns out to be false. There are many varied situations where this is so and it is not possible to describe them all.[129]

13.73 Where the defendant and the publishee have an existing and established relationship it is necessary to look at the nature of that relationship and the relevance to the relationship to what is being communicated. It is important that the publisher and

---

[121] Defamation Act 1996, s 14 – note that if the report is not published contemporaneously with the proceedings it will attract qualified privilege, as to which see below.
[122] *Taylor v Director of the Serious Fraud Office* [1999] 2 AC 177.
[123] Defamation Act 1996, s 14.
[124] Parliamentary Commissioner Act 1967, s 10.
[125] Competition Act 1980, s 16(2).
[125] *Adam v Ward* [1917] AC 309, at 314.
[127] Lindley LJ in *Stuart v Bell* [1891] 2 QB 341, at 350.
[128] In *Joseph & others v Spiller* [2009] EWHC 1152 (QB), at [61], in a case that concerned the parties' respective contentions regarding a private contractual dispute, it was held that there was no duty on the defendant's part to put the allegations into the public domain and doing so could hardly be said to be 'fairly warranted by the occasion'.
[129] *London Association for Protection of Trade v Greenlands Ltd* [1916] 2 AC 15.

publishee have a reciprocal interest in the subject matter of the publication, but if a defendant replies to a query honestly but erroneously believing that the person raising the query had sufficient interest in the information the defendant may have a defence.[130]

13.74 It is necessary to distinguish cases where the communicator and the communicatee were in an existing and established relationship (irrespective of whether the communications related to reciprocal interests or reciprocal duties or a mixture of both) and cases of communications between strangers where no such relationship is established. In *Kearns v General Council of the Bar*[131] it was said that that distinction was a more helpful categorisation than the distinction between 'common interest' and 'duty-interest' cases and once that distinction is drawn it is understandable that privilege should more readily attach to communications within an existing relationship rather than between strangers. It was held in that case that where the communications were between those in an existing relationship (in contrast to situations where privilege is claimed on the basis of social or moral duty) it was not necessary to verify the quality of the information and the question whether a defamatory publication had been adequately investigated or verified went to the issue of malice, not to the issue of whether the occasion of the communication was privileged. So the Bar Council in the *Kearns* case had given a ruling in the context of an established relationship between it and the Bar and the occasion necessarily attracted qualified privilege.

13.75 It is obviously not easy for the media to rely on the defence of qualified privilege because of the necessity to prove a reciprocal interest on the part of the readership to read the material complained of. There might be cases where someone has been attacked in the media and seeks to refute what has been said by using the press to publish the refutation. This might provide a defence if the publication is bona fide and relevant to what was alleged.[132]

13.76 Section 15(1) of the Defamation Act 1996 provides that the publication of any report or other statement mentioned in Sch 1 to the Act is privileged unless the publication is shown to be made by malice. The defence does not apply to publication to the public or a section of the public of matter which is not of public concern and the publication of which is not for the public benefit. Sch 1 divides reports and statements into those having qualified privilege without explanation or contradiction (Pt I – meaning that a defendant wishing to rely on the privilege is not obliged to publish an explanation or qualification of the words should the claimant request them) and those privileged subject to explanation or contradiction (Pt II). In relation to the matters in Part II there is no defence under the section if the claimant shows that the defendant was requested to publish a reasonable letter or statement by way of explanation or contradiction and refused or neglected to do so.[133]

13.77 Matters in the Defamation Act 1996, Sch 1, Pt I include a fair and accurate report of proceedings in public of a legislature or a court anywhere in the world. Matters in Pt II include a fair and accurate report of proceedings at a general meeting of a UK public company[134] and a fair and accurate report of any finding or decision of a associations formed for the purpose of promoting or safeguarding the interests of trade, business, industry or profession or associations formed for the purpose of promoting or

---

[130] Ibid.
[131] [2003] EWCA Civ 331.
[132] *Laughton v Bishop of Sodor and Man* (1872) LR 4 PC 495.
[133] Defamation Act 1996, s 15(2).
[134] Defamation Act 1996, Sch 1, Pt II, para 13(1).

safeguarding the interests of a game, sport or pastime to the playing or exercise of which members of the public are invited or admitted.[135]

13.78 What has become known as *Reynolds* privilege is concerned to provide an appropriate degree of protection for responsible journalism when reporting matters of public concern. Responsible journalism is the point at which a fair balance is held between freedom of expression on matters of public concern and the reputation of individuals. It has been said that it can be regarded as the price journalists pay for the privilege and if they are to have the benefit of the privilege journalists must exercise due professional skill and care.[136]

Reynolds v Times Newspapers[137]

13.79 The '*Reynolds* defence' is primarily concerned with situations where newspapers publish matters of public interest (and is not restricted to political matters). The House of Lords rejected the argument that the common law should develop 'political information' as a new subject matter category attracting qualified privilege whatever the circumstances. The House of Lords expanded the qualified privilege defence to cover situations where the defendant can establish that publication amounted to 'responsible journalism',[138] holding that (1) there is no protection under general common law for defamatory statements in newspapers simply because they were concerned with political issues or other issues of public interest; but (2) qualified privilege does provide a defence if the circumstances in relation to the publication are such that there was a social duty to publish the material to the public to the extent that it could be said that the public were entitled to have the information. Ten (non exhaustive) matters were listed by the House of Lords as relevant matters to be taken into account:

- the seriousness of the allegation;

- the nature of the information;

- the source of the information;

- the steps taken to verify the information;[139]

- the status of the information;

- the urgency of the matter;

- whether the claimant was invited to comment;

- whether the article contained the gist of the claimant's story;

- the tone of the article; and

- the circumstances and timing of the article.

---

[135]   Defamation Act 1996, Sch 1, Pt II, para 14.
[136]   This appraisal was given by Lord Hoffman in *Bonnick v Morris* [2002] UKPC 31, at [23].
[137]   [2001] 2 AC 127.
[138]   *Loutchansky v Times Newspapers Ltd (Nos 2 to 5)* [2002] 2 WLR 640.
[139]   The importance of this factor was illustrated in *Seaga v Harper* [2008] UKPC 9: see Lord Carswell at [15].

13.80 Fundamentally, the established common law approach (duty to disseminate and interest in receiving the information) continues to apply to political information and there is no new special 'political information' defence. The relevant interest in determining whether the media has a duty to publish is that of freedom of expression and the public interest in a free and vigorous press.

13.81 The requirement in CPR Part 53 PD 17, para 2.7 for a defendant to specify the circumstances he relies on in support of a claim of qualified privilege is particularly important in the context of the *Reynolds* defence because it is usually necessary, especially where the defamation has been widely disseminated, to plead a number of circumstantial matters, such as the seriousness of the allegation and the extent to which it is a matter of public concern, the source and status of the information, the steps taken to verify it, the urgency of the matter and the steps taken to obtain and print the claimant's side of the story, and in addition the reasonable belief of those responsible for publication that the story was true.[140]

Jameel v Wall Street Journal Europe[141]

13.82 In the *Jameel* case the House of Lords emphasised that at its core the *Reynolds* defence was concerned with whether journalistic decisions had been made responsibly and that the defence was to be applied flexibly. It was considered the defence was being applied too cautiously by the lower courts. Lord Hoffman said that it is the material which is being published that is privileged not the occasion on which it is published and that the defence might more appropriately be called the 'Reynolds public interest defence'. Judges are not to use the advantage of 'leisure and hindsight' in determining whether a correct editorial decision was made. The courts should look at the overall thrust of the article to determine whether publication was in the public interest rather than focusing on the particular allegation complained of. To establish the necessary public interest in publication the article, looked at as a whole, must contain information the public were entitled to know. The duty of the publisher is a duty to act responsibly in publishing and it is not a reciprocal duty to publish. The paper must justify the decision to include the particular allegation in the article in the sense that it makes 'a real contribution to the public interest element in the article' but not in the sense that the story needed it to be included. In summary, the all-important reciprocal interest of the readership in publication would be established by showing that, looked at as a whole, the article conveyed information the public were entitled to know. Whether the story is true or false is not relevant to the defence, nor is the fact that the paper cannot prove it to be true at trial. This does not mean, of course, that papers can recklessly publish falsehoods in the hope of relying on the *Reynolds* defence.

13.83 Because the *Reynolds* defence is about responsible journalism various factors determine whether the defence will avail. The focus is upon the state of mind of the journalist at the time of publication so only facts in existence at that time are relevant. Where the truth of the information cannot be verified the journalist must make it clear whether reliance is placed on 'reasonable belief in the truth of matters published, or their implications and where he is not'. It has been said[142] that there are many advantages in trying the issue of privilege (in particular, responsible journalism) without a jury because trial by judge alone dispenses with the problematic question of

---

[140] *Jameel v Wall Street Journal* [2006] 3 WLR 642.
[141] [2006] 3 WLR 642.
[142] At first instance: *Charman v Orion Publishing Group Ltd* [2006] EWHC 1756 (QB), [2007] 1 All ER 622 (see also the judgments in the Court of Appeal at [2007] EWCA Civ 972).

distinguishing issues of law (for the judge alone to decide) and issues of fact (for the jury to decide if there is one). It is increasingly common for issues of qualified privilege to be tried by judge alone.[143]

13.84 The *Reynolds* defence can be defeated if the claimant can show that the defendant did not hold 'a reasonable belief in the truth of the matters published or their implications' or that if the defendant did hold such a belief it was not reasonable.[144] The issue will be whether the claimant accepts what that the journalist says his state of mind was. The claimant should be clear whether he denies the journalist believed what was published was true or whether he contends that the journalist's belief was not reasonable. Where a political story is breaking news and neutral reports are published of what the participants are saying as the story unfolds it is difficult for journalists to verify the truth of everything they have been told. In such cases journalists are given more latitude over failure to verify the truth of everything which is printed.[145]

13.85 It was confirmed by the Privy Council in *Seaga v Harper*[146] that the *Reynolds* defence was not confined to the press and broadcasting media and that there was no valid reason why it should not extend to publications made by any person who publishes material of public interest in any medium, so long as the conditions as being applicable to 'responsible' journalism are satisfied.

Charman v Orion Publishing Group[147]

13.86 The following propositions were set out by Ward LJ from an analysis of recent developments in the law:[148]

- whether or not the matter was properly in the public interest and whether or not the standard of responsible journalism had been met has to be considered in the context of the article as a whole;

- taking steps to verify the information is to be given added emphasis (on the basis that there is no duty to publish and the public have no interest to read material which the publisher has not taken reasonable care to verify and this usually means taking reasonable steps to contact the people named for comments);

- if the public interest is engaged the report is privileged if it satisfies the test of responsible journalism (on the basis that responsible journalism is the point at which a fair balance is held between freedom of expression on matters of public concern and the reputations of individuals, ie whether the defendant has acted fairly and responsibly in gathering and publishing information);

- Lord Nicholls' ten factors are to be treated as pointers to be taken into account in deciding whether the test of responsible journalism had been satisfied and not as a series of hurdles that had to be surmounted;

---

[143] *Galloway v Telegraph Group Ltd* [2006] EWCA Civ 17, [2006] EMLR 11 and *Henry v BBC* [2005] EWHC 2787 (QB).
[144] *Jameel v Wall Street Journal* [2005] EWCA Civ 74.
[145] *Al-Fagih v HH Saudi Research & Marketing (UK) Ltd* [2002] EMLR 215.
[146] [2008] UKPC 9. See Lord Carswell at [11], confirming what Lord Hoffman said in *Jameel*, ibid, at [54].
[147] [2007] EWCA Civ 972.
[148] [2007] EWCA Civ 972, at [66].

- in assessing the responsibility of the article, weight must be given to the professional judgment of the journalist (this is to give due regard to the judgment of the editor making the assessment about running the story and how it is presented absent some indication that the judgment was made in a casual, cavalier, slipshod or careless manner);

- the test is not intended to present an onerous obstacle to the media in the discharge of their function; and

- the *Reynolds* case must be seen as the House of Lord's attempt to 'redress the balance' between Arts 8 and 10 of the European Convention for the Protection of Human Rights and Fundamental Freedoms in favour of greater freedom for the press to publish stories of genuine public interest.

Reportage

13.87 Useful guidance was given by the Court of Appeal in *Charman*[149] with regard to the reportage defence. This defence has been described as a convenient word to describe the neutral reporting of attributed allegations rather than their adoption by the newspaper. In such situations the public was entitled to be informed of such a dispute without having to wait for the publisher, following an attempt at verification, to commit himself to one side or the other.[150] The relationship between the reportage defence and *Reynolds* qualified privilege was addressed by Ward LJ in *Charman* as follows:[151]

> 'As for the law on reportage, the nature of the defence and its place within the *Reynolds* doctrine of qualified privilege was recently examined in *Roberts v Gable* [2007] EWCA Civ 721, [2007] EMLR 457. The critical point of that analysis is that the defence will be established where, judging the thrust of the report as a whole, the effect of the report is not to adopt the truth of what is being said, but to record the fact that the statements which were defamatory were made. The judge's task is akin to the way in which at common law hearsay evidence used to be admitted or excluded. The protection is lost if the journalist adopts what has been said and makes it his own or if he fails to report the story in a fair, disinterested, neutral way. To justify the attack on the claimant's reputation the publication must always meet the standards of responsible journalism as that concept has developed in *Reynolds*'s case, the burden being on the defendants. In that way the balance between art 10 and art 8 is maintained. *Roberts v Gable* was a good example of reportage in that the defendant newspaper simply republished allegation and counter-allegation of two politically opposed factions within the British National Party, each side accusing the other of theft of money collected at their "Grand Rally ... to promote the BNP campaign for the London Mayoral and GLA elections in 2004".'

13.88 Thus the protection afforded by the reportage defence is lost if a journalist adopts what is being reported as his own or if the story is not reported in a fair, disinterested and neutral way. The public interest is beside the point if a journalist simply reports accurately and neutrally defamatory utterances because repeating another's libel is just as bad as making the statement directly oneself. For the reportage defence to apply it is necessary to report only the fact that allegations had been made and the fact that they had been denied. If the report goes beyond that to adopt the statements the reportage defence is lost.

---

[149] [2007] EWCA Civ 972, at [46], per Ward LJ.
[150] See Simon Brown LJ in *Al-Fagih v HH Saudi Research & Marketing (UK) Ltd* [2002] EMLR 215.
[151] [2007] EWCA Civ 972, at [48].

13.89   The following principles relating to what was referred to as the species of defence known as reportage were isolated in *Roberts v Gable*[152] as follows:

•   reportage protects the neutral reporting (ie without adoption, embellishment or subscribing to belief in truth) of attributed allegations of both sides of political and possibly other types of dispute;

•   the report must meet the standards of responsible journalism and the information must be in the public interest for the reportage defence to be available;

•   the defence will be available notwithstanding no steps were taken to verify the accuracy of the statements reported because the report is about the fact statements had been made not that they were true; and

•   the protection of the reportage defence will be lost if the author adopts the report and makes it his own, or if he fails to report the story in a fair, disinterested and neutral way.

13.90   CPR Part 53 PD 21, para 2.9 provides that if the defendant contends that any of the words or matters were published on a privileged occasion and the claimant intends to allege that the defendant acted with malice, the claimant must serve a reply giving details of the facts and matters relied on.

Malice

13.91   The defence of qualified privilege is liable to be defeated if it is shown that the words were published maliciously, ie where a defendant uses the occasion for improper motives and thereby abuses it. The defendant is not deprived of the defence if irrelevant defamatory matter is used on an otherwise privileged occasion but it might well show that the defendant was acting maliciously.[153] Malice in the context of qualified privilege means that the defendant has abused the privileged occasion by using it as a means of getting at the claimant. This means the defendant must use the occasion in furtherance of some legal or moral duty to communicate information not for personal spite. The claimant proves malice by showing that the defendant had a dominant improper motive which is generally inferred if it can be shown that the defendant knew that statement was false when it was made or that the defendant made the statement recklessly, not caring whether it was true or false. Malice can exceptionally be shown even where the defendant believed that the words were true.[154] Even a positive belief in the truth of what is published on a privileged occasion may not be sufficient to negative express malice if it can be proved that the defendant misused the occasion, ie where the defendant's dominant motive is to not to perform the relevant duty but to give vent to personal spite or ill will. In such cases positive belief in the truth of what is published will not give rise to protection.

13.92   Malice is a dead letter in relation to *Reynolds* privilege 'because the propriety of the conduct of the defendant is built into the conditions under which the material is privileged'.[155]

---

[152]   [2007] EWCA Civ 721, [2008] QB 502.
[153]   *Adam v Ward* [1917] AC 309, at 326–327.
[154]   See Lord Diplock in *Horrocks v Lowe* [1975] AC 135, at 149–151 and *Rackham v Sandy* [2005] EWHC 482.
[155]   See Lord Hoffman in *Jameel*, ibid, at [46] and see CPR Part 53 PD 22.

Leave and licence

13.93 It is a defence to a defamation claim that the claimant consented to publication of the particular material complained of.

Innocent dissemination

13.94 This defence is important to those who play a subsidiary role in publication because every person responsible for publication of a defamatory statement risks being sued (eg author, editor, proprietor, printer, distributor, retailer etc) irrespective of whether they knew about the defamatory matter. It is of importance in the internet age because of the vast quantities of material distributed throughout the world wide web network. The defence is of particular importance to those 'information society services', such as internet service providers (ISPs), who might 'cache' or 'host' information containing libellous material. There may be defences under the Defamation Act 1996 or under the Electronic Communications (EC Directive) Regulations 2002,[156] which will be considered later in this section (see **13.98** et seq).[157] Those who play a subsidiary role in publishing defamatory material (other than author, editor or commercial publisher) may have a defence provided that they did not know and had no reason to believe that what they did contributed to the publication of defamatory material.[158] If those involved in publishing defamatory material are put on notice that the material is defamatory they will lose the defence.[159] In *Metropolitan International Schools Ltd v Google*[160] Eady J held that those in control of search engines such as Google Inc would not be regarded publishers of defamatory material which resulted from a search.

Defamation Act 1996, s 1

13.95 Section 1(1) of the Defamation Act 1996 provides that in defamation proceedings a person has a defence if he shows that he was not the author, editor or publisher of the statement complained of; that he took reasonable care in relation to its publication; and he did not know, and had no reason to believe, that what he did caused or contributed to the publication of a defamatory statement. Section 1(5) provides that in determining whether a person took reasonable care or had reason to believe that what he did contributed to the publication of a defamatory statement, regard is had to the extent of his responsibility for the content of the statement or the decision to publish it; the nature and circumstances of the publication; and the previous conduct or character of the author, editor or publisher.[161]

13.96 Section 1(3) of the Defamation Act 1996 provides that a person shall not be considered the author, editor or publisher of a statement if he is only involved in:

---

[156] SI 2002/2013.

[157] Defences under the Act and under the Regulations were considered by Eady J in *Bunt v Tilley* [2006] 3 All ER 336, where it was held that an ISP performed only a passive role in facilitating postings on the internet and in defamation proceedings could not be deemed to be a publisher at common law. The ISP was held not to have knowingly participated in the relevant publications and would not be liable for publication.

[158] A passive medium for publication such as a postal service is not a publisher at all: see *Bunt v Tilley* [2007] 1 WLR 1243.

[159] *Godfrey v Demon Internet Ltd* [1994] 4 All ER 342.

[160] [2009] EWHC 1765 (QB).

[161] The common law defence remains but in practical terms adds nothing to the statute because the claimant is obliged to plead and prove that he was not aware that the publication contained the libel or was of a character to contain libellous material and that his ignorance in this regard was not the result of his own negligence.

- printing, producing, distributing or selling printed material containing the statement;

- processing, making copies of, distributing or selling printed material containing the statement;

- processing, making copies of, distributing or selling any electronic medium in or on which the statement is recorded, or in operating or providing any equipment, system or service by means of which the statement is retrieved, copied, distributed or made available in electronic form;

- broadcasting a live programme containing the statement in circumstances in which he has no effective control over the maker of the statement; or

- operating or providing access to a communication system by means of which the statement is transmitted, or made available, by a person over whom he has no effective control.

13.97 Therefore, in certain, strictly defined circumstances, commercial publishers are given a defence under this section, such as ISPs,[162] live broadcasters, newsagents and libraries, and also under common law.

The Electronic Communications (EC Directive) Regulations 2002[163]

13.98 ISPs (and other 'information society services') may have a defence under the Electronic Communications (EC Directive) Regulations 2002 depending on the extent to which the service provider is involved in the process of publication. It is necessary to distinguish: (1) A mere conduit (for which the defence is absolute); (2) A service provider which 'caches' information which originates from another source within the communications network; and (3) A service provider which 'hosts' material.

13.99 The service provider which 'caches' information must act expeditiously to remove or disable access to the information upon obtaining 'actual knowledge' that the original information has been, has been ordered to be, removed from the network (reg 18).[164]

13.100 The service provider which 'hosts' material has a defence provided: (1) It does not have 'actual knowledge' that the information is 'unlawful' and is not aware of facts or circumstances from which unlawfulness would be apparent; (2) it acts expeditiously to remove or disable access to the information upon obtaining such knowledge or awareness; and (3) the person who provided the information was not acting under its authority or control (reg 19).

---

[162] *Godfrey v Demon* [1999] 4 All ER 342.
[163] SI 2002/2013.
[164] It was held in *Bunt v Tilley* [2006] 3 All ER 336 that reg 18 excluded ISPs from liability from storing material and that its purpose was to protect 'information society service' providers in respect of material for which they were not primary host but which they stored temporarily on their computer systems for enabling the efficient availability of internet material.

Damages

13.101   CPR Part 53 PD 23, para 2.10(b) provides that (1) a claimant must give full details of the facts and matters on which he relies in support of his claim for damages; and (2) if seeking exemplary and aggravated the information specified in CPR, r 16.4(1)(c), namely a statement to that effect and his grounds for claiming them.

13.102   The purpose of an award of damages in defamation cases is:

- compensation for the claimant's personal distress and hurt;

- compensation for the damage to the claimant's reputation; and

- vindication of the claimant's reputation.

13.103   Damages in defamation proceedings are assessed as at the point of assessment and are not assessed at the date of publication, nor are they notionally assessed then.[165] The conduct of the defendant after publication could aggravate or mitigate the damage and therefore any award of damages. It follows, as stated previously, that if an unqualified offer of amends is made and accepted and an agreed apology published there is bound to be substantial mitigation and the likely damages substantially reduced.

13.104   The principles on which damages are awarded in defamation proceedings were referred to by Bingham MR giving the judgment of the court in *John v MGN Ltd*:[166]

> 'The successful plaintiff in a defamation action is entitled to recover, as general compensatory damages, such sum as will compensate him for the wrong he has suffered. That sum must compensate him for the damage to his reputation; vindicate his good name; and take account of the distress, hurt and humiliation which the defamatory publication has caused. In assessing the appropriate damages for injury to reputation the most important factor is the gravity of the libel; the more closely it touches the plaintiff's personal integrity, professional reputation, honour, courage, loyalty and the core attributes of his personality, the more serious it is likely to be. The extent of publication is also relevant: a libel published to millions has a greater potential to cause damage than a libel published to a handful of people. A successful plaintiff may properly look to an award of damages to vindicate his reputation: but the significance of this is much greater in a case where the defendant asserts the truth of the libel and refuses any retraction or apology than in a case where the defendant acknowledges the falsity of what was published and publicly expresses regret that the libellous publication took place. It is well established that compensatory damages may and should compensate for additional injury caused to the plaintiff's feelings by the defendant's conduct of the action, as when he persists in an unfounded assertion that the publication was true, or refuses to apologise, or cross-examines the plaintiff in a wounding or insulting way. Although the plaintiff has been referred to as "he", all this of course applies to women just as much as men.'

13.105   The law will presume that damage has been caused so the claimant is not obliged to give particulars and can simply rely on the averment that by reason of the publication the claimant suffered distress and injury to his reputation. This is damage which *flows* from publication, but where the claimant relies on more he must plead it and inform the defendant of the case he is to meet to enable a payment into court to be made. Damages are awarded for the loss of reputation and for injury to feelings, both of

---

[165]   See May LJ in *Nail v NGN* [2004] EWCA Civ 1708, at [41].
[166]   [1997] QB 586, at 607–608, [1996] 2 All ER 35, at 47–48.

which are presumed to flow from the defamatory statement. In summary, the extent of the award will reflect the gravity of the defamatory statement, the extent of publication and the nature of the defendant's conduct. The sort of factors that are relevant are the impact that the libel had on the claimant, such as hurt to his feelings or being shunned, and the behaviour of the defendant in the whole affair including after publication, such as a refusal to apologise or repeating the libel or other unusual features.[167] If the defamatory statement relates to business activities, general damages can be awarded for general loss of business profits and special damages for loss of specific business. Sometimes the claimant will need to amend his statement of case if the defendant's conduct is continuing.

13.106   In defamation cases damages can be reduced by a variety of matters, such as (1) directly relevant background facts giving context to the defamatory statement; (2) evidence in partial justification of the defamatory statement or in support of a plea of fair comment; (3) evidence showing the claimant has a bad reputation; (4) the claimant's own conduct; (5) apologies and offers of amends; and (6) the fact that the claimant has already received damages for substantially the same defamation.

13.107   Evidence of a claimant's bad reputation is admissible to reduce the damages awarded but evidence of particular bad conduct is generally not admissible.[168] In some cases evidence of directly relevant background context is admissible by way of reduction of damages.[169] It has been held that it does not make sense for juries to consider damages in an evidential vacuum and for this reason evidence of directly relevant factual background will not be excluded. But the evidence must be so clearly relevant to the subject matter of the libel or the claimant's reputation or sensitivity in that part of his life in respect of which the complaint was made that there would be a real risk, if such evidence were excluded, the jury might assess damages 'in blinkers', ie on a false basis and in ignorance of the facts: see *Turner v NGN*.[170] In that case the Court of Appeal held that the rule that evidence of specific acts of misconduct could not be given in evidence was largely to avoid the danger of trials within a trial and was never an absolute principle. The rule was always subject to the major exception where specific acts of misconduct on the part of the claimant might have been put before the court in support of pleas of justification or fair comment which had failed. Care should be exercised when seeking to rely on directly relevant background context. In *Turner* it was said:[171]

> 'I accept the point made in argument that it is somewhat repetitive to use the words "background" and "context" in the phrase "directly relevant background context", but that in itself does not produce obscurity. It is in any event inevitable that cases will occur where it is not easy to determine whether the test in *Burstein*'s case is met or not. That does not mean that the test is an inappropriate one, any more than is that propounded in *Scott v Sampson*: as Viscount Simonds recognised in the *Plato Films* case, the line between evidence of general bad reputation and evidence of specific conduct giving rise to such a reputation is not easy to draw. What constitutes the directly relevant background will vary from case to case, but I would myself accept the need for the courts to proceed, as Mr Browne advocates, with some caution in applying *Burstein*'s case, given that it represents a modification of the long-standing rule in *Scott v Sampson*. As Eady J put it in *Polanski v Conde Nast*

---

[167]   *Slipper v BBC* [1991] 1 QB 283.
[168]   In *Burstein v Times Newspapers Ltd* [2001] 1 WLR 579 it was held that directly relevant background context was admissible but not a roving inquiry into the claimant's life – not always an easy distinction to draw.
[169]   *Burstein v Times Newspapers Ltd* [2001] 1 WLR 579.
[170]   [2006] EWCA Civ 540.
[171]   Keene LJ, at [56].

Publications Ltd (21 October 2003, unreported), one should guard against extending too creatively the concept of "directly relevant background". The Court of Appeal in *Burstein*'s case was concerned to avoid jurors having to assess damages while wearing blinkers. If evidence is to qualify under the principle spelt out in *Burstein*'s case, it has to be evidence which is so clearly relevant to the subject matter of the libel or to the claimant's reputation or sensitivity in that part of his life that there would be a real risk of the jury assessing damages on a false basis if they were kept in ignorance of the facts to which the evidence relates.'

MALICIOUS FALSEHOOD

13.108 A person complaining about a defamatory statement might also be entitled to bring an action for malicious falsehood in respect of the words complained of.[172] In order to maintain a claim for malicious falsehood it is necessary to establish that a false statement has been made, that the statement was made maliciously and that the claimant has suffered actual damage as a result of the statement. This was confirmed by Bowen LJ in *Ratcliffe v Evans* who said:[173]

> 'That an action will lie for written or oral falsehoods, not actionable *per se* nor even defamatory, where they are maliciously published, where they are calculated in the ordinary course of things to produce, and where they do produce, actual damage, is established law.'

13.109 There is an exception to cases where actual damage had to be shown under the Defamation Act 1952, s 3, which provides that it is not necessary to allege and prove special damage if the words upon which the action is founded are calculated to cause pecuniary damage to the claimant and are published in writing or other permanent form[174] or if the words are calculated to cause pecuniary damage to the claimant in respect of any office, profession, calling, trade or business carried on by him at the time of publication.

13.110 For a claim in malicious falsehood to run the words complained of must have been published to a third party. Unlike in defamation the burden of proof lies upon the claimant to prove that the words are false. Despite that the defendant must particularise his version of events if he disagrees with the claimant's version and contends that the words are true. If the words are found to be true the claim will fail.

13.111 The fact that a false statement is made that causes damage to the claimant will not found a claim unless malice is established. The central issue in these claims is invariably proof of malice. The burden is on the claimant to prove malice and if good faith is shown the claim will fail. Behind the concept of malice in this sense lies the concept of improper motive. Malice in the sense of improper motive must be proved as a fact.[175] There are various ways malice might be proved, such as personal spite, an intention to injure the claimant without just cause or excuse or knowledge that what is stated is false. It is to be emphasised that these factors are not malice as such but ways of proving the existence of malice. In *Kaye v Robertson*[176] the Court of Appeal said that malice would be inferred if it was proved that the words were calculated to produce

---

[172] *Joyce v Sengupta* [1993] 1 All ER 897.
[173] [1892] 2 QB 524, at 527.
[174] This includes words which are broadcast – see Broadcasting Act 1990, s 166(2).
[175] An indirect or dishonest motive is an improper motive. As to the ingredients of actual malice see generally Lord Diplock in *Horrocks v Lowe* [1975] AC 135, at 149–150 and the CA in *Spring v Guardian Assurance* [1993] 2 All ER 273.
[176] [1991] FSR 62, at 67, per Glidewell LJ.

damage and the defendant knew when he published them that they were false or was
reckless as to whether they were false or not. It was said on the facts of that case it was
quite apparent that the reporter and photographer, who intruded upon Mr Kaye in his
hospital bed, must have known he was in no condition to give any informed consent to
them. Any subsequent publication of the falsehood would therefore inevitably be
malicious.

13.112   With regard to damages, the Court of Appeal suggested in *Joyce v Sengupta*[177]
that, although in order to succeed in a claim for malicious falsehood a claimant must
show the false statement has caused damage or, in reliance on s 3 of the Defamation
Act 1952 were calculated to cause pecuniary damage, a claimant relying on s 3 of 1952
Act (being unable to prove any compensatable pecuniary loss) is not thereby restricted to
nominal damages.[178] Sir Donald Nicholls said:[179]

> 'This state of the authorities suggests that damages for anxiety and distress are not
> recoverable for malicious falsehood. If that is the law it could lead to a manifestly
> unsatisfactory and unjust result in some cases. Take the example I gave earlier of a person
> who maliciously spreads rumours that his competitor's business has closed down. Or the
> rumour might be that the business is in financial difficulty and that a receiver will soon be
> appointed. The owner of the business suffers severe financial loss. Further, because of the
> effect the rumours are having on his business he is worried beyond measure about his
> livelihood and his family's future. He suffers acute anxiety and distress. Can it be right that
> the law is unable to give him any recompense for this suffering against the person whose
> malice caused it? Although injury to feelings alone will not found a cause of action in
> malicious falsehood, ought not the law to take such injury into account when it is connected
> with financial damage inflicted by the falsehood?'

13.113   The issue of damages for injury to feelings in malicious falsehood cases was
revisited by the Court of Appeal in *Khodaparast v Shad*.[180] It was held there was no
reason in principle why a claimant who was entitled to sue for malicious falsehood
(having proved special damage or met the requirements of the Defamation Act 1952,
s 3) should be prevented from recovering aggravated damages for injury to feelings.
These authorities underline that although mental anxiety, distress and injury to feelings
will not be sufficient to found a claim for malicious falsehood, if such a claim can be
founded on other grounds these heads of damage might be compensated by way of
aggravated damages.

---

[177]   [1993] 1 All ER 897.
[178]   Ibid, at 906 and 908.
[179]   Ibid, at 907.
[180]   [2000] 1 All ER 545, at 556–557 and 559.

Chapter 14

HARASSMENT

INTRODUCTION

14.1   Harassment is a major problem for many celebrities whether in the form of stalking, intrusive press photography or surveillance. The Protection from Harassment Act 1997 (PHA 1997) has gone some way to providing a remedy in such situations. To that extent further protection is given against invasion of an individual's privacy. Parliament has added harassment to the list of civil wrongs because it considered that the existing law provided insufficient protection to victims of harassment. The purpose of the Act is to protect victims of harassment, whatever form the harassment takes, wherever it occurs and whatever its motivation. The Act seeks to provide protection against stalkers, racial abusers, disruptive neighbours, bullying at work and so forth.[1] References in the Act to harassing a person include alarming the person or causing the person distress; a 'course of conduct' must involve conduct on at least two occasions and 'conduct' includes speech.[2]

14.2   Celebrities are particularly afflicted by the press campaigns involving intrusive photography and exposure-type articles. The issue of harassment in such cases cannot be divorced from a detailed consideration of European Convention for the Protection of Human Rights and Fundamental Freedoms (ECHR) and from rights such as freedom of expression and privacy. If a victim of press intrusion has a reasonable expectation of privacy in respect of the *information* contained in photographs then the publication of the image will breach the right to privacy and *publication* of the image can be restrained. That would not, of course, deal directly with the problem of the harassing behaviour on the part of the photographers. Where no right of privacy exists and harassment is present the remedy for the distressed celebrity (provided a course of conduct can be established) is under PHA 1997.[3]

THE PROHIBITION OF HARASSMENT

14.3   PHA 1997, s 1(1) provides that a person must not pursue a course of conduct (a) which amounts to harassment of another and (b) which he knows or ought to know amounts to harassment of the other.

14.4   PHA 1997, s 1(1A) provides that a person must not pursue a course of conduct (a) which involves harassment of two or more persons, (b) which he knows involves the

---

[1]   *Majrowski v Guy's & St Thomas' NHS Trust* [2006] UKHL 34, at [18], per Lord Nicholls.
[2]   See PHA 1997, s 7.
[3]   Claims for misuse of private information and harassment are often brought in one claim: see e g *CC v AB* [2007] EMLR 11. Also such claims may include a claim for breach of the Data Protection Act 1998 such as in the *Campbell* case [2004] UKHL 22, where a claim for misuse for private information was coupled with a claim for breach of the Data Protection Act 1998.

harassment of those persons and (c) by which he intends to persuade any person (whether or not one of those mentioned above) not to do something they are entitled or required to do, or to do something that they are under no obligation to do. This deals with situations where at least two or more people are harassed for the purpose of influencing the conduct of a third party. The third party would not be a victim of the course of conduct and the only remedy the third party would have for this form of harassment is the grant of an injunction (see PHA 1997, s 3A).

14.5   PHA 1997, s 1(2) provides that for the purposes of s 1 the person whose course of conduct is in question ought to know that it amounts to harassment of another if a reasonable person in possession of the same information would think the course of conduct amounted to harassment of the other. The test of whether harassment has been committed is thus objective[4] – ie whether a reasonable person in possession of the same information would think the conduct amounted to harassment. Section 1(3) provides that s 1(1) does not apply to a course of conduct if the person who pursued it shows (a) that it was pursued for the purpose of preventing or detecting crime, (b) that it was pursued under any enactment or rule of law or to comply with any condition or requirement imposed by any person under any enactment or (c) that in the particular circumstances the pursuit of the course of conduct was reasonable. It is tolerably clear that, although the victim must be an individual, the perpetrator may be a corporate body.[5]

14.6   As stated above there must be a course of conduct which must involve at least two incidents. There must be some connection between the incidents if they are to constitute a course of conduct.[6] If the incidents are few and widely spread out it is less likely the court will find a course of conduct,[7] although it depends on the facts and the types of incident involved.[8] It has been said by the Court of Appeal[9] that in order to constitute harassment conduct had to be calculated (that is, likely) to alarm or distress the claimant and the conduct also had to be oppressive and unreasonable. As to reasonableness, the claimant in his pleading must allege conduct which was arguably unreasonable and the mere fact the conduct foreseeably caused distress to an individual was not enough. An arguable case of oppression and unreasonableness had to also be satisfied if the claim was to be maintainable.

THE GRAVITY TEST

14.7   A course of conduct must be grave before the offence or tort of harassment is proved. Harassment is both a civil wrong (PHA 1997, s 3(1)) and a crime (PHA 1997, s 2(1)). It has been held that the only real difference between the crime and the tort was the standard of proof to be applied, namely the balance of probabilities in the case of the tort, and the usual criminal standard in respect of the crime – see *Ferguson v British*

---

4   See *R v C (Sean Peter)* [2001] EWCA Civ 1251: the fact that the defendant is mentally ill would not constitute a defence.
5   *Majrowski v Guy's & St Thomas' NHS Trust* [2006] UKHL 34, at [19].
6   See *Lau v DPP* [2000] All ER (D) 224 where two unconnected incidents 6 months apart were held not to be a course of conduct.
7   See *Pratt v DPP* [2001] EWHC Admin 483.
8   *See Lau v DPP* [2000] All ER (D) 224 – 'the broad position must be that if one is left with only two incidents you have to see whether what happened on those two occasions can be described as a course of conduct', per Schiemann LJ.
9   *Allen v Southwark Borough Council* [2008] EWCA Civ 1478; and see Lord Phillips MR in *Thomas v NGN* [2002] EMLR 78, at [30].

Gas.[10] In a well-documented case there is likely to be little difference between the two tests in practice. It was said by the Court of Appeal in *Ferguson* that it is no defence to say that the victim of the harassment would know that the conduct was unjustified because that is nearly always the case – harassment exists as a tort to protect against a persistent course of unjustified conduct. However, it was recognised in *Ferguson* that in life one has to put up with a certain amount of annoyance and things have to be fairly severe before the law, civil or criminal, will intervene.[11]

14.8 In *Majrowski v Guy's and St Thomas' NHS Trust* Lord Nicholls of Birkenhead observed that:[12]

> 'Courts are well able to separate the wheat from the chaff at an early stage of the proceedings. They should be astute to do so. In most cases courts should have little difficulty in applying the "close connection" test. Where the claim meets that requirement, and the quality of the conduct said to constitute harassment is being examined, courts will have in mind that irritations, annoyances, even a measure of upset, arise at times in everybody's day-to-day dealings with other people. Courts are well able to recognise the boundary between conduct which is unattractive, even unreasonable, and conduct which is oppressive and unacceptable. To cross the boundary from the regrettable to the unacceptable the gravity of the misconduct must be of an order which would sustain criminal liability under s 2.'

14.9 Baroness Hale in *Majrowski* said:[13]

> 'All sorts of conduct may amount to harassment. It includes alarming a person or causing her distress: s 7(2). But conduct might be harassment even if no alarm or distress were in fact caused. A great deal is left to the wisdom of the courts to draw sensible lines between the ordinary banter and badinage of life and genuinely offensive and unacceptable behaviour.'

14.10 These passages were applied by the Court of Appeal in *Conn v Sunderland City Council*,[14] which concerned alleged harassment of one employee by another in the workplace. It was held that two workplace rows between an employee and his superior amounted to a 'course of conduct' but there was no 'harassment' because they were not sufficiently grave. Gage LJ said:

> '[11] … As Baroness Hale put it in her speech, harassment is left deliberately wide. Section 7, to which I have referred, points to elements which are included in harassment, namely alarming or causing distress. Speech is also included as conduct which is capable of constituting harassment. The definition of "course of conduct" means that there must be at least two such incidents of harassment to satisfy the requirements of a course of conduct. It is also in my judgment important to note that a civil claim is only available as a remedy for conduct which amounts to a breach of s.1, and so by s.2 constitutes a criminal offence. The mental element in the offence is conduct which the alleged offender knows, or ought to know, judging by the standards of what the reasonable person would think, amounts to harassment of another.

> [12] It seems to me that what, in the words of Lord Nicholls in *Majrowski*, crosses the boundary between unattractive and even unreasonable conduct and conduct which is oppressive and unacceptable, may well depend on the context in which the conduct occurs. What might not be harassment on the factory floor or in the barrack room might well be

---

10 See *Ferguson v British Gas* [2009] EWCA Civ 46, at [17] and [18].
11 See Jacob LJ, at [18].
12 [2006] UKHL 34, [2006] 4 All ER 395, [2007] 1 AC 224, at [30].
13 Ibid, at [66].
14 [2007] EWCA Civ 1492, [2008] IRLR 324.

harassment in the hospital ward and vice versa. In my judgment the touchstone for recognising what is not harassment for the purposes of ss.1 and 3 will be whether the conduct is of such gravity as to justify the sanctions of the criminal law.'

14.11 Buxton LJ said:

'[18] More fundamentally, however, as my Lord has pointed out, there is no indication at this part of the judgment, and no (I have to say) reason to infer from the terms of the recorder's decision, that he had in mind the guidance given by Lord Nicholls in *Majrowski* as to the type of conduct that crosses the line into harassment. Crucial to that is Lord Nicholls' determination my Lord has referred to that the conduct concerned must be of an order that would sustain criminal liability, and not merely civil liability on some other register. Had the recorder had that requirement in mind when he came to this part of his judgment, it seems to me I have to say completely impossible that he would have concluded that the third incident, as it has been called, the first one relied on, could amount to harassment. But what occurred is a very long way away from anything that, in a sensible criminal regime, would lead to a prosecution, much less to a conviction.'

Example: freedom of the press and publications in the media

14.12 Statutory harassment might include speech so issues of freedom of expression are likely to arise under Art 10 of the ECHR. In *Thomas v NGN*,[15] the Court of Appeal considered whether a series of publications in the *Sun* constituted harassment having regard to press freedom and Art 10. Two police sergeants had been demoted following a complaint about a remark made in private which was considered racist. The claimant's name and address were published and the fact she was black. Parts of readers' letters (about the officers' treatment) and a follow-up article were published. It was claimed that the course of conduct amounted to harassment being intended to provoke hostility towards the claimant on grounds of race. The claimant received hate mail. The argument that 'harassment' did not cover newspapers was rejected as was the argument that the defence of reasonable conduct was insufficient to accommodate press freedom. It was held that even robust press criticism would not usually constitute unreasonable conduct within the natural meaning of harassment. It was also held that the test of whether a series of publications was likely to cause distress and constitute harassment required consideration of whether press freedom was being abused to the extent that the pressing social needs of a democratic society required it to be curbed. The *Sun*'s publications gave rise to an arguable case of harassment in that the racist criticism was foreseeably likely to provoke a racist reaction in the readership and cause distress.

14.13 Lord Phillips MR considered the nature of harassment and the nature of reasonable conduct in *Thomas v NGN* as follows:

'[29] Section 7 of the 1997 Act [PHA 1997] does not purport to provide a comprehensive definition of harassment. There are many actions that foreseeably alarm or cause a person distress that could not possibly be described as harassment. It seems to me that s.7 is dealing with that element of the offence which is constituted by the effect of the conduct rather than with the types of conduct that produce that effect.

[30] The Act does not attempt to define the type of conduct that is capable of constituting harassment. "Harassment" is, however, a word which has a meaning which is generally

15 [2001] EWCA Civ 1233.

understood. It describes conduct targeted at an individual which is calculated to produce the consequences described in s.7 and which is oppressive and unreasonable. The practice of stalking is a prime example of such conduct.

[31]   The fact that conduct that is reasonable will not constitute harassment is clear from s.1(3)(c) of the Act. While that subsection places the burden of proof on the defendant, that does not absolve the claimant from pleading facts which are capable of amounting to harassment. Unless the claimant's pleading alleges conduct by the defendant which is, at least, arguably unreasonable, it is unlikely to set out a viable plea of harassment.'

Example: free speech and use of the internet

14.14   Another instructive case is *R v Debnath*,[16] where the defendant had had a one-night stand with the complainant who thereafter harassed him, wrongly believing he had infected her with an STD. She set up a site on the Internet called '[A]isGay.com' and a large amount of homosexual pornography was sent to the complainant's home. The complainant found he was signed up to a database for those with STDs seeking sexual liaisons and he had also been registered on a 'gay American prisoner exchange' and so forth. A restraining order pursuant to PHA 1997, s 5 which prohibited the defendant from (a) contacting – directly or indirectly the complainant, his fiancée and other named persons; and (b) publishing any information about the complainant or his fiancée whether true or not. The order was considered to be necessary and proportionate, in the context of the defendant's right to freedom of expression under Art 10 of the ECHR. It was held that the purpose of the restraining order was to protect the complainant from further offences; that the order had to be clear and precise so there could be no doubt what the defendant was prohibited from doing and the order had to be practical and proportionate. Freedom of expression was a qualified right and any restriction on it had to be prescribed by law, further a legitimate aim, and be necessary in a democratic society. The wide terms of the order were justified to prevent the defendant committing further offences and to protect the complainant from further harassment.

Example: telephone calls

14.15   In *DPP v Hardy*[17] the Divisional Court of the Queen's Bench Division dealt with a case of criminal harassment where the defendant made 95 phone calls to the complainant within a 90-minute period and was charged with harassment. A decision that there was no case to answer was found to be perverse; it was said that conduct which might have begun as a legitimate inquiry could become harassment within PHA 1997, s 1 as a result of the manner and persistence of its pursuit. It was also a factor that the complainant gave evidence that she had felt intimidated.

Example: sending defamatory letters

14.16   In *Bloom v Robinson-Millar*[18]the claimant was the director of a tenant management company for the defendant's property. The claimant brought libel and harassment proceedings in respect of seven letters the defendant had sent to various individuals and organisations accusing the claimant of serious criminal activity, of lying and of breaches of fiduciary duty. Sharp J ruled that the letters were seriously

---

[16]   [2005] EWCA Crim 3472.
[17]   [2008] All ER (D) 315 (Oct).
[18]   The High Court, 7 October 2009.

defamatory and considered that the defendant's course of conduct amounted to harassment because it crossed the threshold of seriousness and it was legitimate for individuals in the position of the claimant, to obtain the protection of the law from obsessive behaviour targeted against them. The judge said that the corrosive effect of such behaviour could not be underestimated. A global award of £30,000 was made to reflect that and an injunction was granted against the defendant.

REASONABLE CONDUCT AND REPEATED PUBLICATION IN THE PRESS

14.16 Freedom of expression is a highly relevant consideration when determining whether or not a series of publications in the press can amount to harassment.[19] The press cannot be gagged or punished because publication of a series of articles is likely (or even highly likely) to distress someone. For the purposes of harassment whether the press has acted reasonably in publishing an article does not turn on whether opinions contained in the article are reasonably held but turns on weighing the press's ECHR, Art 10 right of freedom of expression against any relevant competing rights such as protection of reputation or privacy. Press exposure or criticism generally is not unreasonable conduct or harassment. Merely alleging in a pleading that a series of articles has caused distress to an individual will probably be struck out on the ground no arguable case of harassment is disclosed. To constitute harassment some exceptional circumstance must be present to justify restricting the paper's right to publish as it sees fit. It might be different if a campaign of vilification in the press against an individual was driven entirely by personal animosity, particularly, for example, if an element of racial hatred were involved. It was conceded in one case that a series of articles calculated to incite racial hatred of an individual provides an example of conduct which is capable of amounting to harassment under PHA 1997.[20]

REASONABLE CONDUCT AND SURVEILLANCE

14.17 Eady J stated in *Howlett v Holding* that a course of conduct which involves having a person watched is capable of amounting to harassment:[21]

> 'To keep someone on tenterhooks, knowing that she is likely to be watched as she goes about her daily life, seems to me remarkably cruel. Just because she does not know, in any given instance, that surveillance is taking place, it does not make it any the less distressing for her. What causes the distress is the awareness that secret surveillance is taking place, or is likely to take place at any moment. I see no reason why that form of besetting should fall outside either the spirit or the letter of the Act.
>
> In the sphere of surveillance by the State there are strict controls provided by the provisions of the Regulation of Investigatory Powers Act 2000. This is an area worthy of substantial safeguards. However I also bear in mind that when considering the question of harassment through surveillance one has to take into account that in any event the first plaintiff is going

---

19 See the useful summary of Stephens J in *Callaghan v Independent News* [2009] NIQB 1.
20 Ibid, where it was recognised that the Convention right of freedom of expression did not extend to protect remarks directly against the Convention's underlying values (see *Jersild v Denmark* (1994) 19 EHRR 1, [1994] ECHR 15890/89, at para 35 of the former report; and *Lehideux and Isorni v France* (1998) 30 EHRR 665, at para 53).
21 [2006] EWHC 41, (2006) *The Times*, February 8, at [23].

to be supervised directly and indirectly by the prison authorities and is therefore being watched by them. It is the additional surveillance by the defendant which is in issue.'

REASONABLE CONDUCT AND THE TAKING OF PHOTOGRAPHS

14.18 It has been held that photographing, surveillance and threatened publication of unpixelated photographs of an individual combined with what has been published and is anticipated will be published in articles about the individual could amount to harassment.[22] This was on the basis that the course of conduct was calculated to incite hatred of and animosity and hostility towards the individual and so capable of amounting to harassment. In that case it was considered that the claim for an injunction restraining the defendant from pursuing any conduct which amounts to harassment was too imprecise. In recent proceedings, which were settled before trial, the actress Sienna Miller sued Big Pictures (an agency of paparazzi photographers) and its founder, Darryn Lyons, over claims of harassment and misuse of private information in respect of what she described as intolerable intrusions by pursuing photographers. In her first legal action she sued for harassment claiming she was pursued for 3 months by photographers resulting in 23 photographs being published. She settled that claim for £37,000 damages plus costs. In a second action, she sued for misuse of private information in respect of photographs of her on a boat in Italy published in the *Sun* and *News of the World*. She settled that claim for £16,000 damages plus costs. The defendants undertook, as part of the settlement, not to pursue her by car, motorcycle or on foot and not to 'doorstep' her at her home or that of her family. They remained free to take pictures when she went to bars, nightclubs or restaurants, or was out in public or at 'red carpet' events.

14.19 It is a defence for a person who has pursued a course of conduct to show that (a) it was pursued for the purpose of preventing or detecting crime, (b) it was pursued under any enactment or rule of law or to comply with any condition or requirement imposed by any person under any enactment or (c) in the particular circumstances the pursuit of the course of conduct was reasonable. It has been held that the defence of preventing crime is not designed 'to enable any Tom, Dick or Harry to set himself up as a vigilante and harass his neighbours under the guise of preventing or detecting crime'.[23]

14.20 A harassment claim can be brought and an injunction claimed not only against those directly responsible for the harassment but also against those likely to aid, abet, counsel or procure others to carry out the course of conduct which amounts to harassment.[24]

Example: abusive behaviour

14.21 In *CC v AB*[25] a claim under PHA 1997 was made primarily based on abusive e-mail and telephone communications from the defendant in the course of a bitter divorce, which were placed in evidence before the court. Eady J said:

---

[22]   *Callaghan v Independent News* [2009] NIQB 1.
[23]   See Eady J in *Howlett v Holding* [2006] EWHC 41, (2006) *The Times*, February 8, at [31].
[24]   See *SmithKline v Avery* [2009] EWHC 1488 (QB).
[25]   [2006] EWHC 3083 (QB).

'All in all, the Defendant's behaviour so far demonstrates the need for an interim order under the Protection from Harassment Act 1997 ... these documents lay a clear foundation for reasonable apprehension that, unless restrained by a court order, the Defendant will publish as many details as he knows about the Claimant's relationship, whatever the consequences likely to flow for the Claimant and his family.'

The offence of harassment

14.22   PHA 1997, s 2 makes provision for an offence of harassment and provides that (1) a person who pursues a course of conduct in breach of s 1 is guilty of an offence; (2) a person guilty of an offence under this section is liable on summary conviction to imprisonment for a term not exceeding 6 months, or a fine not exceeding level 5 on the standard scale, or both.

Civil remedies for harassment

14.23   PHA 1997, s 3 makes provision for a civil remedy and provides that (1) an actual or apprehended breach of s 1 may be the subject of a claim in civil proceedings by the person who is or may be the victim of the course of conduct in question and (2) on such a claim, damages may be awarded for (amongst other things) any anxiety caused by the harassment and any financial loss resulting from the harassment.

14.24   In *Emerson Developments Ltd v Avery*[26] the claimants were a group of companies and an employee of the first claimant, who sued on behalf of the employees of the group who were subject to various acts of criminal damage at the hands of the defendants. It was held that it was permissible and convenient for a company director to bring proceedings on behalf of employees so as to enable the court to protect their interests.

14.25   An employer might be held vicariously liable for the acts of its employees in committing acts of harassment in the course of their employment.[27] This is a particularly important decision in relation to acts of harassment committed, for example, by press photographers and the like acting in the course of their employment.

14.26   The standard of proof in harassment cases was considered in *Jones v Hipgrave*, where Tugendhat J concluded:[28]

> '... that the civil standard of proof should be applied to civil proceedings under s.3 of the [PHA 1997]. The application of this standard will require the strictness appropriate to the seriousness of the matters to be proved and the implications of proving them, or not proving them, that is, the implications not only for the defendant, but also for the claimant.'

Injunctions in harassment claims

14.27   The claim for an injunction should be framed with precision. It should not be claimed broadly as an injunction restraining the defendant from further harassing the defendant; the particular course of conduct complained of should be specified. It is possible to enlarge the ambit of an injunction to cover those who have notice of its terms. This might be of relevance to claims for injunctions in respect of intrusive press

---

[26]   [2004] EWHC 194, Field J.
[27]   *Majrowski v Guy's & St Thomas' NHS Trust* [2006] UKHL 34.
[28]   [2004] EWHC 2901 (QB).

photographers. An injunction has been granted restraining defendants and 'any other person who has been given notice in writing of the terms of the injunction' from continuing or repeating a course of prohibited conduct and from entering exclusion zones to prevent further harassment occurring.[29] The court held in that case, which involved animal rights activists, that it was established an injunction could be granted in these wide terms, to bind persons other than the defendants, to afford effective protection to the victims of threatened illegal action. Also exclusion zones were appropriate where reasonably necessary to protect a claimant's legitimate interests such as to protect the claimants' business.

14.28 PHA 1997, s 3(3) provides that where (a) in such proceedings the High Court or a county court grants an injunction for the purpose of restraining the defendant from pursuing any conduct which amounts to harassment, and (b) the claimant considers that the defendant has done anything which he is prohibited from doing by the injunction, the claimant may apply for the issue of a warrant for the arrest of the defendant. Section 3(4) provides that an application under s 3(3) may be made (a) where the injunction was granted by the High Court, to a judge of that court, and (b) where the injunction was granted by a county court, to a judge or district judge of that or any other county court.

14.29 PHA 1997, s 3(5) provides that the judge or district judge to whom an application under s 3(3) is made may only issue a warrant if (a) the application is substantiated on oath and (b) the judge or district judge has reasonable grounds for believing that the defendant has done anything which he is prohibited from doing by the injunction.

14.30 Furthermore, PHA 1997, s 3(6) provides that where (a) the High Court or a county court grants an injunction for the purpose mentioned in s 3(3)(a), and (b) without reasonable excuse the defendant does anything which he is prohibited from doing by the injunction, that person is guilty of an offence. Section 3(7) provides that where a person is convicted of an offence under s 3(6) in respect of any conduct, that conduct is not punishable as a contempt of court. Section 3(9) provides that a person guilty of an offence under s 3(6) is liable (a) on conviction on indictment, to imprisonment for a term not exceeding 5 years, or a fine, or both or (b) on summary conviction, to imprisonment for a term not exceeding 6 months, or a fine not exceeding the statutory maximum, or both.

14.31 Claims under PHA 1997, s 3 are subject to the Civil Procedure Rules 1998[30] (CPR) Part 8 procedure and must be commenced if in the High Court, in the Queen's Bench Division, and if in the county court, in the court for the district in which the defendant resides or carries on business or the court for the district in which the claimant resides or carries on business (see CPR 65.28). Forms must be issued on Form N208 and they are automatically allocated to multi-track. PD 2B, para 8.1 provides that district judges have jurisdiction to grant injunctions under s 3 but they do not have jurisdiction to make orders committing a person to prison for breach of an injunction made under the Act.[31]

---

[29] *Silverton v Gravett* [2001] All ER (D) 282 (Oct).
[30] SI 1998/3132.
[31] CPR Part 65 PD 2B, para 8.3 and CCR Ord 29, r 1.

Putting people in fear of violence

14.32 PHA 1997, s 4(1) provides that a person whose course of conduct causes another to fear, on at least two occasions, that violence will be used against them is guilty of an offence if he knows or ought to know that his course of conduct will cause the other so to fear on each of those occasions. Section 4(2) provides that for the purposes of s 4, the person whose course of conduct is in question ought to know that it will cause another to fear that violence will be used against him on any occasion if a reasonable person in possession of the same information would think the course of conduct would cause the other so to fear on that occasion. Section 3(3) provides that it is a defence for a person charged with an offence under this section to show that (a) his course of conduct was pursued for the purpose of preventing or detecting crime, (b) his course of conduct was pursued under any enactment or rule of law or to comply with any condition or requirement imposed by any person under any enactment or (c) the pursuit of his course of conduct was reasonable for the protection of himself or another or for the protection of his or another's property.

Penalties

14.33 The penalties are laid down under PHA 1997, s 4(4), which provides that a person guilty of an offence under this s 4 is liable (a) on conviction on indictment, to imprisonment for a term not exceeding 5 years, or a fine, or both or (b) on summary conviction, to imprisonment for a term not exceeding 6 months, or a fine not exceeding the statutory maximum, or both. Section 4(5) provides that if on the trial on indictment of a person charged with an offence under this section the jury find him not guilty of the offence charged, they may find him guilty of an offence under s 2.

Restraining orders

14.34 PHA 1997, s 5(1) provides that a court sentencing or otherwise dealing with a person ('the defendant') convicted of an offence under s 2 or 4 may (as well as sentencing him or dealing with him in any other way) make an order under s 5. Section 5(2) provides that the order may, for the purpose of protecting the victim of the offence, or any other person mentioned in the order, from further conduct which (a) amounts to harassment or (b) will cause a fear of violence, prohibit the defendant from doing anything described in the order. Section 5(3) provides that the order may have effect for a specified period or until further order. Section 5(5) provides that if without reasonable excuse the defendant does anything which he is prohibited from doing by an order under this section, he is guilty of an offence and s 5(6) provides that a person guilty of an offence under this section is liable (a) on conviction on indictment, to imprisonment for a term not exceeding 5 years, or a fine, or both or (b) on summary conviction, to imprisonment for a term not exceeding 6 months, or a fine not exceeding the statutory maximum, or both.

Limitation

14.35 PHA 1997, s 6 provides that in s 11 of the Limitation Act 1980 (special time-limit for actions in respect of personal injuries), after s 11(1) there is inserted: '(1A) This section does not apply to any action brought for damages under section 3 of the Protection from Harassment Act 1997.'

Chapter 15

LIBEL AND THE INTERNET

INTRODUCTION

15.1   The internet provides fertile ground for defamatory material. To bring a claim in respect of material on the internet it is first necessary to establish that the material has been published (ie accessed and seen by at least one individual) and, secondly, it must be shown that the defendant is liable at common law for the publication either as publisher or as the person responsible for publication. This chapter is concerned with the liability of those who facilitate internet communications, such as internet service providers (ISPs) and with identifying those responsible for creating offending material and causing it to be published. ISPs held to be responsible for publication at common law may have a statutory defence under s 1 of the Defamation Act 1996 (DeA 1996) provided they are not an 'author', 'editor' or 'publisher' (as defined in s 1) and can show they took reasonable care in relation to the publication and did not know and had no reason to believe that what they did caused or contributed to the publication of a defamatory statement (s 1(1)(b) and (c)). They might also have a defence under the Electronic Commerce (EC Directive) Regulations 2002.[1]

THE ROLE OF INTERNET SERVICE PROVIDERS

15.2   ISPs provide a route as intermediaries, whereby third parties have access to the internet and are able to pass electronic communications from one computer to another resulting, for example, in a posting to a message board. By analogy with the postal services, ISPs do not participate in the process of publication as such, but merely act as facilitators of the communication. They provide a means of transmitting communications rather than publishing them. Defamatory material might be posted to an ISP via the internet and stored on the ISP's server. The ISP will transmit the material (or facilitate its transmission) to subscribers. Whenever an ISP transmits a defamatory posting or a defamatory posting is transmitted from the storage of an ISP's server the posting is published to any of the ISP's customers who access it. Thus every time an ISP's customer accesses the posting there is a publication to that customer.

15.3   Morland J described the role of ISP – on the facts of the *Godfrey v Demon Internet Ltd*[2] case – as follows:

> 'Three facilities (amongst others) are provided via the Internet: e-mail, the World Wide Web and Usenet. This case is primarily concerned with Usenet.

---

[1]   SI 2002/2013.
[2]   [2001] QB 201, [1999] 4 All ER 342.

1.　E-mail is normally electronic mailing of a message from one sender to one recipient. The sender makes a connection to his own local ISP to whom he transmits his e-mail message. The sender's ISP transmits the message via the Internet to the recipient's ISP. At the recipient's request his local ISP sends the message to the recipient.

2.　The World Wide Web provides a facility for one to many publication. "Web pages" are held at a particular site (usually operated by an ISP) in such a way that they can be accessed by Internet users worldwide. The creator of web pages sends them to his local ISP who stores them. An Internet user can access and download copies of the pages by connecting to his own local ISP and requesting transmission of those pages via the Internet.

3.　Usenet is one to many publication from author to readers round the world. An article (known as a posting) is submitted by its author to the Usenet news-server based at his own local ISP (the originating ISP) who disseminates via the Internet the posting. Ultimately it is distributed and stored on the news-servers of every (or nearly every) ISP in the world that offers Usenet facilities to its customers. Internet users world wide can read and download the posting by connecting to their local ISP's news-servers.

"Usenet News" is the name given to the system by which postings are sent by Internet users to forums known as "newsgroups". A posting is readable anywhere in the world by an Internet user whose own ISP offer access to the newsgroup in question. Newsgroups are organised into broad subject areas known as "hierarchies". One such hierarchy is the "Soc" hierarchy which contains newsgroups in which social issues are discussed, for example the newsgroups "soc.culture.thai" and "soc.culture.british". Postings on newsgroups can be read by the customers of a particular ISP by accessing that ISP's "news server". In reading a Usenet posting an Internet user requests the posting from the ISP's news server and a copy of the posting is then transmitted by the news server to the user's computer where it can be held in the user's computer for as long as he wishes. A posting may originate from anywhere in the world entering the Internet through the author's own ISP and follow a "path" through a succession of news servers before eventually reaching a particular reader.

The Usenet service is hosted by others, who are not parties to these proceedings, such as Google.'

RESPONSIBILITY FOR PUBLICATION AT COMMON LAW: A QUESTION OF FACT

15.4　Publication is a question of fact which depends on the circumstances of each case. Greene LJ stated in *Byrne v Deane*:[3]

'... publication, of course, is a question of fact, and it must depend on the circumstances in each case whether or not publication has taken place ... It may very well be that in some circumstances a person, by refraining from removing or obliterating the defamatory matter, is not committing any publication at all. In other circumstances he may be doing so. The test it appears to me is this: having regard to all the facts of the case is the proper inference that by not removing the defamatory matter the defendant really made himself responsible for its continued presence in the place where it had been put?'

15.5　To impose legal responsibility under the common law for the publication of words it is essential to demonstrate a degree of awareness or at least an assumption of general responsibility, such as has long been recognised in the context of editorial responsibility. In *McLeod v St Aubyn*,[4] where the publication in issue consisted in

---

3　[1937] 1 KB 818, at 837–838.
4　[1899] AC 549.

handing over an unread copy of a newspaper for return the following day, it was held there was insufficient awareness or intention to impose legal responsibility for 'publication'. Lord Morris said:[5]

> 'A printer and publisher intends to publish, and so intending cannot plead as a justification that he did not know the contents. The appellant in this case never intended to publish.'

15.6   To hold a person responsible for a publication there must be knowing involvement in the process of publication of the words in question and not merely a passive instrumental role in the process.[6] In the absence of binding authority, Eady J in *Bunt v Tilley*[7] would not attribute liability for publication at common law to a telephone company or other passive medium of communication, such as an ISP. He said that those:[8]

> '... who truly fulfil no more than the role of a passive medium for communication cannot be characterised as publishers: thus they do not need a defence.'

15.7   An ISP which knowingly permits others to communicate defamatory material where it would be possible to prevent publication is likely to be held liable, as would an ISP which sponsored or authorised the transmission of offending material. ISPs which have no such knowledge are likely to be considered more akin to mere conduit intermediaries analogous to postal services and telephone carriers who facilitate communications but do not create, prepare or expect to control content. A distinction is drawn in the cases between ISPs which are unaware they are transmitting defamatory material and ISPs which are on notice and aware of what they are transmitting.

15.8   The ISP was held to be a publisher at common law in *Godfrey v Demon Internet Ltd*,[9] on the basis that after it had been put on notice that it had received and stored defamatory postings it had continued to transmit them or facilitate their transmission to its subscribers. On the particular facts the ISP was held not to be a passive owner of an electronic device through which postings were transmitted because it had knowledge of the material and control over its transmission. It was held (1) that the ISP had actively chosen to receive and store the exchanges containing the posting, (2) that the posting could be accessed by the ISP's subscribers, (3) that it was in the ISP's power to obliterate the posting (as later happened) and (4) that once the ISP knew of the defamatory content and took the decision not to remove it from its server it could not show that it had taken reasonable care nor could it show that it did not know, and had no reason to believe, that what it did caused or contributed to the publication (and so bring itself within DeA 1996, s 1). Although held to be a publisher at common law the ISP was held not to be a commercial publisher under s 1 of the Act. Morland J concluded that:[10]

> '[The ISP] whenever it transmits and whenever there is transmitted from the storage of its news server a defamatory posting, publishes that posting to any subscriber to its ISP who accesses the newsgroup containing that posting ... every time one of the [ISP's] customers accesses "soc.culture.thai" and sees that posting defamatory of the plaintiff there is a publication to that customer.'

---

5   At 562.
6   *Emmens v Pottle* (1885) 16 QBD 354, at 357, per Lord Esher MR.
7   [2006] EWHC 407 (QB).
8   At [37].
9   [2001] QB 201, [1999] 4 All ER 342.
10   [2001] QB 201, at 208–209, [1999] 4 All ER 342, at 348.

15.9   Where the ISPs were not on notice that they were transmitting defamatory
material, it was held, in *Bunt v Tilley*,[11] that they performed no more than a passive role
in facilitating postings on the internet and could not be deemed to be a publisher or
responsible for publication at common law. It was held that a degree of awareness or at
least an assumption of general responsibility, such as had long been recognised in the
context of editorial responsibility, had to be demonstrated in order to impose legal
responsibility at common law for the publication of words. Although awareness of
defamatory content was not always necessary for liability to arise for defamatory
publication, knowing involvement in the process of publication of the relevant words
was necessary. It was not enough that the ISP had played merely a passive instrumental
role in the process to establish that the ISP had, in any meaningful sense, knowingly
participated in the publishing the offending material.

15.10   The nature of the Google search engine was considered in *Metropolitan
International Schools Ltd v Designtechnica Corporation and Google*.[12] In that case
Google was found not to be liable as publisher even though it had been notified of the
defamatory content of certain material thrown up on searches. The court explained that
searches on a search engine involved no human input and automatically threw up
snippets on the screen which largely corresponded to what had been typed in.
Furthermore, it was optional whether they were accessed. In the circumstances Google
was found not to be a publisher at common law because it had not authorised or caused
the snippets to appear on the users' screens but merely facilitated their appearance.[13]
Where Google had been notified that snippets contained defamatory material, although
it was possible for URLs to be blocked (ie not displayed when searched), if blocking did
not stop the offending material appearing it was held that Google could not be liable for
having authorised, approved or acquiesced in the publication. It was confirmed that the
defence of innocent dissemination had effectively been superseded by DeA 1996, s 1 but
had not been abolished. Had Google been prima facie liable for publication, it was said
that the defence of innocent dissemination almost certainly would not apply because the
defamatory words had been drawn to Google's attention.

WHAT AMOUNTS TO PUBLICATION?

15.11   The posting of the offending material on the internet had been for a very short
period of time in *Carrie v Tolkien*.[14] It was confirmed that placing material on the
internet was not presumed in law automatically to amount to substantial publication. It
was held always to be necessary for the precise publication complained of to be pleaded
and established by evidence. It was not enough to plead that the posting had been
accessed 'by a large but unquantifiable number of readers' because this is mere assertion
and there must be a solid basis for the inference. Where there is minimal publication the
claim might be classified as an abuse of process because to pursue it would be
disproportionate. There will be occasions when a claim has to be pursued not because
there had been substantial publication but in order to obtain vindication and an
injunction to put an end to the continuing defamation. In such instances there must be
evidence that the defendant will continue to publish defamatory material in the future.[15]

---

11   [2006] EWHC 407 (QB).
12   [2009] EWHC 1765 (QB), Eady J.
13   See *Bunt v Tilley* [2006] EWHC 407 (QB), [2007] 1 WLR 1243 and *Emmens v Pottle* (1885–86) LR 16 QBD
        354, CA.
14   [2009] EWHC 29 (QB), at [17] and [18], Eady J.
15   Ibid, at [19] and [20], Eady J.

15.12 Guidance regarding the extent of internet publication required to found a claim was given by Eady J in *Mardas v New York*:[16]

'[13] ... both generally and in its application to specific cases the law of defamation is concerned to strike a balance between freedom of information, on the one hand, and the protection of the honour and reputations of individual citizens on the other hand ... it is increasingly being recognised in the Strasbourg jurisprudence that the right to protect one's honour and reputation is to be treated as falling within the protection of Article 8: see e g *Radio France v France* (2005) 40 EHRR 29 and *Pfeifer v Austria* (App. No. 12556/03), 15 November 2007, at [35] and [38] ...

[15] What matters is whether there has been a real and substantial tort within the jurisdiction (or, at this stage, arguably so). This cannot depend upon a numbers game, with the court fixing an arbitrary minimum according to the facts of the case. In *Shevill v Presse Alliance* [1996] AC 959, it was thought that there had been a total of some 250 copies of the French newspaper published within the jurisdiction, of which only five were in Yorkshire where Ms Shevill lived and was most likely to be known. She was permitted to seek her remedies here.

[16] The article complained of in the present case has remained on the Defendants' respective websites to this very day. That fact naturally gives rise at least to a possible inference that there has been a continuing, albeit modest, readership. My attention was drawn in this context to the remarks of Lord Phillips MR (as he then was) in *Loutchansky v Times Newspapers Ltd* [2002] QB 783, 817D at [72]:

"... If the defendants were exposed to liability ... they had only themselves to blame for persisting in retaining the offending articles on their website without qualifying these in any way."

[17] It is also pertinent to have in mind the remarks of Callinan J in the High Court of Australia in *Gutnick v Dow Jones* [2002] HCA 56 at [181] and [192] to the following effect:

"A publisher, particularly one carrying on the business of publishing, does not act to put matter on the Internet in order for it to reach a small target. It is its ubiquity which is one of the main attractions to users of it. And any person who gains access to the Internet does so by taking an initiative to gain access to it in a manner analogous to the purchase or other acquisition of a newspaper, in order to read it.

If a publisher publishes in a multiplicity of jurisdictions it should understand, and must accept, that it runs the risk of liability in those jurisdictions in which the publication is not lawful and inflicts damage."

This approach has also been adopted in a number of the decisions in this jurisdiction and, in particular, by the Court of Appeal in *King v Lewis* [2005] EMLR 45 at [29].'

15.13 Qualified privilege was raised as a defence in *Brady v Norman*[17] and an issue arose as to whether it could be presumed that individuals with no legitimate interest in what was published on an internet site would nonetheless have accessed the site and read the offending words. There is generally no rebuttable presumption of law of publication on the internet to a substantial but unquantifiable number of people within the jurisdiction.[18] In an earlier case, *Trumm v Norman*,[19] Tugendhat J (who tried the action

---

[16]   [2008] EWHC 3135 (QB) at [13]–[15].
[17]   [2008] EWHC 2481 (QB).
[18]   See *Al Amoudi v Brisard* [2007] 1 WLR 113.

without a jury) inferred that members of a union would have accessed the website in issue there but did not infer website publication to non-union members. In *Brady* it was held that there was no basis for presuming that anyone without a legitimate interest in doing so would have accessed the website. Whether or not such individuals might have done so was beside the point: there had to be evidence to justify the inference that they had done so. An inference is a conclusion based on evidence and reasoning not guesswork.

CONTINUED PUBLICATION IN NEWSPAPER ARCHIVES

15.14 An issue arose before the European Court of Human Rights (ECtHR) in *Times Newspapers v United Kingdom*[20] in relation to articles published in the newspaper and retained on the newspaper's internet archive website. The issue concerned the rule whereby each time material was downloaded from internet a new cause of action in libel accrued[21] and whether that rule constituted an unjustifiable and disproportionate restriction on the newspaper's right to freedom of expression. The ECtHR found that Art 10 of the European Convention for the Protection of Human Rights and Fundamental Freedoms (ECHR) did not guarantee a wholly unrestricted freedom of expression to the press, even with respect to press coverage of matters of serious public concern. It was accepted that internet archives made a substantial contribution to preserving and making available news and information and constituted an important source for education and historical research. It was also accepted that the press had a valuable secondary role in maintaining and making available to the public archives containing news which had previously been reported. However, the press had less latitude in what they published where news archives of past events, rather than news reporting of current affairs, were concerned. In particular, the press had a higher duty to ensure the accuracy of historical, rather than perishable, information. It was held that the requirement for a newspaper to publish an appropriate qualification to an article contained in an internet archive, where it had been brought to the newspaper's notice that a libel action had been brought in respect of the same article published in the newspaper itself, did not constitute a disproportionate interference with the right to freedom of expression. It was also held that the finding in the domestic courts that the newspaper had libelled the claimant by continued publication on the internet of two articles was a justified and proportionate restriction on the applicant's right to freedom of expression. In *Flood v Times Newspapers Ltd*[22] it was held that (*Reynolds*) qualified privilege in respect of a newspaper article could be lost if the article was kept on the paper's website without modification when the circumstances had changed. An investigation into a policeman had concluded in the policeman's favour so the original story was no longer a fair representation of the case and the failure to remove the article or add a sufficient qualification could not be described as responsible journalism in respect of the continued publication on the internet. The court found that it was not in the public interest or fair to the claimant for material impugning his honesty to continue to be recorded on the internet, and the defence of qualified privilege failed in respect of internet publication after the date the investigation concluded.

---

[19]   [2008] EWHC 116 (QB).
[20]   App Nos 3002/03 and 23676/03, at [2009] EMLR 254.
[21]   *Loutchansky v Times Newspapers* [2002] QB 783.
[22]   16 October 2009 Tugendhat J.

DEFAMATION ACT 1996, S 1

15.15 In the consultation document 'Reforming Defamation Law and Procedure' issued by the Lord Chancellor's Department in July 1995 it was said:

'2.4 The defence of innocent dissemination has never provided an absolute immunity for distributors, however mechanical their contribution. It does not protect those who knew that the material they were handling was defamatory, or who ought to have known of its nature ... the defence is not available to a defendant who knew that his act involved or contributed to publication defamatory of the plaintiff. It is available only if, having taken all reasonable care, the defendant had no reason to suspect that his act had that effect ...

2.5 Although it has been suggested that the defence should always apply unless the plaintiff is able to show that the defendant did indeed have the disqualifying knowledge or cause for suspicion, only the defendant knows exactly what care he has taken. Accordingly, as in most defences, it is for the defendant to show that the defence applies to him.'

15.16 DeA 1996, s 1 provides:

'(1) In defamation proceedings a person has a defence if he shows that –

(a)   he was not the author, editor or publisher of the statement complained of,
(b)   he took reasonable care in relation to its publication, and
(c)   he did not know, and had no reason to believe, that what he did caused or contributed to the publication of a defamatory statement.

(2) For this purpose "author", "editor" and "publisher" have the following meanings, which are further explained in subsection (3) –
  "author" means the originator of the statement, but does not include a person who did not intend that his statement be published at all;
  "editor" means a person having editorial or equivalent responsibility for the content of the statement or the decision to publish it; and
  "publisher" means a commercial publisher, that is, a person whose business is issuing material to the public, or a section of the public, who issues material containing the statement in the course of that business.

(3) A person shall not be considered the author, editor or publisher of a statement if he is only involved –

(a)   in printing, producing, distributing or selling printed material containing the statement ...
(c)   in processing, making copies of, distributing or selling any electronic medium in or on which the statement is recorded, or in operating or providing any equipment, system or service by means of which the statement is retrieved, copied, distributed or made available in electronic form ...
(e)   as the operator of or provider of access to a communications system by means of which the statement is transmitted, or made available, by a person over whom he has no effective control.

In a case not within paragraphs (a) to (e) the court may have regard to those provisions by way of analogy in deciding whether a person is to be considered the author, editor or publisher of a statement ...

(5)   In determining for the purposes of this section whether a person took reasonable care, or had reason to believe that what he did caused or contributed to the publication of a defamatory statement, regard shall be had to –

(a)   the extent of his responsibility for the content of the statement or the decision to publish it,

(b)   the nature or circumstances of the publication, and

(c)   the previous conduct or character of the author, editor or publisher.'

15.17 ISPs are unlikely to be categorised as commercial publishers of material held on their servers and, even if found responsible for publication at common law, may have a defence under DeA 1996, s 1 if they can show they took reasonable care and did not have the requisite knowledge that their actions contributed to the offending publication.

MESSAGE BOARDS: IDENTIFYING AND OBTAINING PARTICULARS ABOUT THE WRONGDOERS

15.18 With internet publications, especially anonymous message boards, it is difficult to discover who is actually responsible for publication of the defamatory material. Those using message boards often have little knowledge of libel or privacy law and feel free to express themselves freely without recrimination. In such circumstances it is usually necessary to issue a claim form naming the website operator as defendant, claiming disclosure and production in a witness statement of the full name and address of the anonymous user and all documents which were or had been in the defendant's possession, custody or power relating to the identity of the user. This application is known as a *Norwich Pharmacal* application, having regard to the decision of the House of Lords in *Norwich Pharmacal Co v Customs and Excise Comrs*.[23]

15.19 The jurisdiction to make such an order is set out at was first established by the case of *Norwich Pharmacal Co v Customs & Excise Commissioners*:[24]

'... if through no fault of his own a person gets mixed up in the tortious acts of others so as to facilitate their wrongdoing, he may incur no personal liability but he comes under a duty to assist the person who has been wronged by giving him information and disclosing the identity of the wrongdoers. I do not think that it matters whether he became so mixed up by voluntary action on his part or because it was his duty to do what he did. It may be that if this causes him expense the person seeking the information ought to reimburse him. But justice requires that he should co-operate in righting the wrong if he unwittingly facilitated its perpetration.'

15.20 Lightman J in *Mitsui Ltd v Nexen Petroleum UK Ltd*[25] identified three conditions which must be satisfied to enable the court to make a *Norwich Pharmacal* order:

- a wrong must have been carried out or arguably carried out by an ultimate wrongdoer;

---

[23]   [1973] 2 All ER 943, [1974] AC 133; and see Civil Procedure Rules 1998, SI 1998/3132 (CPR), r 38.18 and the notes thereto.

[24]   [1974] AC 133: see Lord Reid who described the principle at 175.

[25]   [2005] EWHC 625 (Ch), at [21].

- there must be the need for an order to enable action to be brought against the ultimate wrongdoer; and

- the person against whom the order is sought must (a) be mixed up in the wrongdoing so as to have facilitated it; and (b) be able or likely to be able to provide the information necessary to enable the ultimate wrongdoer to be sued.

15.21 The court nevertheless retains a discretion to make an order and the following matters were identified by at first instance in *Totalise PLC v The Motley Fool Ltd*[26] as relevant to the discretion:

- the strength of the claimant's prima facie case against the wrongdoer;

- the gravity of the defamatory allegations;

- whether the wrongdoer was waging a concerted campaign against the claimant;

- the size and extent of the potential readership;

- the fact that the wrongdoer was hiding behind the anonymity which the website allowed;

- whether the claimant had any other practical means of identifying the wrongdoer; and

- whether the defendant had a policy of confidentiality for users of the website.

15.22 It will also be relevant to the exercise of discretion whether even if strictly defamatory the words were trivial and not to be taken seriously. The Court of Appeal in *Totalise* thought that disclosure of the identity of an alleged wrongdoer might be refused if the attacks were obviously designed to insult rather than carry a realistic risk of harming the claimant in any quantifiable way. It was also said by the Court of Appeal in *Totalise* (a case in which a *Norwich Pharmacal* order had been made) that:[27]

> 'In a case such as the present, and particularly since the coming into force on 2 October 2000 of the Human Rights Act 1998, the court must be careful not to make an order which unjustifiably invades the right of an individual to respect for his private life, especially when that individual is in the nature of things not before the court: see the Human Rights Act 1998, s 6, and Sch 1, Pt 1, arts 10 and (arguably at least) 6(1). There is nothing in art 10 which supports [the] contention that it protects the named but not the anonymous, and there are many situations in which – again contrary to [that] contention – the protection of a person's identity from disclosure may be legitimate.'

Although claims in respect of postings on bulletin or message boards are usually brought in libel in many cases other causes of action are also likely to be relevant such as harassment, misuse of private information or unlawful data processing. The advantage of a privacy claim is that the truth of the offending material will not constitute a defence and it is easier to obtain an interim injunction prior to publication in privacy cases than in defamation cases.

---

[26]   [2001] EMLR 750, at [27], per Owen J.
[27]   [2001] EWCA Civ 1897.

15.23 The nature of bulletin boards was described by Eady J in *Smith v ADVFN plc and others*[28] as follows:

> '[14] ... Particular characteristics which I should have in mind are that they are read by relatively few people, most of whom will share an interest in the subject-matter; they are rather like contributions to a casual conversation (the analogy sometimes being drawn with people chatting in a bar) which people simply note before moving on; they are often uninhibited, casual and ill thought out; those who participate know this and expect a certain amount of repartee or "give and take".
>
> [15] The participants in these exchanges were mostly using pseudonyms (or "avatars"), so that their identities will often not be known to others. This is no doubt a disinhibiting factor affecting what people are prepared to say in this special environment.
>
> [16] When considered in the context of defamation law, therefore, communications of this kind are much more akin to slanders (this cause of action being nowadays relatively rare) than to the usual, more permanent kind of communications found in libel actions. People do not often take a "thread" and go through it as a whole like a newspaper article. They tend to read the remarks, make their own contributions if they feel inclined, and think no more about it.
>
> [17] It is this analogy with slander which led me in my ruling of 12 May to refer to "mere vulgar abuse", which used to be discussed quite often in the heyday of slander actions. It is not so much a defence that is unique to slander as an aspect of interpreting the meaning of words. From the context of casual conversations, one can often tell that a remark is not to be taken literally or seriously and is rather to be construed merely as abuse. That is less common in the case of more permanent written communication, although it is by no means unknown. But in the case of a bulletin board thread it is often obvious to casual observers that people are just saying the first thing that comes into their heads and reacting in the heat of the moment. The remarks are often not intended, or to be taken, as serious. A number of examples will emerge in the course of my judgment.'

15.24 The problem of website message boards was addressed in *Sheffield Wednesday v Hargreaves*.[29] A football club and its chairman sued the owner of a website on which fans posted messages about club affairs. Members agreed not to post false or defamatory messages but used pseudonyms for their postings. Messages could be removed from the site but it was alleged that the defendant allowed a campaign of false and defamatory messages to appear and thereby facilitated and became mixed up in the wrongdoing. The claimant sought a *Norwich Pharmacal* order to assist in discovering the source of the messages. The order was granted because for an action to be brought there was no other means to identify the authors. The defendant was held to have facilitated the wrongdoing by providing the means for users to post messages and was held likely to be able to provide information to enable wrongdoers to be sued. Although it was held disproportionate and unjustifiably intrusive to order disclosure in respect of trivial postings which were barely defamatory or little more than abusive or jokes, it was otherwise held that the right to protect reputation outweighed any right of the authors to remain anonymous or freedom of expression. The judge in the *Hargreaves* case, Mr Richard Parkes QC, said:

> '[9] ... The proposed order will, if granted, disclose to the Claimants the identities, or at least the e-mail addresses, of users of the Defendant's website who must have expected, given

---

[28] [2008] EWHC 1797 (QB). In that case Eady J found the claims totally without merit and upheld civil restraint orders.

[29] [2007] EWHC 2375 (QB).

their use of anonymous pseudonyms, that their privacy would be respected. As the Court of Appeal observed in *Totalise PLC v The Motley Fool Ltd* [ibid] at paragraph 25, in a case where the proposed order will result in the identification of website users who expected their identities to be kept hidden, the court must be careful not to make an order which unjustifiably invades the right of an individual to respect for his private life, especially when that individual is in the nature of things not before the court. Equally, it is clear that no order should be made for the disclosure of the identity of a data subject, whether under the *Norwich Pharmacal* doctrine or otherwise, unless the court has first considered whether the disclosure is warranted having regard to the rights and freedoms or the legitimate interests of the data subject (see paragraph 6 of schedule 2 of the Data Protection Act 1998). As the Court of Appeal pointed out (at paragraph 26 of the judgment) it is difficult for the court to carry out this task if it is refereeing a contest between two parties neither of whom is the person most concerned, that is to say the data subject. This is not a case, as I understand it, where the website operator has informed the relevant website users of what is going on or offered to pass to the court any particular reason why the users should not want their identities revealed. It did not seem to me that this was a case where I should require that the website users be contacted before making an order ...

[18] The postings which I regard as more serious are those which may reasonably be understood to allege greed, selfishness, untrustworthiness and dishonest behaviour on the part of the Claimants. In the case of those postings, the Claimants' entitlement to take action to protect their right to reputation outweighs, in my judgment, the right of the authors to maintain their anonymity and their right to express themselves freely, and I take into account in this context the restrictions on the use of defamatory language which the rules of the Defendant's bulletin board impose, restrictions which in the case of these postings appear to have been breached. I take into account also that the Defendant does not appear to have had any policy of confidentiality for the benefit of his users.'

15.25 Sometimes bloggers want to maintain their anonymity. In *Author of a Blog v Times Newspapers Ltd* Eady J refused to grant an interim injunction to a blogger (known as 'Night Jack') restraining *The Times* from publishing information which could identify him. He was in fact a policeman and feared disciplinary action if his identity was revealed. He claimed that *The Times* owed him an enforceable duty of confidence not to reveal his identity or alternatively that he had a reasonable expectation of privacy in respect of information which might disclose his identity against which there was no countervailing public interest justification for publication. The claimant's identity was in fact uncovered by a journalist's detective work on the internet so no breach of confidence was involved. The question, therefore, was whether or not the claimant had a legally enforceable right to maintain anonymity. The mere fact that he wished to remain anonymous did not mean he had a reasonable expectation of privacy in respect of the information which would unmask him. Nor did it mean that *The Times* owed him an enforceable obligation not to unmask him. Eady J said that the test as to whether or not there is a reasonable expectation of privacy was an objective one (both for privacy and breach of confidence) as recently underlined by the Court of Appeal in *Napier v Pressdram Ltd*,[30] where Toulson LJ said:

'... For a duty of confidentiality to be owed (other than under a contract or statute), the information in question must be of a nature and obtained in circumstances such that any reasonable person in the position of the recipient ought to recognise that it should be treated as confidential. As Cross J observed in Printers and Finishers Ltd v Holloway [1965] RPC 239, 256, the law would defeat its own object if it seeks to enforce in this field standards which would be rejected by the ordinary person. Freedom to report the truth is a precious thing both for the liberty of the individual (the libertarian principle) and for the sake of

---

[30]   [2009] EWCA Civ 443 at 42, [2009] NLJR 859.

wider society (the democratic principle), and it would be unduly eroded if the law of confidentiality were to prevent a person from reporting facts which a reasonable person in his position would not perceive to be confidential.'

15.26 Normally, if there is no pre-existing relationship of confidence, for a reasonable expectation of privacy to arise the information concerned has to be of a strictly personal nature such as sexual relationships, mental or physical health, financial affairs, or the claimant's family or domestic arrangements. *Mahmood v Galloway*[31] was considered to be authority for the proposition that an undercover journalist writing under a pseudonym had no reasonable expectation of privacy in respect of his identity and Eady J considered that an anonymous blogger had no greater justification for a reasonable expectation of anonymity. This was largely because blogging was essentially a public rather than a private activity.

15.27 Eady J went on to consider the public interest and, echoing Mitting J in *Mahmood*, thought that although conclusions on matters of public interest on applications for interim injunctions were not easy to reach, s 12 of the HRA 1998 required the court to take an overall view as to the likelihood of a claimant succeeding at trial. Eady J thought the public had an interest in knowing the source of an opinion or argument when assessing its value. He said that the defendant's Art 10 right of freedom of expression was not conditional upon the defendant establishing a public interest in what was being expressed. It was not accepted that it was part of the court's function to protect police officers who might be acting in breach of police discipline regulations from coming to the attention of their superiors.

15.28 In summarising under s 12 of the HRA 1998 it was held that since the injunction sought would restrain *The Times* from exercising its right of freedom of expression it was unlikely the claimant would restrain *The Times* at trial from publishing the claimant's identity as the author of the blog, whether on grounds of traditional breach of confidence or on grounds of misuse of 'private information'. The information did not have about it the necessary 'quality of confidence' contemplated by Megarry V-C in *Coco v A N Clark (Engineers) Ltd*;[32] nor did it qualify as information in respect of which the claimant has a reasonable expectation of privacy – essentially because blogging was a public activity. In any event any right of privacy the claimant may have had would be outweighed at trial by a countervailing public interest in revealing that a particular police officer has been making the communications.

15.29 In respect of defamatory material published online and archived as indicated above republication is deemed to have occurred each time a reader accesses a piece, with the consequence that the limitation period continues indefinitely in respect of such accessed material.[33] Those responsible for the boards who monitor the content may lose the defence of innocent dissemination provided under the Electronic Commerce (EC Directive) Regulations 2002 (see below). Message board hosts on the basis of the Directive will not have to pay damages for messages posted on their message boards if they do not have actual knowledge of the unlawful activity and act quickly to remove the offending material upon notification.

---

[31]   [2006] EMLR 763.
[32]   [1969] RPC 41, [1968] FSR 415.
[33]   See *Loutchansky v Times Newspapers* [2002] QB 783, at 817D; and see the ECtHR in *Times Newspapers Ltd (Nos 1 and 2) v United Kingdom* (App No 3002/03 and 23676/03) [2009] EMLR 254.

ELECTRONIC COMMERCE (EC DIRECTIVE) REGULATIONS 2002[34]

Summary

15.30 ISPs (and other 'information society services') may have a defence under the Electronic Commerce (EC Directive) Regulations 2002 depending on the extent to which they are involved in the process of publication. It is necessary to distinguish: (1) a mere conduit (for which the defence is absolute); (2) a service provider which 'caches' information which originates from another source within the communications network; and (3) a service provider which 'hosts' material.

15.31 The service provider which 'caches' information must act expeditiously to remove or disable access to the information upon obtaining 'actual knowledge' that the original information has been or has been ordered to be, removed from the network (reg 18).[35]

15.32 The service provider which 'hosts' material has a defence provided: (1) it does not have 'actual knowledge' that the information is 'unlawful' and is not aware of facts or circumstances from which unlawfulness would be apparent; (2) it acts expeditiously to remove or disable access to the information upon obtaining such knowledge or awareness; and (3) the person who provided the information was not acting under its authority or control (reg 19).

The Regulations

15.33 The Electronic Commerce (EC Directive) Regulations 2002 were reviewed in *Bunt v Tilley*,[36] where it was said that the Regulations define the circumstances in which internet intermediaries should be held accountable for material which is hosted, cached or carried by them but which they did not create. It was pointed out that the protection the Regulations afford is not confined to the publication of defamatory material and embraces other illegal material, such as child pornography or the infringement of intellectual property rights.[37]

15.34 The assertion that the ISPs in *Bunt v Tilley* were not intermediary service providers was rejected on the basis that no such restrictive definition appears in the Regulations and it would not accord with the declared policy underlying them.

15.35 One of the objectives of the Regulations was to remove disparities between the law of member states concerning the liability of service providers as intermediaries so as to facilitate cross-border services and prevent distortions of competition. Service providers are sometimes obliged to prevent or stop unlawful activities and it was thought desirable that the position should be made as clear as possible.

---

[34] SI 2002/2013.
[35] It was held in *Bunt v Tilley* [2006] EWHC 407 (QB) that reg 18 excluded ISPs from liability from storing material and that its purpose was to protect 'information society service' providers in respect of material for which they were not primary host but which they stored temporarily on their computer systems for enabling the efficient availability of internet material.
[36] [2006] EWHC 407 (QB), [2006] 3 All ER 336.
[37] Ibid, at [38].

15.36 The relevant provisions apply to 'information society services' which is any service normally provided for remuneration, at a distance, by electronic means and at the individual request of a recipient of services and is likely to cover ISPs, bulletin board operators and web-hosting services.

Mere conduits

15.37 Regulation 17(1) is concerned with the concept of 'mere conduits' and provides as follows:

> '(1)   Where an information society service is provided which consists of the transmission in a communication network of information provided by a recipient of the service or the provision of access to a communication network, the service provider (if he otherwise would) shall not be liable for damages or for any other pecuniary remedy or for any criminal sanction as a result of that transmission where the service provider – (a) did not initiate the transmission; (b) did not select the receiver of the transmission; and (c) did not select or modify the information contained in the transmission.'

15.38 Regulation 17(2) provides that acts of transmission and of provision of access, for the purposes of reg 17(1), would include:

> '... the automatic, intermediate and transient storage of the information transmitted where it takes place for the sole purpose of carrying out the transmission in the communication network, and provided that the information is not stored for any period longer than is reasonably necessary for the transmission.'

15.39 Web-based e-mail services are likely to be viewed as hosts rather than conduits and unlikely to have protection under reg 17. This is because they store their subscribers' e-mail messages to enable their subscribers to view and delete them. The messages are, therefore, stored for a longer period than reasonably required for transmission. Regulation 17 usually protects internet intermediaries who have bulletin board postings and web pages passing through their computer systems en route from one computer to another (subject to the proviso that the intermediary does not store the constituent IP datagrams for any period longer than is reasonably necessary for the transmission).

Caching

15.40 Regulation 18 provides protection in respect of material for which internet intermediaries are not primary hosts but which they store on their systems temporarily to facilitate its availability on the internet. Material passing through the system is protected but material stored for significant periods is not. Regulation 18 provides as follows:

> 'Where an information society service is provided which consists of the transmission in a communication network of information provided by a recipient of the service, the service provider (if he otherwise would) shall not be liable for damages or for any other pecuniary remedy or for any criminal sanction as result of that transmission where – (a) the information is the subject of automatic, intermediate and temporary storage where that storage is for the sole purpose of making more efficient onward transmission of the information to other recipients of the service upon their request, and (b) the service provider – (i) does not modify the information; (ii) complies with conditions on access to the information; (iii) complies with any rules regarding the updating of the information, specified in a manner widely recognised and used by industry; (iv) does not interfere with the lawful use of technology, widely recognised and used by industry, to obtain data on the use

of the information; and (v) acts expeditiously to remove or to disable access to the information he has stored upon obtaining actual knowledge of the fact that the information at the initial source of the transmission has been removed from the network, or access to it has been disabled, or that a court or an administrative authority has ordered such removal or disablement.'

15.41 It *Bunt v Tilley*[38] BT no longer sought to rely on reg 17 and 18 because it was accepted that it hosts Usenet newsgroups on its servers, the postings on which were stored for periods of time, usually a few weeks, to enable its users to access them. Further, although BT did not operate the newsgroups, it had the ability to remove postings from its news group server, although they could still be viewed via other servers.

The process of caching

15.42 The process of caching was explained in evidence in *Bunt v Tilley* by Mr Nigel Hearth, the Director of Technical Operations for AOL as follows:[39]

'The ability to view web pages quickly ... has led to the development of technical solutions by network providers and internet service providers to enable more efficient transmission of that information across the internet. Caching ... is a technical process which enables internet providers ... to speed up the delivery of web pages to internet users by making a temporary copy of a web page that is requested by a user. When a subsequent request is made for the same page, the user can be provided with that content from the local "cached" copy made by the internet service provider, rather than having to go back to the original web site which is the source of that page ... The AOL web cache in effect watches requests for web pages made by individuals and then saves copies of the responses from Google's computers. If there is a subsequent request for the Google Groups London page from an AOL User then that request is fulfilled by delivery of the Google Groups London page from the AOL web cache, rather than via the original location on Google computers ... [The] entire process is entirely automatic and the only reason for it is to make the transmission of web pages more efficient. AOL does not modify the information contained on web pages in any way ... and does not interfere in any way with the lawful use of technology widely used by the industry to obtain data on the use of information ... The storage of such material on AOL's web cache is temporary – permanent storage would be inherently contradictory to the purpose and aim of the AOL web cache ...'

Defence of lack of knowledge etc on part of information society service provider

15.43 Regulation 19 provides a defence to a claim for damages in certain circumstances where an 'innocent' service provider stores information provided by a subscriber. It provides as follows:

'Where an information society service is provided which consists of the storage of information provided by a recipient of the service, the service provider (if he otherwise would) shall not be liable for damages or for any other pecuniary remedy or for any criminal sanction as a result of that storage where – (a) the service provider – (i) does not have actual knowledge of unlawful activity or information and, where a claim for damages is made, is not aware of facts or circumstances from which it would have been apparent to the service provider that the activity or information was unlawful; or (ii) upon obtaining such

---

[38]   Ibid, at [68].
[39]   Ibid, at [52].

knowledge or awareness, acts expeditiously to remove or to disable access to the information, and (b) the recipient of the service was not acting under the authority or the control of the service provider.'

15.44 Regulation 22 provides as follows:

'In determining whether a service provider has actual knowledge for the purposes of regulations 18(b)(v) and 19(a)(i), a court shall take into account all matters which appear to it in the particular circumstances to be relevant and, among other things, shall have regard to – (a) whether a service provider has received a notice through a means of contact made available in accordance with regulation 6(1)(c), and (b) the extent to which any notice includes – (i) the full name and address of the sender of the notice; (ii) details of the location of the information in question; and (iii) details of the unlawful nature of the activity or information in question.'

15.45 Regulation 6(1)(c) provides as follows:

'A person providing an information society service shall make available to the recipient of the service and any relevant enforcement authority, in a form and manner which is easily, directly and permanently accessible, the following information ... (c) the details of the service provider, including his electronic mail address, which make it possible to contact him rapidly and communicate with him in a direct and effective manner ...'

15.46 In order to be able to characterise something as 'unlawful' a person would need to know something of the strength or weakness of available defences. The provisions of reg 19 would prevent any claim for damages, whether in respect of harassment or any other wrongful act.[40]

Injunctive relief not precluded

15.47 Regulation 20(b) provides that nothing affects the right of a party to apply for relief to prevent or stop infringement of any rights and the Regulations do not preclude the grant of an injunction in a proper case. The Regulations are concerned to restrict financial and penal sanctions.

---

[40]   *Bunt v Tilley* [2006] EWHC 407 (QB), at [72] and [76].

Part IV

BRINGING PROCEEDINGS

Chapter 16

INITIATING PRIVACY, DEFAMATION AND HARASSMENT CLAIMS

16.1   The opening shot in most disputes is the letter of claim. This is not intended to signify the commencement of a gladiatorial-style contest between the parties. The underlying purpose of the letter is to start a process whereby the parties exchange information about their respective cases in accordance with the relevant pre-action protocol to enable them, if possible, to sort out their differences at an early stage. The overall theme of the pre-action protocol regime is that litigation is to be viewed as a last resort. The parties should adopt a 'cards on the table' approach and, in particular, are expected to co-operate in exchanging information and to act proportionately in relation to the dispute. Issues should be defined and narrowed before proceedings are issued. This normally means that the parties must conduct a detailed approach to the case at an early stage and identify the key evidence.

16.2   The pre-action protocol relevant to the nature of the claim to be brought must be followed. Where a protocol does not apply to a particular claim, it is, nonetheless, good practice for the claimant's side to send a detailed letter of claim and to wait a reasonable time before issuing proceedings. It is almost always unreasonable conduct to commence proceedings without sending out a letter of claim and likely to result in a cost sanction.

16.3   The pre-action protocol in defamation cases (at para 3.6) provides that in formulating the letter of claim and the letter of response and in taking any subsequent steps the parties should act reasonably to keep costs proportionate to the nature and gravity of the case and the stage the complaint has reached. It is also provided in that protocol (at para 3.7) that the parties should consider whether some form of alternative dispute resolution procedure would be more suitable than litigation.

THE LETTER OF CLAIM

16.4   Pre-action protocols represent best practice but need not always be slavishly adhered to. The letter of claim should always set out the main facts and circumstances of the claim and should identify the cause of action alleged, as well as clearly stating the remedy sought. In the spirit of providing information to the other side key documents will often be enclosed with the letter of claim. Both the letter of claim and letter of response should set out the respective positions comprehensively but they do not have the status of statements of case. If the defendant intends to admit liability he should normally do so clearly and unequivocally at the outset in the letter of response so that further costs will be avoided by the claimant endeavouring to prove the claim.

16.5   Parties who expend costs pre-action have no entitlement to recover them from the other side unless proceedings are actually commenced or there is an agreement made or confirmed in writing whereby one side agrees to pay the other's costs. Where proceedings are commenced *pre-action costs* incurred in respect of issues raised in the proceedings can be recovered in the proceedings. Pre-action costs incurred in respect of issues which are not raised in the proceedings remain irrecoverable.[1]

16.6   Claimants who want to recover pre-action costs must, therefore, specify in the pre-action letter that any settlement must include an agreement that the defendant will pay the claimant's reasonable costs. The Civil Procedure Rules 1998[2] (CPR), r 44.12A provides that where the parties to a dispute have reached an agreement (made or confirmed in writing) on all the issues (including which party is to pay the costs) but have failed to agree the amount of those costs and no proceedings have been served either party may start proceedings under CPR Part 8 for the court to make an order for costs to be determined by detailed assessment. It is, therefore, important for intended claimants to make sure that they get the intended defendant to agree in writing to pay costs of any pre-action settlement which might be reached.

16.7   The protocol for defamation cases aims to improve pre-action communication between the parties by establishing a timetable for the exchange of information relevant to the dispute and by setting standards for the content of correspondence. Compliance enables the parties to make an informed judgment on the merits of their cases earlier than tends otherwise to happen. The important feature to bear in mind in defamation claims which distinguishes them from other claims is that time is of the essence and the limitation period is only one year. The claimant will usually seek an immediate correction and apology as part of the process of restoring his reputation.

16.8   Paragraph 3.1 of the pre-action protocol in defamation claims provides that the claimant should notify the defendant of his claim at the earliest opportunity and the letter of claim should contain the following information:

- the name of the claimant;

- sufficient details to identify the publication or broadcast which contains the words complained of;

- the words complained of and, if known, the date of publication; where possible, a copy or transcript of the words complained of should be enclosed;

- factual inaccuracies or unsupportable comment within the words complained of: the claimant should give a sufficient explanation to enable the defendant to appreciate why the words are inaccurate or unsupportable;

- the nature of the remedies sought by the claimant;

- where relevant the letter of claim should also include (1) any facts or matters which make the claimant identifiable from the words complained of and (2) details of any special facts relevant to the interpretation of the words complained of and/or any particular damage caused by the words complained of; and

- if possible the meanings the claimant attributes to the words complained of.

---

[1]   See e g *McGlinn v Waltham Contractors Ltd* [2005] EWHC 1419.

[2]   SI 1998/3132.

16.9 The defendant's response to the letter of claim should be full and sent as soon as reasonably possible. If it cannot be sent within 14 days the defendant should inform the claimant and give a date by which the response will be sent. The response should include:

- whether or to what extent the claim is accepted, whether more information is required or whether the claim is rejected;

- if the claim is accepted in whole or in part, the defendant should indicate which remedies it is willing to offer;

- if more information is required the defendant should specify precisely what information is needed to enable the claim to be dealt with and why;

- if the claim is rejected, the defendant should explain the reasons why it is rejected, including a sufficient indication of the facts on which the defendant is likely to rely in support of any substantive defence; and

- if possible the meaning(s) the defendant attributes to the words complained of.

COMMENCING THE CLAIM: THE STATEMENTS OF CASE

16.10 Claims are commenced by the issue of a claim form (see CPR, r 7.2). The claim form must contain a concise statement of the nature of the claim, the remedy which the claimant seeks and such other matters as may be set out in a Practice Direction (see CPR, r 16.2). If the particulars of claim are not contained in or served with the claim form the claimant must state on the claim form that the particulars of claim will follow. The defendant may respond by filing a defence and in response to the defence the claimant may file a reply. These documents are now generically described as statements of case and the object of statements of case is to enable the court and the parties to identify and define the real issues in dispute between the parties. Statements of case must be verified by a statement of truth. The particulars of claim should set out the claimant's claim clearly and fully and the same principal applies to the defence.[3] The defence must provide a comprehensive response to the particulars of claim. It is not sufficient simply to deny the matters raised in the claim.

16.11 The rules relating to statements of case in defamation claims are set out in the Practice Direction at CPR Part 53 PD 2. This confirms that statements of case in defamation claims should be confined to the information necessary to inform the other party of the nature of the case he has to meet and stipulates that such information should be set out concisely and in a manner proportionate to the subject matter of the claim.

16.12 In a claim for libel the publication of the subject of the claim must be identified in the claim form. This means that the place where the publication occurred and the date of publication must be clearly identified so that there is no doubt where the offending

---

[3] See the Queen's Bench Guide, at para 1B-28.

material appeared. In a claim for slander the claim form must so far as possible contain the words complained of, and identify the person to whom they were spoken and when.[4]

16.13 Sometimes excessive particulars are pleaded in the statements of case. In *McPhilemy v Times Newspapers Ltd* (a defamation action) Lord Woolf MR gave the following general guidance about the purpose and importance of statements of case:[5]

> 'The need for extensive pleadings including particulars should be reduced by the requirement that witness statements are now exchanged. In the majority of proceedings identification of the documents upon which a party relies, together with copies of that party's witness statements, will make the detail of the nature of the case the other side has to meet obvious. This reduces the need for particulars in order to avoid being taken by surprise ... Pleadings are still required to mark out the parameters of the case that is being advanced by each party. In particular they are still critical to identify the issues and the extent of the dispute between the parties. What is important is that the pleadings should make clear the general nature of the case of the pleader. This is true both under the old rules and the new rules. The Practice Direction to r 16, para 9.3 (Practice Direction – Statements of Case CPR Pt 16) requires, in defamation proceedings, the facts on which a defendant relies to be given. No more than a *concise* statement of those facts is required ...
>
> ... excessive particulars can achieve directly the opposite result from that which is intended. They can obscure the issues rather than providing clarification. In addition, after disclosure and the exchange of witness statements, pleadings frequently become of only historic interest ... Unless there is some obvious purpose to be served by fighting over the precise terms of a pleading, contests over their terms are to be discouraged ...
>
> While under the rules a party cannot be prevented from putting forward an allegation which is central to his or her defence, the court can control the manner in which this is done and thus limit the costs involved.'

16.14 If the statement of case exceeds 25 pages (excluding schedules) an appropriate short summary must also be filed and served (see para 1.4 of the Practice Direction supplementing CPR Part 16).

HUMAN RIGHTS

16.15 The Human Rights Act 1998 is of relevance to privacy claims and also generally to breach of confidence and defamation claims. Any party who seeks to rely on any provision of or right arising under the Human Rights Act 1998 or seeks a remedy available under that Act must state that fact in the statement of case and must in the statement of case give precise details of the Convention[6] right which it is alleged has been infringed and details of the alleged infringement and specify the relief sought (see CPR Part 16 PD 15).

---

4   See CPR Part 53 PD 2, para 2.2(1) and (2).
5   [1999] 3 All ER 775, at 792–794. See also *Bookbinder v Tebbit* [1989] 1 WLR 640, [1989] 1 All ER 1169.
6   European Convention for the Protection of Human Rights and Fundamental Freedoms (ECHR).

KEEPING THE CONTENTS OF STATEMENTS OF CASE PRIVATE

16.16 Sometimes claimants in privacy, breach of confidence, defamation and similar claims do not want the words they are complaining about disseminated further by publicity being given to what is set out in the statements of case. Under CPR, r 5.4C(1) it is a general rule that a person who is not a party to proceedings may obtain from court records a copy of a statement of case (but not any documents filed with or attached to the statement of case or intended to be served with it). This means that claimants in slander actions who (in accordance with the above rule) set out the words complained of in their statements of case run the risk that the media will be able to publish the offending words under the cloak of qualified privilege. This is a particular problem where publication in the first place has been to a limited number of persons and further publication in the media would only serve to aggravate the damage. CPR, r 5.4(4) provides that the court may, on the application of a party or of any person identified in the statement of case, order that a non-party may not obtain a copy of the statement of case under para (1); may restrict the persons or classes of persons who may obtain a copy of a statement of case; may order that persons or classes of persons may only obtain a copy of a statement of case if it is edited in accordance with directions of the court; or may make such order as it thinks fit.

THE PARTICULARS OF CLAIM

16.17 The overriding principle is that the particulars of claim must include a concise statement of the facts on which the claimant relies (see CPR, r 16.4(1)(a)) and a concise statement of the nature of the claim. Points of law relied on can be referred to in the particulars of claim and the name of a witness may be referred to. Copies of documents relied on which are necessary for the claim may also be served with the particulars of claim (see CPR Part 16 PD 13.3(3)).

16.18 In privacy and breach of confidence claims it might be necessary to refer to a contractual document or other agreement. If there is a written contract a copy of the contract or the documents constituting the contract or agreement should be attached to or served with the particulars of claim and the originals made available at the hearing. If the claim is based on an oral agreement the particulars of claim should set out the contractual words used and state by whom, to whom, when and where they were spoken (see CPR Part 16 PD 7.4).

16.19 Any allegations of fraud or illegality or notice or knowledge of a fact should be set out in the particulars of claim if relied on (see CPR Part 16 PD 8.2(1) and (2)).

16.20 In *Carrie v Tolkien*,[7] where the posting of offending material on the internet had been for a very short period of time, it was confirmed that placing material on the internet was not presumed in law automatically to amount to substantial publication and that it was always necessary to identify the precise publication which must be pleaded and established by evidence. If offending material is on the internet for a very short period of time it was not enough to plead that the posting had been accessed 'by a

---

[7]   [2009] EWHC 29 (QB), at [17] and [18], per Eady J.

large but unquantifiable number of readers' because this is mere assertion and there must be a solid basis for drawing the corresponding inference.

16.21 In harassment claims involving the press it is not enough merely to allege in a particulars of claim that a series of damaging articles in the papers was reasonably likely to cause and has caused distress to an individual. This will probably be struck out on the ground no arguable case of harassment is disclosed. To constitute harassment some exceptional circumstance must be present to justify interfering with a paper's Art 10 right to freedom of expression or to publish as it sees fit. Also, when claiming an injunction in harassment cases the claim should be more precise than simply to restrain the defendant from pursuing any conduct which amounts to harassment. The precise conduct complained of must be identified, for example, continuing to take intrusive photographs of X when at home in the privacy of her flat.

MEANING IN DEFAMATION CLAIMS

16.22 In defamation claims words complained of being defamatory on their face are said to be defamatory in their natural and ordinary meaning. Words defamatory only because of special facts known to the persons who read or heard them are said to be defamatory in an innuendo meaning (ie the legal innuendo). In the latter case it is necessary to set out in the pleading the special facts which give rise to the innuendo meaning.

16.23 It is provided in CPR Part 53 PD 5, paras 2.3(1) and (2) that the claimant must specify in the particulars of claim the defamatory meaning he alleges that the words or matters complained of convey both as to their natural and ordinary meaning and as to any innuendo meaning (that is a meaning alleged to be conveyed to some person by reason of knowing facts extraneous to the words complained of). In the case of an innuendo meaning, the claimant must also identify the relevant extraneous facts.

16.24 Pleading the meaning is important because it sets the parameters for the later conduct of the proceedings in defamation cases. No matter how obvious the natural and ordinary meaning appears to be it should nonetheless be pleaded in the particulars of claim. The basic rule is that the claimant should plead a meaning that is as high and specific as the words will properly bear (this means that the meaning pleaded should not be strained or too wide). But there are dangers in pleading high and specific meanings because if the meaning pleaded is too high it might be struck out and if the meaning pleaded is too wide (eg a general charge that the words mean the claimant is a crook) the defendant is given extra scope to justify that meaning by raking over the claimant's past.[8]

16.25 In cases of legal innuendo meaning it is necessary to set out the facts relied on as giving rise to the alleged defamatory meaning which the words bear. This is dealt with more fully in the chapter on defamation (Chapter 13).

16.26 As seen above in cases of slander the words complained of must be set out in the statements of case. CPR Part 53 PD 9, para 2.4 provides that in a claim for slander the precise words used and the names to whom they were spoken and when must, so far as possible, be set out in the particulars of claim if not already contained in the claim form.

---

8   There is a useful illustration of the dangers in *Bookbinder v Tebbit* [1989] 1 WLR 640, [1989] 1 All ER 1169.

The rule that the actual words used in slander must be set out is of long standing but sometimes presents a difficulty where the precise words used cannot be recalled. The rule is that the claimant should always endeavour to set out the words used as precisely as possible and, at least, with reasonable precision and it is not permissible to plead the gist of the words used.[9]

THE DEFENCE

16.27 The defence should be a comprehensive response to the allegations made in the particulars of claim. In the defence the defendant must state which of the allegations in the particulars of claim are denied, which it is not possible to admit or deny but the claimant is required to prove and which allegations are admitted (see CPR, r 16.5(1)). Denials must be explicit. If an allegation is denied the reasons for the denial must be stated in the defence and if the defendant intends to put forward a different version of events from that given by the claimant the version relied on it must be stated in the defence (see CPR, r 16.5(2)). If an allegation is not dealt with in the defence but the defence sets out the nature of the defendant's case in relation to the issue to which the allegation is relevant the claimant will be required to prove the allegation (see CPR, r 16.5(3)). Otherwise a defendant who fails to deal with an allegation shall be taken to admit it (see CPR, r 16.5(5)). As with the particulars of claim, the defence may also refer to any point of law on which it is based or the name of witnesses the defendant intends to call and it may have attached to it or served with it the relevant documents upon which the defendant intends to rely and which are considered essential.

16.28 The defendant may wish to serve a counterclaim (see CPR Part 20). This is done by serving particulars of the counterclaim, which should normally form one document with the counterclaim following on from the defence (see CPR Part 15 PD 3).

16.29 In defamation claims the following rules apply to defences of justification, fair comment and privilege.

JUSTIFICATION

16.30 CPR Part 53 PD 11, para 2.5 provides that where a defendant alleges that the words complained of are true he must:

(1) specify the defamatory meanings he seeks to justify; and

(2) give details of the matters on which he relies in support of that allegation.

16.31 Justification means that the words complained of are true, ie that the defendant was justified in stating them because they are true. In running a defence to a defamation claim the defendant is not obliged to state what he says the words mean. But if the defendant wishes to plead justification (ie show that the words are true) he must state the meaning he seeks to show is true. It is irrelevant whether the defendant thinks the words actually bear that meaning.[10]

---

[9] *Best v Charter Medical of England Ltd* [2001] EWCA Civ 1588; [2002] EMLR 335, CA.

[10] See Nicholls LJ in *Prager v Times Newspapers* [1988] 1 WLR 77, at 91.

16.32 It is, therefore, necessary to determine in what meaning the defendant says he can show that the words are true. The claimant and the defendant might each contend that the words mean different things. The defendant is not bound to justify what the claimant says the words mean. Whether the defendant agrees or disagrees with the claimant as to what the words mean he must specify the defamatory meaning he seeks to justify and give details of the matters relied on in support of that allegation (see CPR Part 53 PD 11). These particulars of the defence case are called '*Lucas-Box*' particulars.[11] At the end of the trial if the defendant justifies the meaning found by the jury the defence of justification will succeed. If the defendant fails to justify the meaning found by the jury the defence of justification will fail. The defendant must, therefore, endeavour to justify a meaning that the jury is likely to find the words mean.

16.33 Two conditions must be fulfilled when the defendant sets out meaning which he seeks to justify:

- the meaning must be a meaning a jury properly directed could find that the words mean;[12] and

- the meaning to be justified must be a defamatory meaning.[13] (If the jury found the words used bore a meaning that was not defamatory the claim would fail anyway so it would be a waste of time justifying on that basis.)

16.34 The *Lucas Box* particulars set out by the defendant will commonly be along the following lines:

> '... the words in the article complained of are true in the following meanings that is to say that the claimant is a serial expense cheater PARTICULARS (1) the claimant claimed the following expenses he was not entitled to when employed at ... (2) when in office as a councillor the claimant continued to claim expenses he was not entitled to claim in respect of fictitious meals out at ...'

16.35 Particulars of justification must not be vague but be clear and unambiguous. They must contain precise detail of factual allegations relied on to support the plea that the words complained of are true.

FAIR COMMENT ON A MATTER OF PUBLIC INTEREST

16.36 CPR Part 53 PD 14, para 2.6 provides that where a defendant alleges that the words complained of are fair comment on a matter of public interest he must:

(1)   specify the defamatory meaning he seeks to defend as fair comment on a matter of public interest; and

(2)   give details of the matters on which he relies in support of that allegation.

16.37 Fair comment must be based on facts that are true but the defendant is not confined to the facts stated in the words complained of by the claimant or even those set

---

[11]   Named after *Lucas-Box v Newsgroup* [1986] 1 WLR 147, CA.
[12]   See *Prager v Times Newspapers* [1988] 1 WLR 77, at 86; and *Polly Peck v Trelford* [1986] QB 1000.
[13]   See *Broadcasting Corporation of NZ v Crush* [1988] 2 NZLR 234, at 237.

out in the publication itself provided they existed at the time of publication[14] and were known in general terms to the person who made the comment upon them which is alleged to be fair.[15] The meaning sought to be defended as fair comment must, in the same way as with justification, be set out. The defendant should identify and set out the matter of public interest to which the comment relates.

QUALIFIED PRIVILEGE

16.38 CPR Part 53 PD 17, para 2.7 provides that where a defendant alleges that the words complained of were published on a privileged occasion he must specify the circumstances he relies on in support of that conclusion.

16.39 The new *Reynolds* defence[16] has made this provision of particular importance because it will be necessary to give particulars of a range of factors identified by Lord Nicholls (which, of course, is not an exhaustive list):

- the seriousness of the allegation;

- the nature of the information;

- the source of the information;

- the steps taken to verify the information;[17]

- the status of the information;

- the urgency of the matter;

- whether the claimant was invited to comment;

- whether the article contained the gist of the claimant's story;

- the tone of the article; and

- the circumstances and timing of the article.

16.40 It is also necessary to give particulars of the reasonable belief of those responsible for publication that what was stated was true.

---

[14] *Lowe v Associated Newspapers* [2006] EWHC 320 (QB), [2007] 1 QB 580 and *Cohen v Daily Telegraph* [1968] 1 WLR 916.

[15] *Lowe v Associated Newspapers* [2006] EWHC 320 (QB), [2007]QB 580.

[16] *Reynolds v Times Newspapers* [2001] AC 127, HL; and see *Jameel v Wall Street Journal* [2006] UKHL 44, [2007] 1 AC 359.

[17] The importance of this factor was illustrated in *Seaga v Harper* [2008] UKPC 9: see Lord Carswell at [15] – failure to take sufficient care to check the reliability of the information.

THE REPLY TO DEFENCE

16.41 The service of a reply is optional. A claimant who does not file a reply to the defence shall not be taken to admit the matters raised in the defence and if a reply is not served or an allegation in the defence is not dealt with the defendant shall be required to prove the allegation (see CPR, r 16.7). The reply must be consistent with what is set out in the particulars of claim and if the claimant wants to set up a different case from what is set out in the particulars of claim the correct procedure is for the claimant to amend the particulars of claim rather than serve a reply. Such a departure from what was originally pleaded will have costs consequences. One of the purposes of serving a reply might be to 'confess and avoid' what is set out in the defence. This means that the claimant is saying that even if what is set out in the defence is correct the defence will not avail the defendant. This is of particular importance in defamation cases where defences of fair comment and qualified privilege will be defeated by proof of malice.

16.42 If the claimant is responding to a defence and counterclaim the reply will be headed 'Reply and defence to counterclaim' and this should normally be in one document. The court's permission is required for the service of a statement of case subsequent to a reply.

THE REPLY IN DEFAMATION PROCEEDINGS WHERE DEFENCES OF JUSTIFICATION, FAIR COMMENT AND PRIVILEGE ARE RAISED

16.43 CPR Part 53 PD 19, para 2.8 provides that where the defendant alleges that the words complained of are true, or are fair comment on a matter of public interest, the claimant must serve a reply specifically admitting or denying the allegation and giving the facts on which he relies.

16.44 CPR Part 53 PD 21, para 2.9 provides that if the defendant contends that any of the words or matters are fair comment on a matter of public interest, or were published on a privileged occasion, and the claimant intends to allege that the defendant acted with malice, the claimant must serve a reply giving details of the facts and matters relied on.

16.45 Malice is not an ingredient of a defamation claim and the falsity of the words complained of is presumed, so there is no reason to plead in the particulars of claim that words were published 'falsely and maliciously'. Malice is not an issue where *Reynolds* privilege is raised because the conditions for raising the defence could never be fulfilled if malice was present. Malice is, however, an answer to a defence of fair comment or qualified privilege and it should be pleaded in the reply. The reply should state that the defendant was actuated by express malice and the facts from which malice can be inferred to support the allegation should be set out fully but succinctly. The sort of malice required is:

- improper motive or knowledge that (or recklessness as to whether) the words were false in qualified privilege cases; and

- proof that the defendant genuinely did not hold the view he expressed (rather than evidence of spite and ill will) in fair comment cases.[18]

PLEADING DAMAGES IN DEFAMATION CASES

16.46 The law generally presumes that damage has been suffered if a wrong is proved but where damage beyond what is presumed to follow from the words complained of is claimed it is necessary to make that clear in the particulars of claim.

16.47 CPR Part 53 PD 23, para 2.10 provides that:

(1)   a claimant must give full details of the facts and matters on which he relies in support of his claim for damages; and

(2)   where a claimant seeks aggravated or exemplary damages he must provide the information specified in CPR, r 16.4(1)(c).

16.48 CPR, r 16.4(1)(c) provides that the particulars of claim must include, if the claimant is seeking aggravated damages or exemplary damages, a statement to that effect and his grounds for claiming them.

THE RULING ON MEANING IN DEFAMATION CASES

16.49 It is common for there to be a trial of a preliminary issue as to the defamatory meanings which the words complained of were capable of bearing. This is helpful because it assists in letting the parties know at an early stage where they stand. It enables the defendant to know what needs to be proved to make out a defence of justification or fair comment and in some cases assists by showing that the claimant has pitched the defamatory meaning too high. The preliminary ruling can break the case for a claimant at an early stage if the pleaded meaning is rejected by the judge. This is critical because if a judge errs in holding words to be incapable of bearing a meaning pleaded by a claimant, then the claimant is deprived of his right to vindicate his reputation before a court. If the judge errs in holding words to be capable of a meaning pleaded by a claimant, then the defendant will be wrongly burdened with defending libel proceedings.[19]

16.50 In defamation strict rules exist which divide the responsibility for deciding particular issues between those which must be decided by the judge and those which must be decided by the jury:

- the question whether words are capable of bearing a particular meaning is a question of law for a judge,[20] who will set limits to the range of possible defamatory meanings which the words may bear which is a question of law;

[18]   Lord Nicholls in *Tse Wai Chun Paul v Albert Cheng* [2001] EMLR 777.
[19]   See Tugendhat J in *John v Guardian News & Media* [2008] EWHC 3066 (QB).
[20]   *Lewis v The Daily Telegraph* [1964] AC 234.

- it is a question of fact for the jury to determine what the words actually mean within that defined range of meanings;[21] and

- the judge may determine whether the words are capable of bearing a defamatory meaning at all[22] or whether they contain two or more distinct stings.[23]

16.51 The law attributes to the words only one meaning (ie the 'single meaning' rule) although different readers will probably read the words in slightly different senses.[24] Given the ambiguity of language, the single meaning rule does represent a fair and workable method of deciding whether the words under consideration should be treated as defamatory.

16.52 Either party may apply to the court for a ruling on meaning.[25] It is possible for a party to apply even in respect of his own meaning.[26] The application should be made as soon as possible. The application is usually listed directly before the judge in charge of the jury list and not before a Master or district judge.

16.53 CPR Part 53 PD 31, para 4.1 provides that at any time the court may decide: (1) whether a statement complained of is capable of having the meaning attributed to it in the statement of case; (2) whether the statement is capable of being defamatory of the claimant; and (3) whether the statement is capable of bearing any other meaning defamatory of the claimant. An application for a ruling on meaning may be made at any time after service of the particulars of claim and should be made promptly. The precise statement must be identified together with the meaning attributed to it.

16.54 No evidence should be admissible on the challenge to the natural and ordinary meaning relied on[27] and, in relation to innuendo, the court should proceed on the assumption that the claimant would succeed in establishing the matters relied on in support of the innuendo[28] and that some readers at least would have knowledge of those matters. Guidance has been given about the court's function when dealing with applications as to meaning where there was an issue over whether or not the words were capable of conveying the pleaded defamatory meaning or any meaning defamatory of the claimant:

- the court's function is to 'delimit' the meanings that the words complained of are capable of bearing;[29]

- the exercise should be one of 'generosity not parsimony';[30] and

---

21   *Mapp v NGN* [1998] QB 520, at 523.
22   *Berkoff v Burchill* [1977] EMLR 139.
23   *Cruise v Express Newspapers* [1999] QB 931.
24   See Diplock LJ in *Slim v Daily Telegraph Ltd* [1968] 2 QB 157, at 171–172; and Lord Hoffman in *Bonnick v Morris* [2003] 1 AC 300, at [21].
25   A claimant may apply in respect of a defendant's '*Lucas-Box*' meaning, ie the meaning that the defendant intends to justify.
26   *Parry v Express Newspapers* (unreported) 9 March 1995, CA.
27   Eady J in *Tiscali v BT Plc* [2008] EWHC 2927.
28   An application under CPR Part 24 might be appropriate if it is sought to establish that the claimant had no realistic prospect of establishing the accuracy of the pleaded facts.
29   *Mapp v NGN* [1998] QB 520, at 526.
30   Per Sedley LJ in *Berezovsky v Forbes* [2001] EMLR 1030, at [16].

- the court should only exclude a meaning if satisfied it would be perverse to uphold the meaning[31] and that the judge's function was confined to 'pre-empting perversity'.

OFFER OF AMENDS IN DEFAMATION PROCEEDINGS (DEFAMATION ACT 1996, S 2)

16.55 The Defamation Act 1996 (DeA 1996), s 2(1) and (2) provides that a person who has published a statement alleged to be defamatory of another may offer to make amends. The offer may be in relation to the statement generally or in relation to a specific defamatory meaning which the person making the offer accepts that the statement conveys (a qualified offer). The offer of amends regime mitigates the normal rule that liability in defamation is strict and provides a means for the parties to resolve defamation claims with the judge fixing compensation if the parties cannot agree. It also allows a defence to an innocent defendant whose offer of amends is rejected unless it can be shown that the defendant knew or had reason to believe that the statement referred to the claimant (or would be understood to do so) and was false and defamatory of the claimant.

16.56 DeA 1996, s 2(3) provides that the offer of amends must be in writing, it must be expressed to be an offer to make amends under s 2 of the Act and must state whether it is a qualified offer and, if so, set out the defamatory meaning in relation to which it is made. Section 2(4) provides that an offer of amends is an offer to make a suitable correction of the statement complained of and a sufficient apology to the aggrieved party, to publish a correction and apology in a manner that is reasonable and practicable in the circumstances and to pay to the aggrieved party such compensation (if any), and such costs, as may be agreed or determined to be payable.

16.57 DeA 1996, s 2(5) provides that an offer to make amends under the section may not be made by a person after serving a defence in defamation proceedings brought against him by the aggrieved party in respect of the publication in question. Section 2(6) provides that an offer to make amends may be withdrawn before it is accepted; and a renewal of an offer which has been withdrawn shall be treated as a new offer.

Accepting an offer to make amends

16.58 DeA 1996, s 3 provides that if an offer to make amends under s 2 is accepted by the aggrieved party the party accepting the offer may not bring or continue defamation proceedings in respect of the publication concerned against the person making the offer, but he is entitled to enforce the offer to make amends as follows. If the parties agree on the steps to be taken in fulfilment of the offer, the aggrieved party may apply to the court for an order that the other party fulfil his offer by taking the steps agreed. If the parties do not agree on the steps to be taken by way of correction, apology and publication, the party who made the offer may take such steps as he thinks appropriate, and may in particular (1) make the correction and apology by a statement in open court in terms approved by the court and (2) give an undertaking to the court as to the manner of their publication. If the parties do not agree on the amount to be paid by way

---

[31]   Per Simon Brown LJ in *Jameel v Wall Street Journal Europe* [2004] EMLR 6, at [4].

of compensation or costs, they shall be determined by the court[32] on the same principles as damages in defamation proceedings and costs in court proceedings.

16.59 It is for the claimant to decide whether or not to accept an offer of amends and a reasonable time will be allowed for the claimant to do so.[33] If an offer of amends is not accepted this may be construed as non-acceptance. No provision is made in the rules for an offer to be rejected – an offer is either accepted or not accepted. Disclosure has been ordered of specific documents (such as a journalist's notes of an interview) which were relevant to whether the defendant knew the words complained of were false and/or defamatory and would assist the claimant in deciding whether to accept an offer of amends.[34] The order for disclosure was made under CPR, r 31.12 on the basis that the notes would be disclosable regardless of whether the offer of amends was accepted and there was no point postponing when disclosure had to be made. Routine or wide-ranging applications for disclosure by claimants faced with a decision whether or not to accept offers of amends were not generally approved.

Failure to accept an offer to make amends

16.60 DeA 1996, s 4(1) and (2) provides that if an offer to make amends under s 2, duly made and not withdrawn, is not accepted by the aggrieved party, the fact that the offer was made is a defence to defamation proceedings in respect of the publication in question (by that party against the person making the offer) save that a qualified offer is only a defence in respect of the meaning to which the offer related.[35]

16.61 In *Loughton Contracts plc v Dun & Bradstreet Ltd*[36] the defendants made an unqualified offer of amends intended to cover the claim as pleaded which was expressed to be a claim for general damages with right to claim special damages expressly reserved. The claimant's letter of acceptance was in fact a counter offer because it asserted a right to claim special damages in the future contrary to the offer which the claimant had made. The claimant was belatedly allowed to accept the offer of amends because the offer had not lapsed, the claimant had made it clear it wished, in principle, to accept and had not acted in bad faith. There would otherwise have been an unjust outcome whereby the claimant would be denied all compensation for having failed to accept an unqualified offer (which provides a complete defence under DeA 1996, s 4).

16.62 DeA 1996, s 4(3) provides that there is no such defence if the person by whom the offer was made knew or had reason to believe that the statement complained of referred to the aggrieved party or was likely to be understood as referring to him and was both false and defamatory of that party but it shall be presumed until the contrary is shown that he did not know and had no reason to believe that was the case. This means the defence is not available where a claimant can prove that the defendant deliberately defamed him or the defendant chose to ignore or shut his mind to information which should have led him to believe (not merely suspect) that the statement referred to the claimant and was false and defamatory. It has been held that 'reason to

---

32   Without a jury (DeA 1996, s 3(10)).
33   See Eady J in *Tesco Stores v Guardian News & Media Limited* [2009] EMLR 90.
34   See Gray J in *Rigg v Associated Newspapers Ltd* [2003] EWHC 710, [2004] EMLR 52.
35   The person who made the offer does not have to rely on it as a defence but if he does he may not rely on any other defence.
36   [2006] EWHC 1224, (QB).

believe' in DeA 1996 did not apply to anything short of recklessness[37] and that in the context of s 4(3) there was no distinct possible meaning of the words 'had reason to believe' lying between recklessness, on the one hand, and constructive or imputed knowledge based on negligence, on the other.

16.63 DeA 1996, s 4(4) provides that the person who made the offer need not rely on it by way of defence, but if he does he may not rely on any other defence (if the offer was a qualified offer, this applies only in respect of the meaning to which the offer related). Section 4(5) provides that the offer may be relied on in mitigation of damages whether or not it was relied on as a defence.

16.64 The intention behind the offer of amends procedure is broadly to allow a defendant who has published a statement alleged to be defamatory to offer to make amends. Different consequences apply depending on whether or not the offer of amends is accepted:

- If the offer is accepted the procedure under DeA 1996, s 3 applies. This provides that the party accepting the offer cannot bring nor continue defamation proceedings against the person who made the offer which was accepted. The remedy is for the offer to be enforced.

- If the offer of amends is not accepted the fact that the offer was made affords a defence (or if the offer was qualified a partial defence) to defamation proceedings brought in respect of the offending words. However, the defendant who made the offer has no defence if he knew or had reason to believe that the offending words referred to the claimant or was likely to be understood as referring to the claimant and that the words were both false and defamatory of the claimant.

16.65 It was said by Eady J in *Milne v Express Newspapers* that:[38]

'The main purpose of the statutory regime is to provide an exit route for journalists who have made a mistake and are willing to put their hands up and make amends.'

And again it was said by Eady J in *Cleese v Associated Newspapers*:[39]

'It is fair to say, perhaps, that the whole of the "offer of amends" regime is predicated upon the parties' willingness to negotiate meaningfully and thus to give and take, where necessary, in order to achieve a reasonable compromise as quickly and inexpensively as the circumstances permit.'

16.66 CPR Part 53 PD 25, para 2.11 provides that a defendant who relies on an offer to make amends under DeA 1996, s 2 as his defence must state in his defence that he is relying on the offer in accordance with s 4(2), and that the offer has not been withdrawn by him or been accepted and attach a copy of the offer he has made with his defence.

16.67 CPR Part 53 PD 27, para 3.1 deals with the court's powers in connection with an offer of amends made in accordance with the offer of amends procedure in DeA 1996,

---

[37]   *Milne v Express Newspapers Ltd* [2004] EWCA Civ 664, at [36], per May LJ. The recklessness referred to is with regard to the truth.
[38]   [2002] EWHC 2564 (QB), [2003] 1 WLR 927, affirmed in the CA: [2004] EWCA Civ 664, [2005] 1 WLR 772, at [41].
[39]   [2003] EWHC 137 (QB), [2004] EMLR 3, at [19].

ss 2–4 (ie the provisions enabling a person who has made a statement alleged to be defamatory to make an offer of amends and the provisions for the court to assist in the process of making amends). Paragraph 3.2 provides that a claim under DeA 1996, s 3 made *other than in existing proceedings* may be made under CPR Part 8:

(1)   where the parties agree on the steps to make amends, and the sole purpose of the claim is for the court to make an order under s 3(3) for an order that the offer be fulfilled; or

(2)   where the parties do not agree:
       (a)   on the steps to be taken by way of correction, apology and publication (see s 3(4)); or
       (b)   on the amount to be paid by way of costs (see s 3(6)).

Applications in *existing* proceedings made under DeA 1996, s 3 must be made in accordance with CPR Part 23, ie by way of ordinary application notice in existing proceedings.

16.68 CPR Part 53 PD 27, para 3.3 provides that a claim or application under DeA 1996, s 3 must be supported by written evidence which must include:

•   a copy of the offer of amends;

•   details of the steps taken to fulfil the offer of amends;

•   details of the publication of the correction and apology;

•   a statement of the amount of any sum paid as compensation;

•   a statement of the amount of any sum paid for costs; and

•   why the offer is unsatisfactory.

Where any step specified in DeA 1996, s 2(4) has not been taken, then the evidence referred to in the last four bullet points must state what steps are proposed by the party to fulfil the offer of amends and the date or dates on which each step will be fulfilled and, if none, that no proposal has been made to take that step.

16.69 In *Warren v Random House*[40] it was held that:

•   where an offer of amends was accepted contractual rights and obligations were not created because the statutory procedure contained express provisions as to what should or should not happen next and the court retained a role; and

•   the court retained a residual discretion to allow a party to resile from an accepted offer to make amends on one of the traditional contractual grounds but it would rarely be exercised to relieve a party of the consequences of a bargain freely entered into with important and well-understood consequences.[41]

---

[40]   [2008] EWCA Civ 834.
[41]   *Flynn v Scougall* [2004] EWCA Civ 873, [2004] 1 WLR 3069 considered.

16.70 In *Abu v MGN*[42] Eady J gave the following indications to be adopted when an 'offer of amends' was made:

- the approach should accord with the modern 'cards on the table' method of litigation;

- the offer must be made and accepted on the basis that the parties understand the full extent of the damage complained of and once the agreement is reached the claimant cannot later reveal elements of pleadable damage not previously mentioned;

- the principles to be applied by the judge in assessing compensation are the same as those in ordinary defamation proceedings; and

- defendants are entitled to require the claimant to prove that the particular element of damage to reputation or hurt to feelings was caused by the specific libel admitted to be untrue and not to some other libel in another publication or by a separate damaging statement within the publication complained of.

16.71 In *Nail v NGN*[43] the following guidance was given by the Court of Appeal as to the way in damages are to be assessed where unqualified offers to make amends under DeA 1996 were accepted:

- damages were to be assessed on the same principles as damages in defamation proceedings, which included taking into account the conduct of the defendant after publication which might tend to mitigate or aggravate the award;

- usually where an unqualified offer is accepted and an agreed apology published there is bound to be substantial mitigation because the claimant's reputation will have been repaired to some extent and the claimant would be relieved of the expense of contested litigation;

- where an unqualified offer of amends is made and accepted claimants should plead the full substance for which they seek redress and defendants wishing to make amends for significantly less should qualify their offer appropriately. Claimants should not, therefore, normally be permitted to significantly enlarge allegations upon which the offer of amends is made and defendants should not be permitted to significantly water down the pleaded allegations significantly;

- claimants should plead the full substance of the allegations for which they want redress and defendants who wish to make amends for significantly less than the full substance sought by the claimant should make the appropriate qualifications to their offer so both sides know precisely what is being compensated by the award.

---

[42] [2002] EWHC 2345 (QB).
[43] [2005] EWCA Civ 1708; and see *Turner v NGN* [2006] EWCA Civ 540 where it was held that evidence of directly relevant background context could be relied on by defendants in the offer of amends procedure as in defamation proceedings.

SUMMARY DISPOSAL

16.72 DeA 1996, s 8 provides that the court may dispose summarily of the claimant's claim as follows: (1) the court may dismiss it if it appears that it has no realistic prospect of success and there is no reason for it to be tried; and (2) the court may give judgment for the claimant and grant him summary relief if it appears there is no defence to the claim which has a realistic prospect of success, and there is no other reason why the claim should be tried (unless the claimant asks for summary relief, the court shall not act under this subsection unless it is satisfied that summary relief will adequately compensate the claimant for the wrong he has suffered).

16.73 The summary relief that the court may grant means: (1) a declaration that the statement was false and defamatory of the claimant; (2) an order that the defendant publish or cause to be published a suitable correction and apology; (3) damages not exceeding £[ ] or such other amount as may be prescribed; (4) an order restraining the defendant from publishing or further publishing the matter complained of.

16.74 Applications are made by CPR Part 23 notice in the usual form but it is to be distinguished from an application for summary judgment under CPR Part 24. CPR Part 53 PD 37, para 5.1 provides that where an application is made for summary disposal the application notice must state that the application is made in accordance with DeA 1996, s 8 and must[44] identify concisely any point of law or provision in a document on which the applicant relies[45] and/or state that it is made because the applicant believes that on the evidence the respondent has no real prospect of succeeding on the claim or issue or (as the case may be) of successfully defending the claim or issue to which the application relates and in either case that the applicant knows of no other reason why the disposal of the claim or issue should await trial.

16.75 It is important to note that DeA 1996, s 8(4) provides that in considering whether a claim should be tried the court shall have regard to (1) whether all persons who are or might be defendants in respect of the publication complained of are before the court, (2) whether summary disposal of the claim against another defendant would be inappropriate, (3) the extent to which there is a conflict of evidence, (4) the seriousness of the alleged wrong (as regards the content of the statement and the extent of publication) and (5) whether it is justifiable in the circumstances to proceed to a full trial.

16.76 Under CPR Part 53 PD 37, para 5.3 where the court has ordered the defendant to agree and publish a correction and an apology as summary relief under DeA 1996, s 8 and the parties are unable to agree its contents within the time specified in the order then the claimant must provide a summary of the judgment given and serve it on the other parties, and if they cannot agree the summary the claimant can apply to the court for the court to settle the summary; the judge who delivered the judgment being summarised will normally do this and the court may direct the defendant to publish the summary.[46]

---

[44]   CPR Part 24 PD 2, para 2.
[45]   The grounds for the application must be set out in clear terms: see *Armstrong v Times Newspapers Ltd* [2005] EWCA Civ 1007, [2005] EMLR 797.
[46]   DeA 1996, s 9(2).

STATEMENT IN OPEN COURT

16.77 CPR Part 53 PD 41, para 6.1 provides that where a party wishes to accept a Part 36 offer or other offer in settlement in relation to a claim for libel or slander he may apply for permission to make a statement in open court before or after he accepts the Part 36 offer in accordance with CPR, r 36.9(1) or other offer to settle the claim.

16.78 The rule further provides that the statement must be submitted for approval of the court and must accompany the notice of application.

16.79 The court may postpone the time for making the statement if other claims relating to the subject matter of the statement are still proceeding.

16.80 Applications must be made in accordance with CPR Part 23 seeking permission to make a statement in terms approved by the court.

16.81 The statement in open court procedure principally applies to one of the following situations:

- Before the claimant accepts a Part 36 or other offer to settle the claim. At this stage the claimant may wish to accept a Part 36 offer but no concluded agreement has been reached about the terms of the statement in court. An application can be made for permission to make a statement in the terms requested.

- After the claimant has accepted the Part 36 or other offer and one of the terms of the settlement is that a statement will be made in court in agreed terms (ie a bilateral statement).

16.82 The statement in open court procedure is useful because it enables a claimant wishing to settle or who has settled his claim to ensure that the record is put straight publicly in such a way that what is said in court is reportable under privilege protecting fair and accurate reports of proceedings in public. Media reports of the statement in open court will, therefore, publicise the fact that the claimant has been vindicated.

16.83 It is not acceptable for a defendant to agree to a bilateral statement whilst at the same time indicating to the court that the statement is not believed to be true. The court will not lend itself to its procedure being used in this way.[47]

16.84 Usually the claimant stipulates that the defendant should accept that the words complained of were false and that the defendant provides suitable words of contrition.

16.85 It is possible for the defendant to oppose the wording of the statement stipulated by the claimant but generally the court will give permission. If a modest sum is offered in respect of a grave libel the right to vindication might appear less deserving and permission may be refused.[48] The costs incurred in the procedure will usually be treated as part and parcel of the costs of the action payable by the defendant. This is so where a defendant makes a payment into court under CPR Part 36. The defendant will

---

[47] See Tugendhat J in *Adelson v Associated Newspapers Ltd (No 3)* [2008] EWHC 278 (QB).
[48] *Church of Scientology v North News* (1973) 117 SJ 566.

normally have to pay the costs of applications for permission to make a unilateral statement as well as the costs of making the statement itself.[49]

16.86 The application for permission to make the statement is made in the first instance to the Senior Master, with the judge retaining the right to approve the statement. The statement will be read in the judge's court. Usually, if the parties agree on the wording of the statement the court will approve it. However, the interests of outsiders to the litigation, or remaining defendants in existing proceedings, might fall to be considered before the court will agree to a statement in open court being made. The court might, for example, refuse to permit a statement in open court until the outstanding proceedings against other defendants have been resolved.

---

[49] See *Phillips v Associated Newspapers* [2004] EWHC 190, at [12] and [15], per Eady J.

Chapter 17

APPLYING FOR AN INJUNCTION IN PRIVACY AND DEFAMATION CASES

17.1   The tests applied when considering whether to grant an interim restraint order (or injunction) in privacy and defamation cases differ from those applied in other cases. This is because, critically, in privacy and defamation cases restraint orders are likely to suppress a fundamental human right: freedom of expression. The High Court has a general jurisdiction to grant an injunction (by way of final or interlocutory order) in all cases where it appears to the court just and convenient to do so.[1] The underlying question asked by the court when deciding in its discretion whether or not to grant an interlocutory or interim injunction in the normal run of cases was laid down in *American Cyanamid v Ethicon Limited*:[2]

(1)   Is there a serious question to be tried (ie the threshold requirement)?

(2)   If the answer is yes:
    (a)   would damages be an adequate remedy for a party injured by the court's grant or its failure to grant an injunction?
    (b)   if not, where does the balance of convenience lie?

17.2   Although the principles in *American Cyanamid* were intended to be of general application they do not apply (at least without substantial variation) to privacy and defamation cases. This is because the court will strive, where possible, to avoid unduly stifling free speech. In the normal run of cases the overriding object of the court hearing an application for an interim injunction is to abstain from expressing an opinion on the merits of the case until the final hearing of the matter. This is consistent with the court's approach not to expend an inordinate amount of time hearing such applications. This approach is adjusted in privacy and defamation cases to enable the court to assess the strength of the claim in order to strike a balance between the claim to suppress publication and the competing claim not to stifle free speech.

THE RESTRICTION OF FREEDOM OF EXPRESSION

17.3   Section 12 of the Human Rights Act 1998 (HRA 1998) comes into play in any case where the court is considering whether to grant relief which, if granted, might affect the Convention[3] right to freedom of expression. This means that s 12 may be engaged in all cases where the court is considering the grant of injunction as a final remedy or as an interim remedy where the grant of the injunction might affect a

---

[1]   This power was confirmed by the Supreme Court Act 1981, s 37(1) and (2): see *Fourie v Le Roux* [2007] UKHL 1, at [25].
[2]   [1975] AC 396, HL.
[3]   European Convention for the Protection of Human Rights and Fundamental Freedoms (ECHR).

defendant's Art 10 rights, ie the right to freedom of expression. Section 12(3) specifically deals with the situation where the interim relief by way of an injunction is sought pending trial and it provides that the injunction should not be granted unless the court is satisfied that the applicant for relief is likely to establish at trial that publication should not be allowed.

17.4   The legislature has determined that, in cases where the right to freedom of speech is involved, that right should be strengthened by the imposing a narrower range of restrictions on publication than would normally apply in other cases. One particular aspect of freedom of expression is the freedom or right to impart information and ideas without interference. In other words, it is harder to get an interim injunction restraining publication before trial in cases where the right to impart information and ideas without interference is involved. Freedom of speech is given added protection because an interim injunction will be granted only in a narrower range of circumstances than in the normal run of cases. The applicant usually has got to show more than a real prospect of success but will have to show that he will probably win at trial. Sometimes, though, a lesser standard will suffice, as explained below.

17.5   Section 12 of HRA 1998 is in the following terms:

(1)   This section applies if the court is considering whether to grant any relief which, if granted, might affect the exercise of the Convention right to freedom of expression.

(2)   If a person against whom an application for relief is made ('the respondent') is neither present nor represented, no such relief is to be granted by the court unless the court is satisfied:
   (a)   that the applicant has taken all practicable steps to notify the respondent; or
   (b)   that there are compelling reasons why the respondent should not be notified.

(3)   No such relief is to be granted to restrain publication before trial unless the court is satisfied that the claimant is likely to establish that publication should not be allowed.

(4)   The court must have particular regard to the importance of the Convention right to freedom of expression and, where the proceedings relate to material which the respondent claims, or which appears to the court, to be journalistic, literary or artistic material (or conduct connected with such material), to:
   (a)   the extent to which:
      (i)   the material has, or is about to, become available to the public; or
      (ii)   it is, or would be, in the public interest for the material to be published; and
   (b)   any relevant privacy code.

17.6   Special considerations, therefore, apply where an injunction (whether interim or final) will have the effect of restricting freedom of expression. The right might still be restricted but in a less restrictive way than would otherwise be the case. The right to freedom of expression is not absolute and is always balanced against other competing rights. As has been noted in previous chapters, the right to freedom of expression, like the right to respect for a private and family life, is a qualified right. Article 10(1) of the ECHR protects the right to freedom of expression but this is qualified by Art 10(2) which recognises the need to protect the rights and freedoms of others (including the right to privacy under Art 8). Likewise, Art 8 protects the right to respect for a private and family life but Art 8(2) makes that right subject to the rights and freedoms of others (including the right to freedom of expression under Art 10).

17.7 Section 12(3) of HRA 1998 is the subsection which deals with the situation where an application is made to court for interim relief. It provides that no such relief is to be granted restraining publication before trial 'unless the court is satisfied that the applicant is likely to establish that publication should not be allowed'. This is a higher threshold test than that laid down in *American Cyanamid* (ie 'a serious question to be tried' or a 'real prospect of success at trial').

17.8 The meaning of the word 'likely' in HRA 1998, s 12(3) (ie whether 'the claimant is likely to establish that publication should not be allowed') has been a matter of debate. It does not bear the meaning of 'more likely than not' or 'probably'. It means that when considering whether an applicant for an interlocutory injunction restraining publication of material is 'likely to establish that the publication should not be allowed' the court must be satisfied that the prospects of success at trial are sufficiently favourable to justify the order being made in the circumstances. Lord Nichols said in *Cream Holdings v Banerjee*, the leading case on s 12(3):[4]

> '[12] As with most ordinary English words "likely" has several different shades of meaning. Its meaning depends upon the context in which it is being used. Even when read in context its meaning is not always precise. It is capable of encompassing different degrees of likelihood, varying from "more likely than not" to "may well". In ordinary usage its meaning is often sought to be clarified by the addition of qualifying epithets as in phrases such as "very likely" or "quite likely". In section 12(3) the context is that of a statutory threshold for the grant of interim relief by a court.'

17.9 Lord Nicholls explained in *Cream Holdings v Banerjee*[5] that the principal purpose of HRA 1998, s 12(3) was to give greater protection to freedom of speech by setting a higher threshold for the grant of interim restraint orders against the media than would be the case by applying the *American Cyanamid* guideline of a 'serious question to be tried' or a 'real prospect' of success at trial. He said that the 'likely' criterion, which applied to all cases of interim prior restraint, was of general application but explained that a threshold of 'more likely than not' in every case would not be workable in practice because it would prevent the court from granting an interim injunction in some cases where it was plain that injunctive relief should be granted as a temporary measure. For example, the judge might need an opportunity to read and consider the evidence and submissions before being in a position to determine the prospects of the applicant succeeding in obtaining a permanent injunction at trial. If the position were not held meanwhile, confidentiality might forever be lost. Also, in cases where an interim relief is refused the court should be able to grant interim relief pending an interlocutory appeal against the refusal. Given such considerations the word 'likely' in s 12(3) was held not to mean 'more likely than not' in all situations because as a test of universal application it would set the degree of likelihood too high and some flexibility was essential.

17.10 The result is that 'likely' in HRA 1998, s 12(3) has an extended meaning which sets as a normal prerequisite to the grant of an interim injunction before trial a likelihood of success at trial higher than the commonplace *American Cyanamid*

---

[4]   [2004] UKHL 44, [2005] AC 253, at [12].
[5]   Ibid, at [12]–[23].

standard of 'real prospect', but permits the court to dispense with this higher standard where particular circumstances make it necessary. It was said in *Cream Holdings* that in order to achieve the necessary flexibility the degree of likelihood of success at trial needed to satisfy s 12(3) depends on the circumstances and that there is no single, rigid standard governing all applications for interim restraint orders. Section 12(3) precludes the court from making an interim restraint order unless it is satisfied the applicant's prospects of success at the trial are sufficiently favourable to justify such an order being made in the particular circumstances of the case. Generally, the courts will be exceedingly slow to make interim restraint orders where the court is not satisfied the applicant will probably ('more likely than not') succeed at the trial. In exceptional cases though, if necessary, the court will accept a lesser degree of likelihood as a prerequisite for the grant of an interim injunction, for example, where the potential adverse consequences of disclosure are particularly grave, or where a short-lived injunction is needed to enable the court to hear and give proper consideration to an application for interim relief pending the trial or any relevant appeal.

17.11 When embarking on an application for an interim restraint order in relation to the proposed publication of information it is essential that:

(1)   it is clearly established that the respondent to the application actually intends to publish the information which is claimed to be private; and

(2)   the precise information which is claimed to be private or confidential is clearly identified and particularised in the notice of application for the interim injunction (and, if the injunction is granted, in the order itself).

17.12 In *Lord Browne of Madingley v Associated Newspapers Ltd*[6] the Court of Appeal emphasised[7] that the judge at first instance is not conducting a trial but considering an application for an interlocutory injunction. Each piece of information in question must be separately considered and under HRA 1998, s 12(3): the question for decision in relation to each such piece of information is whether the court is satisfied that the applicant is likely to establish (presumably at a trial) that publication should not be allowed. Pursuant to s 12(4) the court must have regard to the importance which the ECHR attaches to freedom of expression and s 12(3) proceeds on the footing that where there is uncertainty publication should be permitted unless the claimant can show that he is likely to succeed at the trial, using the word 'likely' in the flexible manner described by Lord Nicholls. In respect of each category of information, the claimant must satisfy the court that the prospects of success at the trial are sufficiently favourable to justify an order being made in the particular circumstances of the case. With regard to the necessity for the claimant to satisfy the court that he will probably ('more likely than not') succeed at the trial, it was said that by 'succeeding at trial' in privacy cases this meant that the claimant is likely to succeed after the court has carried out the relevant balance between the claimant's rights under Art 8 and the newspaper's rights under Art 10. Where there is uncertainty about any aspect of that balancing process which places doubt on the applicant's ability to demonstrate that he is likely to succeed at trial then publication should be permitted.[8]

---

6   [2007] EWCA Civ 295, [2007] EMLR 538, at [63] and [64].
7   Ibid, at [40].
8   See *Lord Browne of Madingly v Associated Newspapers* [2007] EWCA Civ 295, [2007] 3 WLR 289.

17.13 The balancing test carried out in privacy cases was succinctly expressed by Lord Steyn in the House of Lords in the case of *Re S (a child) (identification: restriction on publication)*, who said:[9]

> 'The interplay between arts 8 and 10 has been illuminated in the House of Lords in *Campbell v Mirror Group Newspapers Ltd* ([2004] 2 All ER 995) ... What does ... emerge clearly from the opinions are four propositions.
>
> • First, neither article has *as such* precedence over the other.
> • Secondly, where the values under the two articles are in conflict, an intense focus on the comparative importance of the specific rights being claimed in the individual case is necessary.
> • Thirdly, the justifications for interfering with or restricting each right must be taken into account.
> • Finally, the proportionality test must be applied to each. For convenience I will call this the ultimate balancing test. This is how I will approach the present case.'

17.14 In privacy cases, therefore, where an interim restraint order is sought and the freedom to impart information or ideas is at stake the court will decide the following questions in order to determine whether or not interim injunctive relief should be granted (see Buxton LJ's analysis in *McKennitt v Ash*[10]):

(1) Whether the information is 'private', ie of the sort protected by Art 8.

(2) If the information is plainly not 'private' then the matter goes no further. If the information is found to be of the type considered to be 'private' the question is whether or not, after the balancing exercise is undertaken, placing a restraint on publication is justified on the facts. The balancing exercise involves a determination of whether or not the interests of the person seeking to protect the private information are outweighed by the interests of those seeking to uphold freedom of expression keeping in mind (a) that both rights (privacy and freedom of expression) are qualified rights and that neither right has precedence over the other and (b) that the interference with either right must go no further than is proportionate to the legitimate aim pursued. The ultimate balancing exercise involves considering the proportionality of interfering with the right to privacy against the proportionality of restricting freedom of expression.

(3) Whether or not the claimant's prospects of success (applying the House of Lords' guidance in *Cream Holdings v Banerjee*[11]) in establishing at trial that an injunction restraining publication are sufficiently favourable to justify the order in all the circumstances.

17.15 In cases where interim restraint orders are sought and freedom of expression is at stake the emphasis is upon what the applicant is likely to establish at trial. The applicant must show in such cases that he is likely *at trial* to show that publication should be restrained. In other cases the emphasis on the applicant is to establish that an interim restraint order ought to be granted. The grant of an injunction is a discretionary remedy. Although the test applied at the interim stage is whether the court is satisfied

---

9   [2004] UKHL 47, [2004] 4 All ER 683, [2004] 3 WLR 1129, at [17].
10   [2006] EWCA Civ 1714; [2008] QB 73.
11   [2004] UKHL 44, [2005] 1 AC 253.

that the applicant is likely to establish at trial that publication should not be allowed, even if this is satisfied the court retains a discretion to refuse to grant the injunction.[12]

17.16 Prohibitory injunctions in respect of confidential information, allegedly taken from a shared computer system without authorisation, were granted by Eady J on an application for summary judgment in *Imerman v Tchenguiz and others*.[13] The injunctions prevented disclosure, copying or use. Some of the documents related to the claimant's personal or private life, his financial or business affairs, or the financial or business affairs of his companies or family trusts. Judgment was granted because taking private and confidential information of such a nature was plainly unlawful and the defendants had no lawful right to retain or use the documents. The primary focus was upon the nature of the information and its source. The court rejected the argument that summary judgment should not be given in breach of confidence and/or privacy cases (under Art 8) without first determining whether there was a reasonable expectation of privacy and/or whether the information possessed 'the necessary quality of confidence' and then carrying out the 'ultimate balancing exercise'. The court accepted that 'the outcome of the balancing exercise [was] inevitable' and considered it unnecessary where the claim was for carefully defined injunctive relief. The court thought that information protected by a password would normally be considered 'confidential' irrespective of content and categorised emails and attachments as 'correspondence' in respect of which a claimant was entitled to 'respect' in accordance with Art 8(1). Protection in such cases did not depend on showing 'the necessary quality of confidence' (per Megarry V-C in *Coco v Clark*) because emails and information about internet usage generally attracted prima facie protection.[14] Reference was made in this regard to *Copland v United Kingdom*[15] where it was held (in the ECtHR) to be a violation of an employee's Art 8 rights to monitor email and internet usage. Reference was also made in argument to *Toulson & Phipps on Confidentiality*[16] where it was said that surreptitious access is a relevant factor when determining whether or not the material is protected:

> 'A person who obtains confidential information by dishonest or discreditable means (such as electronic eavesdropping) should be, and is, in no better legal position than if the information had been imparted to him voluntarily in confidence. Equity acts on the conscience, and the conduct of a person who obtains confidential information improperly is as reprehensible to the conscience as that of a person who violates the confidence in which he received it.'

Ultimately, Eady J found it difficult to understand why the claimant was not entitled to have the information back or at any rate taken out of circulation and to restrain its use or onward transmission by others regardless of how it was originally obtained or by whom. He said there were no public interest arguments justifying the continued retention of the material by any of the defendants.

17.17 Applicants for interim restraining injunctions in privacy cases often want the hearing for the injunction to be in private. The whole point of the exercise in privacy cases is likely to be defeated if an order restraining publication is made but the hearing was heard and judgment was given in public. As a general rule all hearings are in public

---

[12]   See *Douglas v Hello!* [2001] QB 967, CA, at [153], per Keene LJ.
[13]   [2009] EWHC 2024 (QB).
[14]   See Gleeson CJ in the High Court of Australia in *Lenah Game Meats v Australian Broadcasting Corp* (2001) 185 ALR 1 at [42] and Henderson J in *Revenue and Customs Commissioners v Bannerjee* [2009] EWHC 1229 (Ch).
[15]   (2007) BHRC 216.
[16]   At 2-023.

(this is provided by Art 6(1) of the ECHR) but r 39.2(3) of the Civil Procedure Rules 1998[17] (CPR) makes provision for hearings or parts of hearings to be in private if:

- publicity would defeat the object of the hearing;

- it involves confidential information (including information relating to personal financial matters) and publicity could damage that confidentiality;

- a private hearing is necessary to protect the interests of any child or protected party;

- it is a hearing of an application made without notice and it would be unjust for any respondent for there to be a public hearing; or

- the court considers this to be necessary, in the interests of justice.[18]

The last of these provisions ('necessary in the interests of justice') gives the court a wide discretion and the overriding objective (at CPR, r 1.1) will be a relevant consideration and in particular the need for the court to deal with cases justly.

17.18 The Practice Direction (at CPR Part 39 PD 1.4) provides that the decision as to whether to hold a hearing in public or in private must be made by the judge conducting the hearing having regard to any representations which may have been made to him. It is also provided (at CPR Part 39 PD 1.12) that when a judgment is given or an order is made in private, if any member of the public who is not a party to the proceedings seeks a transcript of the judgment or a copy of the order, he must seek the leave of the judge who gave the judgment or made the order. Further, (CPR Part 39 PD 1.13) a judgment or order given or made in private, when drawn up, must have clearly marked in the title: 'Before [*insert title and name of judge*] sitting in Private'. A judge, having heard the application for interim relief in private might decide to give judgment in open court, in which case the judgment will be public, but is not obliged to do so and may give a private judgment which is available only to the parties. Sometimes the court will give two judgments in one application: one which is given in public and the other given in private.[19]

17.19 Difficult issues may arise if the hearing is in private but the application for an interim restraint order fails and the judgment is in public rather than kept private. In such cases there is a risk the claimant might appeal successfully and might even succeed in restraining publication at trial. Even in cases where the application fails, therefore, consideration should always be given to requesting that the judgment be kept private at least until the final disposal of any appeal against the refusal.

APPLYING FOR AN INJUNCTION IN A DEFAMATION CASE

17.20 Critical issues of freedom of speech arise in cases where it is sought to restrain what is claimed to be defamatory material, not least because of the serious intrusion on

---

[17] SI 1998/3132.
[18] See also the Practice Direction at CPR Part 39 PD 1.
[19] See *Lord Browne of Madingly v Associated Newspapers* [2007] EWCA Civ 295, [2007] 3 WLR 289, at [4] and [5].

the ability of the press to fulfil its watchdog role in relation to matters of public interest. If injunctions are routinely granted the press can be effectively 'gagged' until a story has lost its topicality, relevance and force. By granting a restraining order the court might be preventing publication of allegations which a jury might later find were in fact true or not libellous or in respect of which there is a good defence.[20]

17.21 Special principles have evolved when the court considers granting interim injunctions in defamation cases because of the value the court places on freedom of speech and freedom of the press when balanced against the reputation of an individual who would have a remedy in damages if wronged. The underlying principle is that the court will not impose a prior restraint on publication unless it is clear that no defence will succeed at trial (this is known as the prior restraint rule). The principles in *American Cyanamid Co v Ethicon*[21] do not apply to such cases.[22]

17.22 HRA 1998[23] has not changed the prior restraint rule (no prior restraint on publication unless it is clear no defence would succeed at trial). The modern law of prior restraint in defamation actions was set out extensively by the Court of Appeal in *Greene v Associated Newspapers Ltd*.[24] It was at the trial of a defamation action that English law showed itself appropriately solicitous of a claimant's right to a fair reputation. At trial the burden lay on defendants to prove that their defamatory statement was true, or that it represented fair comment on a matter of public interest or that it was made on an occasion that attracted privilege.

17.23 In the leading case: *Bonnard v Perryman*[25] it was held that:[26]

'The Court has jurisdiction to restrain by injunction, and even by an interlocutory injunction, the publication of a libel. But the exercise of the jurisdiction is discretionary, and an interlocutory injunction ought not to be granted except in the clearest cases – in cases in which, if a jury did not find the matter complained of to be libellous, the Court would set aside the verdict as unreasonable.

An interlocutory injunction ought not to be granted when the Defendant swears that he will be able to justify the libel, and the Court is not satisfied that he may not be able to do so.'

17.24 It is a principle of long standing that no interim restraining injunction will be granted in respect of material alleged to be defamatory if the defendant raises the defence of justification. Lord Coleridge CJ said in *Bonnard v Perryman*:[27]

20 For a historical perspective as to how the rules governing the grant of interim injunctions in defamation proceedings developed reference should be made to the illuminating judgment of Brooke LJ in *Greene v Associated Newspapers* [2004] EWCA Civ 1462, [2005] 1 All ER 30, at [42] et seq, which is far more comprehensive than could be justified here.
21 [1975] AC 396, HL.
22 Ie where the court considers whether there is (1) a serious question to be tried and (2) that the balance of convenience favours the grant of an injunction.
23 In particular ss 12(3) and 6. Section 12 provides that the court should have regard to the Convention right to freedom of speech when considering the grant of relief that might affect its exercise. Section 12(3) provides that where an injunction is sought to restrain publication before trial it should not be granted 'unless the court is satisfied that the applicant is likely to establish that the publication should not be allowed'.
24 [2005] EWCA Civ 1462.
25 [1891] 2 Ch 269.
26 See the headnote.
27 At 285.

'... it is wiser in this case, as it generally and in all but exceptional cases must be, to abstain from interference until the trial and determination of the plea of justification.'

17.25 In *Herbage v Pressdram*[28] the following principles governing the grant of interim injunctions in defamation cases were approved by Griffiths LJ:

'The principles which it is conceded generally apply to the grant of interim injunctions in defamation actions are:

- First, no injunction will be granted if the defendant raises the defence of justification. This is a rule so well established that no elaborate citation of authority is necessary. It can be traced back to the leading case of *Bonnard v Perryman* [1891] 2 Ch 269, [1891–4] All ER Rep 965.
- Secondly, no injunction will be granted if the defence raises privilege, unless the evidence of malice is so overwhelming that the judge is driven to the conclusion that no reasonable jury could find otherwise that is, that it would be perverse to acquit the defendant of malice.
- Thirdly, that in the face of this long-established practice in defamation actions, the principles enunciated by the House of Lords in *American Cyanamid Co v Ethicon Ltd* [1975] 1 All ER 504, [1975] AC 396 relating to interim injunctions are not applicable in actions for defamation: see *J Trevor & Sons v Solomon* (1977) 248 EG 779.'

17.26 Griffiths LJ said that these principles have evolved because of the value the court has placed on freedom of speech and, he thought, also on the freedom of the press, when balancing it against the reputation of a single individual who, if wronged, can be compensated in damages. He said that the practical effect of applying *American Cyanamid* principles to such cases would be that in very many cases the claimant would obtain an injunction, for on the *American Cyanamid* principles he would often show a serious issue to be tried, that damages would not be realistic compensation and that the balance of convenience would favour restraining repetition of the alleged libel until trial of the action. Griffiths LJ thought that this would be a very considerable incursion into the present rule which is based on freedom of speech.

17.27 In *Greene v Associated Newspapers* Brooke LJ said:[29]

'This survey of the case law shows that in an action for defamation a court will not impose a prior restraint on publication unless it is clear that no defence will succeed at the trial. This is partly due to the importance the court attaches to freedom of speech. It is partly because a judge must not usurp the constitutional function of the jury unless he is satisfied that there is no case to go to a jury. The rule is also partly founded on the pragmatic grounds that until there has been disclosure of documents and cross-examination at the trial a court cannot safely proceed on the basis that what the defendants wish to say is not true. And if it is or might be true the court has no business to stop them saying it. This is another way of putting the point made by Donaldson MR in *Khashoggi's* case, to the effect that a court cannot know whether the plaintiff has a right to his/her reputation until the trial process has shown where the truth lies. And if the defence fails, the defendants will have to pay damages (which in an appropriate case may include aggravated and/or exemplary damages as well).'

17.28 Section 12(3) of HRA 1998 has had no discernable impact on this approach to prior restraint in defamation cases. It is usually impossible to investigate summarily the merits of the defence of justification because it is so often dependent on the credibility of witnesses and the detailed consideration of documents. In *Greene v Associated*

---

28   [1984] 1 WLR 1160, [1992] 2 All ER 769, CA.
29   [2004] EWCA Civ 1462, at [57].

Newspapers[30] it was said that the judicial authors of the rule in *Bonnard v Perryman* recognised this phenomenon when they created the rule in the first place. It was said that the Court of Appeal recognised it a generation ago when it refused to apply the *American Cyanamid* principles in a defamation action and that there is nothing in the ECHR that requires the rule to be done away with.

17.29 The following principles were accepted and approved by the Court of Appeal in *Greene v Associated Newspapers*:[31]

- English law shows itself appropriately solicitous of the claimant's right to a fair reputation. At the trial the burden lies on defendants to prove that their defamatory statement was true, or that it represented fair comment on a matter of public interest or that it was made on an occasion that attracted privilege. If they fail to do so, they have to pay the penalty for infringing the claimant's right, and the claimant thereby sees his reputation vindicated in a very public way. Even if the case is settled before trial, rules of court uniquely allow a statement to be made in open court by way of vindication.

- At the pre-trial stage, the position is different. As Stuart-Smith LJ said in *Lonrho plc v Fayed (No 5)*:[32]

    '... no one has a right to a reputation which is unmerited. Accordingly one can only suffer an injury to reputation if what is said is false. In defamation the falsity of the libel or slander is presumed; but justification is a complete defence.'

- If a claimant were able to stop a defendant from exercising its Art 10 right merely by arguing on paper-based evidence that it was more likely than not that the defendant could not show that what it wished to say about the claimant was true, it would seriously weaken the effect of Art 10. In *Observer v UK* the European Court of Human Rights said:[33]

    '... the dangers inherent in prior restraints are such that they call for the most careful scrutiny on the part of the Court. This is especially so as far as the press is concerned, for news is a perishable commodity and to delay its publication, even for a short period, may well deprive it of all its value and interest.'

- As Donaldson MR observed in *Khashoggi v IPC Magazines Ltd*,[34] once a claimant's right to a fair reputation is put in issue it is the function of the trial, and the duty of the jury, to determine whether he does have a right to be vindicated. One cannot speak sensibly of the violation of the right until it is established at the trial, and at the trial the rules of evidence will favour the claimant.

- In the passage quoted at [31] above the editors of the current edition of *Gatley* correctly refer to:[35]

---

30   Ibid, at [77], referring to the editors of the then current edition of *Gatley*, at p 797, para 25.19.
31   Ibid, at [72]–[77].
32   [1994] 1 All ER 188, at 202, [1993] 1 WLR 1489, at 1502.
33   (1991) 14 EHRR 153, at 191, para 60.
34   [1986] 3 All ER 577, [1986] 1 WLR 1412.
35   At p 797, para 25.19.

'... the usually impossible task of investigating summarily the merits of the defence of justification which is so often dependent on the credibility of witnesses and the detailed consideration of documents.'

17.30 The Court of Appeal in *Boehringer Ingleheim Ltd v Vetplus Ltd*[36] held that the rule in *Bonnard v Perryman* did not apply to trade mark infringement actions brought to protect exclusive proprietary rights conferred on the proprietor of a registered trade mark. Sometimes a rival's trade marks are used in advertisements to disparage the rival trader. Such advertisements will involve the freedom to state what is in the advertisement, ie freedom of expression. The Court of Appeal held that the threshold requirement stipulated in *Banerjee v Cream Holdings* in relation to HRA 1998, s 12(3) applied to such cases, ie the claimant who finds its trade mark disparaged by a rival trader in a comparative advertisement can obtain a prior restraining order only if it can show that it was more likely than not that the disparagement is wrong and misleading. Unless the claimant can do that then its rival, both for its own commercial interests and in the interests of the public, ought to be free to say that which it honestly believes.

17.31 The non-applicability of the rule in *Bonnard v Perryman* in cases concerning the confidentiality of documents was explained in *Greene v Associated Newspapers* in the following way:[37]

'... the confidentiality of the documents will be lost completely if an injunction against disclosure is not granted when appropriate. In cases involving national security, great damage may similarly be done if an injunction is not granted when appropriate. In a defamation action, on the other hand, while some damage may be done by permitting the publication of what may later turn out to be false, everyone knows that it is at the trial that truth or falsehood will be tested and the claimant vindicated if the defendant cannot prove that the sting of the libel is justified or that he has some other defence the law will recognise. The damage that may on occasion be done by refusing an injunction where a less strict rule would facilitate its grant pales into insignificance compared with the damage which would be done to freedom of expression and the freedom of the press if the rule in *Bonnard v Perryman* was relaxed.'

GENERAL PROVISIONS RELATING TO INTERIM INJUNCTIONS

17.32 The Practice Direction at CPR Part 25 PD 1 provides that, save in limited cases (eg consent orders), only a judge who has jurisdiction to conduct the trial of the action has power to grant an injunction. CPR Part 25 PD 2 provides that the application notice for an injunction must state the order sought and the date, time and place of hearing. The application notice must be served as soon as practicable after issue but in any event not less than 3 clear days before the court is due to hear the application. Applications for interim injunctions must be supported by evidence either a witness statement or statement of case verified by a statement of truth unless the court, an Act or a rule or Practice Direction stipulate an affidavit. The evidence must contain all the material facts relied on or of which the court should be made aware.

17.33 In the case of applications made before the issue of a claim form CPR Part 25 PD 4.4 provides that in addition to the requirements as to the documents to be filed set

---

[36]   [2007] EWCA Civ 583, 97 BMLR 1.
[37]   Ibid, at [78].

out in CPR Part 25 PD 4.3, unless the court orders otherwise, either the applicant must undertake to the court to issue a claim form immediately or the court will give directions for the commencement of the claim. Where possible the claim form should be served with the order for the injunction. The names of the intended parties should be referred to as 'the Claimant and the Defendant in an Intended Action'.

URGENT TELEPHONE APPLICATIONS

17.34 With regard to urgent applications made by telephone where it is not possible to arrange a hearing between 10.00 am and 5.00 pm weekdays, CPR Part 25 PD 4.5 provides that the application can be made by telephoning the Royal Courts of Justice on 0207 947 6000 and asking to be put in contact with a High Court judge of the appropriate division available to deal with emergency applications in the High Court matter. Where the application is made outside those hours the applicant should telephone the Royal Courts of Justice on 0207 947 6000 where he will be put in contact with the clerk to the appropriate High Court judge or the appropriate urgent court business officer of the appropriate circuit, who will contact the local duty judge. Where the facility is available it is likely that the judge will require a draft order to be faxed to him and the notice and evidence in support must be filed with the court on the same or the next working day or as ordered, together with two copies of the order for sealing. Injunctions will be heard by telephone only where the applicant is acting by counsel or solicitors.

REQUIREMENTS FOR ORDERS CONTAINING INJUNCTIONS

17.35 Unless the court otherwise orders, any order for an injunction must contain:

- an undertaking by the applicant to the court to pay any damages which the respondent sustains which the court considers the applicant should pay;

- if made without notice to the other party, an undertaking by the applicant to the court to serve on the respondent the application notice, evidence in support and any order made as soon as practicable;

- if made without notice to the other party, a return date for the further hearing at which the other party can be present;

- if made before filing the application notice, an undertaking to file and pay the appropriate fee on the same or the next working day; and

- if made before the issue of the claim form:
  - an undertaking to issue and pay the appropriate fee on the same or next working day; or
  - directions for the commencement of the claim.

17.36 When the court makes an order for an injunction, it should consider whether to require an undertaking by the applicant to pay any damages sustained by a person other than the respondent, including another party to the proceedings or any other person who might suffer loss as a consequence of the order (see CPR Part 25 PD 5.1A). An order for an injunction made in the presence of all parties to be bound by it or made at a hearing of which they have had notice may state that it is effective until trial or further order. Finally, any order for an injunction must set out clearly what the respondent must do or not do.

'SUPER INJUNCTIONS' AND THE *LNS* CASE

17.37 Sometimes in privacy and confidentiality cases orders are made prohibiting the disclosure of the fact that an order has been made and providing for sealing the whole court file. Such orders have been referred to in the media as 'super injunctions'. The grounds for departing from the normal provisions of the CPR must be set out in the evidence in support of the order for the injunction. CPR r 25.3 provides that the court may grant an interim remedy without notice if good reasons are shown for not giving notice in the evidence in support of the application.

17.38 Applications for 'super injunctions' have sought the following: (1) a private hearing; (2) anonymity for those involved; (3) the sealing of the entire court file pursuant to CPR r 5.4C(4); (4) a prohibition against publishing the existence of the proceedings until after trial or further order; (5) release from the requirement (in CPR PD 25 para 9.2) that the applicant provides any third party served with a copy of the order any materials read by the judge and/or a note of the hearing; (6) an order with no return date (contrary to CPR PD 25 para 5); and (7) a general extension of time for service of the claim form until the respondent has been identified (pursuant to CPR r 7.5 and CPR r 7.6(1)).

17.39 Respondents or persons served with orders containing such provisions who wish to contest the making of the order take on the burden of applying to court in circumstances where they would not know the basis on which the order was made or whether or not the court would permit them to see the material upon which it was granted. Those obtaining such orders although likely to notify the order to various parties might never identify and serve a claim form on a respondent and, since no return date is specified, might never bring the matter to a trial. The effect of the order is likely to be that a permanent injunction will be granted binding on any person the claimant chooses to notify of its existence. This will have the effect of depriving the court of the opportunity to hear the case for the other side including, critically, the social utility of whatever it is media respondents might be threatening to publish.

17.40 An application for a 'super injunction' was considered in *LNS v Persons Unknown* [2010] EWHC 119 (QB) which concerned a well-known footballer. In that case a without notice application was made for an injunction along the lines set out above on the basis that the order was likely to be served on media third parties though none were identified. The draft order sought prohibition on publishing information, documents or photographs disclosing the fact of or details of a personal relationship between the footballer and another person or which might identify them. Tugendhat J considered that there was a real prospect that a respondent might submit that publication, at least of the fact of the relationship, ought not to be prohibited on the ground that publication would be in the public interest or the respondent believed it to be so. The judge found that nothing in the relationship appeared to be unlawful and the evidence related only to an alleged threat to publish the fact of the relationship but no more. The judge ultimately was not satisfied the applicant was likely discharge the burden under HRA 1998, s 12(3) of showing he was likely: (1) to defeat a public interest defence if raised; (2)

to establish there had been a breach of a duty of confidence; or (3) to establish that publication of the fact of the relationship should be prohibited on privacy grounds.

17.41 There were other reasons why the court was not satisfied the applicant was likely to establish that publication should be prohibited. There was uncertainty in the law of misuse of private information as to the extent to which, if at all, the belief of a person threatening to make a publication in the media is relevant to the issue of public interest.[38] Also on the facts *Bonnard v Perryman*[39] applied precluding the grant of injunction because the nub of the application was considered to be protection of reputation rather than any other aspect of the applicant's private life.

17.42 Any impression that extensive derogations from open justice should be routine in claims for injunctions in cases involving misuse of private information was dispelled in the judgment.[40] The need for a return date when injunctions were granted was emphasised in the judgment.[41] It was considered that notice should have been given to the newspapers so that the court would have the benefit of arguments in opposition to the application.[42] An interim injunction was not considered necessary or proportionate having regard to the level and gravity of the interference with the applicant's private life which might result from publication of the fact of the relationship. It was not considered on the facts that the applicant could rely on the interference with the private life of anyone else.

17.43 Applications for 'super injunctions' will need to be carefully reviewed in the light of the *LNS* decision and particular attention will need to be given to ensuring that there is no undue interference with the principle of open justice.

---

[38]   At para [70] to [73].
[39]   [1891] 2 Ch 269, [1891–4] All ER Rep 965.
[40]   See paras [107] to [109].
[41]   At para [136].
[42]   At para [149].

Part V

INDIVIDUAL PERSONAL RIGHTS

Note: In this Part the masculine has been used; unless otherwise specified this should be read as referring to both genders.

Chapter 18

COPYRIGHT

INTRODUCTION

18.1 If you hold a book, a DVD of a film or a television series or a top 20 music CD in your hands you are holding not only a tangible object but also something intangible, namely a bundle of intellectual property rights. The words of a song will in all probability be copyright, as will the music. The sound recording of the words and music on the CD will in all probability be copyright, as will the artwork on the cover of the CD and the information and acknowledgments contained in the CD booklet. In addition the performers on the record and the record company will have performer's rights and the composer of the words and the composer of the music will have moral rights in the compositions. It should also be noted that as well as copyright protection the name of the record company and the name of the band performing the music on the CD will in all probability be protected as registered trade marks or where the names are not trade mark registered they might have protection by way of the law of passing off. A purchaser of a book, DVD or CD owns the physical entity but does not own the copyrights or any other intellectual property rights contained therein. Likewise a person who purchases and downloads music to his computer so that it can be played on the computer or his MP3 player does not own the copyrights or any other intellectual property rights in the downloaded material.

Important note

18.2 The Copyright, Designs and Patents Act 1988 (CDPA 1988) came into force on 1 August 1989 and is now the primary Act governing copyright in the UK.

18.3 Part V will examine some of the main areas of CDPA 1988 as it relates to copyright, moral rights and performer's rights, including performer's moral rights which might need to be considered when dealing with the commercial exploitation of a celebrity's status. This chapter examines in detail how a celebrity can create a copyright work in accordance with CDPA 1988 and the rights he has under CDPA 1988 in the copyright work. It will briefly deal with the defences available to a third party who is alleged to have infringed copyright in a celebrity's copyright work and the civil and criminal sanctions available where there is copyright infringement. The following chapters in Part V will also examine in detail a celebrity's moral rights and a performer's rights, including a performer's moral rights in his work.

18.4 The reader is advised to refer to CDPA 1988 for the exact wording and all the provisions of the Act and to specialist works on copyright for a full treatise on copyright. Previous copyright legislation is beyond the scope of this book.

COPYRIGHT

What is capable of copyright protection?

18.5   Part I of CDPA 1988 deals with copyright.

18.6   CDPA 1988, s 1 provides that copyright is a property right which subsists in:

(1)   original literary, dramatic, musical or artistic works (s 1(1)(a));

(2)   sound recordings, films or broadcasts (s 1(1)(b)); and

(3)   the typographical arrangements of published editions (s 1(1)(c)).

18.7   If a work falls within the ambit of CDPA 1988, s 1(1) then, subject to other criteria being satisfied (for which see below), the work will attract copyright protection.

18.8   It should be noted that CDPA 1988, s 1(1)(a) requires the literary, musical or artistic work to be 'original'. The case of *Ladbroke (Football) Ltd v William Hill (Football) Ltd*[1] dealt with the concept of 'original'. The court held that for the work to be 'original' it 'should not be copied but should originate from the author'. The cases of *University of London Press Ltd v University Tutorial Press Ltd*[2] and *Interlego AG v Tyco Industries Inc*[3] also dealt with the concept of 'original'. The cases held that the author of the work did not have to express any original ideas in the work, but that the author had to use his own skill and effort to produce the work. It is therefore possible for an author to use the same source material as another author to produce his work, but he must use his own skill and effort to produce the work and not copy from the source material. It should be noted that a de minimis principle applies and that some types of work such as the name of a person or the title of a newspaper will not qualify for copyright protection as a literary work due to the de minimis principle. See, for example, *Exxon Corporation v Exxon Insurance Consultants International Ltd*.[4]

18.9   CDPA 1988, s 3(2) provides that copyright will not exist in a literary, dramatic or musical work unless and until it is recorded in writing or otherwise. Writing is defined in CDPA 1988, s 178 as any form of notation or code, whether by hand or otherwise and regardless of the method by which, or medium in or on which, it is written. Section 3(3) further provides that it is immaterial whether the work was recorded by the author or with the permission of the author.

18.10   It should be noted that there is no requirement in CDPA 1988 for a copyright work to be registered in order to attract copyright protection. However, in case there is a dispute at some future date as to the originality of the work it would be sensible for the person who created it to either send a copy to himself by recorded delivery post and not open it when it is delivered or send a sealed copy of the work to his solicitor or accountant to hold in safe custody and get the solicitor or accountant to give him a date-stamped receipt for it.

---

[1]   [1964] 1 WLR 273.
[2]   [1916] 2 Ch 601.
[3]   [1988] 3 WLR 678.
[4]   [1982] Ch 119, [1981] 3 All ER 241.

The definition of literary, dramatic, musical, artistic works, sound recordings, films, broadcasts

18.11 CDPA 1988, s 3(1) defines a 'literary work' as any work other than a dramatic or musical work which is written, spoken or sung. The literary work must be original.[5] There is no requirement for it to be a scholarly work, although to qualify for copyright protection as a literary work the author should have used some skill and effort in producing the work. Works which the courts have held to be literary works include letters from one person to another, examination papers and football fixture lists. The courts have held that certain works do not qualify as a literary work because, for example, little or no skill and effort was used in producing the work, or because the work is too brief, or because the work does not give any information, or because it does not provide any instruction or provide any pleasure. (Where a work does not qualify as a literary work it may be possible to register it as a trade mark.) Works which the courts have refused to give copyright protection to include the title of a song[6] and names.[7]

18.12 CDPA 1988, s 3(1) provides that a 'literary work' includes, inter alia, a database. A database is defined in s 3A as 'a collection of independent works, data or other materials which are arranged in a systematic or methodical way and are individually accessible by electronic or other means'. Section 3A(2) further provides that a literary work consisting of a database is original if, and only if, by reason of the selection or arrangement of the contents of the database the database constitutes the author's own intellectual creation.

18.13 CDPA 1988, s 3(1) provides that a 'dramatic work' includes a work of dance or mime.

18.14 CDPA 1988, s 3(1) defines a 'musical work' as a work consisting of music, excluding any words or action intended to be sung, spoken or performed with the music.

18.15 CDPA 1988, s 4(1) defines an 'artistic work'. An artistic work includes, inter alia, under s 4(1)(a) a graphic work or a photograph, irrespective of artistic quality. Section 4(2) defines a 'graphic work' and includes, inter alia, under s 4(2)(a) any painting or drawing. Section 4(2) defines a 'photograph' and means a recording of light or other radiation on any medium on which an image is produced or from which an image may by any means be produced and which is not a film. This means that the design for a record sleeve and the photographs for the record sleeve/inner booklet will be copyright protected as an artistic work. Also a performer's/band's logo may qualify for copyright protection as an artistic work. If a performer's/band's logo does not qualify for copyright protection as an artistic work it may be possible to register the logo as a trade mark.

18.16 CDPA 1988, s 5A(1)(a) and (b) defines a 'sound recording' as a recording of sounds, from which the sounds may be reproduced, or a recording of the whole or any part of a literary, dramatic or musical work, from which sounds reproducing the work or part may be produced, regardless of the medium on which the recording is made or the method by which the sounds are reproduced, for example, CD, MP3 or any other format which when played will reproduce the sounds. Section 5A(2) provides that

[5]　See s 1(1)(a) at **18.6**.
[6]　See *Francis Day & Hunter v Twentieth Century Fox Corporation Limited* [1940] AC 112.
[7]　See *Exxon Corporation v Exxon Insurance Consultants Limited* [1982] Ch 119, [1981] 3 All ER 241.

copyright does not subsist in a sound recording which is, or to the extent that it is, a copy taken from a previous sound recording.

18.17 CDPA 1988, s 5B(1) defines a 'film' as a recording on any medium from which a moving image may by any means be produced. Section 5B(2) provides that the film soundtrack forms part of the film. This means that DVDs, video films and CD-ROMs fall within the definition of 'film'. Section 5B(4) provides that copyright does not subsist in a film which is, or to the extent that it is, a copy taken from a previous film. Section 5B(5) provides that nothing in s 5B affects any copyright subsisting in a film soundtrack as a sound recording.

18.18 It should be noted that CDPA 1988, s 5B(3) provides that without prejudice to the generality of s 5B(2), where s 5B(2) applies:

(1) references to showing a film include playing the film soundtrack to accompany the film (s 5B(3)(a));

(2) references to playing a sound recording, or to communicating a sound recording to the public, do not include playing or communicating the film soundtrack to accompany the film (s 5B(3)(b));

(3) references to copying a work, so far as they apply to a sound recording, do not include copying the film soundtrack to accompany the film (s 5B(3)(c)); and

(4) references to the issuing, rental or lending of copies of a work, so far as they apply to a sound recording, do not include the issuing, rental or lending of copies of the soundtrack to accompany the film (s 5B(3)(d)).

18.19 CDPA 1988, s 6(1) defines a 'broadcast' as an electronic transmission of visual images, sounds or other information which:

(1) is transmitted for simultaneous reception by members of the public and is capable of being lawfully received by them (s 6(1)(a)); or

(2) is transmitted at a time determined solely by the person making the transmission for presentation to members of the public (s 6(1)(b)),

and which is not excepted by s 6(1A).

18.20 CDPA 1988, s 6(1A) provides that an internet transmission is excepted from the definition of 'broadcast' unless it is:

(1) a transmission taking place simultaneously on the internet and by other means (s 6(1A)(a));

(2) a concurrent transmission of a live event (s 6(1A)(b)); or

(3) a transmission of recorded moving images or sounds forming part of a programme service offered by the person responsible for making the transmission, being a service in which programmes are transmitted at scheduled times determined by that person (s 6(1A)(c)).

18.21 CDPA 1988, s 6(2) provides that an encrypted transmission is regarded as capable of being lawfully received by members of the public only if decoding equipment has been made available to members of the public by or with the authority of the person making the transmission or the person providing the contents of the transmission.

18.22 CDPA 1988, s 6(4) deals with the place from which a wireless broadcast is made. Section 6A deals with safeguards in relation to certain satellite broadcasts and applies where the place from which a broadcast by way of satellite transmission is made is located in a country other than an EEA state and the law of that country fails to provide certain listed levels of protection. These matters are beyond the scope of this book.

18.23 CDPA 1988, s 6(5) provides that the reception of a broadcast includes reception of a broadcast relayed by means of a telecommunications system and s 6(5A) provides that relaying a broadcast by reception and immediate re-transmission is regarded as a separate act of broadcasting from the making of the broadcast which is so re-transmitted.

18.24 CDPA 1988, s 6(6) provides that copyright does not subsist in a broadcast which infringes, or to the extent that it infringes, the copyright in another broadcast.

18.25 Having seen what work is capable of attracting copyright protection, it is necessary to look at the other criteria which have to be satisfied before the work will actually qualify for protection.

Other requirements needed before a work can attract copyright protection

18.26 CDPA 1988, s 1(3) states that copyright will not subsist in a work unless certain qualifying requirements have been satisfied. The requirements to be satisfied before copyright protection will be afforded to a work are detailed in CDPA 1988, s 153 onwards and relate to either (a) the author (detailed in s 154), (b) to the country in which the work was first published (detailed in s 155) or (c) in the case of a broadcast, the place of transmission (s 156).

The author requirement – s 154

18.27 An author qualifies if he was a 'qualifying person' at the 'material time'. CDPA 1988, s 9(1) provides that the 'author' of a work is the person who creates it. (There are cases in CDPA 1988 where this assumption does not apply. This is dealt with in more detail later in the chapter.) A qualifying person is defined under CDPA 1988, s 154(1) as any of the following:

(1) a British citizen, a British overseas territories citizen, a British national (overseas), a British overseas citizen, a British subject or a British protected person within the meaning of the British Nationality Act 1981 (s 154(1)(a));

(2) an individual domiciled or resident in the UK or another country to which the relevant copyright provisions extend (s 154(1)(b));

(3) a body incorporated under the law of a part of the UK or of another country to which the relevant copyright provisions extend (s 154(1)(c)); or

(4) if at the material time the author was a citizen or subject of, an individual domiciled or resident in, or a body incorporated under the law of a country to which the relevant provisions of CDPA 1988 have been extended (s 154(2)).[8]

18.28 If the author is a 'qualifying person' he must have been a 'qualifying person' at the 'material time'. The 'material time' is detailed in CDPA 1988, s 154(4) and (5) as:

(1) In relation to a literary, dramatic, musical or artistic work:
    (a) if the work is unpublished, it is when was made or, if the making of the work extended over a period, a substantial part of that period (s 154(4)(a)); and
    (b) if the work has been published, it is when the work was first published or, if the author had died before that time, immediately before his death (s 154(4)(b)).

(2) In relation to other types of work the material time is:
    (a) for a sound recording or film, when the work was made (s 154(5)(a));
    (b) for a broadcast, when the broadcast was made (s 154(5)(b)); and
    (c) for a typographical arrangement of a published edition, when the edition was first published (s 154(5)(d)).

The publication requirement – s 155

18.29 As opposed to qualifying for copyright protection as an author, it is possible for the work to qualify by reference to the place of first publication. CDPA 1988, s 155(1) provides that a literary, dramatic, musical or artistic work, a sound recording or film or the typographical arrangement of a published edition will qualify for copyright protection if it is first published in:

(1) the UK (s 155(1)(a)); or

(2) any country to which to which the relevant provisions of CDPA 1988 extend (s 155(1)(b)) or have been extended (s 155(2)).[9]

18.30 The question arises as to what is meant by the word 'publication'. CDPA 1988 defines publication in s 175(1)(a) as issuing copies to the public and (b) for literary, dramatic, musical or artistic works and includes making them available to the public by way of an electronic retrieval system. Section 175(4) also states that certain acts do not constitute publication, inter alia:

(1) In the case of a literary, dramatic or musical work:
    (a) performing the work; or
    (b) the communication to the public of the work (otherwise than for the purposes of an electronic retrieval system (s 175(4)(a)(i) and (ii)).

(2) In the case of an artistic work:
    (a) exhibiting the work;
    (b) the issue to the public of copies of a film including the work; or
    (c) the communication to the public of the work (otherwise than for the purposes of an electronic retrieval system) (s 175(4)(b)(i), (iii) and (iv)).

---

8   See also CDPA 1988, s 159.
9   See also CDPA 1988, s 159.

(3)   In the case of a sound recording or a film:
    (a)   playing or showing the work in public; or
    (b)   the communication to the public of the work (s 175(4)(c)(i) and (ii)).

18.31   The case of *Francis Day Hunter v Feldman*[10] examined the question of whether sufficient numbers of the work were made available to satisfy the requirement of 'publication'. The case concerned the sheet music to the song 'You Made Me Love You (I Didn't Want To Do It)'. The court looked at the number of copies available on sale and held that the work had been published in the UK because it had satisfied the small anticipated demand for the sheet music. The work must therefore be available 'to satisfy the reasonable requirements of the public' before it will be regarded as published under CDPA 1988. Indeed, s 175(5) specifically states that the requirement for publication is not satisfied if the publication is 'merely colourable and not intended to satisfy the reasonable requirements of the public'. What is 'merely colourable' depends on the facts of each case.

The place of transmission requirement – s 156

18.32   Apart from satisfying the author requirement under CDPA 1988, s 154 it is also possible for a broadcast to qualify for copyright protection if it has been made from a place in:

(1)   the UK (s 156(1)(a)); or

(2)   any country to which to which the relevant provisions of CDPA 1988 extend (s 156(1)(b)), or have been extended (s 156(2)).[11]

Joint authors

18.33   CDPA 1988, s 154(3) provides that a work of joint authorship qualifies for copyright protection if at the material time any of the authors satisfy the requirements of s 154(1) or (2). CDPA 1988, s 10 deals with the definition of a work of joint authorship.[12] However, even if the work qualifies for copyright protection, only those authors who satisfy the author requirement under s 154 will be taken into account when considering matters such as who is the first owner of the copyright[13] and the duration of copyright,[14] which are looked at later in this chapter.

Where does CDPA 1988 apply?

18.34   CDPA 1988 applies to England and Wales, Scotland and Northern Ireland. In addition it applies to the Isle of Man, Hong Kong and Guernsey.

18.35   CDPA 1988 also provides that the Act can be applied to another member state of the EEC or to other countries which are Convention countries. A Convention country is a country which has signed a copyright convention to which the UK is also a signatory. There are several copyright conventions in existence, the most significant being the

[10]   [1914] 2 Ch 728.
[11]   See also CDPA 1988, s 159.
[12]   See **18.37** et seq and **18.39** et seq.
[13]   See **18.48** et seq.
[14]   See **18.75** et seq.

Berne Convention of 1886 (as subsequently revised) (which is more formerly known as the Convention for the Protection of Literary and Artistic Works) and the Universal Copyright Convention, Geneva of 1952 (as subsequently revised). The UK has adopted both the Berne Convention and the Universal Copyright Convention. Most of the countries in the world are signatories to either the Berne Convention and/or the Universal Copyright Convention. The signatories to these conventions will, as well as providing copyright protection to the works of their own nationals, provide copyright protection to the works of nationals from the other signatory countries. In order to secure protection under the Universal Copyright Convention a copyright work must contain the copyright symbol, ©, followed by the name of the copyright owner, followed by the year in which the work was first published. It should be noted that the © symbol and subsequent details are not required for copyright protection under CDPA 1988 but are required only for international protection under the Universal Copyright Convention.

18.36 In addition under CDPA 1988, s 159(3), the Act may also apply to other countries which have made or will make provision under their law for adequate protection of copyright works for copyright owners.

The author and the owner of a copyright work

18.37 CDPA 1988 distinguishes between the concepts of authors and owners. The person who is the author of a book which is capable of copyright protection may not always be the owner of the copyright. The author, even if he is not the copyright owner, may be entitled to moral rights in the work. Moral rights will be examined in Chapter 19, but it should be noted at this stage that if the author is entitled to moral rights, he has these rights notwithstanding somebody else being the owner of the copyright in the work.

18.38 There is a difference between ownership of the copyright and ownership of the item which contains the copyright work(s): for example, if a celebrity writes a letter to a fan, the celebrity owns the copyright in the words as a literary work whereas the fan owns the paper on which the copyright work was written. The fan can not therefore exploit the literary copyright in the letter which was sent to him.

The author of the work

18.39 As mentioned earlier CDPA 1988, s 9(1) provides that the 'author' of a work is the person who creates it. Usually it is clear who actually created the work. For example, the writer of a book would under s 9(1) be regarded as the 'author'.

18.40 In the case of a sound recording the 'author' under CDPA 1988, s 9(2)(aa) is the producer.

18.41 In the case of a film the 'author' under CDPA 1988, s 9(2)(ab) is the producer and the principal director. Section 10(1A) provides that a film shall be treated as a work of joint authorship unless the producer and the principal director are the same person.

18.42 The producer of a sound recording or a film is defined in CDPA 1988, s 178 as the person who makes the necessary arrangements for the making of the sound recording or film.

18.43 In the case of a broadcast the 'author' under CDPA 1988, s 9(2)(b) is the person making the broadcast (for which see s 6(3) below) or, where the broadcast relays another broadcast by reception and immediate re-transmission the 'author' is the person making that other broadcast. Section 10(2) provides that a broadcast shall be treated as a work of joint authorship in any case where more than one person is to be taken as making the broadcast.

18.44 CDPA 1988, s 6(3) deals with who is the person making a broadcast or a transmission which is broadcast. The person making a broadcast, broadcasting a work or including a work in a broadcast is:

(1) the person transmitting the programme if he has responsibility to any extent for its contents (s 6(3)(a)); and

(2) any person providing the programme who makes with the person transmitting it the arrangements necessary for its transmission (s 6(3)(b)).

18.45 CDPA 1988, s 6(3) also provides that references to a 'programme' in the context of broadcasting are to any item included in a broadcast.

18.46 In the case of a typographical arrangement of a published edition the 'author' under CDPA 1988, s 9(1)(d) is the publisher.

18.47 Quite commonly a piece of work is created by more than one person. CDPA 1988, s 10 deals with works of joint authorship. A work of joint authorship is defined in s 10(1) as a work produced by the collaboration of two or more authors where the contribution of each author is not distinct from that of the other author(s). Section 10 is best illustrated by looking at two songwriters working together. If Elton John writes a tune on his own without Bernie Taupin, and Bernie Taupin writes the words to the tune on his own without Elton John, this is not a work of joint authorship. Elton John in this example would be the author of the musical work and Bernie Taupin would be the author of the literary work. If, however, Elton John and Bernie Taupin collaborate with each other so that each contributes to the tune and to the words, this would be a work of joint authorship if their respective contributions were not distinct from each other, in which case they would be the joint authors in the two copyright works, namely the musical copyright and the literary copyright. If, however, Elton John and Bernie Taupin collaborate with each other so that each contributes to the tune and to the words but in this example Elton John writes all the words to the chorus and Bernie Taupin writes all the words to all the verses this is not a joint authorship of the literary work as their contributions are distinct from each other. If one person contributes before[15] or after[16] the work has been created this will not create a work of joint authorship. Suggesting ideas rather than being directly responsible for the copyright work will not create a work of joint authorship.[17] (See also **18.33** for copyright protection where there are joint authors; **18.41** for s 10(1A) for joint authorship and film; and **18.43** for s 10(2) for joint authorship and broadcast.)

---

[15] *Donoghue v Allied Newspapers Ltd* [1937] 3 All ER 503.
[16] *Wiseman v George Weidenfeld & Nicolson Ltd* [1985] FSR 525.
[17] *Robin Ray v Classic FM* (1998) *The Times*, April 8.

The owner of the work

18.48 As seen earlier the general rule set out in CDPA 1988, s 9(1) is that the author of the work is the person who created it. The general rule regarding copyright ownership is stated in s 11(1) and provides that the author of the work is the first owner of the copyright.

18.49 Because of the general rule that the author of the work is the first owner of the copyright special consideration will need to be had in the following situations.

An employer-employee situation

18.50 The employer-employee situation (a contract of service, rather than a contract for services which is self-employment) is dealt with in CDPA 1988, s 11(2). This provides that where a literary, dramatic, musical or artistic work or film is made by an employee in the course of their employment, their employer is the first owner of any copyright in the work unless there is any agreement between the parties to the contrary. A sensible employment contract should specifically deal with this matter.

Where there is a producer of a sound recording

18.51 As mentioned above, the author of a sound recording is under CDPA 1988, s 9(2)(aa) the producer. The producer is defined in s 178 as the person who makes the necessary arrangements for the making of the sound recording. Also, as mentioned above, the general rule regarding copyright ownership is stated in s 11(1), which provides that the author of the work is the first owner of the copyright. The general rule will therefore mean that the producer is the first owner of the copyright in the sound recording.

18.52 Where, which nowadays is unlikely, the producer is an employee of the record company, the owner of the copyright in a sound recording made by the producer in the course of his employment will under CDPA 1988, s 11(2) be the record company.

18.53 Nowadays, the performer will either produce his own recordings or a third party who is not a record company employee will be brought in to produce the recordings. To avoid the application of the general rule under CDPA 1988, s 11(1), the performer's recording agreement will contain a clause which provides that where the performer produces his own recordings he will assign the ownership of the copyright in the sound recording to the record company. Likewise, where a third party who is not a record company employee produces the performer's recordings the producer's agreement will contain a clause which provides that the producer will assign the ownership of the copyright in the sound recording to the record company.

Where there is joint ownership

18.54 If the creators of the work are joint authors as defined in CDPA 1988, s 10(1)[18] the creators will also be joint owners of the work.

---

[18]   See **18.47** for s 10.

18.55 As was mentioned earlier[19] CDPA 1988, s 10(1A) provides that a film shall be treated as a work of joint authorship unless the producer and the principal director are the same person.

18.56 Where the joint authors are employees and the literary, dramatic, musical or artistic work or film was made by employees in the course of their employment, the employer will be the first owner of any copyright in the work unless there is any agreement between the parties to the contrary.[20]

18.57 CDPA 1988, s 173(2) provides that where there is joint ownership of the copyright in a work any licence to use the copyright work requires a licence from all the joint authors.

18.58 Joint authors can hold the ownership as either joint tenants or as tenants in common. If the ownership of the work is held as joint tenants, when one joint tenant dies his share in the work passes automatically to the remaining living joint tenants. If the ownership of the work is held as tenants in common, when one tenant in common dies his share in the work does not pass to the surviving living tenants in common but passes under his estate to the beneficiaries under his will or where there is no will it passes under the intestacy rules. A joint tenancy can be converted into a tenancy in common by a joint tenant severing the joint tenancy during his lifetime, for example, by giving written notice to the other joint tenants.

18.59 Where two or more people intend to create a work together there should be a written agreement between the parties as to whether the ownership of the work will be held as joint tenants or as tenants in common. In the absence of any agreement between the parties the law will usually assume that the ownership of the copyright will be held as tenants in common.

How can the copyright owner exploit the copyright work?

18.60 Having seen what type of work is capable of copyright protection, how a work qualifies for copyright protection, who is the author of the copyright work and who owns the copyright work, the next matter to consider is how the copyright owner can exploit, or, in other words make money out of, the ownership of his work.

18.61 CDPA 1988, s 90(1) provides that copyright owners can deal with their work in the same way as with their personal or moveable property. This means that a copyright work can be transferred by assignment, by will or by the operation of the law. A copyright owner can make money from his copyright work by exploiting the work himself or by permitting others to exploit it.

18.62 A copyright owner can permit others to exploit his work by granting either a licence or an assignment of the copyright work.

---

[19] See **18.41**.
[20] See **18.50**.

LICENCES OF COPYRIGHT

18.63 A licence is a contractual right, a permission, given by the licensor (the copyright owner) to the licensee. A licence should grant specific rights to the licensee and reserve everything else to the licensor. A licence does not pass any title in the work to the licensee. It is a permission from the licensor to use the work in accordance with the licence agreement.

18.64 A licence can be either exclusive or non-exclusive. CDPA 1988, s 92(1) provides that an exclusive licence is a licence in writing signed by or on behalf of the copyright owner, authorising the licensee, to the exclusion of everybody else including the licensor, to exercise the rights granted which would otherwise be exercisable exclusively by the copyright owner. Section 101(1) provides that an exclusive licensee has the same rights as if he had been given an assignment. Section 101(2) provides that the rights and remedies of an exclusive licensee are concurrent with the rights and remedies of the copyright owner. Section 101(3) provides that in an action brought by an exclusive licensee by virtue of s 101 a defendant may avail himself of any defence which would have been available to him if the action had been brought by the copyright owner.

18.65 A non-exclusive licence will be granted by the licensor where the licensor wants to grant the same rights in the work to more than one licensee. A non-exclusive licence does not have to be in writing although it usually would be. If there is any infringement of copyright a non-exclusive licensee can not take legal proceedings for the infringement. A non-exclusive licensee must require the copyright owner to bring proceedings for infringement.

18.66 CDPA 1988, s 90(4) provides that where a licence is granted by the copyright owner it will bind not only the copyright owner but also every successor in title to his copyright, except for a purchaser for valuable consideration acting in good faith and without notice of the licence. In addition, anybody who derives title to the copyright from such a purchaser for value who acted in good faith and without notice of the licence will not be bound by the licence.

ASSIGNMENT OF COPYRIGHT

18.67 CDPA 1988, s 90(3) states that an assignment of copyright is not effective unless it is in writing and signed by or on behalf of the copyright owner, the assignor. Section 176(1) provides that for a limited company the assignment should be signed by using the common seal of the company. If the assignment is by the original copyright owner it will be known as a grant of copyright, whereas subsequent dealings are known as assignments of copyright.

18.68 CDPA 1988, s 91(1) allows for the copyright in works which have yet to be created to be assigned: for example, a publishing agreement will provide that a composer will for the term of the agreement assign the copyright in all the compositions which he will compose to the publisher. Once the work has been created and is capable of copyright protection the purchaser of the future copyright (or a purchaser from him) is entitled to require the copyright in the work to be vested in him.

18.69 An assignment is an actual transfer of ownership of rights in the work. The assignee becomes the owner of rights in the work which have been assigned to him. This means that the assignor of the work can be stopped from doing anything which infringes the rights given to the assignee.

Using an assignment or licence: dealing with the rights in the copyright work

18.70 As stated earlier, a copyright owner can make money from his copyright works by selling copies of the work himself, or by permitting others to sell copies. If the copyright owner permits others to sell copies he will do so by giving another person(s) either an assignment or an exclusive or non-exclusive licence to use the work.

18.71 CDPA 1988, s 90(2) provides that an assignment, licence or any other permitted way of dealing with copyright does not have to be of the whole of the copyright work. It can be limited so that it can apply to:

(1)   one or more, but not all, of the things the copyright owner has the exclusive right to do;[21] and

(2)   part, but not the whole, of the period for which the copyright is to subsist.[22]

18.72 To sum up, the copyright owner can exploit his work by giving a third party an assignment or licence of either:

(1)   all of his rights in the copyright work for either:
       (a)   the whole period for which copyright subsists; or
       (b)   part of the period for which copyright subsists; or

(2)   some of his rights in the copyright work for either:
       (a)   the whole period for which copyright subsists; or
       (b)   part of the period for which copyright subsists.

18.73 There can often be a problem in deciding whether a document is an assignment or an exclusive licence. The document should state whether it is intended to be an assignment or an exclusive licence. However, stating what the document is intended to be does not necessarily make the document what it is called. It will only suggest what the document may be. If the document is described as an assignment but the rights granted are limited to certain territories the document will in fact be a licence. A licence rather than an assignment may be presumed if the assignee has ongoing obligations to comply with under the terms of the agreement, such as the obligation to pay royalties.

18.74 The copyright owner, with his solicitor, will need to decide whether he wants to grant an assignment or a licence to the third party. He will also need to consider in detail exactly what rights he intends to grant to the third party and ensure that only those rights are granted and that all the other rights are retained.

---

[21]   See **18.89** et seq for the exclusive rights of the copyright owner.
[22]   See **18.75** for how long copyright subsists in a work.

DURATION OF COPYRIGHT

18.75 Copyright does not last in perpetuity. CDPA 1988, as amended by the Duration of Copyright and Rights in Performances Regulations 1995[23] and the Copyright and Related Rights Regulations 2003,[24] sets out the duration of copyright for the various types of copyright works in the UK. This section sets out the duration of copyright as amended by the 1995 and 2003 Regulations.

Literary, dramatic, musical or artistic works

18.76 CDPA 1988, s 12(2) provides that for literary, musical or artistic works copyright expires 70 years from the end of the calendar year in which the author dies. Section 12(8)(a)(i) provides that for s 12(2), if the work is one of joint authorship if the identity of all the authors is known the period will expire 70 years from the end of the calendar year of the death of the last of them to die.[25]

18.77 CDPA 1988, s 12(3) deals with unknown authorship and s 12(4) deals with situations where the identity of the author becomes known before the end of the period specified in s 12(3). This is beyond the scope of this book.

Sound recordings

18.78 For sound recordings, CDPA 1988, s 13A(2)(a), (b) and (c) provides that copyright in a sound recording expires:

(1)   50 years from the end of the calendar year in which the recording is made (s 13A(2)(a));

(2)   if during that period the recording is published, 50 years from the end of the calendar year in which the recording is first published (s 13A(2)(b)); or

(3)   if during that period the recording is not published but is made available to the public by being played in public or communicated to the public, 50 years from the end of the calendar year in which the recording is first so made available (s 13A(2)(c)).

18.79 CDPA 1988, s 13A(2) also provides that in determining whether a sound recording has been published, played in public or communicated to the public, no account shall be taken of any unauthorised act.

Films

18.80 CDPA 1988, s 13B(2) provides that for a film, copyright will expire 70 years from the end of the calendar year in which the death occurs of the last to die of the following:

(1)   the principal director (s 13B(2)(a));

---

[23]   SI 1995/3297.
[24]   SI 2003/2498.
[25]   See **18.39** et seq for s 10 works of joint authorship.

(2)   the author of the screenplay (s 13B(2)(b));

(3)   the author of the dialogue (s 13B(2)(c)); or

(4)   the composer of music specially created for and used in the film (s 13B(2)(d)).

18.81 CDPA 1988, s 13B(3) provides that if the identity of one or more of the people in s 13B(2)(a)–(d) is known and the identity of one or more of the others is not, the reference in s 13B(2) to the death of the last of them to die is to be construed as a reference to the death of the last whose identity is known.

18.82 CDPA 1988, s 13B(4) deals with the situation where the identity of the people referred to in s 13B(2)(a)–(d) is unknown. Section 13B(5) deals with the situation where s 13B(4) appears to apply and the identity of any of the people in s 13B(2)(a)–(d) becomes known before the end of the period specified in s 13B(4). This is beyond the scope of this book.

Broadcasts

18.83 CDPA 1988, s 14(2) provides that the duration of copyright in a broadcast is 50 years from the end of the calendar year in which the broadcast was made.

18.84 CDPA 1988, s 14(3) deals with where the author of a broadcast is not a national of an EEA state. This is beyond the scope of this book.

18.85 It should be noted that CDPA 1988, s 14(5) provides that copyright in a repeat broadcast expires at the same time as the copyright in the original broadcast and no copyright arises in respect of a repeat broadcast which is broadcast after the expiry of the copyright in the original broadcast.

Typographical arrangement of published editions

18.86 CDPA 1988, s 15 provides that copyright in the typographical arrangement of a published edition expires at the end of the period of 25 years from the end of the calendar year in which the edition was first published.

EXTENDED COPYRIGHT AND REVIVED COPYRIGHT

18.87 The previous section on duration of copyright (**18.75** et seq) sets out the duration of copyright under CDPA 1988, as amended by the Duration of Copyright and Rights in Performances Regulations 1995[26] and the Copyright and Related Rights Regulations 2003.[27] Any matters relating to the ownership of any extended copyright or revived copyright works due to amendments to the original wording of CDPA 1988 are beyond the scope of this book.

---

[26]   SI 1995/3297.
[27]   SI 2003/2498.

18.88 It should be noted that it is common in agreements which assign copyright for the full period of copyright for the duration clause to be drafted to provide that copyright is assigned for the full period of copyright and for all renewals and extensions of copyright.

THE EXCLUSIVE RIGHTS OF THE COPYRIGHT OWNER

18.89 CDPA 1988, s 16(1) provides that the owner of the copyright in a work has the exclusive right to do the following acts in the UK, namely to:

(1)   copy the work (s 16(1)(a));

(2)   issue copies of the work to the public (s 16(1)(b));

(3)   rent or lend the work to the public (s 16(1)(ba));

(4)   perform, show or play the work in public (s 16(1)(c));

(5)   communicate the work to the public (s 16(1)(d)); and

(6)   make an adaptation of or do any of the above in relation to an adaptation (s 16(1)(e)).

18.90 The above acts are restricted acts, or as CDPA 1988, s 16(1) calls them 'acts restricted by copyright'. Section 16(2) provides that copyright in a work is infringed by a person who without the licence of the copyright owner does, or authorises another to do, any of the acts restricted by the copyright.

18.91 By virtue of CDPA 1988, s 16(3)(a) copyright infringement can occur where a s 16(1) restricted act is done ' in relation to the whole or any substantial part' of the copyright work by a person who does not have permission to do so from the copyright owner. There is no definition in CDPA 1988 of the word 'substantial'. The courts will, as was done in *Ladbroke (Football) Ltd v William Hill (Football) Ltd*,[28] in deciding whether a 'substantial part' of a work has been used, look at the quality of what was taken rather than the quantity of what was taken.

18.92 The case of *Warwick Film Productions v Eisenger*[29] looked at the situation where A had prepared a work which was part original and part copied from another source and B copied from A's work the part that A had copied from another source. The court found that A's work was a copyright work but that B had not copied a substantial part of A's work as A had himself copied that part from another source.

18.93 In the case of *Hawkes & Son (London) Ltd v Paramount Film Service Ltd*[30] the court considered that a defendant who used 20 seconds from a 4-minute tune had used a 'substantial' part of the work and so infringed copyright. It is not possible to say that X

---

[28]   [1964] 1 WLR 273.
[29]   [1969] 1 Ch 508.
[30]   [1934] Ch 593.

number of seconds or minutes will be regarded as 'substantial' for the purposes of infringement. Obviously, the more of the work used the more likely that the court may say that a 'substantial' part has been taken.

18.94 Having seen what the exclusive rights of the copyright owner are, it is necessary to examine these rights in more detail. CDPA 1988, ss 17–21 go into more detail about each exclusive right.

COPYING

18.95 CDPA 1988, s 17 deals with copying and provides that this a restricted act.

18.96 CDPA 1988, s 17(2) provides that copying for a literary, dramatic, musical or artistic work means reproducing the work in any material form, including storing the work in any medium by electronic means.

18.97 CDPA 1988, s 17(4) provides that copying in relation to a film or broadcast includes making a photograph of the whole or any substantial part of any image which forms part of the film or broadcast.

18.98 CDPA 1988, s 17(6) also states that a work is copied where the copies which are made are transient or incidental to some other use of the work.

18.99 Although it is frequently easy to establish whether a work has been copied it should be noted that it is possible for someone to subconsciously copy a work[31] or to copy a work by parody.

ISSUING COPIES

18.100 CDPA 1988, s 18 deals with issuing copies of the work to the public. Section 18(1) provides that this is a restricted act.

18.101 CDPA 1988, s 18(2)(a) and (b) deals with what is meant by issuing copies of a work to the public, whilst s 18(3) deals with what does not constitute issuing copies of a work to the public.

18.102 CDPA 1988, s 18(2) provides that issuing copies of a work to the public means:

(1)   putting into circulation in the EEA copies not previously put into circulation in the EEA by or with the consent of the copyright owner; or

(2)   putting into circulation outside the EEA copies not previously put into circulation in the EEA or elsewhere.

18.103 CDPA 1988, s 18(3) provides that issuing copies of a work to the public does not include:

---

[31]   See *Francis Day & Hunter Ltd v Bron* [1963] Ch 587.

(1)   any subsequent distribution, sale, hiring or loan of those copies previously put into circulation (subject to the s 18A rental or lending right);[32] or

(2)   any subsequent importation of such copies into the UK or another EEA state, except so far as s 18(2)(a) applies to putting into circulation in the EEA copies previously put into circulation outside the EEA.

RENTING OR LENDING COPIES OF THE WORK TO THE PUBLIC

18.104   CDPA 1988, s 18A deals with renting or lending copies of the work to the public. Section 18A(1) provides that this is a restricted act in:

(1)   a literary, dramatic or musical work (s 18A(1)(a));

(2)   an artistic work, other than:
  (a)   a work of architecture in the form of a building or model for a building; or
  (b)   a work of applied art (s 18A(1)(b)); and

(3)   a film or sound recording (s 18A(1)(c)).

18.105   CDPA 1988, s 18A(2)(a) and (b) defines what constitutes 'rental' and 'lending'. Section 18A(2)(a) provides that 'rental' means making a copy of the work available for use, on terms that it will or may be returned, for direct or indirect economic or commercial advantage. Rental therefore means hiring out the work, usually for money. Section 18A(2)(b) provides that 'lending' means making a copy of the work available for use, on terms that it will or may be returned, otherwise than for direct or indirect economic or commercial advantage, through an establishment which is accessible to the public. Lending therefore means loaning a work out at no charge. The lending must be done by an establishment which is accessible to the public, for example, a public library. (Section 18A(5) states that if a charge is made purely to cover the establishment's operating costs the establishment will still be 'lending' under the definition.)

18.106   CDPA 1988, s 18A(3) provides that 'rental' and 'lending' does not include:

(1)   making available for the purpose of public performance, playing or showing in public, or communication to the public;

(2)   making available for the purpose of exhibition in public; or

(3)   making available for on-the-spot reference use.

18.107   CDPA 1988, s 18A(4) also provides that 'lending' does not include making available between establishments which are accessible to the public.

18.108   Any references in CDPA 1988, s 18A to the rental or lending of copies of a work include by virtue of s 18A(6) the rental or lending of the original work.

---

[32]   See below for s 18A.

RENTAL AND THE RIGHT TO EQUITABLE REMUNERATION

18.109   CDPA 1988, s 93B(1) provides that where an author has transferred his rental right concerning a sound recording or a film to the producer of the sound recording or film, he retains the right to equitable remuneration for the rental.

18.110   The authors to whom CDPA 1988, s 93B applies are:

(1)   the author of a literary, dramatic, musical or artistic work (s 93B(1)(a)); and

(2)   the principal director of a film (s 93B(1)(b)).

18.111   CDPA 1988, s 93B(2) provides that the right to equitable remuneration can not be assigned by the author except to a collecting society for the purpose of enabling it to enforce the right on his behalf. (Section 93B(2) does allow for the right to receive equitable remuneration to be transmissible by testamentary disposition or by operation of the law as personal or moveable property, and that the right to receive equitable remuneration may be assigned or further transmitted by any person into whose hands it passes.)

18.112   The person who is liable to pay the equitable remuneration is stated in CDPA 1988, s 93B(3) to be the person who is currently entitled to the rental right, namely the person to whom the right was transferred or any successor in title of his. Section 93B(4) provides that the amount payable for equitable remuneration is the amount agreed by the parties, or in default of such agreement then by virtue of s 93C either party can ask the Copyright Tribunal to determine the amount payable. Section 93B(5) provides that any clause in an agreement purporting to exclude or restrict the right to equitable remuneration will have no effect.

18.113   There are also provisions in CDPA 1988, s 93C(2)(a) and (b) where equitable remuneration is payable, for either party to the agreement to apply to the Copyright Tribunal to:

(1)   vary any agreement as to the amount payable (s 93C(2)(a)); or

(2)   vary any previous determination of the Copyright Tribunal (s 93C(2)(b)).

18.114   Any clause in an agreement purporting to prevent a party questioning the amount of equitable remuneration before the Copyright Tribunal will by virtue of CDPA 1988, s 93C(5) have no effect.

18.115   CDPA 1988, s 93C(4) provides that the remuneration will not be considered inequitable merely because it was paid by way of a single payment or at the time of the transfer of the rental right.

18.116   CDPA 1988, s 93A(1) provides that where an agreement concerning film production is concluded between an author and a film producer, the author shall be presumed, unless the agreement provides to the contrary, to have transferred to the film producer any rental right in relation to the film arising by virtue of the inclusion of a copy of the author's work in the film. Section 93A(2) provides that an author means an author, or prospective author, of a literary, dramatic, musical or artistic work. In addition, s 93A(3) provides that s 93A(1) does not apply to any rental right in relation to the film arising by virtue of the inclusion in the film of the screenplay, the dialogue or music specifically created for and used in the film.

18.117 A detailed examination of the workings of and the powers of the Copyright Tribunal under CDPA 1988 are beyond the scope of this book.

THE PERFORMANCE, SHOWING OR PLAYING OF THE WORK IN PUBLIC

18.118 CDPA 1988, s 19(1) provides that the performance in public of a literary, dramatic or musical work is a restricted act.

18.119 CDPA 1988, s 19(2)(a) and (b) provides that a 'performance' in relation to a literary, dramatic or musical work:

(1)   includes, inter alia, the delivery of lectures (s 19(2)(a)); and

(2)   any visual or acoustic presentation, including presentation by means of a sound recording, film or broadcast of the work (s 19(2)(b)).

18.120 CDPA 1988, s 19(3) provides that the playing or showing in public of a sound recording, film or broadcast is a restricted act.

18.121 The infringement occurs when performing, playing or showing the work in public. There is no infringement if the work is played in private. There is no definition of what constitutes in public. There have been several cases on what 'in public' means. The general attitude taken in these cases by the courts is that if the performance takes place in a situation where people have to pay money to attend or in a commercial environment, for example, a football match or a hotel, this suggests the performance is in public. A private performance is essentially of a domestic nature, ie in the presence of family and friends.

COMMUNICATION TO THE PUBLIC

18.122 CDPA 1988, s 20(1) provides that communication to the public of a:

(1)   literary, dramatic, musical or artistic work (s 20(1)(a));

(2)   sound recording or film (s 20(1)(b)); or

(3)   broadcast (s 20(1)(c)),

is a restricted act.

18.123 CDPA 1988, s 20(2) provides that communication to the public means communication to the public by electronic transmission and in relation to a work include:

(1) broadcasting the work (s 20(2)(a)); and

(2) making the work available to the public by electronic transmission in such a way that members of the public may access it from a place and at a time individually chosen by them (s 20(2)(b)).

18.124 Consent must therefore be obtained from the copyright owner of the works listed in s 20(1)(a)–(c) to communicate the work to the public.

MAKING AN ADAPTATION

18.125 CDPA 1988, s 21(1) provides that it is a restricted act to make an adaptation of a literary, dramatic or musical work. The adaptation is deemed to have been made when it has been recorded, for example, in writing. Writing here means under CDPA 1988, s 178 any form of notation or code, whether by hand or otherwise and regardless of the method by which, or medium in or on which, it is recorded.

18.126 CDPA 1988, s 21(2) provides that doing any of the acts specified in CDPA 1988, ss 17–20 or in s 21(1) in relation to an adaptation of the work is also an act restricted by the copyright in a literary, dramatic or musical work. Section 21(2) provides that it is immaterial whether the adaptation has been recorded in writing or otherwise at the time the act is done. So, for example, if a literary work is adapted and the adaptation is subsequently copied, the copying of the adaptation is an infringement of the copyright in the literary work.

18.127 CDPA 1988, s 21(3) defines what is an adaptation. For a literary work an adaptation includes, inter alia, a translation of the work. For a musical work an adaptation means an arrangement or transcription of the work.

PRIMARY INFRINGEMENT

18.128 Where somebody without a licence from the copyright owner does, or authorises somebody else to do, any of the exclusive CDPA 1988, s 16 restricted acts they will be committing an act of primary infringement. There is no need for any mens rea by the infringer. Doing or authorising somebody else to do any of the s 16 restricted acts is sufficient to be liable for an act of primary infringement.

SECONDARY INFRINGEMENT

18.129 CDPA 1988, ss 22–26 deal with five other of infringing acts called secondary infringement. These acts are usually carried out by the infringers for monetary gain.

18.130 Before any secondary infringement can exist there needs to be some element of knowledge of infringement by the alleged infringer. CDPA 1988 specifically states that there will be secondary infringement if the person commits the infringing act and either (a) knew or (b) had reason to believe (using an objective test) that he had an infringing copy of the work.

The secondary infringing acts

Importing infringing copies

18.131   CDPA 1988, s 22 provides that it is an infringing act if someone without a licence from the copyright owner imports into the UK, except for his private and domestic use, an article which he knows or has reason to believe is an infringing copy of the work.

18.132   An article is an infringing copy:

(1)   if its making constituted an infringement of copyright in the work (s 27(2)); or

(2)   if it has been or is proposed to be imported into the UK (s 27(3)(a)) and its making in the UK would have constituted an infringement of the copyright in the work, or a breach of an exclusive licence agreement relating to that work (s 27(3)(a) and (b)).

18.133   CDPA 1988 makes it perfectly clear in s 27(5) that an article is not an infringing copy if it can be legally imported into the UK due to any enforceable EC provisions within the meaning of s 2(1) of the European Communities Act 1972. Article 28 of the Treaty of Rome makes provisions for the free movement of goods within EC member states. The effect of Art 28 is that once goods have been put on sale in an EC member state (eg France) with the consent of the copyright owner a third party can take these goods and import them into the UK for re-sale without committing any s 22 act of secondary infringement. It should be noted that although Art 28 allows such goods to be imported for re-sale, Art 30 provides a limited exception to Art 28. Article 30 will stop the free movement of goods within EC member states if the restriction can be justified by showing that it is for 'the protection of industrial and commercial property'. It should also be noted that as well as Arts 28 and 30 of the Treaty of Rome there also exists the European Court of Justice's doctrine of exhaustion of rights. The doctrine of exhaustion of rights means that where goods have been lawfully put on sale in an EC member state that the copyright owner cannot stop these goods being imported into other EC member states.

18.134   For further details about Arts 28 and 30 of the Treaty of Rome readers are advised to refer to specialist books on the subject.

Possessing or dealing with an infringing copy

18.135   CDPA 1988, s 23 provides that it is an infringing act if someone without a licence from the copyright owner either:

(1)   possesses in the course of a business (s 23(a));

(2)   sells or lets for hire, or offers or exposes for sale or hire (s 23(b));

(3)   in the course of a business exhibits in public or distributes (s 23(c)); or

(4)   distributes otherwise than in the course of a business to such an extent as to affect prejudicially the owner of the copyright (s 23(d)),

an article which is, and which he knows or has reason to believe is, an infringing copy of the work.

18.136 Section 23 will therefore catch people who trade in pirate CDs. Section 23(d) will also catch people who are not in business but who, for example, are fans who have pirate live CDs of their favourite band and let other fans of the band have copies of the recording for free or for a nominal charge to cover the cost of a blank tape and postage. For s 23(d) to apply two things will have to be shown: first, the infringer knew or had reason to believe he had an infringing copy of the work and, secondly, he used it to such an extent so as to affect prejudicially the owner of the copyright.

Providing the means for making infringing copies

18.137 CDPA 1988, s 24 provides that it is an infringing act if someone without a licence from the copyright owner either:

(1)   makes (s 24(1)(a));

(2)   imports into the UK (s 24(1)(b));

(3)   possesses in the course of a business (s 24(1)(c)); or

(4)   sells or lets for hire, or offers or exposes for sale or hire (s 24(1)(d)),

an article specifically designed or adapted for making copies of that work, knowing or having reason to believe that it is to be used to make infringing copies.

18.138 CDPA 1988, s 24(2) states that copyright in a work is infringed by a person who without the licence of the copyright owner transmits the work by a telecommunications system (other than by communication to the public), knowing or having reason to believe that infringing copies of the work will be made by means of the reception of the transmission in the UK or elsewhere. (A telecommunications system is defined in CDPA 1988, s 178 as a system to convey visual images, sounds or other information by electronic means.)

18.139 This section covers the machinery used to make copies of the work. For example, it will cover CD and DVD pressing plants. The pressing plant will have to make inquiries of its customers before pressing up the CDs and DVDs to ensure that it is not pressing up infringing copies.

Permitting the use of premises for infringing performances

18.140 CDPA 1988, s 25(1) provides that where the copyright in a literary, dramatic or musical work is infringed by a performance at a place of public entertainment, any person who gave permission for that place to be used for the performance is also liable for the infringement unless when he gave permission he believed on reasonable grounds that the performance would not infringe copyright.

18.141 CDPA 1988, s 25(2) provides that a place of public entertainment includes premises which are occupied mainly for other purposes but are from time to time made available for hire for the purposes of public entertainment

18.142 CDPA 1988, s 25 can possibly catch the owner of the venue where the musical work is performed in concert. It does not apply to venue owners playing a record on a jukebox or on a hi-fi as the section does not deal with sound recordings.

Provision of apparatus for infringing performances

18.143 CDPA 1988, s 26(1) provides that where copyright is infringed by a public performance of the work, or by the playing or showing of the work in public, by means of apparatus for:

(1) playing sound recordings (s 26(1)(a));

(2) showing films (s 26(1)(b)); or

(3) receiving visual images or sounds conveyed by electronic means (s 26(1)(c)).

The following persons are also liable for the infringement:

(1) a person who supplied the apparatus, or any substantial part of it, is liable if when he supplied the apparatus or part (s 26(2)):
   (a) he knew or had reason to believe that the apparatus was likely to be used to infringe copyright (s 26(2)(a)); or
   (b) in the case of apparatus whose normal use involves a public performance, playing or showing, he did not believe on reasonable grounds that it would not be used so as to infringe copyright (s 26(2)(b));

(2) an occupier of premises who gave permission for the apparatus to be brought onto the premises is liable if when he gave permission he knew or had reason to believe that the apparatus was likely to be used to infringe copyright (s 26(3)); and

(3) a person who supplied a copy of a sound recording or film used to infringe copyright is liable if when he supplied it he knew or had reason to believe that what he supplied, or a copy made directly or indirectly from it, was likely to be used to infringe copyright (s 26(4)).

PERMITTED ACTS/DEFENCES

18.144 It is not possible for a solicitor to decide if there has been any copyright infringement without first asking several questions. The checklist of questions he should work through include:

(1) Is the work which has been allegedly infringed one that is capable of copyright protection? If so:

(2) Who is the author of the work?

(3) Is the author the owner of the work? If not, who is the owner?

(4) Is the work still within the relevant copyright protection period?

(5)　Has there been an act of primary infringement?

(6)　Has there been an act of secondary infringement?

(7)　Are there any valid defences available to the alleged infringer?

18.145　It is this last question that we now briefly turn our attention to.

18.146　CDPA 1988, ss 28–76 set out the 'permitted acts' which can be done with a work by a third party even though copyright exists in the work. These permitted acts control to some considerable extent the rights of the copyright owner. There may well have been a prima facie infringement of one of the copyright owner's exclusive rights, but the prospective defendant may be able to use one or more of the CDPA 1988 permitted acts as a defence which, if established, would mean that there has been no infringement of copyright.

18.147　What follows below is a brief reference to and an examination of some of the permitted acts which might be used as a defence in a copyright infringement action. An examination of all the permitted acts is beyond the scope of this book. A full list of the permitted acts in CDPA 1988, ss 28–76 is set out below.

Permitted acts/defences under the CDPA 1988

Section number	Permitted act/defence
28	Introductory provisions
28A	Making of temporary copies
29	Research and private study
30	Criticism, review and news reporting
31	Incidental inclusion of copyright material
31A	Making a single accessible copy for personal use
31B	Multiple copies for visually impaired persons
31C	Intermediate copies and records
31D	Licensing schemes
31E	Limitations, etc. following infringement of copyright
31F	Definitions and other supplementary provision for sections 31A to 31E
32	Things done for purposes of instruction or examination
33	Anthologies for educational use
34	Performing, playing or showing work in course of activities of educational establishment
35	Recording by educational establishments of broadcasts and cable programmes
36	Reprographic copying by educational establishments of passages from published works
36A	Lending of copies by educational establishments

Section number	Permitted act/defence
37	Libraries and archives: introductory
38	Copying by librarians: articles in periodicals
39	Copying by librarians: parts of published works
40	Restriction on production of multiple copies of the same material
40A	Lending of copies by libraries or archives
41	Copying by librarians: supply of copies to other libraries
42	Copying by librarians or archivists: replacement copies of works
43	Copying by librarians or archivists: certain unpublished works
44	Copy of work required to be made as condition of export
44A	Legal deposit libraries
45	Parliamentary and judicial proceedings
46	Royal Commissions and statutory inquiries
47	Material open to public inspection or on official register
48	Material communicated to the Crown in the course of public business
49	Public records
50	Acts done under statutory authority
50A	Back up copies
50B	Decompilation
50BA	Observing, studying and testing of computer programs
50C	Other acts permitted to lawful users
50D	Acts permitted in relation to databases
51	Design documents and models
52	Effect of exploitation of design derived from artistic work
53	Things done in reliance on registration of design
54	Use of typeface in ordinary course of printing
55	Articles for producing material in particular typeface
56	Transfers of copies of works in electronic form
57	Anonymous or pseudonymous works: acts permitted on assumptions as to expiry of copyright or death of author
58	Use of notes or recordings of spoken words in certain cases
59	Public reading or recitation
60	Abstracts of scientific or technical articles
61	Recordings of folksongs
62	Representation of certain artistic works on public display
63	Advertisement of sale of artistic work

Section number	Permitted act/defence
64	Making of subsequent works by same artist
65	Reconstruction of buildings
66	Lending to public of copies of certain works
66A	Films: acts permitted on assumptions as to expiry of copyright, &c
67	Playing of sound recordings for purposes of club, society, &c
68	Incidental recording for purposes of broadcast or cable programme
69	Recording for purposes of supervision and control of broadcasts and cable programmes
70	Recording for purposes of time-shifting
71	Photographs of television broadcasts or cable programmes
72	Free public showing or playing of broadcast or cable programme
73	Reception and re-transmission of broadcast in cable programme service
73A	Royalty or other sum payable in pursuance of section 73(4)
74	Provision of sub-titled copies of broadcast or cable programme
75	Recording for archival purposes
76	Adaptations

Making of temporary copies – s 28A

18.148 CDPA 1988, s 28A provides that copyright in a literary work, other than a computer program or a database, or in a dramatic, musical or artistic work, the typographical arrangement of a published edition, a sound recording or a film, is not infringed by the making of a temporary copy which is transient or incidental, which is an integral and essential part of a technological process and the sole purpose of which is to enable:

(1) a transmission of the work in a network between third parties by an intermediary (s 28A(a)); or

(2) a lawful use of the work (s 28A(b)),

and which has no economic significance.

Fair dealing for research and private study and fair dealing for criticism, review and news reporting – ss 29 and 30

18.149 The permitted act of fair dealing is available in two circumstances:

(1) fair dealing for research and private study (s 29); and

(2)   fair dealing for the purpose of criticism, review and news reporting (s 30).

18.150   There is no definition in CDPA 1988 of what is fair dealing. There has been some considerable case-law on this matter. Lord Denning in *Hubbard v Vosper*[33] set out criteria for deciding what is fair dealing. His criteria and other case-law has shown that what constitutes fair dealing depends on the facts of each case. There are many factors that the courts will take into account, including how much of the work was copied or used and the purpose behind the use of the work.

Research and private study – s 29

18.151   CDPA 1988, s 29(1) provides that fair dealing with a literary, dramatic, musical or artistic work for research for a non-commercial purpose does not infringe any copyright in the work provided that it is accompanied by a sufficient acknowledgement. Section 29(1B) provides that no acknowledgement is required in connection with fair dealing for the purposes mentioned in s 29(1) where this would be impossible for reasons of practicality or otherwise.

18.152   CDPA 1988, s 29(1C) provides that fair dealing with a literary, dramatic, musical or artistic work for the purposes of private study does not infringe any copyright in the work. It should be noted that the defence of fair dealing for private study does not require an acknowledgement to be given.

18.153   CDPA 1988, s 29(2) provides that fair dealing with the typographical arrangement of a published edition for the purposes of research or private study does not infringe any copyright in the arrangement.

18.154   It should be noted that the fair dealing defence for research and private study does not apply to dealing with a sound recording, film or broadcast.

18.155   CDPA 1988, s 29(3) provides that copying by a person other than the researcher or student himself is not fair dealing if:

(1)   in the case of a librarian, or person acting on behalf of a librarian, he does anything which regulations under s 40 would not permit to be done under s 38 or 39 (s 29(3)(a)); or

(2)   in any other case, the person doing the copying knows or has reason to believe that it will result in copies of substantially the same material being provided to more than one person at substantially the same time and for substantially the same purpose (s 29(3)(b)).

18.156   An examination of CDPA 1988, ss 38, 39 and 40 is beyond the scope of this book.

Criticism, review and news reporting – s 30

18.157   CDPA 1988, s 30(1) provides that:

---

[33]   [1972] 2 QB 84.

'Fair dealing with a work for the purpose of criticism or review, of that or another work or of a performance of a work, does not infringe copyright in the work provided that it is accompanied by a sufficient acknowledgement and provided that the work has been made available to the public.'

18.158 CDPA 1988, s 30(1A) provides that for the purposes of s 30(1) a work has been made available to the public if it has been made available by any means, including:

(1) the issue of copies to the public (s 30(1A)(a));

(2) making the work available by means of an electronic retrieval system (s 30(1A)(b));

(3) the rental or lending of copies of the work to the public (s 30(1A)(c));

(4) the performance, exhibition, playing or showing of the work in public (s 30(1A)(d));

(5) the communication to the public of the work (s 30(1A)(e)),

but in determining generally for the purposes of s 30(1) whether a work has been made available to the public no account shall be taken of any unauthorised act.

18.159 CDPA 1988, s 30(2) provides that:

'Fair dealing with a work (other than a photograph) for the purpose of reporting current events does not infringe any copyright in the work provided that it is accompanied by a sufficient acknowledgement.'

18.160 CDPA 1988, s 30(3) provides that:

'No acknowledgement is required in connection with the reporting of current events by means of a sound recording, film or broadcast where this would be impossible for reasons of practicality or otherwise.'

18.161 CDPA 1988, s 178 defines 'sufficient acknowledgement' as:

'... an acknowledgement identifying the work in question by its title or other description, and identifying the author unless (a) in the case of a published work, it is published anonymously or (b) in the case of an unpublished work, it is not possible for a person to ascertain the identity of the author by reasonable inquiry.'

18.162 CDPA 1988, s 30(1) and (1A) will enable a magazine music reviewer to review music that 'has been made available to the public' for a magazine and to use extracts of the lyrics in the review to show, for example, the incisiveness or otherwise of the lyricist's style. If the reviewer quotes from the lyrics in his review he must ensure that there is a 'sufficient acknowledgement', namely identifying the work in question by its title or other description and the identity of the lyricist.

Incidental inclusion of copyright material – s 31

18.163 CDPA 1988, s 31(1) provides that:

'Copyright in a work is not infringed by its incidental inclusion in an artistic work, sound recording, film or broadcast.'

18.164   CDPA 1988, s 31(2) goes on to say:

'Nor is copyright infringed by the issue to the public of copies, or the playing, showing, or communication to the public of anything whose making was, by virtue of section 31(1), not an infringement of the copyright.'

18.165   CDPA 1988, s 31(3) further provides that:

'A musical work, words spoken or sung with music, or so much of a sound recording, or broadcast as includes a musical work or such words, shall not be regarded as incidentally included in another work if it is deliberately included.'

18.166   CDPA 1988, s 31 is easier to understand by looking at an illustration. If we take as an example an MP who is being interviewed live for the TV news in the street outside the House of Commons. Whilst the MP is being interviewed a car drives by slowly with music blaring from the car radio. The music from the car radio gets picked up on the film of the interview. The defence of incidental inclusion under s 31(1) and (2) will probably be available for the broadcasting company concerning the inclusion of the music from the car as it could not control the car going by at that time. It could be argued that if the interview was recorded and not live the defence may very possibly not be available as the interview could have been re-recorded.

18.167   On a film set the director has control of all the events going on set. If the director wants to film a scene of the characters in the film talking whilst a well-known pop song plays on the radio in the background, the defence of incidental inclusion under s 31(1) and (2) will not be available because the pop song has under s 31(3) been deliberately included. The director has control of all the events on set and therefore chose to include the pop song in the filming. To enable the pop song to be used in the background without infringing copyright, licences to use the music in the film should have been obtained from the owner of the copyright in the words and music of the song and from the owner of the copyright in the sound recording.

Education – ss 32–36A

18.168   CDPA 1988, ss 32–36A deal with permitted acts for educational purposes.

18.169   The permitted act of things done for the purposes of instruction or examination is dealt with in s 32; the performing, playing, showing a work in the course of the activities of an educational establishment is dealt with in s 34; the right for educational establishments to record broadcasts for educational purposes is dealt with in s 35; and the right to reprographically copy passages from published literary, dramatic or musical works for the purpose of instruction is dealt with in s 36.

Libraries – ss 37–44A

18.170   CDPA 1988, ss 37–44A deal with the permitted acts for libraries.

18.171   The permitted act allowing a librarian under certain circumstances to copy part of a literary, dramatic or musical work other than an article in a periodical is dealt with in s 39.

Clubs and societies – s 67

18.172   CDPA 1988, s 67 permits the playing of a sound recording as part of the activities of, or for the benefit of, a club, society or other organisation if certain conditions are met.

Recording for purposes of time shifting – s 70

18.173   CDPA 1988, s 70(1) provides that:

> 'The making in domestic premises for private and domestic use of a recording of a broadcast solely for the purpose of enabling it to be viewed or listened to at a more convenient time does not infringe any copyright in the broadcast or in any work included in it.'

18.174   CDPA 1988, s 70(2) provides that where a copy which would otherwise be an infringing copy is made in accordance with this section but is subsequently dealt with:

(1)   it shall be treated as an infringing copy for the purposes of that dealing (s 70(2)(a)); and

(2)   if that dealing infringes copyright, it shall be treated as an infringing copy for all subsequent purposes (s 70(2)(b)).

18.175   The words 'dealt with' in s 70(2) are defined in s 70(3) as meaning 'sold or let for hire, offered or exposed for sale or hire or communicated to the public'.

18.176   CDPA 1988, s 70(1) enables somebody to record a television programme at home to watch at a more convenient time.

COMMON LAW AND OTHER DEFENCES

18.177   It should be noted that although CDPA 1988 has created these permitted acts, there are common law defences available as well. These include the defence that the work is not protected on the grounds of public policy: for example, the original work is obscene. Indeed, CDPA 1988 specifically provides in s 171(3) that nothing in Pt I of the Act (Copyright) affects any rule of law preventing or restricting the enforcement of copyright on grounds of public interest or otherwise.[34]

18.178   There is also the possibility of using the European defences under the Treaty of Rome such as using the defence of Art 28 dealing with the free movement of goods.

---

[34]   See also *Hyde Park Residence Ltd v Yelland* [2001] Ch 143, [2000] 3 WLR 215, CA and *Ashdown v Telegraph Group Ltd* [2001] 3 WLR 1368, [2001] 4 All ER 666, CA.

REMEDIES FOR INFRINGEMENT

18.179　What follows below is a list of some of the civil and criminal remedies available for the copyright owner where infringement has occurred. A detailed examination of these remedies is beyond the scope of this book, although in some places comments have been added to explain or expand upon a relevant remedy. The reader is referred to CDPA 1988 for full details.

Civil remedies

18.180　CDPA 1988, s 96(1) provides that copyright infringement is actionable by the copyright owner, and under s 96(2) the copyright owner can seek damages, injunctions, an account of profits or any other remedy which is available for the owner of a property right.

Damages

18.181　Damages are available as a remedy for the copyright owner but CDPA 1988, s 97 can control the amount of damages awarded.

18.182　CDPA 1988, s 97(1) provides that if the defendant did not know, nor had any reason to believe at the time of the infringement, that copyright existed in the work, the claimant owner is not entitled to damages. This does not preclude the claimant pursuing other legal remedies.

18.183　By contrast CDPA 1988, s 97(2) allows the court to take account of all the circumstances surrounding the infringement, and in particular to see whether the defendant flagrantly infringed copyright and to look at any benefit the defendant may have got from infringing. Having looked at all the circumstances the court may then award the claimant additional damages. The courts can use s 97(2) as an additional punishment against the defendant for their behaviour in using the copyright work.

Injunctions against service providers

18.184　CDPA 1988, s 97A(1) provides that the High Court has the power to grant an injunction against a service provider where the service provider has actual knowledge of another person using its service to infringe copyright.

18.185　CDPA 1988, s 97A(2) provides that in determining whether a service provider has actual knowledge the court shall take into account all matters which appear in the particular circumstances to be relevant and amongst other things shall have regard to:

(1)　whether a service provider has received a notice through a means of contact made available in accordance with reg 6(1)(c) of the Electronic Commerce (EC Directive) Regulations 2002[35] (s 97A(2)(a)); and

(2)　the extent to which any notice includes (s 97A(2)(b)):
　　(a)　the full name and address of the sender of the notice (s 97A(2)(b)(i)); and
　　(b)　details of the infringement in question (s 97A(2)(b)(ii)).

---

[35]　SI 2002/2013.

18.186   CDPA 1988, s 97A(3) provides that the words 'service provider' have the meaning given to it by reg 2 of the Electronic Commerce (EC Directive) Regulations 2002.

18.187   An examination of the Electronic Commerce (EC Directive) Regulations 2002 is beyond the scope of this book.

Delivery up of infringing articles

18.188   CDPA 1988, s 99(1) covers the situation where the defendant:

(1)   has an infringing copy in his possession, custody or control in the course of a business (s 99(1)(a)); or

(2)   has in his possession, custody or control an article specifically designed or adapted for making copies of a copyright work, knowing or having reason to believe that it has been or is to be used to make infringing copies (s 99(1)(b)).

18.189   In such a situation the copyright owner can apply to court for an order that the infringing copy or article is delivered up to him or to any other person whom the court directs.

Right to seize infringing copies and other articles

18.190   CDPA 1988, s 100 is aimed at trying to catch street traders who sell pirate CDs and DVDs.

18.191   CDPA 1988, s 100(1) provides that an infringing copy of a work which is found exposed or otherwise immediately available for sale or hire, and in respect of which the copyright owner would be entitled to apply for an order under s 99,[36] may be seized and detained by him or by a person authorised by him. The right to seize and detain is exercisable subject to the following conditions and subject to any decision of the court under s 114:[37]

(1)   before anything is seized notice of the time and place of the proposed seizure must be given to a local police station (s 100(2));

(2)   a person may for the purpose of exercising the right enter premises to which the public has access but may not seize anything in the possession, custody or control of a person at a permanent or regular place of business of theirs, and may not use any force (s 100(3)); and

(3)   at the time when anything is seized there shall be left at the place where it was seized a notice in the prescribed form containing the prescribed particulars as to the person by whom or on whose authority the seizure is made and the grounds on which it is made (s 100(4)).

---

[36]   For s 99 see **18.188**.
[37]   For s 114 see **18.197**.

18.192 CDPA 1988, s 100(5) provides that 'premises' includes land, buildings, moveable structures, vehicles, vessels, aircraft and hovercraft.

18.193 CDPA 1988, s 100(5) provides that 'prescribed' means prescribed by order of the Secretary of State.

18.194 Since CDPA 1988, s 100(3) precludes the use of force, it would be sensible when informing the police of the proposed seizure to request that they are present when the seizure takes place.

Customs and Excise treating infringing copies as prohibited goods

18.195 CDPA 1988, s 111 enables the copyright owner of a published literary, dramatic, musical work, sound recording or film to request Customs and Excise to treat infringing copies as prohibited goods, although s 111(3A) provides that Customs and Excise can treat as prohibited goods only those infringing copies which arrive in the UK from outside the EEA, or from within the EEA but not those goods which have entered the UK under the doctrine of exhaustion of rights. Section 111(4) makes it clear that the importation of a copy of a work for private and domestic use is not prohibited by the copyright owner using this procedure.

18.196 As well as s 111 consideration needs to be had of the existence of Council Regulation 1383/2003/EC of 22 July 2003 concerning customs action against goods suspected of infringing certain intellectual property rights and the measures to be taken against goods found to have infringed such rights. Under the Regulation, an intellectual property rights holder who thinks that goods infringing its intellectual property rights might be imported into a member state may make 'an application for Customs action' to the designated customs authority in the member state concerned. Assuming the application is in order, the customs authority concerned should 'suspend release of the goods or detain them'. If the intellectual property rights holder pursues infringement proceedings against the owner of the goods in question, the relevant national tribunal can order their destruction. Where the intellectual property rights holder has not given advance warning, customs authorities can detain the goods if they suspect that they are infringing intellectual property rights. The customs authority concerned will contact the intellectual property rights holder, who has 3 days to lodge an application for customs action.

Order as to disposal of infringing copy or other article

18.197 CDPA 1988, s 114 allows for an application to be made to court for an infringing copy or other article which has been delivered up pursuant to s 99[38] or under s 107,[39] or seized and detained under s 100[40] to be:

(1)   forfeited to the copyright owner (s 114(a)); or

(2)   destroyed or dealt with as the court thinks fit (s 114(b)),

or for a decision that no order should be made.

---

[38]   For s 99 see **18.188**.
[39]   For s 107 see **18.210** et seq.
[40]   For s 100 see **18.190** et seq.

18.198 This section allows the copyright owner once he has made a seizure from a street trader under s 100 to go to court to have the pirate CDs and tapes destroyed.

Other civil remedies

18.199 It should be remembered that other civil remedies such as an account of profits, a search order or an interlocutory injunction should be considered as remedies that may be of use to the copyright owner as well as the civil remedies set out in CDPA 1988.

COPYRIGHT PRESUMPTIONS

18.200 CDPA 1988, s 104(1) and (2) creates a rebuttable presumption in relation to proceedings concerning a literary, dramatic, musical or artistic work. Under s 104(2) where a name purporting to be that of the author appears on copies of the published work or on the work when made, the person whose name appears is presumed, until the contrary is proven, to be the author of the work and that it was not made in the course of his employment or in circumstances which fall within s 163, 165 or 168 of CDPA 1988. Sections 163, 165 and 168, which deal with Crown copyright, parliamentary copyright and copyright of certain international organisations, are beyond the scope of this book.

18.201 It should be noted that CDPA 1988, s 105 creates a rebuttable presumption in relation to proceedings concerning sound recordings and films.

RIGHTS AND REMEDIES OF AN EXCLUSIVE LICENSEE

Infringements which are actionable by a non-exclusive licensee

Exercise of concurrent rights

18.202 CDPA 1988, s 101(1) provides that an exclusive licensee has, except against the copyright owner, the same rights and remedies in respect of matters occurring after the grant of the licence as if the licence had been an assignment. Section 101(2) provides that the exclusive licensee's rights and remedies are concurrent with those of the copyright owner.

18.203 CDPA 1988, s 101A(1) provides that a non-exclusive licensee may bring an action for infringement of copyright if:

(1) the infringing act was directly connected to a prior licensed act of the licensee (s 101A(1)(a)); and

(2) the licence:
    (a) is in writing and is signed by or on behalf of the copyright owner (s 101A(1)(b)(i)); and
    (b) expressly grants the non-exclusive licensee a right of action under s 101A.

18.204 CDPA 1988, s 101A(2) provides that in an action brought under s 101A the non-exclusive licensee has the same rights and remedies available to him as the copyright owner would have had if he had brought the action. Section 101A(3) provides that the rights granted under s 101A are concurrent with those of the copyright owner.

18.205 CDPA 1988, s 101A(5) provides that s 102(1), (2), (3) and (4)[41] applies to a non-exclusive licensee who has a right of action by virtue of s 101A as it applies to an exclusive licensee.

18.206 CDPA 1988, s 101A(6) provides that a 'non-exclusive licensee' means the holder of a licence authorising the licensee to exercise a right which remains exercisable by the copyright owner.

18.207 CDPA 1988, s 102(1) provides that where an action for infringement of copyright brought by the copyright owner or an exclusive licensee relates (wholly or partly) to an infringement in respect of which they have concurrent rights of action, the copyright owner or, as the case may be, the exclusive licensee may not, without leave of the court, proceed with the action unless the other is joined as a claimant or added as a defendant. Section 102(2) provides that a copyright owner or exclusive licensee who is added as a defendant in pursuance of s 102(1) is not liable for any costs in the action unless he takes part in the proceedings. Section 102(3) provides that s 102(1) does not affect the granting of interlocutory relief on an application by the copyright owner or an exclusive licensee alone.

18.208 CDPA 1988, s 102(4) provides that where an action for infringement of copyright is brought which relates (wholly or partly) to an infringement in respect of which the copyright owner and an exclusive licensee have or had concurrent rights of action:

(1) the court shall in assessing damages take into account:
    (a) the terms of the licence (s 102(4)(a)(i)); and
    (b) any pecuniary remedy already awarded or available to either of them in respect of the infringement (s 102(4)(a)(ii));

(2) no account of profits shall be directed if an award of damages has been made, or an account of profits has been directed, in favour of the other of them in respect of the infringement (s 102(4)(b)); and

(3) the court shall if an account of profits is directed apportion the profits between them as the court considers just, subject to any agreement between them (s 102(4)(c)),

and these provisions apply whether or not the copyright owner and the exclusive licensee are both parties to the action.

18.209 CDPA 1988, s 102(5)provides that the copyright owner shall notify any exclusive licensee having concurrent rights before applying for an order under s 99[42] or exercising the right conferred by s 100,[43] and the court may on the application of the

---

41 For s 102 see **18.207** et seq.
42 For s 99 see **18.188**.
43 For s 100 see **18.190** et seq.

licensee make such order under s 99 or, as the case may be, prohibiting or permitting the exercise by the copyright owner of the right conferred by s 100, as it thinks fit having regard to the terms of the licence.

CRIMINAL REMEDIES

Criminal liability for making or dealing with infringing articles etc

18.210 CDPA 1988, s 107(1) creates an offence where someone without a licence:

(1)   makes for sale or hire (s 107(1)(a));

(2)   imports into the UK other than for his private and domestic use (s 107(1)(b));

(3)   possesses in the course of a business with a view to committing any act infringing copyright (s 107(1)(c));

(4)   in the course of a business:
    (a)   sells or lets for hire (s 107(1)(d)(i));
    (b)   offers or exposes for sale or hire (s 107(1)(d)(ii));
    (c)   exhibits in public (s 107(1)(d)(iii)); or
    (d)   distributes (s 107(1)(d)(iv)); or

(5)   distributes other than in the course of a business to such an extent as to affect prejudicially the copyright owner (s 107(1)(e)),

an article which is, and which he knows or has reason to believe is an infringing copy of a copyright work.

18.211 CDPA 1988, s 107(2) provides that a person commits an offence who:

(1)   makes an article specially designed or adapted for making copies of a particular copyright work (s 107(2)(a)); or

(2)   has such an article in his possession (s 107(2)(b)),

knowing or having reason to believe that it is to be used to make infringing copies for sale or hire or for use in the course of a business.

18.212 CDPA 1988, s 107(2A) provides that a person who infringes copyright in a work by communicating the work to the public:

(1)   in the course of a business (s 107(2A)(a)); or

(2)   otherwise than in the course of a business to such an extent as to affect prejudicially the copyright owner (s 107(2A)(b)),

commits an offence if he knows or has reason to believe that, by doing so, he is infringing copyright in that work.

18.213   CDPA 1988, s 107(3) provides that where copyright is infringed (other than by reception of a communication to the public):

(1)   by the public performance of a literary, dramatic or musical work (s 107(3)(a)); or

(2)   by the playing or showing in public of a sound recording or film (s 107(3)(b)),

any person who caused the work to be performed, played or shown is guilty of an offence if he knew or had reason to believe that copyright would be infringed.

18.214   CDPA 1988, s 107(4) provides that a person guilty of an offence under s 107(1)(a), (b), (d)(iv) or (e) is liable:

(1)   on summary conviction to imprisonment for a term not exceeding 6 months or a fine not exceeding the statutory maximum, or both (s 107(4)(a)); and

(2)   on conviction on indictment to a fine or imprisonment for a term not exceeding 10 years, or both (s 107(4)(b)).

18.215   CDPA 1988, s 107(4A) provides that a person guilty of an offence under s 107(2A) is liable:

(1)   on summary conviction to imprisonment for a term not exceeding 3 months or a fine not exceeding the statutory maximum, or both (s 107(4A)(a)); and

(2)   on conviction on indictment to a fine or imprisonment for a term not exceeding 2 years, or both (s 107(4A)(b)).

18.216   CDPA 1988, s 107(5) provides that a person guilty of any other offence under s 107 is liable on summary conviction to imprisonment for a term not exceeding 6 months or a fine not exceeding level 5 on the standard scale, or both.

18.217   CDPA 1988, s 107(6) provides that the presumptions in ss 104 and 105[44] which apply in civil cases do not apply in criminal proceedings under s 107.

18.218   The mens rea for criminal infringement under s 107 is of an objective standard.

18.219   As well as the above criminal remedies there are provisions in CDPA 1988, s 108 for the court when hearing a s 107 offence to order the delivery up of an infringing copy or article, for the police under s 109 to obtain a search warrant to look for infringing material relating to offences under s 107(1), (2) or (2A) and for a constable in executing a warrant under s 107(1), (2) or (2A) to seize an article if he reasonably believes that any offence under s 107(1), (2) or (2A) has been or is about to be committed.

18.220   There are other offences which may apply, inter alia, CDPA 1988, s 110 relating to the liability of officers of a company, and under the Trades Descriptions Act 1968 and the Trade Marks Act 1994. These and any other offences are beyond the scope of this book.

---

[44]   For ss 104 and 105 see **18.200–18.201**.

Chapter 19

MORAL RIGHTS

19.1   Moral rights are a European concept which have been incorporated into English law by the Copyright, Designs and Patents Act 1988 (CDPA 1988) with the intention of protecting the creative process. Moral rights under the Act originally protected the author of a work and protected the privacy of certain photographs and films.[1] By virtue of the Performances (Moral Rights, etc) Regulations 2006[2] moral rights protection has been extended in CDPA 1988 to protect the performers of a work.[3]

19.2   Moral rights are dealt with in Part I of CDPA 1988, which deals with copyright, and in Part II, which deals with rights in performances.

19.3   As we have seen earlier the author, if he is the owner of the work, can licence or assign the copyright. CDPA 1988, s 94 provides that moral rights cannot be assigned by the author. They can, however, be waived by the author.[4]

WHAT ARE MORAL RIGHTS?

19.4   CDPA 1988 provides for four moral rights and two performers' moral rights. These are:

(1)   a paternity right (the right to be identified as the author or director) (s 77);

(2)   an integrity right (the right to object to derogatory treatment of a work) (s 80);

(3)   a right to object to the false attribution of a work (s 84);

(4)   the right to privacy of certain photographs and films (s 85);

(5)   a right to be identified as the performer (s 205C);[5] and

(6)   a right to object to derogatory treatment of a performance (s 205F).[6]

---

[1]   For the author of a work see Chapter 18 at **18.37** et seq and **18.39** et seq.
[2]   SI 2006/18.
[3]   For performers see Chapter 20; for performers' moral rights see Chapter 22.
[4]   See **19.43** et seq.
[5]   For s 205C see Chapter 22.
[6]   For s 205F see Chapter 22.

19.5   CDPA 1988, s 86 deals with the duration of moral rights. The paternity right, the integrity right and the right to privacy of certain photographs last for as long as copyright exists in the work (s 86(1)). The right to object to false attribution lasts until 20 years after a person's death (s 86(2)).[7]

THE RIGHT TO BE IDENTIFIED AS THE AUTHOR – THE PATERNITY RIGHT

19.6   CDPA 1988, s 77(1) provides that the author of a copyright literary, dramatic, musical or artistic work, and the director of a copyright film, has the right to be identified as the author or director of the work but the right is not infringed unless it has been asserted in accordance with s 78.[8]

19.7   CDPA 1988, s 77(2) provides that the author of a literary work (other than words intended to be sung or spoken with music) or a dramatic work has the right to be identified whenever:

(1)   the work is published commercially, performed in public or communicated to the public (s 77(2)(a)); or

(2)   copies of a film or sound recording including the work are issued to the public (s 77(2)(b)),

and that right includes the right to be identified whenever any of those events occur in relation to an adaptation of the work as the author of the work from which the adaptation was made.

19.8   CDPA 1988, s 77(3) provides that the author of a musical work, or a literary work consisting of words intended to be sung or spoken with music, has the right to be identified whenever:

(1)   the work is published commercially (s 77(3)(a));

(2)   copies of a sound recording of the work are issued to the public (s 77(3)(b)); or

(3)   a film of which the sound-track includes the work is shown in public or copies of such a film are issued to the public (s 77(3)(c)),

and that right includes the right to be identified whenever any of those events occur in relation to an adaptation of the work as the author of the work from which the adaptation was made.

19.9   CDPA 1988, s 77(4) provides that the author of an artistic work has the right to be identified whenever:

(1)   the work is published commercially or exhibited in public, or a visual image of it is communicated to the public (s 77(4)(a)); or

---

[7]   See also **19.42**. For the duration of the performers' moral rights see Chapter 22.
[8]   For s 78 see **19.15–19.17**.

(2)   a film including a visual image of the work is shown in public or copies of such a film are issued to the public (s 77(4)(b)).

19.10 CDPA 1988, s 77(4)(c) deals with a work of architecture and is beyond the scope of this book.

19.11 CDPA 1988, s 77(6) provides that the director of a film has the right to be identified whenever the film is shown in public or communicated to the public or copies of the film are issued to the public.

19.12 CDPA 1988, s 77(7) provides that the author or director has the right:

(1)   in the case of commercial publication or the issue to the public of copies of a film or sound recording, to be identified in or on each copy or, if that is not appropriate, in some other manner likely to bring his identity to the notice of a person acquiring a copy (s 77(7)(a)); or

(2)   in any other case, to be identified in a manner likely to bring his identity to the attention of a person seeing or hearing the performance, exhibition, showing or communication to the public in question (s 77(7)(c)),

and the identification must in each case be clear and reasonably prominent.

19.13 CDPA 1988, s 77(7)(b) deals with identification on a building and is beyond the scope of this book.

19.14 Some writers or directors work under a pseudonym or initials. In such a case CDPA 1988, s 77(8) provides that the identification of the author or director will be the pseudonym, initials of other form of identification he uses. If he is not identified in this way the subsection allows for any other reasonable form of identification to be used to show that he is the author or director.

19.15 It is important to note that CDPA 1988, ss 77(1) and 78(1) provide that although there is a paternity right it is only infringed where the author or director has asserted his right. Assertion is usually achieved by inserting a clause into the document assigning the copyright. If such a clause is inserted into the assignment, s 78(4)(a) provides that the assignee and anyone claiming through him is bound by it, whether or not he knew of the assertion. It is possible to make the assertion by letter from the author or director to the person permitted to deal with the work. If a letter is written asserting the paternity right, s 78(4)(b) provides that the persons bound by it are anyone to whose notice the assertion is brought.

19.16 A sensible writer or director will almost always want to assert his paternity right and will want a note of his paternity right inserted in every copy of the work.

19.17 It should be noted that the paternity right may also be asserted where there is a public exhibition of an artistic work. This is dealt with in CDPA 1988, s 78(3)(a) and (b) and (4)(c) and (d). This is beyond the scope of this book.

19.18 The paternity right does not apply or is not infringed in certain cases listed in CDPA 1988, s 79. These include:

(1)   where anything is done by or with the authority of the copyright owner where the copyright in the work originally vested in the author's or director's employer by virtue of s 11(2)[9] (s 79(3));

(2)   where copyright would not be infringed by virtue of, for example:
      (a)   s 30, fair dealing so far as it relates to reporting current events by means of a sound recording, film or broadcast[10] (s 79(4)(a)); and
      (b)   s 31, incidental inclusion of a work in an artistic work, sound recording, film, or broadcast[11] (s 79(4)(b));

(3)   where any work is made for the purpose of reporting current events (s 79(5)); and

(4)   the publication in:
      (a)   a newspaper, magazine or similar periodical (s 79(6)(a)); or
      (b)   an encyclopaedia, dictionary, yearbook or other collective work of reference (s 79(6)(b)),
      of a literary, dramatic, musical or artistic work made for the purposes of such publication or made available with the consent of the author for the purposes of such publication.

THE RIGHT TO OBJECT TO DEROGATORY TREATMENT – THE INTEGRITY RIGHT

19.19   CDPA 1988, s 80(1) provides that the author of a copyright literary, dramatic, musical or artistic work, and the director of a copyright film, has the right in certain circumstances not to have his work subjected to derogatory treatment.

19.20   The 'treatment' of a work is defined in CDPA 1988, s 80(2)(a) as any addition to, deletion from or alteration to or adaptation of the work other than:

(1)   a translation of a literary or dramatic work (s 80(2)(a)(i)); or

(2)   an arrangement or transcription of a musical work involving no more than a change of key or register (s 80(2)(a)(ii)).

19.21   Under CDPA 1988, s 80(2)(b) a treatment of a work is derogatory if it amounts to a distortion or mutilation of the work or is otherwise prejudicial to the honour or reputation of the author or director.

19.22   CDPA 1988, s 80(3) provides that in the case of a literary, dramatic or musical work the right is infringed by someone who:

(1)   publishes commercially, performs in public or communicates to the public a derogatory treatment of the work (s 80(3)(a)); or

---

[9]   For s 11(2) see Chapter 18 at **18.50** et seq.
[10]   For s 30 see Chapter 18 at **18.149** et seq.
[11]   For s 31 see Chapter 18 at **18.163** et seq.

(2)   issues to the public copies of a film or sound recording of, or including, a derogatory treatment of the work (s 80(3)(b)).

19.23 CDPA 1988, s 80(4) provides that in the case of an artistic work the right is infringed by a person who:

(1)   publishes commercially or exhibits in public a derogatory treatment of the work, or communicates to the public a visual image of a derogatory treatment of the work (s 80(4)(a)); or

(2)   shows in public a film including a visual image of a derogatory treatment of the work or issues to the public copies of such a film (s 80(4)(b)).

19.24 CDPA 1988, s 80(4)(c) deals with, inter alia, works of architecture in the form of a model for a building and is beyond the scope of this book.

19.25 CDPA 1988, s 80(6) provides that in the case of a film the right is infringed by a person who:

(1)   shows in public or communicates to the public a derogatory treatment of the film (s 80(6)(a)); or

(2)   issues to the public copies of a derogatory treatment of the film (s 80(6)(b)).

19.26 It should be noted that by virtue of CDPA 1988, s 80(7) the right to object to derogatory treatment of a work extends to the treatment of parts of a work resulting from a previous treatment by a person other than the author or director, if those parts are attributed to, or are likely to be regarded as the work of, the author or director.

19.27 CDPA 1988, s 83(1) provides that the right is also infringed by a person who:

(1)   possesses in the course of a business (s 83(1)(a));

(2)   sells or lets for hire, or offers or exposes for sale or hire (s 83(1)(b));

(3)   in the course of a business exhibits in public or distributes (s 83(1)(c)); or

(4)   distributes other than in the course of a business so as to affect prejudicially the honour or reputation of the author or director (s 83(1)(d)),

an article which is, and which he knows, or has reason to believe is, an infringing article.

19.28 The right to object to derogatory treatment does not apply or is not infringed in certain cases listed in CDPA 1988, s 81. These include:

(1)   where any work is made for the purpose of reporting current events (s 80(3));

(2)   the publication in:
    (a)   a newspaper, magazine or similar periodical (s 81(4)(a)); or
    (b)   an encyclopaedia, dictionary, yearbook or other collective work of reference (s 81(4)(b)),

of a literary, dramatic, musical or artistic work made for the purposes of such publication or made available with the consent of the author for the purposes of such publication. Nor does the right apply in relation to any subsequent exploitation elsewhere of such a work without any modification of the published version; and

(3)   where in the case of the BBC anything is done for the purpose of avoiding the inclusion in a programme broadcast by it of anything which offends against good taste or decency or which is likely to encourage or incite to crime or to lead to disorder or to be offensive to public feeling, provided where the author or director is identified at the time of the relevant act or has previously been identified in or on published copies of the work, that there is sufficient disclaimer (s 81(6)(c)).

19.29 CDPA 1988, s 82(1)(a) provides that where copyright originally vested in the author's or director's employer by virtue of s 11(2)[12] that under s 82(2) the right to object to derogatory treatment does not apply to anything done in relation to such a work by or with the authority of the copyright owner unless the author or director:

(a)   is identified at the time of the relevant act (s 82(2)(a)); or

(b)   has previously been identified in or on published copies of the work (s 82(2)(b)),

and where in such a case the right does apply, it is not infringed if there is a sufficient disclaimer.

19.30 In the case of *Morrison Leahy Music Ltd and another v Lightband Limited*[13] George Michael obtained an injunction to stop the release of a megamix of some of his songs. He argued that as the author of the songs he had suffered derogatory treatment in the megamix. The case did not get to trial although at an interlocutory hearing the judge agreed that George Michael had an arguable case that his work had been subject to derogatory treatment.

THE RIGHT TO OBJECT TO FALSE ATTRIBUTION OF A WORK

19.31 CDPA 1988, s 84(1) provides that a person has the right:

(1)   not to have a literary, dramatic, musical or artistic work falsely attributed to him as author (s 84(1)(a)); and

(2)   not to have a film falsely attributed to him as director (s 84(1)(b)).

19.32 Attribution is defined in CDPA 1988, s 84(1) as 'a statement (express or implied) as to who is the author or director'.

---

[12]   For s 11(2) see Chapter 18 at **18.50**.
[13]   [1992] 1 Ent LR.

19.33 CDPA 1988, s 84(2) provides that the right is infringed by a person who:

(1) issues to the public copies of a work of any of those descriptions in or on which there is a false attribution (s 84(2)(a)); or

(2) exhibits in public an artistic work, or a copy of an artistic work, in or on which there is a false attribution (s 84(2)(b)).

19.34 CDPA 1988, s 84(3) provides that the right is infringed by a person who:

(1) in the case of a literary, dramatic or musical work, by a person who performs the work in public, or communicates it to the public as being the work of a person (s 84(3)(a)); or

(2) in the case of a film, shows it in public, or communicates it to the public as being directed by a person (s 84(3)(b)),

knowing or having reason to believe the attribution to be false.

19.35 CDPA 1988, s 84(4) provides that the right is also infringed by the issue to the public or public display of material containing a false attribution in connection with any of the acts mentioned in s 84(2) or (3).

19.36 CDPA 1988, s 84(5) states that the right is also infringed by a person who in the course of a business:

(1) possesses or deals with a copy of a work of any of the descriptions mentioned in s 84(1) in or on which there is a false attribution (s 84(5)(a)); or

(2) in the case of an artistic work, possesses or deals with the work itself when there is a false attribution in or on it (s 84(5)(b)),

knowing or having reason to believe that there is such an attribution and that it is false.

19.37 CDPA 1988, s 84(6) provides that in the case of an artistic work the right is also infringed by a person who in the course of a business:

(1) deals with a work which has been altered after the author parted with possession of it as being the unaltered work of the author (s 84(6)(a)); or

(2) deals with a copy of such a work as being a copy of the unaltered work of the author (s 84(6)(b)),

knowing or having reason to believe that that is not the case.

19.38 CDPA 1988, s 84(7) provides that references to dealing are references to selling or letting for hire, offering or exposing for sale or hire, exhibiting in public or distributing.

19.39 CDPA 1988, s 84 applies where contrary to the fact:

(1) a literary, dramatic or musical work is falsely represented as being an adaptation of the work of a person (s 84(8)(a)); or

(2) a copy of an artistic work is falsely represented as being a copy made by the author of the artistic work (s 84(8)(b)),

as it applies where the work is falsely attributed to the person as author.

RIGHT TO PRIVACY OF CERTAIN PHOTOGRAPHS AND FILMS

19.40 CDPA 1988, s 85(1) provides that a person who for private and domestic purposes commissions the taking of a photograph or the making of a film has, where copyright subsists in the resulting work, the right not to have:

(1) copies of the work issued to the public (s 85(1)(a));

(2) the work exhibited or shown in public (s 85(1)(b)); or

(3) the work communicated to the public,

and except as mentioned in s 85(2), a person who does or authorises the doing of any of those acts infringes that right.

19.41 The right to privacy of certain photographs and films is not infringed in certain cases listed in CDPA 1988, s 85(2). This includes where there is an incidental inclusion of the work in an artistic work, film or broadcast (s 85(2)(a)).

DURATION OF MORAL RIGHTS

19.42 CDPA 1988, s 86 deals with the duration of moral rights. As mentioned earlier,[14] the paternity right, the integrity right and the right to privacy of certain photographs last for as long as copyright exists in the work (s 86(1)). The right to object to false attribution lasts until 20 years after a person's death (s 86(2)).

CONSENT AND WAIVER

19.43 CDPA 1988, s 87(1) provides that it is not an infringement of moral rights to do any act to which the person entitled to the right has consented.

19.44 CDPA 1988, s 87(2) provides that any moral rights can be waived in writing signed by the person giving up the right.

---

[14] See **19.4–19.5**.

19.45 A waiver may relate to a specific work, to works of a specified description or to works generally and may also relate to existing or future works (s 87(3)(a)). A waiver may also be conditional or unconditional and may be expressed to be subject to revocation (s 87(3)(b)). Section 87(3) also provides that if a waiver is made in favour of the owner or the prospective owner of the copyright in the work or works to which it relates that it is presumed to extend to his licensees and successors in title unless a contrary intention is expressed.

19.46 CDPA 1988, s 87(4) allows for the possibility of an informal waiver, in which case the general law of contract or estoppel will apply. Notwithstanding s 87(4), for the sake of clarity any waiver should be recorded in writing and signed by the person waiving the rights, for example, if the author agreed to a waiver it would be included in the document effecting a copyright assignment.

JOINT AUTHORS

19.47 CDPA 1988, s 88 deals with joint authors and moral rights.

Joint authors and the paternity right

19.48 CDPA 1988, s 88(1) provides that the paternity right where there is a work of joint authorship is a right of each joint author to be identified as a joint author. Each joint author must assert the right to be identified in relation to himself.

Joint authors and the integrity right

19.49 CDPA 1988, s 88(2) provides that the integrity right where there is a work of joint authorship is a right of each joint author. An author's integrity right is satisfied if he consents to the treatment of the work.

19.50 CDPA 1988, s 88(3) provides that a waiver under s 87 of the rights by one joint author does not affect the rights of the other joint authors.

Joint authors and false attribution

19.51 CDPA 1988, s 88(4) provides that the right of false attribution is infringed:

(1)   by any false statement as to the authorship of a work of joint authorship (s 88(4)(a)); and

(2)   by the false attribution of joint authorship in relation to a work of sole authorship (s 88(4)(b)),

and such a false attribution infringes the right of every person to whom authorship of any description is, whether rightly or wrongly, attributed.

19.52 CDPA 1988, s 88(5) provides that the provisions of s 88 also apply (with any necessary adaptations) in relation to a film which was, or is alleged to have been, jointly directed, as they apply to a work which is, or is alleged to be, a work of joint authorship.

19.53 CDPA 1988, s 88(5) further provides that a film is 'jointly directed' if it is made by the collaboration of two or more directors and the contribution of each director is not distinct from that of the other director or directors.

19.54 CDPA 1988, s 88(6) provides that the right to privacy of certain photographs and films is, in the case of a work made in pursuance of a joint commission, a right of each person who commissioned the making of the work, so that:

(1)   the right of each is satisfied if they consent to the act in question (s 88(6)(a)); and

(2)   a waiver under s 87 by one of them does not affect the rights of the others (s 88(6)(b)).

PART OF A WORK

19.55 CDPA 1988, s 89(1) provides that the paternity right and the right to privacy of certain photographs and films applies in relation to the whole or a substantial part of a work.

19.56 CDPA 1988, s 89(2) provides that the integrity right and the right to object to false attribution applies in relation to the whole or to any part of a work.

REMEDIES

19.57 The remedies available for infringing moral rights are set out in CDPA 1988, s 103(1) and (2).

19.58 Under CDPA 1988, s 103(1) an infringement of a moral right is actionable as a breach of a statutory duty owed to the person entitled to that right. An infringement will enable the author to seek damages and an injunction.

19.59 CDPA 1988, s 103(2) deals with the integrity right and provides that the court may, if it thinks it is an adequate remedy, grant an injunction prohibiting the doing of any act unless a disclaimer is made, in such terms and in such a manner as may be approved by the court, disassociating the author or director from the treatment of the work.

MORAL RIGHTS ON THE DEATH OF THE AUTHOR

19.60 CDPA 1988, s 95(1) deals with what happens to the paternity and integrity rights and the right to privacy of certain photographs and films on the death of a person entitled to the right(s). Section 95(1)(a) allows the person entitled to the right(s) to leave them as a specific bequest under his will. If there is no such bequest of these rights then, under s 95(1)(b), if the copyright in the work forms part of the estate, these rights belong to the person to whom the copyright passes. Where these rights do not pass under s 95(1)(a) or (b) then, by virtue of s 95(1)(c), they are exercisable by the deceased's personal representatives.

19.61 CDPA 1988, s 95(2) provides that where copyright forming part of a person's estate passes in part to one person and in part to another, where, for example, a bequest is limited so as to apply:

(1)   to one or more, but not all, of the things the copyright owner has the exclusive right to do or authorise (s 95(2)(a));[15] or

(2)   to part, but not the whole, of the period for which copyright is to subsist (s 95(2)(b)),[16]

any right which passes with the copyright by virtue of s 95(1) is correspondingly divided.

19.62 CDPA 1988, s 95(3) provides that where by virtue of s 95(1)(a) or (b) a right becomes exercisable by more than one person:

(1)   it may in the case of the paternity right,[17] be asserted by any of them (s 95(3)(a));

(2)   it is, in the case of the integrity right[18] or the right to privacy of certain photographs and films,[19] a right exercisable by each of them and is satisfied in relation to any of them if he consents to the treatment or act in question (s 95(3)(b)); and

(3)   any waiver[20] of the right in accordance with s 87 by one of them does not affect the rights of the others (s 95(3)(c)).

19.63 CDPA 1988, s 95(4) provides that a consent or waiver previously given or made binds any person to whom a right passes under s 95(1).

19.64 CDPA 1988, s 95(5) provides that any infringement after a person's death relating to a false attribution of a work is actionable by the deceased's personal representatives.

19.65 CDPA 1988, s 95(6) provides that any damages recovered by the deceased's personal representatives for infringement of moral rights after a person's death will pass as part of the estate as if the right of action had subsisted in the person immediately before his death.

CONCLUSION

19.66 In any contractual negotiations for an assignment or licence of copyright, the author/director will want to assert his paternity right and will not want to waive his other moral rights. The assignee or licensee will usually be prepared for the author/director to assert his paternity right (or will require the author/director to waive his statutory paternity right and replace it with a similar contractual right) but will usually require the author/director to waive his other moral rights.

---

[15]   See Chapter 18.
[16]   See Chapter 18.
[17]   For paternity right (s 77) see **19.6** et seq.
[18]   For integrity right (s 80) see **19.19** et seq.
[19]   For right to privacy of certain photographs and films (s 85) see **19.40–19.41**.
[20]   For waiver (s 87) see **19.43** et seq.

19.67   Moral rights are a valuable protection for the author/director. They advertise and protect the author/director's image and professional reputation and should certainly not be regarded as something that is to be given away lightly. Most if not all authors/directors will want to assert their statutory paternity right and they should only agree not to do so where the contractual right on offer is as good as the statutory protection they would have if they were to assert their right under CDPA 1988. As for the other moral rights which an author/director has he should only waive these where he is satisfied that the contractual rights being offered in their place are sufficient to protect his image and reputation. There certainly may be valid reasons why an assignee or licensee may want an author/director to waive his statutory moral rights, in which case the assignee or licensee should offer in their place contractual provisions which adequately replace the statutory rights which the author/director is being asked to waive.

Chapter 20

RIGHTS IN PERFORMANCES

INTRODUCTION AND DEFINITIONS

20.1　As we have seen earlier, the Copyright, Designs and Patents Act 1988 (CDPA 1988) creates copyright protection for a composition consisting of words and music and for a sound recording of a composition. We have also seen that CDPA 1988 protects the author(s) of a composition consisting of words and music by giving the author(s) moral rights. CDPA 1988 also protects:

(1)　the right for performers to consent to the exploitation of their performances (ss 182, 182A, 182B, 182C, 182CA, 183 and 184 detail the different ways in which a performance can be exploited, each of which requires the performer's consent);[1] and

(2)　the performer's moral rights, namely a right to be identified as the performer (s 205C) and a right to object to derogatory treatment of a performance (s 205F);[2] and

(3)　the person, which is usually a record company, who has an exclusive recording contract with a performer, by giving that person rights in the performer's performances (ss 185, 186, 187 and 188 detail these rights).[3]

20.2　CDPA 1988, s 180(1)(a) provides that the consent of the performer is needed to exploit his performances.

20.3　CDPA 1988, s 180(1A) further provides that moral rights are also conferred on the performer, namely a right to be identified as the performer (s 205C) and a right to object to derogatory treatment of a performance (s 205F).[4]

20.4　CDPA 1988, ss 182, 182A, 182B, 182C, 182CA, 183 and 184 detail the different ways in which a performance can be exploited, each of which requires the performer's consent.[5] The necessary consents required under these sections will be given by the performer in the recording contract with his record company, or where a session musician appears on a record the necessary consents will be given by the session musician in the session musician contract with the record company. (The session musician contract that will generally be used will be the standard session musician contract which was agreed by the Musician's Union and British Phonographic Industry Limited.)

---

[1]　See Chapter 21 for these sections.
[2]　For ss 205C and 205F see Chapter 22.
[3]　For ss 185, 186, 187 and 188 see Chapter 21 at **21.58** et seq.
[4]　For ss 205C and 205F see Chapter 22.
[5]　See Chapter 21 for these sections.

20.5   CDPA 1988, s 180(1)(b) provides that the person who has recording rights in relation to a performance, for example, a record company, has rights in relation to recordings made without his consent or the consent of the performer. To be entitled to such rights the person who has recording rights in relation to a performance must have an exclusive recording contract with the performer. CDPA 1988, ss 185–188 deal with the rights of the person having recording rights.[6]

20.6   A 'performance' is defined in CDPA 1988, s 180(2) as:

(1)   a dramatic performance (which includes dance and mime);

(2)   a musical performance;

(3)   a reading or recitation of a literary work; or

(4)   a performance of a variety act or any similar presentation, which is, or so far as it is, a live performance given by one or more individuals.

20.7   The word live is used in the widest sense and includes a performance in concert before an audience or it could a performance in private in the confines of a recording studio. There is no definition of performer in CDPA 1988, but anybody who gives a performance under s 180(2) will be regarded as a performer, for example, a singer, session musicians and musicians in a group.

20.8   CDPA 1988, s 180(2) provides that a 'recording' in relation to a performance means a film or sound recording:

(1)   made directly from the live performance;

(2)   made from a broadcast of the performance; or

(3)   made, directly or indirectly, from another recording of the performance.

20.9   CDPA 1988, s 180(4)(a) stresses that the rights in a performance are independent of any copyright or moral rights that may exist.

20.10   CDPA 1988, s 181 provides that a performance is a qualifying performance in relation to performer's rights if it is given by a qualifying individual or takes place in a qualifying country.

20.11   A qualifying country is defined in CDPA 1988, s 206(1) and includes:

(1)   the UK;

(2)   another member state of the EC; and

(3)   a country where an Order in Council is made under s 208 acknowledging reciprocal protection of performers' rights.

---

6   See Chapter 21 at **21.58** et seq.

20.12 This will include:

(1)   a Convention country (s 208(1)(a)); and

(2)   a country as to which Her Majesty is satisfied that provision has been or will be made under its law giving adequate protection for British performances (s 208(1)(b)).

20.13 CDPA 1988, s 208(2) defines a Convention country as a country which is a party to a convention relating to performers' rights to which the UK is also a party.

20.14 CDPA 1988, s 208(3)(a) and (b) defines a British performance as a performance given by an individual who is a British citizen or resident in the UK, or a performance which takes place in the UK.

20.15 A qualifying individual is defined in CDPA 1988, s 206(1) as a citizen or subject of, or an individual resident in, a qualifying country. Section 206(2) further provides that the reference in the definition of 'qualifying individual' to a person being a citizen or subject of a qualifying country shall be construed:

(1)   in relation to the UK, as a reference to his being a British citizen; and

(2)   in relation to a colony of the UK, as a reference to his being a British overseas territories citizen by connection with that colony.

20.16 A qualifying person is defined in CDPA 1988, s 206(1) as a qualifying individual or a body corporate or other body having legal personality which:

(1)   is formed under the law of a part of the UK or another qualifying country; and

(2)   has in any qualifying country a place of business at which substantial business activity is carried on.

20.17 CDPA 1988, s 206(3) provides that in determining for the purpose of the definition of 'qualifying person' whether substantial business activity is carried on at a place of business in any country, no account shall be taken of dealings in goods which are at all material times outside that country.

Chapter 21

PERFORMERS' RIGHTS AND INFRINGEMENT OF A PERFORMER'S RIGHTS

21.1   The Performances (Moral Rights, etc) Regulations 2006,[1] which amended the Copyright, Designs and Patents Act 1988 (CDPA 1988) make clear that the rights set out in Ch 2 of Pt II of the Act in ss 182–205B are 'Economic Rights'. Part II of CDPA 1988 deals with rights in performances. A performer's rights are infringed by a person who, without the consent of the performer:

(1)   makes a recording of the whole or any substantial part of a qualifying performance directly from the live performance (s 182(1)(a));

(2)   broadcasts live the whole or any substantial part of a qualifying performance (s 182(1)(b));

(3)   makes a recording of the whole or any substantial part of a qualifying performance directly from a broadcast of the live performance (s 182(1)(c));[2]

(4)   makes a copy of a recording of the whole or any substantial part of a qualifying performance (s 182A(1));[3]

(5)   issues to the public copies of a recording of the whole or any substantial part of a qualifying performance (s 182B(1));[4]

(6)   rents or lends to the public copies of a recording of the whole or any substantial part of a qualifying performance (s 182C(1)) (this is referred to as the 'rental right' and the 'lending right');[5]

(7)   makes available to the public a recording of the whole or any substantial part of a qualifying performance by electronic transmission in such a way that members of the public may access the recording from a place and at a time individually chosen by them (s 182CA);[6]

(8)   either:
      (a)   shows or plays in public the whole or any substantial part of a qualifying performance (s 183(a)); or

---

[1]   SI 2006/18.
[2]   For s 182(1)(a)–(c) see **21.2**.
[3]   See **21.3**.
[4]   See **21.5** et seq.
[5]   See **21.9** et seq.
[6]   See **21.16**.

(b)   communicates to the public the whole or any substantial part of a qualifying performance, (s 183(b)),

by means of a recording which was, and which that person knows or has reason to believe was, made without the performer's consent;[7] or

(9)   either:

(a)   imports into the UK other than for his private and domestic use (s 184(1)(a)); or

(b)   in the course of a business possesses, sells or lets for hire, offers or exposes for sale or hire, or distributes (s 184(1)(b)),

a recording of a qualifying performance which is, and which that person knows or has reason to believe is, an illicit recording.[8]

21.2   CDPA 1988, s 182(3) provides that damages for infringement under s 182(1)(a), (b) and (c) will not be awarded where the defendant can show that at the time of the infringement he believed on reasonable grounds that consent had been given.

21.3   CDPA 1988, s 182A(1A) provides that making a copy of a recording includes making a copy which is transient or is incidental to some other use of the original recording. Section 182A(2) provides that it is immaterial whether the copy is made directly or indirectly.

21.4   CDPA 1988, s 182A(3) provides that the right of a performer to authorise or prohibit the making of such copies is the 'reproduction right'.

21.5   CDPA 1988, s 182B(2) provides that references to the issue to the public of copies of a recording are to:

(1)   the act of putting into circulation in the EEA copies not previously put into circulation in the EEA by or with the consent of the performer (s 182B(2)(a)); or

(2)   the act of putting into circulation outside the EEA copies not previously put into circulation in the EEA or elsewhere (s 182B(2)(b)).

21.6   CDPA 1988, s 182B(3) provides that references to the issue to the public of copies of a recording do not include:

(1)   any subsequent distribution, sale, hiring or loan of copies previously put into circulation[9] (s 182B(3)(a));[10] or

(2)   any subsequent importation of such copies into the UK or another EEA state (s 182B(3)(b)),

except so far as s 182B(2)(a) applies to putting into circulation in the EEA copies previously put into circulation outside the EEA.

---

7   See **21.17** et seq.
8   See **21.17** et seq.
9   But see s 182C.
10   Also see below for s 182C.

21.7   CDPA 1988, s 182B(4) provides that references to the issue of live copies of a performance include the issue of the original recording of the live performance.

21.8   CDPA 1988, s 182B(5) provides that the right of a performer to authorise or prohibit the issue of copies to the public is 'the distribution right'.

21.9   CDPA 1988, s 182C(2)(a) provides that 'rental' means making a copy of a recording available for use, on terms that it will or may be returned, for direct or indirect economic or commercial advantage.

21.10   CDPA 1988, s 182C(2)(b) provides that 'lending' means making a copy of a recording available for use, on terms that it will or may be returned, otherwise than for direct or indirect economic or commercial advantage, through an establishment which is accessible to the public.

21.11   CDPA 1988, s 182C(3) provides that 'rental' and 'lending' does not include:

(1)   making available for the purpose of public performance, playing or showing in public or communication to the public (s 182C(3)(a));

(2)   making available for the purpose of exhibition in public (s 182C(3)(b)); or

(3)   making available for on-the-spot reference use (s 182C(3)(c)).

21.12   CDPA 1988, s 182C(4) also provides that 'lending' does not include making available between establishments which are accessible to the public.

21.13   CDPA 1988, s 182C(5) provides that where lending by an establishment accessible to the public gives rise to a payment the amount of which does not go beyond what is necessary to cover the operating costs of the establishment, there is no direct or indirect economic or commercial advantage for the purposes of s 182C.

21.14   CDPA 1988, s 182C(6) provides that references to the rental or lending of copies of a recording of a performance include the rental or lending of the original recording of the live performance.

21.15   CDPA 1988, s 182C(7) provides that:

(1)   'rental right' means the right of a performer to authorise or prohibit the rental of copies to the public; and

(2)   'lending right' the right of a performer to authorise or prohibit the lending of copies to the public.

21.16   CDPA 1988, s 182CA(2) provides that the right of a performer to authorise or prohibit the making available to the public a recording is the 'making available right'.

21.17   CDPA 1988, s 184(2) provides that where an infringement action is brought under s 184, if the defendant can show the illicit recording was innocently acquired by him, or a predecessor in title of his, the only remedy available against him in respect of the infringement is damages not exceeding a reasonable payment in respect of the act complained of.

21.18 CDPA 1988, s 197(2) provides that for the purposes of a performer's rights, a recording of the whole or any substantial part of a performance of his is an illicit recording if it is made, otherwise than for private purposes, without his consent.

21.19 CDPA 1988, s 184(3) provides that 'innocently acquired' under s 184(2) means that the person acquiring the recording did not know and had no reason to believe that it was an illicit recording.

THE WORD 'SUBSTANTIAL'

21.20 CDPA 1988, ss 182, 182A, 182B, 182C, 182CA, 182D and 183 refer to a 'substantial' part of a qualifying performance. There is no definition in the Act of the word 'substantial'. It is likely that 'substantial' will have the same meaning as has been applied by the courts to the word 'substantial' in copyright infringement cases.[11]

DURATION OF PERFORMERS' RIGHTS

21.21 CDPA 1988, s 191(2) provides that the performers' rights expire:

(1)   at the end of the period of 50 years from the end of the calendar year in which the performance takes place (s 191(2)(a)); or

(2)   if during that period a recording of the performance is released, 50 years from the end of the calendar year in which it is released (s 191(2)(b)).

21.22 CDPA 1988, s 191(3) provides that a recording is released when it is first published, played or shown in public or communicated to the public, but in determining whether a recording has been released no account shall be taken of any unauthorised act.

21.23 Where the performer is not a national of an EEA state the duration of his performers' rights is that which the performance is entitled to in the country of which he is a national, provided that this does not exceed the period which would apply under CDPA 1988, s 191(2) and (3). This is provided for in s 191(4). Where the application of s 191(4) would be at variance with an international obligation to which the UK became subject to prior to 29 October 1993, the duration of the rights are as specified in s 191(2) and (3). This is provided for in s 191(5).

---

[11]   See Chapter 18 at **18.91–18.93**.

PERFORMER'S PROPERTY RIGHTS AND NON-PROPERTY RIGHTS

21.24 CDPA 1988, s 191A(1) states that the rights of the performer under ss 182A, 182B, 182C and 182CA are property rights.

21.25 CDPA 1988, s 191A(3) provides that where different persons (whether in consequence of a partial assignment or otherwise) are entitled to different aspects of a performer's property rights in relation to a performance, the rights owner for the purposes of Pt II of CDPA 1988 (Rights in Performances) is the person who is entitled to the aspect of those rights relevant for that purpose.

21.26 CDPA 1988, s 191A(4) provides that where a performer's property rights (or any aspect of them) is owned by more than one person jointly, references for the purposes of Part II CDPA 1988 (Rights in Performances) to the rights owner are to all the owners, so that, in particular, any requirement of the licence of the rights owner requires the licence of all of them.

21.27 CDPA 1988, s 192A(1) states that the rights of the performer under ss 182, 183 and 184 are non-property rights.[12]

Performer's property rights

21.28 CDPA 1988, s 191B(1) provides that a performer's property rights are transmissible by assignment, by testamentary disposition or by operation of the law, as personal or moveable property.

21.29 CDPA 1988, s 191B(2) provides that an assignment or other transmission of a performer's property rights may be partial, that is limited so as to apply:

(1)   to one or more, but not all, of the things which require the consent of the rights owner (s 191B(2)(a)); and

(2)   to part, but not the whole, of the period for which the rights subsist (s 191B(2)(b)).

21.30 CDPA 1988, s 191B(3) states that an assignment of a performer's property rights is not effective unless it is in writing and signed by or on behalf of the assignor. (For a body corporate this will be satisfied by affixing its seal (s 210A).)

21.31 By virtue of CDPA 1988, s 191B(4) a licence granted by the owner of a performer's property rights binds every successor in title to his interest in the rights, except for a purchaser in good faith for valuable consideration and without actual or constructive notice of the licence or a person deriving title from such a purchaser.

21.32 CDPA 1988, s 191C(1) allows for there to be an assignment in the whole or in part of a performer's property rights relating to the future recording of a performance. Such assignment should be signed by or on behalf of the performer. (For a body corporate this will be satisfied by affixing its seal (s 210A).) Section 191C(2) provides that if on the rights coming into existence the assignee or a person claiming under him

---

[12]   For these sections see **21.1**, **21.2**, **21.17** and **21.37**.

would be entitled as against all other persons to require the rights to be vested in him, they will vest in the assignee or his successor in title. Section 191C(3) provides that a licence granted by a prospective owner of a performer's property rights is binding on every successor in title to his interest (or prospective interest) in the rights, except a purchaser in good faith for valuable consideration and without actual or constructive notice of the licence or a person deriving title from such a purchaser. Section 191C(4) provides that a prospective purchaser in relation to a performer's property rights means a person who is prospectively entitled to those rights by virtue of such an agreement as is referred to in s 191C(1).

21.33 CDPA 1988, s 191D allows for an exclusive licence of a performer's property rights to be granted. Section 191D(1) provides that an exclusive licence means a licence in writing signed by or on behalf of the owner of a performer's property rights authorising the licensee to the exclusion of all other persons, including the person granting the licence, to do anything requiring the consent of the rights owner. (For a body corporate this will be satisfied by affixing its seal(s 210A).) Section 191D(2) provides that the licensee under an exclusive licence has the same rights against a successor in title who is bound by the licence as he has against the person granting the licence.

21.34 The provisions of CDPA 1988, s 191E, which deal with whether a performer's property rights in an unpublished original recording passes under a will, and s 191F, which deals with the presumption of the transfer of the rental right in the case of a film production agreement, are beyond the scope of this book.

Performer's non-property rights

21.35 CDPA 1988, s 192A(1) provides that a performer's non-property rights[13] cannot be assigned nor are they transmissible. However, under s 192A(2) on the death of a person entitled to non-property rights, the rights can pass by will to any chosen beneficiary (s 192A(2)(a)) or, if there is no such direction in the will, the rights are exercisable by the deceased's personal representatives (s 192A(2)(b)). Section 192A(4) provides that where by s 192A(2)(a) a right becomes exercisable by more than one person, it is exercisable by each of them independently of the other(s). Any damages which are recoverable by the personal representatives for infringement of a performer's non-property rights after a person's death devolve as part of the estate as if the right of action had subsisted and vested in that person before his death (s 192A(5)).

21.36 CDPA 1988, s 192A(3) provides that references for the purposes of Pt II of CDPA 1988 (Rights in Performances) to the performer, in the context of the person having such right, shall be construed as references to the person for the time being entitled to exercise those rights.

21.37 CDPA 1988, s 193 deals with the issue of consent. The performer's non-property rights are infringed where acts are done without the performer's consent. Section 193(1) provides that consent for non-property rights can be given for a specific performance, a specified description of performances or for performances in general. It is also possible under s 193(1) for consent to relate to past or future performances. Section 193(3) provides that where a performer's non-property right passes to another person, any

---

[13]   For the performer's non-property rights under ss 182, 183 and 184 see Chapter 18.

consent binding on the person previously entitled binds the person to whom the right passes in the same way as if consent had been given by him.

21.38 Consent does not have to be given in writing. Like any permission it is better for it to be recorded in writing so the parties are clear what can and cannot be done. Indeed, consent may have been impliedly given due to the conduct or actions of the performer. To avoid disputes any consents which are required from the performer will be dealt with in a recording agreement between the performer and the record company. All agreements will or should specifically make it clear that the performer agrees to the recording, to making copies of the recording and to the sale of recordings of his performance.

21.39 The question of whether consent has or has not been given can be contrasted by two cases. In the case of *Mad Hat Music v Pulse 8 Records Ltd*[14] it was held that consent given by a performer to make a recording of a performance meant that there was no need for consent to be given by the performer to make records of that performance. In the case of *Bassey v Icon Entertainment*[15] it was held that that consent to make records of a performance was required notwithstanding the fact that consent had been given to the recording of the performance. These cases were decided before the insertion into CDPA 1988 of s 182A, which now makes it clear that the performer's consent is needed to make a copy of a recording of the whole or any substantial part of a qualifying performance.[16] These cases illustrate the point that disputes can arise over whether a performer has given the necessary consent(s) and that a written agreement should specifically detail what the performer is consenting to.

THE RIGHT FOR PERFORMERS TO RECEIVE EQUITABLE REMUNERATION FOR THE EXPLOITATION OF A SOUND RECORDING

21.40 A performer has the right to equitable remuneration where his performance is exploited by way of a sound recording. This is under CDPA 1988, s 182D.

21.41 CDPA 1988, s 182D(1) provides that where a commercially published sound recording of the whole or any substantial part of a qualifying performance is:

(1)   played in public (s 182D(1)(a)); or

(2)   is communicated to the public other than it being made available to the public in the way mentioned in s 182CA(1)[17] (s 182D(1)(b)),

the performer is entitled to equitable remuneration from the owner of the copyright in the sound recording.

---

[14]   [1993] EMLR 172.
[15]   [1995] EMLR 596.
[16]   For s 182A see **21.1**, **21.3** and **21.4**.
[17]   For s 182CA see **21.1** and **21.16**.

21.42 CDPA 1988, s 182D(1A) provides that the reference in s 182D(1) to publication of a sound recording includes making it available to the public by electronic transmission in such a way that members of the public may access it from a place and at a time individually chosen by them.

21.43 By virtue of CDPA 1988, s 182D the record company as the copyright owner in the sound recording will have to pay equitable remuneration to all the performers on the record in the circumstances provided for in s 182D(1)(a) and (b).

21.44 The mechanics of how equitable remuneration is paid by the record company to performers where a sound recording is played in public or is communicated to the public other than where s 182D applies is beyond the scope of this book.

21.45 CDPA 1988, s 182D(2) provides that the right to receive equitable remuneration cannot be assigned by the performer except to a collecting society which will enforce the right on the performer's behalf. Section 182D(2) does, however, allow for the right to receive equitable remuneration to be transmissible by testamentary disposition or by operation of the law as personal or moveable property, and it may be assigned or further transmitted by any person into whose hands it passes. Section 182D(8) provides that for the purposes of s 182D 'collecting society' means a society or other organisation which has as its main object, or one of its main objects, the exercise of the right to equitable remuneration on behalf of more than one performer.

21.46 A discussion of the music industry collecting societies is beyond the scope of this book.

21.47 CDPA 1988, s 182D(3) provides that the amount of equitable remuneration payable is that which is agreed between the parties. The Act does not set out any guidelines as to what constitutes equitable remuneration, although the following sections provide some help to the parties:

(1) s 182D(4), which states that if the parties cannot agree the amount of equitable remuneration that should be paid either party can apply to the Copyright Tribunal to determine the amount that should be paid; and

(2) s 182D(5), which states that where equitable remuneration is payable either party can apply to the Copyright Tribunal to vary any agreement as to the amount payable (s 182D(5)(a)). There is also a provision in s 182D(5) to apply to the Copyright Tribunal to vary any previous decision made by it (s 182D(5)(b)).

21.48 A detailed discussion of the powers of the Copyright Tribunal under CDPA 1988 is beyond the scope of this book.

21.49 There is a provision in CDPA 1988, s 182D(7) that any clause in an agreement between the parties excluding or restricting the right to equitable remuneration (s 182D(7)(a)) or preventing a person questioning the amount of equitable remuneration or restricting the powers of the Copyright Tribunal (s 182D(7)(b)) will have no effect.

THE RIGHT FOR PERFORMERS TO RECEIVE EQUITABLE REMUNERATION WHERE THE S 182C RENTAL RIGHT IN THE SOUND RECORDING HAS BEEN TRANSFERRED

21.50 CDPA 1988, s 191G(1) provides that where a performer has transferred his rental right in a sound recording or a film to the producer of the sound recording or film, the performer retains the right to receive equitable remuneration for the rental. Section 191G(2) provides that the right to equitable remuneration cannot be assigned by the performer except to a collecting society to enable it to enforce the right on his behalf. Section 191G(2) does, however, allow for the right to receive equitable remuneration to be transmissible by testamentary disposition or by operation of the law as personal or moveable property, and that the right to receive equitable remuneration may be assigned or further transmitted by any person into whose hands it passes.

21.51 A discussion of the music industry collecting societies is beyond the scope of this book.

21.52 The person who is liable to pay the equitable remuneration is stated in CDPA 1988, s 191G(3) to be the person who is currently entitled to the rental right. Section 191G(4) provides that the amount of equitable remuneration payable is the amount agreed between the parties, or in default of such agreement then by virtue of s 191H(1) either party can ask the Copyright Tribunal to determine the amount payable. Section 191G(5) provides that any clause in an agreement purporting to exclude or restrict the right to equitable remuneration will have no effect.

21.53 There are also provisions in CDPA 1988, s 191H(2)(a) and (b) where equitable remuneration is payable, for either party to the agreement to apply to the Copyright Tribunal to:

(1)   vary any agreement as to the amount payable (s 191H(2)(a)); or

(2)   vary any previous determination of the Copyright Tribunal as to the amount payable (s 191H(2)(b)).

21.54 CDPA 1988, s 191H(2) also provides that except with special leave of the Copyright Tribunal no such application may be made within 12 months from the date of a previous determination and that an order made under s 191H(2) has effect from the date on which it is made or such later date as may be specified by the Copyright Tribunal.

21.55 CDPA 1988, s 191H(4) provides that the remuneration will not be considered inequitable merely because it was paid by way of a single payment or at the time of the transfer of the rental right.

21.56 CDPA 1988, s 191H(5) provides that an agreement is of no effect in so far as it purports to prevent a person questioning the amount of equitable remuneration or purports to restrict the powers the Copyright Tribunal has under s 191H.

21.57 Save where briefly dealt with, a detailed examination of the workings of and the powers of the Copyright Tribunal under CDPA 1988 are beyond the scope of this book.

EXCLUSIVE RECORDING CONTRACTS AND THE PEOPLE WHO HAVE THE RIGHT TO MAKE RECORDINGS

21.58 As mentioned earlier,[18] CDPA 1988 gives rights to people who have the benefit of an exclusive recording contract with a performer(s), for example, a record company or a production company which signs artists to record exclusively for it.

21.59 CDPA 1988, s 185(1) defines an exclusive recording contract as a contract between a performer and another person under which that person is entitled to the exclusion of all other persons (including the performer) to make recordings of one or more of his performances with a view to their commercial exploitation.

21.60 CDPA 1988, s 185(4) provides that 'with a view to commercial exploitation' means with a view to the recordings being sold or let for hire, or shown or played in public.

21.61 CDPA 1988, s 185(2) provides that the references to 'the person having recording rights' in relation to a performance are (subject to s 185(3)) to a person:

(1) who is a party to and has the benefit of an exclusive recording contract to which the performance is subject (s 185(2)(a)); or

(2) to whom the benefit of such a contract has been assigned (s 185(2)(b)),

and who is a qualifying person.[19]

21.62 CDPA 1988, s 185(3) provides that if a performance is subject to an exclusive recording contract but the person mentioned in s 185(2) is not a qualifying person the references in the Act to 'a person having recording rights' in relation to a performance are to any person:

(1) who is licensed by such a person to make recordings of the performance with a view to their commercial exploitation (s 185(3)(a)); or

(2) to whom the benefit of such a licence has been assigned (s 185(3)(b)),

and who is a qualifying person.[20]

21.63 By virtue of CDPA 1988, s 185(3)(a) if, for example, record company A is not a qualifying person under the Act and has the benefit of an exclusive recording contract with a performer and licences record company B to make recordings of the performer, record company B will be entitled to the rights conferred by CDPA 1988, provided record company B is a qualifying person. Using the same scenario, by virtue of s 185(3)(b), where the benefit of the licence has been assigned by record company B to record company C, record company C will be entitled to the rights conferred by CDPA 1988, provided record company C is a qualifying person.

---

[18]   See also s 180(1)(b) in Chapter 20 at **20.5**.
[19]   For the definition of 'qualifying person' see s 206(1) in Chapter 20 at **20.11–20.12**.
[20]   Ibid.

21.64 CDPA 1988, s 192B(1) provides that the rights of a person having recording rights are not assignable or transmissible. However, s 192B(2) does provide that the provisions of s 192B(1) does not affect s 185(2)(b) or(3)(b) so far as s 185(2)(b) or(3)(b) confer rights on a person to whom the benefit of a contract or licence is assigned. The effect of s 192B(2) is that, for example, an assignee who is a qualified person who has the benefit of an exclusive recording contract will be entitled to the rights conferred by CDPA 1988.

THE RIGHTS OF THE PERSON HAVING RECORDING RIGHTS

21.65 The rights of a person having recording rights in a performance subject to an exclusive contract are infringed where a person does any of the following acts:

(1) Without the consent of the person having recording rights in a performance or the consent of the performer makes a recording of the whole or any substantial part of the performance (s 186(1)).
It is provided in s 186(2) that where there is an action for infringement under s 186(1) damages will not be awarded where a defendant can show that at the time of the infringement he believed on reasonable grounds that consent had been given.

(2) Without the consent of the person having recording rights in a performance or, in the case of a qualifying performance, without the consent of the performer:
(a) shows or plays in public the whole or any substantial part of the performance (s 187(1)(a)); or
(b) communicates to the public the whole or any substantial part of the performance (s 187(1)(b)),
by means of a recording which was, and which that person knows or has reason to believe was made without the appropriate consent.

(3) Without the consent of the person having recording rights in a performance, or in the case of a qualifying performance, without the consent of the performer:
(a) imports into the UK other than for his private and domestic use (s 188(1)(a)); or
(b) in the course of a business possesses, sells or lets for hire, offers or exposes for sale or hire, or distributes (s 188(1)(b)),
a recording of the performance which is, and which that person knows or has reason to believe is, an illicit recording.

21.66 CDPA 1988, s 197(3) provides that for the purposes of the rights of a person having recording rights, a recording of the whole or any substantial part of a performance subject to the exclusive recording contract is an illicit recording if it is made, otherwise than for private purposes, without that person's consent or that of the performer.

21.67 CDPA 1988, s 188(2) provides that where a defendant can show that the illicit recording was innocently acquired by him or a predecessor in title of his, the only remedy available against him in respect of the infringement is damages not exceeding a reasonable payment in respect of the act complained of. Section 188(3) provides that 'innocently acquired' means that the person acquiring the recording did not know and had no reason to believe that it was an illicit recording.

21.68 As mentioned earlier,[21] CDPA 1988, s 193 deals with the issue of consent. The rights of a person who has recording rights are infringed where acts are done without the consent of the person who has the recording rights or are done without the consent of the performer. Section 193(1) provides that consent can be given for a specific performance, a specified description of performances or for performances generally. It is also possible under s 193(1) for consent to relate to past or future performances. Section 193(2) provides that a person having recording rights in a performance is bound by any consent given by a person through whom he derives his rights under the exclusive recording contract or licence, in the same way as if consent had been given by him.

21.69 It should be noted that CDPA 1988, ss 186, 187 and 188[22] require the consent to be given by either the record company or the performer. This means that where the performer gives his consent to the recording of a performance by a third party when he is bound by an exclusive recording contract, the record company will be bound by the consent given by the performer. The record company could, however, sue the performer for breaching his record contract, and it might possibly be able to sue the third party for inducing a breach of contract.

21.70 CDPA 1988, ss 186 and 187 refer to any 'substantial' part of the performance. There is no definition in the Act of the word 'substantial'. It is likely that 'substantial' will have the same meaning as has been applied by the courts to the word 'substantial' in copyright infringement cases.[23]

PERMITTED ACTS/DEFENCES

21.71 As with copyright, performers' rights are by virtue of CDPA 1988, s 189 subject to various permitted acts. Where a permitted act is done this will mean that the performers' rights have not been infringed. The permitted acts are set out in detail in Sch 2 to CDPA 1988. The permitted acts correspond broadly, but not exactly, to the copyright permitted acts.

21.72 The permitted acts in CDPA 1988, Sch 2 include:

(1) fair dealing with a performance or recording for criticism, review and news reporting;

(2) incidental inclusion of a performance or recording;

(3) playing or showing a sound recording, film or broadcast at an educational establishment for the purposes of instruction before an audience consisting of teachers and pupils at the establishment and other persons directly connected with the activities of the establishment;

---

[21] See **21.35** et seq.
[22] For ss 186, 187 and 188 see **21.65** et seq.
[23] For s 16(3) see Chapter 18 at **18.91** et seq.

(4) playing a sound recording as part of the activities of, or for the benefit of, a club, society or other organisation; and

(5) making in domestic premises for private and domestic use a recording of a broadcast solely for the purpose of enabling it to be viewed or listened to at a more convenient time.

21.73 A detailed examination of these and other permitted acts is beyond the scope of this book. The reader is referred to CDPA 1988, Sch 2 (Rights in performance: permitted acts) for full details.

21.74 CDPA 1988, s 190(1) provides that the Copyright Tribunal may, on the application of a person wishing to make a copy of a recording of a performance, give consent where the identity or whereabouts of the person entitled to the reproduction right cannot be ascertained by reasonable inquiry.

21.75 CDPA 1988, s 190(2) provides that consent given by the Copyright Tribunal has effect as the consent of the person entitled to the reproduction right for the purposes of:

(1) the provisions relating to performers' rights (s 190(2)(a)); and

(2) s 198(3)(a) (s 190(2)(b)),

and may be given subject to any conditions specified in the Tribunal's order.[24]

21.76 CDPA 1988, s 190(3) provides that the Copyright Tribunal shall not give consent under s 190(1)(a) except after service or publication of such notices as may be required by rules made under s 150 or as the Copyright Tribunal may in that particular case direct.

21.77 CDPA 1988, s 150 deals with general procedural rules. This is beyond the scope of this book.

21.78 CDPA 1988, s 190(5) requires the Copyright Tribunal to take into account the following factors:

(1) whether the original recording was made with the performer's consent and is lawfully in the possession or control of the person proposing to make the further recording (s 190(5)(a)); and

(2) whether the making of the further recording is consistent with the obligations of the parties to the arrangements under which, or is otherwise consistent with the purposes for which, the original recording was made (s 190(5)(b)).

21.79 CDPA 1988, s 190(6) provides that where the Copyright Tribunal gives consent under s 190 it shall, in default of agreement between the applicant and the person entitled to the reproduction right, make such order as it thinks fit as to the payment to be made to that person in consideration of consent being given.

---

[24] For s 198(3)(a) see **21.109** et seq.

21.80　Save where briefly dealt with, a detailed examination of the workings of and the powers of the Copyright Tribunal under CDPA 1988 are beyond the scope of this book.

REMEDIES FOR INFRINGEMENT OF PERFORMERS' RIGHTS

21.81　Civil and criminal remedies are available where there has been an infringement of a performer's rights.

Civil remedies

21.82　CDPA 1988, s 194 provides that an infringement of a performer's non-property rights (s 194(a)) or any right of a person having recording rights (s 194(b)) is actionable by the person entitled to the right as a breach of statutory duty. An infringement will enable the person entitled to the right to seek damages and an injunction. Also available are an order for delivery up under s 195 and the right to seize illicit recordings under s 196.[25]

21.83　As mentioned earlier, CDPA 1988, s 182(3) provides that damages for infringement under s 182(1)(a), (b) and (c) will not be awarded where the defendant can show that at the time of the infringement he believed on reasonable grounds that consent had been given. Also as mentioned earlier, s 184(2) provides that where an infringement action is brought under s 184, if the defendant can show the illicit recording was innocently acquired by him, or by a predecessor in title of his, the only remedy available against him in respect of the infringement is damages not exceeding a reasonable payment in respect of the act complained of.[26]

21.84　CDPA 1988, s 191I(1) makes it clear that an infringement of a performer's property rights (namely the rights under ss 182A, 182B, 182C and 182CA) is actionable by the rights owner. Section 191I(2) also provides that in an action for infringement of a performer's property rights all such relief by way of damages, injunctions, account of profits or otherwise is available to the claimant as is available in respect of the infringement of any other property right.[27]

21.85　CDPA 1988, s 191J(1) provides that where in an action for infringement of a performer's property rights it is shown that at the time of the infringement the defendant did not know and had no reason to believe that the rights subsisted in the recording to which the action relates, the claimant is not entitled to damages but this is without prejudice to any other remedy.

21.86　CDPA 1988, s 191J(2) provides that the court may in an action for infringement of a performer's property rights, having regard to all the circumstances, and in particular to:

(1)　the flagrancy of the infringement (s 191J(2)(a)); and

(2)　any benefit accruing to the defendant by reason of the infringement (s 191J(2)(b)),

---

[25]　See **21.96** et seq for s 195 and **21.101** et seq for s 196.
[26]　For s 182(1)(a), (b), (c), 182(3) and 184 see **21.1, 21.2** and **21.17**.
[27]　For sections 182A, 182B, 182C and 182CA see **21.1, 21.3, 21.4, 21.5, 21.6, 21.7, 21.8** and **21.9–21.16**.

award such additional damages as the justice of the case may require.

21.87 CDPA 1988, s 191JA(1) provides that the High Court has the power to grant an injunction against a service provider, where that service provider has actual knowledge of another person using its service to infringe a performer's property rights.

21.88 CDPA 1988, s 191JA(2) provides that in determining whether a service provider has actual knowledge for s 191JA(1), a court shall take into account all matters which appear to it in the particular circumstances to be relevant and, amongst other things, shall have regard to:

(1)   whether a service provider has received a notice through a means of contact made available in accordance with reg 6(1)(c) of the Electronic Commerce (EC Directive) Regulations 2002[28] (s 191JA(2)(a)); and

(2)   the extent to which any notice includes:
    (a)   the full name and address of the sender of the notice (s 191JA(2)(b)(i)); and
    (b)   details of the infringement in question (s 191JA(2)(b)(ii)).

21.89 CDPA 1988, s 191JA(3) provides that a 'service provider' has the same meaning given to it by reg 2 of the Electronic Commerce (EC Directive) Regulations 2002.

21.90 An examination of the Electronic Commerce (EC Directive) Regulations 2002 is beyond the scope of this book.

21.91 CDPA 1988, s 191K deals with the situation where in proceedings against a defendant for infringement of a performer's property rights in respect of which a licence is available as of right under CDPA 1988, Sch 2A, para 17 (powers exercisable in consequence of competition report) the defendant undertakes to take a licence on terms. The provisions of s 191K and Sch 2A, para 17 are beyond the scope of this book.

21.92 CDPA 1988, s 191L(1) provides that an exclusive licensee has, except against the owner of a performer's property rights, the same rights and remedies in respect of matters occurring after the grant of the licence as if the licence had been an assignment. Section 191L(2) provides that an exclusive licensee's rights and remedies are concurrent with those of the rights owner. Section 191L(3) provides that in an action brought by an exclusive licensee by virtue of s 191L a defendant may avail himself of any defence which would have been available to him if the action had been brought by the rights owner.

21.93 CDPA 1988, s 191M(1) provides that where an action for infringement of a performer's property rights brought by the rights owner or an exclusive licensee relates (wholly or partly) to an infringement in respect of which they have concurrent rights of action, the rights owner or, as the case may be, the exclusive licensee may not, without leave of the court, proceed with the action unless the other is joined as a claimant or added as a defendant. Section 191M(2) provides that a rights owner or exclusive licensee who is added as a defendant in pursuance of s 191M(1) is not liable for any costs in the action unless he takes part in the proceedings. Section 191M(3) provides that s 191M(1) does not affect the granting of interlocutory relief on an application by the rights owner or exclusive licensee alone.

---

[28]   SI 2002/2013.

21.94 CDPA 1988, s 191M(4) provides that where an action for infringement of a performer's property rights is brought which relates (wholly or partly) to an infringement in respect of which the rights owner and an exclusive licensee have or had concurrent rights of action:

(1)   the court shall in assessing damages take into account:
(a)   the terms of the licence (s 191M(4)(a)(i)); and
(b)   any pecuniary remedy already awarded or available to either of them in respect of the infringement (s 191M(4)(a)(ii));

(2)   no account of profits shall be directed if an award of damages has been made, or an account of profits has been directed, in favour of the other of them in respect of the infringement (s 191M(4)(b)); and

(3)   the court shall if an account of profits is directed apportion the profits between them as the court considers just, subject to any agreement between them (s 191M(4)(c)),

and these provisions apply whether or not the rights owner and the exclusive licensee are both parties to the action.

21.95 CDPA 1988, s 191M(5) provides that the owner of a performer's property rights shall notify any exclusive licensee having concurrent rights before applying for an order under s 195 (order for delivery up) or exercising the right conferred by s 196 (right of seizure); and the court may on the application of the licensee make such order under s 195 or, as the case may be, prohibiting or permitting the exercise by the rights owner of the right conferred by s 196, as it thinks fit having regard to the terms of the licence.[29]

Delivery up

21.96 CDPA 1988, s 195(1) provides that where a person has in his possession, custody or control in the course of a business an illicit recording of a performance, a person having performer's rights or recording rights in relation to the performance may apply to the court for an order that the recording is delivered up to him or to such other person as the court directs.

21.97 CDPA 1988, s 195(2) provides that an application shall not be made after the end of the period specified in s 203; and that no order shall be made unless the court also makes, or it appears to the court that there are grounds for making, an order under s 204.

21.98 CDPA 1988, s 203 deals with the period after which the remedy of delivery up is not available. Section 204 deals with an application to court for an order as to the disposal of an illicit recording of a performance. The details of ss 203 and 204 are beyond the scope of this book.

21.99 CDPA 1988, s 195(3) also provides that a person to whom a recording is delivered up in pursuance of an order under s 195 shall, if an order under s 204 is not made, retain it pending the making of an order or the decision not to make an order under s 204.

---

[29]   For s 195 see **21.96** et seq and for s 196 see **21.101** et seq.

21.100 CDPA 1988, s 195(4) provides that nothing in s 195 affects any other power of the court.

Right to seize illicit recordings

21.101 CDPA 1988, s 196, like s 100, is aimed at trying to catch street traders who sell pirate CDs and DVDs.[30]

21.102 Under CDPA 1988, s 196(1) where a person is entitled to seek a court order for delivery up under s 195,[31] he, or someone authorised by him, may if an illicit recording of a performance is exposed or is immediately available for sale or hire seize and detain the recording.

21.103 CDPA 1988, s 196(1) also provides that the right to seize and detain an illicit recording[32] of a performance is subject to the conditions set out in s 196 and is subject to any decision of the court under s 204. The provisions of s 204 dealing with an application to court for an order as to the disposal of an illicit recording of a performance are beyond the scope of this book.

21.104 CDPA 1988, s 196(2) provides that before anything is seized under s 196 notice of the time and place of the proposed seizure must be given to a local police station.

21.105 CDPA 1988, s 196(3) provides that a person may for the purpose of exercising the right conferred by s 196 enter premises to which the public have access but may not seize anything in the possession, custody or control of a person at a permanent or regular place of business of his and may not use any force.

21.106 CDPA 1988, s 196(4) provides that at the time when anything is seized under s 196 there shall be left at the place where it is seized a notice in the prescribed form containing the prescribed particulars as to the person by whom or on whose authority the seizure is made and the grounds on which it is made.

21.107 CDPA 1988, s 196(5) provides that 'premises' includes land, buildings, fixed or moveable structures, vehicles, vessels, aircraft and hovercraft.

21.108 CDPA 1988, s 196(5) provides that 'prescribed' means prescribed by order of the Secretary of State.

Criminal remedies

21.109 CDPA 1988 provides that in some cases a criminal offence is committed where there is an infringement of the performer's rights. The criminal offences in the Act are similar to those which exist for copyright infringement.[33] The criminal offences are:

---

[30] For s 100 see Chapter 18 at **18.190** et seq.
[31] For s 195 see **21.96** et seq.
[32] Section 197(2) defines an illicit recording for the purposes of a performer's rights. Section 197(3) defines an illicit recording for the purposes of the rights of a person having recording rights. For s 197(2) see **21.18**; for s 197(3) see **21.65** et seq.
[33] See also Chapter 18 at **18.210** et seq.

(1)   Under s 198(1), which provides that an offence is committed where a person without sufficient consent:
(a)   makes for sale or hire (s 198(1)(a));
(b)   imports into the UK other than for his private and domestic use (s 198(1)(b));
(c)   possesses in the course of a business with a view to committing any act infringing the rights conferred by CDPA 1988, Pt II (Rights in Performances) (s 198(1)(c)); or
(d)   in the course of a business:
(i)   sells or lets for hire (s 198(1)(d)(i));
(ii)   offers or exposes for sale or hire (s 198(1)(d)(ii)); or
(iii) distributes (s 198(1)(d)(iii)),
a recording which is, and which he knows or has reason to believe is, an illicit recording.

(2)   Under s 198(1A), which provides that an offence is committed where a person infringes a performer's making available right:
(a)   in the course of a business (s 198(1A)(a)); or
(b)   otherwise than in the course of a business to such an extent as to affect prejudicially the owner of the making available right (s 198(1A)(b)),
if he knows or has reason to believe that, by doing so, he is infringing the making available right in the recording.[34]

(3)   Under s 198(2), which provides that an offence is committed where a person causes a recording of a performance made without sufficient consent to be:
(a)   shown or played in public (s 198(2)(a)); or
(b)   communicated to the public (s 198(2)(b)),
thereby infringing any of the rights conferred by CDPA 1988, Pt II (Rights in Performances), if he knows or has reason to believe that those rights are infringed.

(4)   Under s 201(1), which provides that it is an offence for a person to represent falsely that he is authorised by any person to give consent for the purposes of CDPA 1988, Pt II (Rights in Performances) in relation to a performance, unless he believes on reasonable grounds that he is so authorised.

21.110   CDPA 1988, s 197(4) provides that for the purposes of s 198 a recording is an illicit recording if it is an illicit recording for the purposes mentioned in s 197(2) or (3).[35]

21.111   CDPA 1988, s 198(3) provides that 'sufficient consent' for the purposes of s 198(1) and (2) means:

(1)   in the case of a qualifying performance, the consent of the performer (s 198(3)(a)); and

(2)   in the case of a non-qualifying performance subject to an exclusive recording contract:
(a)   for the purposes of s 198(1)(a) (making of recording), the consent of the performer or the person having recording rights (s 198(3)(b)(i)); and

[34]   For the s 182CA making available right see **21.1**, **21.20** and **21.24**.
[35]   Section 197(2) defines an illicit recording for the purposes of a performer's rights. Section 197(3) defines an illicit recording for the purposes of the rights of a person having recording rights. For s 197(2) see **21.18**; for s 197(3) see **21.65** et seq.

(b)   for the purposes of s 198(1)(b), (c) and (d) and s 198(2) (dealing with or using recording), the consent of the person having recording rights (s 198(3)(b)(ii)).

21.112   CDPA 1988, s 198(5) provides that a person guilty of an offence under s 198(1)(a), (b) or (d)(iii) is liable:

(1)   on summary conviction to imprisonment for a term not exceeding 6 months or a fine not exceeding the statutory maximum, or both (s 198(5)(a)); or

(2)   on conviction on indictment to a fine or imprisonment for a term not exceeding 10 years, or both (s 198(5)(b)).

21.113   CDPA 1988, s 198(5A) provides that a person guilty of an offence under s 198(1A) is liable:

(1)   on summary conviction to imprisonment for a term not exceeding 3 months or a fine not exceeding the statutory maximum, or both (s 198(5A)(a)); or

(2)   on conviction on indictment to a fine or imprisonment for a term not exceeding 2 years, or both (s 198(5A)(b)).

21.114   CDPA 1988, s 198(6) provides that a person guilty of any other offence under s 198 is liable upon summary conviction to a fine not exceeding level 5 on the standard scale or imprisonment for a term not exceeding 6 months, or both.

21.115   CDPA 1988, s 201(2)[36] provides that a person guilty an offence under s 201 is liable on summary conviction to imprisonment for a term not exceeding 6 months or a fine not exceeding level 5 on the standard scale, or both.

21.116   CDPA 1988 also has provisions requiring every local weights and measures authority to enforce within its area the provisions of CDPA 1988, s 198 (s 198A); for the court to order delivery up where criminal proceedings are brought under s 198 (s 199); for the police to obtain a search warrant (s 200); for the possible liability of the officers of a body corporate where the company has committed an offence (s 202); for an application to court for an order as to the disposal of an illicit recording of a performance (s 204); and for an application by a person in connection with the investigation or prosecution of a relevant offence for an order for the forfeiture of illicit recordings where the illicit recordings have come into the possession of that person (s 204A). The provisions of ss 198A, 199, 200, 202, 204 and 204A are beyond the scope of this book.

---

[36]   See **21.109**.

Chapter 22

PERFORMERS' MORAL RIGHTS

22.1 As was mentioned earlier[1] moral rights are a European concept which have been incorporated into English law by the Copyright, Designs and Patents Act 1988 (CDPA 1988) with the intention of protecting the creative process. Moral rights under CDPA 1988 originally protected the author of a work and protected the privacy of certain photographs and films.[2] By virtue of the Performances (Moral Rights, etc) Regulations 2006[3] moral rights protection has been extended in CDPA 1988 to protect the performers of a work.[4]

22.2 Moral rights are dealt with in Pt I of CDPA 1988, which deals with Copyright and in Pt II, which deals with Rights in Performances.

22.3 It should be noted that performers' moral rights under CDPA 1988 do not apply in relation to any performance that took place before the Performances (Moral Rights, etc) Regulations 2006 came into force on 1 February 2006.

22.4 Like moral rights, CDPA 1988, s 205L provides that a performer's moral rights cannot be assigned. Also like moral rights, a performer's moral rights can be waived.[5]

WHAT ARE PERFORMERS' MORAL RIGHTS?

22.5 There are two performers' moral rights provided for in CDPA 1988. These are:

(1) the right to be identified as the performer (s 205C); and

(2) the right to object to the derogatory treatment of a performance (s 205F).

22.6 CDPA 1988, s 205I deals with the duration of performers' moral rights. Section 205I(1) provides that a performer's moral rights in relation to a performance subsist so long as that performer's rights under ss 182–205B (the economic rights) subsist in relation to the performance. As was mentioned earlier[6] s 191(2) provides that a performer's rights in a performance expire:

(1) at the end of the period of 50 years from the end of the calendar year in which the performance takes place (s 191(2)(a)); or

---

[1] See Chapter 19 at **19.4–19.5**.
[2] For the author of a work see Chapter 18 at **18.39** et seq.
[3] SI 2006/18.
[4] For performers see Chapter 20.
[5] See **22.26** et seq.
[6] See Chapter 21 at **21.21** et seq.

(2)   if during that period a recording of the performance is released, 50 years from the end of the calendar year in which it is released (s 191(2)(b)).[7]

22.7   CDPA 1988, s 205I(2) provides that 'performers' rights' as referred to in s 205I(1) includes the rights of a performer which are vested in his successor.

THE RIGHT TO BE IDENTIFIED AS THE PERFORMER

22.8   CDPA 1988, s 205C(1) provides that whenever a person:

(1)   produces or puts on a qualifying performance that is given in public (s 205C(1)(a));

(2)   broadcasts live a qualifying performance (s 205C(1)(b));

(3)   communicates to the public a sound recording of a qualifying performance (s 205C(1)(c)); or

(4)   issues to the public copies of such a recording (s 205C(1)(d)),

the performer has the right to be identified as such.[8]

22.9   CDPA 1988, s 205C(2) provides that the right of the performer under s 205 is:

(1)   in the case of a performance that is given in public, to be identified in any programme accompanying the performance or in some other manner likely to bring his identity to the notice of a person seeing or hearing the performance (s 205C(2)(a));

(2)   in the case of a performance that is broadcast, to be identified in a manner likely to bring his identity to the notice of a person seeing or hearing the broadcast (s 205C(2)(b));

(3)   in the case of a sound recording that is communicated to the public, to be identified in a manner likely to bring his identity to the notice of a person hearing the communication (s 205C(2)(c)); or

(4)   in the case of a sound recording that is issued to the public, to be identified in or on each copy or, if that is not appropriate, in some other manner likely to bring his identity to the notice of a person acquiring a copy (s 205C(2)(d)),

or (in any of the above cases) to be identified in such other manner as may be agreed between the performer and the person mentioned in s 205C(1).

---

[7]   See also Chapter 21 at **21.21** et seq for s 191(3), (4) and (5).
[8]   For the definition of 'qualifying performance' see s 181 in Chapter 20 at **20.10**.

22.10 CDPA 1988, s 205C(3) deals with the situation where a performance is given by a group and provides that the right to be identified as the performer in relation to a performance given by a group (or so much of a performance as is given by a group) is not infringed:

(1) in a case falling within s 205C(2)(a), (b) or (c) (s 205C(3)(a)); or

(2) in a case falling within s 205C(2)(d) in which it is not practicable for each member of the group to be identified (s 205C(3)(b)),

if the group itself is identified as specified in s 205C(2).

22.11 CDPA 1988, s 205C(4) provides that the word 'group' means two or more performers who have a particular name by which they may be identified collectively.

22.12 It is important to note that although a performer has the right to be identified as the performer, CDPA 1988 requires him to assert his right to be identified. Section 205D(1) provides that a person does not infringe the performer's right to be identified as the performer unless the right has been asserted in accordance with the provisions of s 205D(2).

22.13 CDPA 1988, s 205D(2) provides that the right to be identified as the performer may be asserted generally, or in relation to any specified act or description of acts:

(1) by instrument in writing signed by or on behalf of the performer (s 205D(2)(a)); or

(2) on an assignment of a performer's property rights, by including in the instrument effecting the assignment a statement that the performer asserts in relation to the performance his right to be identified (s 205D(2)(b)).

(For a body corporate the s 205D(2)(a) requirement will be satisfied by a signature on behalf of the company or by affixing its seal (s 210A).)

22.14 CDPA 1988, s 205D(3) provides that the persons bound by an assertion of the rights under s 205D(2) are:

(1) in the case of an assertion under s 205D(2)(a), anyone to whose notice the assertion is brought (s 205D(3)(a)); and

(2) in the case of an assertion under s 205D(2)(b), the assignee and anyone claiming through him, whether or not he has notice of the assertion (s 205D(3)(b)).

22.15 CDPA 1988, s 205C(5) provides that if the assertion specifies a pseudonym, initials or some other particular form of identification, that form shall be used; otherwise any reasonable form of identification may be used.

22.16 A sensible performer will almost always want to be identified as the performer and care should be taken to ensure that the assertion is made so that his moral right to be identified is protected.

EXCEPTIONS TO THE RIGHT TO BE IDENTIFIED AS THE PERFORMER

22.17 CDPA 1988, s 205E sets out the situations where the right to be identified as the performer does not apply.

22.18 The right to be identified as the performer does not apply in the following situations:

(1) where it is not reasonably practicable to identify the performer (or where identification of a group is permitted by virtue of s 205C(3)) (s 205E(2));

(2) in relation to any performance given for the purposes of reporting current events (s 205E(3));

(3) in relation to any performance given for the purposes of advertising any goods or services (s 205E(4)); and

(4) where the following permitted acts in CDPA 1988, Sch 2 occur (s 205E(5)):
   (a) (under para 2(1A) of Sch 2) news reporting (s 205E(5)(a));
   (b) (under para 3 of Sch 2) incidental inclusion of a performance or recording (s 205E(5)(b));
   (c) (under para 4(2) of Sch 2) things done for the purposes of examination (s 205E(5)(c));
   (d) (under para 8 of Sch 2) parliamentary and judicial proceedings (s 205E(5)(d)); and
   (e) (under para 9 of Sch 2) Royal Commissions and statutory inquiries (s 205E(5)(e)).

22.19 A detailed examination of these permitted acts is beyond the scope of the book. The reader is referred to Sch 2 (Rights in Performances: Permitted Acts) to CDPA 1988 for full details.

RIGHT TO OBJECT TO THE DEROGATORY TREATMENT OF A PERFORMANCE

22.20 CDPA 1988, s 205F(1) provides that the performer of a qualifying performance has a right which is infringed if:

(1) the performance is broadcast live (s 205F(1)(a)); or

(2) by means of a sound recording the performance is played in public or communicated to the public (s 205F(1)(b)),

with any distortion, mutilation or other modification that is prejudicial to the reputation of the performer.[9]

---

[9] For the definition of 'qualifying performance' see s 181 in Chapter 20 at **20.10**.

22.21   The right to object to the derogatory treatment of a performance is also infringed under CDPA 1988, s 205H by a person who:

(1)   possesses in the course of business (s 205H(1)(a));

(2)   sells or lets for hire, or offers or exposes for sale or hire (s 205H(1)(b)); or

(3)   distributes (s 205H(1)(c)),

an article which is, and which he knows or has reason to believe is, an infringing article.

22.22   An 'infringing article' is defined in CDPA 1988, s 205H(2) as a sound recording of a qualifying performance with any distortion, mutilation or other modification that is prejudicial to the reputation of the performer.

EXCEPTIONS TO THE RIGHT TO OBJECT TO THE DEROGATORY TREATMENT OF A PERFORMANCE

22.23   CDPA 1988, s 205G(1) provides that the right to object to derogatory treatment of performance does not apply or is not infringed in the following situations:

(1)   in relation to any performance given for the purposes of reporting current events (s 205G(2));

(2)   by modifications made to a performance which are consistent with normal editorial or production practice (s 205G(3)); and

(3)   under s 205G(4) and subject to s 205G(5), the right is not infringed by anything done for the purpose of:
 (a)   avoiding the commission of an offence (s 205G(4)(a));
 (b)   complying with a duty imposed by or under an enactment (s 205G(4)(b)); or
 (c)   in the case of the BBC, avoiding the inclusion in a programme broadcast by them of anything which offends against good taste or decency or which is likely to encourage or incite crime or lead to disorder or to be offensive to public feeling (s 205G(4)(c)).

22.24   CDPA 1988, s 205G(5) provides that where:

(1)   the performer is identified in a manner likely to bring his identity to the notice of a person seeing or hearing the performance as modified by the act in question (s 205G(5)(a)); or

(2)   he has previously been identified in or on copies of a sound recording issued to the public (s 205G(5)(b)),

s 205G(4) applies only if there is a sufficient disclaimer.

22.25   A 'sufficient disclaimer' as referred to in CDPA 1988, s 205G(5) is defined in s 205G(6) and means in relation to an act capable of infringing the right, a clear and reasonably prominent indication:

(1)   given in a manner likely to bring it to the notice of a person seeing or hearing the performance as modified by the act in question (s 205G(6)(a)); and

(2)   if the performer is identified at the time of the act, appearing along with the identification (s 205G(6)(b)),

that the modifications were made without the performer's consent.

CONSENT AND WAIVER OF PERFORMERS' MORAL RIGHTS

22.26 CDPA 1988, s 205J(1) provides that there is no infringement where consent has been given by or on behalf of the person entitled to the right. Section 205J(2) provides that any of the performer's moral rights may be waived by instrument in writing signed by or on behalf of the person giving up the right. (For a body corporate this will be satisfied by a signature on behalf of the company or by affixing its seal (s 210A).)

22.27 A waiver of a performer's moral rights may relate to a specific performance, to performances of a specified description or to performances in general, and may relate to existing or future performances (s 205J(3)(a)). In addition, a waiver may be conditional or unconditional and may be expressed to be subject to revocation (s 205J(3)(b)). Section 205J provides that where a waiver is made in favour of the owner or prospective owner of a performer's property rights in the performance or performances to which it relates, it shall be presumed to extend to his licensees and successors in title unless a contrary intention is expressed.

22.28 CDPA 1988, s 205J(4) makes clear that, notwithstanding the provisions in s 205J, CDPA 1988 does not preclude the operation of the law of contract or estoppel in relation to an informal waiver or any other transaction relating to a performer's moral rights.

THE APPLICATION OF THE RIGHT TO BE IDENTIFIED AS THE PERFORMER AND THE RIGHT TO OBJECT TO THE DEROGATORY TREATMENT IN RELATION TO PART OF A PERFORMANCE

22.29 CDPA 1988 provides that the right to be identified as the performer applies to the whole or any substantial part of a performance (s 205K(1)) and the right to object to the derogatory treatment of a performance applies in relation to the whole or any part of a performance (s 205K(2)).

PERFORMER'S MORAL RIGHTS ON THE DEATH OF THE PERFORMER

22.30 CDPA 1988, s 205M deals with what happens to the performer's moral rights on the death of the person entitled to the rights. Section 205M(1) provides that where this occurs:

(1)   the right passes to such person(s) as may be specifically directed by testamentary disposition (s 205M(1)(a));

(2)   if there is no such direction but the performer's property rights in respect of the performance in question form part of the estate, the right passes to the person to whom the property rights pass (s 205M(1)(b)); and

(3)   if or to the extent that the right does not pass under s 205M(1)(a) or (b) it is exercisable by the personal representatives (s 205M(1)(c)).

22.31 CDPA 1988, s 205M(2) provides that where a performer's property rights pass in part to one person and in part to another, as, for example, where a bequest is limited to apply:

(1)   to one or more, but not all, of the things to which the owner has the right to consent (s 205M(2)(a)); or

(2)   to part, but not the whole, of the period for which the rights subsist (s 205M(2)(b)),

any right which by virtue of s 205M(1) passes with the performer's property rights is correspondingly divided.

22.32 CDPA 1988, s 205M(3) provides that where under s 205M(1)(a) or (b) a right becomes exercisable by more than one person:

(1)   it is, in the case of the right to object to the derogatory treatment of a performance, a right exercisable by each of them and is satisfied in relation to any of them if he consents to the treatment or act in question (s 205M(3)(a)); and

(2)   any waiver of the right in accordance with s 205J by one of them does not affect the rights of the others (s 205M(3)(b)).

22.33 CDPA 1988, s 205M(4) provides that a consent or waiver which has previously been given or made binds any person to whom a right passes under s 205M(1).

22.34 CDPA 1988, s 205M(5) provides that any damages recovered by the personal representatives under s 205M in respect of an infringement after a person's death devolves as part of his estate as if the right of action had subsisted and been vested in him immediately before his death.

REMEDIES FOR INFRINGEMENT OF PERFORMERS' MORAL RIGHTS

22.35 CDPA 1988, s 205N(1) provides that an infringement of a performer's moral right is actionable as a breach of statutory duty owed to the person entitled to the right.

22.36 CDPA 1988, s 205N(2) deals with the situation where a person falsely claims to act on behalf of a performer and provides that where:

(1)　　there is an infringement of a performer's moral right (s 205N(2)(a));

(2)　　a person falsely claiming to act on behalf of a performer consented to the relevant conduct or purported to waive the right (s 205N(2)(b)); and

(3)　　there would have been no infringement if he had been so acting (s 205N(2)(c)),

that person shall be jointly and severally liable in respect of the infringement by virtue of s 205N(1), as if he had infringed the right.

22.37　CDPA 1988, s 205N(3) provides that it is a defence in infringement proceedings to prove that:

(1)　　a person claiming to act on behalf of the performer consented to the defendant's conduct or purported to waive the right (s 205N(3)(a)); and

(2)　　the defendant reasonably believed that the person was acting on behalf of the performer (s 205N(3)(b)).

22.38　The court may under CDPA 1988, s 205N(4), in proceedings for the infringement of the right to object to the derogatory treatment of a performance, if it thinks it is an adequate remedy in the circumstances, grant an injunction prohibiting the doing of any act unless a disclaimer is made, in such terms and in such manner as may be approved by the court, dissociating the performer from the broadcast or sound recording of the performance.

22.39　CDPA 1988, s 205D(4) provides that in an action for the infringement of the right to be identified as the performer the court shall, in considering the appropriate remedies, take into account any delay in asserting the right.

A LOOK TO THE FUTURE

22.40　Since writing this book the European Parliament has endorsed a proposal to extend the copyright term for copyright protection for record producers and performers from the current 50 years to 70 years. In addition, there are proposals that session musicians should receive 20% of the record labels offline and online sales revenue; that performers can obtain the copyright after 50 years if the producer does not exploit the sound recording; and that a new 'clean slate' will come into existence which will stop record producers from making deductions to the royalties paid to the performer.[10]

---

[10]　See Press Release IP/09/627 'Commission welcomes Parliament vote on copyright term', 23 April 2009, available at Europa – The European Union On-Line, europa.eu.

Part VI

EXPLOITING INDIVIDUAL RIGHTS

Note: In this Part the masculine has been used; unless otherwise specified this should be read as referring to both genders.

Chapter 23

CELEBRITY PERSONALITY AND IMAGE

PROTECTING THE CELEBRITY IMAGE

23.1   Advertising, merchandising and endorsement present lucrative opportunities for well-known celebrities and are of considerable commercial value. Sometimes famous images or names are purloined and used commercially without consent. Celebrities, however, do not have a monopoly in respect of the use of their image or character. No 'image right' or 'character right' as such has been developed in our law and attempts to forge such rights have been firmly rejected. Simon Brown LJ explained in *Re Elvis Presley Trade Marks*[1] that celebrities do not enjoy any exclusive broad free-standing general right to image or character exploitation:

> '... all the English cases upon which [the appellant] seeks to rely (Mirage Studios not least) can be seen to have turned essentially upon the need to protect copyright or to prevent passing off (or libel). None creates the broad right for which in effect [counsel for the appellant] contends here, a free standing general right to character exploitation enjoyable exclusively by the celebrity. As Robert Walker L.J. has explained, just such a right, a new "character right" to fill a perceived gap between the law of copyright (there being no copyright in a name) and the law of passing off was considered and rejected by the Whitford Committee in 1977. Thirty years earlier, indeed, when it was contended for as a corollary of passing off law, it had been rejected *in McCulloch v. Lewis A. May*.[2] I would assume to reject it. In addressing the critical issue of distinctiveness there should be no a priori assumption that only a celebrity or his successors may ever market (or licence the marketing of) his own character. Monopolies should not be so readily created.'

23.2   It is nevertheless the case that arrangements are frequently made in respect of celebrities' image rights. Such arrangements are a popular means for celebrities (particularly professional sportsmen and women) to create an important income stream. This is usually done by the individual assigning rights in the image to a third party, for example, to his club or a company which will exploit the image right. In the case of footballers, where this is particularly prevalent, routinely clauses are inserted in players' contracts which enable the club to exploit the player's image. This will often require an agreement with any third party owning the rights to the image in question. It is not always easy to discern precisely what it is that is being assigned by the celebrity notwithstanding that vast sums are sometimes paid over for the rights covered by the assignment.

23.3   Trade mark law does not provide a comprehensive means of protecting a celebrity's image or name. Registration of a celebrity's image as a trade mark is likely to be problematical because it is usually difficult to show that the celebrity's image is distinctive for trade mark purposes. Names let alone images are unlikely to be registered

---

[1]   [1999] RPC 567, at 597–598.
[2]   [1947] 2 All ER 845, (1947) 65 RPC 58.

unless they have acquired distinctiveness through use. In 1999 the Patent Office rejected an application to register a number of images of the Princess of Wales, although the grounds for the decision are not known. The images may have been considered as lacking distinctiveness given that she was so well known around the world or it may have been that no trade connection between her image and any of the goods in respect of which it was to be registered was established.

23.4 Revised advice was given to the United Kingdom Patent Office examiners regarding registering the names of famous people and groups as trade marks.[3] When dealing with an application to register the name of a celebrity what had to be considered was:

> '... whether the famous name put forward for registration is so descriptive in relation to the goods/services for which registration is sought that it could not be perceived by consumers as anything more than a description of the subject matter of the goods/services.'

23.5 Posters of pop or football stars would be an example of goods where the pop star's name would be considered as descriptive of the goods in question (eg a poster of a well-known celebrity) rather than as an indication that the goods were authorised by the celebrity. Posters and goods of this type are treated and referred to as 'image carriers'. The position might be different in relation to music or sports videos in the celebrity's field of activity because the celebrity would be considered to have a reputation in relation to such goods. Registration of names usually succeeds in relation to badges of allegiance (such as scarves for football clubs) and registration can be used to prevent the sale of unofficial product.

23.6 Sometimes third parties who have no connection with the celebrity wish to register the celebrity's name in relation to goods and services without consent. With regard to bad faith applications the main issue is whether the celebrity has a connection or an association with the goods or services in respect of which the name is to be registered. If there is such a connection or association the registration is likely to be refused because the applicant would be taking advantage of the celebrity's reputation. Even where there is no connection (and, therefore, no clear attempt to take advantage of the celebrity's reputation in respect of such goods or services) the application might still be rejected on the grounds of passing off. It was emphasised that where the reputation of a famous individual is non commercial (such as a famous politician) care should be taken not to accept applications for registration without that person's consent.

23.7 The question remains as to precisely what personality right it is that celebrities routinely assign for substantial consideration. The reality is that the celebrity grants permission to the third party to do something (using and exploiting his image) that the celebrity would otherwise object to. Whether or not the celebrity strictly has the right in law to prevent the activity is often beside the point.

23.8 By ordinary standards unauthorised use of another's image or character is likely to be viewed as unfair and lacking in honesty and in the past judges have used the action for passing off to ensure a limited degree of honesty and fairness in the way trade is conducted in this regard. Lord Morris of Borth-Y-Gest said in *Parker-Knoll Ltd v Knoll International Ltd*:[4]

---

3   Practice Amendment Notice 5/04.
4   [1962] RPC 265, at 278.

'... in the interests of fair trading and in the interests of all who may wish to buy or to sell goods the law recognises that certain limitations upon freedom of action are necessary and desirable. In some situations the law has had to resolve what might at first appear to be conflicts between competing right. In solving the problems which have arisen there has been no need to resort to any abstruse principles but rather, I think, to the straightforward principle that trading must not only be honest but must not even unintentionally be unfair.'

PASSING OFF

23.9   The law of passing off has been used to provide a remedy in some situations where the celebrity image has been used without authorisation. Laddie J stated in *Irvine v Talksport*[5] that the law of passing off is not designed to protect traders from fair competition and does not create or protect a monopoly in a name or get-up. Parker J clearly stated this in *Burberrys v JC Cording & Co Ltd*:[6]

'... apart from the law as to trade marks, no one can claim monopoly rights in the use of a word or name. On the other hand, no one is entitled to the use of any word or name, or indeed in any other way, to represent his goods as being the goods of another to that other's injury. If an injunction be granted restraining the use of a word or name, it is no doubt granted to protect property, but the property, to protect which it is granted, is not property in the word or name, but property in the trade or good-will which will be injured by its use.'

23.10   Goodwill is property a claimant is entitled to protect from damage and passing off provides a remedy to vindicate the claimant's exclusive right to goodwill. The nature of goodwill was described by Lord Macnaghton in *IRC v Muller & Co's Margarine Ltd* as:[7]

'... a thing very easy to describe, very difficult to define. It is the benefit and advantage of the good name, reputation, and connection of a business. It is the attractive force which brings in custom ... It is very difficult ... to say that goodwill is not property. Goodwill is bought and sold every day. It may be acquired, I think, in any of the different ways in which property is usually acquired. When a man has got it he may keep it as his own. He may vindicate his exclusive right to it if necessary by process of law. He may dispose of it if he will – of course under the conditions attaching to property of that nature.'

23.11   A claim in passing off will lie even where there is no immediate damage to the claimant's goodwill. For example, it lies in situations where instead of benefiting from exclusive rights to his property the claimant finds someone else squatting on it. The remedy is there to give the owner of goodwill the right to maintain, raise or lower the quality of his reputation or to decide who can use it alongside him. This control is compromised if others can freely use the claimant's reputation or goodwill without permission.

---

5   [2002] EWHC 367 (Ch), at [31].
6   (1909) 26 RPC 693, at 701.
7   [1901] AC 217, at 223–224, [1900–1903] All ER Rep 413, at 416.

FALSE ENDORSEMENT

23.12 In *Irvine v Talksport Ltd*[8] Laddie J saw that the law had developed to the extent that if someone acquires a valuable reputation or goodwill, the law of passing off will protect it from unlicensed use by other parties:[9]

- the law will vindicate the claimant's exclusive right to the reputation or goodwill and will not allow others to so use goodwill as to reduce, blur or diminish its exclusivity;

- it is not necessary to show the claimant and the defendant share a common field of activity or that sales of products or services will be diminished either substantially or directly, at least in the short term;

- there is still a need to demonstrate a misrepresentation because it is that which enables the defendant to make use or take advantage of the claimant's reputation;

- the court takes judicial notice of the fact that it is common for famous people to exploit their names and images by way of endorsement not only in their own field of expertise but, depending on the extent of their fame or notoriety, wider afield also;

- for many sportsmen, for example, income received from endorsing a variety of products and services represents a very substantial part of their total income;

- large sums are paid for endorsement because, no matter how irrational it may seem, those in business have reason to believe that the lustre of a famous personality, if attached to their goods or services, will enhance the attractiveness of those goods or services to their target market;

- the endorsee is taking the benefit of the attractive force which is the reputation or goodwill of the famous person;

- there is nothing which prevents an action for passing off succeeding in a false endorsement case; and

- to succeed in a false endorsement case the burden on the claimant includes a need to prove at least two, interrelated, facts: (1) that at the time of the acts complained of the claimant had a significant reputation or goodwill; and (2) that the actions of the defendant gave rise to a false message which would be understood by a not insignificant section of his market that his goods have been endorsed, recommended or are approved of by the claimant.

23.13 In false endorsement cases the claimant cannot succeed simply by showing that his image was used by the defendant for commercial purposes; the claimant must go further and show that there was an implicit representation of endorsement. The question is whether, on a balance of probabilities, a significant proportion of the target

---

8   [2002] EWHC 367 (Ch).
9   At [38], [39] and [46].

audience would think that the claimant had endorsed or recommended the defendant's products or services. In *Irvine v Talksport* Laddie J concluded on the evidence:[10]

> '... part at least of the intention was to convey the message to the audience that Talk Radio was so good that it was endorsed and listened to by Mr Irvine. Mr Irvine's support of Talk Radio would make it more attractive to potential listeners with the result that more would listen to its programmes and that would make Talk Radio an attractive medium in which to place advertisements.
>
> ...
>
> Mr Irvine has a property right in his goodwill which he can protect from unlicensed appropriation consisting of a false claim or suggestion of endorsement of a third party's goods or business. The fact ... he might not be free to engage in a particular form of endorsement when wearing particular clothes or because of some other contractual restraint ... does not alter the fact that the goodwill remains his and can be protected against intruders.'

23.14 Jonathan Parker LJ on appeal in *Irvine v Talksport Ltd* in the Court of Appeal thought it:[11]

> '... difficult to conceive of a clearer way of conveying, by way of a quasi-photographic image, the message that a celebrity has endorsed a particular radio station than by depicting the celebrity listening intently to a radio bearing the station's logo.'

CHARACTER MERCHANDISING

23.15 Separate issues arise in character merchandising cases, where the defendant's activities do not imply any endorsement of their products or services by the claimant. In *Re Elvis Presley Trade Marks*[12] (a trade mark registration case where there was no question of endorsement because Elvis Presley was dead) the issue arose over whether or not the claimant had merchandising rights in Elvis Presley's name or image so as to give the right to restrain others from selling products bearing the name and photographs. The court would not accede to an attempt to create a quasi-copyright in the name and images. Robert Walker LJ said:[13]

> '... this appeal is not an appropriate occasion on which to attempt to define precisely how far the law of passing off has developed in response to the growth of character merchandising, still less to express views as to how much further it should develop or in what direction.'

THE MEASURE OF DAMAGES IN FALSE ENDORSEMENT CASES

23.16 It was held in *Irvine v Talksport*[14] that a reasonable endorsement fee in a false endorsement cases is the fee which, on a balance of probabilities, the defendant *would*

---

[10] [2002] EWHC 367 (Ch), at [72] and [75].
[11] [2003] EWCA Civ 423, at [82].
[12] [1999] RPC 567.
[13] Ibid, at [582].
[14] *Irvine and others v Talksport Ltd* [2003] EWCA Civ 423, at [106], per Parker LJ.

have had to pay in order to obtain lawfully that which it in fact obtained unlawfully. It is not the fee the defendant *could have afforded* to pay and hence the defendant's financial situation is irrelevant.

23.17 The assessment of damages takes into account licences actually granted and the rates of royalty fixed by them. The relevance and comparability of the licences granted must be estimated in relation to the facts of particular cases. The court, so far as possible, will seek to determine the hypothetical bargain that would have been made. To the extent that evidence of existing licences does not provide a figure on which the damage can be measured, the court must consider any other evidence, according to its relevance and weight, on which a royalty rate which would have been agreed can be fixed.

23.18 The assessment of damages in *Irvine v Talksport* proceeded by way of analogy with awards in patent cases. In *General Tire and Rubber Co v Firestone Tyre and Rubber Co Ltd*[15] Lord Wilberforce referred to three groups of cases indicating the approach to typical situations arising in patent infringement cases:

- Where the infringer makes a profit from exploiting the invention, thereby diverting sales from the owner of the patent to the infringer, the measure of damages is normally the profit the owner of the patent would have made if the sales had been made by him.

- Where patents are exploited through the granting of licences in consideration of royalty payments the measure of the damages will be the royalty the infringer would have paid if instead of acting illegally, he had acted legally. The amount of the royalty is essentially and exclusively established by evidence – what has to be ascertained is the amount the infringer would have had to pay if he had come to be licensed under the patent. In cases where the patentee only licensed the patent the rates he charged will be so prima facie the price or royalty the infringer would have had to pay. Before a 'going rate' of royalty can be taken as the basis on which an infringer should be held liable, it must be shown that the circumstances in which the going rate was paid are the same as or comparable to those in which the patentee and the infringer are assumed to strike their bargain.

- Where it cannot be proved either what profit the patentee has lost as a result of the infringement or that there is a 'going rate' of royalty the claimant must adduce evidence of the practice, as regards royalty, in the relevant trade or analogous trades. This might be expert opinion, evidence of the profitability of the invention or any other factor to determine the measure of loss. Such evidence is likely to be of little use in the face of direct type evidence referred to in connection with the second group of cases but there is no rule of law preventing the court (even where there is evidence of licensing practice) from taking these more general considerations into account. The ultimate process is one of judicial estimation of the available indications.

23.19 Lord Wilberforce cited from the judgment of Fletcher Moulton LJ in *Meters Ltd v Metropolitan Gas Meters Ltd*[16] as expressing 'the true principle' governing cases within the third group. In that passage, Fletcher Moulton LJ said this:

---

15   [1976] RPC 197, [1975] 2 All ER 173.
16   (1911) 28 RPC 157, at 164–165.

'It is the duty of the defendant to respect the monopoly rights of the plaintiff … But I am not going to say a word which will tie down future judges and prevent them from exercising their judgment, as best they can in all the circumstances of the case, so as to arrive at that which the plaintiff has lost by reason of the defendant doing certain acts wrongfully instead of either abstaining from doing them, or getting permission to do them rightfully.'

IMAGE RIGHTS AND CELEBRITY EVENTS

23.20 Although the law has not developed separate protection for the celebrity image or created an image right, participants in 'celebrity events' can protect their personality and image by imposing a duty of confidence upon those attending such events. In this way celebrities can exercise control over the publication of information about themselves, contained in photographs and otherwise, at such events (be they celebrity weddings or private parties or gigs). By imposing obligations of confidence on all those attending such functions celebrities can sell the right to publish the confidential material (images of themselves in celebrity magazines) for substantial sums.

23.21 Celebrities, like anyone else, cannot complain simply of being photographed. However, in cases where a duty of confidence is imposed at an event, *information* contained in photographs (eg images of celebrities attending the event) will be confidential and the use or publication of such photographs can be restrained on that ground and substantial damages can be awarded if the confidence is breached. Where information in photographs is not subject to an obligation of confidence it might still be possible to restrain *publication* of photographs containing celebrity images on the grounds of privacy. We are primarily concerned here with the former situation, ie where the *information* in photographs is subject to an obligation of confidence. It is, of course, possible that the same information will be protected both by the law of confidence and the law of privacy. The right to enforce confidential obligations can be licensed (as happened in the *Douglas*[17] case) but privacy is a personal right and the right to enforce it cannot be licensed or assigned and it thus does not have commercial value.

23.22 The extent of protection given to image at celebrity events and generally was considered authoritatively by the House of Lords in *OBG v Allan*,[18] one of the appeals which concerned the celebrity magazine *OK!*. *OK!* had contracted for the exclusive right to publish photographs of the Douglases' celebrity wedding in the United States. All other photography was forbidden. Photographs were surreptitiously taken by an unauthorised photographer pretending to be a waiter or guest and were published by the rival celebrity magazine *Hello!*. *OK!* was held to be entitled to claim damages for breach of its equitable right to confidentiality in photographic images of the wedding. (*OK!* also sued on the basis that the conduct constituted an interference by unlawful means with its contractual or business relations but this part of its appeal failed.) The claim succeeded on the basis of breach of confidence and that it 'is … necessary to avoid being distracted by the concepts of privacy and personal information'.[19]

23.23 The following was said in the House of Lords generally in relation to the creation of an image right in English law, by Lord Hoffman:[20]

---

[17] *Douglas v Hello!* [2003] EWHC 2629 (Ch).
[18] [2007] UKHL 21.
[19] Lord Hoffman, ibid, at [118].
[20] Ibid, at [124].

'There is in my opinion no question of creating an "image right" or any other unorthodox form of intellectual property. The information in this case was capable of being protected, not because it concerned the Douglases' image any more than because it concerned their private life, but simply because it was information of commercial value over which the Douglases had sufficient control to enable them to impose an obligation of confidence. Some may view with distaste a world in which information about the events of a wedding, which Warren and Brandeis in their famous article on privacy "The Right to Privacy" (1890) 4 Harvard LR 193 regarded as a paradigm private occasion, should be sold in the market in the same way as information about how to make a better mousetrap. But being a celebrity or publishing a celebrity magazine are lawful trades and I see no reason why they should be outlawed from such protection as the law of confidence may offer.'

And by Lord Walker:[21]

'Although the position is different in other jurisdictions, under English law it is not possible for a celebrity to claim a monopoly in his image, as if it were a trademark or brand. Nor can anyone (whether celebrity or nonentity) complain simply of being photographed. There must be something more: either that the photographs are genuinely embarrassing (*Theakston v MGN Ltd* [2002] EMLR 398) or that their publication involves a misuse of official powers (*Hellewell v Chief Constable of Derbyshire* [1995] 1 WLR 804) or that they disclose something which merits temporary protection as a commercial secret (*Shelley Films Ltd v Rex Features Ltd* [1994] EMLR 134, in which a photograph of Robert De Niro in the guise of Frankenstein's creature would no doubt have been worth a thousand words of description).'

23.24 It was said by Lord Brown in the House of Lords in relation to the Douglases' right to control the publication of information about themselves (and others) at their celebrity event wedding:[22]

'Nobody disputes that the Douglases were perfectly entitled, quite irrespective of any right of privacy, to sell the exclusive right to publish photographs of their wedding, and nobody doubts that the right was worth the £1m which "OK!" paid for it. Indeed "Hello!" had earlier made an unsuccessful bid for the same right in the same sum. It is no less plain that in publishing as they did the rogue photographs deceitfully taken by an infiltrator at the wedding, "Hello!" not only lent themselves to this outwitting of the strenuous efforts made by the Douglases to safeguard "OK!'s" exclusive but intentionally destroyed the very right itself ... Having paid £1m for an exclusive right it seems to me that "OK!" ought to be in a position to protect that right and to look to the law for redress were a third party intentionally to destroy it ... I would uphold "OK!'s" claim, as Lindsay J did at first instance, on the ground of breach of confidence.'

23.25 The House of Lords held that *OK!*'s complaint was about *Hello!*'s breach of its exclusive right to publish *authorised* photographs and was not about *Hello!* having published images which no one had a right to publish and about which only the Douglases had a right to complain. The latter point was considered to overlook the fact that the Douglases had granted the exclusive right to publish any photographic images of the wedding to *OK!* and had undertaken to do their best to ensure that no photographs were taken by anyone else so that nobody else could defeat *OK!*'s exclusive right. (If the Douglases had been magazine publishers wishing to market the visual images of their wedding as an exclusive in their own magazine it could not be suggested they had no right to complain about *Hello!*'s behaviour.)[23]

---

21   Ibid, in a dissenting speech, at [293].
22   Ibid, at [323] and [325].
23   Lord Brown, ibid, at [327] and [328].

23.26 *Hello!* was held to be liable to *OK!* in damages for breach of confidence assessed at £1,026,706 for loss of profit from the exploitation of unauthorised photographs. It had been concluded at first instance that the full losses from all unauthorised publication of the photographs were sufficiently consequential upon the breach and sufficiently foreseeable as to make '*Hello!* liable for them in the ordinary way':[24]

> 'I do not regard the newspaper publications of the pictures as so remote a consequence of Hello!'s publication as not to be laid at Hello!'s door and plainly the newspaper publications would not have occurred as they did but for Hello!'s publication of the unauthorised photographs.'

23.27 *Hello!* was held liable,[25] applying the well-known criteria for breach of confidence claims summarised by Megarry J in *Coco v AN Clark (Engineers) Ltd*:[26]

> 'First, the information itself ... must have the necessary quality of confidence about it. Secondly, that information must have been imparted in circumstances importing an obligation of confidence. Thirdly, there must be an unauthorised use of that information to the detriment of the party communicating it.'

23.28 The information was identified as being *photographic images* of the wedding and not information about the wedding generally. The obligation of confidence was owed in respect of photographic images. Lindsay J held that the three conditions in *Coco* were satisfied and was upheld by the majority in the House of Lords:

- Photographs of the wedding were confidential information in the sense that none were publicly available:[27]

  > 'What is the information to which the confidence here attached? Plainly the information as to how the wedding looked–the photographic images which bring the event to life and make the viewer a virtual spectator at it. How can one doubt that this was commercially confidential information or, if one prefers, a trade secret? It was, after all, secret information for which "OK!" had been prepared to pay £1m, in the expectation, obviously, that it was to remain secret until they chose to make use of it. And that is certainly how it would also have been perceived by "Hello!" (who had themselves hoped to acquire and exploit the secret in the same way).'

- It had been made clear that anyone admitted to the wedding was not to make or communicate photographic images. They allowed people to witness their marriage, but only on the basis that the information which the spectators thereby obtained was not communicated in the form of a photographic image. *Hello!*'s conscience was tainted and it was not acting in good faith nor by way of fair dealing.

- *Hello!* knew *OK!* had an exclusive contract which would include provisions intended to preclude intrusion and unauthorised photography and that a large sum would have been paid for the exclusive rights. These facts were such that a duty of confidence should be inferred from them. *Hello!* knew of the reputation of the paparazzi for being able to intrude and the unauthorised pictures plainly indicated they were taken surreptitiously. *Hello!* kept its eyes shut lest it saw what would have become apparent to it.

---

24   *Douglas v Hello!* [2003] EWHC 2629 (Ch), at [53], per Lindsay J.
25   [2003] 3 All ER 996.
26   [1969] RPC 41, at 47.
27   Lord Brown, ibid, at [326].

23.29 Lord Hoffman thought[28] the central point was that *OK!* paid £1m for the benefit of the obligation of confidence imposed upon all those present at the wedding in respect of *any* photographs of the wedding and was entitled to enforce it. The case was straightforward, he thought, provided 'one keeps one's eye firmly on the money and why it was paid'.

23.30 The decision in *OBG v Allan* was not concerned with privacy or the protection of the Douglases' privacy; it was about the protection of confidential information. The reasoning was as follows:

- The Douglases had separately recovered damages for an invasion of their privacy and *OK!* had no claim to privacy under Art 8 nor could it make a claim which was parasitic upon the Douglases' right to privacy.

- To make commercial sense the obligation of confidence imposed in favour of *OK!* was not only in respect of the photographs supplied by the Douglases but *any* photographs of the wedding. That was the essential purpose of the security arrangements and the prohibition of unauthorised photography.

- The information in (all) photographic images of the Douglases' wedding was information of commercial value protected as commercially confidential information. The fact the information happened to have been about the Douglases' personal life (their marriage) was irrelevant; the information could have been about anything a newspaper would pay for.

- The Douglases arranged their wedding in such a way as to impose an obligation of confidence on those in attendance in respect of *any* photographic images of their wedding which they exclusively controlled. The Douglases were able to impose a suitably limited obligation of confidence on those attending the wedding (to treat all information contained in photographs of the wedding as confidential). *OK!* paid the Douglases for doing this and for the right to be the only source of that particular form of information.

- The obligation of confidence, it was clear to everyone involved, was imposed for the benefit of *OK!* as well as the Douglases and *Hello!*'s photographs fell within a generic class of commercially confidential information which *OK!* was entitled to protect.

- The fact that the information in certain photographic images of the wedding was not to remain secret but was to be published to the world by *OK!* did not mean an obligation of confidence could not be imposed for enabling someone to be the only source of publication if that was worth paying for.[29] *OK!* paid the Douglases to impose (and enforce) such an obligation of confidence on all those attending the wedding. *OK!* bought the benefit of the obligation of confidence imposed by the Douglases on those present at the wedding and was entitled to protect the right to that benefit against those who intentionally destroyed it and this was regardless of the fact that others were free to communicate other forms of information about the wedding.

[28] Ibid, at [117].
[29] Lord Hoffman, ibid, at [120].

- The photographs simply contained information of commercial value. A newspaper, for example, would be entitled to impose confidentiality on its journalists, subeditors etc to whom such information was communicated awaiting publication. (Such an obligation would not bind someone in receipt of information otherwise than under an obligation of confidence.)

- The photographer (Mr Thorpe) was subject to an obligation of confidence in respect of the pictures which he took surreptitiously and by reason of the circumstances in which they were acquired. *Hello!* was subject to the same obligation which could not be destroyed by *OK!* having published other photographs a few hours earlier.

23.31 Whether information, once in the public domain, can be the subject of confidence depends on the nature of the information and on the facts:

- Where the point of the transaction was that each picture of the wedding (regardless of who took it) would be treated as a separate piece of information which *OK!* would have the exclusive right to publish the fact that pictures published by *OK!* were in the public domain did not mean other pictures were also in the public domain merely because they resembled *OK!*'s pictures:[30]

  > 'The secret consists no less of each and every visual image of the wedding than of the wedding as a whole. Assume, for example, that "OK!" had chosen to publish photographs of the bride and groom in one issue, the guests in the next, and the presents later still. The confidence would, I think, continue throughout and I see no reason why at some point bootlegged photographs should suddenly become acceptable on the grounds that the look of the wedding was now in the public domain so that no confidentiality in its photographic image remained to be protected.'

- The photographic images of the wedding were undoubtedly a secret unless and until *OK!* chose to publish the images authorised by the Douglases and *Hello!* did its best to break what it knew was a secret.[31]

- In relation to copies of its own pictures *OK!* would have to rely on the law of copyright, not the law of confidence, to prevent their reproduction.

- There were indicators suggesting that *Hello!*'s pictures should be treated as subject to an obligation of confidence and as not being in the public domain: (1) *Hello!* was willing to pay the photographer a lot of money for them (which it presumably would not do if they were in the public domain); and (2) their publication undoubtedly caused substantial financial loss to *OK!*.

- The information in the photographs would be treated as in the public domain, for example, if the purpose of publishing was simply to convey information that the Douglases had married or about the bride's wedding dress and so forth as would a description of the event.

23.32 There was resistance in the House of Lords to this approach. In his dissenting speech Lord Walker thought that allowing *OK!*'s claim would create a 'character right' in respect of the celebrity's name and image which is something that had always been

---

[30] Lord Brown, ibid, at [329].
[31] Baroness Hale, ibid, at [307].

rejected in English law. Lord Walker worked on the fundamental premise that 'the confidentiality of information must depend on its nature, not on its market value' and thought that extending the law of confidence as Lord Hoffman suggested would 'go some way to creating an unorthodox and exorbitant form of intellectual property'. He said there was nothing about the photographs that was confidential and the fact that security measures were taken and that money was paid for them did not alter the fundamental premise that the photographs were not, by the nature of the information in them, confidential.

23.33 In summary, it is possible under English law to impose obligations of confidence on those attending celebrity events in respect of photographs (and other media) containing images of those attending. The right to enforce the obligation of confidentiality is capable of being sold (licensed) and, therefore, has commercial value. Those attending the event might also have a personal right to protect against their image being published under the law of privacy but this right cannot be sold.

Chapter 24

THE COMMERCIAL EXPLOITATION OF A CELEBRITY'S IMAGE

INTRODUCTION

24.1   A celebrity's status in the public eye does not have an infinite length. A celebrity's career can last for a very short period of time or may last for many years. It can be very hard to predict how long a person's popularity will last. Throughout their time in the public eye a celebrity's popularity will go through peaks and troughs. To some extent a career trough may occur because the celebrity actively seeks to take himself away from the public glare for a period of time for personal reasons or because he does not have a product to promote such as a record or a film. Some celebrities are so media savvy that in order to maximise their popularity and shelf life they consciously withdraw from the public eye for a period of time because they are aware that if they do not do so the public would tire of them and their career in the spotlight will possibly permanently fade away due to overexposure. In many cases a career trough will happen because the celebrity falls out of fashion for a while and the work they are offered dries up accordingly. Whether the celebrity is an A-list celebrity actor or a celebrity whose talent extends to being famous for no particular reason there is one thing that they all have in common and that is they need to earn money to live. Apart from earning money from the field in which they are known such as in film, television or sport there are many other subsidiary ways in which a celebrity can boost their income. Sometimes the sums a celebrity will earn from subsidiary earnings may be far greater than the money they earn from their main career. One example where this might occur is a where well-known television actor has a subsidiary career as a voice-over for a successful, long-running television advert campaign. This begs the question, in such a situation why would a celebrity continue to work in their main, lesser-paid career when they can earn more from their subsidiary career? The answer to that question is twofold. First, the celebrity may want to carry on with their main career because this is what they enjoy doing. Secondly, it may be that the subsidiary career only exists because of the fame which comes from the main career and if the celebrity gives up the main career the subsidiary career would come to a swift end.

24.2   In some cases a celebrity might take on in addition to his full-time career a time-consuming subsidiary career. For example, a Premier League football manager might at the same time as being a football manager also take on the role of a regular television sports pundit, analysing competitors' football matches for Sky or the BBC. Usually, however, the subsidiary ways a celebrity earns money away from his full-time work does not require an inordinate amount of his time. The main ways a celebrity earns money away from his main career is through sponsorship, merchandising and endorsement deals. The celebrity will be required to spend time working with the sponsor, merchandiser or endorsement company but the time he will be required to spend will be far less time than the time he is required to spend in his main career.

SPONSORSHIP, MERCHANDISING AND ENDORSEMENT – WHAT IS THE DIFFERENCE?

24.3   Before examining the main areas which have to be considered when entering a sponsorship, merchandising or endorsement agreement it is important to define what is meant by sponsorship, merchandising and endorsement.

Sponsorship

24.4   Sponsorship is where a sponsor, usually a company, wants to raise its profile to the general public or to a specific section of the general public and seeks to promote its name and a particular product(s) or service for which it known or for which it wants to become known. The sponsor will look to find a celebrity who it believes is closely associated with its target audience and seek to enter an agreement with the celebrity to promote itself via the celebrity. The celebrity when entering a sponsorship agreement is not actively promoting or recommending the sponsor's goods or services. He is, for want of a better description, allowing the sponsor to advertise itself via him. An example where a sponsorship is commonly used is in the music business for concert tours. Due to the huge cost of touring and due to the fact that many record companies do not want to provide tour support monies to bands/artists it has become quite common for bands/artists to defray all or part of the cost of touring by entering sponsorship deals with companies. The sponsoring company will be given, in exchange for providing money to help defray or pay for the tour costs, the right to promote its name and its goods or services on, inter alia, the band's/artist's concert posters, concert adverts, tickets and concert programmes.

Merchandising

24.5   There is a potentially lucrative income to be earned by a celebrity in using his name, likeness, biographical details, signature, voice and any trade mark(s) which he has on assorted goods and paraphernalia such as T-shirts, sweat shirts, posters, mugs and key rings. Such merchandising is commonly called character merchandising. The most common example of where merchandising of a celebrity occurs is in the music business. A pop star or a band can often earn considerable money from the sale of merchandise items. Indeed, with the general decline in record sales it is now becoming more common for a pop star or a band to make more money in the music industry from touring and from sales of tour merchandise than from the royalties from record sales. A celebrity would rarely if ever have the expertise, time or the contacts to set about manufacturing, distributing and selling merchandised items himself. Celebrities will usually either enter an agreement in their own name or their own limited companies, which deal with their merchandising agreements, will contract with third parties to allow the third parties to manufacture, distribute and arrange for the sale of the merchandise or to allow third parties to enter licences with others to manufacture, distribute and sell such items. A celebrity would receive from the third party royalties calculated on the sale of each of the items and may also receive an advance from the third party which would be recoupable against sales of the items.

Endorsement

24.6   As was mentioned above, where a celebrity is sponsored by a company he is not actively promoting or recommending the sponsor's goods or services. The situation is different with celebrity endorsement. Endorsement occurs where a celebrity actively promotes and recommends a company's particular product or product range. The terms of the endorsement agreement will require the celebrity actually to promote and be seen to use the product which he is endorsing. The celebrity will allow the company to use his name, likeness, biographical details, signature, voice and any trade mark(s) which he has to promote, advertise and sell the product on, for example, radio, television and in newspaper adverts and the right to use his name, likeness, signature and any trade mark(s) which he has for use on the packaging of the goods which he is endorsing or on the goods themselves. The company which is seeking to use the celebrity to endorse a product will have selected that celebrity because it believes that the relationship between its product range and the celebrity will strike a positive connection with the general public and will increase the sales of that particular product. Some celebrity endorsements will not only promote an existing range of the company's products but will also be used to promote a new range of products which have been designed (sometimes by the celebrity himself) and manufactured as that particular celebrity's own product range. For example, a sportsman may endorse a company's existing range of tennis rackets and/or he may also endorse a new range of tennis rackets which has his name on and which have been designed by him for use by the general public. Although endorsement agreements are common with sportsmen they are entered into by many types of celebrity, for example, a rock musician may endorse a particular range of guitars or a pop star, film actress or reality television celebrity might endorse a perfume which has been designed in consultation with the celebrity and made in conjunction with the perfume house and is named after the celebrity or named after something that has a connection with the celebrity.

24.7 Having briefly outlined the differences between sponsorship, endorsement and merchandising we will now examine the key terms which are to be found in each type of agreement.

PRELIMINARY CONSIDERATIONS BEFORE NEGOTIATING A SPONSORSHIP, MERCHANDISING OR ENDORSEMENT AGREEMENT

24.8 Before negotiating a sponsorship, merchandising or endorsement agreement for a celebrity it is vital that the celebrity's solicitor checks with his client whether he has entered any other sponsorship, merchandising or endorsement agreements in the past. If the celebrity has, the solicitor should examine any such agreements to check the following:

(1)   Is the agreement still in existence?

(2)   If an agreement is in existence are there any contractual restrictions which will stop the celebrity from entering the proposed new agreement? For example:
    (a)   Is there a clause in the existing agreement which prohibits the celebrity from entering an agreement with a competitor company or a competing product?
    (b)   Does the existing agreement allow the sponsoring/merchandising/ endorsement company an option to extend the existing agreement which would prohibit the celebrity from entering an agreement with another company? If so, the existing agreement should be examined to see how the option can be exercised. The existing company might, for example, have the

right to extend the agreement on a matching rights basis. If this is the case the terms of the matching rights clause would need to be complied with, giving the existing company the right to decide whether it wants to continue its contractual relationship with the celebrity – if it does this might prohibit the celebrity from entering an agreement with another company.

(3)   Even if the term of the sponsorship/merchandising/endorsement agreement has expired it should be checked to see whether notwithstanding the expiry of the term there is a run off period in the agreement which would enable, for example, a merchandising company a period of time to sell off any remaining merchandise. The terms of the run off clause might prohibit the celebrity from entering an agreement with another company until this period has expired. In the event that there is a run off period in the agreement and the celebrity is free to contract with a different company during this period, the celebrity should where the run off period is still in existence disclose this to the proposed new company with whom he is negotiating as the new company might not want to enter an agreement with the celebrity or for it to start whilst there is an existing run off period under a previous agreement.

(4)   Where the term has expired it should be checked that any intellectual property rights such as trade marks which might have been assigned by the celebrity for the term of the agreement are reassigned to the celebrity and the necessary details have been registered with the trade mark registry. In addition, any intellectual property rights which were created by the sponsoring/merchandising/endorsement company to promote the agreement and which under the terms of the agreement are to belong to the celebrity are assigned to him.

(5)   Where the term has expired any sub-licences which might have been entered into by the sponsoring/merchandising/endorsement company under the terms of the agreement must be checked to ensure that they have terminated.

24.9   Also any employment contract(s) which the celebrity may have must be checked to see what restrictions there are on the celebrity which might affect his ability to enter a sponsorship, endorsement or merchandising agreement. This will be particularly important where the celebrity is a sportsman as his employer club (and where he is also an international player, his country) will in all probability have entered various sponsorship, endorsement and merchandising agreements which may in turn due to the celebrity's employment contract restrict whether, where or how the celebrity can enter an agreement with, for example, a competitor sponsor to his club's sponsor. For example, it might mean that the celebrity can endorse a competing product to that which his club endorses but can only do it as an individual and not as a sportsman who plays for 'X United' and that the celebrity can endorse the product wearing ordinary clothing but not wearing his club's playing strip. In addition, the rules of a particular playing tournament and television broadcasting regulations may also affect celebrity's ability to enter a sponsorship, endorsement or merchandising agreement.

Chapter 25

SPONSORSHIP AGREEMENT

INTRODUCTION

25.1   As was mentioned above,[1] sponsorship is commonly used in the music business to help defray or pay for the cost of a band/artist's concert tour especially where the record company is not prepared to advance tour support monies to the band/artist. It should be noted that as well as a company agreeing to sponsor a concert tour the company may also at the same time possibly enter a merchandising agreement and/or an endorsement agreement with the band/artist which the company is sponsoring. For example, a musical instrument manufacturer might sponsor a band's tour and at the same time enter an endorsement agreement with the band members, either individually or as a group, to use on tour and in the recording studio and to promote before, during and after the tour the company's guitars, drums and synthesizer equipment. Alternatively, a sponsor might sponsor the band/artist's concert tour and at the same time enter a merchandising agreement with the band/artist to manufacture, distribute and sell the band/artist's concert tour merchandise. Indeed, very recently there has been a tendency for some of the most famous and best-selling recording artists such as Madonna and Jay-Z to enter joint recording, touring and merchandising agreements with the same company (in this case with Live Nation). Where a band/artist intends to enter a recording, tour sponsorship and merchandising agreement with the same company or with related companies it is vitally important from a commercial position to consider each part of the deal in isolation from the other parts. When an arm's length consideration is taken to each element of such a deal this should ensure that the band/artist secures the best terms possible at the best possible price for each element of the agreement so that the band/artist does not give away one part of the deal at a discount to its real value because it is entering other deals at the same time with the company.

25.2   The sponsoring company will from its position ideally want total exclusivity or at the least some degree of exclusivity with the celebrity it is sponsoring. This will enable the sponsor to look to maximise its investment return in the sponsorship of the celebrity. The sponsor wants the public to believe that only it, or a very limited select group of companies, is promoting the celebrity. The more sponsors involved the less the effect of the sponsorship return may be. The sponsoring company may therefore require the celebrity it is sponsoring to agree that he will not enter any other sponsorship deals during the period of their sponsorship agreement. Such a restriction may well be unacceptable to the celebrity. Alternatively, the sponsoring company may require the celebrity not to enter a sponsorship agreement with another company which manufactures, distributes or sells similar goods or provides similar services to the sponsoring company. Where the sponsoring company is, for example, a multinational company which manufactures, distributes or sells many different unrelated products it

---

[1]   See Chapter 24 at **24.3** et seq.

may be too restrictive for the celebrity to agree not to enter a sponsorship agreement with another company which provides similar goods and services to the sponsoring company because of the diversity of the products sold by the sponsoring company. In this case it may be better for the celebrity to agree that he will not enter a sponsorship agreement with a company which manufactures, distributes or sells a particular range of products. This will allow the celebrity to negotiate sponsorship with other non-competing companies.

25.3	Where a celebrity is very successful and is looking for sponsorship for, say, a concert tour, he may be able to accept sponsorship from a few companies and separate the sponsors into primary and secondary sponsors. The difference between a primary and secondary sponsor is that the primary sponsor will provide more sponsorship money than a secondary sponsor and will therefore obtain greater rights in return for the larger cash injection. The primary sponsor would, for example, look to receive a specified sized billing and perhaps the name of the company and possibly the designation as primary sponsor on all concert posters, concert adverts, tickets, concert programmes and tour merchandise as well as receiving a specified number of free or discounted tickets in the best part of the concert venue or in a specially designated VIP area which the sponsor can use for hospitality or for distribution to the general public, who might enter a competition organised by the sponsor to win tickets to the concert tour. A primary sponsor may also want a part of the venue set aside away from the general public for corporate hospitality prior to and after the concert and may also want the right for a few members of the company or competition winners to meet the celebrity either before or after the concert. A secondary sponsor provides less sponsorship money than a primary sponsor and so the package of rights offered would be less than that on offer to a primary sponsor. Commonly a secondary sponsor is a provider of a particular product on the concert tour, such as of a particular type of drink. Such a sponsor will often be given the designation 'Official Supplier' of that particular product for the concert tour. Where sponsors are divided into primary and secondary categories any sponsor, whether primary or secondary, will want to ensure that no other competitor will be able to sponsor the celebrity. The key throughout is for the celebrity to maximise sponsorship revenue and for the sponsor to ensure that its investment is not diluted in value by the appointment of any competing companies.

THE MAIN TERMS

25.4	As was mentioned above,[2] before negotiating a sponsorship agreement for a celebrity it is vital that the celebrity's solicitor checks with his client whether he has entered any other sponsorship agreements in the past and also checks any employment contract(s) as they may restrict whether, where or how the celebrity can enter a sponsorship agreement.

25.5	The main terms which would need to be dealt with in a sponsorship agreement are:

(1)	the parties to the sponsorship agreement;

(2)	the event which is being sponsored;

2	See Chapter 24 at **24.8** et seq.

(3) the territory;

(4) the sponsorship term;

(5) the sponsorship fee;

(6) the sponsor's rights;

(7) the sponsor's obligations;

(8) the celebrity's obligations;

(9) termination of the agreement;

(10) intellectual property rights; and

(11) warranties, indemnities and other clauses.

25.6   We will now examine briefly the key areas which need to be considered and will examine them on the basis that the celebrity is a pop singer who is going on tour to promote a new album and is obtaining tour sponsorship from one or more companies.

THE PARTIES TO THE SPONSORSHIP AGREEMENT

25.7   There will usually be no problem regarding the contracting parties as they will be the celebrity who is the sponsored party and the company which is the sponsor.

25.8   It may be that the celebrity enters all his agreements through limited companies which have been set up to deal with various aspects of his career. For example, he may have one limited company set up to deal with his recording agreement, a separate limited company to deal with his song-writing and publishing, a third which deals with his concert tours and a fourth which deals with his merchandising. Where a celebrity enters contractual arrangements via limited companies the sponsor should ideally consider obtaining a side letter signed by the celebrity himself providing that should his company not comply with its obligations then he will personally be responsible for the contractual obligations and will perform them or will be a party to the agreement itself as guarantor that his company will comply with its obligations and that if it does not then he will personally be responsible for and will perform his company's contractual obligations.

25.9   Consideration should also be had from the celebrity's position as to the financial status of the sponsoring company. If the sponsor is effectively underwriting the whole or a substantial cost of a tour it is imperative that the sponsor is able to pay the sponsorship fee and be able to pay it on time. If the sponsor fails to do so the tour may have to be cancelled, with subsequent loss of income for the celebrity and with substantial damage done to the celebrity's public reputation. If there is concern about the financial position of the proposed sponsoring company then consideration should be had as to what financial guarantees could be provided by the sponsor company, for example, a parent company could be asked to guarantee the financial obligations of a subsidiary sponsoring company.

THE EVENT WHICH IS BEING SPONSORED

25.10 The agreement should set out in detail what event(s) the company is sponsoring. If the sponsor company is sponsoring a celebrity's concert tour the agreement should set out the dates and the venues where the concerts are to be held. Provision should also be made in the agreement as to whether any extra concert dates which might be added to the proposed tour or an extension beyond the proposed original concert tour schedule will be covered by the sponsorship deal. The sponsor will in all probability want the sponsorship deal to cover any extra added tour dates or extension to the proposed original concert tour schedule especially as this will increase the exposure of the sponsor's name/product(s) to the general public and will be of added value to the sponsoring company. Extra concert dates are commonly added to tours as ticket demand frequently outstrips supply and it is a ploy of some tour promoters to want to sell out a small number of select venues before adding extra dates to a tour itinerary. Provision should also be made as to whether concerts which are moved to larger or more prestigious venues or are rearranged dates due to cancellation of existing tour dates are covered by the sponsorship agreement, which again in all probability they will be. Notwithstanding listing the actual tour dates covered by the agreement, provision should be made as to the proposed start and end dates of the sponsorship agreement. This will enable the sponsoring company to start promoting its sponsorship involvement with the celebrity. The proposed start date will usually be some time before the tour actually commences and the end date will usually be a short time after the tour has actually ended. This enables the sponsoring company to have a lead in time to promote its sponsorship of the tour before the first concert date and enables it to wind down its sponsorship promotion for a short period after the last concert date. It might be that the celebrity decides at some later stage to do an extra tour date(s) after the agreement has ended. This might be, for example, because there has been a sudden unpredicted upturn in the celebrity's image leading to a public demand for more concerts. The agreement should cover whether the sponsoring company has the right to sponsor these dates and, if so, how the parties are to deal with this possibility should it arise.[3] It may be that the celebrity intends or is invited to appear at one or more music festivals during the proposed tour. It is quite common for a festival organiser to have its own sponsorship deals in place, and possibly with a competitor to the celebrity's sponsoring company. To avoid any potential problems arising the sponsorship agreement should deal with the possibility of the celebrity appearing at a music festival. From the celebrity's position a sponsorship agreement for his concert tour should not cover his appearance at a music festival (which will need to be carefully defined in the agreement or a list of music festivals which are not covered by the sponsorship agreement should be listed in a schedule to the agreement).

THE TERRITORY

25.11 The agreement should set out the territory which the sponsorship agreement covers. This will usually be the territory in which the concerts take place. However, as was previously mentioned,[4] the tour may be extended or other dates may be added, some of which may go into other territories. Careful consideration will therefore need to be had as to defining the territory covered by the agreement.

---

3   See **25.12** and **25.13**.
4   See **25.10**.

THE SPONSORSHIP TERM

25.12 The sponsorship agreement will set out, often in some detail, the length of the sponsorship term.[5] The term will usually be either a fixed term, a fixed term subject to any extensions which might occur under the agreement (to cover any extra added concerts which have been added or rescheduled for after the original proposed tour),[6] or a fixed term subject to any renewal option.[7] Where the term is defined as a fixed term subject to any extensions which might occur under the agreement there should be a long stop date provision in the agreement because the celebrity will want to ensure that he knows the latest date the agreement can end as this will enable him to seek a new sponsorship deal with other competing companies from the long stop date.

THE SPONSORSHIP FEE

25.13 The following are some of the matters that need to be considered when negotiating and subsequently drafting the sponsorship fee clause:

(1)   Is the sponsorship fee to cover a one-off event or a series of events?

(2)   Is the sponsorship fee to be paid in advance of the event, after the event or in stages?

(3)   If the sponsorship fee is to be paid in stages what are the stages that trigger each payment? Are equal payments to be made at each stage or are different amounts to be paid at each stage?

(4)   If the sponsorship fee is to cover a series of events over, say, 2 or 3 years will the amount of the sponsorship fee increase each year? If so, what mechanism is to be used to calculate the amount payable each year? There may be a straight uplift of £x each year or a formula may be set out in the agreement which can be used to calculate how much will be payable.

(5)   Will any bonus payments be payable if certain targets are achieved by the celebrity? For example, the sponsorship fee might be increased by a certain amount if the celebrity's new album gets to number 1 or gets into the top 5 or the top 10 in the UK charts during a specified period of time. If the celebrity is a footballer his sponsorship fee might be increased if during a specified period of time he makes x number of first team appearances for his club in Premier League games or if he scores x number of goals for his club in the Premier League or if he makes x number of appearances during a specified period of time for his national football team.

(6)   Will the sponsor be able to withhold any payments if the celebrity fails to achieve certain targets? For example, if the celebrity cancels x number of concerts on his tour and does not reschedule them the sponsor can withhold £x per cancelled concert from the sponsorship fee.

---

[5]   See **25.10**.
[6]   See **25.10**.
[7]   See point (9) at **25.13**.

(7)   If there are bonus or penalty targets in the sponsorship agreement notwithstanding these provisions is there to be a minimum and/or a maximum sum which the sponsor has to pay the celebrity?

(8)   To whom is the fee payable? For example, it may be payable to the celebrity in person, to his own limited company, to his manager or agent or to his accountant.

(9)   Will the sponsor have an option to extend the sponsorship agreement? If so, the terms of how the sponsor can exercise or decline the option needs to be detailed in the agreement. The clause will need to provide a formula to calculate the sponsorship fee should the sponsor decide to exercise the option to extend the sponsorship agreement. The sponsorship fee under the option clause might provide for the existing sponsorship fee in the last year of the existing agreement to be uplifted by a specified amount or by a certain percentage or the sponsor might be given a matching rights option. A matching rights option will enable the celebrity to look for another sponsor but the celebrity will not be able to sign a new agreement with another sponsor unless the existing sponsor has had a chance to and decides not to match the terms offered by the proposed new sponsor. If the sponsor declines the chance to match the offer the celebrity will then be able to enter the agreement with the proposed new sponsor. It should be noted that the terms of a matching rights clause must be set out in detail in the agreement and should cover every eventuality. For example, the matching rights clause should deal with the possibility of what will happen where the existing sponsor has declined the chance to match an offer from a proposed new sponsor only for the proposed new sponsor to subsequently decide not to proceed. Does this allow the celebrity to sign a sponsorship agreement with another party on lesser terms than those offered to the original sponsor under the matching rights clause or would these new lesser terms have to be offered to the existing sponsor to match?

THE SPONSOR'S RIGHTS

25.14 As was mentioned earlier,[8] where a celebrity is sponsored by a company he is not actively promoting or recommending the sponsor's goods or services. The situation is different with celebrity endorsement. Endorsement occurs where a celebrity actively promotes and recommends a company's particular product or product range. A sponsor will nonetheless still want to promote its association with the celebrity to the general public and in particular to that section of the public which buys its goods or uses its services. In exchange for payment of sponsorship money the sponsor will be granted a number of rights to enable it to promote its sponsorship of the celebrity.

25.15 The sponsorship agreement will set out whether the sponsor is the sole sponsor, the primary sponsor, a secondary sponsor and/or a secondary sponsor with the designation of 'Official Supplier' of a particular product such as a brand of lager. The sponsor wants the right to some form of exclusivity with the celebrity under the sponsorship agreement. The extent of the exclusivity being granted must be set out in the sponsorship agreement so that the sponsor will be able to ensure that no competitor will also be sponsoring the celebrity at the same time.

---

[8]   See Chapter 24 at **24.3** et seq.

25.16 Apart from the right to some form of exclusivity the sponsor will also want other rights granted to it to maximise the promotion of its sponsorship deal with the celebrity. Whether the sponsor will be granted these rights depends substantially upon whether the sponsor is the sole exclusive sponsor, in which case the celebrity may be prepared to grant all the rights being sought by the sponsor, or whether, where there are several sponsors involved, the sponsor is a primary or secondary sponsor. A primary sponsor will pay more for the right to be a primary sponsor and so will want more rights than those which will be granted to a secondary sponsor. Where a celebrity has primary and secondary sponsors he will put together a package of rights which he will be prepared to give to each category of sponsor. The following are some of the rights which the sponsor may want to secure in the agreement:

(1) To have the company name and/or its product on the concert tickets.

(2) To have an advert in the tour programme. If this is agreeable other matters such as the positioning of the advert in the programme, its wording and size should be set out in the agreement. The agreement should also provide whether the advert is to be free of charge or whether the sponsor will be given a reduced advertising rate to that which it is proposed will be charged to non-sponsor advertisers.

(3) To have the sponsor's name and/or its product placed on all advertising, publicity and promotional material for the celebrity's tour. If this is agreeable the positioning, wording and size of the sponsor's name and/or product should be set out in the agreement.

(4) To have a stated number of advertising hoardings at the concert venue(s) advertising the sponsor's name and/or its products. In addition to the number of signs permitted the agreement would also need to deal with their size and their positioning at the venue(s).

(5) To produce promotional material to give away in competitions to promote its sponsorship of the celebrity. The celebrity may not be prepared or able to grant such a right especially where he has or intends to enter a merchandising agreement. Should the celebrity be prepared to allow the sponsor to produce promotional material he should only allow it under strict conditions as he will want to ensure that nothing is produced which might damage or lessen his image to the public. For example, the celebrity would want the right to approve any proposed promotional material and its packaging so that he can check its quality and suitability and will want to ensure that the sponsor has product liability insurance in place, preferably with the celebrity's name noted on the policy.[9] The celebrity should also ensure that where his name, image and/or logo is used by the sponsor on any promotional material the relevant copyright notices and trade mark notices are credited.

(6) To use the celebrity's name, image and/or logo in any publicity or promotional material produced by the sponsor to promote its sponsorship of the celebrity. Where the celebrity agrees to this he must ensure that he only allows the non-exclusive use by the sponsor of his name, image and/or logo as he will want to grant other companies with whom he has other commercial agreements the right to use his name, image and/or logo. In addition, to ensure control of his image the

---

[9] See also point (6) below concerning the celebrity's name, image and/or logo.

celebrity must reserve the right to approve the use of his name, image and/or logo on any proposed promotional material. The celebrity should also ensure that where his name, image and/or logo are used by the sponsor the relevant copyright notices and trade mark notices are credited.

(7) To require the celebrity to attend a press conference or a launch party and/or promotional events to promote the sponsorship agreement. If the celebrity agrees to this the agreement should provide that he will attend at an agreed date and venue (or at a date and venue which will be notified to him e g 8 weeks in advance of the proposed date) for a specified period of time and that he will attend subject to his overriding work commitments with his employer. A provision that he will attend subject to his work commitments would be needed to cover a situation where, for example, the celebrity is a Premier League footballer and he is required by his club to travel with the team to play in a rescheduled league or cup game on the day of his proposed promotional appearance for the sponsor. Where the celebrity agrees to appear at a press conference, launch party or promotional events he will want to ensure the sponsor pays his reasonable travel, food and where necessary hotel accommodation expenses and in addition he may also require an additional appearance fee. These matters should also be dealt with in the agreement.[10]

(8) To use on a non-exclusive basis (either for free or paid for by the sponsor) the hospitality facilities at the venue(s). Where hospitality is to be provided the celebrity will want the sponsor to provide a guest list so that gatecrashers do not get in.

(9) To meet the celebrity with a specified number of guests (namely the sponsor's employees, the sponsor's guests or winners of a competition to meet the celebrity which has been organised by the sponsor to promote its sponsorship) before or after the concert.

(10) The right to a specified number of free top priced tickets to the concert(s) for the sponsor, the sponsor's guests or competition winners of a competition organised by the sponsor to promote its sponsorship. The sponsor may also want a specified number of backstage or VIP passes to the concert(s). It may also want the right to a specified number of top priced tickets at a discount price to the ticket face value. Where the celebrity allows the sponsor to have tickets to the concert(s) he should ensure that a clause is put in the agreement that these tickets are to be given away to the sponsor's employees, its guests and its competition winners but are not allowed to be resold. The celebrity may also require a provision in the agreement requiring the sponsor to provide his manager or concert promoter with the names of the people who will be using the free tickets so that it can be checked that only the named people (who will have to provide proof of identity at the event) will be allowed in.

THE SPONSOR'S OBLIGATIONS

25.17 The following are some of the obligations which the sponsor might be required to comply with:

---

[10] See also point (2) at **25.17** and point (11) at **25.18**.

(1)   To pay the sponsorship money and any bonus payments (and where relevant VAT on the sponsorship money and any bonus payments) in accordance with the payment schedule in the agreement. The sponsor will want the celebrity to invoice it for the monies and will usually want a receipted invoice for the payment. Provision should also be made in the agreement for the sponsor to pay interest at a specified rate to the celebrity for late payment(s). The sponsor will want a provision inserted stating that where the celebrity is in material breach of contract and has been notified of it by the sponsor and the breach has not been remedied by the celebrity to the reasonable satisfaction of the sponsor within a stated period of time, the sponsor will not be liable to make further sponsorship payments to the celebrity. This clause would be in addition to the sponsor's right to sue the celebrity for breach of contract.

(2)   Where the celebrity is required to attend a press conference, launch party and/or promotional events to promote the sponsorship agreement the sponsor will pay him the agreed appearance fee and reimburse expenses which have been reasonably incurred by him for his appearance.[11]

(3)   To actively promote the sponsorship with the celebrity in accordance with the rights granted to the sponsor in the agreement.

(4)   Not to do or permit anything to be done which damages or might damage the name, reputation or image of the celebrity or any of the celebrity's copyrights or trade marks or other intellectual property rights. In addition, the celebrity will want a provision included in the agreement that the sponsor will immediately notify him of any infringements which it becomes aware of.

(5)   Where the celebrity is a sportsman the sponsor will be required to ensure that it complies with the domestic and international sports governing bodies' rules and regulations which apply to the celebrity's sport.

(6)   That the sponsor cannot use the rights granted to it in the agreement to run joint promotions with others.

(7)   To provide samples of any promotional material and packaging to the celebrity so that he can examine them to decide whether he is prepared to approve them.[12] In addition, the sponsor will be required to ensure that product liability insurance is in place, preferably with the celebrity's name noted on the policy and that where the celebrity's name, image and/or logo is used that the relevant copyright notices and trade mark notices are credited.

(8)   Where the sponsor is to provide goods/services to the celebrity the agreement should deal with this. The agreement should also provide whether the goods/services are provided to the celebrity for free or at a discount or full price and whether any such goods can be retained for free by the celebrity at the end of the agreement or whether he can purchase them at an agreed price or whether they are to be returned to the sponsor. Other provisions may need to be considered such as who is to maintain and service any such goods and at whose cost and

---

[11]   See point (7) at **25.16** and point (11) below.
[12]   See also point (7) at **25.16**.

whether insurance is required to be taken out to maintain and service the goods and who is to pay the insurance premiums.

THE CELEBRITY'S OBLIGATIONS

25.18 The celebrity will be required by the sponsor to comply with various obligations in consideration of the sponsorship fee paid by the sponsor to him. The following are some of the obligations which the celebrity may be required to comply with:

(1) To perform at the sponsored event(s) in a professional manner.

(2) To comply with his obligations in the agreement and to comply with his obligations to others with whom he contracts in relation to the sponsored event(s).

(3) To confirm that he is in good health and, if required, to undergo a medical to satisfy the sponsor or the sponsor's insurers that this is the case. In addition, the celebrity will be required to take reasonable steps to ensure that he remains in good health.

(4) Not to participate during the term of the agreement in any dangerous or hazardous activities which might prevent him from carrying out his contractual obligations.

(5) At all times to keep the sponsor informed of his whereabouts and supply the sponsor with his personal mobile and landline telephone numbers so that the sponsor can contact him as and when required. As an alternative to supplying his personal telephone numbers to the sponsor, other contact numbers such as that of his personal manager may be acceptable.

(6) Where the celebrity is a sportsman, to comply with his club's and his national and international governing bodies' rules and regulations.

(7) Not to do or permit anything to be done which damages or might damage his own name, reputation or image and not to do or permit anything to be done which damages or might damage his own copyrights or trade marks or other intellectual property rights.

(8) Not to do or permit anything to be done which damages or might damage the sponsor's name, reputation or image or the name, reputation or image of its goods/services and not to do or permit anything to be done which damages or might damage the sponsor's copyrights or trade marks or other intellectual property rights.

(9) Not to enter or purport to enter any agreement(s) with third parties in the sponsor's name.

(10) Where the celebrity is actually staging the event(s) for which he is sponsored, he will stage the event professionally and will ensure that all necessary insurance cover is in place and that any necessary consent(s) is/are obtained, for example, from the local authority, to hold the event. In addition, the sponsor will also

require the celebrity to comply with all relevant regulations which have to be complied with to hold the event(s), such as compliance with fire and crowd safety regulations and any relevant trade union regulations. The celebrity will also be required to ensure that where a third party is staging the event at which he is appearing the third party will comply with these requirements.

(11)   To attend a press conference or a launch party and/or promotional events to promote the sponsorship agreement.[13]

(12)   Where the celebrity is promoting the sponsorship agreement, for example, by making a personal appearance or filming a promotional advert, he will comply with all relevant regulations such as fire, health and safety and crowd safety regulations and any relevant trade union regulations.

(13)   When promoting the sponsored event(s) the celebrity will be required to mention the name of the sponsor and/or its goods/services in interviews with the press and other broadcast media. He may also be required to wear clothes displaying the sponsor's name and logo on for promotional interviews and may be required to ensure that there is wherever possible a backdrop with the sponsor's name, logo, goods/services emblazoned on it at press conferences or other promotional events held to which the press are invited to attend to promote the event(s).

(14)   The sponsor may want the celebrity to use its product(s) and wear its company logo on his clothing in his professional career. This could be a problem where, for example, the celebrity is a sportsman as his employment contract with his club or the rules of his playing association or particular tournament rules or television broadcaster regulations may limit or prohibit particular types of advertising or may limit the size and positioning of advertising logos. The agreement should therefore provide that the celebrity will use the sponsor's product(s) and wear the company's logo on his clothing in his professional career subject to any constraints that he is under in his professional career.

TERMINATION OF THE AGREEMENT

25.19 The agreement should contain specific provisions which if breached would enable the innocent party to terminate. For example, a well-drafted agreement should contain a 'morality clause' providing that the celebrity will not do anything which damages or might damage the sponsor's name, reputation or image or the name, reputation or image of its goods/services. Where the celebrity does something which might bring the sponsor's name into disrepute, for example, getting arrested for or charged with a serious crime, the sponsor will then be able to terminate the agreement under the morality clause provision.

25.20 The sponsorship agreement ideally should not only contain relevant provisions which allow for termination of the agreement in circumstances where there is a serious or substantial breach of contract, but also set out what happens where one party terminates the agreement due to the other party's breach. For example, the agreement would usually provide that the sponsor has no liability to the celebrity for future sponsorship fees or for future obligations from the date of the celebrity's breach

---

[13]   See also point (7) at **25.16** and point (2) at **25.17**.

although both parties would retain their existing contractual rights and liabilities up to the date of termination. The agreement may also need to deal with what is to happen to any goods/services which have been supplied by the sponsor to the celebrity where the agreement has been terminated due to breach of contract by the celebrity. For example, the agreement may provide that where the sponsor has terminated the agreement due to the celebrity's breach any goods supplied to him by the sponsor will be returned at the celebrity's expense in the condition in which they were originally delivered.[14]

25.21 Where the agreement is for a fixed term but contains a provision for the sponsor to renew, the procedure for exercising the option should be set out in detail so that both parties know whether the agreement will continue or will terminate at the end of the proposed fixed term. A written notice procedure between the parties should be provided for in the agreement. For example, the agreement may require the celebrity to notify the sponsor in writing of his right to exercise an option 3 months before the proposed termination date of the agreement and allow the sponsor a period of 14 days from service of the notice to decide whether to exercise the option or whether to let the agreement end. Where the sponsor has a matching rights option the agreement should also set out the terms the sponsor must match to be able to exercise the option and what information the celebrity is to supply to the sponsor to enable it to decide whether to exercise the option.[15] If the sponsor decides not to renew the agreement having had a chance to do so the celebrity can then safely treat the existing agreement as terminated and look for a new sponsor.

25.22 The agreement might be for a fixed term with a break clause allowing one of the parties to terminate the agreement early by exercising the break clause provision. The details of how and when a break clause can be exercised must be set out in the agreement. For example, a 3-year sponsorship agreement might contain a provision which allows the sponsor to terminate the agreement at the end of the first year, to be exercised by the sponsor giving written notice of termination to the celebrity by first class post to his home address and the notice being sent not less than 3 months before the end of the first year of the agreement. If the break clause is not exercised or not correctly exercised as prescribed in the agreement then the agreement will continue until the end of the term or until the next break clause is exercised (if there is another break clause provided for in the agreement). If the break clause is validly exercised by the sponsor the agreement should provide that any sponsorship monies payable which would have been payable in the future are no longer payable, although any monies still owing to the celebrity for the period up to the termination date are still payable. The agreement should also provide that all liabilities and obligations until the date of termination still exist notwithstanding the exercise of the break clause.

25.23 A clause(s) may be of such importance to the sponsor that it goes to the 'essence' of the agreement. For example, the sponsor may only want to be associated with the celebrity because he is a high-profile actor playing a particular role in a television soap opera whereas other potential sponsors would have been prepared to contract with the celebrity for the person he is rather than for the character he plays in the television soap opera. In a situation such as where the sponsor has contracted with the celebrity purely because of the role he plays in a television soap opera and it is imperative to the sponsor that he remains in the role during the term of the agreement, a provision should be

---

[14] See point (8) at **25.17**.
[15] See point (2)(b) in Chapter 24 at **24.8** and point (9) at **25.13**.

included in the agreement to this effect and that it is 'of the essence' of the contract. This will enable the sponsor to terminate the agreement should the celebrity leave the soap opera.

25.24 The agreement will often provide that where one party is in material breach of contract the other party must notify it in writing of the breach and require the breach to be remedied within a period of time and if the breach has not been remedied in that time the agreement is automatically terminated. The agreement should also provide that where termination has occurred due to a material breach by one of the parties the parties' contractual rights, liabilities and obligations until the date of termination still exist notwithstanding termination (save for the obligation by the sponsor to pay any outstanding sponsorship fee to the celebrity where it is the celebrity who has been in material breach of contract).

25.25 It should be noted that cancellation of a sponsored event(s) may entitle the sponsor to terminate the agreement. The agreement should deal with what is to happen where an event(s) is cancelled. Likewise the agreement should also deal with what is to happen where an event(s) is postponed. Dependent on the wording of the agreement cancellation or postponement of an event(s) may entitle the innocent party to terminate the agreement.

25.26 Whether the term expires due to effluxion of time or due to the sponsor's breach of contract the sponsor should be required to return any photographs and other items which were supplied by the celebrity to enable the sponsor to promote the sponsorship agreement. There should also be a provision in the agreement stating that upon termination all the celebrity's intellectual property rights which were licensed to the sponsor revert to the celebrity and that the sponsor will execute any documents which are required to ensure the intellectual property rights revert to the celebrity.[16]

25.27 The agreement should contain a force majeure clause, which should list all the events beyond the control of the contracting parties, for example, act of God, civil war, terrorism, strikes, lock outs, and which if any of them occur will excuse the party who cannot perform its contractual obligations due to the force majeure event. The clause should provide that the party who cannot perform its contractual obligations will not be in breach of contract for non-performance where this is due to a force majeure event. The clause should require the party who cannot perform its obligations due to a force majeure event to give notice to the other party of the existence of the force majeure event and that it prevents it from performing its contractual obligations. The force majeure clause should provide that the agreement is suspended whilst the force majeure event exists and that the agreement will recommence once the force majeure event has ended. As the suspension could last for a long time there should be a long stop provision in the agreement allowing one party to serve written notice on the other party terminating the agreement where the agreement is suspended for a specified period of time due to a force majeure event. Where termination occurs due to a force majeure event, the agreement should deal with what is to happen in these circumstances.

---

[16] See also point (5) at **25.29**.

INTELLECTUAL PROPERTY RIGHTS

25.28 One party will often allow the other the right to use its copyrights or trade marks or other intellectual property rights to promote the agreement. Where this is permitted, provisions should be made in the agreement to ensure that the parties' intellectual property rights are protected.[17]

25.29 The celebrity and the sponsor will also need to ensure the following:[18]

(1)   Before one party contracts to allow the other party to use any of its intellectual property rights it must check that the other party actually owns the relevant rights which it intends to license. It may be, for example, that a logo was commissioned by the celebrity from a third party in which case the celebrity should check that he has taken a full assignment of the copyright in the design of the logo from the third party before he enters the sponsorship agreement allowing the sponsor the right to use it.

(2)   That the use of their intellectual property rights is strictly controlled in the agreement. There should be a provision in the agreement which states that a party is granting the other a non-exclusive licence to use the relevant right(s). The extent to which the licensee has to use the rights granted must also be set out precisely in the agreement.[19]

(3)   That the licensee of the intellectual property rights cannot allow anyone else to use the licensor's intellectual property rights without the express written permission of the licensor. Where it is intended that the licensee can permit others to use the licensor's intellectual property rights the agreement should set out in detail the circumstances in which this is permitted.

(4)   That where one party has been granted a licence to use the other's intellectual property rights it will immediately inform the other where it knows there is or suspects there may be an infringement of these rights by a third party. The clause in the agreement may also require the licensee to assist the licensor to protect the licensor's rights where they have been or are suspected to have been infringed by third parties and possibly to pay for or contribute towards taking legal action to protect them.

(5)   Where the term expires due to effluxion of time or due to the sponsor's breach of contract the sponsor will return any photographs and any other items which were supplied by the celebrity to enable the sponsor to promote the sponsorship agreement. There should also be a provision in the agreement stating that upon termination all the celebrity's intellectual property rights which were licensed to the sponsor revert to the celebrity and that the sponsor will execute any documents which are required to ensure that the intellectual property rights revert to the celebrity.[20]

---

[17]   See point (6) at **25.16**; point (4) at **25.17**; point (5) at **25.18**; and **25.30** et seq. See also Chapter 18 on Copyright.
[18]   See also Chapter 18 on Copyright.
[19]   See **25.14** et seq; **25.17** et seq; and **25.19** et seq. For the difference between a licence and an assignment see Chapter 24 at **24.3** et seq. See also Chapter 18 on Copyright.
[20]   See also **25.19** et seq.

(6) If any new intellectual property rights are created during the agreement term, for example, a new logo is created to advertise the sponsorship, there should be a provision as to who will own the intellectual property rights and that any necessary documents will be executed to ensure an effective creation and transfer of ownership in these rights and that any third parties will be required to execute any necessary documentation to ensure the transfer of ownership.[21]

(7) In the unlikely event that the celebrity is required to make audio and/or audio-visual recordings to promote the sponsorship agreement the copyright, moral rights and performers' rights issues need to be considered in relation to the recordings.[22]

WARRANTIES, INDEMNITIES AND OTHER CLAUSES

25.30 The agreement should contain a warranty where the sponsor is allowed to use the sponsored party's trade mark to promote the sponsorship that the sponsored party's trade mark is original, that he is the sole and absolute owner of the trade mark and that the trade mark does not infringe the rights of any third party. A similar warranty should also be given in the agreement where the sponsored party is allowing the sponsor to use any other of his intellectual property rights. Likewise, similar warranties should be given by the sponsor to the sponsored party where the sponsored party is given the right to use the sponsor's intellectual property rights to promote the sponsorship.

25.31 Where one party is granting the other a right to use its intellectual property rights the party granting the right should indemnify the other party in the agreement from any expense or liability which might be incurred where the warranty relating to the intellectual property rights proves to be incorrect.

25.32 The agreement should contain a warranty by each party that it is free and able to enter the agreement that it is able to perform its contractual obligations and it has not entered any agreements which might compete or conflict. The sponsor might seek to widen the scope of this warranty to provide that the celebrity will not during the term of the agreement except where expressly provided for enter any competing or conflicting agreement.

25.33 Other provisions which should be dealt with in the agreement include, inter alia:

(1) That both parties will keep the terms of the agreement confidential and will not disclose them to anyone other than their professional advisers or as may be required by law.

(2) That the agreement between the parties does not constitute a joint venture, partnership or employment relationship.

(3) That the agreement reflects the whole of the agreement between the parties and replaces any earlier oral or written agreement.

---

[21] See also Chapter 18 on Copyright.
[22] See Chapter 27 at **27.40** et seq.

(4)   That the sponsored party will not hold itself out as representing the sponsor. A
       similar provision should also be made by the sponsor to the sponsored party.

(5)   Where the sponsor is merely sponsoring the celebrity and not staging the
       sponsored event(s) the sponsored party should indemnify the sponsor for any
       liability for any claims by third parties concerning the running of the event(s). The
       agreement should also provide that appropriate insurance cover should be taken
       out to cover possible third party claims.[23]

(6)   (Possibly) a provision enabling the parties to limit the extent of any indemnity
       which has been given to the other party.

(7)   Which legal system will apply (in nearly all cases this will be the law of England
       and Wales) and the method to be used to resolve any disputes between the parties,
       namely alternative dispute resolution, arbitration or legal proceedings in the High
       Court or county court.

(8)   (Possibly) a clause prohibiting assignment of the agreement. Where assignment is
       to be permitted in certain circumstances and/or is permitted subject to certain
       conditions the clause should detail the relevant circumstances and conditions.

(9)   A clause providing that if the sponsor becomes bankrupt or enters into a
       voluntary arrangement or any company through which the sponsor is operating
       goes into compulsory or voluntary liquidation (save for the purposes of
       reconstructing or amalgamating a solvent company), or becomes insolvent or has
       a receiver, manager, or administrative receiver or provisional liquidator or
       administrator appointed, the agreement will automatically terminate. Provision
       should also be made in the clause as to the reassignment of any intellectual
       property rights which may have been licensed between the parties and to deal with
       the position of any new intellectual property rights which may have come into
       existence between the parties under the agreement.

(10)   A provision stating that the celebrity has received independent legal advice on the
       terms of the agreement from a solicitor with experience in dealing with
       sponsorship agreements.

(11)   A notice clause. A notice clause should be included to deal with the procedure to
       be followed where the agreement requires one party to give notice to the other
       party to activate a contractual clause, for example, to activate an option clause. A
       notice clause should provide how the notice should be given, namely in writing to
       the other party, and should provide how it is to be sent, for example, by personal
       delivery, fax, first class or recorded delivery post, when it is deemed to have been
       delivered, for example, for first class post it will usually be deemed to have been
       delivered on the first or second business day after it has been posted, and the
       address to which it should be sent, for example, to the address set out in the
       agreement or to the registered office or to such other address as may previously
       have been notified in writing by one party to the other.

---

[23]   See point (7) at **25.18**.

Chapter 26

MERCHANDISING AGREEMENT

INTRODUCTION

26.1   As was mentioned above,[1] merchandising can be a potentially lucrative source of income for a celebrity. Character merchandising is the use by a celebrity of his name, likeness, biographical details, signature, voice and any trade mark(s) which he has on assorted goods and paraphernalia such as T-shirts, sweat shirts, posters, mugs and key rings. Character merchandising differs from endorsement in that endorsement occurs where a celebrity actively promotes and recommends a company's particular product or product range.

26.2   The range of character merchandising has expanded beyond all recognition in the last 10 to 15 years, along with the income that the celebrity can earn from using their fame to exploit these products. The merchandise that was available used to be at the cheap and cheerful end of the market. Nowadays things have changed considerably. There are still the usual T-shirts, mugs and key rings available for the public to buy but now it is possible to buy a much larger range of merchandise. For example, it is possible to buy wine made from Sir Cliff Richard's vineyard or from Sting's vineyard, food produce grown on Sting's estate or clothes from Jay-Z's clothing range. Perhaps the most extreme example of character merchandising is that offered by the band Kiss, which has Kiss coffins for fans to buy.

26.3   It is certainly not unknown for a celebrity to earn more from the sale of merchandise products than he earns from the area in which he is famous. Indeed, if a particular product becomes so established it may in time become more associated in the public's eye with the celebrity than his 'main' career. One particular example of this is Loyd Grossman (whose name is a registered trade mark), who is probably now far more famous as the person associated with the highly successful range of Italian, Indian and Thai food sauces than for his career as a television presenter, chef, writer and musician.

THE MAIN TERMS

26.4   As was mentioned above,[2] before negotiating a merchandising agreement for a celebrity it is vital that the celebrity's solicitor checks with his client whether he has entered any other merchandising agreements in the past and also checks any employment contract(s) as they may restrict whether, where or how the celebrity can enter a merchandising agreement.

---

[1]   See Chapter 24 at **24.3** et seq.
[2]   See Chapter 24 at **24.8** et seq.

26.5   The main terms which would need to be dealt with in a merchandising agreement are:

(1)   the parties to the merchandising agreement;

(2)   the territory;

(3)   the term;

(4)   the advance, royalties and accounting;

(5)   the merchandiser's exclusive and non-exclusive rights;

(6)   the merchandiser's obligations;

(7)   the celebrity's obligations;

(8)   termination of the agreement;

(9)   intellectual property rights; and

(10)   warranties, indemnities and other clauses.

THE PARTIES TO THE MERCHANDISING AGREEMENT

26.6   As was mentioned above, a celebrity would rarely if ever have the expertise, time or contacts to set about manufacturing, distributing and selling merchandised items himself. The celebrity will usually enter an agreement in his own name or his own limited company which deals with his merchandising agreements will contract with a third party to allow the third party to manufacture, distribute and arrange the sale of the merchandise or to allow the third party to enter licences with others to manufacture, distribute and sell such items. The celebrity would receive from the third party royalties calculated on the sale of each of the items and he may also receive an advance from the third party which would be recoupable against sales of the items.

26.7   The third party would look to earn for providing its services to the celebrity a fee of between 20 and 30% of the net receipts from the merchandise licences it enters into.

26.8   It may be that the celebrity enters all his agreements through limited companies which have been set up to deal with various aspects of his career. Where a celebrity enters contractual arrangements via limited companies the merchandiser should ideally consider obtaining a side letter signed by the celebrity himself providing that should his company not comply with its obligations then he will personally be responsible for and will perform the contractual obligations or will be a party to the agreement itself as guarantor providing that his company will comply with its obligations and that if it does not then he will personally be responsible for and will perform the company's contractual obligations.

26.9   The celebrity may be concerned when contracting with the third party as to the third party's financial status. For example, the third party might be a fairly new company or may be a subsidiary of a larger, more established company. The celebrity should in such circumstances seek a guarantor to ensure that where the third party does not comply with the terms of the agreement that the guarantor will do so instead.

THE TERRITORY

26.10 The agreement should set out the territory in which the third party is allowed to manufacture, distribute and sell the merchandised items. The agreement will be subject to EU competition law, in particular the prohibition on anti-competitive agreements contained in Art 101(1) of the Treaty on the functioning of the European Union (Art 81(1) TEC).[3] Whilst the celebrity may prevent the third party actively selling into territories allocated to other third parties or reserved to the celebrity, the celebrity will not be able to prevent passive sales by the third party into other territories, ie sales made as a result of unsolicited orders.

THE TERM

26.11 The term might be a fixed term, a fixed term subject to sales targets being achieved, such as the term being for 4 years with sales targets having to be achieved each year before the contract will continue into the next year, or a fixed term with an option to renew. The option to renew might be subject to a matching rights clause.[4] The option to renew might, however, depend upon minimum sales targets being achieved during the term of the agreement and also subject to a further advance being paid on the exercise of the option and on each anniversary thereafter and an increase in the royalties payable for the option period with a minimum royalty payable each year irrespective of sales.[5] Alternatively, the term might be for a fixed term but would continue until any advance which has been paid to the celebrity has been recouped, subject to a long stop provision for the agreement to end if the advance has not been recouped by the long stop date.

THE ADVANCE, ROYALTIES AND ACCOUNTING

26.12 The agreement will commonly provide for an advance to be paid to the celebrity upon entering the agreement. The advance will usually be stated to be non-refundable and should only be recoupable from earnings generated from the agreement. The agreement may provide for further advances to be paid on every anniversary of the agreement, in which case the celebrity will want to ensure that the agreement provides for the advance to be paid in full even if the previous advance has not been recouped. The agreement may set out different advance figures to be paid for different merchandise products, for example, £10,000 advance for T-shirts, £5,000 advance for

---

[3] The TEC is the Treaty establishing the European Community and is basically the Treaty of Rome. The official title of the Treaty of Rome was the Treaty Establishing the European Economic Community. Following the Maastricht Treaty its name was changed to the Treaty establishing the European Community, as the European Economic Community was renamed the European Community. The Lisbon Treaty scraps the European Community, and the whole entity becomes the European Union. If it comes into force, as planned, the TEC will be renamed as the Treaty on the Functioning of the European Union (TFEU).
The Lisbon Treaty changes all the article numbers so Art 81(1) in the TEC will become Art 101(1) in the TFEU.

[4] See Chapter 25 at **25.13** point (9) for how a matching rights option operates.

[5] See Chapter 25 at **25.13** point (9) for how a matching rights option operates.

badges and £3,000 for cups and mugs. If the advance is set out in this way the celebrity should ideally ensure that recoupment for each tranche of the total advance payable is recoupable against those products for which the advance is paid. This is because, using the example above, if the advance for T-shirts has been recouped but the advances for badges and cups and mugs have not been recouped further sales of T-shirts will generate royalties which will actually be paid to the celebrity as that part of the advance has been recouped. Royalties would not be actually paid to the celebrity for badges and cups and mugs until their respective advances have been recouped. If a total global advance is payable for all merchandise then no royalties would actually be paid until the total advance has been recouped. If there is an option which is exercised and a further advance(s) is payable the celebrity will want to ensure that the agreement provides that the advance(s) payable will be paid irrespective of whether the previous advance(s) has been recouped. The licensee will have to recoup the outstanding unrecouped advance(s) and the advance(s) paid on exercising the option from future sales of merchandise.

26.13 As is all too common fame can be very transient. As quickly as a celebrity star rises so can it wane. If the celebrity begins to loose his allure the sales of merchandise product will fall away. An experienced merchandiser will be too aware of this possibility and if, say, in the second year of a 3-year agreement sales slide due to the decline in the celebrity's popularity, the merchandiser will not want to promote and manufacture the merchandise as vigorously in the third year of the agreement as it did in the past. This would mean with sales falling there would be a substantial reduction in royalties for the celebrity. In order to ensure that the merchandiser actively promotes the merchandise throughout the whole term of the agreement, the celebrity would want to have a minimum royalty payment clause in the agreement. The minimum royalty might be payable in addition to the advance, although the merchandiser would in all probability not agree to this. More likely would be that the minimum royalty would be based on the difference between the advance paid and the minimum royalty payable and would only be payable if actual royalties generated were less than the minimum royalty payable. This figure would be calculated at the end of each relevant accounting period. For example, if the agreement provided for a global £10,000 advance in the first year which is non-refundable but recoupable with a minimum royalty payable in the first year of £12,000 and merchandise sales in the first year were only £8,000, the celebrity would be due to be paid after the first accounting period an extra £2,000 even though the celebrity is still in an unrecouped position.

26.14 It is possible that the merchandiser has failed to achieve the minimum royalty payable not because of a decline in the celebrity's status but because the merchandiser has not done a good job promoting the merchandise or manufacturing enough merchandise to satisfy demand. The agreement could be drafted to protect the celebrity in this situation by providing either that where the merchandiser fails to achieve sufficient sales to reach the minimum royalty figure the celebrity can terminate the agreement or, if the agreement gave the merchandiser an exclusive right to sell particular products in a particular territory for a particular period of time, that the agreement will automatically become a non-exclusive agreement so that the celebrity can look to appoint others to sell the products in that territory(ies). It should be questioned whether another merchandiser would want to enter a non-exclusive agreement with the celebrity for the same products in the same territory for the same period of time and compete with the existing merchandiser which has failed to reach its sales targets, and even if another merchandiser would be prepared to do so, what advance and royalty rate would it be prepared to pay for an non-exclusive as opposed to an exclusive agreement?

26.15 The agreement will also need to define the word 'royalties'. Royalties will commonly be defined as the wholesale price of the merchandise sold excluding VAT or any other sales tax. An alternative to using the wholesale price of the merchandise sold to calculate the royalty payable fee could be to base it upon a percentage of the suggested retail sales price excluding VAT or any other sales tax. The royalty rate might, for example, be 10–15% of the suggested retail sales price excluding VAT or any other sales tax for all merchandise or there might be different royalty rates for different types of merchandise. (The royalty rate will be higher if the wholesale price is used as the basis for the royalty calculation.) Whatever definition is used, the agreement should provide that the royalty payable to the celebrity is exclusive of VAT and that VAT will only be payable in addition to the royalty payable where the celebrity is VAT registered and supplies the merchandiser with a VAT invoice. The celebrity will want to ensure the agreement does not allow the merchandising company to withhold royalties as a reserve against possible stock returns or to withhold payments as a set off in respect of any claims there might be. There should also be a provision for interest to be paid to the celebrity where royalty payments are made late. In addition, where all or some of the payments are made in a foreign currency the agreement should provide that where there is late payment of royalties the celebrity can choose whether the exchange rate used to calculate the royalty payable is to be the exchange rate on the date the royalty payment is due, namely the date prescribed in the agreement, or the date it is actually paid. This will enable the celebrity to ensure that he does not loose money due to him because of currency exchange variations.

26.16 The agreement should also deal with discounts from the wholesale price or the retail sales price which might be given by the merchandiser to third parties. Royalties should be calculated and paid to the celebrity on the wholesale price or the retail sales price and any discounts given by the merchandiser should only be given where the discount has been given in the normal course of business on an arm's length basis to someone unconnected to the merchandiser. The agreement should provide that if a discount is given outside of these circumstances, for example, by the merchandise company to its subsidiary company, then the royalty rate would be paid at the full rate. The agreement should also provide the amount of the discount which the merchandiser is permitted to offer and that if the merchandiser discounts below this sum that the royalty is payable at the discount rate as set out in the merchandise agreement.

26.17 The agreement should set out the accounting dates and the dates when the advance and royalty payments will be made. The accounting dates will usually be either twice a year on 30 June and 31 December or four times a year on the usual quarter days. The agreement should provide that an accounting statement will be prepared and sent to the celebrity within 21 days of the accounting date along with the royalty payment. The currency in which payment is made should also be set out in the agreement. Where all or some of the payments are made in a foreign currency the exchange rate should be the date that payment is due under the agreement unless (as was mentioned above) there is late payment of royalties, in which case the celebrity should be able to choose whether the exchange rate used to calculate the royalty payable is to be the exchange rate on the date the royalty payment is due or the date it is actually paid. This will enable the celebrity to ensure that he does not loose money due to him because of currency exchange variations. As was also mentioned above, interest should be paid where payment is made later than the agreed payment date and the agreement should provide for this and set out the rate of interest payable.

26.18 The celebrity will want to ensure the agreement between himself and the merchandiser provides that the accounting periods and payment dates in any sub-licences which may be entered into by the merchandiser are such that that the celebrity is paid the royalties due from any sub-licence agreements at the earliest possible date. This means ensuring that the merchandising agreement provides that the accounting periods and the payment dates in the merchandising agreement and in any sub-licences will be the same.

26.19 The agreement should also require the merchandising company to keep detailed, accurate accounts and allow the celebrity and/or his appointed agent/financial or legal adviser to carry out an audit of the accounts and a stock check no more than once a year upon giving written reasonable (say 14 days') notice. The merchandising company should be required to co-operate with the celebrity and/or his appointed agent/financial or legal adviser where an audit or stock check occurs and should be required to help the celebrity and/or his appointed agent/financial or legal adviser to check the accuracy of the sales figures with any sub-licensees, manufacturers or retail sales outlets which the merchandising company has dealt with. Any audit or stock check should be paid for by the celebrity unless there is an underpayment by the merchandising company of, say, 5%, in which case the cost of the audit should be borne by the merchandising company. The agreement will usually allow the merchandiser a run off period of 6 or 12 months after the end of the term to sell off any excess merchandise. The agreement should, because of the run-off period, allow the celebrity and/or his appointed agent/financial or legal adviser to have access to the accounts during this period and to carry out an audit or stock check on the same basis as if the agreement was still ongoing.

26.20 There is a possibility that a country where merchandise is sold has currency restrictions prohibiting money being sent out of the country. The agreement should contain a provision that where this situation occurs the merchandiser will inform the celebrity in writing that there is a currency restriction in place in that country and that the merchandiser will open a bank account for the celebrity in that country and deposit the royalties due to him into the account. The agreement should also require the merchandiser where withholding tax has been deducted on royalty payments in a foreign country to provide the celebrity with a tax deduction certificate which can be used by the celebrity to claim if possible the benefit of any double tax convention.

THE MERCHANDISER'S EXCLUSIVE AND NON-EXCLUSIVE RIGHTS

26.21 The agreement should set out what rights are being granted by the celebrity to the merchandiser and whether they are exclusive or non-exclusive rights. Some rights being granted will be exclusive whilst others will be non-exclusive. For example, the merchandiser may be granted:

(1) The non-exclusive right to use the celebrity's registered and non-registered trade marks(s) and other intellectual property rights in the ways permitted in the agreement. The reason why a non-exclusive right would be granted is because the celebrity will want to allow others to use his registered and non-registered trade marks(s) and other intellectual property rights so maximising the economic value

of his celebrity status.[6] To ensure control of his image the celebrity must reserve the right to approve the use of his name, image and/or logo on any proposed merchandise, on any promotional or advertising material and on any packaging which the company wants to use to promote the sale of the merchandise. The celebrity should also ensure that where his name, image and/or logo are used by the company the relevant copyright and trade mark notices are credited and that the company will immediately inform him of any infringements of which it becomes aware. As is mentioned below,[7] the merchandiser will be required to provide the celebrity with samples of the full range of the merchandise product and its packaging for the celebrity's written approval of its quality and design before it goes into production. The celebrity will want to ensure that he has the right to require changes to the quality and design of the merchandise and packaging before it goes into production. The merchandiser will resist the right for the celebrity to have total control over this approval and will usually only agree for the clause to allow the celebrity to make changes where they are reasonably required and for the celebrity's consent not to be unreasonably withheld. The merchandiser may also want to use quotes which are attributed to the celebrity to promote the merchandise in an advertising campaign. These should ideally be detailed in the agreement or the agreement should provide that the celebrity will allow the company to use any such attributed quotes which the company requires to promote the merchandise, subject to the celebrity's right to approve such quotes with his approval not to be unreasonably withheld.

(2)   The non-exclusive right to manufacture particular products. This allows other merchandisers who have contracted with the celebrity to be able to manufacture their products should they want to do so in the same territory as other merchandisers who have contracted with the celebrity.

(3)   The exclusive right to promote and sell particular products in a particular territory for a particular period of time.

26.22 It should be noted that the products should be defined in detail in the agreement to avoid any doubt as to what the merchandiser is permitted to manufacture, promote and sell.

THE MERCHANDISER'S OBLIGATIONS

26.23 The following are some of the obligations which the merchandiser might be required to comply with:

(1)   To pay the advance and royalties to the celebrity and to comply with the accounting provisions as detailed in the agreement.[8]

(2)   Where the celebrity is required to attend a press conference or a launch party and/or promotional events to promote the merchandise agreement the company

---

[6]   See **26.36** et seq.
[7]   See point (4) at **26.23**.
[8]   See **26.12** et seq.

will pay the celebrity the agreed appearance fee and reimburse the expenses which have been reasonably incurred by the celebrity for his appearance.[9]

(3)   To ensure the products which it is allowed to manufacture will be manufactured to the highest industry standards, in particular, that the products are made to a proper standard of worksmanship, do not use dangerous or defective materials and that they will comply with all relevant laws and regulations including safety and labelling regulations.

(4)   To manufacture, promote and sell the products throughout the whole term of the agreement and to ensure that adequate supplies are available during the term to meet anticipated sales demand. The merchandiser should also be required actively to promote the merchandise during the term of the agreement to the best of its ability in order to promote interest and increase sales.

       The merchandiser will be required to ensure that all advertising will comply with all legal and industry requirements such as those published by the Advertising Standards Authority.

(5)   To provide samples of the full range of the merchandise product and its packaging for the celebrity's written approval of their quality and design before they go into production. The celebrity will want to ensure that he has the right to require changes to the quality and design of the merchandise and packaging before it goes into production. The merchandiser will resist the right for the celebrity to have total control over its approval and will usually only agree for the clause to allow the celebrity to require changes to be made where they are reasonably required and for the celebrity's consent not to be unreasonably withheld. Samples of the products which have been manufactured for sale should also be sent to the celebrity on a regular basis or as and when reasonably required by the celebrity so that he can check the quality is of a consistent satisfactory standard, and where it is not the celebrity will want the right to request changes to be made to ensure that it is. The samples submitted for approval must be of the same quality and design as the intended final sale product. The clause should also provide that the merchandiser will take all necessary steps to remedy the situation where the merchandise for some reason does not come up to standard and that it will immediately cease manufacture, distribution and sales of any such defective merchandise until the defects have been remedied.

       One area that may need to be addressed is the possibility of a change in the celebrity's persona during the term of the agreement. For example, if the celebrity is a musician he might change the style of his music and accordingly his image several times throughout his career, like David Bowie has consistently done or as Rod Stewart has done in recent years, moving from being a rock singer to a more middle of the road/jazz singer with his interpretations of the Great American Songbook. Where the celebrity changes his image during the term of the agreement he may no longer want merchandise being manufactured and sold which shows his previous image and may want merchandise manufactured to reflect the new image. The celebrity will therefore want the agreement to provide that where he changes his image the merchandise will be altered accordingly to reflect the new image. In such a case the agreement would require the celebrity to submit images reflecting his new persona and to inform the merchandiser some time before the proposed image change to allow what will quickly become

---

[9]   See also point (6) at **26.26**.

outdated and potentially unsaleable stock to be sold off and for the new image merchandise to be manufactured in time for the launch of the celebrity's new persona. The merchandiser may, however, want a clause providing that where there is a substantial change of image it can terminate the agreement if it considers the new image is not as marketable as the previous image. Alternatively or in addition, the merchandiser may want the right to terminate the agreement if the celebrity changes his image more than once during the term of the agreement as it would be difficult to offload outdated stock and prepare new image stock on a regular basis.

(6) To supply to the celebrity for his own use free of charge or at a nominal cost a certain amount or a reasonable quantity of the final version of each type of the merchandise items. The merchandiser will want to ensure that the clause states the merchandise is for the celebrity's own use and is not for resale or to be given away in a promotional campaign and that these items are royalty free.

(7) Not do or permit anything to be done which damages or might damage the name, reputation or image of the celebrity or any of the celebrity's copyrights or trade marks or other intellectual property rights. In addition, the celebrity will want a provision included in the agreement that the merchandiser will immediately notify him of any infringements of which it becomes aware.

(8) Where the merchandiser has an exclusive licence to promote and sell the merchandise in a particular territory the merchandiser may be required under the terms of the agreement to take legal action against anyone who has or appears to have infringed the celebrity's intellectual property rights in the merchandise items.[10] Where the agreement contains such a clause the merchandiser should be required to notify the celebrity before commencing or threatening any such legal action and there similarly should be a requirement for the celebrity to notify the merchandiser of any potential infringements of which he is aware. Although the merchandiser may be required to take legal action for such infringement, the clause may provide that the merchandiser is only required to take such action if the merchandiser has a favourable legal opinion from a solicitor or barrister specialised in intellectual property litigation. As for who is to pay the cost of any such legal opinion and/or legal action, this should be dealt with in the agreement. Also the question of whether the merchandiser is required to take a second legal opinion if the first opinion is not favourable or whether the merchandiser is required to appeal an unfavourable court decision and, if so, how far it is required to appeal the decision, for example, is the merchandiser required to proceed to an appeal to the Court of Appeal, the Supreme Court or to the European courts, should be dealt with in the agreement.

(9) To ensure that all merchandise will have where relevant trade mark and copyright notices placed on them along with a statement that the merchandise is manufactured under licence from the right's owner.

(10) To ensure that product liability insurance is in place, preferably with the celebrity's name noted on the policy. The merchandiser will also be required to indemnify the celebrity for any claim, loss damage, liability or expense relating to any defective or allegedly defective merchandise.

---

[10] See Chapter 18 on Copyright.

(11) To submit all the advertising and promotional material to the celebrity for approval. The merchandiser will want the celebrity's approval not to be unreasonably withheld. The celebrity may want the merchandiser to guarantee that a minimum amount will be spent each year promoting the merchandise, in which case this should be set out in the agreement.

(12) Not to sell merchandise as remainder goods or as seconds or to give merchandise away for free or as premium or promotional goods. The celebrity may also want the merchandiser not to offer any merchandise on a sale or return basis, although the merchandiser may not be prepared to accept such a provision where it is usual for it to conduct its business or a substantial part of it on a sale or return basis.

(13) To comply with the terms of the agreement. Where the merchandiser intends to appoint another company to manufacture the merchandise the clause should also provide that the merchandiser will ensure that the manufacturer complies with the restrictions in the agreement between the celebrity and the merchandiser.

THE CELEBRITY'S OBLIGATIONS

26.24 As was mentioned earlier,[11] some intellectual property rights such as trade marks are protected by registration. The celebrity should be required to ensure that such intellectual property rights are protected by registration and that the registration of these rights is not allowed to lapse.[12]

26.25 As was mentioned above,[13] where the merchandiser has an exclusive licence to promote and sell the merchandise in a particular territory it may be required under the terms of the agreement to take appropriate legal action against anyone who has or appears to have infringed the celebrity's intellectual property rights in the merchandise items. It may be that the merchandiser either does not want to take on such an onerous responsibility or that the celebrity wants to retain the right for himself. If this is the case, the agreement should place the responsibility to do so on the celebrity, in which case there should be a requirement on the celebrity to notify the merchandiser before commencing or threatening any such legal action and there should be a requirement for the merchandiser to notify the celebrity of any potential infringements of which it is aware. Although the celebrity may be required to take relevant legal action for infringement of his intellectual property rights in the merchandise, the clause may provide that the celebrity is only required to take such action where he has a favourable legal opinion from a solicitor or barrister specialised in intellectual property litigation. As for who is to pay the cost of any such legal opinion and/or legal action, this should be dealt with in the agreement. Also the question of whether the celebrity is required to take a second legal opinion if the first opinion is not favourable or whether the celebrity is required to appeal an unfavourable court decision and, if so, how far he is required to appeal the decision, for example, is the celebrity required to proceed to an appeal to the Court of Appeal, the Supreme Court or to the European courts, should be dealt with in the agreement.

---

[11]   See Chapter 18 on Copyright.
[12]   See **26.36** et seq.
[13]   See point (7) and (8) at **26.23**.

26.26 The following are some other obligations which the celebrity may be required to comply with:

(1)   To comply with his obligations in the agreement.

(2)   To perform his obligations in a professional manner.

(3)   To confirm that he is in good health and, if required, to undergo a medical to satisfy the merchandiser or the merchandiser's insurers that this is the case. In addition, the celebrity will be required to take reasonable steps to ensure that he remains in good health.

(4)   Not to participate during the term of the agreement in any dangerous or hazardous activities which might prevent him from carrying out his contractual obligations.

(5)   At all times to keep the merchandiser informed of his whereabouts and supply it with his personal mobile and landline telephone numbers so that the merchandiser can contact him as and when required. As an alternative to supplying his personal telephone numbers to the merchandiser other contact numbers such as that of his personal manager may be acceptable.

(6)   To attend a press conference, launch party and/or promotional events to promote the merchandised products. If the celebrity agrees to this, the agreement should provide that he will attend at an agreed date and venue (or at a date and venue which will be notified to him eg 8 weeks in advance of the proposed date) for a specified period of time and that he will attend subject to his overriding work commitments with his employer. A provision that the celebrity will attend subject to his work commitments would be needed to cover a situation where, for example, the celebrity is a Premier League footballer and he is required by his club to travel with the team to play in a rescheduled league or cup game on the day of his proposed promotional appearance for the merchandiser. Where the celebrity agrees to appear at a press conference, launch party or promotional events he will want to ensure the company pays his reasonable travel, food and where necessary hotel accommodation expenses and in addition he may also require an additional appearance fee. These matters should also be dealt with in the agreement.[14]

(7)   Where the celebrity is promoting the merchandising agreement, for example, by making a personal appearance or filming a promotional advert, he will comply with all relevant regulations such as fire, health and safety and crowd safety regulations and any relevant trade union regulations.

(8)   Where the celebrity is a sportsman, he will be required to comply with his club's and national and international governing bodies' rules and regulations.

(9)   Not to do or permit anything to be done which damages or might damage his own name, reputation or image and not to do anything or permit anything to be done which damages or might damage his own copyrights or trade marks or other intellectual property rights.

---

[14]   See also point (2) at **26.23**.

(10)   Not do anything or permit anything to be done which damages or might damage the merchandiser's name, reputation or image or the name, reputation or image of its products and not to do or permit anything to be done which damages or might damage the merchandiser's copyrights or trade marks or other intellectual property rights.

(11)   Not to enter or purport to enter any agreement(s) with third parties in the merchandiser's name.

(12)   When promoting the merchandise, to mention the name of the merchandise company and/or its goods/services in interviews with the press and other broadcast media. The celebrity may also be required to wear clothes with the merchandiser's name and logo on for promotional interviews.

(13)   The merchandiser will usually want the celebrity to use its product(s) and wear its company logo on his clothing in his professional career. This could be a problem where, for example, the celebrity is a sportsman, as his employment contract with his club or the rules of his playing association or particular tournament rules or television broadcaster regulations may limit or prohibit particular types of advertising or may limit the size and positioning of advertising logos. The agreement should therefore provide that the celebrity will use the merchandiser's product(s) and wear its logo on his clothing in his professional career subject to any constraints that he is under in his professional career.

TERMINATION OF THE AGREEMENT

26.27   It is possible that the merchandiser might fail to achieve the minimum royalty payment target provided for in the agreement. In such a situation there could be a provision in the agreement allowing the celebrity to terminate the agreement.[15] The celebrity may also want the right to terminate where the merchandiser has substantially (eg by 25%) under-accounted for royalties on, for example, two occasions. The agreement may also provide that the celebrity is permitted to terminate where the merchandiser ceases to carry out its merchandising business.

26.28   The agreement should also deal with what is to happen with existing merchandise following termination of the agreement. Where the agreement expires by effluxion of time, the agreement should allow the merchandiser a period of time following the end of the agreement term to sell any remaining merchandise which it has left. The agreement should provide that during the sell off period the merchandiser only has a non-exclusive licence to sell the remaining merchandise which it has left and that it can no longer manufacture any further stock during this period. The clause may also provide that the merchandiser cannot sell the remaining stock at a discount price and, in addition, that it will inform the celebrity in writing immediately before the commencement of the sell off period of the amount of merchandise it has left in stock. (It should be remembered that where the celebrity enters a merchandising agreement with another company immediately after the termination of the previous agreement, where the previous agreement has a non-exclusive sell off right the celebrity can only grant the new merchandiser a non-exclusive right to sell whilst the previous merchandiser still has the right to sell its remaining stock and only after this period has expired can the celebrity

---

[15]   See **26.12** et seq.

grant the new merchandiser an exclusive right to sell.) Where there is a sell off period clause there should be an additional provision in the agreement requiring the merchandiser to destroy any stock which remains after the sell off period has expired. Alternatively or in addition, the agreement may provide that the celebrity can buy the remaining stock from the merchandiser at the end of the term at either wholesale, retail or a discount price. To ensure an excessive amount of merchandise is not manufactured by the merchandiser towards the end of the term a clause should be included which requires the merchandiser not to manufacture during, for example, the last year of the term more than the average amount of merchandise which was produced during the first year of the agreement. Where the agreement expires due to a breach of contract by the merchandiser the agreement should provide that the merchandiser's rights cease automatically and it has no right to manufacture, distribute and/or sell the merchandise. Whether the term expires due to effluxion of time or due to the merchandiser's breach of contract a provision should be included in the agreement requiring the merchandiser to return any photographs and other items which were supplied by the celebrity to enable the merchandiser to produce the merchandise. There should also be a provision in the agreement stating that upon termination all the celebrity's intellectual property rights which were licensed to the merchandiser revert to the celebrity and that the merchandiser will execute any documents which are required to ensure that the intellectual property rights revert to the celebrity.

26.29 The agreement should contain specific provisions which if breached would enable the innocent party to terminate. For example, a well-drafted agreement should contain a 'morality clause' providing that the celebrity will not do anything which damages or might damage the merchandiser's name, reputation or image or the name, reputation or image of its goods/services. Where the celebrity does something which might bring the merchandiser's name into disrepute, for example, he gets arrested for or charged with a serious crime, the merchandiser will then be able to terminate the agreement under the morality clause provision.

26.30 The agreement should ideally not only contain relevant provisions which allow for termination of the agreement in circumstances where there is a serious or substantial breach of contract, but also set out what happens where one party terminates the agreement due to the other party's breach. For example, the agreement would usually provide that the innocent party has no liability to the other party for future obligations from the date of the breach, although both parties would retain their existing contractual rights and liabilities up to the date of termination.

26.31 Where the agreement is for a fixed term but contains a provision for the merchandiser to renew, the procedure as to how to exercise the option should be set out in detail so that both parties know whether the agreement will continue or will terminate at the end of the proposed fixed term. A written notice procedure between the parties should be provided for in the agreement. For example, the agreement may require the celebrity to notify the merchandiser in writing of his right to exercise an option 3 months before the proposed termination date of the agreement and allow the merchandiser a period of 14 days from service of the notice to decide whether to exercise the option or whether to let the agreement end. Where the merchandiser has a matching rights option the agreement should also set out the terms the merchandiser must match to be able to exercise the option and what information the celebrity is to supply to the merchandiser to enable it to decide whether to exercise the option.[16] If the

---

[16] See point (2)(b) in Chapter 24 at **24.8** and point (9) at **25.13**.

merchandiser decides not to renew the agreement having had a chance to do so the celebrity can then safely treat the existing agreement as terminated and look for a new merchandiser.

26.32 The agreement might be for a fixed term with a break clause allowing one of the parties to terminate the agreement early by exercising the break clause provision. The details of how and when a break clause can be exercised must be set out in the agreement. For example, a 3-year agreement might contain a provision which allows the merchandiser to terminate the agreement at the end of the first year, which would be exercised by the merchandiser giving written notice of termination to the celebrity by first class post to his home address with the notice being sent not less than 3 months before the end of the first year of the agreement. If the break clause is not exercised or not correctly exercised as prescribed in the agreement then the agreement will continue until the end of the term or until the next break clause is exercised (if there is another break clause provided for in the agreement). If the break clause is validly exercised by the merchandiser the agreement should provide that any further advances which would have been payable in the future are no longer payable, although any monies still owing to the celebrity for the period up to the termination date and any royalty payments which will become due on any outstanding stock which is sold after the termination date are still payable. The agreement should also provide that all liabilities and obligations until the date of termination still exist notwithstanding the exercise of the break clause.

26.33 A clause(s) may be of such importance to the merchandiser that it goes to the 'essence' of the agreement. For example, the merchandiser may only want to be associated with the celebrity because he is a high-profile actor playing a particular role in a television soap opera, whereas other potential merchandisers would have been prepared to contract with the celebrity for the person he is rather than for the character he plays in the television soap opera. In a situation such as where the merchandiser has contracted with the celebrity purely because of the role he plays in a television soap opera and it is imperative to the merchandiser that he remains in the role during the term of the agreement, a provision should be included in the agreement to this effect and that it is 'of the essence' of the contract. This will enable the merchandiser to terminate the agreement should the celebrity leave the soap opera.

26.34 The agreement will often provide that where one party is in material breach of contract the other party must notify it in writing of the breach and require the breach to be remedied within a period of time and that if the breach has not been remedied in that time the agreement is automatically terminated. The agreement should also provide where termination has occurred due to a material breach by one of the parties that the parties' contractual rights, liabilities and obligations until the date of termination still exist notwithstanding termination (save for the obligation by the merchandiser to pay any outstanding advance to the celebrity where it is the celebrity who has been in material breach of contract).

26.35 The agreement should contain a force majeure clause. A force majeure clause should list all the events beyond the control of the contracting parties, for example, act of God, civil war, terrorism, strikes, lock outs, which if any occur will excuse the party who cannot perform its contractual obligations due to the force majeure event. The clause should provide that the party who cannot perform its contractual obligations will not be in breach of contract for non-performance where this is due to a force majeure event. The clause should require the party who cannot perform its obligations due to a force majeure event to give notice to the other party of the existence of the force majeure event and that it prevents it from performing its contractual obligations. The force majeure clause should provide that the agreement is suspended whilst the force majeure event exists and that the agreement will recommence once the force majeure event has ended. As the suspension could last for a long time there should be a long stop provision in the agreement allowing one party to serve written notice on the other party terminating the agreement where the agreement is suspended for a specified period of time due to a force majeure event. Where termination occurs due to a force majeure event, the agreement should deal with what is to happen in these circumstances.

INTELLECTUAL PROPERTY RIGHTS

26.36 The celebrity will need to ensure the following:[17]

(1) Before entering the contract, that he has checked that he does actually own the relevant rights which he is intending to license. It may be, for example, a logo was commissioned by the celebrity from a third party in which case the celebrity should check that he has taken a full assignment of the copyright in the design of the logo from the third party before he enters the merchandising agreement allowing the merchandiser the right to use it.

(2) That the use of his intellectual property rights is strictly controlled in the agreement. There should be a provision in the agreement which states that the celebrity is granting the merchandiser a non-exclusive licence to use the relevant right(s). The extent to which the merchandiser can use the rights granted must also be set out precisely in the agreement.[18] The celebrity will also want a provision included in the agreement that the merchandiser will immediately notify him of any infringements of which the merchandiser becomes aware.

(3) That the merchandiser cannot, save where the agreement provides, allow anyone else to use the celebrity's intellectual property rights without the express written permission of the celebrity. Where it is intended that the merchandiser can permit others to use the celebrity's intellectual property rights the agreement should set out in detail the circumstances in which this is permitted.

(4) If any new intellectual property rights might be created during the agreement term, for example, new photographs are taken of the celebrity by the merchandiser for a product range, then there should be a provision as to who will own the intellectual property rights and that any necessary documents will be executed to ensure an effective creation and transfer of ownership in these rights and that any third parties will be required to execute any necessary documentation to ensure the transfer of ownership.

(5) In the unlikely event that the celebrity is required to make audio and/or audio-visual recordings to promote the merchandise agreement the copyright,

---

[17] See also Chapter 18 on Copyright.
[18] See **26.21** et seq, **26.23** and **26.27** et seq. For the difference between a licence and an assignment see above. See also Chapter 18 on Copyright.

moral rights, performers' rights and performers' moral rights issues need to be considered in relation to the recordings.[19]

26.37 There should be a provision in the agreement stating that upon termination all the celebrity's intellectual property rights which were licensed to the merchandiser revert to the celebrity and that the merchandiser will execute any documents which are required to ensure that the intellectual property rights revert to the celebrity.[20] Some intellectual property rights such as trade marks are protected by registration. The celebrity should be required to ensure that such intellectual property rights are protected by registration and that the registration of these rights is not allowed to lapse.[21]

26.38 The agreement should also deal with who is responsible for taking legal action where the celebrity's intellectual property rights have been infringed.[22] and for the merchandiser to ensure that all merchandise will have where relevant trade mark and copyright notices placed on them along with a statement that the merchandise is manufactured under licence from the right's owner.[23]

26.39 The agreement should also contain a warranty from the celebrity that any trade mark he has licensed to the merchandiser is original, that he is the sole and absolute owner of the trade mark and that any such trade mark does not infringe the rights of any third party. A similar warranty should also be given in the agreement where the celebrity is allowing the merchandiser to use any other of his intellectual property rights. The agreement should also provide that the celebrity will indemnify the merchandiser from any expense or liability which might be incurred where the warranty relating to his intellectual property rights proves to be incorrect.[24]

WARRANTIES, INDEMNITIES AND OTHER CLAUSES

26.40 As mentioned above,[25] the agreement should contain a warranty from the celebrity that any trade mark he has licensed to the merchandiser is original, that he is the sole and absolute owner of the trade mark and that any such trade mark does not infringe the rights of any third party. A similar warranty should also be given in the agreement where the celebrity is allowing the merchandiser to use any other of his intellectual property rights. The agreement should also provide that the celebrity will indemnify the merchandiser from any expense or liability which might be incurred where the warranty relating to his intellectual property rights proves to be incorrect.[26]

26.41 The agreement should contain a warranty by each party that they are free and able to enter the agreement, that they are able to perform their contractual obligations and that neither party has entered any agreements which might compete or conflict. The merchandising company might seek to widen the scope of this warranty to provide that the celebrity will not during the term of the agreement except where expressly provided for enter any competing or conflicting agreement.

---

[19]   See Chapter 27 at **27.40** et seq for details. See also Chapter 18 on Copyright.
[20]   See also **26.27** et seq.
[21]   See also **26.24** et seq and Chapter 18 on Copyright.
[22]   See also point (6) at **26.23** and **26.24** et seq.
[23]   See also point (8) at **26.23**.
[24]   See **26.21–26.22** and **26.40** et seq.
[25]   See **26.36** et seq.
[26]   See **26.21–26.22**.

26.42 Other provisions which should be dealt with in the agreement include, inter alia:

(1)   That both parties will keep the terms of the agreement confidential and will not disclose them to anyone other than their professional advisers or as may be required by law.

(2)   That the agreement between the parties does not constitute a joint venture, partnership or employment relationship.

(3)   That the agreement reflects the whole of the agreement between the parties and replaces any earlier oral or written agreement.

(4)   That the celebrity will not hold himself out as representing the merchandiser. A similar provision should also be made by the merchandiser to the celebrity.

(5)   Which legal system will apply (in nearly all cases this will be the law of England and Wales) and the method to be used to resolve any disputes between the parties, namely alternative dispute resolution, arbitration or legal proceedings in the High Court or county court.

(6)   (Possibly) a provision enabling the parties to limit the extent of any indemnity which has been given to the other party.

(7)   (Possibly) a clause prohibiting assignment of the agreement. Where assignment is to be permitted in certain circumstances and/or is permitted subject to certain conditions the clause should detail the relevant circumstances and conditions.

(8)   A clause providing that if the merchandiser becomes bankrupt or enters into a voluntary arrangement or any company through which the merchandiser is operating goes into compulsory or voluntary liquidation (save for the purposes of reconstructing or amalgamating a solvent company), or becomes insolvent or has a receiver, manager, or administrative receiver or provisional liquidator or administrator appointed, the agreement will automatically terminate. Provision should also be made in the clause as to the reassignment of any intellectual property rights which may have been licensed between the parties and to deal with the position of any new intellectual property rights which may have come into existence between the parties under the agreement.

(9)   A clause stating that the celebrity has received independent legal advice on the terms of the agreement from a solicitor with experience in dealing with merchandising agreements.

(10) A notice clause. A notice clause should be included to deal with the procedure to be followed where the agreement requires one party to give notice to the other party to activate a contractual clause, for example, to activate an option clause. A notice clause should provide how the notice should be given, namely in writing to the other party, and should provide how it is to be sent, for example, by personal delivery, fax, first class or recorded delivery post, when it is deemed to have been delivered, for example, for first class post it will usually be deemed to have been delivered on the first or second business day after it has been posted, and the address to which it should be sent, for example, to the address set out in the

agreement or to the registered office or to such other address as may previously have been notified in writing by one party to the other.

Chapter 27

ENDORSEMENT AGREEMENT

INTRODUCTION

27.1   As was mentioned above,[1] endorsement occurs where a celebrity actively promotes and recommends a company's particular product or product range. The terms of the endorsement agreement will require the celebrity actually to promote and be seen to use the product which he is endorsing. The celebrity will allow the company to use his name, likeness, signature, biographical details, voice and any trade mark(s) which he has in advertising the product on, for example, radio, television and in newspaper adverts and his name, likeness, signature, and any trade mark(s) which he has for use on the packaging of the goods which he is endorsing or on the goods themselves. The company which is seeking to use the celebrity to endorse a product will have selected that celebrity because it believes that the relationship between its product range and the celebrity will strike a positive connection with the general public and will increase the sales of that particular product. Some celebrity endorsements will not only promote an existing range of the company's products but will also be used to promote a new range of products which have been designed (sometimes by the celebrity himself) and manufactured as that particular celebrity's own product range. For example, a sportsman may endorse a company's existing range of tennis rackets and/or he may also endorse a new range of tennis rackets which has his name on and which have been designed by him for use by the general public. Although endorsement agreements are common with sportsmen they are entered into by many types of celebrity, for example, a rock musician may endorse a particular range of guitars or a pop star, film actress or reality television celebrity might endorse a perfume which has been designed in consultation with the celebrity and made in conjunction with the perfume house and is named after the celebrity or named after something that has a connection with the celebrity.

THE MAIN TERMS

27.2   As was mentioned above,[2] before negotiating an endorsement agreement for a celebrity it is vital that the celebrity's solicitor checks with his client whether the celebrity has entered any other endorsement agreements in the past and also checks any employment contract(s) as they may restrict whether, where or how the celebrity can enter an endorsement agreement.

27.3   The main terms which would need to be dealt with in an endorsement agreement are:

---

[1]   See **24.3** et seq.
[2]   See **24.8–24.9**.

(1)   the parties to the endorsement agreement;

(2)   the territory;

(3)   the term and exclusivity;

(4)   the endorsement fee and the endorsed product(s);

(5)   the company's exclusive and non-exclusive rights;

(6)   the company's obligations;

(7)   the celebrity's obligations;

(8)   termination of the agreement;

(9)   intellectual property rights; and

(10) warranties, indemnities and other clauses.

THE PARTIES TO THE ENDORSEMENT AGREEMENT

27.4   A celebrity will enter an agreement with a company which wants him to endorse its product(s) either in his own name or via his own limited company. Where the celebrity enters an endorsement agreement via a limited company which has been set up to deal with his endorsement deals, he will be required to either sign a side letter providing that should that company not comply with its obligations then he will personally be responsible for and will perform the contractual obligations or be a party to the agreement itself as guarantor that his company will comply with its obligations and that if it does not then he will personally be responsible for and will perform his company's contractual obligations.

27.5   The celebrity may be concerned when contracting with a company as to the company's financial status. For example, the company might be a fairly new company or may be a subsidiary of a larger more established company. The celebrity should in such circumstances seek a guarantor to ensure that where the company does not comply with the terms of the agreement the guarantor will do so instead.

THE TERRITORY

27.6   The agreement should set out the territory/territories in which the celebrity is contracting to endorse the company's product(s).

THE TERM AND EXCLUSIVITY

27.7   The agreement will usually be for a fixed term of at least a year often with an option for the company to renew.[3] Where the endorsement is of a personalised product range such as the 'Anne Smith' perfume, the agreement would be for a fairly long period of time to enable the company to make a return on the manufacture and marketing of the special personalised product range.[4] The company will want some degree of exclusivity with the celebrity with reference to the product(s) he is endorsing. The company will at the minimum require the celebrity to endorse the product(s) which are the subject of the agreement exclusively for the term of the agreement. The company may also want the right after the term has ended to have an additional short period of time to wind down any advertising or promotional campaigns which it has been running and the right to dispose of any outstanding endorsed stock free from the competition of any competing products which the celebrity might subsequently endorse with another company. Where a run off period is required by the company the celebrity will not during this period be able actively to advertise or promote or permit another company to advertise, promote or sell competing products unless the original company is prepared to accept a non-exclusive right to advertise, promote and sell the outstanding stock during the run off period and unless, which is extremely unlikely, the competing company is also prepared to accept a non-exclusive right to advertise, promote and sell its product during the run off period and thereafter the non-competing company's non-exclusive right will become an exclusive right.

27.8   The word 'product(s)' must be defined in detail so that it is clear what the celebrity is exclusively endorsing.[5] The exclusivity clause in the agreement should be one that is fair and reasonable to both parties. Certainly, the company will not want the celebrity endorsing products which compete directly or indirectly with those which are the subject of the agreement and the celebrity will not want to be barred from endorsing non-competing products with other companies, although it may be appropriate to do so if the endorsement period is for a very short period of time. Any exclusivity should also be limited to the territory in which the endorsed product(s) are sold.

THE ENDORSEMENT FEE AND THE ENDORSED PRODUCT(S)

27.9   As was mentioned above,[6] the word 'product(s)' must be defined in detail so that it is clear what the celebrity is exclusively endorsing. Generally, the endorsement will be either one particular product range or one product in that product range, although it may be an endorsement of all the company's products. In addition to or as opposed to any existing product range, the endorsement might be of a new product, namely a personalised product such as the 'John Smith' golf clubs or golf wear, or the 'Anne Smith' perfume which will be brought out when the celebrity enters the agreement.

27.10   Most endorsement deals pay a flat fee often paid over the term of the agreement to the celebrity rather than a royalty based upon the number of endorsed items sold. Where the agreement is for a period of years the celebrity should ideally ensure that the

---

[3]   See point (9) at **25.13** for how a matching rights option operates.
[4]   See **27.9** et seq.
[5]   See **27.9** et seq.
[6]   See **27.7–27.8**.

fee payable increases at the start of each year of the term and should certainly seek an increase in the fee where the merchandiser wants to exercise an option clause. The celebrity could also seek additional fees where the endorsement is promoted in specific ways, for example, he may want an increase in the fee where the merchandiser decides to promote the product(s) by way of a television campaign and will also want repeat fees to be paid for such adverts.

27.11 In addition, it is possible that the company might be prepared to pay the celebrity an increased fee should sales of the endorsed product exceed a stated figure. It should, however, be noted that it is not that common for an increased fee to be paid by the company as the company is paying the celebrity to endorse a product which is already being sold and the object of the endorsement is to increase the sales of an existing product. From the company's position the endorsement fee is meant to pay the celebrity to help increase existing sales of the products. However, the company may be prepared to pay an increased fee or perhaps royalties where a new product line is launched from scratch and should pay royalties where a celebrity personalised product range is launched to tie in with the endorsement such as the 'John Smith' golf clubs. Where a royalty is payable the company will usually want the royalty to be calculated on sales at the net invoice value excluding VAT.

27.12 Where the celebrity enters an endorsement agreement which includes a personalised product range as well as the endorsement fee which he will be paid there will be in addition a royalty fee payable on sales of the personalised items. Where a royalty is to be paid to the celebrity he may want the company to pay an advance on the anticipated sales of the personalised product range.

27.13 The endorsement fee may be a flat fee which will increase dependent upon performance levels achieved by the celebrity in the field for which he is renowned. For example, the celebrity might be a footballer and the endorsement fee might be increased should he achieve certain targets with his club and/or country such as finishing as the top scorer in the Premier League at the end of the season or scoring goals in World Cup qualifying games for his international team.

27.14 Where the celebrity or the company through which he provides his services is registered for VAT the agreement should provide that all monies due to him or that company under the agreement will be subject to VAT and that the endorsement company will be supplied by him or that company with a VAT invoice.

THE COMPANY'S EXCLUSIVE AND NON-EXCLUSIVE RIGHTS

27.15 The company will want some degree of exclusivity with the celebrity with reference to the product(s) he is endorsing. The company will at the minimum require the celebrity to endorse the product(s) which are the subject of the agreement exclusively for the term of the agreement. The company may also want the exclusivity period to extend for a short period after the agreement term so that it can finish its advertising campaign and dispose of any outstanding endorsed stock free from competition from any competing products which the celebrity might subsequently endorse with another company. As was mentioned earlier, the word 'product(s)' must be defined in detail so that it is clear what the celebrity is exclusively endorsing.[7] The exclusivity clause in the

---

[7]   See **27.9** et seq.

agreement should be one that is fair and reasonable to both parties. Certainly, the company will not want the celebrity endorsing products which compete directly or indirectly with those which are the subject of the agreement and the celebrity will not want to be barred from endorsing non-competing products with other companies, although it may be appropriate to do so if the endorsement period is for a very short period of time. Any exclusivity should also be limited to the territory in which the endorsed product(s) is sold for the agreement term.

27.16 The company will require the exclusive right to use the celebrity's name, likeness, biographical details, signature, voice and any trade mark(s) which he has to promote, advertise and sell the endorsed product(s) on, for example, radio, television and in newspaper adverts and the right to use the celebrity's name, likeness, signature and any trade mark(s) which he has for use on the packaging of the goods which he is endorsing or on the goods themselves. Except in very few cases, such as possibly where the endorsement period is for a very short period of time, the celebrity should ensure that he is only granting the company the exclusive right to use his name, likeness, biographical details, signature, voice and any trade mark(s) which he has for the purpose of endorsing the products which are the subject of the agreement as he may want to grant the use of these rights to other companies for other commercial purposes so maximising the economic value of his celebrity status.

27.17 To ensure control of his image the celebrity must reserve the right to approve the use of his name, image and/or logo on any proposed material, such as any promotional or advertising material, and on any packaging which the company wants to use to promote the sale of the product(s). The celebrity should also ensure that where his name, image and/or logo are used by the company the relevant copyright notices and trade mark notices are credited and that there is a provision in the agreement that the company will immediately notify the celebrity of any infringements of his name, image and/or logo of which the company becomes aware. The company will also want to use quotes which are attributed to the celebrity to promote the endorsed product(s) in the advertising campaign. These should ideally be detailed in the agreement or the agreement should provide that the celebrity will allow the company to use any such attributed quotes which the company requires to promote the endorsed product(s) subject to the celebrity's right to approve such quotes with his approval not to be unreasonably withheld.

THE COMPANY'S OBLIGATIONS

27.18 The celebrity will be concerned that the endorsed product(s) do not in any way damage his reputation and might leave him possibly open to a legal claim from a third party or to damaging publicity due to his recommendation of the product(s) should they be of poor quality or defective or where they cause injury or death. To this end the agreement will require the company to ensure that the endorsed product(s) and the packaging will comply with all relevant safety legislation, regulations and industry standards. The celebrity will also want to ensure that where the company is allowed to licence the rights all licensees will be required to adhere to these requirements. The agreement should therefore provide that the company will ensure that any licensees will comply with these requirements.

27.19 Where the endorsement includes any personalised product such as the 'John Smith' golf clubs or golf wear as well as the company's usual product range, there should be a provision in the agreement that any such personalised product range will be at the premium end of the company's product range. This is because the celebrity will have a certain reputation, image and status to live up to and will want his personalised product range to reflect that and will also want to portray the image that his personalised product range is at the very least the equal to any of the product ranges he is endorsing for the company.

27.20 The company may require the celebrity to use any personalised products such as the 'John Smith' golf clubs in professional tournaments. Where this is the case the agreement should provide that the company will at its own expense alter the products the celebrity is actually using in tournaments to the celebrity's personal needs. This is because sports equipment for professional sportsmen is tailor-made or adapted to suit their individual needs.

27.21 The celebrity will usually want the company to let him have a specified amount of the endorsed product free of charge. The company will want to limit the amount it is obliged to provide free of charge to the celebrity and will want to ensure that it is for the celebrity's own personal use and will not be resold by him. In addition, the celebrity may want the right to purchase additional amounts of the endorsed product from the company at cost price or at a discount to the wholesale or suggested retail price. The company will again want to ensure that where it agrees to this there is a limit on the amount the celebrity can purchase at a discount and that it is for the celebrity's own personal use and will not be resold by him. In addition, where the celebrity is receiving either free or discounted product from the company the company will require the agreement to provide that these items are not royalty bearing.

27.22 As the company will be advertising the endorsed products using the celebrity's name, likeness, biographical details, signature, voice and any trade mark(s), the agreement should provide that all advertising relating to the endorsed products will comply with all relevant laws and regulations such as the Advertising Standards Authority Code of Practice and that the celebrity will not be portrayed in a way that would damage his reputation. In addition, the celebrity will want all advertising and promotional material to be submitted to him for approval. The endorsement company will want to ensure that the agreement provides that the celebrity's approval will not be unreasonably withheld.[8]

27.23 If, for example, the celebrity is a professional golfer he may be concerned that the company might decide to enter an endorsement agreement with another professional golfer to promote the same or similar products to those which the celebrity is endorsing whilst he is himself under contract to the company. If this is the case the agreement should provide that the company will not during the term of the agreement enter an endorsement agreement with another professional golfer for the same or similar products. Where such a provision is required by the celebrity it should be limited from the company's point of view to the territory for which the celebrity has contracted to endorse the product(s).

27.24 As was mentioned earlier,[9] the company will want a short period of time after the end of the term to finish its advertising campaign and dispose of any outstanding endorsed stock free from competition from any competing products which the celebrity

---

[8] The ASA Code is beyond the scope of this book.
[9] See **27.7–27.8**.

might subsequently endorse with another company. The agreement should provide that at the end of the run off period any surplus stock which still remains will be destroyed. Alternatively, the celebrity may allow the company to give any surplus unsold stock to charity.

27.25 The company may require the celebrity to make personal appearances to help promote the endorsed product(s). Where this is the case the celebrity may require the company to make an additional payment for each personal appearance and will certainly require the company to reimburse him for all the reasonable expenses he incurs such as travel, food and where necessary hotel accommodation in promoting the company's products.[10] The agreement should therefore deal with the company's obligations towards the celebrity where he is required by it to make personal appearances to promote the endorsed product(s).

27.26 The following are some other obligations which the endorsement company might be required to comply with:

(1)   To pay the endorsement fee and where there is an advance and royalties the advance and royalties to the celebrity and to comply with the accounting provisions as detailed in the agreement.[11]

(2)   To ensure the products which it is allowed to manufacture will be manufactured to the highest industry standards and, in particular, that the products are made to a proper standard of worksmanship, do not use dangerous or defective materials and that they will comply with all relevant laws and regulations, including safety and labelling regulations.

(3)   To manufacture, promote and sell the endorsed products throughout the whole term of the agreement and to ensure that adequate supplies are available during the term to meet anticipated sales demand. The endorsement company should also be required actively to promote the products during the term of the agreement to the best of its ability in order to promote interest and increase sales.

(4)   The endorsement company will be required to ensure that all advertising will comply with all legal and industry requirements such as those published by the Advertising Standards Authority.

(5)   To provide samples of the full range of the endorsed products and their packaging to the celebrity before they go into production. The endorsement company will not agree to the celebrity having approval rights in relation to an existing product's quality and design which the celebrity will be endorsing, although the company may be prepared to grant the celebrity the right to approve the packaging on an existing product where the packaging bears the name or identity of the celebrity on it. In addition, the company may be prepared to grant the celebrity approval rights over the quality and design where a personalised product is to be manufactured under the terms of the agreement. In any event, should the company agree to the celebrity having any form of approval rights it will only agree to allow the celebrity to require changes to be made where they are reasonably required and for the celebrity's consent not to be unreasonably

---

[10]   See also Chapter 25 at **25.16** point (7) and point (6) at **26.26**.
[11]   See **27.9** et seq.

withheld. Samples of the products which have been manufactured for sale should also be sent to the celebrity on a regular basis or as and when reasonably required by the celebrity so that he can check the quality is of a consistent satisfactory standard and where it is not the celebrity will want the right to require changes to be made to ensure that it is. The samples submitted for approval must be of the same quality and design as the intended final sale product. The clause should also provide that the endorsement company will take all necessary steps to remedy the situation where the endorsed products for some reason do not come up to standard and that it will immediately cease manufacture, distribution and sales of any such defective products until the defects have been remedied.

One area that may need to be addressed is the possibility of a change in the celebrity's persona during the term of the agreement. For example, if a celebrity musician might change the style of his music and accordingly his image several times throughout his career, like David Bowie has consistently done or as Rod Stewart has done in recent years moving from being a rock singer to a more middle of the road/jazz singer with his interpretations of the Great American Songbook. Where the celebrity changes his image during the term of the agreement he may no longer want his previous image to be used to promote the endorsed products and will want the packaging on the endorsed products and the attendant advertising to reflect the new image. The celebrity will therefore want the agreement to provide that where he changes his image the packaging on the endorsed products and the attendant advertising will be altered accordingly to reflect the new image. If the company is prepared to agree to such a provision in the agreement then the agreement would need to provide that the celebrity will submit images of his new persona to the endorsement company and will inform the endorsement company some time before the proposed image change to enable the necessary changes to be made to the product packaging and to any future advertisements featuring the celebrity's image. The endorsement company may, however, want a clause providing that where there is a substantial change of image it can terminate the agreement if it considers the new image is not as marketable as the previous image. Alternatively or in addition, the endorsement company may want the right to terminate the agreement if the celebrity changes his image more than once during the term of the agreement. In all probability an endorsement company will not agree to a provision requiring it to change its packaging and advertising due to the celebrity changing his image. In all probability it is far more likely that the endorsement company will require the celebrity not to change his image during the term of the agreement due to the inconvenience and expense it would cost it to change the packaging and advertising to accommodate the celebrity. It is after all the celebrity who is endorsing the product not the endorsement company that is marketing the celebrity. Contrast this with tour merchandise where the merchandise company is making its money out of the celebrity's image on products such as badges and T-shirts which would not ordinarily sell without the image on them.

(6)   Not to do or permit anything to be done which damages or might damage the name, reputation or image of the celebrity or any of the celebrity's copyrights or trade marks or other intellectual property rights.

(7)   (Possibly) a provision requiring the endorsement company to take legal action against anyone who has or appears to have infringed the celebrity's intellectual property rights due to the manufacture, distribution, promotion or selling of the

endorsed products.[12] Where the agreement contains such a clause the endorsement company should be required to notify the celebrity before commencing or threatening any such legal action and there similarly should be a requirement for the celebrity to notify the endorsement company of any potential infringements of which he is aware. Although the endorsement company may be required to take legal action for such infringement, the clause may provide that the endorsement company is only required to take such action if the endorsement company has a favourable legal opinion from a solicitor or barrister specialised in intellectual property litigation. As for who is to pay the cost of any such legal opinion and/or legal action, this should be dealt with in the agreement. Also the question of whether the endorsement company is required to take a second legal opinion if the first opinion is not favourable or whether the endorsement company is required to appeal an unfavourable court decision and if so how far the company is required to appeal the decision, for example, is the company required to proceed to an appeal to the Court of Appeal, the Supreme Court or the European courts should be dealt with in the agreement.

(8)   As the endorsement company will be using the celebrity's name, image, and/or logo and perhaps some attributed quotes from the celebrity, the agreement should require the endorsement company to ensure the relevant copyright notices and trade mark notices are credited where the celebrity's intellectual property rights are used.

(9)   To ensure that product liability insurance is in place, preferably with the celebrity's name noted on the policy. The endorsement company will also be required to indemnify the celebrity for any claim, loss damage, liability or expense relating to any defective or allegedly defective products.

(10)   Not to sell any of the endorsed products as remainder goods or as seconds or to give any away for free or as premium or promotional goods. The celebrity may also want the company not to offer any of the goods on a sale or return basis, although the company may not be prepared to accept such a provision where it is usual for it to conduct its business or a substantial part of it on a sale or return basis.

(11)   To comply with the terms of the agreement. Where the endorsement company intends to appoint another company to manufacture some or all of the products the clause will also provide that the endorsement company will ensure that the manufacturer complies with the restrictions in the agreement between the celebrity and the endorsement company.

THE CELEBRITY'S OBLIGATIONS

27.27 The company will want some degree of exclusivity with the celebrity with reference to the product(s) he is endorsing. The celebrity will therefore be required to:

(1)   Endorse the product(s) which are the subject of the agreement exclusively for the term of the agreement.

---

[12]   See also Chapter 18 on Copyright.

(2)   Allow the company the right to use his name, likeness, biographical details, signature, voice and any trade mark(s) which he has to promote, advertise and sell the endorsed products.

(3)   Allow the company to use his name, image and/or logo on any proposed material such as any promotional or advertising material and on any packaging which the company wants to use to promote the sale of the product(s).

(4)   Actively help promote the product(s).

27.28 For more detail concerning these points see **27.15** et seq.

27.29 As was mentioned above,[13] the agreement may require the endorsement company to take legal action against anyone who has or appears to have infringed the celebrity's intellectual property rights due to the manufacture, distribution, promotion or selling of the endorsed products. It may be that the endorsement company either does not want to take on such an onerous responsibility or that the celebrity wants to retain the right for himself. If this is the case, the agreement should place the responsibility to do so on the celebrity, in which case there should be a requirement on the celebrity to notify the endorsement company before commencing or threatening any such legal action and there should be a requirement for the endorsement company to notify the celebrity of any potential infringements of which it is aware. Although the celebrity may be required to take relevant legal action for infringement of his intellectual property rights in the endorsed products, the clause may provide that the celebrity is only required to take such action where he has a favourable legal opinion from a solicitor or barrister specialised in intellectual property litigation. As for who is to pay the cost of any such legal opinion and/or legal action, this should be dealt with in the agreement. Also the question of whether the celebrity is required to take a second legal opinion if the first opinion is not favourable or whether the celebrity is required to appeal an unfavourable court decision and, if so, how far he is required to appeal the decision, for example, is he required to proceed to an appeal to the Court of Appeal, the Supreme Court or the European courts should be dealt with in the agreement.

27.30 The following are some other obligations which the celebrity may be required to comply with:

(1)   To comply with his obligations in the agreement.

(2)   To perform his obligations in a professional manner.

(3)   To confirm that he is in good health and, if required, to undergo a medical to satisfy the endorsement company or its insurers that this is the case. In addition, the celebrity will be required to take reasonable steps to ensure that he remains in good health.

(4)   Not to participate during the term of the agreement in any dangerous or hazardous activities which might prevent him carrying out his contractual obligations.

---

[13]   See point (7) at **27.26**.

(5)   At all times to keep the company informed of his whereabouts and supply it with his personal mobile and landline telephone numbers so that the company can contact him as and when required. As an alternative to supplying his personal telephone numbers to the company other contact numbers such as that of his personal manager may be acceptable.

(6)   To attend a press conference, launch party and/or promotional events to promote the endorsed products. If the celebrity agrees to this the agreement should provide that he will attend at an agreed date and venue (or at a date and venue which will be notified to him eg 8 weeks in advance of the proposed date) for a specified period of time and that he will attend subject to his overriding work commitments with his employer. A provision that the celebrity will attend subject to his work commitments would be needed to cover a situation where, for example, the celebrity is a Premier League footballer and he is required by his club to travel with the team to play in a rescheduled league or cup game on the day of his proposed promotional appearance for the endorsement company.[14] Where the celebrity agrees to appear at a press conference, launch party or promotional events he will want to ensure the company pays his reasonable travel, food and where necessary hotel accommodation expenses and in addition he may also require an additional appearance fee. These matters should also be dealt with in the agreement.

(7)   Where the celebrity is promoting the endorsement agreement, for example, by making a personal appearance or filming a promotional advert, he will comply with all relevant regulations such as fire, health and safety and crowd safety regulations and any relevant trade union regulations.

(8)   Where the celebrity is a sportsman he will be required to comply with his club's and his national and international governing bodies' rules and regulations.

(9)   Not to do or permit anything to be done which damages or might damage his own name, reputation or image and not to do anything or permit anything to be done which damages or might damage his own copyrights or trade marks or other intellectual property rights.

(10)   Not do anything or permit anything to be done which damages or might damage the endorsement company's name, reputation or image or the name, reputation or image of its products and not to do or permit anything to be done which damages or might damage the endorsement company's copyrights or trade marks or other intellectual property rights.

(11)   Not to enter or purport to enter any agreement(s) with third parties in the endorsement company's name.

(12)   When promoting the product(s), to mention the name of the endorsement company and/or its good/services in interviews with the press and other broadcast media. The celebrity may also be required to wear clothes with the endorsement company's name and logo on for promotional interviews.

---

[14]   See also **27.18** et seq.

(13) The company will usually want the celebrity to use the product(s) and wear the company's logo on his clothing in his professional career. This could be a problem where, for example, the celebrity is a sportsman as his employment contract with his club or the rules of his playing association or particular tournament rules or television broadcaster regulations may limit or prohibit particular types of advertising or may limit the size and positioning of advertising logos. The agreement should therefore provide that the celebrity will use the product(s) and wear the company's logo on his clothing in his professional career subject to the constraints that he is under in his professional career.

TERMINATION OF THE AGREEMENT

27.31 The agreement should contain specific provisions which if breached would enable the innocent party to terminate. For example, a well-drafted agreement should contain a 'morality clause' providing that the celebrity will not do anything which damages or might damage the endorsement company's name, reputation or image or the name, reputation or image of its goods/services. Where the celebrity does something which might bring the endorsement company's name into disrepute, for example, he gets arrested for or charged with a serious crime, the endorsement company will then be able to terminate the agreement under the morality clause provision.

27.32 The agreement should ideally not only contain relevant provisions which allow for termination of the agreement in circumstances where there is a serious or substantial breach of contract, but also set out what happens where one party terminates the agreement due to the other party's breach. For example, the agreement would usually provide that the innocent party has no liability to the other party for future obligations from the date of the breach, although both parties would retain their existing contractual rights and liabilities up to the date of termination.

27.33 Where the agreement is for a fixed term but contains a provision for the company to renew, the procedure as to how to exercise the option should be set out in detail so that both parties know whether the agreement will continue or will terminate at the end of the proposed fixed term. A written notice procedure between the parties should be provided for in the agreement. For example, the agreement may require the celebrity to notify the company in writing of his right to exercise an option 3 months before the proposed termination date of the agreement and allow the company a period of 14 days from service of the notice to decide whether to exercise the option or whether to let the agreement end. Where the company has a matching rights option the agreement should also set out the terms the company must match to be able to exercise the option and what information the celebrity is to supply to the company to enable it to decide whether to exercise the option.[15] If the company decides not to renew the agreement having had a chance to do so the celebrity can then safely treat the existing agreement as terminated.

27.34 The agreement might be for a fixed term with a break clause allowing one of the parties to terminate the agreement early by exercising the break clause provision. The details of how and when a break clause can be exercised must be set out in the agreement. For example, a 3-year agreement might contain a provision which allows the company to terminate the agreement at the end of the first year which would be

---

[15]   Chapter 24 at **24.8** point (2)(b), Chapter 25 at **25.13** point (9) and Chapter 26 at **26.31**.

exercised by the company giving written notice of termination to the celebrity by first class post to his home address, with the notice being sent not less than 3 months before the end of the first year of the agreement. If the break clause is not exercised or not correctly exercised as prescribed in the agreement then the agreement will continue until the end of the term or until the next break clause is exercised (if there is another break clause provided for in the agreement). If the break clause is validly exercised by the company the agreement should provide that any further advances which would have been payable in the future are no longer payable, although any monies still owing to the celebrity for the period up to the termination date and, where royalties are payable, any royalty payments which will become due on any outstanding stock which is sold after the termination date are still payable. The agreement should also provide that all liabilities and obligations until the date of termination still exist notwithstanding the exercise of the break clause.

27.35 A clause(s) may be of such importance to the sponsor that it goes to the 'essence' of the agreement. For example, the company may only want to be associated with the celebrity because he is a high-profile actor playing a particular role in a television soap opera whereas other potential endorsement companies would have been prepared to contract with the celebrity for the person he is rather than for the character he plays in the television soap opera. In a situation such as where the company has contracted with the celebrity purely because of the role he plays in a television soap opera and it is imperative to the company that he remains in the role during the term of the agreement, a provision should be included in the agreement to this effect and that it is 'of the essence' of the contract. This will enable the company to terminate the agreement should the celebrity leave the soap opera.

27.36 The agreement will often provide that where one party is in material breach of contract the other party must notify them in writing of the breach and require it to be remedied within a period of time and if the breach has not been remedied in that time the agreement is automatically terminated. The agreement should also provide where termination has occurred due to a material breach by one of the parties that the party's contractual rights, liabilities and obligations until the date of termination still exist notwithstanding termination (save for the obligation by the company to pay any outstanding fee and/or advance to the celebrity where it is the celebrity who has been in material breach of contract).

27.37 The agreement should contain a force majeure clause. A force majeure clause should list all the events beyond the control of the contracting parties, for example, act of God, civil war, terrorism, strikes, lock outs, which if any of them occur will excuse the party who cannot perform its contractual obligations due to the force majeure event. The clause should provide that the party who cannot perform its contractual obligations will not be in breach of contract for non-performance where this is due to a force majeure event. The clause should require the party who cannot perform its obligations due to a force majeure event to give notice to the other party of the existence of the force majeure event and that this prevents it from performing its contractual obligations. The force majeure clause should provide that the agreement is suspended whilst the force majeure event exists and that the agreement will recommence once the force majeure event has ended. As the suspension could last for a long time there should be a long stop provision in the agreement allowing one party to serve written notice on the other party terminating the agreement where the agreement is suspended for a specified period of time due to a force majeure event. Where termination occurs due to a force majeure event, the agreement should deal with what is to happen in these circumstances.

27.38 Where the celebrity is endorsing a personalised range of products and is to be paid a royalty on their sales he may want the right to terminate where the endorsement company has substantially under-accounted (eg by 25%) for royalties on, for example, two occasions.

27.39 The agreement should also deal with what is to happen with existing endorsed products following termination of the agreement. Where the agreement expires by effluxion of time the agreement should allow the company a period of time following the end of the agreement term to sell any remaining endorsed products. The agreement should provide that during the sell off period the company only has a non-exclusive licence to sell the remaining endorsed product and that it can no longer manufacture any such further stock during this period. The clause may also provide that the company cannot sell the remaining stock at a discount price and also that it will inform the celebrity in writing immediately before the commencement of the sell off period of the amount of endorsed products it has left in stock. (It should be remembered that where the celebrity enters an endorsement agreement with another company immediately after the termination of the previous agreement where the previous agreement has a non-exclusive sell off right the celebrity can only grant the new company a non-exclusive right to sell whilst the previous company still has the right to sell its remaining stock and only after this period has expired can the celebrity grant the new endorsement company an exclusive right to sell.) Where there is a sell off period clause there should be an additional provision in the agreement requiring the endorsement company to destroy any stock which remains after the sell off period has expired. Alternatively or in addition, the agreement may provide that the celebrity can buy the remaining stock from the endorsement company at the end of the term at either wholesale, retail or a discount price. To ensure an excessive amount of stock is not manufactured by the company towards the end of the term a clause should be included which requires the company not to manufacture during, for example, the last year of the term more than the average amount of stock which was produced during the first year of the agreement. Where the agreement expires due to a breach of contract by the endorsement company the agreement should provide that the company's rights cease automatically and it has no right to manufacture, distribute and/or sell the endorsed products. Whether the term expires due to effluxion of time or due to the endorsement company's breach of contract a provision should be included in the agreement requiring the company to return any photographs and other items which were supplied by the celebrity to enable the company to produce the stock. There should also be a provision in the agreement stating that upon termination all the celebrity's intellectual property rights which were licensed to the endorsement company revert to the celebrity and that the endorsement company will execute any documents which are required to ensure that the intellectual property rights revert to the celebrity.

INTELLECTUAL PROPERTY RIGHTS

27.40 The celebrity will need to ensure the following:[16]

(1) Before entering the contract, that he has checked that he does actually own the relevant rights which he is intending to license. It may be, for example, a logo was commissioned by the celebrity from a third party, in which case the celebrity should check that he has taken a full assignment of the copyright in the design of the logo from the third party before he enters the endorsement agreement allowing the endorsement company the right to use it.

(2) That the use of his intellectual property rights is strictly controlled in the agreement. There should be a provision in the agreement which states that the celebrity is granting the endorsement company a non-exclusive licence to use the relevant right(s). The extent to which the endorsement company has to use the rights granted must also be set out precisely in the agreement.[17] The celebrity will also want a provision included in the agreement that the company will immediately notify him of any infringements of which the company becomes aware.

(3) That the endorsement company cannot, save where the agreement provides, allow anyone else to use the celebrity's intellectual property rights without the express written permission of the celebrity. Where it is intended that the endorsement company can permit others to use the celebrity's intellectual property rights the agreement should set out in detail the circumstances in which this is permitted.

(4) If any new intellectual property rights might be created during the agreement term, for example, new photographs are taken of the celebrity by the merchandiser for a product range, then there should be a provision as to who will own the intellectual property rights, and that any necessary documents will be executed to ensure an effective creation and transfer of ownership in these rights and that any third parties will be required to execute any necessary documentation to ensure the transfer of ownership.

(5) There should be a provision in the agreement stating that upon termination all the celebrity's intellectual property rights which were licensed to the endorsement company revert to the celebrity and that the endorsement company will execute any documents which are required to ensure that the intellectual property rights revert to the celebrity.[18] Some intellectual property rights such as trade marks are protected by registration. The celebrity should be required to ensure that such intellectual property rights are protected by registration and that the registration of these rights is not allowed to lapse.[19]

27.41 The agreement should also deal with who is responsible for taking legal action where the celebrity's intellectual property rights have been infringed[20] and provide for

---

[16] See also Chapter 18 on Copyright.
[17] See **27.15** et seq, **27.18** et seq and **27.31** et seq. For the difference between a licence and an assignment see above. See also Chapter 18 on Copyright.
[18] See also **27.31** et seq.
[19] See also **27.27** et seq. And see also Chapter 18 on Copyright.
[20] See point (7) at **27.26** and **27.27** et seq.

the endorsement company to ensure that all endorsed products will have where relevant trade mark and copyright notices placed on them.[21]

27.42 The agreement should also contain a warranty from the celebrity that any trade mark he has licensed to the endorsement company is original, that he is the sole and absolute owner of the trade mark and that any such trade mark does not infringe the rights of any third party. A similar warranty should also be given in the agreement where the celebrity is allowing the endorsement company to use any other of his intellectual property rights. The agreement should also provide that the celebrity will indemnify the endorsement company from any expense or liability which might be incurred where the warranty relating to his intellectual property rights proves to be incorrect.[22]

27.43 The celebrity may be required to make audio and/or audio-visual recordings for use on radio and/or television to help promote the product(s). The following are some of the matters that may need to be considered in relation to any such recordings:

(1) The celebrity will be required by the company to consent to the use of his performer's non-property rights and to assign his performer's property rights in the recordings.[23]

(2) The celebrity will be required by the company to waive the moral rights and the performer's moral rights which he has in the recordings.[24]

(3) The company will usually require the copyright in any audio or audio-visual recordings made with the celebrity to promote the product(s) to vest in it. If the celebrity is a musician and has an exclusive recording agreement with a record company and/or a publishing agreement for his songs it will be necessary to check the celebrity's recording and publishing agreements before he enters an endorsement contract as he will probably need the consent of his record company to make any audio and/or audio-visual recordings for the company and from his music publisher for the use of any his songs whether they are newly created, existing songs or adapted from existing songs or where he contributes to the script for an advert.

(4) Similar considerations should be had as for point (3) where the celebrity is, for example, a film, television or radio presenter, an actor with a contract with a television or film company or an author with a publishing agreement.

WARRANTIES, INDEMNITIES AND OTHER CLAUSES

27.44 As mentioned above,[25] the agreement should contain a warranty from the celebrity that any trade mark he has licensed to the endorsement company is original, that he is the sole and absolute owner of the trade mark and that any such trade mark does not infringe the rights of any third party. A similar warranty should also be given

---

[21] See point (8) at **27.26**.
[22] See **27.15** et seq and **27.44** et seq.
[23] See also Chapter 18 on Copyright.
[24] See also Chapter 18 on Copyright.
[25] See **27.40** et seq.

in the agreement where the celebrity is allowing the endorsement company to use any other of his intellectual property rights. The agreement should also provide that the celebrity will indemnify the endorsement company from any expense or liability which might be incurred where the warranty relating to his intellectual property rights proves to be incorrect.[26]

27.45 The agreement should contain a warranty by each party that they are free and able to enter the agreement that they are able to perform their contractual obligations and that neither party has entered any agreements which might compete or conflict. The endorsement company might seek to widen the scope of this warranty to provide that the celebrity will not during the term of the agreement except where expressly provided for enter any competing or conflicting agreement.

27.46 Other provisions which should be dealt with in the agreement include, inter alia:

(1)   That both parties will keep the terms of the agreement confidential and will not disclose them to anyone other than their professional advisers or as may be required by law.

(2)   That the agreement between the parties does not constitute a joint venture, partnership or employment relationship.

(3)   That the agreement reflects the whole of the agreement between the parties and replaces any earlier oral or written agreement.

(4)   That the celebrity will not hold himself out as representing the endorsement company. A similar provision should also be made by the endorsement company to the celebrity.

(5)   Which legal system will apply (in nearly all cases this will be the law of England and Wales) and the method to be used to resolve any disputes between the parties, namely alternative dispute resolution, arbitration or legal proceedings in the High Court or county court.

(6)   (Possibly) a provision enabling the parties to limit the extent of any indemnity which has been given to the other party.

(7)   (Possibly) a clause prohibiting assignment of the agreement. Where assignment is to be permitted in certain circumstances and/or is permitted subject to certain conditions the clause should detail the relevant circumstances and conditions.

(8)   A clause providing that if the endorsement company becomes bankrupt or enters into a voluntary arrangement or any company through which the endorsement company is operating goes into compulsory or voluntary liquidation (save for the purposes of reconstructing or amalgamating a solvent company), or becomes insolvent or has a receiver, manager, or administrative receiver or provisional liquidator or administrator appointed, the agreement will automatically terminate. Provision should also be made in the clause as to the reassignment of any intellectual property rights which may have been licensed between the parties and

---

[26]   See **27.15** et seq.

to deal with the position of any new intellectual property rights which may have come into existence between the parties under the agreement.

(9) A provision stating that the celebrity has received independent legal advice on the terms of the agreement from a solicitor with experience in dealing with endorsement agreements.

(10) A notice clause. A notice clause should be included to deal with the procedure to be followed where the agreement requires one party to give notice to the other party to activate a contractual clause, for example, to activate an option clause. A notice clause should provide how the notice should be given, namely in writing to the other party, and should provide how it is to be sent, for example, by personal delivery, fax, first class or recorded delivery post, when it is deemed to have been delivered, for example, for first class post it will usually be deemed to have been delivered on the first or second business day after it has been posted, and the address to which it should be sent, for example, to the address set out in the agreement or to the registered office or to such other address as may previously have been notified in writing by one party to the other.

Chapter 28

PUBLISHING AGREEMENT

INTRODUCTION

28.1   In recent years there has been a trend for some celebrities to exploit their celebrity status by selling the right to cover their day-to-day lives along with accompanying photos to weekly celebrity magazines. There is a proliferation of stories and photos of celebrities on holiday, celebrating their weddings, births of their children, break ups of their marriages and myriad other events both large and small no matter how personal and at times tragic. The demand by the public for its weekly update on celebrity life has lead book publishers to realise that there is an enormous market for books written by celebrities. Of course, autobiographies have always been a staple part of many publishers' catalogues, but the proliferation of such books nowadays seems to be far greater than ever before. Some people, whether justified or not, might argue that an autobiography written by a young person who has played top flight football for a couple of years or who has become famous because they have won a reality television programme or because they have dated or married a famous sportsman would be of little interest as they have not had much life experience to relate. However, there is a demand for such books and they do sell. As such, books written by celebrities are commissioned by publishers in ever-increasing numbers. Indeed, some celebrities have within a few years of their autobiography being published written a second or even a third volume. The autobiography may be written by the celebrity himself, although frequently a celebrity autobiography is written in collaboration with an experienced writer who will put the 'autobiography'[1] together in collaboration with the celebrity.

28.2   Some celebrities may use their celebrity status to write books on subjects that are not related to the area in which they are commonly known, for example a pop star or actor might write a cook book or a diet book following well-publicised weight loss or, as Madonna and Geri Halliwell have done, a celebrity might write a children's book(s). Other areas in which celebrities have marketed their celebrity status include novels purportedly written by them but which are actually written by others after the celebrity has explained in detail the plot line to the actual author and miscellany/humorous quotes books which go under the name of the celebrity and which relate to their area of celebrity status. One other massively popular publishing theme is the celebrity chef cookbooks, such as those written by the Roux Brothers, Raymond Blanc, Heston Blumenthal, Gordon Ramsay and Jamie Oliver, which may or may not tie in with a television series. These books have a massive market and can prove to be a very lucrative way to increase the commercial income of some of the best and most famous chefs.

28.3   This chapter will examine the key terms that need to be considered when a celebrity is being commissioned by a publisher to write a book such as an autobiography in his own name. It does not consider the Minimum Terms Agreement which has been

---

[1]   A book written in collaboration with an experienced writer is not strictly speaking an autobiography.

developed by the Society of Authors and the Writers Guild of Great Britain. It is suggested that when looking at the proposed publishing agreement the Minimum Terms Agreement is looked at alongside the proposed agreement to ensure the terms being offered are at least as favourable as those in the Minimum Terms Agreement. Where the terms are not as favourable the author's[2] legal representative can use the Minimum Terms Agreement as an argument as to why the proposed terms should be improved.

THE MAIN TERMS

28.4	Before negotiating a publishing agreement for an author it is vital that the author's solicitor checks with his client whether he has entered any other publishing agreements in the past and also checks any employment contract(s), as they may restrict whether the author can enter a publishing agreement and may where he can enter the agreement limit what he is permitted to write about or disclose. For example, the author may have previously assigned or licensed to another publisher the intellectual property rights in the work he is now intending to write or update, the rights to which remain with the previous publisher or the author may want to use in his book extracts from works he created in his time as an employee and the intellectual property rights in these works belong to his employer.[3]

28.5	The main terms which would need to be dealt with in a publishing agreement are:

(1)	the parties to the publishing agreement;

(2)	the term, territory and exclusivity;

(3)	the description of and the nature and length of the book;

(4)	the rights granted to the publisher;

(5)	intellectual property rights;

(6)	the delivery date and publication;

(7)	advances, royalties and exploitation of the book;

(8)	accounting;

(9)	termination of the agreement; and

(10)	warranties, indemnities and other clauses.

---

[2]	The word 'celebrity' has been changed to 'author' in most instances in this chapter as this is the term used in a publishing agreement.

[3]	See Chapter 18 on Copyright.

THE PARTIES TO THE PUBLISHING AGREEMENT

28.6   There will usually be no problem regarding the contracting parties as they will be the author who is the author and a publishing company which is the publisher.

28.7   It may be that the author enters all his agreements through limited companies which have been set up to deal with various aspects of his career. For example, an author may have one limited company set up to deal with his recording agreement, a separate limited company to deal with his song-writing and publishing, a third which deals with his concert tours and a fourth which deals with his merchandising. Where an author enters contractual arrangements via limited companies, the publisher should ideally consider obtaining a side letter signed by the author himself providing that should his company not comply with its obligations then he will personally be responsible for and will perform the contractual obligations or be a party to the agreement itself as guarantor that the company will comply with its obligations and that if it does not then he will personally be responsible for and will perform the company's contractual obligations.

28.8   Consideration should also be made, from the author's position, as to the financial status of the publishing company. If there is concern about the financial position of the proposed publishing company then consideration should be made as to what financial guarantees could be provided by the publishing company, for example, a parent company could be asked to guarantee the financial obligations of a subsidiary publishing company.

THE TERM, TERRITORY AND EXCLUSIVITY

28.9   The term of the agreement being sought by the publisher will vary from publisher to publisher. Some publishers may seek an assignment of the rights in the book (or assignment of future copyright where the book has yet to be written) for the full term of copyright plus any extensions or renewals thereof or an assignment of copyright for a comparatively short period of time, such as for a period of 7 years. Other publishers may be prepared to accept a grant of a licence for a period of time as opposed to an assignment of copyright.[4] Many publishers will want the right to publish the book throughout the world. Whether the author is prepared to grant this right will depend upon many factors, such as the size of the advance being offered for the rights, the royalty rate offered, what rights the publisher is seeking over the book,[5] the proposed term of the agreement and whether the publisher is capable of publishing and promoting the book throughout the world or, if not, what contacts it has with publishers in other territories to publish and promote the book. (For example, the publisher might be part of a group of publishing companies under the control of a large parent company and the publisher intends to sub-licence the publishing rights to related publishers for those territories in which it does not actively publish.) It should be stressed that the author should, if he is prepared to grant the publisher the right to publish throughout the world, ensure that the publisher is capable of either publishing throughout the world on its own or where it is not that the publisher is capable of sub-licensing the rights to other capable publishers in those territories in which it is not active.

---

4   See Chapter 18 on Copyright. See also **28.14** et seq and **28.34** et seq.
5   See **28.14** et seq and **28.56** et seq for the ways a book can be exploited by a publisher.

28.10 Those publishers not seeking the right to publish throughout the world will instead usually want the right to publish either in the UK and other named English-speaking countries or seek the right to publish in the US. The agreement should specify the territory(ies) for which the publisher has the right to publish the book so that there is no dispute between the author and the publisher as to the territorial scope of the publisher's rights under the agreement.

28.11 Whether the publisher is seeking an assignment of copyright for the full copyright term or for a shorter period or a licence for a period of time, whether the publisher is seeking the right to publish throughout the world or in the UK and other named English-speaking countries or the right to publish in the US, the one thing the publisher will always want is for the author to grant it these rights on a sole and exclusive basis.

THE DESCRIPTION OF AND THE NATURE AND LENGTH OF THE BOOK

28.12 In the situation where the author's book has already been written the agreement will contain details of the proposed title of the book and its length, detailed by the number of pages and/or by the number of words. More commonly the author will not have written the book until some time after he has entered the publishing agreement. Indeed, it is most likely that the author will not have written any of it by the time he has signed the agreement and at most might have prepared a short outline detailing what he intends to cover in the book. In the situation where the author has either not finished or not started writing the book before he has entered the agreement, the book will be described in the agreement by way of the proposed title or its working title and by the estimated number of pages it will contain and/or the estimated number of words. In addition, the agreement will set out a treatment of the work, for example, the treatment may provide that the author will write an autobiography which will cover a specified period in his life and will focus in detail on those things for which he is renowned and on specified episodes and events in his life and also any exposes about the author's personal and private life which the publisher specifically wants the author to include. In addition, and in particular where the author is writing his autobiography, the book will usually contain a selection of photographs showing the author growing up at various stages of his life and at various important times in his career. Where photographs are to be included in the book the agreement should detail whether the author owns the copyright in them and, if not, who owns the copyright so that appropriate copyright clearance can be obtained to include them in the book. In addition, the agreement should detail whether the author will have the choice of which photographs are to be included or, as is more likely, whether the choice of photographs which are to be included will be made by the author in collaboration with the publisher. Where illustrations are to be included in the book, as would commonly occur where the author writes a children's book, similar details will need to be included in the agreement.[6]

28.13 The agreement will commonly provide that where the author intends to use someone's copyright material, such as extracts or quotations from someone else's work, words from songs (including lyrics he has written and the copyright in which he has assigned to a third party), photographs taken by a third party and illustrations drawn by a third party, it is the author's responsibility to obtain the appropriate copyright

---

[6]   See Chapter 18 on Copyright. See also **28.14** et seq and **28.34** et seq.

clearance to use these works and the agreement will commonly provide that the publisher will pay the costs involved in getting copyright clearance to use such works. An author may prefer simply to identify in the agreement those third party works he wishes to use and require the publisher to obtain the appropriate release as well as pay the costs involved. This is something the publisher may be prepared to agree to do, and in many cases it would be easier for the publisher to arrange for the appropriate clearances rather than pass the responsibility for them on to the author, especially where the publisher is paying the costs involved in obtaining clearances. The publisher may want to put a ceiling on the amount of costs it is prepared to spend on obtaining clearances and may require this to be put into the agreement along with a provision that where the cost of clearances exceeds this amount that it is the responsibility of the author to pay the excess costs involved. Whoever is responsible for obtaining the third party's permission, it should be ensured that the permission covers all the ways for which it is intended the book will be exploited.[7]

THE RIGHTS GRANTED TO THE PUBLISHER AND THE PUBLISHER'S OBLIGATIONS

28.14 Some publishers will want either an assignment of the rights in the book (or an assignment of future copyright where the book has yet to be written) for the full term of copyright plus any extensions or renewals thereof or an assignment of copyright for a comparatively short period of time, such as for a period of 7 years. Other publishers may be prepared to accept a grant of a licence for a period of time as opposed to an assignment of copyright. It should be noted that the clause dealing with the rights which are being granted should be read in conjunction with the clauses dealing with the term and territory so that it is clear for how long and where in the world the publisher has these rights. In addition, it should be checked whether (which would usually be the case) the rights granted are exclusive to the publisher.[8]

28.15 It should be remembered that the intellectual property rights which exist in a book go far beyond the right to publish the book itself, and that some of these rights may be infinitely more valuable than the right to publish and sell hardback and paperback editions of the book. For example, there might be the potential for the book to be turned into a successful radio or television series or a series of motion pictures, along with merchandising the characters in the book. Careful consideration will need to be had as in any agreement dealing with intellectual property rights as to exactly what intellectual property rights which exist in the book (or where the book is still to be written when the agreement has been entered into, will exist once the book has been written) are to be granted to the publisher. Factors which the author will need to take into account in deciding what rights he is prepared to grant the publisher include whether the publisher is personally experienced in dealing with the relevant rights, the size of the advance being offered and the royalty rates payable for the rights.[9] The agreement should therefore set out in detail exactly what rights are being granted to the publisher. The rights which are granted to the publisher will need to be detailed in the agreement along with the royalty rates payable for each of these rights. It is common for

---

[7]   See Chapter 18 on Copyright. See also **28.14** et seq and **28.34** et seq.
[8]   See Chapter 18 on Copyright. See also **28.9** et seq and **28.34** et seq.
[9]   See **28.34** et seq. See also Chapter 18 on Copyright.

the rights granted clause, rather than set out the rights in detail, to state that the rights which are granted are those which are set out in the royalties clause.[10]

28.16 The publisher will usually want the sole and exclusive right to copy, produce, publish and sell the book and all editions, abridged versions, adaptations and amendments of the book in hardback and paperback, along with the right to publish the book in electronic form (which would include, inter alia, online and offline electronic storage, CD-ROM and CD-I) for the term of the agreement and for the territory(ies) which it has been granted by the author. In addition, the publisher may need the right to translate the book into various foreign languages. The agreement should provide whether the publisher has the right to copy, produce, publish and sell an English language version of the book and/or the right to translate the book into foreign languages, in which case the languages the publisher has the right to translate the book into should be specified in the agreement.

28.17 Where the author is a member of the Authors' Licensing and Collecting Society Limited the publisher may be prepared to allow the author to reserve the reprographic right in the work. This is because the Copyright Licensing Agency will collect in the money due under the licences it grants to photocopy and scan extracts from magazines, books, journals and digital publications and arrange for the money to be sent to the Authors' Licensing and Collecting Society Limited and the Publishers' Licensing Society, which then arrange to pay the author and publisher respectively. Whether the reprographic right is reserved to the author or is granted to the publisher, the author should become a member of the Authors' Licensing and Collecting Society Limited so that he receives his share of the reprographic rights monies paid by the Copyright Licensing Agency to the Authors' Licensing and Collecting Society Limited.

28.18 It should be noted that some publishers will agree for the reprographic right to be reserved to the author whereas some publishers will not. Where the publisher does not agree to the reprographic right being reserved to the author the publisher will usually agree to split the money earned from the reprographic right with the author on a 50:50 basis, although the publisher will want to set the author's share against any unrecouped advance which has been paid to the author.

28.19 The author will want to ensure the agreement provides that the public lending right (which is a property right and, as such, can be given away, sold or bequeathed by will) is excluded from the rights granted to the publisher as the public lending right is a right for authors, editors, illustrators and translators to receive payment (from Public Lending Right) for the loan of their books by public libraries. (For contact details for the Authors' Licensing and Collecting Society Limited, the Publishers' Licensing Society, the Copyright Licensing Agency Limited and Public Lending Right see Appendix 4.)

28.20 The publisher will require the author to grant it the right to edit the book. The publisher requires this right because the book will need to be altered in places by the editor to correct any errors, to ensure consistency of content and style throughout the work and to put it into the publisher's house style. The publisher will also need the right to edit the book where the book is to be translated into another language and for any changes which are required should the book be, inter alia, potentially libellous, infringe another person's privacy, breach a duty of confidentiality, blasphemous or obscene, in

---

[10]   See **28.34** et seq and **28.56** et seq.

breach of official secrets or where it comes to light that any statements that were believed by the author to be facts are inaccurate.

28.21 As was mentioned above,[11] it is common for the rights granted clause, rather than set out the rights in detail, to state that the rights which are granted are those which are set out in the royalties clause.

28.22 The publisher will require the right to use the author's name, image and/or logo in any publicity material to promote the book in the territory covered by the agreement and for the term of the agreement. The author should ensure that the publisher is only allowed to use these rights for the promotion of the book and not for any other purposes, as he will in all probability want to use these rights himself for other valuable commercial activities. The author will want to reserve the right to approve the use of his name, image and/or logo on any proposed promotional material. The author should also ensure that where his name, image and/or logo are used by the publisher the relevant copyright notices and trade mark notices are credited in the publicity material.

28.23 The agreement will also set out what exactly the author is expected to deliver to the publisher. The publisher will usually require the author to deliver on or before the delivery date a hard copy typed manuscript along with a copy on disk in Word or some other specified format or as an e-mail attachment and will also require the author to retain a hard copy of the typed manuscript and a copy of it on disk in his own possession for safekeeping in case the manuscript and/or the computer disk gets lost in transit to or whilst in the possession of the publisher. The agreement will also usually provide that the publisher will not be liable to the author in the event that the material sent by the author is lost.[12]

28.24 Most books will also contain an index. The preparation of an index is a special skill and is something that authors will in nearly all cases not be able to do. The agreement will usually provide that where an index for the book is required this will be arranged by the publisher and the costs of its preparation will usually be borne by the publisher.

28.25 Any book which is delivered to a publisher in its final form will need to be edited by a professional editor and once this has been done it will need to be read through thoroughly by the author to ensure that he is happy with the changes the editor has made and to make any necessary amendments to the editor's proof. The agreement will contain provisions requiring the author to read, check, amend where necessary and approve (with the approval not to be unreasonably withheld) the editor's proof and where required by the publisher to make changes which the publisher requires within a period of 21 days of receipt of the editor's proof. The agreement will usually provide that where the author is unable or unwilling to do this the publisher can appoint a third party to read the editor's proof and make the necessary changes and to charge the author for the costs involved. The agreement will frequently require the author to reimburse the publisher for these costs out of his own pocket or alternatively the agreement might provide that the costs involved would be recoverable by the publisher by deducting the costs from future advances and royalties payable under the agreement, and where the costs have not been recouped by the publisher within one year from any future advances or royalties then the author would be personally liable to pay the

---

[11] See **28.15**.
[12] See also **28.44** et seq.

outstanding balance due to the publisher out of his own pocket. As well as requiring the author to read and make any necessary changes to the editor's proof the agreement will contain a provision stating that where the changes to the typesetting exceed more than 10% of the book the author is responsible for the excess costs involved. The agreement should provide that in calculating whether more than 10% of the typesetting has been changed any editors' errors, printing errors and any changes which have been required due to changes in the law or in changes in practice which have been dealt with by the book and which have been introduced or changed since the author wrote the book will not count towards the 10% figure. Where the author is liable to pay these costs the agreement will provide whether the author is to pay them out of his own pocket immediately they fall due or whether they will be deducted from future monies payable to him under the agreement with a long stop provision requiring the author personally to pay the outstanding balance due to the publisher where the publisher has not been fully repaid from monies payable to the author under the agreement.

28.26 As for the book itself, the author will require his name on its front cover and spine and, where the book is a hardback edition, on the dust jacket. In addition, the author will require his name to appear inside the book itself on the title page and in the legal notices section at the front of book. The author will want to ensure the agreement provides for the assertion of the author's moral rights in the book. The publisher should ensure that when the book is published the author's moral rights are set out in the legal notices section at the front of the book along with all the appropriate copyright and, where relevant, any trade mark notices.[13] The agreement should deal with these requirements and should also deal with the prominence of the author's name on the front cover, the book spine and the dust jacket.

28.27 The publisher should be required to consult with the author about the illustrations to be included in the book and the book's front and back cover and dust jacket design. In addition, the author will want to be consulted about the introduction to the book (where he has not written it) and the back cover notes. In all probability the author will want the right to approve all these matters rather than the right to be consulted, and where the publisher agrees to let the author have approval rights it will want to ensure the agreement provides that the author's approval will not to be unreasonably withheld or delayed.

28.28 The author will want the publisher to require any licensee of the publisher to be under similar obligations to those imposed upon the publisher concerning the assertion of the author's moral rights, copyrights and trade marks. The publisher will usually have no problem agreeing to such a requirement, but it will usually want a proviso that where it enters a licensing agreement it will not be liable for any accidental or inadvertent failure by the licensee or any third party to include any such notices and that where there has been an accidental or inadvertent failure that this will not be a breach of the publishing agreement or of the author's rights.

28.29 Where the work is a work of fiction the author should ensure the publisher and any licensee of the publisher is required to put a note in the legal notices section that the work is a work of fiction and that the names and characters in the book are the product of the author's imagination and that any resemblance to any actual person or persons whether living or dead is entirely coincidental. Any good publisher will automatically

---

[13]   See Chapter 18 on Copyright. See also **28.34** et seq.

include such a provision in the book, but the author should check that this will be done in an attempt to prevent possible libel action.[14]

28.30 Many books 'written' by a celebrity are in fact written by or co-written with a ghost writer. The publishing agreement with the publisher, the celebrity and the ghost writer will need to deal with, inter alia, the prominence and positioning of the ghost writer's name on the book cover, jacket and title page and the ghost writer's copyright and moral rights (which he will want to assert) in the work.[15] It should be noted that where a ghost writer is involved in writing the book the publishing agreement will need to deal not only with the contractual rights and responsibilities of the celebrity but also with the contractual rights and responsibilities of the ghost writer.

28.31 Where a celebrity's book is written by a ghost writer the agreement will need to deal with how the royalties and any advance are divided between the celebrity and the ghost writer. In addition, the agreement will need to deal with the royalties and any advances which are payable where the celebrity is unwilling or unable to update, revise or write a new edition of the book and another author is employed by the publisher to do the work.[16]

28.32 The agreement will usually provide that the publisher can request the author to update, revise or write a new edition of the book. The agreement will usually provide that where the author declines to do so or fails to do so under the timetable provided for in the agreement the publisher can employ another author or editor to do this. When this happens the publisher will usually want the right to add the name of the new author or editor on the book cover, jacket and title page and in the legal notices section (concerning the new author's copyright and moral rights in the work), and the right to alter the size of, change the positioning of, or remove the name of the author from the book. The author will in most cases not be prepared to accept the alteration, positioning or removal of his name from the book and will at most only be prepared to accept that the name of the new author/editor will be added in a smaller font size to his own name and positioned in such a way as not to take prominence away from his own name. In addition, as the publisher will want the right to employ another author or editor to update, revise or write a new edition of the book when the author declines or fails to do so, the agreement will contain a provision allowing the publisher the right in such circumstances to add to, remove or rewrite the author's words. It may be that the author due to time constraints is not able to update, revise or write a new edition and may be perfectly happy for the publisher to employ another author or editor so to do. However, the author will be concerned whether or not he is happy for the book to be amended by another person to ensure that the alterations to the book will not cause him any upset, embarrassment or distress. For this reason, the author should ensure the publishing agreement provides that any such alterations will be subject to his approval, which the publisher will require not to be unreasonably withheld or delayed.

28.33 Usually the agreement will provide how the costs of employing another author or editor will be paid for when the author declines or fails to update, revise or write a new edition. The publisher will usually require the costs of employing another author or editor to be paid for by the author out of any future advance and royalties payable to him under the agreement. Alternatively, the publisher may seek a provision stating that except for residual sales of the then current and previous editions of the work, when the

---

[14]   See Chapter 13 on Defamation.
[15]   See Chapter 18 on Copyright.
[16]   See also **28.56** et seq.

author is unable or unwilling to update, revise or write a new edition of the book, subsequent advances and royalties will cease to be paid to him for sales of updated, revised or new editions which have been written by someone employed by the publisher. The author will in all probability not be prepared to forgo these payments in their entirety or at all where he is unwilling or unable to update, revise or write a new edition of the book and this clause will have to be negotiated between the parties to find a compromise solution.

INTELLECTUAL PROPERTY RIGHTS

28.34 As was mentioned earlier,[17] before negotiating a publishing agreement it is vital that the author's solicitor checks with his client whether he has entered any other publishing agreements in the past and also checks any employment contract(s) as they may restrict whether the author can enter a publishing agreement and may, where he can enter the agreement, limit what he is permitted to write about or disclose. For example, the author may have previously assigned or licensed to another publisher the intellectual property rights in the work he is now intending to write or update the rights to which remain with the previous publisher or he may want to use in his book extracts from works he created in his time as an employee and the intellectual property rights in these works belong to his employer.[18]

28.35 It should be remembered that the intellectual property rights which exist in a book go far beyond the right to publish the book itself, and that some of these rights may be infinitely more valuable than the right to publish and sell hardback and paperback editions of the book. For example, there might be the potential for the book to be turned into a successful radio or television series or a series of motion pictures, along with merchandising the characters in the book. Careful consideration will need to be had in any agreement dealing with intellectual property rights as to exactly what intellectual property rights which exist in the book (or where the book is still to be written, when the agreement has been entered into will exist once the book has been written) are to be granted to the publisher. Factors which the author will need to take into account in deciding what rights he is prepared to grant the publisher include whether the publisher is personally experienced in dealing with the relevant rights, the size of the advance being offered and the royalty rates payable for the rights. As was mentioned previously, the rights which are granted to the publisher will need to be detailed in the agreement along with the royalty rates payable for each of these rights. As was also mentioned previously, it is common for the rights granted clause rather than set out the rights in detail to state that the rights which are granted are those which are set out in the royalties clause.[19]

28.36 In addition to considering what rights in the book are to be granted to the publisher, attention should also be had as to the proposed term and territory for which the intellectual property rights are being granted and whether the rights are being dealt with by way of an assignment of copyright or the grant of a licence.[20]

---

[17] See Chapter 24 at **24.8–24.9** and **28.4–28.5**.
[18] See Chapter 18 on Copyright.
[19] See **28.14** et seq and **28.56** et seq. See also Chapter 18 on Copyright.
[20] See **28.9** et seq and **28.14** et seq. See also Chapter 18 on Copyright.

28.37 In addition to clauses dealing with the rights which are granted to the publisher, there should also be a provision in the agreement dealing with what will happen where the rights which have been granted by the author to the publisher are infringed by a third party. The author will want his intellectual rights in the work to be protected and will, as he will have granted either an assignment or an exclusive licence of these rights in the work to the publisher, require legal action to be taken against any infringers by the publisher and will also require the publisher to be responsible for paying the legal costs and expenses incurred in taking legal action.[21]

28.38 The author will also want a provision included in the agreement that the publisher will immediately notify the author of any infringements which the publisher becomes aware of and will keep the author actively informed about developments in any proceedings against any infringers. The publisher will where it is required to fund the legal costs and expenses incurred pursuing any infringer want the right to compromise or settle any such action. In order to ensure that any such compromise or settlement of any action against a copyright infringer has acceptable terms, the author should require the publisher to obtain a written opinion from a solicitor or barrister that the terms of the proposed compromise or settlement are commercially acceptable. The agreement will also need to deal with how any compensation which has been obtained in pursuing an infringer is to be divided between the author and the publisher. As well as the author requiring the publisher to inform him immediately of any infringements of which the publisher is aware, the publisher will require a similar obligation to be imposed upon the author so that the publisher can take appropriate action to protect the commercial value of the rights in the work against any infringers of which it might be unaware which are drawn to its attention by the author.

28.39 Where a third party's copyright work is to be used, such as might happen with extracts or quotations from someone else's work, words from songs (including lyrics which the author has written himself or with someone else and the copyright in which the author has assigned to a third party), photographs taken by a third party and illustrations drawn by a third party, approval should be obtained for the third party's work to be used in the book and it should be ensured that the permission which is obtained covers all the ways for which it is intended the book will be exploited.

28.40 The publisher will, as mentioned earlier, require the right to use the author's name, image and/or logo in any publicity material to promote the book in the territory covered by the agreement and for the term of the agreement. The agreement should contain a warranty from the author that any trade mark he has licensed to the publisher is original, that he is the sole and absolute owner of the trade mark and that any such trade mark does not infringe the rights of any third party. A similar warranty should also be given in the agreement where the author is allowing the publisher to use any other of his intellectual property rights. The agreement should also provide that the author will indemnify the publisher from any expense or liability which might be incurred where the warranty relating to his intellectual property rights proves to be incorrect.[22]

28.41 The author should ensure that the publisher is only allowed to use these rights for the promotion of the book and not for any other purpose, as the author will in all probability want to use these rights himself for other valuable commercial activities. The

---

[21] See **28.12–28.13** et seq and **28.14** et seq. See also Chapter 18 on Copyright.
[22] See also **28.91** et seq.

author will want to reserve the right to approve the use of his name, image and/or logo on any proposed promotional material. The author should also ensure that where his name, image and/or logo are used by the publisher the relevant copyright notices and trade mark notices are credited in the publicity material and that there is a provision in the agreement that the publisher will notify the author of any infringements of his name, image and/or logo of which the publisher becomes aware.[23] There should also be a provision in the agreement stating that upon termination all the author's intellectual property rights which were licensed to the publisher revert to the author and that the publisher will execute any documents which are required to ensure that the intellectual property rights revert to the author.[24]

28.42 The author will want to ensure the agreement provides for the assertion of his moral rights in the book. The publisher should ensure that when the book is published the author's moral rights are set out in the legal notices section at the front of the book along with all the appropriate copyright and, where relevant, any trade mark notices. In addition, where a ghost writer is employed to help write the book the ghost writer's moral rights will also need to be asserted.[25]

28.43 As was mentioned earlier,[26] the author will want the publisher to require any licensee of the publisher to be under similar obligations to those imposed upon the publisher concerning the assertion of the author's moral rights, copyrights and trade marks. The publisher will usually have no problem agreeing to such a requirement but it will usually want a proviso that where it enters a licensing agreement it will not be liable for any accidental or inadvertent failure by the licensee or any third party to include any such notices and that where there has been an accidental or inadvertent failure that this will not be a breach of the publishing agreement or of the author's rights.

THE DELIVERY DATE AND PUBLICATION

28.44 The agreement should contain a list of and a timetable for the author's and the publisher's respective responsibilities to enable the book to be written and published on the proposed publication date. The timetable should not provide for time to be of the essence. Indeed, the timetable for the author's and publishers' responsibilities should allow for reasonable extensions of time to be permitted as creative writing cannot always even with the best of intentions work to a rigid timetable. The timetable should contain a long stop provision so that if there is any significant delay by one party in complying with its obligations under the timetable the other party has the right to terminate the agreement.[27]

28.45 As was mentioned earlier,[28] the publisher will usually require the author to deliver on or before the delivery date a hard copy typed manuscript along with a copy on disk in Word or some other specified format or as an e-mail attachment and will also require the author to retain a hard copy of the typed manuscript and a copy of it on disk in his own possession for safekeeping in case the manuscript and/or the computer

---

[23]   See **28.14** et seq. See also Chapter 18 on Copyright.
[24]   See also **28.84** et seq.
[25]   See also **28.14** et seq. See also Chapter 18 on Copyright.
[26]   See **28.14** et seq.
[27]   See also **28.84** et seq.
[28]   See also **28.14** et seq.

disk gets lost in transit to or whilst in the possession of the publisher. The agreement will also usually provide that the publisher will not be liable to the author in the event that the material sent by the author is lost.

28.46 The agreement will usually contain a clause providing that if the author does not deliver the work by the delivery date then the publisher can if it so desires decide not to publish it.[29] The agreement will also contain a clause providing that even where the author has delivered the work in accordance with the timetable the publisher has the right to decline acceptance of the work if it does not conform to the agreed length, or if in its reasonable opinion the work is not of the standard or detail or covers the matters outlined in the treatment, or if in the publisher's reasonable opinion after taking legal advice the book is potentially libellous, infringes another person's privacy, might breach a duty of confidentiality, is blasphemous or obscene, is in breach of official secrets or it comes to light that any statements that were believed by the author to be facts are inaccurate and editing out the requisite passages would not make the book a commercially viable prospect. Alternatively or in addition, the agreement may provide that the publisher may accept the work provided certain changes are made so that the book reflects the treatment agreed to.[30] The agreement should ideally allow the author a reasonable period of time to make any necessary changes required by the publisher to remedy the situation where the publisher has declined to accept the work because the delivered work was not what was expected or where the publisher requires certain changes before it will accept it.

28.47 The agreement should provide a period of time in which the publisher has to decide whether or not to accept the work and the publisher should be required to notify the author in writing whether or not it accepts the work.

28.48 The publisher will want the right to appoint someone to make any necessary changes where the author is unable or unwilling to do this and will want the right to deduct the costs of employing someone to make the necessary changes out of any future advance and royalties payable to the author under the agreement and that where the costs have not been recouped by the publisher within one year from any future advances or royalties then the author would be liable personally to pay the outstanding balance due to the publisher out of his own pocket. In addition, the agreement will usually provide that the publisher will require the author to approve any changes which have been made to the proof with the author's approval not to be unreasonably withheld or delayed.

28.49 The publisher will require a clause providing that where it has not accepted the work or it has terminated the agreement within a year of the agreed delivery date the author will not within one year from the later of these events allow or permit the book (or an expanded, amended or abridged version of it) to be published without giving the publisher a first option to publish it on the same terms as the original publishing agreement. The agreement should provide a time-limit in which the publisher has to decide whether to exercise the option. Should the publisher decide not to exercise the option then the author would be free to offer it to others to publish.

28.50 Once the publisher has accepted the work, it should arrange for the work to be edited by the editor and the proof should be sent to the author for him to read, amend

---

[29]   See **28.44**.
[30]   See also **28.12–12.13**.

where necessary and approve. Once the author has read, amended where necessary and approved the proof it should be returned to the publisher for it to publish. All these tasks should be completed within the timescale set out in the timetable for the parties' respective responsibilities.[31]

28.51 The timetable should allow the publisher a reasonable period of, say, 6 months to one year to publish the work. Where the work is of current public interest and may only remain so for a relatively short period of time the timetable in which the publisher should be required to publish the work should be much shorter so as to capitalise on the current public interest in the subject matter of the work. Notwithstanding the period of time in which the publisher has to publish the book the agreement should provide that the publisher will give the author notice of the actual proposed publication date.

28.52 The agreement will usually require the publisher to consult with the author about the design of the book cover and about how the book will be promoted. Where the author has approval rights the publisher should ensure that author's approval will not to be unreasonably withheld or delayed.[32] Apart from those matters specifically detailed in the agreement where the author has approval rights or the right to be consulted relating to the publication of the work, all other matters relating to the publication of the book and which are in the publisher's expertise, such as the inclusion of an index, the typographical arrangement and binding of the book, will be the responsibility of the publisher to deal with and should, except in rare cases, be left for the publisher to deal with without the need for the author to be consulted or to approve.

28.53 If the agreement requires the author to make personal appearances in book stores, on radio and television programmes or at a press conference or launch party to promote the book, the agreement should provide that the author will attend at agreed dates and venues (or at dates and venues which will be notified to the author eg 8 weeks in advance of the proposed dates) for a specified period of time and that the author will attend subject to his overriding work commitments with his employer. A provision that the author will attend subject to his work commitments would be needed to cover a situation where, for example, the author is a Premier League footballer and he is required by his club to travel with the team to play in a rescheduled league or cup game on the day of his proposed promotional appearance. Where the celebrity agrees to appear at a press conference, launch party or promotional events he will want to ensure the company pays his reasonable travel, food and where necessary hotel accommodation expenses and in addition he may also require an additional appearance fee. These matters should also be dealt with in the agreement.

28.54 The agreement may provide an indication of the number of books the publisher intends to print for the first printing of the hardback and paperback editions and the anticipated retail sale price of both editions. If the agreement does contain these provisions it will also provide that these are indications only and are not obligations on the publisher to print these numbers or that the book will be sold at the prices stated in the clause.

28.55 The publisher may, where the book proves over the course of time to be a good seller, want an updated, revised or a new edition to be written. Updated and revised

---

[31] For the author's requirement to read, check, amend where necessary and approve the proof and for where the author is unable or unwilling to do this and for liability for the costs of changing the typesetting see **28.14** et seq. See also **28.44**.

[32] See also **28.14** et seq.

editions are now becoming more common where the hardback edition has proved successful and the publisher wants an added chapter or two for the paperback edition to help increase interest and sales of the title in paperback form. The agreement will contain a provision that where the publisher wants an updated, revised or a new edition of the book written it will notify the author in writing. The author will then have a period of, say, 28 days to decide whether he wants to write an updated, revised or a new edition and to notify the publisher of his decision. If the author is prepared to update, revise or write a new edition he will have a period of, say, 6 months in which to write and deliver the work to the publisher.[33] If the author is unwilling or unable to update, revise or write a new edition the agreement will provide that the publisher can employ someone else to do so.[34]

ADVANCES, ROYALTIES AND EXPLOITATION OF THE BOOK

28.56 Note: Where percentage figures are given below these are indications only. The actual percentage figures will vary from agreement to agreement.

28.57 As was mentioned previously, the rights which are granted to the publisher will need to be detailed in the agreement along with the royalty rates payable for each of these rights. It is common for the rights granted clause, rather than set out the rights in detail, to state that the rights which are granted are those which are set out in the royalties clause.[35]

28.58 An advance may be paid to the author for writing the book. The publisher will require the advance to be recoupable against all monies which are payable under the agreement, namely it will be recoupable against royalties and any one-off payments where a one-off payment is made for a particular type of exploitation of the book rather than a payment of royalties. The author should ensure that the agreement does not allow any outstanding unrecouped advance to be recoupable against any future advances which may become payable, such as where a further advance becomes payable, for example, where the publisher exercises an option for the author to write another book.

28.59 Where an advance is payable it may be paid in full upon signing the agreement or, more commonly, it will be payable in stages. Usually an advance which is to be paid to the author upon signing the agreement will be paid in instalments in equal parts, upon signing the agreement, upon delivery of the work to the publisher and upon publication of the work. An advance may be a small sum, such as £500 to £1,000, paid as a sign of good faith by the publisher or it may be a sum which reflects the amount of royalties the publisher anticipates the author will receive for sales of the book. Where the advance is paid reflecting the author's anticipated royalties the amount the author should expect to receive for the advance is in the region of 60% of his anticipated royalty receipts.

28.60 The royalty rate which is payable on book sales is calculated on the retail sale price of the book in hardback and paperback form less VAT. Royalty rates normally

---

[33] For what is meant by delivery see **28.14** et seq and **28.44** et seq.
[34] For the situation where the publisher employs someone other than the original author to update, revise or write a new edition and for the costs situation and the possible effect on the original author's future advances and royalties see **28.14** et seq.
[35] See **28.14** et seq and **28.34** et seq.

range from 7.5% to 15% (with a sliding scale between) based on net receipts. There should from the author's position be no deductions from the retail sale price other than VAT or any sales or similar tax or duties. Sometimes publishers sell books on a sale or return basis, in which case there may be a provision in the agreement that the publisher can retain a certain percentage of the royalties payable as a reserve against returns. If there is a reserve provision there should also be a provision providing for a time period by which if the reserve or any part of it has not been used up it will be liquidated and paid over to the author.

28.61 The royalty rate will usually increase once sales have exceeded a certain number. For example, the royalty rate for the hardback edition might be 10% for the first 2,000 copies sold, 12.5% for the next 2,000 and 15% for subsequent sales. The royalty rate for a paperback edition might be 7.5% of the published price (or if the royalty is based upon the trade price it might be 8 or 9% of the trade price), rising after sales of 15 or 20,000 copies to 10% of the published price (or if the royalty is based upon the trade price it might be 10.5 or 11.5% of the trade price). The increase in the royalty rate for a paperback edition will be based upon higher sales numbers since the retail and trade price is considerably less for a paperback than for a hardback and the profit margin for the publisher for a paperback is often less per copy than for a hardback. Some agreements contain a provision that where the publisher reprints a small number of copies these copies will attract the lowest royalty rate and also that these copies will not count towards the numbers sold for calculating whether a higher royalty rate becomes payable. The publisher's argument for this may be based on the fact that a small print run is expensive to arrange and that the costs of setting up a print run are the same for a large or a small run and that the profit on a small print run is considerably less than it would normally be for these copies had they been part of a larger print run. The author should resist any such provision in the agreement as by doing so he is effectively helping to subsidise the publisher's print run cost.

28.62 Once a higher royalty rate has become payable, the author may seek to make it be retrospective to the first copy, in other words once a higher royalty becomes payable that increase in the royalty rate will apply to all the copies previously sold at the lower royalty rate. Using the previous numbers used in **28.61** this would mean an extra 2.5% royalty on the hardback edition for the first 2,000 copies once sales exceed 2,000 copies. Whether the publisher is prepared to agree to the increased royalties being retrospective to the first copy will depend upon the negotiating strengths of the parties.

28.63 It should be noted that royalties paid on book club and mail order sales will usually be lower than the royalty rate payable for hardback and paperback retail shop sales. For example, the royalty rate for book club sales may start at 6 or 7% of the book club list price for the first 8,000 or 10,000 copies and increase on subsequent sales. Alternatively, the royalty for book club sales might be 10 to 12.5% of the receipts by the publisher on copies of the book which are sold to the book club or 55 to 60% of the receipts by the publisher on copies of the book which have been printed by the book club under licence.

28.64 The agreement should provide the royalty rates payable where the publisher licences specific rights to a third party. For example, the agreement may provide that where the publisher grants a licence to publish a hardback or paperback edition the author will receive of 60% of the publisher's receipts increasing to 70% once sales exceed a certain number (or the author will be paid a royalty based on sales starting at 10% and increasing to a top royalty rate of 15%) or where the publisher licences the rights to translate the work into a language other than English or licences the right to reproduce extracts from the book in a magazine or another work the royalty might be 10% of the amount received by the publisher rising to 12.5% once sales exceed a certain number. The author may seek the royalty in these situations to be based on the amount which is payable to the publisher by the licensee after specific listed agreed deductions (if any) rather than on the amount actually received by the publisher. This will ensure the author, publisher and any licensees know what can be deducted from the monies due to the publisher and will also ensure the author is entitled to be paid the royalty where the publisher has not been paid by the licensee.

28.65 The agreement may also provide that no royalty is payable where the work is used for a non-commercial purpose and no payment is made to the publisher for its use, such as where it is translated into Braille or an audio recording of the work is made for the use of those people who are print handicapped. In addition, the agreement will often provide that no royalty is payable where copies of the book have been destroyed by fire, water or in transit.

28.66 Whether or not the reprographic right has been reserved to the author, the agreement should provide a statement that the publisher has mandated the Publishers' Licensing Society to permit the Copyright Licensing Agency Limited to grant licences to photocopy and scan extracts from magazines, books, journals and digital publications. By doing this the publisher will receive its share of the reprographic rights monies received by the Publishers' Licensing Society from the Copyright Licensing Agency Limited. The author should become a member of the Authors' Licensing and Collecting Society Limited so that he receives his share of the reprographic rights monies paid by the Copyright Licensing Agency Limited to the Authors' Licensing and Collecting Society Limited.[36]

28.67 As was mentioned above,[37] the author will want to ensure the agreement provides that the public lending right is excluded from the rights granted to the publisher as the public lending right is the right for authors, editors, illustrators and translators to receive payment (from Public Lending Right) for the loan of their books by public libraries. The author should ensure that he registers the book with Public Lending Right so that he receives the monies which he is entitled to for the loan of the book by public libraries.[38]

28.68 The agreement will also provide that the author is entitled to a certain number of free copies of the book when it has been published and where the book is published in electronic form to a certain number of free copies of the book in electronic form. The agreement will also usually allow the author to purchase extra copies of the work for his own personal use and not for resale at trade price. The agreement will also usually provide that where the author is unwilling or unable to write an updated, revised or new edition of the book he will not be entitled to any free copies of the updated, revised or new edition. The agreement will usually provide that no royalty is payable to the author on review copies, on copies distributed for publicity purposes or which have been given to the author under the terms of the agreement, and that these copies will not count towards the sale numbers in calculating when a higher royalty rate is payable. The

---

[36] For contact details for the Authors' Licensing and Collecting Society Limited, the Publishers' Licensing Society and the Copyright Licensing Agency Limited see Appendix 4 and see also **28.14** et seq.
[37] See **28.19**.
[38] For contact details for the Authors' Licensing and Collecting Society Limited, the Publishers' Licensing Society and the Copyright Licensing Agency Limited see Appendix 4 and see also **28.14** et seq.

author should ideally try to limit the number of royalty free copies which the publisher can give away for review or publicity purposes.

28.69 Some publishers will draft the agreement in such a way as to provide that the royalty payable is calculated on the number of copies of the book which have been sold and for which they have received payment. The author will want the agreement to provide that the royalty payable is calculated solely on the basis of the number of copies of the book which have been sold. The author should resist a provision in the agreement which calculates the royalty on the basis of the number of copies of the book which have been sold and for which the publisher has received payment.

28.70 Where a celebrity's book is written by a ghost writer the agreement will need to deal with how the royalties and any advances are divided between the celebrity and the ghost writer. In addition, the agreement will need to deal with the royalties and any advances which are payable where the celebrity is unwilling or unable to update, revise or write a new edition of the book and someone else is employed by the publisher to do the work.[39] The agreement will usually provide that where someone other than the celebrity is used by the publisher to update, revise or write a new edition of the book the celebrity's right to receive royalties will cease, although the celebrity will still continue to receive royalties for any residual sales of the previous edition(s) of the book. A complete loss of entitlement for the celebrity to receive royalty payments for a new version of the book written by someone else is something the celebrity should strongly resist. The publisher may have a good argument for the celebrity's share of the royalty payment to be reduced where someone else is employed to update, revise or write a new edition, especially as the person employed to produce the new version will want to be paid royalties for sales of the new version, but it should be borne in mind that where an updated, revised or new edition is prepared a lot of the existing work will continue to be used in the new version for which the celebrity should continue to be paid, and it can be very strongly argued by the celebrity that sales of the new version will be based substantially on the goodwill generated by the previous version and he should be paid for the goodwill which has carried forward into sales of the new version of the book.

28.71 Other rights which might be granted to the publisher and the percentage royalty which the author might expect to be paid by the publisher include, inter alia:

(1) The right to publish the book in electronic form, for which the author might expect to receive in the region of 15 % of the money payable to or received by the publisher.

(2) Film and television rights, for which the author might expect to receive in the region of 90% of the money payable to or received by the publisher.

(3) Merchandising rights, for which the author might expect to receive in the region of 85% of the money payable to or received by the publisher.

(4) First serialisation of the book, for which the author might expect to receive in the region of 90% of the money payable to or received by the publisher.

---

[39] See also **28.14** et seq.

(5) Serialisation of the book other than first serialisation rights, for which the author might expect to receive in the region of 75% of the money payable to or received by the publisher.

(6) Where the publisher has granted a licence to publish the book in the US, the author might expect to receive in the region of 80% of the money payable to or received by the publisher.

28.72 As was mentioned at the start of this section, where percentage figures are given above these are indications only. The actual percentage figures will vary from agreement to agreement. As was also previously mentioned,[40] it should be remembered that the intellectual property rights which exist in a book go far beyond the right to publish the book itself and that some rights, such as film and television and merchandising rights, may be infinitely more valuable than the right to publish and sell hardback and paperback editions of the book. Careful consideration will need to be had as to which rights should be granted to the publisher. Factors which the author will need to take into account in deciding what rights he is prepared to grant the publisher include whether the publisher is personally experienced in dealing with the relevant rights, the size of the advance being offered and the royalty rates payable for the rights.

28.73 One area that needs to be considered is the possibility of the book being published in a format which does not currently exist or which no one has currently envisaged might exist. In the music business it was common for recording agreements to contain a provision that the record company could release a group's sound recording in formats which did not currently exist at half the royalty rate which was payable to the group for long playing vinyl records. The argument which was put forward to justify a half royalty rate was that any new technology which might come about would be very expensive for the record company to invest in and so paying a royalty equal to half the royalty payable for long playing vinyl records would help the record company to recoup the massive expenditure involved in investing in the new technology needed to release the group's sound recording in that format. Also it was not envisaged that new technology would affect in any way sales of long playing vinyl records. Moving forward to the end of the 1970s suddenly compact discs come on to the market, a new form of technology which was not in existence or even thought about when many groups signed their record deal. Compact disc sales took over from long playing vinyl records and the cost of producing them, due to economies of scale, went down from somewhere in the region of £1 to a few pence per disc. Record companies had a windfall re-releasing old records on compact disc and many of the groups were paid only half the royalty rate they were receiving for long playing vinyl records. The moral of this story is that consideration should be given to the possibility of the book being exploited in some new technology which does not currently exist or which no one has currently envisaged might exist. If the publisher is to be granted these rights, which is what the publisher will want, the royalty rate should be a figure that is not less than the royalty rate payable for the hardback or the paperback version of the book, with escalations based on realistic sales targets, or it should be an amount which is to be agreed with the author and which in any event will not be less than the royalty rate payable for the hardback or the paperback version of the book with escalations based on realistic sales targets.

---

[40] See **28.34** et seq.

28.74 As is dealt with below,[41] the agreement should deal with what the publisher can do with any stock which it has left following termination of the agreement. The agreement should deal with the royalty rate payable on any remaining stock which the publisher has when the agreement has expired by effluxion of time. Where the book is sold in the usual way after the term has ended the normal royalty rate should be payable. Where the publisher is permitted to sell any remainder stock at the end of the agreement at a discount rate as remainder stock the publisher may seek to pay no royalties on such sales. The author should resist any such provision and seek ideally the full royalty rate payable under the agreement for such hardback and paperback books. As a compromise half royalty rate on such hardback and paperback sales or a percentage of the price which the publisher sells the remainder stock for might be an acceptable compromise rate payable by the publisher for remainder stock sold at or after the end of the agreement term.

ACCOUNTING

28.75 The agreement should set out the accounting dates and the dates when the advance (if any) and royalty payments will be made. The accounting dates will usually be twice a year on 30 June and 31 December. The agreement should provide that an accounting statement will be prepared and sent to the author within 90 days of the accounting dates along with the royalty payment. If possible the author should seek a reduction in the 90-day period so that he receives the royalty payment as close to the accounting dates as possible. As the royalty paid to the author is exclusive of VAT, there should also be a provision that VAT will be payable in addition to the royalty payment where the author supplies the publisher with a VAT invoice.

28.76 The currency in which payment is to be made should also be set out in the agreement. In most if not all cases this will be pounds sterling. Where all or some of the payments are made in foreign currency the exchange rate should be the date that the payment is due under the agreement, although where late payment is made to the author he should be able to choose whether the exchange rate used to calculate the royalty payable is the exchange rate on the date the royalty payment is due or the date it is actually paid. This will enable the author to ensure he does not lose money due because of currency exchange variations.

28.77 The agreement should provide that interest at a specified rate will be payable where payment is made later than the agreed payment date.

28.78 The author may require the advance (if any) and all royalty payments to be sent to his manager or agent (under the terms of his management or agent's agreement) or to his accountant.

28.79 Where the author requires payment to a third party, such as to his manager or agent, the publishing agreement should provide that a receipt by the third party is deemed to be the receipt of the author.

28.80 The agreement should also require the publisher to keep detailed, accurate accounts and allow the author and/or his appointed agent/financial or legal adviser to carry out an audit of the accounts no more than once a year upon giving written

---

[41] See **28.84** et seq.

reasonable (say 14 days') notice. The publisher should be required to co-operate with the author and/or his appointed agent/financial or legal adviser where an audit occurs and should require the publisher to help the author and/or his appointed agent/financial or legal adviser to check the accuracy of the sales figures with any licensees or retail sales outlets which the publisher has dealt with. Any audit should be paid for by the author unless there is an underpayment by the publisher of, say, 15% in which case the cost of the audit should be borne by the publisher.

28.81 As mentioned previously,[42] where the agreement expires by effluxion of time the agreement should allow the publisher a period of time following the end of the agreement term to sell off any remaining stock which it has left. As the agreement will allow the publisher a period of time by way of a non-exclusive licence to sell off any remaining stock, there should be a provision in the agreement allowing the author and/or his appointed agent/financial or legal adviser to have access to the accounts during this period to carry out an audit or stock check on the same basis as if the agreement was still ongoing.

28.82 There is a possibility that a country where rights have been licensed by the publisher might have currency restrictions in place prohibiting money being sent out of the country. The agreement should contain a provision that where this situation occurs that the publisher will inform the author in writing that there is a currency restriction in place in that country and that the publisher will open a bank account for the author in that country and deposit the royalties due to him into the account. The agreement should also require the publisher where withholding tax has been deducted on royalty payments in a foreign country to provide the author with a tax deduction certificate which can be used by the author to claim if possible the benefit of any double tax convention.

TERMINATION OF THE AGREEMENT

28.83 The agreement should contain specific provisions which if breached would enable the innocent party to terminate. For example, a well-drafted agreement should contain a 'morality clause' providing that the author will not do anything which damages or might damage the publisher's name, reputation or image. Where the author does something which might bring the publisher's name into disrepute, for example, getting arrested for or charged with a serious crime, the publisher will then be able to terminate the agreement under the morality clause provision.

28.84 The agreement may contain a provision which enables the publisher to exercise an option requiring the author to write another book(s).[43]

28.85 The agreement might be for a series of books with a provision allowing the publisher to terminate the agreement early by exercising a break clause. A break clause might be included in the agreement where, for example, the publisher has signed a young sportsman to write a series of books detailing his career as it progresses. The publisher may want a break clause allowing it to terminate the requirement for the sportsman to write further books in the series if the publisher decides that in light of

---

[42] See **28.56** et seq and **28.84** et seq.
[43] See Chapter 24 at **24.8** point (2)(b), Chapter 25 at **25.19** et seq, Chapter 26 at **26.27** et seq and Chapter 27 at **27.31** for further details about the exercising of an option clause.

sales of previous books in the series the commercial demand for them has waned. The details of how and when a break clause can be exercised and the situation concerning past, present and future liabilities and obligations of the parties must be set out in detail in the agreement.[44]

28.86 The agreement should deal with what is to happen with any books which the publisher has left in stock following termination of the agreement. Where the agreement expires by effluxion of time, the agreement should allow the publisher a period of time following the end of the agreement term to sell off any remaining stock which it has left. The agreement should provide that during the sell off period the publisher only has a non-exclusive licence to sell the remaining books which it has left and that it cannot print any more copies of the book during this period. The agreement will usually permit the publisher to sell off the remaining stock at full price or as remainder stock and will usually provide that the publisher can pulp or otherwise dispose of the remaining stock and will, where the book is to be remaindered, pulped or otherwise disposed of, give the author one month's notice in writing of the intention to do so. The agreement should also provide that at the end of the sell off period any stock which remains will be pulped by the publisher. The agreement should also require the publisher to inform the author immediately before the commencement of the sell off period of the number of hardback and paperback copies of the book it has left in stock. The author may be concerned that the sale of his books at remainder or pound shops might damage his reputation or image and may want a provision in the agreement prohibiting the sale of any remaining stock to remainder or pound shops and/or may want first option to buy any remaining stock from the publisher at the end of the term at either wholesale or discount price. (It should be remembered that if the author enters a publishing agreement with another publisher to publish the book or an updated version of the book immediately after the termination of the previous agreement, where the previous agreement has continuing non-exclusive rights the author can only grant a new publisher similar rights for the book until the non-exclusive rights period in the previous publishing agreement has expired. Only after the non-exclusive rights period in the previous publishing agreement has expired can these rights be converted in the new agreement to exclusive rights.) To ensure that an excessive number of copies of the book are not printed towards the end of the agreement, the agreement should contain a formula limiting the amount of copies which the publisher can print in the last year of the agreement. For example, on the assumption that the book sales will gradually diminish during the term of the agreement the agreement might provide that the publisher will not print during the last year of the term more than the 50% of the average amount that was printed during the first year of the agreement. The agreement should also deal with the royalty rate payable where any remaining stock is sold by the publisher at a discount as remainder stock.[45]

28.87 Whether the term expires due to effluxion of time or due to the publisher's breach of contract a provision should be included in the agreement requiring the publisher to return any photographs and other items which have been supplied by the author to enable the publisher to publish and promote the book. There should also be a provision in the agreement stating that upon termination all the author's intellectual property rights which were licensed to the publisher revert to the author and that the publisher will execute any documents which are required to ensure that the intellectual property rights revert to the author.[46]

---

[44] See Chapter 25 at **25.19** et seq, Chapter 26 at **26.27** et seq and Chapter 27 at **27.31** for further details about exercising a break clause.

[45] See **28.56** et seq.

[46] See also **28.34** et seq.

28.88 As was mentioned earlier,[47] the agreement should contain a list of and a timetable for the author's and the publisher's respective responsibilities to enable the book to be written and published on the proposed publication date. The timetable should allow for reasonable extensions of time to be permitted by the parties, with a long stop provision so that if there is any significant delay by one party in complying with its obligations under the timetable the other party has the right to terminate the agreement.

28.89 The agreement may also provide for termination, inter alia:

(1)   Where there is a serious or substantial breach of contract. The clause should also deal with what happens where one party terminates the agreement due to the other party's breach.[48]

(2)   Where a particular matter is of such importance that it goes to the 'essence' of the agreement. For example, the publisher may only want the celebrity to write the book because he is a known celebrity and has contracted to participate at some time in the near future in a celebrity reality television programme and it is the fact that the celebrity is going to participate in the reality television programme that makes the idea of publishing a book written by him commercially viable. If it is imperative that the celebrity participates in the television programme before the publication of the book a provision should be included in the agreement to this effect and that it is 'of the essence' of the contract. This will enable the publisher to terminate the agreement should the celebrity fail to participate in the television programme.

(3)   Where one party is in material breach of contract the other party must notify them in writing of the breach and require the breach to be remedied within a period of time, and if the breach is not remedied in that time the agreement is automatically terminated. Where termination has occurred due to a material breach by one of the parties, the agreement should also provide that the parties' contractual rights, liabilities and obligations until the date of termination still exist notwithstanding termination (save for the obligation by the publisher to pay any outstanding or further advance to the author where it is the author who has been in material breach of contract).

(4)   A force majeure clause. A force majeure clause should list all the events beyond the control of the contracting parties, for example, act of God, civil war, terrorism, strikes, lock outs, which if any of them occur will excuse the party who cannot perform its contractual obligations due to the force majeure event. The clause should provide that the party who cannot perform its contractual obligations will not be in breach of contract for non-performance where this is due to a force majeure event. The clause should require the party who cannot perform its obligations due to a force majeure event to give notice to the other party of the existence of the force majeure event and that it prevents that party from performing its contractual obligations. The force majeure clause should provide that the agreement is suspended whilst the force majeure event exists and that the agreement will recommence once the force majeure event has ended. As the

---

[47]   See **28.44** et seq.
[48]   See Chapter 25 at **25.19** et seq, Chapter 26 at **26.27** et seq and Chapter 27 at **27.31** for further details about exercising a break clause.

suspension could last for a long time there should be a long stop provision in the agreement allowing one party to serve written notice on the other terminating the agreement where the agreement is suspended for a specified period of time due to a force majeure event. Where termination occurs due to a force majeure event, the agreement should deal with what is to happen in these circumstances.

WARRANTIES, INDEMNITIES AND OTHER CLAUSES

28.90 The agreement should contain a warranty by the author that he is the sole legal owner of the copyright in the work and that he has the power to enter the agreement. In addition, the author should warrant that the book is an original work, that it does not infringe any other person's copyright or breach any agreements which he may have previously entered into and that there is no current or prospective claim or litigation concerning the contents of the book and/or the title of the book or its ownership. This warranty should be modified so that it does not apply to those parts of the work which have been identified by the author to the publisher as belonging to a third party and for which copyright clearance has been or will be obtained to use in the work.[49] The author will also be required to warrant that the work has not been previously published and that he will not write a competing work which substantially reproduces the whole or a substantial part of the work which he has contracted to deliver to the publisher or which is likely to substantially decrease the number of sales of the work. There should also be a warranty from the author that the work does not contain anything which is defamatory, which infringes another person's privacy, which might breach a duty of confidentiality, which is blasphemous or obscene or which is in breach of any official secrets and that all the statements purporting to be facts are true.

28.91 As mentioned above,[50] the publisher will require the right to use the author's name, image and/or logo in any publicity material to promote the book in the territory covered by the agreement and for the term of the agreement. The agreement should also contain a warranty from the author that any trade mark he has licensed to the publisher is original, that he is the sole and absolute owner of the trade mark and that any such trade mark does not infringe the rights of any third party. A similar warranty should also be given in the agreement where the author is allowing the publisher to use any other of his intellectual property rights. The agreement should also provide that the author will indemnify the publisher from any expense or liability which might be incurred where the warranty relating to his intellectual property rights proves to be incorrect.[51]

28.92 Other provisions which should be dealt with in the agreement include, inter alia:

(1)   That both parties will keep the terms of the agreement confidential and will not disclose them to anyone other than their professional advisers or as may be required by law.

(2)   That the agreement between the parties does not constitute a joint venture, partnership or employment relationship.

---

[49]   See also **28.34** et seq.
[50]   See also **28.34** et seq.
[51]   See also **28.34** et seq.

(3)   That the agreement reflects the whole of the agreement between the parties and replaces any earlier oral or written agreement.

(4)   That the author will not hold himself out as representing the publisher. A similar provision should also be made by the publishing company to the author.

(5)   Which legal system will apply (in nearly all cases this will be the law of England and Wales) and the method to be used to resolve any disputes between the parties, namely alternative dispute resolution, arbitration or legal proceedings in the High Court or county court.

(6)   (Possibly) a provision enabling one party to limit the extent of any indemnity which has been given to the other party.

(7)   (Possibly) a clause prohibiting assignment of the agreement. Where assignment is to be permitted in certain circumstances and/or is permitted subject to certain conditions the clause should detail the relevant circumstances and conditions.

(8)   A clause providing that if the publisher becomes bankrupt or enters into a voluntary arrangement or any company through which the publisher is operating goes into compulsory or voluntary liquidation (save for the purposes of reconstructing or amalgamating a solvent company), or becomes insolvent or has a receiver, manager, or administrative receiver or provisional liquidator or administrator appointed, the agreement will automatically terminate. Provision should also be made in the clause as to the reassignment of any intellectual property rights which may have been licensed between the parties and to deal with the position of any new intellectual property rights which may have come into existence between the parties under the agreement.

(9)   A provision stating that the author has received independent legal advice on the terms of the agreement from a solicitor with experience in dealing with publishing agreements.

(10) A notice clause. A notice clause should be included to deal with the procedure to be followed where the agreement requires one party to give notice to the other party to activate a contractual clause, for example, to activate an option clause. A notice clause should provide how the notice should be given, namely in writing to the other party, and should provide how it is to be sent, for example, by personal delivery, fax, first class or recorded delivery post, when it is deemed to have been delivered, for example, for first class post it will usually be deemed to have been delivered on the first or second business day after it has been posted, and the address to which it should be sent, for example, to the address set out in the agreement or to the registered office or to such other address as may previously have been notified in writing by one party to the other.

Chapter 29

MANAGEMENT AGREEMENT

INTRODUCTION

29.1 Note: The word 'manager' is used in this chapter as an alternative to the word 'agent' to describe the person who oversees the running of a celebrity's career.

29.2 Note: This chapter has been written on the basis that an individual celebrity is looking to appoint someone to manage his career. The additional provisions which relate to the situation where several people are looking to appoint someone to manage their career(s), such as would occur with a rock or pop group, are beyond the scope of this book.

29.3 The first question that needs to be asked is does a celebrity need a manager? The answer to that question is invariably yes. Most celebrities do not have the time, the interest, the contacts or the experience to be able to manage their career successfully. Managing a successful celebrity's career can take up a lot of time and may even be a full-time job in itself. Unless the celebrity employs his own staff to look after his career he will need to find a manager to deal with the ins and outs of the various aspects of his career.

29.4 Probably the most important person in a celebrity's career, with the obvious exception of the celebrity himself, is his manager. The main responsibility of a manager is to develop, promote and supervise the celebrity's career. In addition, the manager takes on other responsibilities, and will have to be the celebrity's 'father figure', friend and mentor. He may have to deal with the celebrity's legal and financial problems even though he may not be a lawyer or an accountant. The roles that a manager may have to take on for a celebrity mean that he has to be prepared to be a jack of all trades. A manager must be a good businessman and understand the workings of the entertainment business and must be able to develop contacts to help get the celebrity work in the entertainment industry. Above all, he must be able to retain the trust of the celebrity.

29.5 The management agreement is probably the first, and arguably the most important, agreement a celebrity will sign in his career. Johnny Rogan wrote a book about music business managers called *Starmakers and Svengalis*. In many respects the title of the book sums up what a manager is. Hopefully, a good manager is a starmaker and a svengali in only the positive meaning of the words. A good manager should be able to open doors for the celebrity and give him the chance to be a star. A bad manager will not be able to do this and he may be the reason why a very talented celebrity does not make it in the entertainment industry.

29.6 The choice of whom to appoint as manager is one of the most important decisions that a celebrity will have to make. The celebrity should only appoint someone whom he believes he can trust. However, should the celebrity only appoint someone with previous managerial expertise? There is obviously a lot to be said for appointing someone with experience as he will have a lot of contacts in the entertainment industry which can be used to develop the celebrity's career, and the celebrity may be regarded with more credibility by others if he is represented by a known manager. However, there is a possible problem in that if an experienced manager has a roster of clients on his books, he may not be able to spend the time required servicing each of his clients' needs and demands adequately. The problems which exist with appointing an inexperienced manager are that he may be learning the business at the celebrity's expense and he probably will not have the necessary contacts to develop the celebrity's career. However, what an inexperienced manager may have is time and enthusiasm, which if used effectively may be of more use to a celebrity than representation by an experienced manager who does not have the time to spend on the celebrity's career.

29.7   It is rare for the manager-celebrity relationship to be one of employer and employee. The manager-celebrity relationship is usually one of principal and agent, with the celebrity as principal and the manager as agent. As the celebrity is the principal and the manager the agent, where the manager has validly negotiated an agreement for the celebrity with a third party[1] it will be the celebrity and not the manager who is contracting with the third party, and the manager will not be liable for any breach by the celebrity under the agreement with the third party. However, it should be noted that if the manager not only negotiates but also purports to enter an agreement between the celebrity and a third party, the celebrity will only be bound by the contract with the third party if there was actual or apparent authority for the manager to enter the agreement. If the third party is not sure that the manager has actual or apparent authority, it should make inquiries about the manager's authority to see whether the celebrity will be bound by such an agreement. As will be seen below,[2] the celebrity will want the management agreement to provide that only the celebrity can sign agreements with third parties.

29.8   There is no need for there to be a written agreement for a manager to represent the celebrity. An oral management agreement can exist and may operate successfully until there is a contractual dispute between the parties. It is, however, always best for the agreement terms to be set out in writing. The manager should ensure that the celebrity receives independent legal advice on the contents of the proposed management agreement from a solicitor with experience of management agreements.

ORAL MANAGEMENT AGREEMENT

29.9   As mentioned above, there is no need for there to be a written agreement in order for a manager to represent the celebrity. An oral management agreement can exist and may operate successfully until there is a contractual dispute between the parties. Indeed, before a written agreement is prepared the manager may have been providing his services to the celebrity for some period of time on the basis of an oral agreement. If there is no written agreement or if a written or oral agreement does not cover a particular matter(s), the law will imply terms into a management agreement. These implied terms include that:

---

[1]   See **29.30** et seq for negotiating and signing agreements.
[2]   See **29.30** et seq for negotiating and signing agreements.

(1) the manager will personally carry out his obligations to the celebrity and will do so with due skill and care;

(2) the manager will not allow a conflict of interest to arise between himself and the celebrity;

(3) the manager will not misuse any confidential information concerning the celebrity that he becomes aware of. This duty exists not only whilst he is manager but will continue after he ceases to represent the celebrity;

(4) the manager will keep accounts of all income and expenditure relating to the celebrity; and

(5) the manager is entitled to be indemnified by the celebrity for any expenses which he incurs on the celebrity's behalf, but the manager is not entitled to be paid a salary or commission for providing his services to the celebrity.

29.10 An oral management agreement will probably deal with the key terms and, in particular, the matter of the manager's remuneration, but will not always cover all the terms of the agreement. However, as mentioned above, if any terms are not dealt with in an oral or written agreement the law will imply terms into the agreement. It is always best for the parties to agree all the terms they want rather than leave them to be implied by law, and it is certainly a good idea to put any oral agreement into writing as soon as possible.

THE MAIN TERMS

29.11 The main terms which would need to be dealt with in a management agreement are:

(1) the appointment of the manager;

(2) the territory;

(3) the management term;

(4) the rights and activities clause;

(5) the celebrity's warranties and obligations;

(6) the indemnity clause by the celebrity;

(7) the manager's obligations;

(8) the indemnity clause by the manager;

(9) the manager's remuneration clause;

(10) the manager's remuneration after the agreement has ended;

(11) termination of the agreement;

(12) suspension of the agreement; and

(13) other clauses.

THE APPOINTMENT OF THE MANAGER

29.12 Where the celebrity had a previous management agreement which he believes has expired, that agreement should be checked to confirm it has actually expired, so that the celebrity can validly enter a new management agreement with someone else, and to check whether the previous manager is still entitled to earn commission from the celebrity's earnings notwithstanding the fact that the previous manager no longer represents the celebrity.

29.13 When negotiating a management agreement both parties should remember that it is the celebrity who is appointing the manager and not the other way round. The celebrity will appoint the manager to be his sole exclusive manager in a defined territory(ies)[3] to represent him for all or some of his activities in the entertainment industry and the manager will be required to spend as much time as is necessary to develop the celebrity's career. The agreement is an agreement for the provision of personal services by the manager for the celebrity for which the manager will earn commission on the celebrity's earnings from those areas in which the manager represents the celebrity.

29.14 The appointment clause should make it expressly clear what the manager is appointed to do. The manager would ideally like to see the appointment clause drafted widely so that he is appointed to represent the celebrity in all his activities in the entertainment business. The celebrity may well seek to limit the scope of the manager's appointment because the manager only has expertise in a particular field of the entertainment industry or because the celebrity already has a manager or agent representing him in certain areas of the entertainment business or because certain areas of the entertainment industry are particularly specialised and require the services of someone with the contacts in that field of the entertainment business. For example, a celebrity who is a sportsman may already have an agent representing him in sports-related matters, in which case the appointment of a manager to represent him in the entertainment industry should specifically exclude the right to represent him in those areas already being dealt with by his agent, which may mean excluding the right for the new manager to represent the celebrity in sponsorship, merchandising and endorsement deals.

29.15 It may be that the celebrity is appointing a large management company to be his manager because he wants a particular employee at the management company to handle his affairs. Where this is the case the celebrity should try to obtain a key man clause in the management agreement providing that if the person he wants to handle his affairs leaves the company or no longer personally handles his affairs then he will be free to terminate the management agreement. A large management company may not, however,

---

[3]   See **29.19** et seq for the territory.

be prepared to agree to a key man clause. Its attitude may be that although a capable employee may have left its employment it has other equally capable employees who can handle the celebrity's affairs properly.

29.16 A management company may be the vehicle through which the manager operates his business affairs. Where a manager runs his business affairs via his own management company, a celebrity who wants to appoint the manager will contract not with the manager but with the manager's company. The celebrity should in this situation obtain a key man clause in the management agreement or a side letter from the manager, which should provide that if the management company ceases to exist or the manager leaves the company or the manager no longer personally handles the celebrity's affairs at the company, the manager will personally represent the celebrity for the remainder of the term of the management agreement.

29.17 It may be that the celebrity operates his business affairs through his own company, in which case it will be the celebrity's company which will contract with the manager/management company. Where the celebrity's company enters a management agreement with the manager/management company, the manager/management company should ensure that that there is a side letter from the celebrity guaranteeing the performance of the agreement by the celebrity's company.

29.18 The appointment clause should be examined alongside the clauses dealing with the term and territory.[4] If the manager represents the celebrity throughout the world, the manager may want the right to appoint agents in other countries to help him. The celebrity may not want the manager to appoint agents in other countries to help manage his affairs, but if he is prepared to let the manager do so, he may want the right to be consulted about the proposed agents, or he may want the right to approve the manager's choices. If the manager appoints agents in other countries to help him manage the celebrity's affairs he will want these costs to be paid for by the celebrity. If these costs are to be paid for by the celebrity they will be dealt with in the agreement in the clauses which deal with the manager's commission.[5]

THE TERRITORY

29.19 The celebrity will need to consider the territory(ies) in which the manager will represent him and the agreement must contain a clause which deals with this. It used to be fairly common that a celebrity had several managers. Each manager would be appointed to be the exclusive manager for the celebrity in specific countries. Frequently this would lead to the celebrity being given conflicting career advice, disputes would arise between each manager over what the celebrity should be doing at a particular time and one manager would often blame another manager when something went wrong or when the celebrity became dissatisfied. It is quite possible and on occasion may be sensible for the celebrity to have two or three managers, each representing him exclusively in specific countries. However, for this to succeed there has to be some sensible channel of communication between all parties. Nowadays it is becoming more common for the celebrity to appoint just one manager to represent him throughout the world.

---

4   See **29.19** et seq and **29.23** et seq for details.
5   See also **29.49** et seq and **29.19** et seq.

29.20 The celebrity will need to establish whether his manager is capable of representing him efficiently and effectively throughout the world or whether the manager is only capable of representing him properly in certain territories. Some managers may have the contacts and the set-up to represent the celebrity in the EC but have no experience or contacts elsewhere in the world. If this is the case the celebrity should appoint the manager to represent him in the territories in which the manager has expertise, and appoint managers with requisite experience in other territories.

29.21 It is possible that the manager may not have a worldwide set-up but can still manage the celebrity throughout the world by delegating some of his responsibilities to others. The celebrity may be prepared to allow this if the agreement provides that the manager will be responsible for the running of his career throughout the world and that the manager will ensure that any work he delegates will be properly supervised and carried out. Also, as mentioned earlier,[6] the celebrity may want the right to be consulted about any proposed agents to whom the manager wishes to delegate work, or he may require the right to approve the manager's choice of agents.[7]

29.22 If the celebrity has previously appointed a manager to represent him in a particular territory(ies) and that agreement is still in existence, a management agreement with a new manager should exclude those territory(ies) which are already being managed.

THE MANAGEMENT TERM

29.23 The length of the manager's appointment must be included in the agreement.

29.24 If the manager has a limited or no proven management track record the celebrity may only want to appoint him for a trial period of 6 months. If the celebrity is satisfied at the end of the trial period with the manager's performance the manager will continue for a longer period as detailed in the agreement. If, however, the celebrity wishes to terminate the agreement so that it does not continue beyond the 6-month trial period he should be required to give 30 days' notice to the manager. The agreement should provide how and when the celebrity can serve the notice, for example, by first class post to the manager at his last known address and that it cannot be sent until the end of the fifth month of the agreement. The clause should ensure that time is not of the essence for serving the notice of termination. If the clause provides that time is of the essence for serving the notice of termination, this would mean that if the celebrity did not serve the notice on time the agreement has not been validly terminated and it automatically continues.

29.25 Most managers would not be happy to agree to a trial period which can be terminated at the whim of the celebrity. A manager may, however, be prepared to agree to a trial period based upon a performance target which if is achieved would mean the agreement would continue (see below for performance targets).

29.26 The agreement could be for a fixed term of between, say, 3 to 5 years. The celebrity would most probably like the fixed term to be for 3 years whilst the manager would like it to be for 5 years. The celebrity would prefer a shorter fixed term because

---

[6]   See **29.12** et seq.
[7]   See **29.49** et seq.

this will enable him, should he become successful in this period, to negotiate a new agreement at an early date with his existing manager or with another manager on more favourable terms, or, where he has not become successful in this period, it will enable him to look for another manager who may be more effective in developing his career. The manager would like a longer fixed term because it takes time to build up a celebrity's career and earnings potential and he will want a chance to be fully rewarded for as long as possible for all his efforts on behalf of the celebrity.

29.27 The term could be for an initial period of one year with perhaps four separate one-year options exercisable by the manager. The celebrity would want to provide that the options are only exercisable if the manager achieves stated performance targets. For example, in the first year the manager would be required to use his expertise to obtain agreements which would in total earn a certain amount of money for the celebrity. If the manager achieves the target figure he would be allowed to exercise the option to extend the agreement for another year. In the second and subsequent years the manager would be given new, higher targets to achieve before he could exercise the next option. If the manager fails to achieve the target set for the year he would not be able to exercise the option and the management agreement would terminate.[8] As opposed to or in addition to setting financial targets for the manager to achieve, the manager might be set a target of obtaining, for example, a music recording agreement or a book publishing agreement for the celebrity. Where a target such as a music recording agreement or a book publishing agreement is set, care should be taken to define the target to be achieved. For example, does a music recording agreement mean an agreement for one single only with any record company, which would therefore include some fly-by-night record company set up by a friend of the manager, or does it mean an agreement for, say, up to three albums with a 'major record company' (as itself defined in the agreement)?

29.28 A potential problem that needs to be considered by the manager is what should happen if he is given a financial target to achieve and the celebrity turns down work, thereby hindering the manager in achieving his target and also depriving him of commission. The manager should ensure the target clause is drafted to include a provision that if the celebrity turns down any offers of work submitted by the manager the value of this work is included in the calculation of the target figure. The celebrity may resist such a provision but he may possibly agree to it being counted towards the target figure if the work is type of work he has previously done or is seeking to do and the remuneration reflects the amount that would be expected to be paid to a celebrity of his standing. As for the manager not receiving commission on the work he has offered the celebrity, the manager would want the commission clause to include a provision that he receives commission on work he obtains for the celebrity but which the celebrity turns down. The celebrity may again resist such a clause, but may possibly agree that the manager should be paid commission if the work is the type of work he has previously done or is seeking to do and the remuneration reflects the amount that would be expected to be paid to a celebrity of his standing.[9]

29.29 The agreement should provide a time-limit within which the manager may exercise any option he has to extend the term. The time-limit the manager has should not be too long as the celebrity will want the opportunity to appoint another manager as soon as possible should the option not be exercised. Sometimes there may be a provision that if the manager has not informed the celebrity whether or not he intends to take up

---

[8] Notwithstanding termination of the agreement the manager and celebrity will still have ongoing responsibilities to each other. See **29.76–29.77**.

[9] See **29.49** et seq for the manager's remuneration clause.

the option, before the agreement can terminate the celebrity must notify the manager of this whereupon the manager will have a period of time from the celebrity notifying him to decide whether to exercise the option. Such a clause is unacceptable to the celebrity as the agreement continues until he takes positive action to terminate it. In any event, why should the manager be given a second chance to exercise his option if he has forgotten to do so?

THE RIGHTS AND ACTIVITIES CLAUSE

29.30 As mentioned earlier,[10] the agreement should make it specifically clear in what areas the manager represents the celebrity. A performance criteria may also be inserted into the agreement for the manager to achieve for the celebrity.[11]

29.31 The celebrity should ensure the agreement provides that the manager will use his best endeavours in representing and promoting the celebrity. Any alternative promise offered should be resisted by the celebrity.

29.32 The parties will need to decide whether the manager is authorised to negotiate and sign agreements on behalf of the celebrity. Certainly the manager would like such authority. The celebrity should resist giving the manager such wide authority as these agreements relate to his career and the celebrity will want the final say on them, after he has been advised by his manager and if necessary by his solicitor and accountant. The celebrity will probably want the clause to provide that the manager can negotiate agreements but that they can only be signed by the celebrity. Where the management agreement provides that the manager can negotiate agreements on behalf of the celebrity and that the celebrity will sign them, the manager will want a clause in the management agreement that the celebrity will not unreasonably refuse to sign an agreement which the manager has negotiated for the celebrity.

29.33 The only time the celebrity should possibly consider allowing the manager actually to sign an agreement for him is for a one-off engagement. Even then the celebrity would want the manager to use his best endeavours to try to consult him first before the manager can sign an agreement for him.

29.34 The manager will require the celebrity to refer any offers of employment to him which relate to the scope of his appointment and which have been made directly to the celebrity and not to the manager. Such a clause should be accepted by the celebrity as the manager needs to be able to consider all offers made to the celebrity to carry out his responsibilities properly.

29.35 The manager may seek a clause giving him the right to require the celebrity to sign any documents which he wants the celebrity to sign. The celebrity should resist such a clause as it is his career and the manager should not be allowed to dictate to the celebrity in this way. The final say should be with the celebrity not the manager.

29.36 The manager may seek a clause giving him the right to require the celebrity to attend any promotional interviews which the manager has arranged for him. The celebrity should modify any such clause to provide that he will be consulted in advance

[10]   See **29.12** et seq.
[11]   See **29.23** et seq.

about whether he is prepared to or is available to attend any such interviews. If the management agreement gives the celebrity control over giving interviews, the manager will usually require the clause to be drafted so that the celebrity will not unreasonably refuse to do promotional interviews. If the celebrity acts unreasonably he may be in breach of the management agreement because he may be hindering the manager's ability to carry out his management responsibilities.

29.37 The manager will want the right to use the celebrity's name, likeness, biographical details, and any trade mark(s) belonging to the celebrity in order to promote him. This should be acceptable to the celebrity provided it is made clear in the agreement that the manager only has the right to use the celebrity's name and likeness etc to promote the celebrity in those areas in which the manager is appointed to represent him and not for any other purpose. The celebrity will want the right to approve any proposed use of his name and likeness etc by the manager in any proposed promotional material, although the manager would prefer the agreement to provide that he only has to consult with the celebrity rather than seek the celebrity's approval for this. Where the agreement provides for the celebrity to have approval rights the manager will usually want the celebrity to only have qualified approval rights, ie that the celebrity will have the right to approve any proposed use of his name and likeness etc in any proposed promotional material with such approval not to be unreasonably withheld or delayed.

THE CELEBRITY'S WARRANTIES AND OBLIGATIONS

29.38 The management agreement should contain provisions dealing with the celebrity's warranties and obligations. These will include that:

(1)   he is not a minor;

(2)   he is free to enter the agreement;

(3)   he is not suffering from any disability which prevents him from providing his services;

(4)   he will carry out any services which he is required to provide under the agreement or any agreement which the manager has obtained for him professionally and to the best of his ability;

(5)   he has appointed the manager as his sole and exclusive manager in the territory(ies) stated in the agreement to represent him in all his activities in the entertainment industry. (If this is not the case the clause will need to be drafted to reflect the situation);[12]

(6)   he has taken independent legal advice from a solicitor with experience of entertainment management agreements;

(7)   he will keep the contents of the agreement confidential. The clause should allow the celebrity to disclose the contents of the agreement to his lawyer, accountant, bank and financial adviser or as may be required by law;

---

[12]   See also **29.12** et seq and **29.19** et seq.

(8)   he will inform the manager of all past professional agreements which he is bound by or may still be bound by;

(9)   he will not enter any other conflicting management agreement(s) for the territory(ies) in which the manager is appointed;

(10) he will not subsequently vary the terms of any agreement which the manager has negotiated and which he has previously agreed to;

(11) he will not do anything which will bring himself or the manager into disrepute;

(12) he will keep himself, so far as it is possible to do so, in good health and will pay attention to his personal appearance when in public;

(13) if the manager takes out any life, health or other insurance on the celebrity, the celebrity will comply with the reasonable requirements of the insurance company(ies);

(14) he will keep the manager informed as to his whereabouts and his availability to perform;

(15) he will not change his image or his professional stage name;

(16) he will undergo any reasonable training that may be necessary so that he can provide his services professionally;

(17) he will not give any interviews without the manager's consent. Such a clause would be unacceptable for a celebrity and should be deleted from any draft management agreement as it is his career and he should not be beholden to the manager over giving interviews;

(18) any employment offers he receives which fall within the scope of the manager's activities will be referred by him to the manager;

(19) any intellectual property rights which he has licensed the manager to use to promote him are original, that he is the sole and absolute owner of the rights and that any such rights do not infringe the rights of any third party. The agreement should also provide that the celebrity will indemnify the manager from any expense or liability which might be incurred where the warranty relating to his intellectual property rights proves to be incorrect; and

(20) he will join any relevant collecting societies. This clause will be required because the manager wants to ensure the celebrity receives the monies due to him from the relevant collecting societies so that the manager can take his commission from these monies. A discussion of collecting societies is beyond the scope of the book.

THE INDEMNITY CLAUSE BY THE CELEBRITY

29.39 The management agreement should contain an indemnity clause requiring the celebrity to indemnify the manager for all the costs, liabilities, losses and damage incurred by the manager due to any breach or non-performance by the celebrity of the management agreement. The celebrity should try to limit the scope of the indemnity so that he will only be liable to indemnify the manager for specific breaches. In addition, the celebrity should try to limit liability for the manager's costs to the reasonable costs which have been reasonably incurred by the manager, or to the manager's reasonable legal and other professional costs.

29.40 The manager may want a provision included in the agreement allowing him, where he collects the celebrity's income, to withhold the celebrity's money where legal proceedings have been threatened or commenced against the celebrity by a third party in which the manager is or might become involved.[13] This would enable the manager to directly offset the celebrity's money which he is withholding against any loss or damage which he incurs, rather than have to pursue the celebrity for the money due to him under an indemnity clause. The celebrity should not agree to such a provision. The celebrity may possibly be prepared to agree to a similar provision which will allow the manager to withhold his money, provided:

(1) any such legal action involves a substantial breach of the celebrity's obligations; and

(2) a limit is put on the amount of money which the manager can withhold; and

(3) any money withheld will be put on deposit to earn interest; and

(4) that where the threat of legal proceedings does not lead to the issue of court proceedings within a specified time the money which has been withheld will be returned to the celebrity together with accrued interest.

THE MANAGER'S OBLIGATIONS

29.41 The management agreement will not usually restrict the number of artists whom the manager can represent. The management agreement will, however, require the manager to use his best endeavours to represent the celebrity, to spend such time as is necessary to represent the celebrity properly, and will require the manager not to act where a conflict of interest arises between the celebrity and any other people whom he manages.

29.42 In order for the manager to carry out his responsibilities properly he may need to consult others to carry out certain tasks. For example, the manager may need to use a solicitor to examine an agreement and an accountant to give tax advice. The management agreement will provide that such costs will be paid for by the celebrity. The celebrity may want to put a monetary limit on the amount of such costs for which he is responsible. The manager will usually resist this as he will not want to be personally liable to pay the difference between the amount of the costs incurred and the amount the celebrity has contracted to be responsible for. As opposed to putting a monetary limit on the amount of costs, the clause might be drafted so that the celebrity is responsible for any reasonable fees which have been reasonably incurred by the manager.

---

[13] See **29.49** et seq for who is entitled to collect the celebrity's income.

29.43 The celebrity should ensure the management agreement contains a clause which specifically provides that the manager cannot assign the agreement. The only variation on assignment that the celebrity may be prepared to accept would be to allow the agreement to be assigned to a management company which is owned and controlled by the manager. This may be acceptable to the celebrity provided there is a suitable key man clause or suitable side letter from the manager.[14]

29.44 The manager may seek to limit the times that he is required to provide his services to the celebrity. For example, he may seek to provide his services during normal office hours from Monday to Friday. Such times will probably be unsuitable, especially as the celebrity may need to speak to the manager at weekends and in the evenings. The celebrity should resist any restrictions on the times the manager is available, and he should seek a clause that provides that the manager will be available to provide his services as and when required. A compromise may be that the manager will provide his services to the celebrity during normal office hours on Mondays to Fridays and at such other times as is reasonably required. The agreement may also provide that the manager will be available to be contacted as and when necessary on a mobile phone and that the number will be given to the celebrity and others so that the manager can properly carry out his responsibilities to the celebrity.

29.45 The agreement will also specifically oblige the manager to negotiate (and, if the agreement permits, sign) agreements relating to the celebrity. There will also be a specific obligation on him to provide the services in which he has been appointed to represent the celebrity.[15]

29.46 The agreement should contain a clause which requires the manager to keep the contents of the agreement confidential. The confidentiality clause should allow the manager to disclose the contents of the agreement to his lawyer, accountant, bank and financial adviser or as may be required by law.

29.47 The agreement will usually provide that the manager's obligations are subject to the performance by the celebrity of his obligations.

THE INDEMNITY CLAUSE BY THE MANAGER

29.48 The management agreement should contain an indemnity clause requiring the manager to indemnify the celebrity for all the celebrity's costs, liabilities, losses and damage incurred by the celebrity due to any breach or non-performance by the manager of the management agreement. The manager should try to limit the scope of the indemnity so that he will only be liable to indemnify the celebrity for specific breaches. In addition, the manager should try to limit liability for the celebrity's costs to the reasonable costs which have been reasonably incurred by the celebrity, or to the celebrity's reasonable legal and other professional costs.

---

[14] See **29.12** et seq for the key man clause and the side letter.
[15] See **29.12** et seq.

THE MANAGER'S REMUNERATION CLAUSE

29.49 The celebrity will only want to pay commission to the manager on income received from agreements which the manager has negotiated. The celebrity will not want the manager to be entitled to commission on income received from agreements which existed prior to the manager's appointment and which is received during the term of the management agreement. The celebrity will only want to pay commission to the manager during the term of the management agreement (which will include any options exercised by the manager) and once the management agreement has expired the celebrity will want the manager's entitlement to commission to cease.

29.50 The manager will want his commission to be calculated on all the gross income due to the celebrity (including income from agreements which were not negotiated by him) without deduction of any of the celebrity's expenses. In addition, the manager will want his commission to continue to be payable for as long as possible after the management agreement has expired in respect of any agreements he has negotiated or substantially negotiated for the celebrity.

29.51 The manager and the celebrity will have to negotiate a halfway house between the celebrity attempting to limit the commission payable for as short a period as possible and the manager attempting to get the commission payable for as long as possible. The parties will also have to negotiate the rate at which commission will be paid.

29.52 The usual commission rate is between 15 and 25% of the celebrity's gross income which is derived from the areas in which the manager is appointed to represent the celebrity before any deduction of the celebrity's expenses. (The agreement will need to be clear whether the commission is calculated on the income which is actually received by or on behalf of the celebrity or the income which is due to the celebrity.) There are certain deductions, such as the manager's expenses, which will be deducted from the gross figure before the manager's commission is calculated (see below for details). The general rule of thumb is that less well-known celebrities will pay a higher commission rate than better-known celebrities. Many agreements provide for a fixed commission rate, but there are many other methods which could be adopted to calculate the commission payable to the manager; for example, it could be agreed that the manager will receive:

(1)　15% for the first £100,000 income, 20% on the income from £100,000.01 to £200,000 and 25% on the income from £200,000.01; or

(2)　25% for the first £100,000 income, 20% on the income from £100,000.01 to £200,000 and 15% on the income from £200,000.01; or

(3)　25% on income from music recordings, 20% on income from music publishing, 18% on income from live performances, 15% on income from merchandising; or

(4)　20% on all activities in which the manager represents the celebrity but the total commission payable in the first year of the management agreement cannot exceed £150,000, in the second year it cannot exceed £300,000, in the third year it cannot exceed £600,000 and so on.

29.53 It is possible that the manager may not be paid commission but be paid a salary or a salary with a performance-related bonus. Some established international celebrities may even consider dispensing with a manager and hire staff to run their daily affairs, with their business affairs being run by their solicitor or accountant, who will be paid for the time they spend at their hourly charging out rate. In the music industry some managers may, instead of being on commission, be paid as if they were a member of the band and be paid an equal share of the band's net profits. If the manager is to receive an equal share of a band's net profits instead of commission, care should be taken to define in the management agreement what exactly is meant by 'net'.

29.54 The management agreement should be checked to ensure that if the celebrity provides his services via a limited company the commission payable to the manager is only calculated on the income due to or received by the celebrity's company. The celebrity will be paid a salary from his company and the manager should not commission this as well because this would amount to the manager receiving double commission, namely from the celebrity's company and from the celebrity's salary.

29.55 The celebrity should also ensure the agreement provides that the manager will be entitled to commission on any advances which are payable under any agreements between the celebrity and a third party, for example, a music recording agreement, but that the manager is not entitled to receive commission on any royalties which are used to recoup the advance. If the manager were allowed to commission the advance and any royalties which were used to recoup the advance this would amount to the manger receiving double commission. The advance is effectively a loan to the celebrity by the third party which will be recouped by the third party from future royalties, and the celebrity will not actually receive any royalties until such time as the advance has been fully recouped.

29.56 The celebrity will want the agreement to provide that the manager will only be paid commission on money which has been 'received', whereas the manager will seek commission to be paid upon money which has been received or is still 'due'. The manager will argue that notwithstanding the fact that money is still due he has brought in the work for the celebrity, that it is not his fault if a third party has not yet paid the celebrity for his services and that he should be paid his commission and not be penalised for the failure of the third party to pay. The celebrity will argue that it may be true that the manager obtained the work for him, but he should not have to pay the manager commission for work he has provided and not been paid for, as this would mean not only has he presently provided his services for free with the possibility of never being paid if the third party goes into liquidation or bankruptcy, but until such time as he is actually paid it is causing him a financial loss as he is paying commission on money which he has not yet, and may not ever, receive. As to whether the manger is paid on income which is still 'due' will depend on the negotiating strengths of the parties.

29.57 The agreement should provide that it is the manager's own responsibility to pay for those costs which are directly attributable to the running of his own business. The manager will therefore be expected to pay for his own office expenses, which will include rent, business rates, heating, lighting, stationery and staff. This is different to the costs which the manager incurs specifically for the benefit of the celebrity. Those costs which are incurred by the manager specifically for the benefit of the celebrity should be recoverable from the celebrity's income. The celebrity will want a clause in the agreement which requires the manager to provide receipts for any expenses which he wants to reclaim and in addition the celebrity will want to limit the amount which the manager can reclaim. Commonly, rather than put a monetary figure on the amount which the manager can reclaim, the agreement will provide that the manager will only be repaid for his reasonable expenses which have been reasonably incurred by the manager specifically for the benefit of the celebrity. Another limitation which the celebrity might seek to put into the agreement concerning the manager's expenses would be to require the manager to obtain prior authority from him before incurring expenses above a certain figure. The celebrity will also want a clause in the agreement which provides that the manager can only reclaim his expenses out of the income from which he represents the celebrity and not from any other income which the celebrity receives. Also, if the manager can appoint agents to help manage the celebrity the agreement should deal with whether the agent's costs are an expense recoverable from the celebrity's income.

29.58 It should be noted that if commission is calculated on the celebrity's gross income the manager's expenses should be deducted from the gross figure before commission is calculated.

29.59 Sometimes the manager will find suitable offers of work for the celebrity which the celebrity for no apparent reason decides to turn down. This means that the manager will lose the chance to earn commission. The manager will not want to work for nothing and will want a clause in the agreement which provides that he will be entitled to be paid commission on work which he finds for the celebrity which the celebrity turns down. The celebrity will resist such a clause in the management agreement on the basis that it is his career and if he does not feel that a particular offer is suitable he has the right to turn it down. The manager will argue that the work is of the type the celebrity is seeking and that he should be paid commission if the celebrity has a flight of fancy and rejects suitable offers of work. If, which is unlikely, the celebrity is prepared to agree that the manager should be paid commission for work which he turns down, he should ensure the management agreement is drafted in such a way that it provides that the work the manager has obtained is similar to the work, in terms of pay and conditions, which he has done in the past and which would be expected to be carried out by a celebrity of his standing or, if it is of a type which he has not previously been involved in, it is in an area in which he has expressed an interest in becoming involved, and which reflects his professional standing in the field in which he is known.

29.60 On rare occasions a celebrity might be given a gift, such as a Ferrari or a Bentley, by a grateful promoter at the end of a concert tour, or by a record company to reflect its pleasure at his record sales. The manager will want to commission payments in kind and personal gifts which have been made to the celebrity. The celebrity will probably resist the manager having the right to commission personal gifts. The manager will argue that he should be paid commission upon any personal gifts the celebrity might receive from grateful third parties on the basis that the manager obtained the agreement which led to the relationship between the celebrity and the third party and therefore if it had not been for the manager the celebrity would not have received the gift. Also, the manager might argue that the gift is an equivalent to a further advance or a higher royalty, albeit in the complete discretion of the donor, and is therefore commissionable, or he could argue that it is a sweetener to the celebrity to try to buy his loyalty in the future which may persuade him to want to stay with the donor at the end of the agreement on possibly less favourable terms than might be offered by another person.

29.61 The manager should be entitled to commission payments in kind because a payment in kind is an alternative method for the celebrity to be paid for providing his services. The agreement should, however, provide a method for calculating at what stage a payment in kind is commissioned, for example, is it commissioned on the value when the celebrity takes delivery of the payment in kind or when he sells it? The agreement should also provide what deductions can be made from the payment in kind before the manager can commission it, for example, the celebrity should be allowed to deduct from the agreed value of the payment in kind the costs he incurs in selling it.

29.62 As mentioned above, the manager's commission is usually between 15 and 25% of the celebrity's gross income which is derived from the areas in which the manager is appointed to represent the celebrity before any deduction of the celebrity's expenses.[16] There are certain deductions or exclusions which should be made from the celebrity's gross income before the manager's commission is calculated. The deductions or exclusions include:

(1)   VAT.

(2)   Where the celebrity is going on tour to promote a record:
    (a)   tour support if it is given by the record company to the celebrity. Tour support is money which may be given to the celebrity by his record company to enable him to perform live in concert to promote a record. The manager should not be able to commission tour support as it is not money which is due to the celebrity, but is money paid to the celebrity to offset a tour's financial losses;
    (b)   where a tour makes a profit, receipted tour costs, for example, the travel and hotel expenses of the celebrity and his road crew, his road crew's wages and any money which the celebrity has to pay an established band to be the opening act for him on tour;
    (c)   tour agent's costs (these are usually in the region of between 10 and 15% of the gross tour receipts); and
    (d)   any hire fee paid by a promoter to the celebrity for the use of the celebrity's own sound and lighting equipment on tour.

(3)   Where the manager has already received commission on an advance which has been paid by a third party to the celebrity, any royalties which would have been payable by the third party to the celebrity but which are used by the third party to recoup the advance paid to the celebrity should be excluded.

(4)   Any monies paid by the celebrity's record company to an independent record producer or engineer. If the celebrity is also the producer and/or engineer of his album he will be paid an additional sum(s) to perform these functions by the record company, in which case these monies belong to the celebrity and would be commissionable. However, if the celebrity is not the record producer and/or if he is not the engineer these monies do not belong to the celebrity and so should not be commissionable by the manager.

(5)   Recording costs and video recording costs paid for by the record company or paid for by the celebrity out of any recording costs advance or video recording costs advance which the celebrity received from a record company (see also (5) above). Like tour support (see (2)(a) above), these are monies which are paid by a record company to enable the celebrity to make a record and to make any accompanying videos. These are not monies which belong to the celebrity and so should not be commissioned by the manager.

---

[16]   See **29.56**.

(6) The costs which the manager has incurred specifically for the benefit of the celebrity.

29.63 Another area which must specifically be dealt with in the management agreement is who is entitled to collect the celebrity's income. There are several ways of dealing with who collects the celebrity's income, for example:

(1) The manager will collect the income. Obviously, this is what the manager wants. However, the celebrity should resist this as it is his money, save for the manager's 15 to 25% commission. The celebrity will be concerned that the manager might possibly either run off with his money or go into liquidation or bankruptcy. If the manager insists on collecting the income and the celebrity is prepared to agree to this, the manager should be required to account to the celebrity monthly or at least quarterly, and in the event that the manager receives large sums such as recording or book publishing advances or royalties he should be required to account to the celebrity within 7 days of their receipt. There should be a provision that any money received by the manager will be paid into a bank account before any commission is deducted. The bank account should not be the manager's bank account, but should be a separate trust bank account either in the name of the celebrity or in the names of the celebrity and the manager. Any interest earned on the money should belong to the celebrity, although the manager will want to be able to commission the interest earned. The celebrity and the manager should both be required to sign any cheques issued on the account, although there may be provision allowing the manager to be the sole signatory for small cheques of, say, up to £100. The celebrity will be paid his money from the trust bank account either by way of a cheque or by a direct transfer from the trust bank account to his personal bank account. Where the payment is by way of a direct bank transfer the agreement should set out the name of the celebrity's bank, the account name and number and the sort code to enable the payment to be made directly into the account.

(2) The manager will collect the income from those areas which it is anticipated will not generate the majority of the celebrity's income, but he will not collect the income from those areas which it is anticipated will generate the majority of the celebrity's income. If, for example, the celebrity is expected to earn the majority of his income from book publishing and merchandising the management agreement would not permit the manager to collect the income earned from these areas, although the manager would be permitted to collect the income from the other areas in which he represents the celebrity.

(3) The manger will collect the income for the first year or 2 years of the agreement (if it is anticipated that the celebrity will not earn substantial sums during that period) and thereafter the celebrity or the celebrity's accountant will collect the income. An extra safety valve could be inserted to provide that if during the time the manager collects the income the celebrity signs a music recording or a book publishing agreement or any other agreement which will bring in sizeable income, any monies which from these agreements will not be collected by the manager but by the celebrity or the celebrity's accountant.

(4)   The manager will collect the income during the agreement term (in which case the matters discussed at (1) above will still be relevant), and after the agreement has ended the celebrity will collect the income and account to the manager for his commission.

(5)   The celebrity will collect the income and will pay the manager his commission. The manager will certainly resist any such suggestion as he will be concerned that the celebrity might run off with his commission or that celebrity might become bankrupt before he has been paid his commission, or where he has contracted with the celebrity's company rather than the celebrity in person that the celebrity's company might go into liquidation before he has been paid his commission.

(6)   The celebrity's accountant will collect the income and will pay the manager his commission. This may be acceptable to the manager if he cannot persuade the celebrity to let him collect the money.

29.64 Where the manager collects the celebrity's income there should be a provision in the agreement requiring the manager to maintain proper accounts relating to the celebrity's income, to be kept at the manager's registered office or main place of business. In addition, the manager will be required to send the celebrity a detailed statement of account when paying the celebrity the money which is due to him. The manager may insert a clause giving the celebrity, for example, one year from receipt of the accounts to object to their accuracy. The celebrity should not accept any clause which allows the manager to reduce the 6-year contractual limitation period to object to the accounts. The agreement should also contain an audit clause which will allow the celebrity or his professionally qualified accountant to inspect, audit and take copies of the manager's books and records to determine the accuracy of the accounts. The clause will usually require the celebrity to give notice of his intention to carry out the audit, and will limit the inspection to one inspection a year at the celebrity's expense. In addition, the clause will usually provide that the audit will take place at the manager's registered office or main place of business and will take place during the manager's normal business hours. There may be an additional restriction that the accountant carrying out the audit for the celebrity is not presently engaged on another audit of the manager on behalf of another celebrity.

29.65 The audit clause should contain a provision that the information disclosed to the celebrity and/or his accountant is confidential information and will not be disclosed to anyone other than the celebrity's professional advisers or as may be required by law. The manager will usually require a copy of the celebrity's final audit report to be sent to him.

29.66 The agreement should provide that where the celebrity has been underpaid by a specified sum, for example, he has been underpaid by at least £5,000, or has been underpaid by a specified percentage, for example, 10%, whichever is greater, that the cost of the audit will be paid for by the manager. The agreement should provide that where the celebrity has been underpaid the manager will account to the celebrity for the underpayment. The celebrity should ensure that the clause is drafted so that the manager accounts for any underpayment immediately and that the manager pays interest on any underpaid sum at 3 or 4 % above a stated bank's base rate from time to time in force.

29.67 The manager may insert a clause in the agreement which allows him, where he collects the celebrity's income, to retain such amount of the celebrity's money as he deems necessary as a reserve for future expenses which he anticipates he will incur for the celebrity. Where the celebrity's money is collected by the celebrity or his accountant, the manager may want a clause giving him the right to be sent such amount of the celebrity's money as he deems necessary for him to hold for such a reserve. The celebrity will not want his money to be retained and will resist such a clause. At most the celebrity might be persuaded to agree to a clause which will either allow a 'reasonable' reserve or a specified sum to be retained.

29.68 Where the celebrity or his accountant collects the income, the manager will want a detailed statement of account sent to him with his commission and will require audited accounts to be sent to him once a year. The matters discussed in the above paragraphs concerning where the accounts are to be kept, the right to audit, the mechanics and cost of the audit, underpayment, that the information is confidential and requiring a copy of the final audit report to be sent to the audited party are also relevant in this situation. Likewise, any attempt by the celebrity to cut back the 6-year contractual limitation period for the manager to object to the accounts should not be accepted by the manager.

29.69 The celebrity's solicitor should try to obtain a provision in the agreement that notwithstanding who collects the celebrity's income, the manager's right to receive commission is conditional upon the celebrity not terminating the agreement because of the manager being in substantial breach of contract. The manager will strongly resist any such provision being included in the agreement.

29.70 Occasionally the celebrity may find that a party with whom he has contracted is delaying or refusing to pay him for his services. The celebrity should ensure that the management agreement does not allow the manager to commence legal proceedings in his name. The decision to litigate should rest solely with the celebrity after consultation with the manager. This is because of the time, expense and possible publicity involved for the celebrity in litigating.

THE MANAGER'S REMUNERATION AFTER THE AGREEMENT HAS ENDED

29.71 As mentioned earlier, the celebrity will only want to pay commission to the manager during the term of the management agreement (which will include any options exercised by the manager) and once the management agreement has expired he will want the manager's entitlement to commission to cease. In contrast, the manager will want his commission to continue to be payable for as long as possible after the management agreement has expired in respect of any agreements that he has negotiated or substantially negotiated for the celebrity. The manager will often have to put a lot of effort into obtaining suitable agreements for the celebrity and he should be financially rewarded for his work. Imagine the situation where with 6 months left to run on the management agreement the manager obtains a long-term worldwide music recording agreement or a Hollywood three-film acting contract for the celebrity. The manager will be entitled to commission any advance paid to the celebrity during the term of the management agreement, but if his right to receive commission were to cease automatically at the expiration of the management agreement, he will lose the chance to commission any further advances and royalties the celebrity would receive from the agreements which he had secured for the celebrity. The celebrity will want to cut off the manager's right to receive commission at the end of the management agreement because any new manager he appoints will want to commission all the income he earns from the activities in which the new manager represents him. If the celebrity is not careful he could find himself paying two sets of commission at full rate on the same income, namely to his previous manager if the previous manager is entitled to receive commission beyond the term of the management agreement and to the new manager under the new management agreement.

29.72 The celebrity will obviously not want to pay two sets of commission at full rate on his income. To protect against this problem a clause should be included in any management agreement which will ensure that the celebrity will not pay commission at full rate twice on the same income or, if he does, that it will only be for a short period of time. The clause which should be inserted to deal with this situation should ideally provide that the commission payable after the end of the term to the manger will be tapered so that it will reduce from a 100% entitlement to a zero entitlement over a period of time. There are many ways this clause could be drafted: for example, the agreement might provide that the manager will be paid commission on the monies earned in respect of any agreements that he has negotiated or substantially negotiated for the celebrity:

(1) at full rate commission for the first 2 years after the end of the term; thereafter

(2) 80% of the full rate commission rate for the next 2 years; thereafter

(3) 60% of the full rate commission rate for the next 2 years; thereafter

(4) 40% of the full rate commission rate for the next 2 years; thereafter

(5) 20% of the full rate commission rate for the next 2 years, thereafter the manager will no longer be entitled to commission any of the celebrity's income.

29.73 A tapering clause will enable the manager to continue to commission the celebrity's income from those areas in which he represented the celebrity for a period of time after the management agreement has ended, albeit the commission rate will reduce over a period of time, and will enable the celebrity to move on and earn money without having to pay the manager commission in perpetuity.

29.74 If the celebrity subsequently appoints a new manager and agrees to pay him commission on income arising from agreements entered into prior to the new manager's appointment, he should try to ensure that the new manager accepts a lower but gradually increasing commission rate on this income. The objective for the celebrity is to try to ensure that the total commission which he pays to his previous manager and to his new manager on this income does not amount to more than the 100% of the commission which he would pay to one manager.

29.75 A new manager would seek and should be entitled to commission at full rate in respect of any agreements he subsequently negotiates or substantially negotiates for the celebrity. There may, however, be some scope in attempting to negotiate a reduced commission rate payable to a new manager where the new manager negotiates the exercise of an option relating to a contract which was originally negotiated by a previous manager or where a brand new contract is negotiated by the new manager which is in essence the equivalent to the exercise of an option of an existing contract which was originally negotiated by a previous manager. The reason why there may be some scope for trying to reduce the commission rate in these circumstances is because it is arguable that the new manager is merely continuing to develop a relationship which was brought to fruition by a previous manager and has not found that work for the celebrity. However, to counter that argument the new manager would say that he has had to use his skill in negotiating the best terms for the celebrity and that he has helped ensure the relationship between the celebrity and the third party has continued to the point where the third party wants to extend its working relationship with the celebrity.

TERMINATION OF THE AGREEMENT

29.76 The agreement should contain provisions as to when the management agreement will automatically terminate. The agreement should also contain provisions as to when an aggrieved party has the right to elect to terminate the management agreement. The agreement may provide that where a terminating event occurs which entitles an aggrieved party to elect to terminate the agreement, before he can elect to terminate the agreement he must serve a notice on the other party giving notice of the terminating event and requiring it to be remedied within a period of 30 days, and only if the terminating event has not been remedied within that time can he then terminate the agreement. The circumstances where termination will or may occur include:

(1)   Where one party has been in substantial breach of contract the other party has the right to terminate the agreement.

(2)   Where one party becomes either bankrupt or enters into a voluntary arrangement or any company through which the party operates goes into compulsory or voluntary liquidation (save for the purposes of reconstructing or amalgamating a solvent company), or becomes insolvent or has a receiver, manager, or administrative receiver or provisional liquidator or administrator appointed, the agreement will automatically terminate.

(3)   Where one party has been convicted of a criminal offence the other party has the right to terminate the agreement. The provision should be drafted so that it only allows for termination to occur where there has been a serious criminal conviction. The definition of 'serious conviction' must be included in the agreement so that both parties are in no doubt as to what will or will not give rise to a right to terminate.

(4)   The celebrity has the right to terminate where the manager has failed to meet any performance targets placed upon him.

(5)   At the end of the contractual term the agreement will automatically terminate whereupon the celebrity will be free to sign with another manager.

29.77 The termination clause will usually contain a provision that notwithstanding termination both parties must continue to comply with the clauses of the management agreement to the extent that they are not affected by termination. For example, if the agreement is terminated by the celebrity due to a substantial breach of contract by the manager, although the celebrity can terminate the agreement both parties will still be bound by any clause in the agreement providing for confidentiality.

SUSPENSION OF THE AGREEMENT

29.78 The agreement will usually contain a clause allowing the manager to suspend rather than terminate the agreement whilst there is a breach of contract existing which has arisen through no fault of the manager. If there is a suspension clause there should be a provision in the agreement that before suspension can occur the manager must give the celebrity notice that the agreement will be suspended if the celebrity has not rectified the breach within a period of time, for example, 28 days. The agreement should also list the circumstances where the manager can invoke a suspension clause.

29.79 Where the agreement is suspended the term is frozen from the date of suspension. The term recommences once the breach has been rectified. A suspension clause may provide that the manager does not have to make any payment of monies due to the celebrity until the breach has been rectified. The celebrity's solicitor should not agree to a provision in the suspension clause which provides that the manager can withhold the celebrity's money during a period of suspension.

29.80 The circumstances where suspension may occur include:

(1) Where the celebrity refuses to provide his services under the agreement the manager may suspend the agreement.

(2) Where the celebrity is in breach of his contractual obligations the manager may suspend the agreement.

(3) Where a force majeure event occurs.

29.81 The agreement may provide that notwithstanding the right which the manager has to suspend the agreement that for certain specified events, for example, if the celebrity refuses to provide his services, the manager may elect to terminate the agreement immediately, whereas for other events, for example, force majeure, termination can only occur 14/21/28 days after the agreement has been suspended and the event which gave rise to suspension has not been rectified.

29.82 The suspension and termination clauses should be drafted to make it clear that any legal right or remedy which existed prior to suspension and/or termination is not affected by suspension and/or termination.[17]

OTHER CLAUSES

29.83 Other provisions which should be dealt with in the agreement include inter alia:

(1) A clause which allows the manager to promote himself to others that he is the celebrity's manager.

(2) A clause making it clear that the manager has the right to represent other people as well as the celebrity.

---

[17] See also **29.83** for a non-waiver clause.

(3)   A clause confirming that the management agreement does not constitute a joint venture, partnership or employment relationship between the manager and the celebrity.

(4)   A clause confirming that the agreement reflects the whole of the agreement between the parties and replaces any earlier oral or written agreement.

(5)   A force majeure clause. A force majeure clause should list all the events beyond the control of the contracting parties, for example, act of God, civil war, terrorism, strikes, lock outs, which if any of them occur will excuse the party who cannot perform his contractual obligations due to the force majeure event. The clause should provide that the party who cannot perform his contractual obligations will not be in breach of contract for non-performance where this is due to a force majeure event. The clause should require the party who cannot perform his obligations due to a force majeure event to give notice to the other party of the existence of the force majeure event and that it prevents him from performing his contractual obligations. The force majeure clause should provide that the agreement is suspended whilst the force majeure event exists and that the agreement will recommence once the force majeure event has ended. As the suspension could last for a long time there should be a long stop provision in the agreement allowing one party to serve written notice on the other party terminating the agreement where the agreement is suspended for a specified period of time due to a force majeure event. Where termination occurs due to a force majeure event, the agreement should deal with what is to happen in these circumstances.

(6)   Which legal system will apply (in nearly all cases this will be the law of England and Wales) and the method to be used to resolve any disputes between the parties, namely alternative dispute resolution, arbitration or legal proceedings in the High Court or county court.

(7)   A notice clause. A notice clause should be included to deal with the procedure to be followed where the agreement requires one party to give notice to the other party to activate a contractual clause, for example, to activate an option clause. A notice clause should provide how the notice should be given, namely in writing to the other party, and should provide how it is to be sent, for example, by personal delivery, fax, first class or recorded delivery post, when it is deemed to have been delivered, for example, for first class post it will usually be deemed to have been delivered on the first or second business day after it has been posted, and the address to which it should be sent, for example, to the address set out in the agreement or to the registered office or to such other address as may previously have been notified in writing by one party to the other.

Chapter 30

RECORDING AGREEMENT

INTRODUCTION – PART 1

30.1   The way music is now listened to has changed in the last 10 years beyond all recognition. Until the advent of the internet and the availability to download music there was an effective business model which most record companies adopted very successfully to sell records. The record companies were able to adapt very quickly whenever any new technology came on stream and were often able to use it to their advantage to make more money not only from current artists' recordings but also from back catalogue recordings of those artists whose careers had all but ended. Perhaps the best and most recent example of this was the advent of the compact disc in the early 1980s. Until Sony and Phillips brought out their CD players, most recorded music from the mid-1960s was either sold on 45 or 33 1/3 rpm vinyl or on cassette. When the CD format came out it was seen as a revolutionary way in which to listen to music. For a start you could get up to 80 minutes' playing time on a CD (although the original marketing of CDs suggested the playing time was somewhere in the region of 60 to 70 minutes), the sound quality was supposedly superior (although there was and still is some argument about this amongst hi fi fanatics and sound engineers) and CDs were supposedly almost indestructible and so would be playable no matter how badly they were handled. Once the price of the hardware came down and more recordings became available on CD this became the format of choice for the consumer to use to listen to their music. People who had their records on vinyl or cassette (or on other formats such as reel-to-reel or eight track) went out and bought them again on CD. Not only have people bought them on CD having already got them in a different format in the past, but over the last 20-plus years many people have also bought subsequent reissues of the same CDs because they have been re-mastered (so that the sound quality is even better than it was originally on CD) and/or they have been reissued with extra tracks or as a double CD with a DVD of a live concert performance or of the promotional videos that accompanied the songs when they were originally released or with remixed or extended versions or radio sessions or demo versions of the songs included.

30.2   With the advent of the home computer and the internet the record industry has seen its established business model thrown into chaos. For whatever reasons, nearly all the record industry was caught off guard and did not adapt from the start to the fact that people would want their music more portable than it currently was. As opposed to leading the vanguard of selling music via the internet, the record companies seemed to be caught off guard and did not establish or effectively promote their own platforms to sell recorded music via the net. At the same time illegal sites were springing up far quicker than they were being closed down. In addition, successful non-record company owned legal downloading sites were opening and selling music for the I-Pod and the mobile phone generation. The record industry was from the start playing catch up and to a large extent still is. Due to the nature of the internet the music industry will always have a fight on its hands as illegal sites and file sharers can operate very easily anywhere in the world (and often do so in parts of the world where copyright protection either does not apply or is not properly enforced) and illegal sites and file sharers can be very hard to trace and close down. The effect of the internet is that in recent years record sales in non-MP3 formats have been in decline, some would say in terminal decline. In addition, record stores have been going out of business at an alarming rate. In the last few years the independent record shop on the high street seems to have all but disappeared and several large multiple record shops and at least one general store which carried some back catalogue and current chart records have also disappeared. The Virgin store sold out to Zavvi, which is no longer in existence, MVC was closed down by its parent company Woolworths, Fopp went into administration and only a few of these stores now remain (owned by HMV) and Woolworths, which carried a selection of CDs along with chart CDs, is no more. WH Smith, although still selling CDs in some stores, has contracted back its selection to almost exclusively chart CDs, Borders have gone into administration, and food chains such as Tesco and Sainsbury's sell mainly chart CDs. Apart from the very few remaining specialist independent stores, the only large national chain to sell chart and non-chart CDs is HMV. Even HMV, with the exception of their flagship stores in Oxford Street, London, appears to have cut back its CD selection in stores, preferring to use store space to sell DVDs, computer games, books and selected entertainment hardware items such as games consoles, MP3 players and DAB radios. This has meant that there are very few places which now sell CDs on the high street. The 7-inch or CD single is effectively no more and has been replaced by the digital download single, and the CD album is now more available either as a download album or as a physical CD which can be bought over the internet.

30.3   The advent of the internet along with the current economic climate means that the business model which most record companies adopted very successfully to sell records in the past is no more. There appears to be no standard business model which the record companies are using to sell their recordings. We are in a situation where the record companies are trying different methods to see what does and does not work. Currently, many major and independent record companies are not signing artists in the numbers that they had previously due to the decline in income from record sales. In addition, many artists who have had some success in the past rather than being retained by the record companies have found themselves being released from their contract when the record company has to decide whether to exercise an option to extend the agreement. To compound the record companies' problems, current successful artists are often choosing to leave their record companies at the end of their deal rather than accept the offer of a new contract. Successful artists are often choosing to release their records in ways which 5 or 10 years ago they would not have considered or had the opportunity to do, as they can make more money even with less sales numbers and also have more artistic freedom than if they were signed to an established record label.

30.4   The types of deals now being done by recording artists vary in the extreme. For example, several artists, such as Madonna and Jay-Z, have signed 360 degree deals with Live Nation which not only covers their recordings but also live concert appearances and merchandising. Prince, McFly and UB40 each signed one-off deals with the *Mail on Sunday* to give away for free with the newspaper their latest album which had until then not been commercially available. Several leading artists have released their latest album either exclusively or for a period of time exclusively via a record label set up by the Starbucks coffee shop chain which could only be purchased at Starbucks coffee shops. Radiohead released their latest album via the internet on a 'pay what you think it is worth' basis before it was commercially released. Other ways in which artists are releasing their recordings include paying for the recordings themselves and then licensing them to a record company, giving the latest record away with a ticket to their concert, releasing live recordings of each of their live concerts within 24 hours of each concert, agreeing to a sponsorship deal which includes giving away for free downloads of their record via the sponsor's website, getting fans to pay £50 each to finance the recording with a guarantee that the fan will be sent a copy of the album when it is released along with their name being credited in the album booklet and/or including a guarantee that the fan will receive not only the album but also a copy of all subsequent recordings made in addition to the album for a year.

30.5   As can be seen from the above, the recording industry is in a great state of flux. Record companies are now far more cautious than before about signing an artist to a record deal and are far more careful about how much money they will be prepared to spend on recording and promoting an artist. In addition, due to the availability of the option clause in the agreement the record company will be more likely to release the artist from the agreement than to take up the next option.

INTRODUCTION – PART 2

30.6   Note: This chapter has been written on the basis that the celebrity is not an established musician but has achieved his celebrity status in some other area of the entertainment industry. He is an adult over the age of 18, is a solo singer (known to have a good singing voice), does not play in a group and assumes that he does not write and will not write or co-write songs.[1] His reputation in his field of the entertainment industry is such that there has been a bidding war between a couple of major record companies and he has personally signed (and has not contracted via his own limited company) a record contract for the UK and Europe only which gives the record company options to extend the agreement several times so that if all the options are exercised the record deal will be a long-term multi album deal.[2] This scenario will enable an examination of the key terms which may need to be considered in a recording agreement. The scenario means that the key terms in a recording agreement which relate to a band are beyond the scope of this book, as is a detailed examination of the controlled composition clause which is found mainly in recording agreements which relate to the US and Canada, although such a clause may be found in recording agreements which relate to other territories. (A controlled composition is often defined as a composition which has been written by, or is owned by or is controlled by, the recording artist. A controlled composition clause in a recording agreement is used to limit the amount the record company has to pay the copyright owner of a composition for a mechanical licence to record, manufacture and distribute for retail sale copies of the recording of the composition on record, CD etc.) As the scenario provides that the celebrity is signing directly with a major record company an examination of a production agreement is beyond the scope of this book. (A production agreement is an agreement whereby a performer enters an agreement exclusively to record for a company which is not owned by him and the company licences the recordings to the record company.) In addition, as the scenario provides that he does not and will not write or co-write songs, the terms of a music publishing agreement are not dealt with in this book.

---

[1]   It should be noted that points (11) and (15) at **30.44** deal with the possibility that he might write songs which he will record. In addition, there is also a brief reference to the celebrity writing songs at **30.70** et seq and some consideration is given to the possibility of the celebrity writing songs at **30.84–30.85** et seq.

[2]   It should be noted that point (7) at **30.78** considers the situation where the territory of the recording agreement covers not only the UK and Europe but also the rest of the world.

30.7   Although some record agreements are extremely long, running to many dozens of pages, and contain complex provisions, the basics of a recording agreement are simple to understand. Essentially, the celebrity, in exchange for royalties and an advance which is recoupable against royalties, agrees to record exclusively for the record company and allows the record company to record, manufacture, distribute and sell his recordings. In addition, the record company provides the money to make the recordings, the cost of which will be recoupable against the celebrity's royalties, and the record company will agree to release the recordings for sale to the public, although it will reserve the right not to do so in certain circumstances such as where it believes they are not in its opinion commercially acceptable to release.

30.8   The record company will want the copyright in the sound recordings to be owned by them for the full copyright term and for any renewals and extensions of copyright. As was seen earlier,[3] s 11(1) of the Copyright, Designs and Patents Act 1988 (CDPA 1988) provides the general rule that the author of a copyright work is the first owner of the work, and s 9(2)(aa) provides that the author of a sound recording is the producer. The producer is defined in s 178 as the person who makes the necessary arrangements for the creation of the sound recording. The record company will require a clause in the recording agreement providing that where the copyright in the sound recordings vests in the celebrity he will assign the ownership of the copyright in the sound recordings to the record company. This clause will be in the agreement in case the celebrity produces his own recordings. Where, as is very common, a third party who is not a record company employee is brought in to produce the celebrity's recording sessions, the third party producer will in the producer's agreement be required to assign the ownership of the copyright in the sound recordings to the record company. (An examination of the clauses in a producer's agreement is beyond the scope of this book.)

30.9   As will be seen later, recording costs are paid for by the record company but are recoupable from the celebrity's royalties. Assuming the celebrity has recouped his advance, recording costs and any other recoupable sums, he will have paid for the sound recordings although they will be owned by the record company. It is only fair that the record company, which is making a substantial economic investment in the celebrity, should be able to earn back its costs and earn a return on its investment. There is an argument that a celebrity who is fully recouped and has therefore paid for the sound recordings should own the sound recordings after the record company has had a reasonable period of time to earn a return on their investment. As sound recordings are a valuable asset, the celebrity's solicitor should try to negotiate a clause in the recording agreement which provides for the copyright in the sound recordings to be assigned or reassigned to the celebrity, and for the physical property of the master tapes to be handed over to the celebrity, say, 10 or 15 years after the end of the contractual term. Although the celebrity's solicitor should seek such a clause in the recording agreement, most record companies will reject out of hand any such provision. In the unlikely event that the record company agrees to assign or reassign the copyright in the sound recordings to the celebrity, it will usually only be prepared to do so if the celebrity is recouped or is prepared to repay the record company any unrecouped sums, and provided the celebrity pays its reasonable legal fees for the assignment or reassignment and a nominal sum of, say, £250 per master track. Where the record company has agreed to assign or reassign the copyright in the sound recordings to the celebrity, the recording

---

[3]   See Chapter 18 on Copyright at **18.48–18.49**.

agreement should provide that the assignment or reassignment is subject to and with the benefit of any licences which the record company has granted to third parties to use the sound recordings.[4]

30.10 Perhaps the most complex area in any recording agreement is the royalty clause. The reason why the royalty clause is so complex is threefold. First, there are many different formats and ways in which recorded performances can be sold to the public, each of which may generate different royalty rates, for example, LP, CD, downloading from the internet, licensing the recording for a television advert or for a film soundtrack or using the recording on a compilation with other performers' recordings, such as on the NOW series. Secondly, there are different price ranges in which the same recording may at some time be sold to the public, for example, usually a CD will initially be brought out on the record company's top line label at full price, after a period of time it may be released at mid-price and at a later date it may be released at budget price. Thirdly, there are various deductions, such as for packaging, which need to be taken into account before the royalty payable can be calculated.

30.11 The celebrity may be swayed to sign with record company A rather than record company B because of the 'higher' royalty rate being offered on sales of his records on record company A's top line full price label. However, one cannot take royalty rates being offered at face value because there will be various deductions which need to be taken into account and there will be different royalty rates for recordings released on different formats and different royalty rates for recordings on full price, mid-price and budget price releases. For this reason, the celebrity's solicitor and his manager should look closely at the royalty rates on offer and calculate what it they are really worth based on hypothetical sales figures and advise the celebrity what the deal on offer is actually worth. It is very possible that a 16% royalty rate offered by record company A may in fact be worth less than a 12% royalty rate offered by record company B.

THE MAIN TERMS

30.12 The main terms which would need to be dealt with in a recording agreement are:

(1)   the parties to the recording agreement;

(2)   the territory;

(3)   the minimum commitment – the term – options;

(4)   the grant of rights by the celebrity;

(5)   the celebrity's warranties and obligations;

(6)   the indemnity clause by the celebrity;

(7)   the record company's obligations;

(8)   the indemnity clause by the record company;

---

4   See also **30.96**.

(9)   advances;

(10) royalties;

(11) deductions from the gross royalty;

(12) items which should not be deducted from the gross royalty;

(13) reserves against returns;

(14) royalty rates for different formats and different types of exploitation;

(15) escalating the royalty rate;

(16) accounting and auditing;

(17) termination of the agreement;

(18) suspension provisions; and

(19) other clauses.

THE PARTIES TO THE RECORDING AGREEMENT

30.13 The parties to the recording agreement will be the record company and the celebrity.

30.14 Where session musicians are used they will give their consent to the record company to record and exploit their performances under the standard Musicians Union agreement.

THE TERRITORY

30.15 The recording agreement must set out the territories in which the record company can exploit the celebrity's recordings. The celebrity must ensure that he only grants the record company the right to exploit the recordings in those territories which he is capable of giving. If, for example, a record company were seeking worldwide rights and the celebrity has an existing recording agreement with another company covering North America and Canada then these territories should be excluded from any recording agreement he enters with another record company.

THE MINIMUM COMMITMENT – THE TERM – OPTIONS

30.16 The term during which the celebrity will make recordings for the record company will usually be defined in the recording agreement as a period of time, with options for the record company to extend the agreement. The clause will be drafted so that it interrelates with the number of recordings which the record company requires from the celebrity. The number of recordings the record company requires during the initial term and during each option period is known as the minimum commitment or the minimum recording commitment.[5] The minimum commitment during the initial term might, for example, be enough recordings for two singles, and in addition at the request of the record company enough recordings for a long playing record.[6]

30.17 It should be noted that the term of the agreement relates to the period during which the celebrity will make recordings for the record company and not to the length of time which the record company has to exploit the recordings. The record company will want the right to exploit the recordings made by the celebrity for the full copyright term and for any renewals and extensions of copyright.[7]

30.18 The celebrity's solicitor should attempt to get the record company during the initial term to require an album's-worth of recordings from the celebrity rather than only one, two or three singles with an option for the record company to require an album. The celebrity will want a guarantee that he will be able to record and release at least one album rather than let the record company decide upon the success or failure of a couple of singles as to whether it wants to continue its relationship with him and require an album from him. If the record company refuses to agree to a minimum commitment of an album and will only commit to a couple of singles, the celebrity's solicitor should try to get the record company to agree to spend a minimum guaranteed sum promoting the singles and he should try to get the record company to guarantee (rather than have an option) that it will require an album if a single achieves a certain number of sales or a top 30 chart place within a specified period of time after it has been released in a designated territory.

30.19 A single may, for example, be defined as three recordings of different compositions, none of which are either instrumentals or have been previously recorded by the celebrity. In addition, the record company will require each of the compositions to be of a certain minimum and maximum length. A long playing record may be defined, for example, as not less than ten recordings of different compositions, none of which are instrumentals, none of which have been previously recorded by the celebrity, each lasting, for example, not less than 3 minutes nor more than 6 minutes 30 seconds, and together lasting not less than 35 minutes. In addition, where the celebrity is a songwriter the record company may require the recordings to be of compositions which have been written by him. The agreement should be checked to ensure it does not provide that if more than a certain number of compositions are on the long playing record it will be defined as a double album. The effect of this is that the celebrity may need the consent of the record company to release a double album, and it will affect the royalty rate payable to the celebrity.[8]

30.20 The minimum commitment will often state that neither a live recording of the celebrity in concert nor the release of a 'greatest hits' or 'best of' record will count toward the minimum commitment. The record company may insert a clause into the recording agreement to provide that double albums will only count as a single album for the purposes of the minimum commitment requirement. The reason why a record

---

[5]   See below for how an initial term clause might be drafted.
[6]   See below for what is a long playing record.
[7]   See Chapter 18 on Copyright at **18.78–18.79**. See also **30.6** et seq, **30.33** et seq, point (1) at **30.47** and point (3) at **30.96**.
[8]   See **30.78**. See also below as a double album may be counted as one album for the purposes of the minimum commitment.

company will count a double album in this way is because there is a tendency for them to sell in lesser quantities than single albums and they are usually priced at far less than twice the price of a single album. The celebrity will want a live/greatest hits/best of album to count towards the minimum commitment, but the record company will not agree to this as the compositions have previously been recorded by the celebrity. In addition, the record company will often not want to release a live album as these do not usually sell in such quantities as studio recorded material. The celebrity's solicitor may be able to persuade the record company that any compositions which have been included on a live/greatest hits/best of album which have not been previously released should count towards the minimum commitment. It is becoming common for live albums to contain material which the celebrity has not released before, and for greatest hits/best of albums to contain two or three newly recorded tracks to entice fans who have all the other material on the album to purchase the compilation.

30.21 The agreement will require the recordings made by the celebrity to be master recordings. A master recording will be defined in the agreement. Put very basically, a master recording is the original tape recording or any other method which is used to record music professionally, for example, computer disk. The lead vocals, backing vocals and each instrument will be recorded onto separate tracks on the tape. Once the performances have been recorded onto the tape it is then edited, mixed (the levels between each of the instruments and the vocals on the tracks are balanced), and equalized (simply balancing the treble, bass and mid-range). From the edited, mixed and equalized tape another tape is made which will be used in the manufacture process of LPs and CDs.

30.22 The record company should be aware that the length of the term needs to be sufficient to enable it to make a financial return on its investment in the celebrity whilst ensuring that the term is not so long that it might be held by the courts to be in restraint of trade. It should be remembered that the courts will look at all the terms of the agreement, including how long the whole of the agreement will last if all the options are exercised, together with any extensions of time provided for in the agreement for late delivery of the minimum commitment by the celebrity. Whether an agreement is likely to be in restraint of trade will vary from case to case and will depend upon all the terms of the particular recording agreement. As a guideline, restraint of trade cases seem to suggest that the maximum acceptable length of term including options is 7 years.

30.23 As was mentioned above, the term during which the celebrity will make recordings for the record company will usually be defined in the recording agreement as a period of time, with options for the record company to extend the agreement, during which time the celebrity will be required to satisfy the minimum commitment requirement.

30.24 The length of the initial term for which the celebrity will be required to make recordings for the record company can be drafted in several ways. For example:

(1)   the term will last for a period of one year during which time the celebrity will satisfy the minimum recording commitment;

(2)   the term will last until 180 days after the delivery of the minimum recording commitment but in any event the term will last not less than one year nor last for more than 18 months in total; or

(3)   the term will last until 180 days after the release in the UK of the minimum recording commitment but in any event the term will last not less than one year nor last for more than 18 months in total.

30.25 It should be noted that in (2) above the term is defined by reference to delivery, whereas in (3) above the term is defined by reference to release. The release of the record by the record company may be easily 6 to 9 months after the delivery of the record by the celebrity to the record company and therefore a term clause based on the release of the recording will last longer than if it were based on the delivery of the recording to the record company.

30.26 Some record agreements provide that where the record company has not exercised an option the agreement will continue until the celebrity has given it notice that it has not exercised the option and the record company will then have an extra period of time, for example, 4 weeks from the celebrity's notice to decide whether or not to take the option up. If the record company does not take up the option within the time period given under the celebrity's notice, the celebrity will only then be free to enter a recording agreement with another record company. The celebrity's solicitor should delete any clause requiring the celebrity to give notice and extra time to the record company to decide whether to exercise the option. It is the record company's and not the celebrity's responsibility to keep an eye on when an option clause in favour of the record company becomes exercisable.

30.27 It is quite common for the celebrity to fall behind in the recording sessions and so be unable to deliver the minimum commitment on time. The record company will often require a right allowing it to elect to terminate the agreement if the celebrity does not deliver the minimum commitment on time. In addition, where the celebrity has not delivered the minimum commitment on time the agreement will provide that the term will automatically be extended. The celebrity should only agree to the automatic extension of the term where the delay is his fault. Due to the possibility of the agreement being in restraint of trade, the record company should insert a long stop date beyond which the automatic extension cannot run, for example, if the celebrity does not deliver the minimum commitment during the initial period, the initial period will automatically continue until the minimum commitment has been delivered, although the initial period shall not exceed a period of 2 years. In addition, where there has been late delivery of the minimum commitment the agreement will usually provide for an extension of time for the record company to exercise any option it might have. It is only fair that where the celebrity has not delivered the minimum commitment the record company should have an extension of time to decide whether to exercise an option to retain the celebrity. To do so it needs to evaluate the recordings, which it cannot do until it has received them from the celebrity. The extension provided for in the agreement to exercise the option may easily be in the region of 180 days following delivery of the minimum commitment. The celebrity's solicitor should ensure where the agreement provides for an extension of time to exercise an option that this only operates where the delay in delivering the minimum commitment is the celebrity's fault. In addition, the celebrity's solicitor should try to cut back the time period allowed for the record company to decide whether to exercise the option. The record company should not require too long an extension to decide whether to exercise the option due to the possibility of the agreement being in restraint of trade.

30.28 The agreement should be drafted to make it clear that where an option is not taken up all subsequent options will automatically lapse and the agreement is automatically terminated, enabling the celebrity to look for another deal with another record company.

30.29 Stories often abound in newspapers and magazines that a celebrity has signed a record deal for five albums for a £1,000,000 advance. In reality what the celebrity has most likely signed is a recording agreement for one or two albums for a £50,000 advance with the record company having a series of options Where the record company exercises each option it will pay the celebrity a further advance. If all the options are exercised the record deal will be for a total of five albums for £1,000,000. As the record company will have a series of options over the celebrity's recording services, it can at each option date decide either to exercise the option where the celebrity is still popular or not to take up the option where the celebrity's popularity has declined. This will enable the record company to drop the celebrity once he loses his popularity and will save it the substantial costs involved in recording and releasing his albums.

30.30 The celebrity should ensure that any option clause is drafted so that he will receive an increased advance on the exercise of each option by the record company. For example, if the record agreement was for an initial one-year term with an advance of £50,000 with four options of one year each, the celebrity might seek a further advance of £100,000 on the exercise of the first option, £150,000 on the exercise of the second option, £200,000 on the exercise of the third option and £250,000 on the exercise of the fourth option. There are other ways that the celebrity can provide for an increased advance on the exercise of the option.[9] In addition, when each option is exercised the celebrity should ensure the recording budget, his royalty rate and any royalty escalations also increase.[10]

30.31 The record company will usually insert a clause into the agreement providing that the celebrity cannot start recording his second or subsequent albums until he has delivered his previous recording to it, and that the celebrity cannot deliver the new recording until 9 months after he has delivered his previous recording. This enables the record company to ensure that it only receives one record at a time to promote and that these recordings are the celebrity's current style of performance and, from the record company's point of view, hopefully still in touch with current music fashion trends. In addition, this will prevent the celebrity signing a long-term agreement with the record company and presenting it with the whole of his contractual commitment in one go whereupon he will be free to leave and sign with another record company.

30.32 Sometimes a celebrity might record an album, deliver it to the record company then almost immediately disappear out of the public spotlight for several years and then reappear saying he is ready to record his new album. To protect against the possibility of a celebrity who may have gone out of fashion suddenly reappearing and wanting to make a new album, the record company will usually insert a clause into the agreement providing that if the celebrity has not delivered his next album within, say, 18 months of delivering his previous album it can terminate the recording agreement. The celebrity's solicitor should ensure that any such clause is not drafted to allow the record company to terminate the recording agreement where the celebrity has not delivered his next album for legitimate reasons, such as when he has been promoting and/or touring the

---

9   See **30.49** et seq and **30.57** et seq.
10 See **30.49** et seq and **30.57** et seq.

current album either for the record company in the territory covered by the agreement or for another record company where it has been released in other territories.

THE GRANT OF RIGHTS BY THE CELEBRITY

30.33 It is important the recording agreement provides that the grant of rights by the celebrity is conditional upon the record company complying with its contractual obligations.

30.34 The celebrity will usually grant the record company the exclusive right to his services as an audio and audio-visual recording artist in the defined territory for the defined term. However, there may be a problem for the celebrity agreeing to provide his services to the record company as an audio-visual recording artist. This is because an audio-visual recording includes film, television and video and so will include the celebrity's work not only as a musician but also as a film actor or television presenter. Even though the record company would usually give its consent for the celebrity to work as a film actor or television presenter, if the celebrity is presently engaged in such activities or it is envisaged that he may want to do so in the future, the clause should be amended to specifically exclude these activities being granted to the record company.

30.35 In addition to having the right to record the celebrity's performances, the record company will need the right to manufacture, distribute and sell copies of the recordings of the celebrity's performances on LP, CD and any other formats which are now known or which may come into existence in the future. As was seen earlier, the celebrity has rights in his performances under CDPA 1998, ss 182, 182A, 182B, 182C, 182CA, 183 and 184.[11] The recording agreement will contain a provision giving the celebrity's consent for the record company to exploit his performances in accordance with the provisions of ss 182, 182A, 182B, 182C, 182CA, 183 and 184. The consent will be given to enable the record company to exploit the recordings both during and after the agreement term as it will want the right to exploit the recordings for the full copyright term and for any renewals and extensions of copyright. In addition, the celebrity should ensure his performers' moral right to be identified as the performer under CDPA 1998, s 205C is asserted in the recording agreement.[12]

30.36 The record company will require the right to adapt, add material to, alter, delete material from and rearrange material on the sound recordings which contain the celebrity's performances. Whether the record company will be granted all or some of these rights or whether these rights will be granted in a modified form will depend upon negotiation between the parties. The celebrity should seek a restriction in the recording agreement that the record company will not adapt, add material to, alter, delete material from, or rearrange material on the sound recordings where any such adaptation etc would or might be a derogatory treatment of an author's literary or musical work under CDPA 1998, s 80 (unless the author has consented to any such adaptation etc) and that the record company will not distort, mutilate or modify the sound recordings of his performances in such a way that is prejudicial to his reputation (which is effectively extending the CDPA 1998, s 205F right to object to derogatory treatment of a performance directly to the sound recordings themselves).[13] If possible, the celebrity

---

[11]   See Chapter 21 on Performers' Rights and Infringement of a Performer's Rights.
[12]   See Chapter 22 at **22.8** et seq.
[13]   See Chapter 19 at **19.19** et seq and Chapter 22 at **22.20**.

should try to ensure the record company can only adapt, add material to, alter, delete material from, and rearrange material on the sound recordings subject to the celebrity's consent. The record company will not agree to what amounts to total control by the celebrity but it may be prepared to agree to a clause allowing the celebrity to have qualified consent, ie it can adapt, add material to, alter, delete material from and rearrange material on the sound recordings subject to the celebrity's consent, such consent not to be unreasonably withheld or delayed. Notwithstanding any such permission which may be granted by the celebrity to adapt etc the sound recordings which contain the celebrity's performances, the record company will need to be aware that any adaptation etc of a sound recording may amount to a derogatory treatment of an author's literary or musical work in the underlying composition comprised on the sound recording. Where this would or might amount to a derogatory treatment the record company should ensure it has the permission of the author(s) of the work to make the adaptation etc.

30.37 The recording agreement will give the record company the right to lease, licence and sell the recordings. This will enable the record company and not the celebrity to allow others to use the recordings in, for example, an advertisement, a television programme or a film. A celebrity may not want the recordings to be used to advertise certain products, for example, he may not want his recordings to be used to promote the sale of meat if he is a vegetarian, or to be associated with particular television or film scenes, for example, he may not want his music being used in a sex scene. The celebrity should, where he has strong preferences against the recordings being used in certain situations, either seek a total bar on such use or require the record company to seek his approval before they can be used. A record company will usually be sensitive to a celebrity's feelings on such matters and will often agree to prohibitions on the use of the recordings in these circumstances.

30.38 The exclusive nature of the record company's rights to the celebrity's services means that the celebrity cannot make recordings for other companies whilst he is under contract to the record company. Sometimes a celebrity is invited to contribute to a recording made by a performer who is contracted to another record company. The celebrity may want to make a 'guest' appearance on another performer's record, but will need his own record company's permission to do so because he is exclusively contracted to his own record company. The celebrity's solicitor should ensure the record agreement allows the celebrity to make 'guest' appearances on other performer's records. The record company will often agree to this, but on terms such as:

(1)   the record company will be credited on the cover or inner sleeve of the record for letting the celebrity make a 'guest' appearance, ie 'John Smith appears courtesy of ABC12 Record Company Ltd';

(2)   the celebrity will only 'guest' and not be a 'featured artist' on the record and will only be credited on the record sleeve, record packaging and adverts for the record as a 'guest';

(3)   the size of any 'guest' credit on the record sleeve, record packaging and adverts for the record will be the same size as any 'guest' credits for other performers on the record;

(4)   no photographs of the celebrity can be included on the record sleeve or record packaging nor on any adverts for the record;

(5)   any 'guest' appearance will not interfere with any commitment the celebrity has under his recording agreement.

30.39   The exclusive nature of the record company's rights to the celebrity's services also means that if the celebrity wants to record some of his songs for radio or television, for example, for a BBC Radio 1 session or for a specially recorded concert for radio or television he will need his record company's permission to do so. The record company will normally allow the celebrity to record his songs for radio or television as it is good free publicity. However, the record company will usually only allow the celebrity to record his songs for broadcast purposes only. The record company will not usually allow the celebrity's recordings which were made to be broadcast on radio or television to be released for sale to the public by the radio or television company or by any other record company which has an agreement with the radio or television company to release recordings from its archives. The celebrity would like to be able to record his compositions for radio or television for broadcast purposes only without the need to seek the prior consent of the record company. If the record company will not agree to amend the agreement to allow for this, the celebrity's solicitor should try to obtain as an alternative amendment that the record company's consent to allow the celebrity to make recordings for broadcast purposes only will not be unreasonably withheld or delayed.

30.40   The rights clause will also provide that where the sound recording copyright, ie the master tapes, vests in the celebrity he will assign the copyright to the record company. This clause will be in the agreement in case the celebrity produces his own recordings.[14]

30.41   The celebrity will be required to grant the record company the right to use his name, image, logo, biographical details and any trade mark or service mark belonging to him to promote and exploit the recordings. Unless the celebrity is giving the record company merchandising rights (for which see below), he should ensure the record company only has the right to use his name, image etc to promote and exploit the recordings and not for any other purpose. The celebrity will want the record company to submit any proposed promotional material which bears his name, image etc to him for his approval. The majority of record companies will often only be prepared to consult the celebrity about the proposed use and content of any proposed promotional material which bears the celebrity's name, image etc. Where a record company is prepared to let the celebrity have approval rights the record company will usually only agree to the celebrity having qualified approval rights, ie that the celebrity's approval will not be unreasonably withheld or delayed.

30.42   Some record companies will try to obtain the celebrity's merchandising rights so that they can licence them to merchandising companies, collect the royalty income from the merchandising companies, take a percentage of the royalty income for themselves and account to the celebrity with the balance. In addition, the record company will be able to earn interest on the celebrity's share of the merchandising royalties until it has to account to the celebrity. The recording agreement may also contain a provision that the record company can use the celebrity's share of the merchandising royalties to recoup any sums which are unrecouped under the recording agreement. If the celebrity were to allow the record company to have his merchandising rights he should not agree to any provision allowing the record company to use his merchandising royalties to recoup any sums which are unrecouped under the recording agreement. Because of the potential

---

[14]   See **30.6** et seq for the sound recording copyright. See also Chapter 18 at **18.48–18.49**.

value of merchandising, a celebrity should strongly resist giving the record company his merchandising rights. The celebrity should ideally contract directly with a merchandising company of his own choice. If the celebrity does give the record company his merchandising rights they should only be given on terms, including the royalty rate payable to the celebrity, which would usually be given to a merchandising company which is not connected to the record company.

30.43 Some record companies with a related merchandising company might try to get the celebrity to sign a separate merchandising agreement with their related merchandising company. If the celebrity agrees to give his merchandising to a merchandising company which is related to the record company he should only do so on terms, including the royalty rate payable to the celebrity, which would usually be given to a merchandising company which is not connected to the record company. In addition, neither the merchandising or recording agreement should contain a provision allowing for cross-collateralising between the agreements. Cross-collateralisation is the offsetting of monies which are owing to the celebrity under one agreement against any unrecouped position of the celebrity in the other agreement.

THE CELEBRITY'S WARRANTIES AND OBLIGATIONS

30.44 The warranties and obligations of the celebrity which will frequently be included in the agreement include that:

(1)   The celebrity is a qualifying person under CDPA 1998.[15]

(2)   The celebrity is not a minor.

(3)   The celebrity is free to enter the agreement.

(4)   The celebrity is not suffering from any disability which prevents him from providing his services.

(5)   The celebrity has taken independent legal advice from a solicitor with experience of music agreements.

(6)   The material which the celebrity records will not be obscene, defamatory, blasphemous or infringe any copyright or any third party's rights.

(7)   The recordings will be original recordings of the celebrity made specifically for the record company under the agreement and the compositions comprised in the recordings have not been previously recorded by the celebrity.

(8)   Where he is required to assign any rights to the record company that he is free to assign them to the record company.

(9)   The celebrity is free to use his professional name.

---

[15]   For the qualifying person see Chapter 18 at **18.27–18.28**.

(10) The celebrity will keep the terms of the agreement confidential and will not disclose them to anyone other than his professional advisers or as may be required by law.

(11) The celebrity will waive, or where waiver is not permitted by law he will not assert, his moral rights. It should be noted that the wording in a standard recording agreement provides for all moral rights and performers' moral rights to be waived, or where waiver is not permitted by law that they will not be asserted, by the performer and does not refer to the moral and performer's rights individually. The wording in a standard recording agreement will additionally include a provision that the performer will receive a credit as the performer of the recording in accordance with CDPA 1998, s 205C. The celebrity should not waive the moral rights which he has where he is the author of a literary or musical work and should ensure that the recording agreement does contain a provision that he will be identified as the performer in accordance with s 205C. Indeed, the celebrity should actually assert his CDPA 1988, s 77 paternity right and if the recording agreement does not contain a provision identifying him as a performer under s 205C he should ensure that he actually asserts his s 205C right. In addition, he should if possible look to extend the scope of s 205F so that it applies to the sound recordings themselves.[16]

(12) The celebrity will not record with any other performer without firstly obtaining the record company's permission.[17]

(13) The celebrity will deliver the minimum commitment required within the time provided for in the agreement.[18]

(14) The celebrity will not sample any recordings for inclusion on his recordings unless the record company has been informed beforehand and cleared their use.[19]

(15) Where the celebrity writes his own compositions, he will only record his own original compositions. The clause will also provide that the compositions must be new material and must not have been previously recorded. It may be that the celebrity will want to record some compositions written by other composers. This clause prohibits this. The celebrity's solicitor should amend the clause to allow the celebrity to record other people's compositions, although if the record company is signing the celebrity because he is a singer-songwriter rather than as a vocal interpreter of other people's compositions, it may put a limit upon the number of other people's compositions which he may record.

(16) The celebrity cannot start recording his second or subsequent albums until he has delivered his previous recording to the record company, and he cannot deliver the new recording until 9 months (or some other stated period of time) after he has delivered his previous recording.[20]

---

[16] See Chapter 19 at **19.6** et seq, **19.19** et seq, **19.31** et seq, **19.40** et seq and Chapter 22 at **22.8** et seq and **22.20**. See also **30.33** et seq.
[17] See also **30.38** et seq for 'guest' appearances and how this can be dealt with in the agreement.
[18] For the minimum commitment see **30.16** et seq.
[19] See Chapter 18 at **18.89** et seq and **18.95** et seq.
[20] For the minimum commitment see **30.16** et seq.

(17) The celebrity recordings will be 'technically and commercially' acceptable. The celebrity will want to resist any reference to the recordings being 'commercially' acceptable. There will frequently be a requirement in the agreement, especially for non-established performers, that the record company will, or the record company and the performer will together, select the material which will be recorded. Where the record company selects the material to be recorded or selects it together with the celebrity, the celebrity may possibly be able to persuade the record company to remove the words 'commercially acceptable' on the basis that, as the record company is either selecting or helping to select the material which will be recorded, it believes this material is, or will be, 'commercially acceptable', and so the reference to these words is unnecessary.

(18) The celebrity will perform the material at the recording studios and with the producer selected by the record company. The celebrity will not want the record company to have the right to select the material, the recording studios or the producer. The celebrity would ideally want the right to decide these matters for himself. The record company may be prepared to allow its established, successful performers the freedom to select their material, the recording studios and the producer, although the record company would still want either the right to be consulted about or to approve the celebrity's decisions. Because of its substantial financial investment, the record company will in most cases not allow such important decisions to be made by the performer alone. Most performers will only be able to obtain either the right to be consulted about or the right to approve such matters, with such approval not to be unreasonably withheld or delayed.

(19) The celebrity will re-record those recordings which the record company has deemed under the terms of the agreement to be unacceptable, for example, where they are not technically acceptable.

(20) The celebrity will, as and when required by the record company, participate in the making of promotional videos to accompany his recordings.[21]
      Where a promotional video is made, the agreement should provide who has control over, for example, the video storyline, its producer and director. As the record company is initially paying for the substantial video recording costs, it will in nearly all cases require total control over the making of the video, although the celebrity may be able to negotiate either the right of approval, with such approval not to be unreasonably withheld or delayed, or the right to be consulted by the record company about making the video.[22]

(21) The celebrity will carry out the services which he is required to provide under the agreement professionally and to the best of his ability.

(22) The celebrity will perform under his professional name and will not use any other name to perform under. (Perhaps, following the case of Prince, who is now using that name again, but who a few years ago changed his name to The Artist Formerly Known As Prince aka TAFKAP, and then later became known to the public as Symbol when he changed his professional name to a sort of hieroglyphic which nobody knew how to translate, spell or pronounce in English, the

---

[21] See also point (5) at **30.47** and **30.57** et seq for how the cost of making videos is dealt with in the agreement.
[22] See point (5) at **30.47** and see **30.57** et seq for how the cost of making any videos and royalties payable on sales of videos will be dealt with in the agreement.

clause should be extended to provide that the celebrity will not use any other professional name, nor adopt any symbol or hieroglyphic as a professional name.)

(23) The celebrity will not change his musical style or his professional image. The record company will want this clause to prevent what it perceives could be an inappropriate change of musical direction by the celebrity, for example, it would have serious misgivings if the celebrity was a long-haired, heavy metal celebrity whose professional image was that of a typical heavy metal celebrity suddenly deciding that he wanted to perform in the style of and adopt the image of a jazz singer. The celebrity will not want the record company completely controlling his musical style or his professional image and will resist a very restrictive clause. It may be possible to agree a less restrictive clause which will allow the record company some control over the celebrity's musical style and image thereby allaying its concerns that the celebrity will not suddenly attempt to recreate himself in a completely new and unrelated field of music, whilst allowing the celebrity to have some latitude to change his musical style and image as his career develops and as public tastes change. A clause that might be acceptable to both the record company and the celebrity could be one which provides a list of musical styles in which the celebrity can perform that are deemed to be acceptable, with an acceptance that the professional image may change to reflect the musical style being performed. In addition, the clause could provide a list of musical styles which are not acceptable to the record company.

(24) The celebrity will endeavour to stay in good health. The record company may require a best endeavours or a reasonable endeavours clause from the celebrity.

(25) (If the record company wants to take out insurance on the celebrity) the celebrity will attend any medical and will comply with any requirements of the insurance company to ensure that the insurance policy remains in force.

(26) The celebrity is a member of, or will join, the Musicians Union.

(27) The celebrity will not do anything which will bring himself or the record company into disrepute. This is commonly known as a morals clause. Certainly, many celebrities' behaviour in public or their behaviour in private which might become public knowledge would or might breach a morals clause. Some celebrities would be offended by the record company requiring a morals clause in a record agreement and would not want it included in the agreement. It does appear that hardly anything seems to shock a record company and, despite a morals clause being inserted in the agreement, little save for the most foul criminal behaviour (or to be cynical a severe drop in popularity and record sales) would encourage a record company to terminate a record agreement. Bad behaviour will very rarely have any real adverse effect on a celebrity's career, and in an industry where the adage 'there is no such thing as bad publicity' seems to be true, the record company will either agree to the removal of the clause or, if not, will usually not enforce any breach of the clause by the celebrity save in the most extreme circumstances. The one occasion where the record company will usually refuse to remove the clause and may even act upon a breach of it is where a celebrity is aimed at the pre-teenage market and he has a particular clean-cut image but his behaviour goes totally against the image being portrayed and will therefore hasten a decline in record sales.

(28) The celebrity will inform the record company of his current address and landline and mobile telephone numbers and will keep them informed as to where he can be contacted.

(29) The celebrity will keep the record company informed of his proposed professional plans and engagements both within and outside of the music industry. This will enable the record company to tie in record releases, national and local special promotions and local radio and television personal appearances and advertisement campaigns to increase record sales. The record company may additionally require the celebrity to arrange a concert tour around the release of a single or album, and it may even want to approve or consult with the celebrity over the proposed dates, venues and tour budgets. This is not only to enable the record company to promote the records in the locality around the time of the concerts, but also because it may be giving tour support to the celebrity.[23]

(30) The celebrity will make himself available, and will attend, co-operate and participate as and when required, at the recording sessions (including rehearsals for the recording sessions and at the mixing and editing stages of the recording process), and at the recording of any promotional videos. The celebrity will want the clause to provide that he will be available subject to other prior personal or professional commitments and that he will be given a period of notice, for example, 7 days, before he is needed.

(31) The celebrity will make himself available and will attend, co-operate and participate as and when required at promotional photo shoots. The celebrity will want the clause to provide that he will be available subject to other prior personal or professional commitments and that he will be given a period of notice, for example, 7 days, before he is needed.

(32) The celebrity will make himself available and will attend, co-operate and participate at personal appearances and interviews which the record company reasonably requires to promote the recordings. The celebrity will want the clause to provide that he will be available subject to other prior personal or professional commitments, that he will be given a period of notice, for example, 7 days, before he is needed, and that the record company pays his reasonable travel, food and where necessary hotel accommodation. In addition he may require an additional appearance fee.

(33) The celebrity will not re-record any material which he has recorded for the record company for a period of 5 years after the term. The record company require this clause as it does not want the celebrity at the end of the term to walk away from the record company, sign with another company and then re-record all his most popular recordings which the new record company can release to compete with the previous record company's recordings. This clause is an attempt to protect and maximise the economic value of the recordings, enabling the previous record company to exploit them for 5 years after the term without any competition from similar recordings by the new record company. After the 5-year period has expired the celebrity can freely re-record his previous recordings for his new record company, which will compete for sales with similar recordings made for the previous record company. The celebrity will certainly want to try to cut back a

---

[23]   See **30.57** et seq for tour support.

5-year re-recording restriction period and may be able to cut the time period back to 3 years. In addition, the celebrity may be able to obtain a provision that he can re-record any recordings made by him but which have not been released by the record company one year after the end of the term of the agreement.

(34) (Where advances and royalties are to be paid by the record company directly into the celebrity's bank account) the celebrity will supply the record company with the name of his bank, the account name and number and the sort code to enable payments to be made directly into the account.[24] (If the celebrity requires his advances and royalties to be paid directly into a third party's account, such as to his accountant, the agreement should require the celebrity to give the record company all the relevant bank account details. In addition, where the celebrity requires advances and royalties to be paid into a third party's account the agreement will provide that payment into the third party's account will satisfy the record company's obligation to make payment to the celebrity.)

THE INDEMNITY CLAUSE BY THE CELEBRITY

30.45 The recording agreement should contain an indemnity clause by the celebrity requiring him to indemnify the record company for all the record company's costs, liabilities, losses and damage incurred due to any breach or non-performance by him of the recording agreement. The celebrity should try to limit the scope of the indemnity so that he will only be liable to indemnify the record company for specific breaches. In addition, the celebrity should try to limit liability for the record company's costs to the reasonable costs which have been reasonably incurred by the record company, or to the record company's reasonable legal and other professional costs.

30.46 The record company may want a provision allowing it to withhold the celebrity's royalties in the event of there being any legal action or threat of legal action concerning the celebrity in which it is involved. This would enable the record company to offset the money it is withholding against any loss or damage which it incurs, rather than having to pursue the celebrity for the money due to it under an indemnity clause. The celebrity should not agree to such a provision. The celebrity may possibly be prepared to agree to a similar provision which will allow the record company to withhold his royalties provided:

(1) the legal action involves a substantial breach of the celebrity's obligations;

(2) a limit is put on the amount of money which the record company can withhold;

(3) any money withheld will be put on deposit to earn interest; and

(4) that where the threat of legal proceedings does not lead to the issue of court proceedings within a specified time the money which has been withheld will be returned to the celebrity together with accrued interest.

---

[24] See also point (8) at **30.47**.

THE RECORD COMPANY'S OBLIGATIONS

30.47 The obligations of the record company include the following:

(1)   The record company will release the recordings and make them commercially available to the public. The clause should provide that it will release those recordings which are 'acceptable' within a specified period of time, for example, within a period of 6 months after they have been delivered to the record company.[25] It should be remembered that an agreement which does not contain an obligation to release the recordings may be in restraint of trade. The clause should provide that the recordings will initially be released to the public on the record company's top line label at full price. The record company will usually guarantee a release in the UK but will frequently not guarantee to release the record in other territories for which the celebrity is contracted to the record company . The celebrity may be able to negotiate that the record company will guarantee release in additional territories apart from the UK, or may be able to get a guaranteed release in some other territories if, for example, the record achieves a top 10 placing or sales of 50,000 within 3 months of being put on sale in the UK.

Where, for example, the celebrity has not delivered the required minimum commitment, or the recordings are not technically acceptable, the record company can rely upon the fact that the celebrity is in breach of his contractual obligations and can legitimately refuse to comply with its obligation to release the recordings. The record company may, however, decide not to release the recordings for invalid reasons, for example, the people in the record company who believe in the celebrity may have left (as is quite common in such a fast-moving industry) and been replaced by other people who do not have the same interest or belief in the celebrity. To allow for the possibility that the record company may, without any valid contractual reason, decide not to release the record, the celebrity should require a clause in the agreement which enables him to serve a notice on the record company requiring it to release the record within a specified time period, and that if the record company does not release the record in the time period provided for in the notice, then the celebrity can either:

(a)   serve another notice on the record company terminating the agreement (which will include any future options), whereupon the record company will hand over the master tapes of the unreleased recordings to the celebrity and will assign/reassign the copyright in them to the celebrity; or

(b)   serve another notice on the record company, whereupon the record company will hand over the master tapes of the unreleased recordings to the celebrity and will assign/reassign the copyright in them to the celebrity. The difference from (a) above is that in this scenario the agreement is not terminated.

Although (a) and (b) above provide for the celebrity to obtain the unreleased recordings, the record company will not give them up just like that. If (and it is a big if) it is prepared to let the celebrity obtain the unreleased recordings it will want the celebrity to repay the record company for the recording costs which have been incurred, and for its reasonable legal fees incurred in assigning the copyright in the sound recording and a nominal sum of, say, £250 per master track. Most record companies will not accept a clause which enables the celebrity to obtain any unreleased recordings. A record company might instead agree to a clause which provides that where the record has not been released in a particular territory(ies), if another record company is interested in releasing these recordings on terms

---

[25]   See point (17) at **30.44** for what is an 'acceptable' recording.

which are similar to those contained in the celebrity's record agreement, it will grant a licence to that record company to release them, but only in the territory(ies) where the record has not been released. The record company will also want the licensed record company to pay all the royalties to it. The royalty money received will be divided between the celebrity and the record company in the proportions set out in the recording agreement as if it and not the licensed record company had released the record, and it will in due course pay the celebrity his share, provided of course he is recouped, otherwise this money will be used to reduce his account deficit with the record company. Finally, in addition to the record company taking a share of the royalty income from sales of the licensed recordings, the record company will take an additional override royalty (which is a percentage of between 2 and 5% which the record company deducts out of the royalty money it receives from the licensed record company before it is divided up between it and the celebrity). Essentially, this is a fee for the record company agreeing to and implementing the clause in the agreement relating to licensing the unreleased recordings to another record company.

In addition to dealing with the release of the recordings, the agreement should deal with who will select and prepare the artwork for the record covers. Where a performer is not an established artist the agreement will provide that the record company will do this, although the performer may be able to get consultation rights. The record company may agree to an established performer having the right to select and prepare the artwork for the record, although the record company will usually want consultation rights. Some established performers may be able to get the right to select and prepare the artwork without any need to consult the record company, although the record company will want the performer to warrant that the artwork is neither obscene, blasphemous nor defamatory, nor infringes any copyright or any other third party rights. If possible a performer should attempt to get the record company to agree that a guaranteed minimum budget will be available for the artwork for each release, and may be able to get it to agree to raise the guaranteed minimum for each subsequent release or where an option is exercised by the record company.

(2) Having released the recordings on its top line label at full price, the record company will not bring the record out on any mid-price label or budget price label for an agreed minimum period of time, for example, it will not bring out the record on any mid-price label until a period of 2 years after the initial release of the record on its top line label, and it will not bring out the record on any budget price label until a period of 4 years after the initial release of the record on its top line label. (It should be noted that not all record companies will agree to such a provision.)

(3) The record company will provide the recording facilities for the celebrity and will pay for the costs of the recording. The clause will provide that the recording costs will be paid for by the record company as an additional advance. This means that although the record company initially pays the recording costs, it is recoupable from the celebrity's royalties, and if the celebrity is successful he and not the record company will in the end pay for the recording costs. Recording costs are recoupable from royalties due to the celebrity from all of the recordings made during the term of the agreement. This means that if an album has flopped the unrecouped recording costs can be recovered out of the royalties due to the celebrity from hit albums recorded during the agreement.

The definition of recording costs must be examined very closely to ensure that only those items relating to recording costs are recoupable from the celebrity.[26]

It may be possible for the celebrity to obtain a guarantee that the record company will make a minimum amount available to record each album and that the guaranteed minimum amount will increase for each album or will be increased should the record company exercise an option.

(4)   The released recordings will contain a credit naming the celebrity as a performer. As was mentioned earlier,[27] the celebrity should assert his performers' moral right to be identified as a performer under CDPA 1998, s 205C. Having included a clause in the recording agreement asserting his s 205C right, a corresponding obligation should be inserted in the agreement to ensure the record company is reminded of the need to place a credit on the released recordings naming the celebrity as a performer in accordance with s 205C.[28]

(5)   The record company will, at its own expense, promote the celebrity and his recordings. The celebrity would ideally want the record company to agree to use its best endeavours to promote the celebrity and his recordings. The record company will usually only agree to a reasonable endeavours clause.

As noted above, promotion is paid for by the record company. However, it will only agree to pay for its normal promotional activities. The agreement may provide that any costs incurred by the record company promoting the celebrity in a way that it would not usually do, such as running a national radio and/or television campaign, will be shared between the record company and the celebrity. Where this happens the record company would pay the costs incurred but half of these costs would be recoupable from the celebrity.[29] Where there is such a provision in the agreement, if the celebrity cannot get the record company to remove it, then he should try to:

(a)   reduce his percentage contribution;

(b)   get the right for him to approve the content of the campaign, or at the least he should try to get consultation rights; and

(c)   get the right for him to approve the campaign budget.

In addition, the celebrity should check that the royalty rate payable is not affected by such advertising. It may be that the royalty rate payable is reduced by the record company for records sold in the territory(ies) where the promotion took place during the time of the special promotional campaign.[30] The celebrity would not want to be responsible for half of the special promotional campaign costs and also have the royalty rate on the records sold during the time of a special promotional campaign reduced. If the celebrity pays half of the special promotional campaign costs he should ensure, if at all possible, that his royalty is not reduced on the records sold during the time of the special campaign. If the record company wants to do a special campaign at its own expense then it may be acceptable for the royalty rate to be reduced on sales of those recordings for the period of the special promotional campaign.

One area of promotion which is commonly used by a record company to promote a record and the celebrity is the use of promotional videos. Promotional videos are notoriously expensive to produce. A single video may easily cost more

---

26   See **30.57** et seq for what are recording costs.
27   See point (11) at **30.44**.
28   See Chapter 22 at **22.8** et seq.
29   See also **30.57** et seq, point (8) at **30.63**, point (4) at **30.64**, and point (19) at **30.78**.
30   See point (19) at **30.78**.

to make than the cost of recording a whole album. Although promotional videos may be commercially exploited by being put on sale to the public on DVD or included as an added extra with the album release, the money made from them will rarely recoup the video recording costs. Due to the cost of making promotional videos the celebrity will usually have to negotiate a clause in the agreement requiring the record company to make them. Usually, a record company will want to make promotional videos to accompany the single releases from the album; however, it would prefer to do so at its discretion rather than be required to do so under the terms of the recording agreement. The more established the performer the more likely the record company will be prepared to commit to making promotional videos to accompany the release of the recordings, although it will usually only be prepared to commit to making promotional videos to accompany single releases from the album and perhaps for a maximum of one or two other tracks per album.[31] Where a video is made the record company will pay for the video recording costs but will want them to be recoupable from the celebrity. The record company will try to make all the video recording costs recoupable from the celebrity's record royalties and/or from his video royalties (which are likely to be very small in comparison with his record royalties). This will mean that a successful selling celebrity may well find 100% of the video recording costs are offset against his record royalties, which would substantially reduce the record royalties payable to him. The celebrity's solicitor should, where it is proposed that video recording costs are recoupable from both record and video royalties, amend the clause to ensure that they are only recoupable from video royalties (which the record company will rarely if ever agree to), or where the record company will not agree to this he should look to amend the clause to provide that a maximum of, say, 50% of the video recording costs will be recoupable from his record royalties with the remainder of the video recording costs recoupable only from the celebrity's video royalties.[32]

(6)   Where the record company is under an obligation to make a certain number of videos the celebrity may possibly get the record company to agree to spend a minimum amount to record each video.[33] The celebrity's solicitor might also be able to obtain a clause in the agreement that the record company will not only spend a minimum amount to record each video but it will also increase the minimum amount it has guaranteed throughout the term of the agreement, for example, the minimum guarantee spend will be higher for videos made to accompany the second album than for videos made to accompany the first album.

(7)   The record company will pay for tour support. Most record companies will agree to some sort of tour support provision in the agreement. Tour support is money which is given by the record company to pay for the losses incurred by the performer whilst on tour. Many performers, such as The Rolling Stones, earn considerable sums out of a concert tour. However, most performers starting out on their career cannot afford to tour. Some established performers actually charge the support band, who may be known performers themselves, to tour with them as it helps to reduce their tour costs or increases their tour profits. Some venues, far from paying performers, will require the celebrity to pay them for playing in their venue. Most performers need to tour to promote their records. The reason why a record company will often agree to provide tour support is because touring is

---

[31]   See point (20) at **30.44**.
[32]   See point (7) at **30.63**.
[33]   See also point (20) at **30.44**.

promotion, and promotion helps sell records. If the celebrity cannot tour because he cannot afford to, this will seriously affect record sales, if not even kill the celebrity's career before it has had a chance to get off the ground. If the record company agrees to provide tour support there will be conditions placed upon such support. The record company will probably want to approve the proposed concert dates, venues and most matters concerning the concert including, most importantly, the proposed tour costs. To enable the record company to establish whether the tour has made a loss and so require it to pay tour support, the agreement will detail exactly what are the allowable expenses which can be deducted from tour income, for example, receipted travel, hotel accommodation and equipment hire up to a certain amount will be regarded as legitimate expenses, whilst, for example, commission on tour income payable by the celebrity to his manager will not be a legitimate deductible expense. The record company will not agree to an open-ended liability to pay for any tour losses and will put a limit on the amount it will provide. The record company may, where it is prepared to pay tour support, want the tour support to be recoupable from the celebrity's royalties. The celebrity should resist tour support being recoupable from his royalties and should ensure that it is treated as a record company expense on the basis that it is standard promotion cost for the record.

(8) The record company will pay the advances specified in the agreement, and will both during and after the agreement term collect the income from exploiting the recordings and pay the celebrity his royalties at the rates set out in the royalty clause.[34] Where the record company is directed by the celebrity to send the advances/royalties to a third party such as his accountant, the clause will provide that the third party's receipt will satisfy the record company's duty to pay the celebrity. As was mentioned above,[35] where advances and/or royalties are paid by the record company directly into the celebrity's or a third party's bank account, the agreement will provide that payment into the relevant account will satisfy the record company's obligation to make payment to the celebrity. The agreement will usually provide that the record company's obligation to make these payments will be subject to the celebrity complying with his contractual obligations.

(9) The record company will keep accounts detailing the number of the celebrity's recordings sold, the income received from other uses of the recordings, for example, from licensing a recording for use in a television advert, and the amount of royalties which are due to the celebrity.[36]

(10) The record company will keep the contents of the agreement confidential and will not disclose them to anyone other than its professional advisers or as may be required by law.

THE INDEMNITY CLAUSE BY THE RECORD COMPANY

30.48 The recording agreement should contain an indemnity clause by the record company requiring the record company to indemnify the celebrity for all the celebrity's costs, liabilities, losses and damage incurred by the celebrity due to any breach or

---

[34] See **30.57** et seq for details.
[35] See **30.33** et seq.
[36] See **30.88** et seq.

non-performance by the record company of the recording agreement. The record company should try to limit the scope of the indemnity so that it will only be liable to indemnify the celebrity for specific breaches. In addition, the record company should try to limit liability for the celebrity's costs to the reasonable costs which have been reasonably incurred by the celebrity, or to the celebrity's reasonable legal and other professional costs.

ADVANCES

30.49 A celebrity will want to ensure he can get as large an advance from the record company as possible. Indeed, many performers are more concerned about the size of the advance than the royalty rates they will be paid for sales and other uses of their recordings. It is impossible to predict exactly the size of the advance a record company will offer a celebrity. The amount depends upon the status of the celebrity and whether he has a successful track record in the music business, how many record companies are chasing the celebrity for his signature and the type of music the celebrity intends to play, for example, a jazz musician may not necessarily expect to get as large an advance as a rock musician because jazz music does not sell in such numbers as rock music. Indeed, some performers may not even be offered an advance at all. As an extremely rough guide, an established celebrity who is new to the music business may get an advance from a token figure up to £100,000. It must be stressed that a sum approaching the upper figure would be rare. The advance figure will usually be toward the bottom end of the spectrum. For an established celebrity with a successful track record in the music business, the size of the advance will to a considerable extent depend upon his past sales and how much the record company believes his sales record will continue in the future. An established celebrity with a successful track record in the music business may be able to command a sizable advance, with the top end being in the region of £250,000. For superstars, they may be able to name not only their price but also the terms of the agreement.

30.50 A recording advance is non-returnable but recoupable against royalties, ie the celebrity will not be required to return the advance or any part of it if the record company does not recoup the advance out of the income earned from exploiting the recordings. Where a celebrity is being chased by more than one record company or is an established celebrity or superstar, he may be able to get, in addition to an advance, a signing on fee which will not be recoupable, or may be able to negotiate that part of the advance is paid as a non-recoupable signing on fee.

30.51 In only a few cases will the whole of the advance be paid to the celebrity on signing the agreement. The record company will usually pay the advance in stages throughout the term of the agreement. The record company will provide that a percentage of the advance will be paid upon signing the agreement, a percentage when the celebrity starts recording, a percentage on delivery of the recordings and a percentage on the release of the recordings.

30.52 The celebrity's solicitor should consider negotiating ways in which the advance can be increased in the future. For example, a further sum might be payable by way of advance if the record achieves either a particular number of sales or a particular chart placing within a specified period of time after its release in the UK, or where the actual recording costs are less than the minimum amount guaranteed by the record company the difference between the two will be paid to the celebrity as an additional advance.

30.53 The celebrity's solicitor should ensure that where the record company exercises an option an additional advance is paid and that this advance is higher than the previous advance. Rather than have a fixed money figure in the agreement, there may be a provision allowing for a formula to be used to calculate the advance payable when an option is exercised. The formula can also be subject to a floor and ceiling. For example, the agreement may provide that where an option is exercised an additional advance is payable (which will be paid in specified stages) and that the additional advance will be 50% of the royalties earned on sales in the UK on the company's top line label during the first 9 months of release of the album which was released prior to the exercise of the option (provided it was not a greatest hits or best of album, in which case it will be based on royalties of the album which was released prior to the greatest hits or best of album), with in any event the advance payable being not less than £75,000 nor more than £175,000.

30.54 The celebrity's solicitor may also be able to get a further advance if the record company releases a greatest hits or best of album of the celebrity. Where the record company agrees to pay an advance if it releases a greatest hits or best of album, it will usually provide that any money which is unrecouped at the date the further advance is due will be deducted from the further advance, although the celebrity's solicitor may be able to get the record company to agree a floor, for example, if the further advance is £60,000 less any amount unrecouped but with a floor of £20,000, if the celebrity is unrecouped by £50,000 he will receive an advance of £20,000 and not £10,000 as he has a guaranteed minimum advance of £20,000 irrespective of the amount unrecouped.

30.55 The record company will either pay the performer an additional sum of money as an advance to cover the recording costs and leave it to him to pay for them or the record company will pay for the recording costs itself on behalf of the performer. Where the record company pays the celebrity an additional sum of money as an advance to cover the recording costs and the agreement provides that advances are payable in stages, the agreement should be checked to ensure the recording costs advance will be paid to the celebrity sufficiently in advance to ensure he has enough money to pay these costs as and when they fall due. Whichever method is used to pay for the recording costs the agreement will provide that they are an expense incurred by the record company on behalf of the performer and are recoupable from the performer's royalties.

30.56 The celebrity's solicitor should try to ensure the agreement provides that when the record company exercises an option any advance payable upon exercising the option is payable in full (albeit in stages) and cannot be used by the record company towards recouping any unrecouped balance on the celebrity's account.

ROYALTIES

30.57 Usually royalties are paid on a percentage of the sale proceeds of the recordings. It is important that the celebrity's solicitor checks exactly what is meant in the agreement by 'sale proceeds'. Sale proceeds will usually be either:

(1)   the wholesale price of the recordings (also commonly called dealer price or published dealer price, 'PDP') excluding VAT; or

(2)   a fictional retail price. The fictional retail price of a CD is created by taking the wholesale price of the CD excluding VAT and multiplying it by 129%.

30.58 It should be noted that recording agreements more commonly use a royalty calculation based upon PDP than on a fictional retail price. In addition, most recording agreements provide that royalties are paid on the sale proceeds which the record company has received, so ensuring the record company will not be required to pay royalties where it has not been paid itself.

30.59 Although royalties are usually paid on a percentage of PDP or the fictional retail sale proceeds of the recordings, before the actual amount of royalties due to the celebrity can be calculated the cost of the record packaging will be deducted. For CDs the packaging deduction is 25%. The reason why packaging is deducted is because record companies say they are paying the celebrity for sales of the recordings and not for sales of the recordings and the packaging in which the recording is contained. The packaging deduction is an industry standard figure and does not reflect the actual cost of packaging, which in reality is less than the 25% figure. The celebrity should try to negotiate a lower figure for the packaging deduction, although the record company will probably not agree to a lower packaging deduction rate. If the record company will not agree to reduce the packaging deduction, the celebrity's solicitor should try to negotiate an increase in the royalty rate by an amount which cancels out the figure the celebrity is seeking for packaging deduction and the figure the record company proposes. The recording agreement will specify how the recordings will be packaged, for example, it will set out the number of pages the CD booklet can have. If the celebrity wants special packaging, for example, he wants a coloured CD plastic case as opposed to the standard clear plastic case or wants extra pages in the CD booklet the record company will, if it agrees to the request charge a higher packaging deduction and/or seek to reduce the royalty rate for the record.[37] The figure which is reached after the packaging costs have been deducted is called the royalty base.

30.60 The criteria for the royalty rate the record company is prepared to pay the celebrity is the same as that used in deciding the size of the advance it is prepared to pay the celebrity. The royalty rate recommended by the Musicians' Union for a new performer where the royalty calculation is based upon PDP is between 15 and 20% of PDP. It should be noted that where the royalty calculation is based upon a fictional retail price the royalty rate payable will be in the region of 30% lower than the royalty rate payable where the calculation is based upon PDP. This is because the PDP is about 30% lower than the fictional retail price.[38]

30.61 The royalty base should be multiplied by the royalty rate to give the royalty rate per record. The royalty rate per record should then be multiplied by the number of records sold which will give the gross royalty due to the celebrity.[39]

30.62 It should be noted that some independent record companies instead of paying royalties on a percentage of the sale proceeds will instead pay the celebrity a royalty based upon the 'net profit' before VAT from the exploitation of the recordings. The celebrity can expect to negotiate a royalty in the region of 40 to 60% of the net profit. The celebrity's solicitor must check what items the record company proposes to deduct from the gross income and that these items are acceptable deductions. Essentially, the acceptable deductible items from gross income are the actual costs which are payable by

---

[37] See also **30.78**.
[38] See also **30.78**.
[39] See **30.76** for a worked example.

the record company to others, for example, recording costs. The record company's own operating expenses, for example, rent, staffing, heating, lighting, are not acceptable deductions.

DEDUCTIONS FROM THE GROSS ROYALTY

30.63 The celebrity does not get paid the gross royalty. There are certain deductions which will be made from the gross royalty. The deductions are for:

(1)   Free copies. It is common for a recording agreement to contain a provision that between 5 and 10% of the gross royalties will be deducted to account for free copies which the record company will send to record shops to encourage them to stock more copies of the record. Although in recent years a celebrity's solicitor would often agree to a deduction figure of between 5 and 10% for free copies, it is arguable that he should seek an even lower percentage figure now that there are fewer record shops on the high street to which the record company will need to send free copies and in addition the majority of sales will probably be from downloads rather than from high street sales. The record company will no doubt try to counter the argument on the basis that as there are fewer record shops on the high street it needs to send more free copies to the remaining shops to encourage them to stock the record and that it also will need to send free copies to internet stores which will stock the record. As with breakages,[40] it is doubtful that the record company will easily agree to reduce the figure for free copies below 5 to 10% because it reduces the actual royalty rate payable to the celebrity. If the record company will not agree to reduce the figure for free copies, the celebrity's solicitor should try to negotiate an increase in the royalty rate by an amount which cancels out the difference between the figure the celebrity is seeking as a deduction for free copies and the figure the record company proposes.

(2)   Promotional copies. The record companies will send copies of the record to music magazines for review and to radio and television stations and club disc jockeys to encourage them to play the record.
          Promotional records (called promos) are packaged in either the same packaging as that used for copies which are on retail sale and can only be differentiated by the fact that the CD case and/or the actual CD packaging and/or the CD itself is stamped as a promotional copy, or it may be in less elaborate packaging than the copies which are on retail sale, for example, the CD might just be packaged in a simple, white cardboard sleeve with no artwork and details of the tracks printed on the cover. However the promo record is packaged the record company will not pay a royalty to the celebrity for it.
          Certainly, promo records are a vital way to promote the celebrity and his record and help increase awareness and sales of the record. As promos are given away free and not sold, no royalty is paid on them. Although the celebrity will accept that promos are a necessary and useful marketing tool, he may be concerned about the numbers which are given away. The celebrity may therefore want to insert a limit in the agreement on the number of promos which can be given away and which do not bear a royalty.

---

[40]   See (3) below for breakages.

(3) Breakages. A few record companies try to deduct between 5 and 10% for breakages. The celebrity's solicitor should resist a deduction for breakages. In reality, few if any CDs break easily. The reason why record companies originally made a deduction for breakages is because in the days of 78 rpm records many records were liable to break easily because they were made of shellac. The real reason why a record company might seek a deduction for breakages is because it reduces the actual royalty payable to the celebrity. If the record company wants a deduction for breakages and refuses to delete it, the celebrity's solicitor should try to negotiate an increase in the royalty rate by an amount which cancels out the deduction for breakages.

(4) Some record companies will seek a deduction of between 5 and 10% for returns. The record company only pays royalties on record sales and not on records which it has manufactured and distributed to the record shops for them to sell. The record company may manufacture and distribute 80,000 copies of the record to the shops but that does not mean that 80,000 copies will sell. Certainly, some will be returned by the shops as they cannot sell them, and, in the worst-case scenario if the record is an absolute turkey, 80,000 records may come back to roost with the record company. Some record companies may insert a provision in the recording agreement allowing them to deduct between 5 and 10% for records which have been returned as unsold. Although this might seem on the surface to be an acceptable deduction, the celebrity's solicitor should delete any such clause where the agreement also contains a clause which allows the record company to keep a reserve out of the royalties to allow for returns.[41] Any clause allowing the record company to deduct between 5 and 10% for returns where there is a separate right for the record company to hold back a reserve against returns is unnecessary and is just a way of reducing the royalty due to the celebrity.

(5) The advance paid to the celebrity (including any additional advance given by the record company to the celebrity for him to pay for the recording costs).

(6) The recording costs where the record company actually pays for them instead of advancing extra money to the celebrity for him to pay them.
     Whether the celebrity or the record company actually writes the cheque for the recording costs at the end of the day, they are recoupable from the celebrity's royalties. The agreement should define exactly what is meant by recording costs. It will include the cost of the record producer, the studio engineers, session musicians who are used, hire of the equipment, including the hire of any instruments, recording tape and the studio hire.[42]
     The definition of recording costs may include items such as the cost of remixing the recordings and of cutting. These are items which the celebrity will not want to be responsible for. The celebrity will only want to be liable for those costs which are incurred in making acceptable recordings. The celebrity does not want to be liable for any of the costs such as the cutting costs which have to be incurred in converting and manufacturing the recordings into CD. These costs should be the responsibility of the record company.
     The celebrity will need to pay the costs of mixing the recordings, but he will not want to be responsible for any remixing costs because the recording once mixed, provided it is an acceptable recording, is the finished product from the celebrity's

---

[41] See **30.67** et seq.
[42] See also **30.70** et seq.

point of view. Remixing is the taking of an acceptable finished recording and putting a different musical slant on it. Remixing is very popular, especially for dance music, and in many cases a remix helps to sell records or even makes a record a hit. An acceptable recording can be and often is remixed into many different versions and the celebrity will not want to be liable for these costs as they will substantially reduce his royalty.

(7)   Video recording costs. As mentioned earlier,[43] the record company will try to make all the video recording costs recoupable from the celebrity's record royalties and/or from his video royalties (which are likely to be very small in comparison with his record royalties). This will mean that a successful selling celebrity may well find 100% of the video recording costs offset against his record royalties, which would therefore substantially reduce the record royalties payable to him. The celebrity's solicitor should, where it is proposed that video recording costs are recoupable from both record and video royalties, amend the clause to ensure that they are only recoupable from video royalties (which the record company will rarely if ever agree to), or where the record company will not agree to this he should look to amend the clause to provide that a maximum of, say, 50% of the video recording costs will be recoupable from the celebrity's record royalties, with the remainder of the video recording costs recoupable only from the celebrity's video royalties.[44]

(8)   Promotion costs charged by specialist promotion companies which may be used in addition to the record company's own in-house promotions department, for example, pluggers (individuals who use their contacts with radio producers and programmers to help the record company get the record directly to these people in the hope that they will listen to it and put it on the radio station playlist). Although the record company has its own staff who promote the record, many of the people who have the best contacts do not work as record company employees but work independently of them. Specialist promotion companies can make the difference between the record being a success or failure and are often used by record companies. Where specialist promotion companies are used, half the cost is usually deductible out of the gross royalties. The celebrity should ensure that a ceiling is placed upon the actual amount that can be deducted for specialist promotion costs per single and album, for example, he is liable for half the costs of specialist promotion incurred by the record company up to a maximum of £x per single and £y per album.

Costs charged by specialist promotion companies should be distinguished from record company in-house promotion costs which should not be deducted from the gross royalty.[45]

(9)   Where the record company promotes the celebrity's record in a way that it would not normally use, for example, it runs a national radio and/or television campaign, the record company may deduct half of these costs.[46]

---

[43]   See point (5) at **30.47**.
[44]   See also point (20) at **30.44** and point (7) at **30.63**.
[45]   See point (4) at **30.64**.
[46]   See point (5) at **30.47**, point (4) at **30.64** and point (19) at **30.78**.

ITEMS WHICH SHOULD NOT BE DEDUCTED FROM THE GROSS ROYALTY

30.64 There are certain items which should not be deducted by the record company from the gross royalty. The items which should not be deducted are:

(1)   The cost of designing the artwork for the sleeve.

(2)   The cost incurred in manufacturing the LP or CD.

(3)   The cost of distributing the records.

(4)   The cost of promoting and advertising the recording.
As mentioned above,[47] half of any promotion costs charged by specialist promotion companies is usually deducted from the gross royalty, but in-house promotion costs should not be deducted from the gross royalty as they are a business operating expense which should be borne by the record company. Although the cost of normal record company advertising done by the record company to promote the record is not deducted from the gross royalty, this should be distinguished from advertising which the record company would not normally use, for example, a national radio and/or television campaign, where the record company may deduct half of such costs.[48]

(5)   Any tour support.[49]

(6)   Mechanical licence fees and mechanical royalties.
Mechanical licence fees are the fees payable to the composer/publisher of a composition to enable the composition to be recorded and for copies of the composition to be manufactured, distributed and sold to the public.[50]

30.65 The record company should pay the celebrity royalties for sales of all the recordings. However, some record companies do not pay royalties based on 100% of sales, but pay only on 85 or 90% of sales. The reasoning behind this is that the record company is allowing itself a margin for breakages. If the record company proposes a royalty based upon 85 or 90% of sales, this should be resisted by the celebrity's solicitor, who should either insist on royalties being paid on 100% of sales or ensure that the royalty rate is increased by an amount which cancels out the difference between royalties based on 100% of sales and the sales percentage figure upon which the record company proposes to pay the celebrity.

30.66 Any clause in the agreement dealing with a deduction for breakages,[51] a deduction for returns[52] and for a provision for royalties to be paid on 85 or 90% of sales should be examined by the celebrity's solicitor very closely. There should be no need for the record company to make any deduction for breakages, any deduction for returns or for royalties to be paid on less than 100% of sales as the agreement will usually contain

---

[47]   See point (8) at **30.63**.
[48]   See point (9) at **30.63**, point (5) at **30.47** and point (19) at **30.78**.
[49]   See point (8) at **30.47** for tour support.
[50]   See also **30.84–30.85**.
[51]   See point (3) at **30.63**.
[52]   See point (4) at **30.63**.

a provision which enables the record company to make a reserve against returns.[53] Any attempt by the record company to make deductions for breakages and for returns and to pay only on 85 or 90% of sales where there is a provision allowing the record company to hold a reserve against returns is an unacceptable way of reducing the royalties due to the celebrity.

RESERVES AGAINST RETURNS

30.67 As mentioned above, the record company will want to withhold royalties due to the celebrity as a reserve against returns due to the fact that it only pays royalties on records which have actually been sold and not on records which have been distributed to shops for sale to the public. The recording agreement will allow the record company to withhold royalties from the celebrity until it has become clear whether the records have sold or whether they have been returned. The reserve will be based upon the gross not the net royalties due to the celebrity. It is only fair that the record company should be allowed to withhold some of the celebrity's royalties in case the record which has been distributed does not sell. The agreement may provide that the record company has the right to decide what percentage of royalties it can withhold. The celebrity's solicitor should not allow the record company to have *carte blanche* to decide the amount of the celebrity's royalties which it can withhold against returns. The celebrity's solicitor should ensure there is a maximum percentage figure which can be withheld. The maximum percentage which should be withheld from royalties depends upon the status of the celebrity. A celebrity with no track record in the music business will probably have to accept a 20 to 25% reserve, whereas a celebrity with an established track record in the music business may be able to get a 5 to 10% reserve. Many record companies will set different percentage reserves for each of the formats in which the recordings are released for sale, for example, they may want a 20% reserve for CDs, a 25% reserve for LPs and a 50% reserve for any other format in which the recordings are released, such as on a CD single or 7-inch single. The reason why the record company may want different reserve figures for different formats is because those formats with higher reserves are more likely to be returned. In addition, the record company may want the right to increase the reserve figure if, for example, it has agreed that the celebrity who has been signed to make pop records releases an album in a different style, such as a jazz or classical crossover album, or releases a Christmas themed album which will only sell at Christmas time rather than throughout the year.

30.68 The celebrity's solicitor should ensure the agreement provides that the balance of any reserve withheld by the record company (namely the amount left after deducting from the reserve the royalties which are no longer payable because records have been returned) will be liquidated, ie paid to the celebrity, at the latest 2 years after the record has initially been distributed. The celebrity's solicitor should try to ensure that the balance of any reserve will be liquidated rateably during the 2 years over four accounting periods (ie on 30 June and 31 December each year) rather than wait for 2 years before the balance of any reserve is liquidated.[54]

30.69 In addition, the celebrity's solicitor should try to ensure that any reserve withheld by the record company will be held in a bank account to earn interest, which is payable to the celebrity.

---

[53]　See also **30.67** et seq.
[54]　See **30.88** et seq.

The producer

30.70 The main job of a producer is to use his creative skill and technical ability to professionally record a performer's creative ideas and compositions and turn them into commercial hits. In addition, the producer may help the performer to write the compositions themselves. The choice of a producer can often make the difference between a record being a success or a failure. A top name producer or production team will often be as well known to the public as the performer himself, for example, Sir George Martin, Brian Eno, Quincy Jones, Xenomania, Daniel Lanois and Jay-Z, to name just a few.

30.71 A producer will usually want a fee to produce the celebrity, as well as royalties and a non-returnable but recoupable advance. In addition, the producer will where he helps the celebrity to write compositions for the record want a co-writing credit and a share in the publishing royalties. A successful producer's record royalty will be up to 5% of the fictional retail price. Usually, the producer's record royalty will be in the region of 3% of the fictional retail price. The celebrity's solicitor should try to get the record company to agree that the producer's royalty will not be recoupable from the celebrity's royalties. The record company will in most cases not agree to this, although the celebrity's solicitor may be able to get the record company to agree that a specified amount of the royalty will not be recoupable from the celebrity's royalties. This argument may succeed where the record company wants the celebrity to work with a particular producer and that producer wants more than a 3% royalty. In such a case the record company may possibly agree that it will be responsible for the excess royalty over 3% and that this amount is not recoupable from the celebrity's royalties.

30.72 It should be ensured that the producer does not receive a higher royalty than the celebrity as the celebrity will lose money on every copy of the record sold where the producer's royalty is recoupable from the celebrity's royalty. In addition, care should be taken to ensure the calculation of the producer's royalty in the production agreement contains the same deductions (e g for packaging, free copies and promos) and royalty rate reductions for different types of sales and for sales on different formats as are in the celebrity's recording agreement (although obviously the production agreement will not make deductions from the producer's royalty for any advances given by the record company to the celebrity nor for recording costs), or if the deductions are different that the celebrity's recording agreement has lower deductions and reductions than the production agreement.[55] An examination of the clauses in a production agreement is beyond the scope of this book.

30.73 There is one particular problem the celebrity should be aware of when the producer has negotiated a royalty for his services. The problem is that the celebrity will only be entitled to receive royalties from his record company once he is in a recouped position, namely after any advance, recording costs, half of any video recording costs which are added to his recording account and half the cost of any independent promotion have been repaid to the record company. The producer is entitled to receive royalties on sales of the record once any advance he has been paid has been recouped. This will mean in most cases that the producer will be entitled to receive royalties on sales of the record at an earlier stage than the celebrity.

---

[55]   See also **30.78**.

30.74 The production agreement will often provide that the producer will not be paid the royalty which is due to him until the recording costs have been recouped at a royalty rate which is arrived at by taking the celebrity's royalty rate and deducting from it the producer's royalty rate, ie if the celebrity has a royalty rate of 14% and the producer has a royalty rate of 3%, the producer will not be paid the royalty which is due to him until the celebrity has recouped the recording costs at a royalty rate of 11%. Although the use of this calculation may to some extent help the celebrity, he may still have problems paying the producer his royalties even where the recording costs have been recouped under this formula as the celebrity may not have recouped other items in his recording agreement, such as his advance, and so he will not have any royalties himself out of which to pay the producer. Unless the celebrity has money from another source he may well find that he is unable to pay the producer his royalties. The best solution to this problem is either for the celebrity to ensure he sets money aside from his advance so that he can pay the producer's royalty or he gets the record company to pay the producer his royalty after the producer's advance and the recording costs have been recouped (at the celebrity's royalty rate less the producer's royalty rate) and for the record company to treat the producer's royalty payment as an additional advance to the celebrity which is recoupable from the celebrity's royalties. This will mean the producer gets paid and the celebrity will not have to worry about this problem, although it will increase the monies which are recoupable from the celebrity's royalties and therefore the celebrity will have to wait longer before he is in a recouped position and entitled to receive royalties.

30.75 It should be noted that a prudent producer will obviously be concerned that the celebrity will not be able to pay him any monies which are due to him and so should ensure that the record company is responsible for paying any monies which are due to him.

An example of a royalty calculation

30.76 Having seen in detail how the royalty is calculated it would be useful to see a worked example showing how the pieces fit together. If we assume the following:

(1)   The celebrity has negotiated his first record agreement with a royalty rate for CDs of 12% of the fictional retail price. (Although for the purposes of this example the fictional retail price is used, it should be noted that recording agreements more commonly use a royalty calculation based upon PDP. Where PDP is used the royalty rate payable would be about 30% higher than the royalty rate payable where the calculation is based on a fictional retail price.[56])

(2)   The celebrity receives an advance from the record company of £10,000.

(3)   (For the purposes of this example) the fictional retail price of a CD is £10. (This figure has been reached by taking the wholesale price excluding VAT and multiplying it by 129%.)

(4)   (For the purposes of this example) the first album will only be released on CD on the record company's top line label.

(5)   There is a packaging deduction of 25%.

---

[56]   See also **30.57** et seq.

(6) The producer of the album receives a 2% royalty rate. (The calculation of the producer's royalty which is set out in the production agreement contains the same deductions (eg for packaging, free copies and promos) as are in the celebrity's record agreement (although obviously there are no deductions for any advances given to the celebrity nor for recording costs).) (The record company has agreed to pay the producer's royalty and also agreed that it would not be recoupable from the celebrity. It should be noted that in real life the agreement would provide for the celebrity to be ultimately responsible for paying the producer's royalty. This unusual provision has been included in order to make the calculation easier to follow.)

(7) Recording costs are £100,000.

(8) Video recording costs come to £100,000, but only half of this sum (£50,000) is recoupable from record royalties. The other half is recoupable out of video royalties.

(9) An independent promotion company is used to promote the album and it has charged £40,000, of which only half (£20,000) is recoupable from record royalties.

(10) Free copies and promos total 10% of sales (which was the limit agreed upon by the celebrity and the record company in the record agreement).

(11) There is no deduction for breakages in the agreement.

(12) There is no deduction for returns in the agreement.

(13) Sales of the CD total 350,000 copies.

(14) The record company will retain 20% as a reserve against returns. (The record company withholds the reserve based upon the gross royalty total.) The agreement provides that any unused reserve will be liquidated 2 years after the record has been initially distributed. There is no provision in the agreement for any unused reserve to be liquidated over four accounting periods during the 2-year period.

(Fictional retail) CD price	£10.00
Minus	–
Packaging (25%)	£2.50
Royalty Base	£7.50

Royalty Base	£7.50
Multiplied by	x
Celebrity's royalty rate	12%
Royalty per CD	£0.90

Royalty per CD	£0.90
Multiplied by	x
CD sales	350,000
Gross royalty total	£315,000

Gross royalty total	£315,000
Minus	–
Free copies and promos (10%)	(£31,500)
Recording costs	(£100,000)
Video recording costs	(£50,000)
(50% of £100,000)	
Independent promotion	(£20,000)
(50% of £40,000)	
Advance received from the record company	(£10,000)
Total royalty due to the celebrity from the record company	£103,500*

* See **30.77** below

30.77 Although the celebrity appears to be entitled to a royalty of £103,500 on sales of 350,000 copies of the album, the record company will not pay the whole £103,500 to the celebrity as there is a 20% reserve against returns which is withheld against the gross royalty, namely £63,000, ie 20% of £315,000. The £63,000 which has been withheld as a reserve against returns by the record company will only be liquidated 2 years after the record has been initially distributed. The celebrity is only entitled at this stage to be paid a royalty of £40,500.

ROYALTY RATES FOR DIFFERENT FORMATS AND DIFFERENT TYPES OF EXPLOITATION

30.78 As mentioned earlier,[57] the royalty rate recommended by the Musicians' Union for a new celebrity is between 15 and 20% of PDP. This is the royalty rate for a recording which is sold on the record company's top line label at full price in the UK (which will be called in the examples below 'full rate'). The royalty rate payable will depend upon the

---

[57]   See **30.60** et seq.

format in which the recording is released, for example, different rates may apply to a release of the recording on CD or LP or on an unusual format such as USB disk. A full rate CD might be, say, 14% of PDP, whereas a full rate LP might be, say, 10% of PDP. In addition, if the recording is:

(1)   Released on the record company's mid-price label, the royalty rate will be in the region of 66.6% of the full rate.

(2)   Released on the record company's budget label, the royalty rate will be in the region of 50 to 66.6% of the full rate.

(3)   Sold to the armed forces, the royalty rate will be in the region of 50% of the full rate.

(4)   Sold to libraries or other educational establishments, the royalty rate will be in the region of 50% of the full rate.

(5)   Released as a 12-inch single, the royalty rate will be in the region of 75% of the full rate. The record company may try to get the celebrity to accept that a certain number will be royalty free. The celebrity should try to ensure that all copies will bear a royalty or limit the numbers which are royalty free.

(6)   Released as a single, the royalty rate will be in the region of 75% of the full rate.

(7)   Released in territories outside the UK, the record company will reduce the royalty rate for these territories. The record company may divide the world, excluding the UK, into major territories and the rest of the world. For the major territories, which will need to be defined, the record company will pay a royalty rate in the region of 60 to 85% of the full rate. For the rest of the world, the royalty rate will be in the region of 50 to 60% of the full rate. The celebrity's solicitor should try to get full rate irrespective of where the record is released. However, it is unlikely that the record company will agree to this and the celebrity's solicitor should instead try to raise the percentage figure offered, and ensure that all the major territories where records are sold are included within the definition of major territories. Also, the celebrity's solicitor should ensure that any territory where the celebrity is popular is included within the definition of a major territory.

(8)   Given away as free copies or as promotional copies to radio stations etc, there will be no royalty payable (because the record company has given them away and not sold them). The celebrity will want to put a limit on the number of promotional copies the record company can give away which are not royalty bearing.[58]

(9)   Released on a new format which is not currently used to sell recordings, the royalty rate will be in the region of 50 to 90% of the full rate. In addition, the record company will usually require a higher packaging deduction than that charged for established formats. The record company's attitude is that manufacturing recordings on a new format costs more than for established formats, the packaging is more expensive compared to established formats, sales will for several years at

---

[58]   See also points (1) and (2) at **30.63** for free copies and promos.

least be negligible compared to sales on established formats and there is no guarantee that a new format will become an established way for the public to buy recordings.

The celebrity's solicitor should however try to obtain the full royalty rate for new format sales although the record company will usually not agree to this. The celebrity's solicitor may as an alternative try to limit the time period for which a reduced rate will be paid on new format sales, for example, the celebrity will be paid a reduced rate on new format sales for 3 years after the recording is first released on that format and thereafter he will be paid the full rate, or will be paid a reduced rate until the record company starts to pay other performers full rate on that format, whereupon the celebrity will also be paid full rate.

It should be noted that some very famous performers were for many years after compact disc became established paid a reduced royalty rate on compact disc sales because their recording agreement was signed at a time when compact disc was not in existence and was under the terms of their recording agreement regarded for royalty rate purposes as a new format. This problem was largely sorted out by subsequent negotiations between the performers' solicitors and the record companies when options came to be exercised or by negotiations which led to a variation of the terms of the existing agreement. Great care should be taken when considering whether to accept a reduced royalty rate for sales on new formats because a new format could become in the future an important way to sell recordings.

(10)   Released on a Best Of or Greatest Hits record of the celebrity, the royalty rate will usually be the full rate. Some record companies may only offer 50% of the full rate and try to justify the reduced rate on the basis that it is re-using existing recordings and not using new recordings and that sales of the recordings were paid at full rate when they were originally released. The celebrity's solicitor should resist any such reduction, especially as a greatest hits album may be the celebrity's best selling record.

The tracks on the greatest hits album will come from various stages of the celebrity's career and be taken from albums which may have attracted different royalty rates. The royalty rate for the greatest hits album will be pro rata to the albums from which they were taken. For example, if the greatest hits album contains twelve tracks with four tracks from the first album which attracted a 12% royalty, two tracks from the second album which also attracted a 12% royalty, three tracks from the third album which attracted a 13% royalty and three tracks from the fourth album which attracted a 15% royalty, the royalty rate for the greatest hits album would be 13%. The recording agreement needs to deal with what royalty rate is payable on tracks used for a greatest hits album where the albums from which the recordings were taken had escalating royalty rates. For example, if the first two albums had a royalty rate of 12% and the rate escalated to 13% for sales over 100,000 copies, and further escalated to 14% for sales over 200,000 copies, if the first album sold 120,000 copies and the second album sold 235,000 copies will the royalty rate for the tracks taken off these albums for the greatest hits album be at the basic 12% rate or at the higher rates of 13% for the tracks taken from the first album and 14% for the tracks taken from the second album? The recording agreement should deal with this point. In addition, the celebrity's solicitor should, if possible, get an escalated royalty rate on sales of the greatest hits album.[59]

---

[59]   For escalations see **30.79** et seq.

(11) Released on a compilation record alongside recordings by the record company's other performers and/or or alongside recordings made by performers signed to a related record label, such as on the Now That's What I Call Music series, the royalty rate is pro rata to the number of tracks on the album, for example, if there are 40 tracks on the album and one of these is by the celebrity, the royalty rate is 1/40th of the celebrity's full royalty rate. If the celebrity does not want his recordings used in compilations with other performers' recordings, his solicitor should ensure the agreement contains a provision prohibiting such use.

(12) Released by a record company under licence from the celebrity's record company on a compilation record with other performers' recordings, the royalty will usually be in the region of 50% of the money which the celebrity's record company receives from the licencee for the use of the celebrity's recording.

As in (11) above, if the celebrity does not want his recordings used in compilations with other performers' recordings his solicitor should ensure the agreement contains a provision prohibiting such use.

(13) Released by the record company on a sampler record, with other performers' recordings, for example, XYZ Record Company's New Artists Sampler 2009 Volume 1 which is sold to the public at a cheap price of £1.99, there will be no royalty payable. The record company will not pay a royalty as the use of the recording is to get the public interested in the performers and is a way of promoting them to get the public to go out and buy the records by each performer on the sampler.

If the celebrity does not want his recordings used on a sampler, his solicitor should ensure the agreement contains a provision prohibiting such use.

(14) Sold to jukebox companies for use in jukeboxes, there will be no royalty payable.

(15) Sold as a deletion or sold as a cut-out or sold for scrap, there will be no royalty payable.

The record company will delete an album from its catalogue when it believes the album no longer has any more sales potential as it has been exploited fully at full price, mid-price and finally at budget price. It will notify record shops of its intention to delete the album from its catalogue from a particular date and the record shops can return any copies they have during this period to get a credit. After this date the record company will not accept returns of the album and it is deleted from its catalogue.

Where there has been an overproduction of the album, the record company may sell the album for whatever price it can get for it, and it will cut the album sleeve with a hole puncher, hence the term 'cut out', to show that it is not a full-priced album.

The record company will sell an album at scrap to be melted down and used for some other purpose when it has copies left over which it cannot sell as cut-outs.

The celebrity may want a clause in the record agreement providing that the record company will not cut out the record for 2 or 3 years after it has been initially released. Cut-outs portray the album as a failure and if the celebrity can ensure an album will not be cut out at all or it will not be cut out for a reasonable period of time after it has been initially released, it will help to maintain his public reputation as a successful selling artist. In addition to seeking a clause which provides the album will not be cut out or will not be cut out for a reasonable period of time, the celebrity will usually be able to obtain a clause in the record agreement which will allow him, should he so wish, to buy all the cut-outs from the record company at the best price that the record company has been offered for them.

(16) Licensed by the record company for use in a television advert or for inclusion in a film or television programme, the celebrity will be paid a royalty in the region of 50% of the net money received by the record company. The word 'net' will need to be defined to ensure that only valid deductions from the gross royalty are made.

(17) Promoted by the record company in a way that it would not normally use, for example, if it runs a national radio and/or television campaign, the record company may deduct half of these costs from the gross royalty payable and/or it may reduce the royalty rate payable to the celebrity to something in the region of 50 to 66.6% of the full rate. If the royalty rate is reduced, it should only be reduced for records sold in the territory(ies) where the promotion took place during the time of the special promotional campaign.

As mentioned above,[60] the celebrity will not want to be responsible for half of the special promotional campaign costs and also have the royalty rate on the records sold reduced during the time of a special promotional campaign. If the celebrity pays half of the special promotional campaign costs, he should ensure, if at all possible, that his royalty is not decreased on the records sold during the time of the special campaign. If the record company wants to run a special campaign at its own expense then it may be acceptable for the royalty rate to be reduced on sales of those recordings for a period of time.

(18) Released as a double or triple CD album, the royalty rate is a percentage of the full rate, calculated as the percentage that the selling price of the double or triple CD album bears to two or three times the selling price of a single CD album. For example, if a single CD album sells for £13.99 (£14 for round figures) and the celebrity releases a double CD album and it is sells for £15.99 (£16 for round figures), the royalty rate on the double CD album is 8/14ths of the full rate, ie £16 (for the double CD album), over £28 (twice the price of a single CD album). The reason why the royalty rate is reduced for a multiple CD is that they usually do not sell in such quantities as a single CD album and the selling price of a double CD album is less than the two or three times the selling price of a single CD album, so the record company's profit margin will be less.[61]

(19) Used as a premium, the royalty will be in the region of 50% of the net amount received by the record company from the company wanting to use the recording. The word 'net' will need to be defined to ensure that only valid deductions from gross are made.

A premium is a record which is used to promote another product, for example, send in to a drinks company five ring pulls from a fizzy drink can and for the cost of a stamped addressed envelope the drinks company will send out a CD containing three tracks by the celebrity.

Many performers do not want their recordings used in such a way. As premiums are only a small source of income for the record company, it will usually agree to a clause in the record agreement prohibiting such use of the celebrity's recordings.

---

[60] See point (8) at **30.63**, point (4) at **30.64** and point (5) at **30.47**.
[61] See also **30.16** et seq.

(20) Packaged at the celebrity's request in a way that is not how the record would normally be packaged, the record company will, if it agrees to the celebrity's packaging request, charge a higher packaging deduction and/or may also seek to reduce the royalty rate for the record.[62] Although the recording agreement will detail the normal packaging deductions, it will not set out the special packaging deductions, as the record company is not able to calculate the cost of the special packaging at the time of the agreement as it will not know what type of packaging the celebrity requires, and the celebrity will not know what he wants until a much later date, which is usually about the time he records the single or album which he wants specially packaged. The deductions for special packaging will therefore have to be negotiated between the parties at a later date. The celebrity's solicitor should try to avoid there being any extra packaging deduction in addition to a reduction in the royalty rate.

Some recording agreements allow the celebrity to have some extras over and above the normal packaging specification, so he can, for example, have a couple of extra pages inserted in the CD booklet accompanying his album to enable him to include extra photos of himself and to allow him more space to thank everybody for their help in making the record.

(21) Discounted in price by the record company to shop chains or others who buy records in bulk quantities, the record company will either want to alter the definition of sale proceeds to take into account the discount offered by the record company thereby reducing the royalty payable,[63] or will want to reduce the royalty to reflect the amount of the discount given to the record company. The celebrity's solicitor should resist any clause which allows the record company to reduce the celebrity's royalty where the record company has given a discount on record sales to bulk buyers of the record.

ESCALATING THE ROYALTY RATE

30.79 The celebrity's solicitor should try to get the recording agreement to provide for an escalation in the royalty rate payable for a recording once that recording has achieved certain sales figures. Where the celebrity obtains an escalated royalty rate in his recording agreement it will usually only apply to those recordings which are sold on the record company's top line label at full price and on recordings which attract a full rate royalty.

30.80 The recording agreement could provide, for example, that the royalty rate for the first two albums is 13%, escalating to 14% if the album sells 50,000 copies in the UK (a silver record), 15% if the album sells 100,000 copies in the UK (a gold record) and 16% if the album sells 300,000 copies in the UK (a platinum record). The escalated royalty rate will usually only apply to the particular record which has achieved the sales target. Subsequent records will usually start off at the basic royalty rate and only escalate once they achieve the relevant sales targets. (As opposed to escalating on UK sales, where a performer has signed with the record company for the world it is possible to use worldwide sales as the target, in which case the target figures to achieve an escalated royalty will be in the region of 500,000, 1,000,000 and 2,000,000 sales worldwide.)

---

[62] For normal packaging deductions see **30.57** et seq.
[63] See **30.57** for the definition of sale proceeds.

30.81 Usually, the escalated rate will not apply to all sales of the record but only to those records sold from the target figure onwards, for example, using the royalty rate figures from above, if the first album sold 350,000, the royalty rate on sales of the first 49,999 copies will attract a royalty of 13%, sales from copy number 50,000 to 99,999 will attract a royalty rate of 14%, sales from copy number 100,000 to 299,999 will attract a royalty rate of 15% and sales from copy number 300,000 onwards will attract a royalty rate of 16%. The celebrity's solicitor should when negotiating the agreement try to obtain a provision that any escalation of the royalty rate based on sales is retrospective to the first sale of the record and not from the target figure. The record company will in nearly all cases not agree to a retrospective escalation clause

30.82 An escalated royalty rate can apply to singles as well as albums, but where there is a singles royalty rate escalation the target figure before any escalation applies will usually be much higher than the target figure for an album royalty rate escalation. Escalations for UK single sales will often only apply once sales in the region of 500,000, 750,000 and 1,000,000 have been reached.

30.83 As well as obtaining an escalation based on sales, the celebrity's solicitor should ensure the recording agreement provides that whenever the record company exercises an option the basic and escalated royalty rates for albums and singles recorded during the option period increases.

Mechanical licences

30.84 As was mentioned earlier,[64] a controlled composition is often defined as a composition which has been written by, or is owned by or is controlled by the recording artist. A controlled composition clause in a recording agreement is used to limit the amount the record company has to pay the copyright owner of a composition for a mechanical licence to record, manufacture and distribute for retail sale copies of the recording of the composition on record, CD etc. A detailed examination of the controlled composition clause is beyond the scope of this book, as is an examination of the terms of a music publishing agreement.

30.85 Apart from advances and royalties, the record company will be liable to pay for the right to use the composition on the record and on any accompanying promotional video. The record company will therefore be liable for:

(1) Mechanical licence fees payable to the composer/publisher to enable the compositions to be recorded and for copies to be manufactured, distributed and sold to the public.[65]

Where the celebrity performs his own compositions the recording agreement may limit (and for the US and Canada, will limit) the amount payable for mechanical fees for controlled compositions. The recording agreement will need to be examined very carefully to see what exactly constitutes a controlled composition. If the celebrity is a composer, his publishing agreement must be checked to ensure that his publisher is prepared to grant the composer/celebrity's record company a favourable mechanical rate. If the composer/celebrity's recording agreement provides for a favourable mechanical rate for the record company but his publishing agreement does not contain a similar provision, the

---

[64] See **30.6** et seq.
[65] See also point (6) at **30.64**.

publishing company can and, very likely will, refuse to give the record company a mechanical licence on favourable terms and the record company would have to pay the full rate to use the composition. Where this happens the record company will take the excess it has paid (ie the difference between the full rate the record company paid the publisher and the favourable rate the celebrity contracted that the record company would have to pay for a mechanical licence) from the celebrity's record royalties.

Any clause which gives a favourable mechanical rate to the record company is reducing the royalty which is payable by the record company to the composer/publisher. The celebrity's solicitor should try to negotiate an improvement in any controlled composition terms proposed by the record company. One thing that is certain is that the record company will not agree to the deletion of the clause. The best that the celebrity's solicitor can do is to try to get:

(a)   A provision, where the record company is seeking a favourable mechanical rate for all the territories covered by the recording agreement, that the favourable rate will only apply to the US and Canada. It should be noted that the record company will not usually agree to restrict its favourable mechanical rate to the US and Canada where it is seeking that rate for all territories covered by the recording agreement.

(b)   An increase in the mechanical rate payable based on sales of the record, for example, the rate payable will be 75% of the mechanical rate for the first 500,000 copies sold, 80% for record sales between 500,001 to 1,000,000 copies, and 85% for record sales from 1,000,001 copies onwards.

(c)   An increase in the mechanical rate on later albums, for example, the rate payable will be 75% of the mechanical rate for the first two albums, 80% for the next two albums and 85% for subsequent albums.

If the record company agrees a higher mechanical rate on later albums, the recording agreement should specify whether the release of a greatest hits/best of album will attract the lower mechanical royalty of 75% or whether the royalty rate is determined by when the record is released, ie if it is the fourth album released it will attract an 80% mechanical rate. There are other ways for the mechanical rate to be calculated for a greatest hits/best of album, for example, it might be based upon the total mechanical rate payable for the tracks at the rate paid on the albums from which the tracks were taken before any escalation for sales, divided by the number of tracks on the greatest hits/best of album. If, for example, the mechanical rate for the first two albums was 75%, 80% for the next two albums and 85% on subsequent albums, if the greatest hits/best of album comprises 12 tracks with three tracks taken from the first two albums, four tracks taken from the next two albums and five tracks taken from subsequent albums, the record company will pay an 80.83% mechanical rate (ie $(3 \times 75) + (4 \times 80) + (5 \times 85) \div 12 = 80.83$).

(d)   An increase in the maximum number of compositions per record for which the record company will pay a mechanical royalty.

Some recording agreements provide that all compositions which the performer intends to record (and not just the compositions written by, owned by or controlled by the performer) will be licensed at a favourable mechanical rate. This provision should be resisted by the celebrity's solicitor because in most cases the composer/publisher of a composition not written by, owned by or controlled by the performer will not be prepared to license the composition at a favourable rate. Where there is a favourable mechanical rate for all compositions, the record company will seek to deduct the difference between the licence fee payable and the favourable rate provided for in the recording agreement from the performer's royalties. It should be noted that even if the celebrity's solicitor manages to get the record company to accept that the favourable mechanical rate will not apply to compositions which are not written by, owned by or controlled by the performer, there will still be provisions in the recording agreement which will have an effect on the total amount of mechanicals for which the record company has agreed that it will be responsible. For example, the recording agreement will usually contain a provision that the mechanical rate for the US and Canada will be what is known as the minimum statutory rate. (A discussion of how the mechanical rate is calculated for the US and Canada is beyond the scope of this book.) At the end of the day, if the total amount of mechanicals payable exceeds the total amount for which the record company has agreed to be responsible, the record company will take the excess it pays from the performer's royalties.

(2)   Synchronisation and mechanical licence fees payable to the composer/publisher to enable the recorded compositions to be used on video/DVD. (A synchronisation licence, more commonly called a 'synchro' licence is required from the copyright owner of the composition to use the composition in timed relation (ie synchronised) with visual images such as a film, DVD, a television programme or a television commercial.) The record company will often want a clause in the recording agreement which provides that no licence fees will be payable where recorded compositions are used on a promotional video/DVD. This is because the video/DVD has been made purely to promote sales of the recorded compositions. The record company should, however, be required to pay licence fees where videos/DVDs of the recorded compositions are sold to the public. The celebrity's solicitor should ensure that any favourable synchronisation and mechanical licence fees to use the compositions on video/DVD only apply to controlled compositions (which will need to be defined in the agreement) and not to all compositions (see (1) above for the reason why).

Equitable remuneration

30.86   The right exists for the author of the words (being a literary work under CDPA 1998) and the author of the music (being a musical work under CDPA 1998) to be paid equitable remuneration under CDPA 1998, s 93B[66] for the rental of their work where the rental right under s 18A[67] has been transferred. It should be noted that the Act does not state what will amount to equitable remuneration, although a single payment may suffice.

30.87   The celebrity is entitled to receive equitable remuneration under CDPA 1998, s 191G[68] where he has transferred his s 182C[69] rental right in the sound recording. In addition, the celebrity is entitled to receive equitable remuneration under s 182D[70] where the sound recording is broadcast or played in public. The relevant monies are collected and distributed by Phonographic Performance Limited (PPL). (A discussion of the workings of PPL and other collecting societies is beyond the scope of this book.)

---

[66]   See Chapter 18 at **18.109** et seq.
[67]   See Chapter 18 at **18.104** et seq.
[68]   See Chapter 21 at **21.50** et seq.
[69]   See Chapter 21 at **21.9** et seq.
[70]   See Chapter 21 at **21.40** et seq.

ACCOUNTING AND AUDITING

30.88 The recording agreement should contain an accounting provision clause requiring the record company to keep accounts detailing the number of the celebrity's recordings sold, the income received from other uses of the recordings, for example, from licensing a recording for use in a television advertisement, and the amount of royalties which are due to the celebrity. The record company will be required to keep the accounts at its registered office or its main place of business.

30.89 The recording agreement will usually provide that the record company will send the celebrity a statement of account twice a year, for example, 90 days after 30 June and 31 December, showing full details of all the monies which have been received by the record company for record sales and for other uses of the celebrity's recordings, together with a cheque for the royalties due. The recording agreement will usually provide that royalties will only be paid on record sales and on other uses of the celebrity's recordings for which the record company has been paid and that no royalty will be paid for records which have been sold by the record company and subsequently returned to it. The celebrity will not want to wait 90 days from the end of the accounting period to receive any money due to him. It may be possible to reduce the 90-day period to 60 days, but the record company will resist an attempt to move the time period to account any closer to the actual accounting period. The currency in which payment is made should also be set out in the recording agreement. Where all or some of the payments are made in a foreign currency the exchange rate should be the date that payment is due under the agreement, but where there is late payment of royalties the celebrity should be able to choose whether the exchange rate used to calculate the royalty payable is to be the exchange rate on the date the royalty payment is due or the date it is actually paid. This will enable the celebrity to ensure that he does not loose money due to him because of currency exchange variations.

30.90 The record company may insert a clause giving the celebrity, for example, one year from receipt of the accounts to object to their accuracy. The celebrity should not accept any attempt by the record company to reduce the 6-year contractual limitation period to object to the accounts.

30.91 The recording agreement should always contain an audit clause which allows the celebrity or his professionally qualified accountant to inspect, audit and take copies of the record company's books and records to determine the accuracy of the accounts. The conditions applied to the right to audit will be tightly controlled by the record company. For example, the record company will want to limit the documents to which the auditor has access; it will usually only want to allow the auditor access to its sales ledgers. To enable the auditor to have a more complete picture which will enable him to pick up more easily any irregularities, he will want to have access to other record company documentation, for example, the manufacturing and distribution ledgers, and copies of any licences granted by the record company to use the recordings. This will help the auditor to verify the number of records made, the numbers sold, the numbers returned, the type of sales of these recordings and the amount distributed as free copies.[71]

30.92 The audit clause will usually require the celebrity to give notice of his intention to carry out the audit, and will limit the inspection to one inspection a year at the

---

[71] See **30.78** for how different types of sale of the same record will bear different royalty rates and **30.63** for free goods.

celebrity's expense. In addition, the clause will usually provide that the audit will take place at the record company's registered office or its main place of business and will take place during the record company's normal business hours. There may be an additional restriction that the accountant carrying out the audit for the celebrity is not presently engaged in another audit of the record company on behalf of another celebrity.

30.93 The agreement should provide that where the celebrity has been underpaid by a specified sum, for example, by at least £5,000, or has been underpaid by a specified percentage, for example, 10%, whichever is greater, that the cost of the audit will be paid for by the record company. Where the celebrity has been underpaid the agreement should provide for the record company to account to the celebrity for the underpayment. The celebrity should ensure the clause is drafted so that the record company accounts for any underpayment immediately and that the record company pays interest on any underpaid sum at a specified rate of interest.

30.94 The audit clause should contain a provision that the information disclosed to the celebrity and/or his accountant is confidential information and will not be disclosed to anyone except the celebrity's professional advisers or as may be required by law. The record company will usually require a copy of the celebrity's final audit report to be sent to it.

30.95 The celebrity will need to specify in the agreement the address to which the record company should send the accounts and any royalty cheque. Usually, the address to which they will be sent is the celebrity's home address. The celebrity may want the accounts to be sent to his accountant with the royalty cheque paid by the record company directly into his bank account, in which case the record company will need to be given the name of the celebrity's bank, the account name and number and the sort code to enable payment to be made directly into the account. The celebrity should also insert a provision to allow him to give notice to the record company requiring the accounts and any royalty cheque to be sent to a different address and/or bank account. The recording agreement should also provide that where any payments are made by the record company at the request of the celebrity to his manager or another person, such as his accountant, a receipt by the third party is deemed to be the receipt of the celebrity.

TERMINATION OF THE AGREEMENT

30.96 The agreement should contain provisions as to when the recording agreement will automatically terminate. The agreement should also contain provisions as to when the aggrieved party has the right to elect to terminate the recording agreement. The agreement may provide that where a terminating event occurs which entitles the aggrieved party to elect to terminate, before he can do so he must serve a notice on the other party giving notice of the terminating event and requiring it to be remedied within a period of 30 days, and only if the terminating event has not been remedied within that time can he then terminate the agreement. The circumstances where termination will or may occur include:

(1)   Where one party has been in substantial breach of contract the other party has the right to terminate. The effect of the celebrity terminating the recording agreement is that he will then be free to sign with another record company. The record company with whom he terminated the agreement will still retain the copyright in the sound recordings which the celebrity made for it for the full period of

copyright, ie 50 years and for any renewals and extensions of copyright.[72] The record company will not agree to a clause which provides for the copyright in the sound recordings to be assigned or reassigned to the celebrity where he terminates the agreement. (See also (3) below dealing with whether the copyright in the sound recordings will be assigned to the celebrity where the agreement expires by effluxion of time.)

(2)   Where one party becomes either bankrupt or enters a voluntary arrangement or any company through which he operates goes into compulsory or voluntary liquidation (save for the purposes of reconstructing or amalgamating a solvent company), or becomes insolvent or has a receiver, manager, or administrative receiver or provisional liquidator or administrator appointed, the agreement will automatically terminate.

(3)   At the end of the contractual term the agreement automatically terminates and the celebrity will be free to sign to another record company. As in (1) above, the record company will retain the copyright in the sound recordings which the celebrity made for it for the full period of copyright, ie 50 years, and for any renewals and extensions of copyright.[73] As mentioned at the beginning of this chapter,[74] because sound recordings are a valuable asset, the celebrity's solicitor should try to negotiate a clause in the recording agreement which provides for the copyright in the sound recordings to be assigned or reassigned to the celebrity and for the physical property of the master tapes to be handed over to the celebrity, say, 10 or 15 years after the end of the contractual term. Although the celebrity's solicitor should seek such a clause in the recording agreement, most record companies will flatly refuse such a request. In the unlikely event that the record company agrees to assign or reassign the copyright in the sound recordings to the celebrity, it will usually only be prepared to do so if the celebrity is recouped or is prepared to repay the record company any unrecouped sums, and provided the celebrity pays its reasonable legal fees for the assignment or reassignment and a nominal sum of, say, £250 per master track. Where the record company has agreed to assign or reassign the copyright in the sound recordings to the celebrity, the recording agreement should provide that the assignment or reassignment is subject to and with the benefit of any licences which the record company has granted to third parties to use the sound recordings.

SUSPENSION PROVISIONS

30.97 The agreement will usually contain a clause allowing the record company to suspend rather than terminate the recording agreement whilst there is a breach of contract existing which has arisen through no fault of the record company.

30.98 The circumstances where suspension may occur include:

(1)   where the celebrity refuses to provide his services to the record company;

---

[72]   See Chapter 18 at **18.78–18.79**. See also **30.6** et seq, **30.16** et seq, **30.33** et seq, point (1) at **30.47** and point (3) at **30.96**.

[73]   See Chapter 18 at **18.78–18.79**. See also **30.6** et seq, **30.16** et seq, **30.33** et seq, point (1) at **30.47** and point (3) at **30.96**.

[74]   See **30.6** et seq.

(2)   where the celebrity is unable to perform because of illness or disability; and

(3)   where a force majeure event occurs.[75]

OTHER CLAUSES

30.99 Other provisions which should be dealt with in the recording agreement include, inter alia:

(1)   That both parties will keep the terms of the agreement confidential and will not disclose them to anyone other than their professional advisers or as may be required by law.

(2)   That the agreement between the parties does not constitute a joint venture, partnership or employment relationship.

(3)   That the agreement reflects the whole of the agreement between the parties and replaces any earlier oral or written agreement.

(4)   That the celebrity will not hold himself out as representing the record company. A similar provision should also be made by the record company to the celebrity.

(5)   Which legal system will apply (in nearly all cases this will be the law of England and Wales) and the method to be used to resolve any disputes between the parties, namely alternative dispute resolution, arbitration or legal proceedings in the High Court or county court.

(6)   (Possibly) a provision enabling the parties to limit the extent of any indemnity which has been given to the other party.

(7)   A clause prohibiting assignment of the agreement. Where assignment is to be permitted in certain circumstances and/or is permitted subject to certain conditions the clause should detail the relevant circumstances and conditions.

(8)   A clause providing that the celebrity has received independent legal advice on the terms of the agreement from a solicitor with experience of dealing with music business agreements.

(9)   A notice clause. A notice clause should be included to deal with the procedure to be followed where the agreement requires one party to give notice to the other party to activate a contractual clause, for example, to activate an option clause. A notice clause should provide how the notice should be given, namely in writing to the other party, and should provide how it is to be sent, for example, by personal delivery, fax, first class or recorded delivery post, when it is deemed to have been delivered, for example, for first class post it will usually be deemed to have been delivered on the first or second business day after it has been posted, and the address to which it should be sent, for example, to the address set out in the

---

[75]   See point (10) at **30.99** for force majeure.

agreement or to the registered office or to such other address as may previously have been notified in writing by one party to the other.

(10) A force majeure clause. A force majeure clause should list all the events beyond the control of the contracting parties, for example, act of God, civil war, terrorism, strikes, lock outs, which if any of them occur will excuse the party who cannot perform its contractual obligations due to the force majeure event. The clause should provide that the party who cannot perform its contractual obligations will not be in breach of contract for non-performance where this is due to a force majeure event. The clause should require the party who cannot perform its obligations due to a force majeure event to give notice to the other party of the existence of the force majeure event and that it prevents it from performing its contractual obligations. The force majeure clause should provide that the agreement is suspended whilst the force majeure event exists and that the agreement will recommence once the force majeure event has ended. As the suspension could last for a long time there should be a long stop provision in the agreement allowing one party to serve written notice on the other party terminating the agreement where the agreement is suspended for a specified period of time due to a force majeure event. Where termination occurs due to a force majeure event, the agreement should deal with what is to happen in these circumstances.

Part VII

PRECEDENTS

GUIDANCE AND SAMPLE PRECEDENTS FOR INITIATING PRIVACY, HARASSMENT AND DEFAMATION CLAIMS

PRIVACY CASES

Guidance

The following is a list of salient points to be used as a checklist when drafting a letter before action, application to the Court or pleading (statement of case):

- The cause of action is misuse of private *information*.

- The information in issue, therefore, must be identified and must be private.

- The cause of action is breach of confidence but is called misuse of private information.

- No pre-existing relationship of confidence need be shown but normally the person who has received the information must have known or should have known fairly and reasonably that the information is confidential.

- In privacy cases the claimant must show a reasonable expectation of privacy in respect of the information in the particular circumstances of the case.

- This means a person of ordinary sensibilities placed in the claimant's position would reasonably expect the information would not be published.

- Absent a pre-existing relationship of confidence the focus is on the nature of the information.

- If information is obviously private this should be emphasised especially if the defendant should have known that to be the case.

- Where there is a pre-existing relationship of confidence (eg marriage or an intimate personal relationship) focus first and foremost on that relationship. The nature of the information remains relevant though.

- The information usually must not generally be available to the public.

- All relevant circumstances should be identified and set out.

- The information alleged to be confidential and/or private should be defined in the statement of case with as much precision as possible.

- If the claimant does not wish the information to be disclosed in the statement of case it is permissible for the information to be set out in a separate schedule (having obtained an undertaking that it will be kept private) on the basis that an application will be made that it should not be read out in court or otherwise disclosed to the public.

- Publication will be allowed if the right to privacy is outweighed by the factors in Article 8(2) particularly the right to freedom of expression.

- This means the right to privacy will prevail unless there is a relevant countervailing public interest in respect of the information.

- There is usually little public interest justifying publication of private photographs particularly those obtained intrusively.

- Those who commission photographs (in which copyright subsists)for private or domestic purposes have a *moral* right not to have the photographs made public and a claim for breach of statutory duty if that right is infringed.

- If an injunction is sought to restrain publication before trial it must be shown that the claimant is *likely* at trial to prevent publication which is not always easy if freedom of expression is at stake.

PRECEDENT 1

Letter before action in a misuse of private information case [Clancy Delany]

Dear Sir

Re: Clancy Delany

We act on behalf of the above-named who is a well known film actor and screen star. Our client has recently published a best-selling autobiography. This letter is written in compliance with the pre-action protocol regime.

It has come to our client's attention that you imminently propose to publish, in this Sunday's edition of your newspaper "Publish and Be Damned", revelations by our client's former girlfriend (Ms Catherine Kittle) concerning the intimate sexual relationship she shared with him when they were both teenagers. Your pre-publication publicity suggests that a series of articles containing lurid details about the relationship will be published and that our client will be revealed as sexually deviant and hypocritical. It is also suggested that graphic photographs will accompany the story, although it is not indicated who took them.

Publication of this story (and of the photographs) amounts to a breach of confidence and breaches our client's right to privacy. Given the urgency of the matter we expect you to confirm *by return* that you will not run the story or publish the photographs. If an application can be heard in time the Court is likely to restrain publication.

It is understood that old acquaintances of our client and Ms Kittle have disclosed to your newspaper details of the intimate relationship between our client and Ms Kittle based on what they were allegedly told by them years ago. Any such disclosures were confidential and no one has the unilateral right to disclose the details to the press.

The information in question is confidential and obviously private and our client reasonably expects it to remain so. Your pre-publication publicity suggests the revelations have been made to "set the record straight" after our client's best-selling autobiography. Our client did not allude to his relationship with Ms Kittle in his autobiography and there is no ground for revealing details of this part of his private life.

There is no legitimate public interest in what you are proposing to publish. It is a simple kiss and tell story in exchange for money.

The photographs were taken in private circumstances where a relationship of trust and confidence existed between those involved. In fact our client was unaware such photographs were being taken and does not consent to publication now.

We put you on notice that if this material is published our client will suffer serious upset, humiliation and distress and his career will be damaged.

On these facts our client is likely to be granted an injunction restraining publication at trial of what you propose to publish and, therefore, the criteria for pre-trial restraint are met.

In the circumstances we require you to undertake (by your directors, officers, servants or agents or otherwise howsoever):

(1)   Not to publish or further publish any information concerning our client's relationship with Ms Catherine Kittle other than to confirm that he did once have a relationship with her many years ago when they were both teenagers.

(2)   Not to publish, license or sell any photographs or images concerning our client's relationship with Ms Kittle or permit publication of such photographs or images in the future.

(3)   To deliver up to this firm all of the photographs, negatives or images or copies in your possession whether or not the same have been published.

(4)   To delete all the images from your database and website and to confirm the deletion by way of affidavit sworn by one of your directors within two days.

(5)   To make proposals for compensating our client in damages or at our client's option to provide an account of the profits in respect of the disclosure of private information you have made about our client referred to above.

(6)   To pay our client's reasonable legal costs in relation to this matter.

We expect a satisfactory response to this letter by return and by no later than 12 noon today otherwise we shall immediately apply for an injunction without further reference to you. All our client's rights are reserved.

Yours faithfully

Signed

PRECEDENT 2

Particulars of claim in a breach of confidence and misuse of private information case

IN THE HIGH COURT OF JUSTICE   **Case Number**

CHANCERY DIVISION

BETWEEN:

CLANCY DELANY

Claimant

and

PUBLISH AND BE DAMNED GROUP NEWSPAPERS

Defendant

PARTICULARS OF CLAIM

1. The Claimant is a well known film actor and screen star.

2. The Defendant is the publisher of the Sunday Newspaper "Publish and Be Damned".

3. In the Sunday 27th September 2009 edition of "Publish and Be Damned" the Defendant published an article containing revelations by the Claimant's former girlfriend (Ms Catherine Kittle) about her intimate sexual relationship with the Claimant at a time when they were both teenagers ("the Article").

4. The Article also contained disclosures by acquaintances of the Claimant and Ms Kittle ("the Acquaintances") of intimate details of the said relationship they claimed to have learned from the Claimant and Ms Kittle.

5. The Article was accompanied by photographs of the Claimant and Ms Kittle of a graphic sexual nature ("the Photographs").

6. The information about the relationship between the Claimant and Ms Kittle in the Article and the Photographs is referred to below as "the Information". A copy of the Article and Photographs is attached hereto. The Article contained the following words which referred to the Claimant:
"[set out the words of the Article complained of]"

7. The Information was confidential and private.

Particulars of the Private and Confidential Information

(1)   The Information was derived from pre-existing relationships of confidence existing between Ms Kittle, the Acquaintances and the Claimant. Each fairly and reasonably would have known of the confidential and private nature of Information and that it was not for publication.

(2)   Intimate details of a personal sexual relationship are obviously private.

(3)   The Defendant either knew or should have known that the Claimant would fairly and reasonably regard the Information as confidential and private.

(4)   It is primarily contended that all the information is confidential and in particular the following parts of the Article which it is contended are highly confidential [set out extracts]

8.   The Claimant accordingly has a reasonable expectation of privacy in respect of the Information.

9.   The Defendant's publication of the Information constituted a breach of confidence and an unjustified misuse of private information and by reason thereof the Claimant has suffered loss and damage.

Particulars

(1)   The Claimant has suffered distress and anxiety as a result of the exposure of his private life.

(2)   In consequence of the exposure of details of his private life the Claimant has lost at least one major film role.

10.   In support of his claim for aggravated damages the Claimant will rely upon the following:

a.   The fact that the Claimant's solicitor wrote to the Defendant prior to publication asking them to refrain from publication until such time as he could apply for and obtain an interim injunction to restrain publication. The Defendant refused this request and expedited publication and distribution of the offending article before the Claimant could obtain an injunction.

b.   The fact that at the time of publication the Defendant knew that the Claimant objected to the material being published and that it would cause him distress and upset and humiliation but went ahead and published nonetheless.

11.   The Defendant threatens to publish further disclosures of an intimate sexual nature about relationship between the Claimant and Ms Kittle.

12.   The Claimant is entitled to and claims interest on all sums awarded to him pursuant to section 35A of the Supreme Court Act 1981.

And the Claimant claims:

1.   Damages including aggravated damages or at the Claimant's option an account of profits derived from the publication of the Information.

2.   An injunction restraining the Defendant (whether by its directors, agents, employees or otherwise howsoever) from:

    a.   Publishing or further publishing the Information or any details of the Claimant's relationship with Ms Kittle beyond confirming that such a relationship once existed.

    b.   Publishing, licensing or selling for publication any photographs of the Claimant with Ms Kittle or permit publication of such photographs or images in the future.

3.   **[An order that the Defendant delivers up all photographs, negatives or images or copies of the Claimant with Ms Kittle in its possession whether or not the same have been published.]**

4.   **[An order that the Defendant deletes all images from its database and website and to confirm the deletion by way of affidavit sworn by one of its directors].**

5.   The said statutory interest to be assessed.

6.   Costs.

7.   Further or other relief.

PRECEDENT 3

Letter before action in commissioned photograph case breach of statutory duty/moral right (ss 85 and 103 of the CDPA 1988)

Dear Sir

Re: Catherine Kittle

This letter is written by way of compliance with the pre-action protocol regime.

We act on behalf of Catherine Kittle who, since her appearance on "Make Yourself a Celebrity" and her subsequent disclosures about her intimate relationship with Clancy Delany, has become famous in her own right as a personality and celebrity. Ms Kittle has consulted us about the unauthorised publication of a number of photographs of her in various newspapers and magazines. We understand, from the newspapers and magazines concerned that the images in question were supplied by your photographic agency having appeared in your photographic portfolio (published in your portfolio magazine and on your website).

The photographs were taken in May 2005 by Paul Goodview, one of the staff photographers at your agency. Our client commissioned Mr Goodview to take photographs of her for private and domestic purposes, at a time when she was a teenager and embarking on an intended career as a glamour model.

Copyright subsists in the photographs.

Our client has always kept all copies at home and has not disclosed them beyond family and close friends. She does not believe she was given the negatives (or positives). Nor has she given anyone the right to publish the photographs.

She has the moral right not to have copies of the photographs issued to the public or communicated to the public pursuant to section 85 of the Copyright, Designs and Patents Act 1988. Any infringement of that right by virtue of section 103 of the 1988 Act is actionable by her as a breach of statutory duty. You are in breach of that right by issuing copies to the public and communicating to the public.

Copies of the photographs taken of our client pursuant to the commission are attached hereto in a bundle marked at the front "A". When referring to photographs, negatives and images below it is to all of these we are referring.

Copies of the extracts of newspapers and magazines containing reproductions of photographs and images of our client in "A" are attached hereto in a bundle marked on the front: "B".

In the circumstances we also require you to undertake (by your directors, officers, servants or agents or otherwise howsoever):

(1)   Not to publish or further publish, license or sell the photographs or images in question.

(2)   Not to permit the publication of such photographs or images in the future.

(3)   To write to all publishing companies, newspapers and magazines you have contacted about the photographs or images to inform them that the photographs and images in question are no longer available for publication

(4)   To supply a copy of all letters sent pursuant to (5) above for our approval on behalf of our client.

(5)   To make proposals for compensating our client in damages or at our client's option to provide an account of the profits you have made from exploiting the photographs with an undertaking to pay over such profits to our client.

(6)   To pay our client's reasonable legal costs in relation to this matter.

We will expect a satisfactory response to this letter no later than within the next seven days otherwise we shall advise our client to issue proceedings without further reference to you. Meanwhile all of our client's rights are reserved.

Yours faithfully

Signed

[It might also be possible on similar facts to combine the claim for breach of statutory duty with claims for breach of confidence and/or misuse of private information]

PRECEDENT 4

Particulars of claim in a commissioned photograph case

Right to privacy of certain photographs and films s 85 of the CDPA 1988

Breach of moral right/statutory duty under s 103 of the CDPA 1988

IN THE HIGH COURT OF JUSTICE   Case Number

CHANCERY DIVISION

BETWEEN:

CATHERINE KITTLE

Claimant

and

PAUL GOODVIEW AND ASSOCIATES LIMITED

Defendant

PARTICULARS OF CLAIM

1.   The Claimant is a well known personality and celebrity.

2.   The Defendant is limited company incorporated within the jurisdiction which has at all material times carried on business as a photographic agency.

3.   In about May 2005 the Claimant commissioned Paul Goodview, a photographer employed by the Claimant, to shoot a series of photographs of her for her private and domestic purposes ("the Photographs").

4.   Copies of the Photographs (negatives and images) taken of the Claimant pursuant to the commission are attached hereto in a bundle marked at the front "A".

5.   Copyright subsists in the Photographs.

6.   The Claimant has the moral right not to have copies of the Photographs issued to the public or communicated to the public pursuant to section 85 of the Copyright, Designs and Patents Act 1988.

7.   Infringement of the Claimant's moral right is actionable as a breach of statutory duty pursuant to section 103 of the said Act.

8.   In breach of the said statutory duty the Defendant (1) issued copies of the Photographs to the public, (2) exhibited and/or showed the Photographs in public and (3) communicated the Photographs to the public.

Particulars

The Defendant sold the Photographs to various newspaper and magazine publishers and copies of extracts of newspapers and magazines containing reproductions of the Photographs are attached hereto in a bundle marked at the front: "B".

9. By reason of the Defendant's said breach of statutory duty the Claimant has suffered loss and damage:

Particulars

[Insert loss and damage suffered]

10. Alternatively at her option the Claimant is entitled to claim an account of the profits made by the Defendant as a result of the breach of statutory duty.

11. The Claimant is entitled to and claims interest on all sums due or awarded to her pursuant to section 35A of the Supreme Court Act 1981.

AND THE CLAIMANT CLAIMS:

(1) Damages for breach of statutory duty.

(2) Alternatively, at the Claimant's option, an account of profits made by the Defendant as a result of the breach of statutory duty.

(3) An injunction restraining the Defendant whether by itself or its officers, directors, servants, agents or otherwise howsoever from:
     a. Publishing or further publishing, licensing or selling the Photographs.
     b. Permitting the publication of the Photographs.

(4) The said statutory interest to be assessed.

(5) Costs.

(6) Further or other relief.

HARRASSMENT

Guidance

The following is a list of salient points to be used as a checklist when drafting a letter before action, application to the Court or pleading (statement of case):

*   The defendant must have pursued a course of conduct.

*   The claim can be brought against those likely to aid, abet, counsel or procure others to carry out the course of conduct which amounts to harassment.

*   The claim can be brought by a company director on behalf of his company's employees to enable the court to protect their interests.

- The claim can be brought against a company held vicariously liable for the acts of its employees in the course of their employment.

- The course of conduct must *usually* (but not always) have been such as to have caused alarm and distress to the claimant.

- The defendant must have known or ought to have known that his conduct amounted to harassment of the claimant.

- The knowledge must be on the basis that a reasonable person in the possession of the same information as the defendant would think that the course of conduct amounted to harassment of the other (ie an objective test).

- The course of conduct must not have been pursued for the purpose of preventing or detecting crime or under any requirement under an enactment.

- The course of conduct must involve at least two or more incidents.

- There must be a connection between the incidents to make them a course of conduct.

- The conduct must have been calculated to cause alarm or distress to the claimant and oppressive and unreasonable.

- Particulars should be given of what, it is said, makes the conduct unreasonable.

- The mere fact that the conduct foreseeably causes distress is not enough; the conduct must have been oppressive, unreasonable and unacceptable. This may well depend upon the context in which the conduct occurs.

- The conduct must have been grave ie sufficient to constitute a crime.

- *Each* of the incidents relied on as constituting the course of conduct must fulfil these conditions.

- The relief sought must be necessary and proportionate and should not interfere unduly with the defendant's rights eg the right to freedom of expression under Article 10 of the ECHR.

- If a harassment claim is brought against the press freedom of expression is important and the press cannot be gagged simply because a series of articles causes distress. There must be some exceptional circumstance to justify restricting the paper from publishing what might otherwise amount material likely to harass the claimant (eg where it is motivated by personal or racial hatred).

- Photographing, surveillance and threatened publication of photographs might in context amount to harassment.

- The relief sought must be justified on the basis of preventing the defendant from committing further acts of harassment and to protect the claimant from further harassment.

- The claim for an injunction must be framed with precision.

- The injunction can be framed to include those who have notice of its terms e g restraining the defendants from pursuing a particular course of conduct *and any other person who has been given notice in writing of the terms of the injunction.*

- The injunction can specify an exclusion area to prevent further harassment from occurring.

- The injunction may specify a time or be until further order.

- The relief sought can include:
  - o An injunction restraining the defendant from contacting the claimant or other named persons connected with the claimant.
  - o An injunction restraining the defendant from publishing information about the claimant whether true or false.
  - o A claim simply for an injunction to restrain the defendant from pursuing any conduct which amounts to harassment is likely to be held too imprecise.

PRECEDENT 5

Letter before action in a newspaper harassment case

Dear Sir

Re: Ms Pamela Caruso

This letter is written by way of compliance with the pre-action protocol regime.

We act on behalf of Ms Pamela Caruso the well known actress. She has consulted us regarding the intolerable course of conduct which has been pursued by your newspaper and its staff photographers which amounts to harassment. Over the past six months, since her revelations of an intimate relationship with fellow actor Clancy Delany, photographers from your newspaper have conducted a campaign whereby our client has been constantly followed or tailed by photographers travelling by car, on motorcycle or on foot literally wherever she has gone. She has also been "door-stepped" (or under siege from press photographers) at her home.

This conduct fully entitles our client to obtain an order for an injunction to restrain such further harassment and to obtain compensation for what she has suffered.

The cumulative effect of this persistent course of conduct has been to cause our client alarm and distress when confronted by your staff photographers. On at least eight occasions over the six month period photographers from your newspaper have door-stepped and jumped out at Ms Caruso when she has been going about her daily business causing her to suffer considerable alarm and distress. Those responsible must have known or ought to have known that this conduct would amount to harassment and any reasonable person in the position of the photographers responsible would have known that jumping out and taking flash photographs of someone causes alarm and distress.

Your newspaper has plainly targeted Ms Caruso and the resulting behaviour has become oppressive and unreasonable. On our advice Ms Caruso has kept a personal log describing all incidents involving photographs from your newspaper and a commentary on how this has made her feel.

The conduct complained of has endured for a continuous period of at least six months. Full particulars (dates and times etc) are available but essentially the offending conduct is as follows:

- Photographers have waited outside Ms Caruso's home all night, often in concealed positions, in the hope of photographing her.

- Photographers have persistently followed her when she has left her home for social and other engagements.

- Photographers have waited outside locations other than her home for her to reappear and have recommended taking photographs of her.

- Photographers have physically manhandled Ms Caruso on at least three occasions when trying to photograph her and on at least ten occasions have become verbally abusive when she has tried to shield her face from them.

- On at least nine occasions she has been subjected surveillance, both when at home and when at the homes of friends and family members, by photographers who have trained long lenses on rooms she has been in and have threatened publication of the resultant photographs.

The above incidents have each caused our client to suffer considerable alarm and distress. There is no justification on any public interest or other grounds for this intolerable press intrusion and it is necessary and proportionate that she should seek the assistance of the Court to restrain further such behaviour and to protect her from further harassment.

We require you to identify the photographers on your staff or who are paid by your newspaper who are responsible for the above. We intend to seek an order that your newspaper and its employees and agents are restrained by the terms of the injunction we shall seek and we intend to frame the terms of the injunction to include those who have notice of its terms ie restraining your newspaper and any other person who has been given notice in writing of the terms of the injunction from pursuing the course of conduct complained of.

We require you to give the following undertakings regarding the conduct of your photographers:

(1)   Not to come within 100 yards of Ms Caruso's home address at [insert] or the addresses of her friends and family at [insert] for a period of [insert].

(2)   Not to take photographs of Ms Caruso or come within 20 yards of her other than when she is in bars, nightclubs or restaurants or is out in public at red carpet events.

PRECEDENT 6

Particulars of claim in a newspaper harassment case

IN THE BLANKTOWN COUNTY   Case Number
COURT

BETWEEN:

PAMELA CARUSO

Claimant

and

PUBLISH AND BE DAMNED GROUP NEWSPAPERS LIMITED

Defendant

PARTICULARS OF CLAIM

1.   The Claimant is a well known actress.

2.   The Defendant is the publisher of a Sunday tabloid newspaper and employs staff photographers.

3.   Staff photographers in the course of their employment with the Defendant have wrongfully pursued a course of conduct over a period of at least 6 months which amounts to harassment of the Claimant.

Particulars

(1)   Since May 2009 the Defendant's staff photographers have relentlessly followed the Claimant travelling by car, on motorcycle or on foot literally wherever she goes and on at least eight occasions have jumped out in front of her to take photographs causing her to suffer considerable alarm and distress. The eight occasions were on [insert the dates].

(2)   Also since May 2009 staff photographers have "door-stepped" the Claimant in her own home. Photographers have waited outside the Claimant's home all night, often in concealed positions, in the hope of photographing her. Photographers have persistently followed her when she has left her home for social and other engagements. Photographers have waited outside locations other than her home for her to reappear and have recommenced taking photographs of her. The cumulative effect of this persistent course of conduct has caused the Claimant to suffer alarm and distress when unexpectedly confronted by the Defendant's staff photographers. This has occurred on the following occasions [insert the dates]

(3)   Photographers have physically manhandled the Claimant on at least three occasions when attempting to photograph her and on at least ten occasions have become verbally abusive when she has tried to shield her face from them. This has occurred on the following occasions [insert the dates].

(4)   The Claimant has been subjected surveillance, both when at home and when at the homes of friends and family members, by photographers who have trained long lenses on rooms she has been in and have threatened publication of the resultant photographs. On at least five occasions the

Claimant has been alarmed to see photographers training long lenses on her on the following dates [insert the dates].

4. The said course of conduct complained of was oppressive and unreasonable and those responsible knew or ought to have known that the same amounted to harassment and would cause alarm and distress to any reasonable person in the position of the Claimant subjected to it. In the circumstances the course of conduct constitutes harassment of the Claimant contrary to sections 1 and 3 of the Protection from Harassment Act 1997.

5. By reason of the aforesaid harassment the Claimant has suffered loss and damage.

Particulars

(1) Severe anxiety, distress and depression particulars of which will be given by way of a medical report served separately.
(2) [Insert other damage suffered].

6. The Claimant will rely upon the following in support of her claim for aggravated damages:
    (1) The photographers continued to follow, photograph and alarm the Claimant when they knew that she was suffering anxiety and distress as a result of their activities.
    (2) The photographers trespassed on her private property in order to take photographs.
    (3) The photographers used long lenses and invaded the Claimant's privacy when taking shots of her in her home.

7. The Defendant has refused to undertake to the Claimant to cease the course of conduct complained of and unless restrained the Defendant threatens to continue to harass the Claimant.

8. The Claimant is entitled to and claims interest on all sums awarded to her to be assessed pursuant to section 69 of the County Courts Act 1984.

AND THE CLAIMANT CLAIMS:

(1) Damages.

(2) An injunction restraining the Defendant or anyone who has notice in writing of the terms of the injunction whether by themselves (and in the case of corporations their directors or officers) or their servants or agents or otherwise howsoever from:
    a. Further pursuing the course of conduct complained of.
    b. Coming within 100 yards of the Claimant's home address at [insert] or the addresses of her friends and family at [insert] for a period of [insert].
    c. Taking photographs of the Claimant or coming within 20 yards of her other than on public occasions in bars, nightclubs or restaurants or at red carpet events.

(3)   The said statutory interest to be assessed.

(4)   Costs.

DEFAMATION

Guidance

The following is a list of salient points to be used as a checklist when drafting a letter before action, application to the Court or pleading (statement of case):

- Allege that the defamatory material was published.

- Generally libel is concerned with publication in a permanent form and slander in a non-permanent form.

- Internet publication is actionable in libel.

- Slander is not actionable without proof of actual injury (save in special cases).

- The words must refer to the claimant and this can be proved by alleging special facts known at the time of publication and identifying who would have known them.

- As to what is defamatory it is the words that matter, and the reaction of the ordinary reader, not what the defendant thinks.

- Words are defamatory if they tend to lower the claimant in the estimation of right thinking members of society.

- Words must be read in their context.

- All those responsible for publication are liable to be sued.

- Each republication constitutes a separate cause of action.

- The original publisher might be liable for the subsequent foreseeable publications.

- If an Internet Service Provider is to be sued for publishing a libel it is necessary to put the ISP on notice first of the defamatory posting.

- The actual words used should be set out.

- The claimant must allege what the words mean:
  o Either their natural ordinary meaning or
  o Their innuendo meaning (what the words mean to someone who knows of facts extraneous to the words used – words in the same passage are not extraneous but part of the context).

- The pleaded meaning should be neither too wide nor too narrow.

- Where the alleged libel is a statement about investigations into the claimant by the authorities there are three levels of meaning:
  o Chase level one – positive conclusion of guilt.
  o Chase level two – strong grounds to suspect.

    o   Chase level three – reasonable grounds to suspect.

- The following are frequently raised as defences:
  - o   Limitation.
  - o   Not responsible for publication.
  - o   Words incapable of bearing defamatory meaning.
  - o   Words incapable of bearing meaning contended for.
  - o   Words bear different meaning from that contended for.
  - o   Extrinsic facts known to publishees make words innocent.
  - o   Truth.
  - o   Fair comment on a matter of public interest.
  - o   Absolute privilege.
  - o   Qualified privilege.
  - o   Consent to publication.

PRECEDENT 7

Letter before action in a defamation case

Dear Sir

Re: Ms Catherine Kittle

This letter is written by way of compliance with the pre-action protocol regime.

We act on behalf of the above-named who has consulted us in connection with an article about her which appeared on the front page and on pages 4 and 5 of the 4th October 2009 edition of the "Sunday Gossip". The article to which we refer appeared under the title: *"Celebrity – She's no more than a money grubbing witch"* and also has appeared under that title on your newspaper's website since that date. The article stated the following about our client:

> "Catherin Kittle's latest exposures of the rich and famous have shocked the celebrity world. Rather than work to make money like most ordinary people Catherine Kittle has spent her life attempting to bed the rich and famous, with varying degrees of success, in the hope of selling details of her conquests to the tabloid press. Does her cynicism know no bounds?"

These words refer to our client and are defamatory of her.

In their natural and ordinary meaning the words meant that rather than work our client made a career from selling details of her sexual exploits with rich and famous celebrities to the media.

There are no grounds in fact to support the publication of these slurs on our client which constitute a serious libel causing serious damage to her reputation. Further, as a result of publication our client has suffered severe humiliation, anxiety and distress and has been ridiculed, threatened and shunned. In particular our client [set out the matters which support the claim for damages].

In the circumstances our client is entitled to substantial damages in respect of the publication and she expects urgently to receive a full and clear apology and public retraction (in the form set out below or otherwise to be agreed by us) together with a statement in open court and an undertaking that your newspaper will not repeat the above or similar allegations regarding our client. Our client also expects agreement from you that you will be responsible for paying her legal costs.

The apology our client requires is in the following form:

> "In an article about Ms Catherine Kittle in the 4th October 2009 edition of this newspaper under the heading: "Celebrity – She's no more than a money grubbing witch" it was suggested that Ms Catherine Kittle had made a career from cynically having sex with celebrities in order to sell her story to the newspapers. We accept this is not correct and that her relationships with celebrities had only ever been serious and committed. We are happy to put the record straight and apologise for any upset our article may have caused her. We have agreed to pay Ms Kittle her legal costs in this matter and a substantial sum to compensate her for any upset and distress the article may have caused her."

Our client expects a response to this letter without delay and in any event no later than [insert]. In the absence of a satisfactory reply it is our client's intention to commence proceedings in respect of the libel without further notice to you. Our client's rights in this matter are strictly reserved.

Yours faithfully etc.

PRECEDENT 8

Particulars of claim in a defamation case

IN THE HIGH COURT OF JUSTICE   Case Number

QUEEN'S BENCH DIVISION

BETWEEN:

CATHERINE KITTLE

Claimant

and

PUBLISH AND BE DAMNED GROUP NEWSPAPERS LIMITED

Defendant

PARTICULARS OF CLAIM

1.   The Claimant is a well known actress and in particular is well known as [set out any relevant background details relating to that part of the Claimant's reputation particularly damaged by the libel].

2.   The Defendant is the publisher of the Sunday tabloid newspaper "The Sunday Gossip" with a substantial circulation and readership in the jurisdiction of the Court.

3.   On pages 4 and 5 of the 4th October 2009 edition of the "Sunday Gossip" under the title: *"Celebrity – She's no more than a money grubbing witch"* the Defendant published an article accompanied by photographs of the Claimant in which the following words appeared of and concerning the Claimant:

"Catherin Kittle's latest exposures of the rich and famous have shocked the celebrity world. Rather than work to make money like most ordinary people Catherine Kittle has spent her life attempting to bed the rich and famous, with varying degrees of success, in the hope of selling details of her conquests to the tabloid press. Does her cynicism know no bounds?"

4.   The said article in substantially the same terms has also appeared under the same title on the Defendant's website since 4th October 2009.

5.   Copies of the article appearing in the "Sunday Gossip" and on the Defendant's website are annexed to this Particulars of Claim.

6.   The words complained refer to the Claimant and are defamatory of her.

7.   In their natural and ordinary meaning the words meant that rather than work the Claimant made a career from selling details of her sexual exploits with rich and famous celebrities to the media.

8.   By reason of the publication the Claimant has been severely damaged in her character and reputation, has suffered severe humiliation, anxiety and distress and has been ridiculed, threatened and shunned. She has also suffered special damage.

Particulars of Special Damage

[Set out particulars of special damage suffered]

9. The Claimant will rely upon the following facts and matters in support of her claim for general and/or aggravated damages:

Particulars

10. Unless restrained the Defendant threatens to continue to publish the same or similar words defamatory of the Claimant.

AND THE CLAIMANT CLAIMS:

(1) Damages including special and aggravated damages for libel.

(2) Interest to be assessed on special damages pursuant to section 35A of the Supreme Court Act 1981.

(3) An injunction to restrain the Defendant whether by its directors, servants or agents or otherwise howsoever from further publishing or causing to be published the same or similar words defamatory of the Claimant.

Part VIII

APPENDICES

Appendix 1

PCC EDITORS' CODE OF PRACTICE

Reproduced with the kind permission of the Press Complaints Commission (PCC).

The Press Complaints Commission is charged with enforcing the following Code of Practice which was framed by the newspaper and periodical industry and was ratified by the PCC in September 2009 to include changes which took effect from 19 October 2009.

THE EDITORS' CODE

All members of the press have a duty to maintain the highest professional standards. The Code, which includes this preamble and the public interest exceptions below, sets the benchmark for those ethical standards, protecting both the rights of the individual and the public's right to know. It is the cornerstone of the system of self-regulation to which the industry has made a binding commitment.

It is essential that an agreed code be honoured not only to the letter but in the full spirit. It should not be interpreted so narrowly as to compromise its commitment to respect the rights of the individual, nor so broadly that it constitutes an unnecessary interference with freedom of expression or prevents publication in the public interest.

It is the responsibility of editors and publishers to apply the Code to editorial material in both printed and online versions of publications. They should take care to ensure it is observed rigorously by all editorial staff and external contributors, including non-journalists, in printed and online versions of publications.

Editors should co-operate swiftly with the PCC in the resolution of complaints. Any publication judged to have breached the Code must print the adjudication in full and with due prominence, including headline reference to the PCC.

1 Accuracy

i) The Press must take care not to publish inaccurate, misleading or distorted information, including pictures.

ii) A significant inaccuracy, misleading statement or distortion once recognised must be corrected, promptly and with due prominence, and – where appropriate – an apology published.

iii) The Press, whilst free to be partisan, must distinguish clearly between comment, conjecture and fact.

iv)   A publication must report fairly and accurately the outcome of an action for
       defamation to which it has been a party, unless an agreed settlement states
       otherwise, or an agreed statement is published.

2 Opportunity to reply

A fair opportunity for reply to inaccuracies must be given when reasonably called for.

3 *Privacy

i)   Everyone is entitled to respect for his or her private and family life, home, health
       and correspondence, including digital communications.

ii)   Editors will be expected to justify intrusions into any individual's private life
       without consent. Account will be taken of the complainant's own public
       disclosures of information.

iii)   It is unacceptable to photograph individuals in private places without their
       consent.

Note – Private places are public or private property where there is a reasonable
expectation of privacy.

4 *Harassment

i)   Journalists must not engage in intimidation, harassment or persistent pursuit.

ii)   They must not persist in questioning, telephoning, pursuing or photographing
       individuals once asked to desist; nor remain on their property when asked to leave
       and must not follow them. If requested, they must identify themselves and whom
       they represent.

iii)   Editors must ensure these principles are observed by those working for them and
       take care not to use non-compliant material from other sources.

5 Intrusion into grief or shock

i)   In cases involving personal grief or shock, enquiries and approaches must be made
       with sympathy and discretion and publication handled sensitively. This should not
       restrict the right to report legal proceedings, such as inquests.

*ii)   When reporting suicide, care should be taken to avoid excessive detail about the
       method used.

6 *Children

i)   Young people should be free to complete their time at school without unnecessary
       intrusion.

ii)   A child under 16 must not be interviewed or photographed on issues involving their own or another child's welfare unless a custodial parent or similarly responsible adult consents.

iii)   Pupils must not be approached or photographed at school without the permission of the school authorities.

iv)   Minors must not be paid for material involving children's welfare, nor parents or guardians for material about their children or wards, unless it is clearly in the child's interest.

v)   Editors must not use the fame, notoriety or position of a parent or guardian as sole justification for publishing details of a child's private life.

7 *Children in sex cases

1.   The press must not, even if legally free to do so, identify children under 16 who are victims or witnesses in cases involving sex offences.

2.   In any press report of a case involving a sexual offence against a child –
       i)   The child must not be identified.
       ii)   The adult may be identified.
       iii)   The word 'incest' must not be used where a child victim might be identified.
       iv)   Care must be taken that nothing in the report implies the relationship between the accused and the child.

8 *Hospitals

i)   Journalists must identify themselves and obtain permission from a responsible executive before entering non-public areas of hospitals or similar institutions to pursue enquiries.

ii)   The restrictions on intruding into privacy are particularly relevant to enquiries about individuals in hospitals or similar institutions.

9 *Reporting of Crime

(i)   Relatives or friends of persons convicted or accused of crime should not generally be identified without their consent, unless they are genuinely relevant to the story.

(ii)   Particular regard should be paid to the potentially vulnerable position of children who witness, or are victims of, crime. This should not restrict the right to report legal proceedings.

10 *Clandestine devices and subterfuge

i)   The press must not seek to obtain or publish material acquired by using hidden cameras or clandestine listening devices; or by intercepting private or mobile telephone calls, messages or emails; or by the unauthorised removal of documents or photographs; or by accessing digitally-held private information without consent.

ii)   Engaging in misrepresentation or subterfuge, including by agents or intermediaries, can generally be justified only in the public interest and then only when the material cannot be obtained by other means.

11 Victims of sexual assault

The press must not identify victims of sexual assault or publish material likely to contribute to such identification unless there is adequate justification and they are legally free to do so.

12 Discrimination

i)   The press must avoid prejudicial or pejorative reference to an individual's race, colour, religion, gender, sexual orientation or to any physical or mental illness or disability.

ii)   Details of an individual's race, colour, religion, sexual orientation, physical or mental illness or disability must be avoided unless genuinely relevant to the story.

13 Financial journalism

i)   Even where the law does not prohibit it, journalists must not use for their own profit financial information they receive in advance of its general publication, nor should they pass such information to others.

ii)   They must not write about shares or securities in whose performance they know that they or their close families have a significant financial interest without disclosing the interest to the editor or financial editor.

iii)   They must not buy or sell, either directly or through nominees or agents, shares or securities about which they have written recently or about which they intend to write in the near future.

14 Confidential sources

Journalists have a moral obligation to protect confidential sources of information.

15 Witness payments in criminal trials

i)   No payment or offer of payment to a witness – or any person who may reasonably be expected to be called as a witness – should be made in any case once proceedings are active as defined by the Contempt of Court Act 1981.
        This prohibition lasts until the suspect has been freed unconditionally by police without charge or bail or the proceedings are otherwise discontinued; or has entered a guilty plea to the court; or, in the event of a not guilty plea, the court has announced its verdict.

*ii)   Where proceedings are not yet active but are likely and foreseeable, editors must not make or offer payment to any person who may reasonably be expected to be called as a witness, unless the information concerned ought demonstrably to be published in the public interest and there is an over-riding need to make or promise payment for this to be done; and all reasonable steps have been taken to ensure no financial dealings influence the evidence those witnesses give. In no circumstances should such payment be conditional on the outcome of a trial.

*iii) Any payment or offer of payment made to a person later cited to give evidence in proceedings must be disclosed to the prosecution and defence. The witness must be advised of this requirement.

16 *Payment to criminals

i) Payment or offers of payment for stories, pictures or information, which seek to exploit a particular crime or to glorify or glamorise crime in general, must not be made directly or via agents to convicted or confessed criminals or to their associates – who may include family, friends and colleagues.

ii) Editors invoking the public interest to justify payment or offers would need to demonstrate that there was good reason to believe the public interest would be served. If, despite payment, no public interest emerged, then the material should not be published.

The public interest

There may be exceptions to the clauses marked * where they can be demonstrated to be in the public interest.

1. The public interest includes, but is not confined to:

i) Detecting or exposing crime or serious impropriety.

ii) Protecting public health and safety.

iii) Preventing the public from being misled by an action or statement of an individual or organisation.

2. There is a public interest in freedom of expression itself.

3. Whenever the public interest is invoked, the PCC will require editors to demonstrate fully that they reasonably believed that publication, or journalistic activity undertaken with a view to publication, would be in the public interest.

4. The PCC will consider the extent to which material is already in the public domain, or will become so.

5. In cases involving children under 16, editors must demonstrate an exceptional public interest to over-ride the normally paramount interest of the child.

Appendix 2

MAKING A COMPLAINT

Reproduced with the kind permission of the Press Complaints Commission.

INTRODUCTION

The Press Complaints Commission is an independent body, which has been set up to examine complaints about the editorial content of UK newspapers and magazines (and their websites). We are here to help you and our services are free.

This section of our website explains what we can deal with – and what we can't. It explains how our complaints procedures work and sets out what you can expect from us.

If anything is not clear please call us on 0207 831 0022 or 0845 600 2757 (a local-rate number). The FAQs page on this website should help to answer some of the most common questions people ask us. Additionally, this section provides guidance on particular aspects of the Code of Practice, including media harassment, discrimination and court and inquest reporting.

Please remember that we are happy to offer informal advice prior to you lodging an official complaint. Contact us any time. For emergencies only (usually relating to harassment by journalists) please use our 24-hour helpline: 07659 152656.

If your first language is not English, information is available in a range of other languages. Please click here for more information.

Remember too that editors are often happy to deal with complaints directly. You may, therefore, like to try a direct approach before considering a formal complaint to the PCC. Any such approach should be made promptly. If you do not receive a reply within a week – or if you are dissatisfied by the editor's response – please write to us as soon as possible.

OUR REMIT

The PCC deals with all editorially-controlled material in UK newspapers and magazines (and their websites). This can include:

- Articles and pictures

- Words and pictures (including video) on newspaper and magazine websites

- Audio material on newspaper and magazine websites

- Readers' letters

- Edited or moderated reader comments on newspaper and magazine websites

We also deal with the physical behaviour of journalists. This can include:

- Persistent pursuit of individuals

- Refusing requests to stop taking photos or asking questions

- Using hidden cameras to obtain material

- Failing to be sensitive when dealing with cases involving grief and shock

- Failing to obtain the proper consent before speaking to children or people in hospital

Please remember, however:

Complaints have to be judged against the Code of Practice. Before making your complaint we strongly advise that you consult the Code. If you need help in doing this, please contact us for assistance.

We normally accept complaints only from those who are directly affected by the matters about which they are complaining.

We do not generally accept complaints made more than two months after the date of publication (or over two months after the end of direct correspondence between you and the editor, provided that correspondence was entered into straight away). If the article remains available on the publication's website, this rule does not usually apply.

There are some things we don't deal with. For example:

- Complaints about TV and radio (Ofcom is the regulator for the broadcast industry)

- Complaints about advertising (The Advertising Standards Authority is the regulator for the advertising industry)

- Concerns about matters of taste and decency

- Legal or contractual matters that are dealt with more appropriately by the courts

- Complaints about books

- Complaints about online material that is not on newspaper or magazine websites

The Links section of this website provides information about other regulatory and advice bodies that might be able to help.

OUR COMPLAINTS PROCEDURE

When making a complaint please send us a copy of the article in question (if there is one) and a letter or email outlining your concerns. If there are other relevant letters or documents which would help us to assess the complaint, please send us these as well. For us to take your complaint forward it will need to engage one or more of the numbered Clauses of the Code of Practice. We can send you a hard copy of the Code if necessary.

Checklist – what to check before sending in your complaint:

- Have you sent us a copy of the complete article, if available, and a note of the publication date?

- Have you told us the name of the publication concerned?

- Have you provided us with a brief summary of your complaint which explains how you believe the article has breached the Code of Practice?

- Have you included copies of relevant documentation (eg, any previous correspondence with an editor etc)?

In the steps below we take you through the basic stages of our complaints procedure. Please note that each case is treated on its merits and the following guide is not exhaustive.

1. Assessing your complaint

If your complaint falls within our remit – and is neither delayed nor subject to related to legal proceedings – we will assess whether it raises a possible breach of our Code of Practice. If we think it does not, we will explain why. If we think it does, we will initiate an investigation by writing to the editor of the relevant publication.

2. The investigation

When we write to the editor we will send him or her a copy of your complaint and a copy of the article about which concerns have been raised. We will ask the editor to respond to your complaint and a copy of his or her reply will be sent to you. It if still appears that there may have been a breach of the Code, our primary aim will be to a find a satisfactory resolution to your complaint.

3. Resolution by mediation

Depending on the seriousness of the case, there are a variety of ways in which complaints can be resolved. For instance, if a serious error has been published, a correction or apology in the paper may be required.

Alternatively, we can seek assurances about future coverage or perhaps look to have online material amended or deleted. We cannot generally obtain financial compensation. If your complaint is resolved, we will publish a summary of the case on our website. Click here to see examples of complaints that have been resolved to the satisfaction of the complainant.

4. Taking stock

If it proves impossible to find a way of settling your complaint the Commission will evaluate the case. It will first decide whether there has, in fact, been a breach of the Code of Practice. If there has, it will decide whether the newspaper or magazine has taken – or offered – sufficient remedial action.

5. Complaint upheld

If the Commission concludes that the Code has been breached (and the breach has not – or cannot – be remedied) it will uphold your complaint in a public ruling. The newspaper or magazine is obliged to publish the critical ruling in full and with due prominence. This is a serious outcome for any editor and puts down a marker for future press behaviour.

IMPORTANT POINTS TO REMEMBER

When we write to the editor we will have to identify you (unless there are exceptional circumstances). If you do not wish for your address details to be passed on to the newspaper or magazine, please say so at the outset of the complaint. However, you may remain anonymous in any public ruling or summary of your case.

- The Commission can only consider evidence that has been made available to both sides.

- A summary of every resolved complaint will be published on our website as will the full details of all upheld cases.

- Even where the Commission does not rule in your favour, a copy of your complaint (and the Commission's decision) will be sent to the editor of the publication in question.

- All decisions about whether there has been a breach of the Code or about the adequacy of remedial action will be made by the Commission. PCC staff will, however, advise you about likely outcomes.

- Not all decisions made by the Commission are made public. However, all upheld complaints and other case which raise an important point of principle are made public, and can be seen here.

OUR SERVICE COMMITMENTS

When you make an enquiry or complaint to the PCC, we will seek to deal with your concerns as effectively as possible. In particular:

- We will respond quickly to your enquiries. For instance, we will acknowledge complaints we receive in writing within 3 days.

- We will deal with your complaint as quickly as possible. We will explain any delays and keep you informed of the progress of our investigations. Overall, we aim to deal with complaints in an average of 35 working days.

- Our procedures will be transparent.

- We will process your complaint at no cost to you.

- We will be as open and accessible as possible. Our staff will identify themselves by name and be courteous and polite.

These commitments form part of our Complainant's Charter. A copy can also be sent to you on request.

The PCC surveys complainants on an ongoing basis to assess the level of service it provides to complainants. You can see some of the feedback we have received by clicking here [http://www.pcc.org.uk/complaints/form.html].

THE CHARTER COMMISSIONER

If, at the end of the process, you have concerns about the way your complaint has been handled by the Commission and its staff, you should write – within one month of being told the outcome of your complaint – to the independent Charter Commissioner.

He will investigate your concerns and report any finding and recommendations to the Commission. He cannot investigate complaints about the substance of a decision made by the PCC.

Appendix 3

DEALING WITH THE MEDIA

Reproduced with the kind permission of the Press Complaints Commission.

GOVERNMENT, CITIZENS AND RIGHTS: DEALING WITH THE MEDIA

Following a major event in which people have died, press interest in survivors and bereaved families can be intense. Everyone reacts to this interest in different ways – some find the press a valuable way of bringing issues that are concerning them to light, while others prefer no contact. In either case, there are rules and standards the press should follow and help available if you're having problems.

Standards for journalists

Journalists are under an obligation to respect the position of bereaved people and survivors under the Press Complaints Commission (PCC) Code of Practice which states that:

> 'In cases involving personal grief and shock, enquiries and approaches must be made with sympathy and discretion and publication handled sensitively.'

The full code can be found on the Press Complaints Commission website.

[See Appendix 1]

If you do NOT wish to speak to the media

You are under no obligation to speak to the media. Tell them you do not want to speak to them, perhaps saying something like:

> 'I do not wish to speak to the media about this issue. I will not be speaking to you or any other journalist about it. I understand that under the Press Complaints Commission Code of Practice you must not persist in contacting me if I have asked you to stop.'

Unfortunately, this may not be the end of the story; so, for example, if a journalist, paper or TV channel has your phone number, they may continue to ring you. Be consistent and repeat what you have told them. You may also want to consider getting an answering machine; or for a friend, neighbour or relative to answer the phone for you.

If you still feel that you are being harassed, contact the Press Complaints Commission immediately. Their address is:

Press Complaints Commission
Halton House
20/23 Holborn
London EC1N 2JD

Helpline: 0845 600 2757; or 0131 220 6652 (if calling from Scotland); 0292 039 5570 (if calling from Wales).

Email: complaints@pcc.org.uk

Similarly, if the media turn up at your home you are under no obligation to admit them. If you do not wish to answer your door, pin a short note to it saying that you do not wish to speak to journalists and do not want to be disturbed.

If you have been assigned a Police Family Liaison Officer you may want to inform them of any problems you encounter with the media. Otherwise, contact details for your local police can be found by using the link below.

Police services in the UK

If you DO wish to speak to the media

You should consider the following if you decide you do wish to speak to the media:

- always make a note of the person's name and contact phone number at the outset

- consider appointing somebody as a spokesperson for you/your family – this could be a relative or friend or your solicitor. Some support groups have appointed media liaison people who will field questions on behalf of the support group

- don't do anything in a hurry, whatever the journalist says about deadlines. Ask them what they want to talk to you about; ask them to write down the questions they want to ask you; give yourself time to think about what you want to say; write down your answers; ask the journalist to ring you back at a specified time

- ask if you can see what they wish to quote from you before it goes to press – they may not do this, but it will alert them to your concerns about what they are going to publish

- never say anything 'off the record' unless both you and the journalist have a shared understanding of what this means

- remember that a journalist is entitled to report anything you say, so don't mistake them for counsellors or friends

- bring the conversation to a close if you are uncomfortable

Photographs

Sometimes journalists will ask for photographs of you, your loved one, and your family. You may wish to provide these, but remember that you are under no obligation to do so. If you do, ensure that you have a copy and ask for the photographs and any other personal items that you pass on to be returned.

Appendix 4

USEFUL ADDRESSES

It should be noted that the following are, except where briefly referred to in Chapter 28, beyond the scope of the book.

A THE AUTHORS' LICENSING AND COLLECTING SOCIETY LIMITED

The Authors' Licensing and Collecting Society Limited represents all UK writers and aims to ensure writers are fairly compensated for any works that are copied or broadcast and also deals with some foreign public lending rights.

Their contact address is:

The Authors' Licensing and Collecting Society Limited
The Writers' House
13 Haydon Street
London
EC3N 1DB

Telephone: 020 7264 5700
Fax: 020 7264 5755
Website: www.alcs.co.uk

B THE SOCIETY OF AUTHORS

The Society of Authors represents the interests of professional writers. They deal with any query relating to the business of writing. Their services include the confidential, individual vetting of contracts and help with professional disputes.

Their contact address is:

The Society of Authors
84 Drayton Gardens
London
SW10 9SB

Telephone: 020 7373 6642
Fax: 020 7373 5768
Website: www.societyofauthors.org

C THE WRITERS' GUILD OF GREAT BRITAIN

The Writers Guild of Great Britain is the trade union representing writers in TV, radio, theatre, books, poetry, film and video games.

Their contact address is:

The Writers' Guild of Great Britain
15 Britannia Street
London
WC1X 9JN

Telephone: 020 7833 0777
Fax: 020 7833 4777
Website: www.writersguild.org.uk

D THE PUBLISHERS ASSOCIATION

The Publishers Association is the leading trade association serving book, journal and electronic publishers in the UK. Their core service is the representation and lobbying about copyright, rights and other matters relevant to their members who represent roughly 80% of the industry by turnover.

Their contact address is:

The Publishers Association
29b Montague Street
London
WC1B 5BW

Telephone: 020 7691 9191
Fax: 020 7691 9199
Website: www.publishers.org.uk

E PUBLISHERS LICENSING SOCIETY

The sole objective of the Publishers Licensing Society is to serve the UK publishing industry by working to protect publishers' rights and to lead on industry-wide initiatives involving rights management and collective licensing.

Their contact address is:

Publishers Licensing Society
37–41 Gower Street
London
WC1E 6HH

Telephone: 020 7299 7730
Fax: 020 7299 7780
Website: www.pls.org.uk

F THE COPYRIGHT LICENSING AGENCY

The Copyright Licensing Agency licenses organisations to photocopy and scan from magazines, books, journals and digital publications on behalf of authors, publishers and visual creators. It was set up in 1983 by the Authors' Licensing and Collecting Society Limited and the Publishers Licensing Society to perform collective licensing on their behalf and provides a fair and effective way of collecting fees due to authors and publishers for the reproduction of their work.

Their contact address is:

The Copyright Licensing Agency
Head Office
Saffron House
6–10 Kirby Street
London
EC1N 8TS

Telephone: 020 7400 3100
Fax: 020 7400 3101
Website: www.cla.co.uk

G PUBLIC LENDING RIGHT

The Public Lending Right is the right for authors, editors, illustrators, translators and revisers to receive payment under the Public Lending Right legislation for the loan of their books by public libraries. To qualify for payment applicants must apply to register their books with Public Lending Right.

Their contact address is:

Public Lending Right
Richard House
Sorbonne Close
Stockton-on-Tees
TS17 6DA

Telephone: 01642 604699
Fax: 01642 615641
Website: www.plr.uk.com

It is suggested the reader visits the websites of the above bodies for further information as to the advice and services which they offer to their members.

H THE SOCIETY OF EDITORS

The Society of Editors has more than 400 members in national, regional and local newspapers, magazines, broadcasting and new media, journalism, education and media law. It campaigns for media freedom, self regulation, the public's right to know and the maintainance of standards in journalism.

Their contact address is:

The Society of Editors
University Centre
Mill Lane
Cambridge
CB2 1RU

Telephone: 01223 304080
Fax: 01223 304090
Website: www.societyofeditors.org

Appendix 5

STATUTES

DEFAMATION ACT 1952

(1952 c 66)

1 ...

Amendments—Repealed by the Broadcasting Act 1990, s 203(3), Sch 21

2 Slander affecting official, professional or business reputation

In an action for slander in respect of words calculated to disparage the plaintiff in any office, profession, calling, trade or business held or carried on by him at the time of the publication, it shall not be necessary to allege or prove special damage, whether or not the words are spoken of the plaintiff in the way of his office, profession, calling, trade or business.

3 Slander of title, etc

(1) In an action for slander of title, slander of goods or other malicious falsehood, it shall not be necessary to allege or prove special damage –

(a) if the words upon which the action is founded are calculated to cause pecuniary damage to the plaintiff and are published in writing or other permanent form; or

(b) if the said words are calculated to cause pecuniary damage to the plaintiff in respect of any office, profession, calling, trade or business held or carried on by him at the time of the publication.

(2) Section one of this Act shall apply for the purposes of this section as it applies for the purposes of the law of libel and slander.

4 ...

Amendments—Repealed by the Defamation Act 1996, s 16, Sch 2

5 Justification

In an action for libel or slander in respect of words containing two or more distinct charges against the plaintiff, a defence of justification shall not fail by reason only that the truth of every charge is not proved if the words not proved to be true do not materially injure the plaintiff's reputation having regard to the truth of the remaining charges.

6 Fair comment

In an action for libel or slander in respect of words consisting partly of allegations of fact and partly of expression of opinion, a defence of fair comment shall not fail by reason only that the truth of every allegation of fact is not proved if the expression of opinion is fair comment having regard to such of the facts alleged or referred to in the words complained of as are proved.

7 ...

Amendments—Repealed by the Defamation Act 1996, s 16, Sch 2

8 ...

Amendments—Repealed by the Defamation Act 1996, s 16, Sch 2

9 Extension of certain defences to broadcasting

(1) Section three of the Parliamentary Papers Act 1840 (which confers protection in respect of proceedings for printing extracts from or abstracts of parliamentary papers) shall have effect as if the reference to printing included a reference to broadcasting by means of wireless telegraphy.

(2)–(3) ...

Amendments—Repealed by the Defamation Act 1996, s 16, Sch 2

10 Limitation on privilege at elections

A defamatory statement published by or on behalf of a candidate in any election to a local government authority, to the National Assembly for Wales,] [to the Scottish Parliament] or to Parliament shall not be deemed to be published on a privileged occasion on the ground that it is material to a question in issue in the election, whether or not the person by whom it is published is qualified to vote at the election.

Amendments—Government of Wales Act 2006, s 160(1), Sch 10, para 5; Scotland Act 1998, s 125, Sch 8, para 10.

11 Agreements for indemnity

An agreement for indemnifying any person against civil liability for libel in respect of the publication of any matter shall not be unlawful unless at the time of the publication that person knows that the matter is defamatory, and does not reasonably believe there is a good defence to any action brought upon it.

12 Evidence of other damages recovered by plaintiff

In any action for libel or slander the defendant may give evidence in mitigation of damages that the plaintiff has recovered damages, or has brought actions for damages, for libel or slander in respect of the publication of words to the same effect as the words on which the action is founded, or has received or agreed to receive compensation in respect of any such publication.

13 Consolidation of actions for slander, etc

Section five of the Law of Libel Amendment Act 1888 (which provides for the consolidation, on the application of the defendants, of two or more actions for libel by the same plaintiff) shall apply to actions for slander and to actions for slander of title, slander of goods or other malicious falsehood as it applies to actions for libel; and references in that section to the same, or substantially the same, libel shall be construed accordingly

14 Application of Act to Scotland

This Act shall apply to Scotland subject to the following modifications, that is to say: –

   (a)   sections one, two, eight and thirteen shall be omitted;

   (b)   for section three there shall be substituted the following section –

> **3 Actions for verbal injury**
>
> In any action for verbal injury it shall not be necessary for the pursuer to aver or prove special damage if the words on which the action is founded are calculated to cause pecuniary damage to the pursuer.';

       (c)   subsection (2) of section four shall have effect as if at the end thereof there were added the words 'Nothing in this subsection shall be held to entitle a defender to lead evidence of any fact specified in the declaration unless notice of his intention so to do has been given in the defences.'; and

       (d)   for any reference to libel, or to libel or slander, there shall be substituted a reference to defamation; the expression 'plaintiff' means pursuer; the expression 'defendant' means defender; for any reference to an affadavit made by any person there shall be substituted a reference to a written declaration signed by that person; for any reference to the High Court there shall be substituted a reference to the Court of Session or, if an action of defamation is depending in the sheriff court in respect of the publication in question, the sheriff; the expression 'costs' means expenses; and for any reference to a defence of justification there shall be substituted a reference to a defence of veritas.

15...

Amendments—Repealed by the Northern Ireland Constitution Act 1973, s 41(1), Sch 6, Pt I

16 Interpretation

(1) Any reference in this Act to words shall be construed as including a reference to pictures, visual images, gestures and other methods of signifying meaning.

(2) ...

(3) ...

(4) ...

Amendments—Repealed by the Cable and Broadcasting Act 1984, s 57(2), Sch 6; Defamation Act 1996, s 16, Sch 2.

17 Proceedings affected and saving

(1) This Act applies for the purposes of any proceedings begun after the commencement of this Act, whenever the cause of action arose, but does not affect any proceedings begun before the commencement of this Act.

(2) Nothing in this Act affects the law relating to criminal libel.

18 Short title, commencement, extent and repeals

(1) This Act may be cited as the Defamation Act 1952 and shall come into operation one month after the passing of this Act.

(2) This Act shall not extend to Northern Ireland.

(3)...

Amendments—Repealed by the Cable and Broadcasting Act 1984, s 57(2), Sch 6; Defamation Act 1996, s 16, Sch 2.

Schedule

Part I

...

Amendments—Repealed by the Defamation Act 1996, s 16, Sch 2.

Part 2

...

Amendments—Repealed by the Defamation Act 1996, s 16, Sch 2.

Part 3

...

Amendments—Repealed by the Defamation Act 1996, s 16, Sch 2.

DEFAMATION ACT 1996

(1996 c 31)

Responsibility for publication

1 Responsibility for publication

(1) In defamation proceedings a person has a defence if he shows that –

 (a) he was not the author, editor or publisher of the statement complained of,

 (b) he took reasonable care in relation to its publication, and

 (c) he did not know, and had no reason to believe, that what he did caused or contributed to the publication of a defamatory statement.

(2) For this purpose 'author', 'editor' and 'publisher' have the following meanings, which are further explained in subsection (3) –

 'author' means the originator of the statement, but does not include a person who did not intend that his statement be published at all;

 'editor' means a person having editorial or equivalent responsibility for the content of the statement or the decision to publish it; and

 'publisher' means a commercial publisher, that is, a person whose business is issuing material to the public, or a section of the public, who issues material containing the statement in the course of that business.

(3) A person shall not be considered the author, editor or publisher of a statement if he is only involved –

 (a) in printing, producing, distributing or selling printed material containing the statement;

 (b) in processing, making copies of, distributing, exhibiting or selling a film or sound recording (as defined in Part I of the Copyright, Designs and Patents Act 1988) containing the statement;

 (c) in processing, making copies of, distributing or selling any electronic medium in or on which the statement is recorded, or in operating or providing any equipment, system or service by means of which the statement is retrieved, copied, distributed or made available in electronic form;

 (d) as the broadcaster of a live programme containing the statement in circumstances in which he has no effective control over the maker of the statement;

 (e) as the operator of or provider of access to a communications system by means of which the statement is transmitted, or made available, by a person over whom he has no effective control.

In a case not within paragraphs (a) to (e) the court may have regard to those provisions by way of analogy in deciding whether a person is to be considered the author, editor or publisher of a statement.

(4) Employees or agents of an author, editor or publisher are in the same position as their employer or principal to the extent that they are responsible for the content of the statement or the decision to publish it.

(5) In determining for the purposes of this section whether a person took reasonable care, or had reason to believe that what he did caused or contributed to the publication of a defamatory statement, regard shall be had to –

(a)   the extent of his responsibility for the content of the statement or the decision to publish it,

(b)   the nature or circumstances of the publication, and

(c)   the previous conduct or character of the author, editor or publisher.

(6) This section does not apply to any cause of action which arose before the section came into force.

Offer to make amends

2 Offer to make amends

(1) A person who has published a statement alleged to be defamatory of another may offer to make amends under this section.

(2) The offer may be in relation to the statement generally or in relation to a specific defamatory meaning which the person making the offer accepts that the statement conveys ('a qualified offer').

(3) An offer to make amends –

(a)   must be in writing,

(b)   must be expressed to be an offer to make amends under section 2 of the Defamation Act 1996, and

(c)   must state whether it is a qualified offer and, if so, set out the defamatory meaning in relation to which it is made.

(4) An offer to make amends under this section is an offer –

(a)   to make a suitable correction of the statement complained of and a sufficient apology to the aggrieved party,

(b)   to publish the correction and apology in a manner that is reasonable and practicable in the circumstances, and

(c)   to pay to the aggrieved party such compensation (if any), and such costs, as may be agreed or determined to be payable.

The fact that the offer is accompanied by an offer to take specific steps does not affect the fact that an offer to make amends under this section is an offer to do all the things mentioned in paragraphs (a) to (c).

(5) An offer to make amends under this section may not be made by a person after serving a defence in defamation proceedings brought against him by the aggrieved party in respect of the publication in question.

(6) An offer to make amends under this section may be withdrawn before it is accepted; and a renewal of an offer which has been withdrawn shall be treated as a new offer.

3 Accepting an offer to make amends

(1) If an offer to make amends under section 2 is accepted by the aggrieved party, the following provisions apply.

(2) The party accepting the offer may not bring or continue defamation proceedings in respect of the publication concerned against the person making the offer, but he is entitled to enforce the offer to make amends, as follows.

(3) If the parties agree on the steps to be taken in fulfilment of the offer, the aggrieved party may apply to the court for an order that the other party fulfil his offer by taking the steps agreed.

(4) If the parties do not agree on the steps to be taken by way of correction, apology and publication, the party who made the offer may take such steps as he thinks appropriate, and may in particular –

(a) make the correction and apology by a statement in open court in terms approved by the court, and
(b) give an undertaking to the court as to the manner of their publication.

(5) If the parties do not agree on the amount to be paid by way of compensation, it shall be determined by the court on the same principles as damages in defamation proceedings.

The court shall take account of any steps taken in fulfilment of the offer and (so far as not agreed between the parties) of the suitability of the correction, the sufficiency of the apology and whether the manner of their publication was reasonable in the circumstances, and may reduce or increase the amount of compensation accordingly.

(6) If the parties do not agree on the amount to be paid by way of costs, it shall be determined by the court on the same principles as costs awarded in court proceedings.

(7) The acceptance of an offer by one person to make amends does not affect any cause of action against another person in respect of the same publication, subject as follows.

(8) In England and Wales or Northern Ireland, for the purposes of the Civil Liability (Contribution) Act 1978 –

(a) the amount of compensation paid under the offer shall be treated as paid in bona fide settlement or compromise of the claim; and
(b) where another person is liable in respect of the same damage (whether jointly or otherwise), the person whose offer to make amends was accepted is not required to pay by virtue of any contribution under section 1 of that Act a greater amount than the amount of the compensation payable in pursuance of the offer.

(9) In Scotland –

(a) subsection (2) of section 3 of the Law Reform (Miscellaneous Provisions) (Scotland) Act 1940 (right of one joint wrongdoer as respects another to recover contribution towards damages) applies in relation to compensation paid under an offer to make amends as it applies in relation to damages in an action to which that section applies; and
(b) where another person is liable in respect of the same damage (whether jointly or otherwise), the person whose offer to make amends was accepted is not required to pay by virtue of any contribution under section 3(2) of that Act a greater amount than the amount of compensation payable in pursuance of the offer.

(10) Proceedings under this section shall be heard and determined without a jury.

4 Failure to accept offer to make amends

(1) If an offer to make amends under section 2, duly made and not withdrawn, is not accepted by the aggrieved party, the following provisions apply.

(2) The fact that the offer was made is a defence (subject to subsection (3)) to defamation proceedings in respect of the publication in question by that party against the person making the offer.

A qualified offer is only a defence in respect of the meaning to which the offer related.

(3) There is no such defence if the person by whom the offer was made knew or had reason to believe that the statement complained of –

(a)   referred to the aggrieved party or was likely to be understood as referring to him, and

(b)   was both false and defamatory of that party;

but it shall be presumed until the contrary is shown that he did not know and had no reason to believe that was the case.

(4) The person who made the offer need not rely on it by way of defence, but if he does he may not rely on any other defence.

If the offer was a qualified offer, this applies only in respect of the meaning to which the offer related.

(5) The offer may be relied on in mitigation of damages whether or not it was relied on as a defence.

Limitation

5 Limitation of actions: England and Wales

(1)-(5) ...

(6) The amendments made by this section apply only to causes of action arising after the section comes into force.

Amendments—Sub-ss (1)–(5): substitute the Limitation Act 1980, ss 4A, 32A and amend ss 28, 36.

6 Limitation of actions: Northern Ireland

(1)–(4) ...

(5) The amendments made by this section apply only to causes of action arising after the section comes into force.

Amendments—Sub-ss (1)–(4): amend the Limitation (Northern Ireland) Order 1989, SI 1989/1339, arts 6, 48, 51.

The meaning of a statement

7 Ruling on the meaning of a statement

In defamation proceedings the court shall not be asked to rule whether a statement is arguably capable, as opposed to capable, of bearing a particular meaning or meanings attributed to it.

Summary disposal of claim

8 Summary disposal of claim

(1) In defamation proceedings the court may dispose summarily of the plaintiff's claim in accordance with the following provisions.

(2) The court may dismiss the plaintiff's claim if it appears to the court that it has no realistic prospect of success and there is no reason why it should be tried.

(3) The court may give judgment for the plaintiff and grant him summary relief (see section 9) if it appears to the court that there is no defence to the claim which has a realistic prospect of success, and that there is no other reason why the claim should be tried.

Unless the plaintiff asks for summary relief, the court shall not act under this subsection unless it is satisfied that summary relief will adequately compensate him for the wrong he has suffered.

(4) In considering whether a claim should be tried the court shall have regard to –

(a) whether all the persons who are or might be defendants in respect of the publication complained of are before the court;

(b) whether summary disposal of the claim against another defendant would be inappropriate;

(c) the extent to which there is a conflict of evidence;

(d) the seriousness of the alleged wrong (as regards the content of the statement and the extent of publication); and

(e) whether it is justifiable in the circumstances to proceed to a full trial.

(5) Proceedings under this section shall be heard and determined without a jury.

9 Meaning of summary relief

(1) For the purposes of section 8 (summary disposal of claim) 'summary relief' means such of the following as may be appropriate –

(a) a declaration that the statement was false and defamatory of the plaintiff;

(b) an order that the defendant publish or cause to be published a suitable correction and apology;

(c) damages not exceeding £10,000 or such other amount as may be prescribed by order of the Lord Chancellor;

(d) an order restraining the defendant from publishing or further publishing the matter complained of.

(2) The content of any correction and apology, and the time, manner, form and place of publication, shall be for the parties to agree.

If they cannot agree on the content, the court may direct the defendant to publish or cause to be published a summary of the court's judgment agreed by the parties or settled by the court in accordance with rules of court.

If they cannot agree on the time, manner, form or place of publication, the court may direct the defendant to take such reasonable and practicable steps as the court considers appropriate.

(2A) The Lord Chancellor must consult the Lord Chief Justice of England and Wales before making any order under subsection (1)(c) in relation to England and Wales.

(2B) The Lord Chancellor must consult the Lord Chief Justice of Northern Ireland before making any order under subsection (1)(c) in relation to Northern Ireland.

(2C) The Lord Chief Justice may nominate a judicial office holder (as defined in section 109(4) of the Constitutional Reform Act 2005) to exercise his functions under this section.

(2D) The Lord Chief Justice of Northern Ireland may nominate any of the following to exercise his functions under this section –

(a)   the holder of one of the offices listed in Schedule 1 to the Justice (Northern Ireland) Act 2002;

(b)   a Lord Justice of Appeal (as defined in section 88 of that Act).

(3) Any order under subsection (1)(c) shall be made by statutory instrument which shall be subject to annulment in pursuance of a resolution of either House of Parliament.

Amendments—Sub-ss (2A)–(2D): inserted by the Constitutional Reform Act 2005, s 15(1), Sch 4, Pt 1, para 255.

10 Summary disposal: rules of court

(1) Provision may be made by rules of court as to the summary disposal of the plaintiff's claim in defamation proceedings.

(2) Without prejudice to the generality of that power, provision may be made –

(a)   authorising a party to apply for summary disposal at any stage of the proceedings;

(b)   authorising the court at any stage of the proceedings –
   (i)   to treat any application, pleading or other step in the proceedings as an application for summary disposal, or
   (ii)   to make an order for summary disposal without any such application;

(c)   as to the time for serving pleadings or taking any other step in the proceedings in a case where there are proceedings for summary disposal;

(d)   requiring the parties to identify any question of law or construction which the court is to be asked to determine in the proceedings;

(e)   as to the nature of any hearing on the question of summary disposal, and in particular –
   (i)   authorising the court to order affidavits or witness statements to be prepared for use as evidence at the hearing, and
   (ii)   requiring the leave of the court for the calling of oral evidence, or the introduction of new evidence, at the hearing;

(f)   authorising the court to require a defendant to elect, at or before the hearing, whether or not to make an offer to make amends under section 2.

11 Summary disposal: application to Northern Ireland

In their application to Northern Ireland the provisions of sections 8 to 10 (summary disposal of claim) apply only to proceedings in the High Court.

Evidence of convictions

12 Evidence of convictions

(1) ...

The amendments made by this subsection apply only where the trial of the action begins after this section comes into force.

(2) ...

The amendments made by this subsection apply only for the purposes of an action begun after this section comes into force, whenever the cause of action arose.

(3) ...

The amendments made by this subsection apply only where the trial of the action begins after this section comes into force.

Amendments—Sub-s (1): words omitted amend the Civil Evidence Act 1968, s 13; Sub-s (2): words omitted amend the Law Reform (Miscellaneous Provisions) (Scotland) Act 1968, s 12; Sub-s (3): words omitted amend the Civil Evidence Act (Northern Ireland) 1971, s 9.

Evidence concerning proceedings in Parliament

13 Evidence concerning proceedings in Parliament

(1) Where the conduct of a person in or in relation to proceedings in Parliament is in issue in defamation proceedings, he may waive for the purposes of those proceedings, so far as concerns him, the protection of any enactment or rule of law which prevents proceedings in Parliament being impeached or questioned in any court or place out of Parliament.

(2) Where a person waives that protection –

    (a)   any such enactment or rule of law shall not apply to prevent evidence being given, questions being asked or statements, submissions, comments or findings being made about his conduct, and

    (b)   none of those things shall be regarded as infringing the privilege of either House of Parliament.

(3) The waiver by one person of that protection does not affect its operation in relation to another person who has not waived it.

(4) Nothing in this section affects any enactment or rule of law so far as it protects a person (including a person who has waived the protection referred to above) from legal liability for words spoken or things done in the course of, or for the purposes of or incidental to, any proceedings in Parliament.

(5) Without prejudice to the generality of subsection (4), that subsection applies to –

    (a)   the giving of evidence before either House or a committee;

    (b)   the presentation or submission of a document to either House or a committee;

    (c)   the preparation of a document for the purposes of or incidental to the transacting of any such business;

    (d)   the formulation, making or publication of a document, including a report, by or pursuant to an order of either House or a committee; and

    (e)   any communication with the Parliamentary Commissioner for Standards or any person having functions in connection with the registration of members' interests.

In this subsection 'a committee' means a committee of either House or a joint committee of both Houses of Parliament.

Statutory privilege

14 Reports of court proceedings absolutely privileged

(1) A fair and accurate report of proceedings in public before a court to which this section applies, if published contemporaneously with proceedings, is absolutely privileged.

(2) A report of proceedings which by an order of the court, or as a consequence of any statutory provision, is required to be postponed shall be treated as published contemporaneously if it is published as soon as practicable after publication is permitted.

(3) This section applies to –

(a)   any court in the United Kingdom,
(b)   the European Court of Justice or any court attached to that court,
(c)   the European Court of Human Rights, and
(d)   any international criminal tribunal established by the Security Council of the United Nations or by an international agreement to which the United Kingdom is a party.

In paragraph (a) 'court' includes any tribunal or body exercising the judicial power of the State.

(4)...

Amendments—Sub-s (4): amends the Rehabilitation of Offenders Act 1974, s 8(6) and the Rehabilitation of Offenders (Northern Ireland) Order 1978, SI 1978/1908, art 9(6).

15 Reports, &c protected by qualified privilege

(1) The publication of any report or other statement mentioned in Schedule 1 to this Act is privileged unless the publication is shown to be made with malice, subject as follows.

(2) In defamation proceedings in respect of the publication of a report or other statement mentioned in Part II of that Schedule, there is no defence under this section if the plaintiff shows that the defendant –

(a)   was requested by him to publish in a suitable manner a reasonable letter or statement by way of explanation or contradiction, and
(b)   refused or neglected to do so.

For this purpose 'in a suitable manner' means in the same manner as the publication complained of or in a manner that is adequate and reasonable in the circumstances.

(3) This section does not apply to the publication to the public, or a section of the public, of matter which is not of public concern and the publication of which is not for the public benefit.

(4) Nothing in this section shall be construed –

(a)   as protecting the publication of matter the publication of which is prohibited by law, or
(b)   as limiting or abridging any privilege subsisting apart from this section.

Supplementary provisions

16 Repeals

The enactments specified in Schedule 2 are repealed to the extent specified.

17 Interpretation

(1) In this Act –

'publication' and 'publish', in relation to a statement, have the meaning they have for the purposes of the law of defamation generally, but 'publisher' is specially defined for the purposes of section 1;

'statement' means words, pictures, visual images, gestures or any other method of signifying meaning; and

'statutory provision' means –

(a)   a provision contained in an Act or in subordinate legislation within the meaning of the Interpretation Act 1978,

(aa)   a provision contained in an Act of the Scottish Parliament or in an instrument made under such an Act, or

(b)   a statutory provision within the meaning given by section 1(f) of the Interpretation Act (Northern Ireland) 1954.

(2) In this Act as it applies to proceedings in Scotland –

'costs' means expenses; and

'plaintiff' and 'defendant' mean pursuer and defender.

Amendments—Definition inserted by the Scotland Act 1998, s 125, Sch 8, para 33(2).

General provisions

18 Extent

(1) The following provisions of this Act extend to England and Wales –

section 1 (responsibility for publication),
sections 2 to 4 (offer to make amends), except section 3(9),
section 5 (time limit for actions for defamation or malicious falsehood),
section 7 (ruling on the meaning of a statement),
sections 8 to 10 (summary disposal of claim),
section 12(1) (evidence of convictions),
section 13 (evidence concerning proceedings in Parliament),
sections 14 and 15 and Schedule 1 (statutory privilege),
section 16 and Schedule 2 (repeals) so far as relating to enactments extending to England and Wales,
section 17 (interpretation),

this subsection,

section 19 (commencement) so far as relating to provisions which extend to England and Wales, and

section 20 (short title and saving).

(2) The following provisions of this Act extend to Scotland –

section 1 (responsibility for publication),
sections 2 to 4 (offer to make amends), except section 3(8),
section 12(2) (evidence of convictions),
section 13 (evidence concerning proceedings in Parliament),
sections 14 and 15 and Schedule 1 (statutory privilege),
section 16 and Schedule 2 (repeals) so far as relating to enactments extending to Scotland,
section 17 (interpretation),
this subsection,

section 19 (commencement) so far as relating to provisions which extend to Scotland, and
section 20 (short title and saving).

(3) The following provisions of this Act extend to Northern Ireland –

section 1 (responsibility for publication),
sections 2 to 4 (offer to make amends), except section 3(9),
section 6 (time limit for actions for defamation or malicious falsehood),
section 7 (ruling on the meaning of a statement),
sections 8 to 11 (summary disposal of claim),
section 12(3) (evidence of convictions),
section 13 (evidence concerning proceedings in Parliament),
sections 14 and 15 and Schedule 1 (statutory privilege),
section 16 and Schedule 2 (repeals) so far as relating to enactments extending to Northern Ireland,
section 17(1) (interpretation),
this subsection,
section 19 (commencement) so far as relating to provisions which extend to Northern Ireland, and
section 20 (short title and saving).

19 Commencement

(1) Sections 18 to 20 (extent, commencement and other general provisions) come into force on Royal Assent.

(2) The following provisions of this Act come into force at the end of the period of two months beginning with the day on which this Act is passed –

section 1 (responsibility for publication),
sections 5 and 6 (time limit for actions for defamation or malicious falsehood),
section 12 (evidence of convictions),
section 13 (evidence concerning proceedings in Parliament),
section 16 and the repeals in Schedule 2, so far as consequential on the above provisions, and
section 17 (interpretation), so far as relating to the above provisions.

(3) The provisions of this Act otherwise come into force on such day as may be appointed –

(a)   for England and Wales or Northern Ireland, by order of the Lord Chancellor, or
(b)   for Scotland, by order of the Secretary of State,

and different days may be appointed for different purposes.

(4) Any such order shall be made by statutory instrument and may contain such transitional provisions as appear to the Lord Chancellor or Secretary of State to be appropriate.

20 Short title and saving

(1) This Act may be cited as the Defamation Act 1996.

(2) Nothing in this Act affects the law relating to criminal libel.

Schedule 1
Qualified Privilege

Section 15

PART I
STATEMENTS HAVING QUALIFIED PRIVILEGE WITHOUT EXPLANATION OR CONTRADICTION

1

A fair and accurate report of proceedings in public of a legislature anywhere in the world.

2

A fair and accurate report of proceedings in public before a court anywhere in the world.

3

A fair and accurate report of proceedings in public of a person appointed to hold a public inquiry by a government or legislature anywhere in the world.

4

A fair and accurate report of proceedings in public anywhere in the world of an international organisation or an international conference.

5

A fair and accurate copy of or extract from any register or other document required by law to be open to public inspection.

6

A notice or advertisement published by or on the authority of a court, or of a judge or officer of a court, anywhere in the world.

7

A fair and accurate copy of or extract from matter published by or on the authority of a government or legislature anywhere in the world.

8

A fair and accurate copy of or extract from matter published anywhere in the world by an international organisation or an international conference.

PART II
STATEMENTS PRIVILEGED SUBJECT TO EXPLANATION OR CONTRADICTION

9

(1) A fair and accurate copy of or extract from a notice or other matter issued for the information of the public by or on behalf of –

    (a)   a legislature in any member State or the European Parliament;

    (b)   the government of any member State, or any authority performing governmental functions in any member State or part of a member State, or the European Commission;

    (c)   an international organisation or international conference.

(2) In this paragraph 'governmental functions' includes police functions.

10

A fair and accurate copy of or extract from a document made available by a court in any member State or the European Court of Justice (or any court attached to that court), or by a judge or officer of any such court.

11

(1) A fair and accurate report of proceedings at any public meeting or sitting in the United Kingdom of –

    (a)   a local authority or local authority committee;

    (aa)   in the case of a local authority which are operating executive arrangements, the executive of that authority or a committee of that executive;

    (b)   a justice or justices of the peace acting otherwise than as a court exercising judicial authority;

    (c)   a commission, tribunal, committee or person appointed for the purposes of any inquiry by any statutory provision, by Her Majesty or by a Minister of the Crown a member of the Scottish Executive, the Welsh Ministers or the Counsel General to the Welsh Assembly Government or a Northern Ireland Department;

    (d)   a person appointed by a local authority to hold a local inquiry in pursuance of any statutory provision;

    (e)   any other tribunal, board, committee or body constituted by or under, and exercising functions under, any statutory provision.

(1A) In the case of a local authority which are operating executive arrangements, a fair and accurate record of any decision made by any member of the executive where that record is required to be made and available for public inspection by virtue of section 22 of the Local Government Act 2000 or of any provision in regulations made under that section.

(2) In sub-paragraph (1)(a)-In sub-paragraphs (1)(a), (1)(aa) and (1A) –

'local authority' means –

    (a)   in relation to England and Wales, a principal council within the meaning of the Local Government Act 1972, any body falling within any paragraph of section 100J(1) of that Act or an authority or body to which the Public Bodies (Admission to Meetings) Act 1960 applies,

(b)   in relation to Scotland, a council constituted under section 2 of the Local Government etc (Scotland) Act 1994 or an authority or body to which the Public Bodies (Admission to Meetings) Act 1960 applies,

(c)   in relation to Northern Ireland, any authority or body to which sections 23 to 27 of the Local Government Act (Northern Ireland) 1972 apply; and

'local authority committee' means any committee of a local authority or of local authorities, and includes –

(a)   any committee or sub-committee in relation to which sections 100A to 100D of the Local Government Act 1972 apply by virtue of section 100E of that Act (whether or not also by virtue of section 100J of that Act), and

(b)   any committee or sub-committee in relation to which sections 50A to 50D of the Local Government (Scotland) Act 1973 apply by virtue of section 50E of that Act.

(2A) In sub-paragraphs (1) and (1A) –

'executive' and 'executive arrangements' have the same meaning as in Part II of the Local Government Act 2000.

(3) A fair and accurate report of any corresponding proceedings in any of the Channel Islands or the Isle of Man or in another member State.

Amendments—SI 2001/2237; SI 2002/808; SI 2002/1057.

12

(1) A fair and accurate report of proceedings at any public meeting held in a member State.

(2) In this paragraph a 'public meeting' means a meeting bona fide and lawfully held for a lawful purpose and for the furtherance or discussion of a matter of public concern, whether admission to the meeting is general or restricted.

13

(1) A fair and accurate report of proceedings at a general meeting of a UK public company.

(2) A fair and accurate copy of or extract from any document circulated to members of a UK public company –

(a)   by or with the authority of the board of directors of the company,

(b)   by the auditors of the company, or

(c)   by any member of the company in pursuance of a right conferred by any statutory provision.

(3) A fair and accurate copy of or extract from any document circulated to members of a UK public company which relates to the appointment, resignation, retirement or dismissal of directors of the company.

(4) In this paragraph 'UK public company' means –

(a)   a public company within the meaning of section 4(2) of the Companies Act 2006, or

(b)   a body corporate incorporated by or registered under any other statutory provision, or by Royal Charter, or formed in pursuance of letters patent.

(5) A fair and accurate report of proceedings at any corresponding meeting of, or copy of or extract from any corresponding document circulated to members of, a public company formed under the law of any of the Channel Islands or the Isle of Man or of another member State.

Amendments—SI 2009/1941.

14

A fair and accurate report of any finding or decision of any of the following descriptions of association, formed in the United Kingdom or another member State, or of any committee or governing body of such an association –

(a) an association formed for the purpose of promoting or encouraging the exercise of or interest in any art, science, religion or learning, and empowered by its constitution to exercise control over or adjudicate on matters of interest or concern to the association, or the actions or conduct of any person subject to such control or adjudication;

(b) an association formed for the purpose of promoting or safeguarding the interests of any trade, business, industry or profession, or of the persons carrying on or engaged in any trade, business, industry or profession, and empowered by its constitution to exercise control over or adjudicate upon matters connected with that trade, business, industry or profession, or the actions or conduct of those persons;

(c) an association formed for the purpose of promoting or safeguarding the interests of a game, sport or pastime to the playing or exercise of which members of the public are invited or admitted, and empowered by its constitution to exercise control over or adjudicate upon persons connected with or taking part in the game, sport or pastime;

(d) an association formed for the purpose of promoting charitable objects or other objects beneficial to the community and empowered by its constitution to exercise control over or to adjudicate on matters of interest or concern to the association, or the actions or conduct of any person subject to such control or adjudication.

15

(1) A fair and accurate report of, or copy of or extract from, any adjudication, report, statement or notice issued by a body, officer or other person designated for the purposes of this paragraph –

(a) for England and Wales or Northern Ireland, by order of the Lord Chancellor, and

(b) for Scotland, by order of the Secretary of State.

(2) An order under this paragraph shall be made by statutory instrument which shall be subject to annulment in pursuance of a resolution of either House of Parliament.

PART III
SUPPLEMENTARY PROVISIONS

16

(1) In this Schedule –

'court' includes any tribunal or body exercising the judicial power of the State;

'international conference' means a conference attended by representatives of two or more governments;

'international organisation' means an organisation of which two or more governments are members, and includes any committee or other subordinate body of such an organisation; and

'legislature' includes a local legislature.

(2) References in this Schedule to a member State include any European dependent territory of a member State.

(3) In paragraphs 2 and 6 'court' includes –

(a) the European Court of Justice (or any court attached to that court) and the Court of Auditors of the European Communities,

(b) the European Court of Human Rights,

(c) any international criminal tribunal established by the Security Council of the United Nations or by an international agreement to which the United Kingdom is a party, and

(d) the International Court of Justice and any other judicial or arbitral tribunal deciding matters in dispute between States.

(4) In paragraphs 1, 3 and 7 'legislature' includes the European Parliament.

17

(1) Provision may be made by order identifying –

(a) for the purposes of paragraph 11, the corresponding proceedings referred to in sub-paragraph (3);

(b) for the purposes of paragraph 13, the corresponding meetings and documents referred to in sub-paragraph (5).

(2) An order under this paragraph may be made –

(a) for England and Wales or Northern Ireland, by the Lord Chancellor, and

(b) for Scotland, by the Secretary of State.

(3) An order under this paragraph shall be made by statutory instrument which shall be subject to annulment in pursuance of a resolution of either House of Parliament.

Schedule 2
Repeals

Section 16

Chapter	Short title	Extent of repeal
1888 c 64	Law of Libel Amendment Act 1888	Section 3
1952 c 66	Defamation Act 1952	Section 4Sections 7, 8 and 9(2) and (3). Section 16(2) and (3) The Schedule

Chapter	Short title	Extent of repeal
1955 c 20	Revision of the Army and Air Force Acts (Transitional Provisions) Act 1955	In Schedule 2, the entry relating to the Defamation Act 1952
1955 c 11(NI)	Defamation Act (Northern Ireland) 1955	Section 4
		Sections 7, 8 and 9(2) and (3) Section 14(2) The Schedule
1972 c 9 (NI)	Local Government Act (Northern Ireland) 1972	In Schedule 8, paragraph 12
1981 c 49	Contempt of Court Act 1981	In section 4(3), the words 'and of section 3 of the Law of Libel Amendment Act 1888 (privilege)'
1981 c 61	British Nationality Act 1981	In Schedule 7, the entries relating to the Defamation Act 1952 and the Defamation Act (Northern Ireland) 1955
1985 c 43	Local Government (Access to Information) Act 1985	In Schedule 2, paragraphs 2 and 3
1985 c 61	Administration of Justice Act 1985	Section 57
SI 1986/594 (NI 3)	Education and Libraries (Northern Ireland) Order 1986	Article 97(2)
SI 1990 c 42	Broadcasting Act 1990	Section 166(3) In Schedule 20, paragraphs 2 and 3

HUMAN RIGHTS ACT 1998

(1998 c 42)

Introduction

1 The Convention Rights

(1) In this Act, 'the Convention rights' means the rights and fundamental freedoms set out in –

(a) Articles 2 to 12 and 14 of the Convention, and
(b) Articles 1 to 3 of the First Protocol, and
(c) Article 1 of the Thirteenth Protocol,

as read with Articles 16 to 18 of the Convention.

(2) Those Articles are to have effect for the purposes of this Act subject to any designated derogation or reservation (as to which see sections 14 and 15).

(3) The Articles are set out in Schedule 1.

(4) The Secretary of State may by order make such amendments to this Act as he considers appropriate to reflect the effect, in relation to the United Kingdom, of a protocol.

(5) In subsection (4) 'protocol' means a protocol to the Convention –

(a) which the United Kingdom has ratified; or
(b) which the United Kingdom has signed with a view to ratification.

(6) No amendment may be made by an order under subsection (4) so as to come into force before the protocol concerned is in force in relation to the United Kingdom.

Amendments—SI 2003/1887; SI 2004/1574.

2 Interpretation of Convention rights

(1) A court or tribunal determining a question which has arisen under this Act in connection with a Convention right must take into account any –

(a) judgment, decision, declaration or advisory opinion of the European Court of Human Rights,
(b) opinion of the Commission given in a report adopted under Article 31 of the Convention,
(c) decision of the Commission in connection with Article 26 or 27(2) of the Convention, or
(d) decision of the Committee of Ministers taken under Article 46 of the Convention,

whenever made or given, so far as, in the opinion of the court or tribunal, it is relevant to the proceedings in which that question has arisen.

(2) Evidence of any judgment, decision, declaration or opinion of which account may have to be taken under this section is to be given in proceedings before any court or tribunal in such manner as may be provided by rules.

(3) In this section 'rules' means rules of court or, in the case of proceedings before a tribunal, rules made for the purposes of this section –

(a) by the Lord Chancellor or the Secretary of State, in relation to any proceedings outside Scotland;

(b) by the Secretary of State, in relation to proceedings in Scotland; or

(c) by a Northern Ireland department, in relation to proceedings before a tribunal in Northern Ireland –

(i) which deals with transferred matters; and

(ii) for which no rules made under paragraph (a) are in force.

Amendments—SI 2003/1887; SI 2005/3429.

Legislation

3 Interpretation of legislation

(1) So far as it is possible to do so, primary legislation and subordinate legislation must be read and given effect in a way which is compatible with the Convention rights.

(2) This section –

(a) applies to primary legislation and subordinate legislation whenever enacted;

(b) does not affect the validity, continuing operation or enforcement of any incompatible primary legislation; and

(c) does not affect the validity, continuing operation or enforcement of any incompatible subordinate legislation if (disregarding any possibility of revocation) primary legislation prevents removal of the incompatibility.

4 Declaration of incompatibility

(1) Subsection (2) applies in any proceedings in which a court determines whether a provision of primary legislation is compatible with a Convention right.

(2) If the court is satisfied that the provision is incompatible with a Convention right, it may make a declaration of that incompatibility.

(3) Subsection (4) applies in any proceedings in which a court determines whether a provision of subordinate legislation, made in the exercise of a power conferred by primary legislation, is compatible with a Convention right.

(4) If the court is satisfied –

(a) that the provision is incompatible with a Convention right, and

(b) that (disregarding any possibility of revocation) the primary legislation concerned prevents removal of the incompatibility,

it may make a declaration of that incompatibility.

(5) In this section 'court' means –

(a) the Supreme Court;

(b) the Judicial Committee of the Privy Council;

(c) the Court Martial Appeal Court;

(d) in Scotland, the High Court of Justiciary sitting otherwise than as a trial court or the Court of Session;

(e) in England and Wales or Northern Ireland, the High Court or the Court of Appeal.

(f) the Court of Protection, in any matter being dealt with by the President of the Family Division, the Vice-Chancellor or a puisne judge of the High Court.

(6) A declaration under this section ('a declaration of incompatibility') –

(a)   does not affect the validity, continuing operation or enforcement of the provision in respect of which it is given; and

(b)   is not binding on the parties to the proceedings in which it is made.

Amendments—Mental Capacity Act 2005, s 67(1), Sch 6, para 43; Constitutional Reform Act 2005, s 40(4), Sch 9, Pt 1, para 66(1), (2); Armed Forces Act 2006, s 378(1), Sch 16, para 156.

5 Right of Crown to intervene

(1) Where a court is considering whether to make a declaration of incompatibility, the Crown is entitled to notice in accordance with rules of court.

(2) In any case to which subsection (1) applies –

(a)   a Minister of the Crown, or
(b)   a member of the Scottish Executive,
(c)   a Northern Ireland Minister,
(d)   a Northern Ireland department,

is entitled, on an application made to the court in accordance with rules of court, to be joined as a party to the proceedings.

(3) An application under subsection (2) may be made at any time during the proceedings.

(4) A person who has been made a party to criminal proceedings (other than in Scotland) as the result of an application under subsection (2) may, with leave, appeal to the Supreme Court against any declaration of incompatibility made in the proceedings.

(5) In subsection (4) –

'criminal proceedings' includes all proceedings before the Court Martial Appeal Court; and
'leave' means leave granted by the court making the declaration of incompatibility or by the Supreme Court.

Amendments—Constitutional Reform Act 2005, s 40(4), Sch 9, Pt 1, para 66(1), (3); Armed Forces Act 2006, s 383(2).

Public authorities

6 Acts of public authorities

(1) It is unlawful for a public authority to act in a way which is incompatible with a Convention right.

(2) Subsection (1) does not apply to an act if –

(a)   as the result of one or more provisions of primary legislation, the authority could not have acted differently; or
(b)   in the case of one or more provisions of, or made under, primary legislation which cannot be read or given effect in a way which is compatible with the Convention rights, the authority was acting so as to give effect to or enforce those provisions.

(3) In this section, 'public authority' includes –

(a)   a court or tribunal, and
(b)   any person certain of whose functions are functions of a public nature,

but does not include either House of Parliament or a person exercising functions in connection with proceedings in Parliament.

(4) ...

(5) In relation to a particular act, a person is not a public authority by virtue only of subsection (3)(b) if the nature of the act is private.

(6) 'An act' includes a failure to act but does not include a failure to –

(a)   introduce in, or lay before, Parliament a proposal for legislation; or
(b)   make any primary legislation or remedial order.

Amendments—Constitutional Reform Act 2005, ss 40(4), 146, Sch 9, Pt 1, para 66(1), (4), Sch 18, Pt 5.

7 Proceedings

(1) A person who claims that a public authority has acted (or proposes to act) in a way which is made unlawful by section 6(1) may –

(a)   bring proceedings against the authority under this Act in the appropriate court or tribunal, or
(b)   rely on the Convention right or rights concerned in any legal proceedings,

but only if he is (or would be) a victim of the unlawful act.

(2) In subsection (1)(a) 'appropriate court or tribunal' means such court or tribunal as may be determined in accordance with rules; and proceedings against an authority includes a counterclaim or similar proceeding.

(3) If the proceedings are brought on an application for judicial review, the applicant is to be taken to have a sufficient interest in relation to the unlawful act only if he is, or would be, a victim of that act.

(4) If the proceedings are made by way of a petition for judicial review in Scotland, the applicant shall be taken to have title and interest to sue in relation to the unlawful act only if he is, or would be, a victim of that act.

(5) Proceedings under subsection (1)(a) must be brought before the end of –

(a)   the period of one year beginning with the date on which the act complained of took place; or
(b)   such longer period as the court or tribunal considers equitable having regard to all the circumstances,

but that is subject to any rule imposing a stricter time limit in relation to the procedure in question.

(6) In subsection (1)(b) 'legal proceedings' includes –

(a)   proceedings brought by or at the instigation of a public authority; and
(b)   an appeal against the decision of a court or tribunal.

(7) For the purposes of this section, a person is a victim of an unlawful act only if he would be a victim for the purposes of Article 34 of the Convention if proceedings were brought in the European Court of Human Rights in respect of that act.

(8) Nothing in this Act creates a criminal offence.

(9) In this section 'rules' means –

    (a)   in relation to proceedings before a court or tribunal outside Scotland, rules made by the Lord Chancellor the Secretary of State for the purposes of this section or rules of court,

    (b)   in relation to proceedings before a court or tribunal in Scotland, rules made by the Secretary of State for those purposes,

    (c)   in relation to proceedings before a tribunal in Northern Ireland –

        (i)   which deals with transferred matters; and

        (ii)   for which no rules made under paragraph (a) are in force,

rules made by a Northern Ireland department for those purposes,

and includes provision made by order under section 1 of the Courts and Legal Services Act 1990.

(10) In making rules regard must be had to section 9.

(11) The Minister who has power to make rules in relation to a particular tribunal may, to the extent he considers it necessary to ensure that the tribunal can provide an appropriate remedy in relation to an act (or proposed act) of a public authority which is (or would be) unlawful as a result of section 6(1), by order add to –

    (a)   the relief or remedies which the tribunal may grant; or

    (b)   the grounds on which it may grant any of them.

(12) An order made under subsection (11) may contain such incidental, supplemental, consequential or transitional provision as the Minister making it considers appropriate.

(13) 'The Minister' includes the Northern Ireland department concerned.

Amendments—SI 2003/1887; SI 2005/3429.

8 Judicial remedies

(1) In relation to any act (or proposed act) of a public authority which the court finds is (or would be) unlawful, it may grant such relief or remedy, or make such order, within its jurisdiction as it considers just and appropriate.

(2) But damages may be awarded only by a court which has power to award damages, or to order the payment of compensation, in civil proceedings.

(3) No award of damages is to be made unless, taking account of all the circumstances of the case, including –

    (a)   any other relief or remedy granted, or order made, in relation to the act in question (by that or any other court), and

    (b)   the consequences of any decision (of that or any other court) in respect of that act,

the court is satisfied that the award is necessary to afford just satisfaction to the person in whose favour it is made.

(4) In determining –

    (a)   whether to award damages, or

    (b)   the amount of an award,

the court must take into account the principles applied by the European Court of Human Rights in relation to the award of compensation under Article 41 of the Convention.

(5) A public authority against which damages are awarded is to be treated –

    (a)   in Scotland, for the purposes of section 3 of the Law Reform (Miscellaneous Provisions) (Scotland) Act 1940 as if the award were made in an action of damages in which the authority has been found liable in respect of loss or damage to the person to whom the award is made;

    (b)   for the purposes of the Civil Liability (Contribution) Act 1978 as liable in respect of damage suffered by the person to whom the award is made.

(6) In this section –

'court' includes a tribunal;
'damages' means damages for an unlawful act of a public authority; and
'unlawful' means unlawful under section 6(1).

9 Judicial acts

(1) Proceedings under section 7(1)(a) in respect of a judicial act may be brought only –

    (a)   by exercising a right of appeal;
    (b)   on an application (in Scotland a petition) for judicial review; or
    (c)   in such other forum as may be prescribed by rules.

(2) That does not affect any rule of law which prevents a court from being the subject of judicial review.

(3) In proceedings under this Act in respect of a judicial act done in good faith, damages may not be awarded otherwise than to compensate a person to the extent required by Article 5(5) of the Convention.

(4) An award of damages permitted by subsection (3) is to be made against the Crown; but no award may be made unless the appropriate person, if not a party to the proceedings, is joined.

(5) In this section –

'appropriate person' means the Minister responsible for the court concerned, or a person or government department nominated by him;
'court' includes a tribunal;
'judge' includes a member of a tribunal, a justice of the peace (or, in Northern Ireland, a lay magistrate) and a clerk or other officer entitled to exercise the jurisdiction of a court;
'judicial act' means a judicial act of a court and includes an act done on the instructions, or on behalf, of a judge;
'rules' has the same meaning as in section 7(9).

Amendments—Justice (Northern Ireland) Act 2002, s 10(6), Sch 4, para 39.

Remedial action

10 Power to take remedial action

(1) This section applies if –

    (a)   a provision of legislation has been declared under section 4 to be incompatible with a Convention right and, if an appeal lies –
        (i)   all persons who may appeal have stated that they do not intend to do so;
        (ii)   the time for bringing an appeal has expired and no appeal has been brought within that time; or

(iii) an appeal brought within that time has been determined or abandoned; or

(b) it appears to a Minister of the Crown or Her Majesty in Council that, having regard to a finding of the European Court of Human Rights made after the coming into force of this section in proceedings against the United Kingdom, a provision of legislation is incompatible with an obligation of the United Kingdom arising from the Convention.

(2) If a Minister of the Crown considers that there are compelling reasons for proceeding under this section, he may by order make such amendments to the legislation as he considers necessary to remove the incompatibility.

(3) If, in the case of subordinate legislation, a Minister of the Crown considers –

(a) that it is necessary to amend the primary legislation under which the subordinate legislation in question was made, in order to enable the incompatibility to be removed, and

(b) that there are compelling reasons for proceeding under this section,

he may by order make such amendments to the primary legislation as he considers appropriate.

(4) This section also applies where the provision in question is in subordinate legislation and has been quashed, or declared invalid, by reason of incompatibility with a Convention right and the Minister proposes to proceed under paragraph 2(b) of Schedule 2.

(5) If the legislation is an Order in Council, the power conferred by subsection (2) or (3) is exercisable by Her Majesty in Council.

(6) In this section 'legislation' does not include a Measure of the Church Assembly or of the General Synod of the Church of England.

(7) Schedule 2 makes further provision about remedial orders.

Other rights and proceedings

11   Safeguard for existing human rights

A person's reliance on a Convention right does not restrict –

(a) any other right or freedom conferred on him by or under any law having effect in any part of the United Kingdom, or

(b) his right to make any claim or bring any proceedings which he could make or bring apart from sections 7 to 9.

12   Freedom of expression

(1) This section applies if a court is considering whether to grant any relief which, if granted, might affect the exercise of the Convention right to freedom of expression.

(2) If the person against whom the application for relief is made ('the respondent') is neither present nor represented, no such relief is to be granted unless the court is satisfied –

(a) that the applicant has taken all practicable steps to notify the respondent; or

(b) that there are compelling reasons why the respondent should not be notified.

(3) No such relief is to be granted so as to restrain publication before trial unless the court is satisfied that the applicant is likely to establish that publication should not be allowed.

(4) The court must have particular regard to the importance of the Convention right to freedom of expression and, where the proceedings relate to material which the respondent claims, or which appears to the court, to be journalistic, literary or artistic material (or to conduct connected with such material), to –

    (a)   the extent to which –
        (i)   the material has, or is about to, become available to the public; or
        (ii)   it is, or would be, in the public interest for the material to be published;
    (b)   any relevant privacy code.

(5) In this section –

'court' includes a tribunal; and
'relief' includes any remedy or order (other than in criminal proceedings).

13 Freedom of thought, conscience and religion

(1) If a court's determination of any question arising under this Act might affect the exercise by a religious organisation (itself or its members collectively) of the Convention right to freedom of thought, conscience and religion, it must have particular regard to the importance of that right.

(2) In this section 'court' includes a tribunal.

Derogations and reservations

14 Derogations

(1) In this Act, 'designated derogation' means –

any derogation by the United Kingdom from an Article of the Convention, or of any protocol to the Convention, which is designated for the purposes of this Act in an order made by the Secretary of State.

(2) ...

(3) If a designated derogation is amended or replaced it ceases to be a designated derogation.

(4) But subsection (3) does not prevent the Secretary of State from exercising his power under subsection (1)... to make a fresh designation order in respect of the Article concerned.

(5) The Secretary of State must by order make such amendments to Schedule 3 as he considers appropriate to reflect –

    (a)   any designation order; or
    (b)   the effect of subsection (3).

(6) A designation order may be made in anticipation of the making by the United Kingdom of a proposed derogation.

Amendments—SI 2001/1216; SI 2003/1887.

15 Reservations

(1) In this Act, 'designated reservation' means –

    (a)   the United Kingdom's reservation to Article 2 of the First Protocol to the Convention; and

    (b)   any other reservation by the United Kingdom to an Article of the Convention, or of any protocol to the Convention, which is designated for the purposes of this Act in an order made by the Secretary of State.

(2) The text of the reservation referred to in subsection (1)(a) is set out in Part II of Schedule 3.

(3) If a designated reservation is withdrawn wholly or in part it ceases to be a designated reservation.

(4) But subsection (3) does not prevent the Secretary of State from exercising his power under subsection (1)(b) to make a fresh designation order in respect of the Article concerned.

(5) The Secretary of State must by order make such amendments to this Act as he considers appropriate to reflect –

    (a)   any designation order; or

    (b)   the effect of subsection (3).

Amendments—SI 2003/1887.

16   Period for which designated derogations have effect

(1) If it has not already been withdrawn by the United Kingdom, a designated derogation ceases to have effect for the purposes of this Act –

at the end of the period of five years beginning with the date on which the order designating it was made.

(2) At any time before the period –

    (a)   fixed by subsection (1), or

    (b)   extended by an order under this subsection,

comes to an end, the Secretary of State may by order extend it by a further period of five years.

(3) An order under section 14(1) ceases to have effect at the end of the period for consideration, unless a resolution has been passed by each House approving the order.

(4) Subsection (3) does not affect –

    (a)   anything done in reliance on the order; or

    (b)   the power to make a fresh order under section 14(1)

(5) In subsection (3) 'period for consideration' means the period of forty days beginning with the day on which the order was made.

(6) In calculating the period for consideration, no account is to be taken of any time during which –

    (a)   Parliament is dissolved or prorogued; or

    (b)   both Houses are adjourned for more than four days.

(7)   If a designated derogation is withdrawn by the United Kingdom, the Secretary of State must by order make such amendments to this Act as he considers are required to reflect that withdrawal.

Amendments—SI 2001/1216; SI 2003/1887.

17 Periodic review of designated reservations

(1) The appropriate Minister must review the designated reservation referred to in section 15(1)(a) –

(a)   before the end of the period of five years beginning with the date on which section 1(2) came into force; and

(b)   if that designation is still in force, before the end of the period of five years beginning with the date on which the last report relating to it was laid under subsection (3).

(2) The appropriate Minister must review each of the other designated reservations (if any) –

(a)   before the end of the period of five years beginning with the date on which the order designating the reservation first came into force; and

(b)   if the designation is still in force, before the end of the period of five years beginning with the date on which the last report relating to it was laid under subsection (3).

(3) The Minister conducting a review under this section must prepare a report on the result of the review and lay a copy of it before each House of Parliament.

Judges of the European Court of Human Rights

18 Appointment to European Court of Human Rights

(1) In this section 'judicial office' means the office of –

(a)   Lord Justice of Appeal, Justice of the High Court or Circuit judge, in England and Wales;

(b)   judge of the Court of Session or sheriff, in Scotland;

(c)   Lord Justice of Appeal, judge of the High Court or county court judge, in Northern Ireland.

(2) The holder of a judicial office may become a judge of the European Court of Human Rights ('the Court') without being required to relinquish his office.

(3) But he is not required to perform the duties of his judicial office while he is a judge of the Court.

(4) In respect of any period during which he is a judge of the Court –

(a)   a Lord Justice of Appeal or Justice of the High Court is not to count as a judge of the relevant court for the purposes of section 2(1) or 4(1) of the Senior Courts Act 1981 (maximum number of judges) nor as a judge of the Senior Courts for the purposes of section 12(1) to (6) of that Act (salaries etc);

(b)   a judge of the Court of Session is not to count as a judge of that court for the purposes of section 1(1) of the Court of Session Act 1988 (maximum number of judges) or of section 9(1)(c) of the Administration of Justice Act 1973 ('the 1973 Act') (salaries etc);

(c)   a Lord Justice of Appeal or a judge of the High Court in Northern Ireland is not to count as a judge of the relevant court for the purposes of section 2(1) or 3(1) of the Judicature (Northern Ireland) Act 1978 (maximum number of judges) nor as a judge of the Senior Courts of Northern Ireland for the purposes of section 9(1)(d) of the 1973 Act (salaries etc);

(d)   a Circuit judge is not to count as such for the purposes of section 18 of the Courts Act 1971 (salaries etc);

(e)   a sheriff is not to count as such for the purposes of section 14 of the Sheriff Courts (Scotland) Act 1907 (salaries etc);

(f)   a county court judge of Northern Ireland is not to count as such for the purposes of section 106 of the County Courts Act (Northern Ireland) 1959 (salaries etc).

(5) If a sheriff principal is appointed a judge of the Court, section 11(1) of the Sheriff Courts (Scotland) Act 1971 (temporary appointment of sheriff principal) applies, while he holds that appointment, as if his office is vacant.

(6) Schedule 3 makes provision about judicial pensions in relation to the holder of a judicial office who serves as a judge of the Court.

(7) The Lord Chancellor or the Secretary of State may by order make such transitional provision (including, in particular, provision for a temporary increase in the maximum number of judges) as he considers appropriate in relation to any holder of a judicial office who has completed his service as a judge of the Court.

The following paragraphs apply to the (7A) making of an order under subsection (7) in relation to any holder of a judicial office listed in subsection (1)(a) –

(a)   before deciding what transitional provision it is appropriate to make, the person making the order must consult the Lord Chief Justice of England and Wales;

(b)   before making the order, that person must consult the Lord Chief Justice of England and Wales.

The following paragraphs apply to the (7B) making of an order under subsection (7) in relation to any holder of a judicial office listed in subsection (1)(c) –

(a)   before deciding what transitional provision it is appropriate to make, the person making the order must consult the Lord Chief Justice of Northern Ireland;

(b)   before making the order, that person must consult the Lord Chief Justice of Northern Ireland.

The Lord Chief Justice of England and (7C) Wales may nominate a judicial office holder (within the meaning of section 109(4) of the Constitutional Reform Act 2005) to exercise his functions under this section.

The Lord Chief Justice of Northern Ireland (7D) may nominate any of the following to exercise his functions under this section –

(a)   the holder of one of the offices listed in Schedule 1 to the Justice (Northern Ireland) Act 2002;

(b)   a Lord Justice of Appeal (as defined in section 88 of that Act).

Amendments—Constitutional Reform Act 2005, ss 15(1), 59(5), Sch 4, Pt 1, para 278, Sch 11, Pts 1–3, paras 1(2), 4(1), (3), 6(1), (3).

Parliamentary procedure

19 Statements of compatibility

(1) A Minister of the Crown in charge of a Bill in either House of Parliament must, before Second Reading of the Bill –

(a) make a statement to the effect that in his view the provisions of the Bill are compatible with the Convention rights ('a statement of compatibility'); or

(b) make a statement to the effect that although he is unable to make a statement of compatibility the government nevertheless wishes the House to proceed with the Bill.

(2) The statement must be in writing and be published in such manner as the Minister making it considers appropriate.

Supplemental

20 Orders etc under this Act

(1) Any power of a Minister of the Crown to make an order under this Act is exercisable by statutory instrument.

(2) The power of the Lord Chancellor or the Secretary of State to make rules (other than rules of court) under section 2(3) or 7(9) is exercisable by statutory instrument.

(3) Any statutory instrument made under section 14, 15 or 16(7) must be laid before Parliament.

(4) No order may be made by the Lord Chancellor or the Secretary of State under section 1(4), 7(11) or 16(2) unless a draft of the order has been laid before, and approved by, each House of Parliament.

(5) Any statutory instrument made under section 18(7) or Schedule 4, or to which subsection (2) applies, shall be subject to annulment in pursuance of a resolution of either House of Parliament.

(6) The power of a Northern Ireland department to make –

(a) rules under section 2(3)(c) or 7(9)(c), or

(b) an order under section 7(11),

is exercisable by statutory rule for the purposes of the Statutory Rules (Northern Ireland) Order 1979.

(7) Any rules made under section 2(3)(c) or 7(9)(c) shall be subject to negative resolution; and section 41(6) of the Interpretation Act Northern Ireland) 1954 (meaning of 'subject to negative resolution') shall apply as if the power to make the rules were conferred by an Act of the Northern Ireland Assembly.

(8) No order may be made by a Northern Ireland department under section 7(11) unless a draft of the order has been laid before, and approved by, the Northern Ireland Assembly.

Amendments—SI 2003/1887, SI 2005/3429.

21 Interpretation, etc

(1) In this Act –

'amend' includes repeal and apply (with or without modifications);

'the appropriate Minister' means the Minister of the Crown having charge of the appropriate authorised government department (within the meaning of the Crown Proceedings Act 1947);

'the Commission' means the European Commission of Human Rights;

'the Convention' means the Convention for the Protection of Human Rights and Fundamental Freedoms, agreed by the Council of Europe at Rome on 4th November 1950 as it has effect for the time being in relation to the United Kingdom;

'declaration of incompatibility' means a declaration under section 4;

'Minister of the Crown' has the same meaning as in the Ministers of the Crown Act 1975;

'Northern Ireland Minister' includes the First Minister and the deputy First Minister in Northern Ireland;

'primary legislation' means any –

> (a)   public general Act;
> (b)   local and personal Act;
> (c)   private Act;
> (d)   Measure of the Church Assembly;
> (e)   Measure of the General Synod of the Church of England;
> (f)   Order in Council –
>> (i)   made in exercise of Her Majesty's Royal Prerogative;
>> (ii)   made under section 38(1)(a) of the Northern Ireland Constitution Act 1973 or the corresponding provision of the Northern Ireland Act 1998; or
>> (iii)   amending an Act of a kind mentioned in paragraph (a), (b) or (c);

and includes an order or other instrument made under primary legislation (otherwise than by Welsh Ministers, the First Minister for Wales, the Counsel General to the Welsh Assembly Government, a member of the Scottish Executive, a Northern Ireland Minister or a Northern Ireland department) to the extent to which it operates to bring one or more provisions of that legislation into force or amends any primary legislation;

'the First Protocol' means the protocol to the Convention agreed at Paris on 20th March 1952;

...

'the Eleventh Protocol' means the protocol to the Convention (restructuring the control machinery established by the Convention) agreed at Strasbourg on 11th May 1994;

'the Thirteenth Protocol' means the protocol to the Convention (concerning the abolition of the death penalty in all circumstances) agreed at Vilnius on 3rd May 2002;

'remedial order' means an order under section 10;

'subordinate legislation' means any –

> (a)   Order in Council other than one –
>> (i)   made in exercise of Her Majesty's Royal Prerogative;
>> (ii)   made under section 38(1)(a) of the Northern Ireland Constitution Act 1973 or the corresponding provision of the Northern Ireland Act 1998; or
>> (iii)   amending an Act of a kind mentioned in the definition of primary legislation;
> (b)   Act of the Scottish Parliament;
> (ba)   Measure of the National Assembly for Wales;
> (bb)   Act of the National Assembly for Wales;

(c) Act of the Parliament of Northern Ireland;

(d) Measure of the Assembly established under section 1 of the Northern Ireland Assembly Act 1973;

(e) Act of the Northern Ireland Assembly;

(f) order, rules, regulations, scheme, warrant, byelaw or other instrument made under primary legislation (except to the extent to which it operates to bring one or more provisions of that legislation into force or amends any primary legislation);

(g) order, rules, regulations, scheme, warrant, byelaw or other instrument made under legislation mentioned in paragraph (b), (c), (d) or (e) or made under an Order in Council applying only to Northern Ireland;

(h) order, rules, regulations, scheme, warrant, byelaw or other instrument made by a member of the Scottish Executive, Welsh Ministers, the First Minister for Wales, the Counsel General to the Welsh Assembly Government, a Northern Ireland Minister or a Northern Ireland department in exercise of prerogative or

other executive functions of Her Majesty which are exercisable by such a person on behalf of Her Majesty;

'transferred matters' has the same meaning as in the Northern Ireland Act 1998; and 'tribunal' means any tribunal in which legal proceedings may be brought.

(2) The references in paragraphs (b) and (c) of section 2(1) to Articles are to Articles of the Convention as they had effect immediately before the coming into force of the Eleventh Protocol.

(3) The reference in paragraph (d) of section 2(1) to Article 46 includes a reference to Articles 32 and 54 of the Convention as they had effect immediately before the coming into force of the Eleventh Protocol.

(4) The references in section 2(1) to a report or decision of the Commission or a decision of the Committee of Ministers include references to a report or decision made as provided by paragraphs 3, 4 and 6 of Article 5 of the Eleventh Protocol (transitional provisions).

(5) Any liability under the Army Act 1955, the Air Force Act 1955 or the Naval Discipline Act 1957 to suffer death for an offence is replaced by a liability to imprisonment for life or any less punishment authorised by those Acts; and those Acts shall accordingly have effect with the necessary modifications.

Amendments—SI 2004/1574; Government of Wales Act 2006, s 160(1), Sch 10, para 56; Armed Forces Act 2006, s 378(2), Sch 17.

22 Short title, commencement, application and extent

(1) This Act may be cited as the Human Rights Act 1998.

(2) Sections 18, 20 and 21(5) and this section come into force on the passing of this Act.

(3) The other provisions of this Act come into force on such day as the Secretary of State may by order appoint; and different days may be appointed for different purposes.

(4) Paragraph (b) of subsection (1) of section 7 applies to proceedings brought by or at the instigation of a public authority whenever the act in question took place; but otherwise that subsection does not apply to an act committed before the coming into force of that section.

(5) This Act binds the Crown.

(6) This Act extends to Northern Ireland.

(7) ...

Amendments—Armed Forces Act 2006, s 378(2), Sch 17.

Schedules

Schedule 1
The Articles

PART I
THE CONVENTION — RIGHTS AND FREEDOMS

Article 2
Right to life

1

Everyone's right to life shall be protected by law. No one shall be deprived of his life intentionally save in the execution of a sentence of a court following his conviction of a crime for which this penalty is provided by law.

2

Deprivation of life shall not be regarded as inflicted in contravention of this Article when it results from the use of force which is no more than absolutely necessary –

    (a)   in defence of any person from unlawful violence;
    (b)   in order to effect a lawful arrest or to prevent the escape of a person lawfully detained;
    (c)   in action lawfully taken for the purpose of quelling a riot or insurrection.

Article 3
Prohibition of torture

No one shall be subjected to torture or to inhuman or degrading treatment or punishment.

Article 4
Prohibition of slavery and forced labour

1

No one shall be held in slavery or servitude.

2

No one shall be required to perform forced or compulsory labour.

3

For the purpose of this Article the term 'forced or compulsory labour' shall not include –

(a)   any work required to be done in the ordinary course of detention imposed according to the provisions of Article 5 of this Convention or during conditional release from such detention;

(b)   any service of a military character or, in case of conscientious objectors in countries where they are recognised, service exacted instead of compulsory military service;

(c)   any service exacted in case of an emergency or calamity threatening the life or well-being of the community;

(d)   any work or service which forms part of normal civic obligations.

Article 5
Right to liberty and security

1

Everyone has the right to liberty and security of person. No one shall be deprived of his liberty save in the following cases and in accordance with a procedure prescribed by law –

(a)   the lawful detention of a person after conviction by a competent court;

(b)   the lawful arrest or detention of a person for non-compliance with the lawful order of a court or in order to secure the fulfilment of any obligation prescribed by law;

(c)   the lawful arrest or detention of a person effected for the purpose of bringing him before the competent legal authority on reasonable suspicion of having committed an offence or when it is reasonably considered necessary to prevent his committing an offence or fleeing after having done so;

(d)   the detention of a minor by lawful order for the purpose of educational supervision or his lawful detention for the purpose of bringing him before the competent legal authority;

(e)   the lawful detention of persons for the prevention of the spreading of infectious diseases, of persons of unsound mind, alcoholics or drug addicts or vagrants;

(f)   the lawful arrest or detention of a person to prevent his effecting an unauthorised entry into the country or of a person against whom action is being taken with a view to deportation or extradition.

2

Everyone who is arrested shall be informed promptly, in a language which he understands, of the reasons for his arrest and of any charge against him.

3

Everyone arrested or detained in accordance with the provisions of paragraph 1(c) of this Article shall be brought promptly before a judge or other officer authorised by law to exercise judicial power and shall be entitled to trial within a reasonable time or to release pending trial. Release may be conditioned by guarantees to appear for trial.

4

Everyone who is deprived of his liberty by arrest or detention shall be entitled to take proceedings by which the lawfulness of his detention shall be decided speedily by a court and his release ordered if the detention is not lawful.

5

Everyone who has been the victim of arrest or detention in contravention of the provisions of this Article shall have an enforceable right to compensation.

Article 6
Right to a fair trial

1

In the determination of his civil rights and obligations or of any criminal charge against him, everyone is entitled to a fair and public hearing within a reasonable time by an independent and impartial tribunal established by law. Judgment shall be pronounced publicly but the press and public may be excluded from all or part of the trial in the interest of morals, public order or national security in a democratic society, where the interests of juveniles or the protection of the private life of the parties so require, or to the extent strictly necessary in the opinion of the court in special circumstances where publicity would prejudice the interests of justice.

2

Everyone charged with a criminal offence shall be presumed innocent until proved guilty according to law.

3

Everyone charged with a criminal offence has the following minimum rights –

(a) to be informed promptly, in a language which he understands and in detail, of the nature and cause of the accusation against him;
(b) to have adequate time and facilities for the preparation of his defence;
(c) to defend himself in person or through legal assistance of his own choosing or, if he has not sufficient means to pay for legal assistance, to be given it free when the interests of justice so require;
(d) to examine or have examined witnesses against him and to obtain the attendance and examination of witnesses on his behalf under the same conditions as witnesses against him;
(e) to have the free assistance of an interpreter if he cannot understand or speak the language used in court.

Article 7
No punishment without law

1

No one shall be held guilty of any criminal offence on account of any act or omission which did not constitute a criminal offence under national or international law at the time when it was committed. Nor shall a heavier penalty be imposed than the one that was applicable at the time the criminal offence was committed.

2

This Article shall not prejudice the trial and punishment of any person for any act or omission which, at the time when it was committed, was criminal according to the general principles of law recognised by civilised nations.

Article 8
Right to respect for private and family life

1

Everyone has the right to respect for his private and family life, his home and his correspondence.

2

There shall be no interference by a public authority with the exercise of this right except such as is in accordance with the law and is necessary in a democratic society in the interests of national security, public safety or the economic well-being of the country, for the prevention of disorder or crime, for the protection of health or morals, or for the protection of the rights and freedoms of others.

Article 9
Freedom of thought, conscience and religion

1

Everyone has the right to freedom of thought, conscience and religion; this right includes freedom to change his religion or belief and freedom, either alone or in community with others and in public or private, to manifest his religion or belief, in worship, teaching, practice and observance.

2

Freedom to manifest one's religion or beliefs shall be subject only to such limitations as are prescribed by law and are necessary in a democratic society in the interests of public safety, for the protection of public order, health or morals, or for the protection of the rights and freedoms of others.

Article 10
Freedom of expression

1

Everyone has the right to freedom of expression. This right shall include freedom to hold opinions and to receive and impart information and ideas without interference by public authority and regardless of frontiers. This Article shall not prevent States from requiring the licensing of broadcasting, television or cinema enterprises.

2

The exercise of these freedoms, since it carries with it duties and responsibilities, may be subject to such formalities, conditions, restrictions or penalties as are prescribed by law and are necessary in a democratic society, in the interests of national security, territorial integrity or public safety, for the prevention of disorder or crime, for the protection of health or morals, for the protection of the reputation or rights of others, for preventing the disclosure of information received in confidence, or for maintaining the authority and impartiality of the judiciary.

Article 11
Freedom of assembly and association

1

Everyone has the right to freedom of peaceful assembly and to freedom of association with others, including the right to form and to join trade unions for the protection of his interests.

2

No restrictions shall be placed on the exercise of these rights other than such as are prescribed by law and are necessary in a democratic society in the interests of national security or public safety, for the prevention of disorder or crime, for the protection of health or morals or for the protection of the rights and freedoms of others. This Article shall not prevent the imposition of lawful restrictions on the exercise of these rights by members of the armed forces, of the police or of the administration of the State.

Article 12
Right to marry

Men and women of marriageable age have the right to marry and to found a family, according to the national laws governing the exercise of this right.

Article 14
Prohibition of discrimination

The enjoyment of the rights and freedoms set forth in this Convention shall be secured without discrimination on any ground such as sex, race, colour, language, religion, political or other opinion, national or social origin, association with a national minority, property, birth or other status.

Article 16
Restrictions on political activity of aliens

Nothing in Articles 10, 11 and 14 shall be regarded as preventing the High Contracting Parties from imposing restrictions on the political activity of aliens.

Article 17
Prohibition of abuse of rights

Nothing in this Convention may be interpreted as implying for any State, group or person any right to engage in any activity or perform any act aimed at the destruction of any of the rights and freedoms set forth herein or at their limitation to a greater extent than is provided for in the Convention.

Article 18
Limitation on use of restrictions on rights

The restrictions permitted under this Convention to the said rights and freedoms shall not be applied for any purpose other than those for which they have been prescribed.

PART II
THE FIRST PROTOCOL

Article 1
Protection of property

Every natural or legal person is entitled to the peaceful enjoyment of his possessions. No one shall be deprived of his possessions except in the public interest and subject to the conditions provided for by law and by the general principles of international law.

The preceding provisions shall not, however, in any way impair the right of a State to enforce such laws as it deems necessary to control the use of property in accordance with the general interest or to secure the payment of taxes or other contributions or penalties.

Article 2
Right to education

No person shall be denied the right to education. In the exercise of any functions which it assumes in relation to education and to teaching, the State shall respect the right of parents to ensure such education and teaching in conformity with their own religious and philosophical convictions.

Article 3
Right to free elections

The High Contracting Parties undertake to hold free elections at reasonable intervals by secret ballot, under conditions which will ensure the free expression of the opinion of the people in the choice of the legislature.

PART III
ARTICLE 1 OF THE THIRTEENTH PROTOCOL

Article 1
Abolition of the death penalty

The death penalty shall be abolished. No one shall be condemned to such penalty or executed.

Amendments—SI 2004/1574.

Schedule 2
Remedial Orders

Orders

1

(1) A remedial order may –

    (a)   contain such incidental, supplemental, consequential or transitional provision as the person making it considers appropriate;

    (b)   be made so as to have effect from a date earlier than that on which it is made;

    (c)   make provision for the delegation of specific functions;

    (d)   make different provision for different cases.

(2) The power conferred by sub-paragraph (1)(a) includes –

    (a)   power to amend primary legislation (including primary legislation other than that which contains the incompatible provision); and

    (b)   power to amend or revoke subordinate legislation (including subordinate legislation other than that which contains the incompatible provision).

(3) A remedial order may be made so as to have the same extent as the legislation which it affects.

(4) No person is to be guilty of an offence solely as a result of the retrospective effect of a remedial order.

Procedure

2

No remedial order may be made unless –

    (a)   a draft of the order has been approved by a resolution of each House of Parliament made after the end of the period of 60 days beginning with the day on which the draft was laid; or

    (b)   it is declared in the order that it appears to the person making it that, because of the urgency of the matter, it is necessary to make the order without a draft being so approved.

Orders laid in draft

3

(1) No draft may be laid under paragraph 2(a) unless –

    (a)   the person proposing to make the order has laid before Parliament a document which contains a draft of the proposed order and the required information; and

    (b)   the period of 60 days, beginning with the day on which the document required by this sub-paragraph was laid, has ended.

(2) If representations have been made during that period, the draft laid under paragraph 2(a) must be accompanied by a statement containing –

    (a)   a summary of the representations; and

    (b)   if, as a result of the representations, the proposed order has been changed, details of the changes.

Urgent cases

4

(1) If a remedial order ('the original order') is made without being approved in draft, the person making it must lay it before Parliament, accompanied by the required information, after it is made.

(2) If representations have been made during the period of 60 days beginning with the day on which the original order was made, the person making it must (after the end of that period) lay before Parliament a statement containing –

    (a)   a summary of the representations; and

(b)   if, as a result of the representations, he considers it appropriate to make changes to the original order, details of the changes.

(3) If sub-paragraph (2)(b) applies, the person making the statement must –

(a)   make a further remedial order replacing the original order; and
(b)   lay the replacement order before Parliament.

(4) If, at the end of the period of 120 days beginning with the day on which the original order was made, a resolution has not been passed by each House approving the original or replacement order, the order ceases to have effect (but without that affecting anything previously done under either order or the power to make a fresh remedial order).

Definitions

5

In this Schedule –

'representations' means representations about a remedial order (or proposed remedial order) made to the person making (or proposing to make) it and includes any relevant Parliamentary report or resolution; and
'required information' means –

(a)   an explanation of the incompatibility which the order (or proposed order) seeks to remove, including particulars of the relevant declaration, finding or order; and
(b)   a statement of the reasons for proceeding under section 10 and for making an order in those terms.

Calculating periods

6

In calculating any period for the purposes of this Schedule, no account is to be taken of any time during which –

(a)   Parliament is dissolved or prorogued; or
(b)   both Houses are adjourned for more than four days.

PROTECTION FROM HARASSMENT ACT 1997

1 Prohibition of harassment

(1) A person must not pursue a course of conduct –

(a)   which amounts to harassment of another, and
(b)   which he knows or ought to know amounts to harassment of the other.

(1A) A person must not pursue a course of conduct –

(a)   which involves harassment of two or more persons, and
(b)   which he knows or ought to know involves harassment of those persons, and
(c)   by which he intends to persuade any person (whether or not one of those mentioned above) –
    (i)   not to do something that he is entitled or required to do, or
    (ii)   to do something that he is not under any obligation to do.

(2) For the purposes of this section, the person whose course of conduct is in question ought to know that it amounts to or involves harassment of another if a reasonable person in possession of the same information would think the course of conduct amounted to or involved harassment of the other.

(3) Subsection (1) or (1A) does not apply to a course of conduct if the person who pursued it shows –

(a)   that it was pursued for the purpose of preventing or detecting crime,
(b)   that it was pursued under any enactment or rule of law or to comply with any condition or requirement imposed by any person under any enactment, or
(c)   that in the particular circumstances the pursuit of the course of conduct was reasonable.

Amendments—Serious Organised Crime and Police Act 2005, s 125(1), (2).

2 Offence of harassment

(1) A person who pursues a course of conduct in breach of section 1(1) or (1A) is guilty of an offence.

(2) A person guilty of an offence under this section is liable on summary conviction to imprisonment for a term not exceeding six months, or a fine not exceeding level 5 on the standard scale, or both.

(3) (*repealed*)

Amendments—Police Reform Act 2002, s 107(2), Sch 8; Serious Organised Crime and Police Act 2005, s 125(1), (3).

3 Civil remedy

(1) An actual or apprehended breach of section 1(1) may be the subject of a claim in civil proceedings by the person who is or may be the victim of the course of conduct in question.

(2) On such a claim, damages may be awarded for (among other things) any anxiety caused by the harassment and any financial loss resulting from the harassment.

(3) Where –

    (a)   in such proceedings the High Court or a county court grants an injunction for the purpose of restraining the defendant from pursuing any conduct which amounts to harassment, and

    (b)   the plaintiff considers that the defendant has done anything which he is prohibited from doing by the injunction,

the plaintiff may apply for the issue of a warrant for the arrest of the defendant.

(4) An application under subsection (3) may be made –

    (a)   where the injunction was granted by the High Court, to a judge of that court, and

    (b)   where the injunction was granted by a county court, to a judge or district judge of that or any other county court.

(5) The judge or district judge to whom an application under subsection (3) is made may only issue a warrant if –

    (a)   the application is substantiated on oath, and

    (b)   the judge or district judge has reasonable grounds for believing that the defendant has done anything which he is prohibited from doing by the injunction.

(6) Where –

    (a)   the High Court or a county court grants an injunction for the purpose mentioned in subsection (3)(a), and

    (b)   without reasonable excuse the defendant does anything which he is prohibited from doing by the injunction,

he is guilty of an offence.

(7) Where a person is convicted of an offence under subsection (6) in respect of any conduct, that conduct is not punishable as a contempt of court.

(8) A person cannot be convicted of an offence under subsection (6) in respect of any conduct which has been punished as a contempt of court.

(9) A person guilty of an offence under subsection (6) is liable –

    (a)   on conviction on indictment, to imprisonment for a term not exceeding five years, or a fine, or both, or

    (b)   on summary conviction, to imprisonment for a term not exceeding six months, or a fine not exceeding the statutory maximum, or both.

Amendments—Serious Organised Crime and Police Act 2005, s 125(1), (4).

3A Injunctions to protect persons from harassment within section 1(1A)

(1) This section applies where there is an actual or apprehended breach of section 1(1A) by any person ('the relevant person').

(2) In such a case –

    (a)   any person who is or may be a victim of the course of conduct in question, or

    (b)   any person who is or may be a person falling within section 1(1A)(c), may apply to the High Court or a county court for an injunction restraining the relevant person from pursuing any conduct which amounts to harassment in relation to any person or persons mentioned or described in the injunction.

(3) Section 3(3) to (9) apply in relation to an injunction granted under subsection (2) above as they apply in relation to an injunction granted as mentioned in section 3(3)(a).

Amendments—Serious Organised Crime and Police Act 2005, s 125(1), (5).

4 Putting people in fear of violence

(1) A person whose course of conduct causes another to fear, on at least two occasions, that violence will be used against him is guilty of an offence if he knows or ought to know that his course of conduct will cause the other so to fear on each of those occasions.

(2) For the purposes of this section, the person whose course of conduct is in question ought to know that it will cause another to fear that violence will be used against him on any occasion if a reasonable person in possession of the same information would think the course of conduct would cause the other so to fear on that occasion.

(3) It is a defence for a person charged with an offence under this section to show that –

    (a)   his course of conduct was pursued for the purpose of preventing or detecting crime,

    (b)   his course of conduct was pursued under any enactment or rule of law or to comply with any condition or requirement imposed by any person under any enactment, or

    (c)   the pursuit of his course of conduct was reasonable for the protection of himself or another or for the protection of his or another's property.

(4) A person guilty of an offence under this section is liable –

    (a)   on conviction on indictment, to imprisonment for a term not exceeding five years, or a fine, or both, or

    (b)   on summary conviction, to imprisonment for a term not exceeding six months, or a fine not exceeding the statutory maximum, or both.

(5) If on the trial on indictment of a person charged with an offence under this section the jury find him not guilty of the offence charged, they may find him guilty of an offence under section 2.

(6) The Crown Court has the same powers and duties in relation to a person who is by virtue of subsection (5) convicted before it of an offence under section 2 as a magistrates' court would have on convicting him of the offence.

5 Restraining orders on conviction

(1) A court sentencing or otherwise dealing with a person ('the defendant') convicted of an offence may (as well as sentencing him or dealing with him in any other way) make an order under this section.

(2) The order may, for the purpose of protecting the victim or victims of the offence, or any other person mentioned in the order, from conduct which –

    (a)   amounts to harassment, or

    (b)   will cause a fear of violence,

prohibit the defendant from doing anything described in the order.

(3) The order may have effect for a specified period or until further order.

(3A) In proceedings under this section both the prosecution and the defence may lead, as further evidence, any evidence that would be admissible in proceedings for an injunction under section 3.

(4) The prosecutor, the defendant or any other person mentioned in the order may apply to the court which made the order for it to be varied or discharged by a further order.

(4A) Any person mentioned in the order is entitled to be heard on the hearing of an application under subsection (4).

(5) If without reasonable excuse the defendant does anything which he is prohibited from doing by an order under this section, he is guilty of an offence.

(6) A person guilty of an offence under this section is liable –

(a)   on conviction on indictment, to imprisonment for a term not exceeding five years, or a fine, or both, or

(b)   on summary conviction, to imprisonment for a term not exceeding six months, or a fine not exceeding the statutory maximum, or both.

(7) A court dealing with a person for an offence under this section may vary or discharge the order in question by a further order.

Amendments—Serious Organised Crime and Police Act 2005, s 125(1), (6); Domestic Violence, Crime and Victims Act 2004, ss 12, (2), (3), (4), 58(1), (2), 59, Sch 10, para 43, Sch 11; SI 2009/2501.

5A Restraining orders on acquittal

(1) A court before which a person ('the defendant') is acquitted of an offence may, if it considers it necessary to do so to protect a person from harassment by the defendant, make an order prohibiting the defendant from doing anything described in the order.

(2) Subsections (3) to (7) of section 5 apply to an order under this section as they apply to an order under that one.

(3) Where the Court of Appeal allow an appeal against conviction they may remit the case to the Crown Court to consider whether to proceed under this section.

(4) Where –

(a)   the Crown Court allows an appeal against conviction, or

(b)   a case is remitted to the Crown Court under subsection (3),

the reference in subsection (1) to a court before which a person is acquitted of an offence is to be read as referring to that court.

(5) A person made subject to an order under this section has the same right of appeal against the order as if –

(a)   he had been convicted of the offence in question before the court which made the order, and

(b)   the order had been made under section 5.

Prospective Amendment—Inserted by the Domestic Violence, Crime and Victims Act 2004, s 12(5).

6 Limitation

In section 11 of the Limitation Act 1980 (special time limit for actions in respect of personal injuries), after subsection (1) there is inserted –

'(1A) This section does not apply to any action brought for damages under section 3 of the Protection from Harassment Act 1997.'

7 Interpretation of this group of sections

(1) This section applies for the interpretation of sections 1 to 5A.

(2) References to harassing a person include alarming the person or causing the person distress.

(3) A 'course of conduct' must involve –

(a)   in the case of conduct in relation to a single person (see section 1(1)), conduct on at least two occasions in relation to that person, or

(b)   in the case of conduct in relation to two or more persons (see section 1(1A)), conduct on at least one occasion in relation to each of those persons.

(3A) A person's conduct on any occasion shall be taken, if aided, abetted, counselled or procured by another –

(a)   to be conduct on that occasion of the other (as well as conduct of the person whose conduct it is); and

(b)   to be conduct in relation to which the other's knowledge and purpose, and what he ought to have known, are the same as they were in relation to what was contemplated or reasonably foreseeable at the time of the aiding, abetting, counselling or procuring.

(4) 'Conduct' includes speech.

(5) References to a person, in the context of the harassment of a person, are references to a person who is an individual.

Amendments—Criminal Justice and Police Act 2001, s 44(1); Serious Organised Crime and Police Act 2005, s 125(1), (7); Domestic Violence, Crime and Victims Act 2004, s 58(1), Sch 10, para 44.

Scotland

8 Harassment

(1) Every individual has a right to be free from harassment and, accordingly, a person must not pursue a course of conduct which amounts to harassment of another and –

(a)   is intended to amount to harassment of that person; or

(b)   occurs in circumstances where it would appear to a reasonable person that it would amount to harassment of that person.

(2) An actual or apprehended breach of subsection (1) may be the subject of a claim in civil proceedings by the person who is or may be the victim of the course of conduct in question; and any such claim shall be known as an action of harassment.

(3) For the purposes of this section –

'conduct' includes speech;
'harassment' of a person includes causing the person alarm or distress; and

a course of conduct must involve conduct on at least two occasions.

(4) It shall be a defence to any action of harassment to show that the course of conduct complained of –

(a)   was authorised by, under or by virtue of any enactment or rule of law;

(b)   was pursued for the purpose of preventing or detecting crime; or

(c)   was, in the particular circumstances, reasonable.

(5) In an action of harassment the court may, without prejudice to any other remedies which it may grant –

(a)   award damages;

(b)   grant –

  (i)   interdict or interim interdict;

  (ii)   if it is satisfied that it is appropriate for it to do so in order to protect the person from further harassment, an order, to be known as a 'non-harassment order', requiring the defender to refrain from such conduct in relation to the pursuer as may be specified in the order for such period (which includes an indeterminate period) as may be so specified,

but a person may not be subjected to the same prohibitions in an interdict or interim interdict and a non-harassment order at the same time.

(6) The damages which may be awarded in an action of harassment include damages for any anxiety caused by the harassment and any financial loss resulting from it.

(7) Without prejudice to any right to seek review of any interlocutor, a person against whom a non-harassment order has been made, or the person for whose protection the order was made, may apply to the court by which the order was made for revocation of or a variation of the order and, on any such application, the court may revoke the order or vary it in such manner as it considers appropriate.

(8) In section 10(1) of the Damages (Scotland) Act 1976 (interpretation), in the definition of 'personal injuries', after 'to reputation' there is inserted ', or injury resulting from harassment actionable under section 8 of the Protection from Harassment Act 1997'.

9 Breach of non-harassment order

(1) Any person who is in breach of a non-harassment order made under section 8 is guilty of an offence and liable –

(a)   on conviction on indictment, to imprisonment for a term not exceeding five years or to a fine, or to both such imprisonment and such fine; and

(b)   on summary conviction, to imprisonment for a period not exceeding six months or to a fine not exceeding the statutory maximum, or to both such imprisonment and such fine.

(2) A breach of a non-harassment order shall not be punishable other than in accordance with subsection (1).

(3) A constable may arrest without warrant any person he reasonably believes is committing or has committed an offence under subsection (1).

(4) Subsection (3) is without prejudice to any power of arrest conferred by law apart from that subsection.

Amendments—Criminal Justice (Scotland) Act 2003, s 49(2)(a), (b).

10 Limitation

(1) After section 18A of the Prescription and Limitation (Scotland) Act 1973 there is inserted the following section –

'18B Actions of harassment

(1) This section applies to actions of harassment (within the meaning of section 8 of the Protection from Harassment Act 1997) which include a claim for damages.

(2) Subject to subsection (3) below and to section 19A of this Act, no action to which this section applies shall be brought unless it is commenced within a period of 3 years after –

    (a)   the date on which the alleged harassment ceased; or

    (b)   the date, (if later than the date mentioned in paragraph (a) above) on which the pursuer in the action became, or on which, in the opinion of the court, it would have been reasonably practicable for him in all the circumstances to have become, aware, that the defender was a person responsible for the alleged harassment or the employer or principal of such a person.

(3) In the computation of the period specified in subsection (2) above there shall be disregarded any time during which the person who is alleged to have suffered the harassment was under legal disability by reason of nonage or unsoundness of mind.'

(2) In subsection (1) of section 19A of that Act (power of court to override time-limits), for 'section 17 or section 18 and section 18A' there is substituted 'section 17, 18, 18A or 18B'.

11 Non-harassment order following criminal offence

After section 234 of the Criminal Procedure (Scotland) Act 1995 there is inserted the following section –

'Non-harassment orders

234A Non-harassment orders

(1) Where a person is convicted of an offence involving harassment of a person ('the victim'), the prosecutor may apply to the court to make a non-harassment order against the offender requiring him to refrain from such conduct in relation to the victim as may be specified in the order for such period (which includes an indeterminate period) as may be so specified, in addition to any other disposal which may be made in relation to the offence.

(2) On an application under subsection (1) above the court may, if it is satisfied on a balance of probabilities that it is appropriate to do so in order to protect the victim from further harassment, make a non-harassment order.

(3) A non-harassment order made by a criminal court shall be taken to be a sentence for the purposes of any appeal and, for the purposes of this subsection 'order' includes any variation or revocation of such an order made under subsection (6) below.

(4) Any person who is found to be in breach of a non-harassment order shall be guilty of an offence and liable –

    (a)   on conviction on indictment, to imprisonment for a term not exceeding 5 years or to a fine, or to both such imprisonment and such fine; and

    (b)   on summary conviction, to imprisonment for a period not exceeding 6 months or to a fine not exceeding the statutory maximum, or to both such imprisonment and such fine.

(5) The Lord Advocate, in solemn proceedings, and the prosecutor, in summary proceedings, may appeal to the High Court against any decision by a court to refuse an application under subsection (1) above; and on any such appeal the High Court may make such order as it considers appropriate.

(6) The person against whom a non-harassment order is made, or the prosecutor at whose instance the order is made, may apply to the court which made the order for its revocation or variation and, in relation to any such application the court concerned may, if it is satisfied on a balance of probabilities that it is appropriate to do so, revoke the order or vary it in such manner as it thinks fit, but not so as to increase the period for which the order is to run.

(7) For the purposes of this section 'harassment' shall be construed in accordance with section 8 of the Protection from Harassment Act 1997.'

General

12 National security, etc

(1) If the Secretary of State certifies that in his opinion anything done by a specified person on a specified occasion related to –

(a)   national security,
(b)   the economic well-being of the United Kingdom, or
(c)   the prevention or detection of serious crime,

and was done on behalf of the Crown, the certificate is conclusive evidence that this Act does not apply to any conduct of that person on that occasion.

(2) In subsection (1), 'specified' means specified in the certificate in question.

(3) A document purporting to be a certificate under subsection (1) is to be received in evidence and, unless the contrary is proved, be treated as being such a certificate.

13 Corresponding provision for Northern Ireland

An Order in Council made under paragraph 1(1)(b) of Schedule 1 to the Northern Ireland Act 1974 which contains a statement that it is made only for purposes corresponding to those of sections 1 to 7 and 12 of this Act –

(a)   shall not be subject to sub-paragraphs (4) and (5) of paragraph 1 of that Schedule (affirmative resolution of both Houses of Parliament), but
(b)   shall be subject to annulment in pursuance of a resolution of either House of Parliament.

14 Extent

(1) Sections 1 to 7 extend to England and Wales only.

(2) Sections 8 to 11 extend to Scotland only.

(3) This Act (except section 13) does not extend to Northern Ireland.

15 Commencement

(1) Sections 1, 2, 4, 5 and 7 to 12 are to come into force on such day as the Secretary of State may by order made by statutory instrument appoint.

(2) Sections 3 and 6 are to come into force on such day as the Lord Chancellor may by order made by statutory instrument appoint.

(3) Different days may be appointed under this section for different purposes.

16 Short title

This Act may be cited as the Protection from Harassment Act 1997.

PROTECTION FROM HARASSMENT ACT 1997

1 Prohibition of harassment

(1) A person must not pursue a course of conduct –

(a)   which amounts to harassment of another, and

(b)   which he knows or ought to know amounts to harassment of the other.

(1A) A person must not pursue a course of conduct –

(a)   which involves harassment of two or more persons, and

(b)   which he knows or ought to know involves harassment of those persons, and

(c)   by which he intends to persuade any person (whether or not one of those mentioned above) –

    (i)   not to do something that he is entitled or required to do, or

    (ii)   to do something that he is not under any obligation to do.

(2) For the purposes of this section, the person whose course of conduct is in question ought to know that it amounts to or involves harassment of another if a reasonable person in possession of the same information would think the course of conduct amounted to or involved harassment of the other.

(3) Subsection (1) or (1A) does not apply to a course of conduct if the person who pursued it shows –

(a)   that it was pursued for the purpose of preventing or detecting crime,

(b)   that it was pursued under any enactment or rule of law or to comply with any condition or requirement imposed by any person under any enactment, or

(c)   that in the particular circumstances the pursuit of the course of conduct was reasonable.

Amendments—Serious Organised Crime and Police Act 2005, s 125(1), (2).

2 Offence of harassment

(1) A person who pursues a course of conduct in breach of section 1(1) or (1A) is guilty of an offence.

(2) A person guilty of an offence under this section is liable on summary conviction to imprisonment for a term not exceeding six months, or a fine not exceeding level 5 on the standard scale, or both.

(3) (*repealed*)

Amendments—Police Reform Act 2002, s 107(2), Sch 8; Serious Organised Crime and Police Act 2005, s 125(1), (3).

3 Civil remedy

(1) An actual or apprehended breach of section 1(1) may be the subject of a claim in civil proceedings by the person who is or may be the victim of the course of conduct in question.

(2) On such a claim, damages may be awarded for (among other things) any anxiety caused by the harassment and any financial loss resulting from the harassment.

(3) Where –

    (a)   in such proceedings the High Court or a county court grants an injunction for the purpose of restraining the defendant from pursuing any conduct which amounts to harassment, and

    (b)   the plaintiff considers that the defendant has done anything which he is prohibited from doing by the injunction,

the plaintiff may apply for the issue of a warrant for the arrest of the defendant.

(4) An application under subsection (3) may be made –

    (a)   where the injunction was granted by the High Court, to a judge of that court, and

    (b)   where the injunction was granted by a county court, to a judge or district judge of that or any other county court.

(5) The judge or district judge to whom an application under subsection (3) is made may only issue a warrant if –

    (a)   the application is substantiated on oath, and

    (b)   the judge or district judge has reasonable grounds for believing that the defendant has done anything which he is prohibited from doing by the injunction.

(6) Where –

    (a)   the High Court or a county court grants an injunction for the purpose mentioned in subsection (3)(a), and

    (b)   without reasonable excuse the defendant does anything which he is prohibited from doing by the injunction,

he is guilty of an offence.

(7) Where a person is convicted of an offence under subsection (6) in respect of any conduct, that conduct is not punishable as a contempt of court.

(8) A person cannot be convicted of an offence under subsection (6) in respect of any conduct which has been punished as a contempt of court.

(9) A person guilty of an offence under subsection (6) is liable –

    (a)   on conviction on indictment, to imprisonment for a term not exceeding five years, or a fine, or both, or

    (b)   on summary conviction, to imprisonment for a term not exceeding six months, or a fine not exceeding the statutory maximum, or both.

Amendments—Serious Organised Crime and Police Act 2005, s 125(1), (4).

3A Injunctions to protect persons from harassment within section 1(1A)

(1) This section applies where there is an actual or apprehended breach of section 1(1A) by any person ('the relevant person').

(2) In such a case –

    (a)   any person who is or may be a victim of the course of conduct in question, or

    (b)   any person who is or may be a person falling within section 1(1A)(c), may apply to the High Court or a county court for an injunction restraining the relevant person from pursuing any conduct which amounts to harassment in relation to any person or persons mentioned or described in the injunction.

(3) Section 3(3) to (9) apply in relation to an injunction granted under subsection (2) above as they apply in relation to an injunction granted as mentioned in section 3(3)(a).

Amendments—Serious Organised Crime and Police Act 2005, s 125(1), (5).

4 Putting people in fear of violence

(1) A person whose course of conduct causes another to fear, on at least two occasions, that violence will be used against him is guilty of an offence if he knows or ought to know that his course of conduct will cause the other so to fear on each of those occasions.

(2) For the purposes of this section, the person whose course of conduct is in question ought to know that it will cause another to fear that violence will be used against him on any occasion if a reasonable person in possession of the same information would think the course of conduct would cause the other so to fear on that occasion.

(3) It is a defence for a person charged with an offence under this section to show that –

    (a)   his course of conduct was pursued for the purpose of preventing or detecting crime,

    (b)   his course of conduct was pursued under any enactment or rule of law or to comply with any condition or requirement imposed by any person under any enactment, or

    (c)   the pursuit of his course of conduct was reasonable for the protection of himself or another or for the protection of his or another's property.

(4) A person guilty of an offence under this section is liable –

    (a)   on conviction on indictment, to imprisonment for a term not exceeding five years, or a fine, or both, or

    (b)   on summary conviction, to imprisonment for a term not exceeding six months, or a fine not exceeding the statutory maximum, or both.

(5) If on the trial on indictment of a person charged with an offence under this section the jury find him not guilty of the offence charged, they may find him guilty of an offence under section 2.

(6) The Crown Court has the same powers and duties in relation to a person who is by virtue of subsection (5) convicted before it of an offence under section 2 as a magistrates' court would have on convicting him of the offence.

5 Restraining orders on conviction

(1) A court sentencing or otherwise dealing with a person ('the defendant') convicted of an offence may (as well as sentencing him or dealing with him in any other way) make an order under this section.

(2) The order may, for the purpose of protecting the victim or victims of the offence, or any other person mentioned in the order, from conduct which –

    (a)   amounts to harassment, or
    (b)   will cause a fear of violence,

prohibit the defendant from doing anything described in the order.

(3) The order may have effect for a specified period or until further order.

(3A) In proceedings under this section both the prosecution and the defence may lead, as further evidence, any evidence that would be admissible in proceedings for an injunction under section 3.

(4) The prosecutor, the defendant or any other person mentioned in the order may apply to the court which made the order for it to be varied or discharged by a further order.

(4A) Any person mentioned in the order is entitled to be heard on the hearing of an application under subsection (4).

(5) If without reasonable excuse the defendant does anything which he is prohibited from doing by an order under this section, he is guilty of an offence.

(6) A person guilty of an offence under this section is liable –

    (a)   on conviction on indictment, to imprisonment for a term not exceeding five years, or a fine, or both, or

    (b)   on summary conviction, to imprisonment for a term not exceeding six months, or a fine not exceeding the statutory maximum, or both.

(7) A court dealing with a person for an offence under this section may vary or discharge the order in question by a further order.

Amendments—Serious Organised Crime and Police Act 2005, s 125(1), (6); Domestic Violence, Crime and Victims Act 2004, ss 12, (2), (3), (4), 58(1), (2), 59 Sch 10, para 43, Sch 11; SI 2009/2501.

5A Restraining orders on acquittal

(1) A court before which a person ('the defendant') is acquitted of an offence may, if it considers it necessary to do so to protect a person from harassment by the defendant, make an order prohibiting the defendant from doing anything described in the order.

(2) Subsections (3) to (7) of section 5 apply to an order under this section as they apply to an order under that one.

(3) Where the Court of Appeal allow an appeal against conviction they may remit the case to the Crown Court to consider whether to proceed under this section.

(4) Where –

    (a)   the Crown Court allows an appeal against conviction, or

    (b)   a case is remitted to the Crown Court under subsection (3),

the reference in subsection (1) to a court before which a person is acquitted of an offence is to be read as referring to that court.

(5) A person made subject to an order under this section has the same right of appeal against the order as if –

    (a)   he had been convicted of the offence in question before the court which made the order, and

    (b)   the order had been made under section 5.

Prospective Amendment—Inserted by the Domestic Violence, Crime and Victims Act 2004, s 12(5).

6 Limitation

In section 11 of the Limitation Act 1980 (special time limit for actions in respect of personal injuries), after subsection (1) there is inserted –

'(1A) This section does not apply to any action brought for damages under section 3 of the Protection from Harassment Act 1997.'

7 Interpretation of this group of sections

(1) This section applies for the interpretation of sections 1 to 5A.

(2) References to harassing a person include alarming the person or causing the person distress.

(3) A 'course of conduct' must involve –

(a)   in the case of conduct in relation to a single person (see section 1(1)), conduct on at least two occasions in relation to that person, or

(b)   in the case of conduct in relation to two or more persons (see section 1(1A)), conduct on at least one occasion in relation to each of those persons.

(3A) A person's conduct on any occasion shall be taken, if aided, abetted, counselled or procured by another –

(a)   to be conduct on that occasion of the other (as well as conduct of the person whose conduct it is); and

(b)   to be conduct in relation to which the other's knowledge and purpose, and what he ought to have known, are the same as they were in relation to what was contemplated or reasonably foreseeable at the time of the aiding, abetting, counselling or procuring.

(4) 'Conduct' includes speech.

(5) References to a person, in the context of the harassment of a person, are references to a person who is an individual.

Amendments—Criminal Justice and Police Act 2001, s 44(1); Serious Organised Crime and Police Act 2005, s 125(1), (7); Domestic Violence, Crime and Victims Act 2004, s 58(1), Sch 10, para 44.

Scotland

8 Harassment

(1) Every individual has a right to be free from harassment and, accordingly, a person must not pursue a course of conduct which amounts to harassment of another and –

(a)   is intended to amount to harassment of that person; or

(b)   occurs in circumstances where it would appear to a reasonable person that it would amount to harassment of that person.

(2) An actual or apprehended breach of subsection (1) may be the subject of a claim in civil proceedings by the person who is or may be the victim of the course of conduct in question; and any such claim shall be known as an action of harassment.

(3) For the purposes of this section –

'conduct' includes speech;
'harassment' of a person includes causing the person alarm or distress; and

a course of conduct must involve conduct on at least two occasions.

(4) It shall be a defence to any action of harassment to show that the course of conduct complained of –

(a)   was authorised by, under or by virtue of any enactment or rule of law;

(b) was pursued for the purpose of preventing or detecting crime; or

(c) was, in the particular circumstances, reasonable.

(5) In an action of harassment the court may, without prejudice to any other remedies which it may grant –

(a) award damages;

(b) grant –

(i) interdict or interim interdict;

(ii) if it is satisfied that it is appropriate for it to do so in order to protect the person from further harassment, an order, to be known as a 'non-harassment order', requiring the defender to refrain from such conduct in relation to the pursuer as may be specified in the order for such period (which includes an indeterminate period) as may be so specified,

but a person may not be subjected to the same prohibitions in an interdict or interim interdict and a non-harassment order at the same time.

(6) The damages which may be awarded in an action of harassment include damages for any anxiety caused by the harassment and any financial loss resulting from it.

(7) Without prejudice to any right to seek review of any interlocutor, a person against whom a non-harassment order has been made, or the person for whose protection the order was made, may apply to the court by which the order was made for revocation of or a variation of the order and, on any such application, the court may revoke the order or vary it in such manner as it considers appropriate.

(8) In section 10(1) of the Damages (Scotland) Act 1976 (interpretation), in the definition of 'personal injuries', after 'to reputation' there is inserted ', or injury resulting from harassment actionable under section 8 of the Protection from Harassment Act 1997'.

9 Breach of non-harassment order

(1) Any person who is in breach of a non-harassment order made under section 8 is guilty of an offence and liable –

(a) on conviction on indictment, to imprisonment for a term not exceeding five years or to a fine, or to both such imprisonment and such fine; and

(b) on summary conviction, to imprisonment for a period not exceeding six months or to a fine not exceeding the statutory maximum, or to both such imprisonment and such fine.

(2) A breach of a non-harassment order shall not be punishable other than in accordance with subsection (1).

(3) A constable may arrest without warrant any person he reasonably believes is committing or has committed an offence under subsection (1).

(4) Subsection (3) is without prejudice to any power of arrest conferred by law apart from that subsection.

Amendments—Criminal Justice (Scotland) Act 2003, s 49(2)(a), (b).

10 Limitation

(1) After section 18A of the Prescription and Limitation (Scotland) Act 1973 there is inserted the following section –

'18B Actions of harassment

(1) This section applies to actions of harassment (within the meaning of section 8 of the Protection from Harassment Act 1997) which include a claim for damages.

(2) Subject to subsection (3) below and to section 19A of this Act, no action to which this section applies shall be brought unless it is commenced within a period of 3 years after –

  (a) the date on which the alleged harassment ceased; or
  (b) the date, (if later than the date mentioned in paragraph (a) above) on which the pursuer in the action became, or on which, in the opinion of the court, it would have been reasonably practicable for him in all the circumstances to have become, aware, that the defender was a person responsible for the alleged harassment or the employer or principal of such a person.

(3) In the computation of the period specified in subsection (2) above there shall be disregarded any time during which the person who is alleged to have suffered the harassment was under legal disability by reason of nonage or unsoundness of mind.'.

(2) In subsection (1) of section 19A of that Act (power of court to override time-limits), for 'section 17 or section 18 and section 18A' there is substituted 'section 17, 18, 18A or 18B'.

11 Non-harassment order following criminal offence

After section 234 of the Criminal Procedure (Scotland) Act 1995 there is inserted the following section –

'Non-harassment orders

234A Non-harassment orders

(1) Where a person is convicted of an offence involving harassment of a person ('the victim'), the prosecutor may apply to the court to make a non-harassment order against the offender requiring him to refrain from such conduct in relation to the victim as may be specified in the order for such period (which includes an indeterminate period) as may be so specified, in addition to any other disposal which may be made in relation to the offence.

(2) On an application under subsection (1) above the court may, if it is satisfied on a balance of probabilities that it is appropriate to do so in order to protect the victim from further harassment, make a non-harassment order.

(3) A non-harassment order made by a criminal court shall be taken to be a sentence for the purposes of any appeal and, for the purposes of this subsection 'order' includes any variation or revocation of such an order made under subsection (6) below.

(4) Any person who is found to be in breach of a non-harassment order shall be guilty of an offence and liable –

  (a) on conviction on indictment, to imprisonment for a term not exceeding 5 years or to a fine, or to both such imprisonment and such fine; and
  (b) on summary conviction, to imprisonment for a period not exceeding 6 months or to a fine not exceeding the statutory maximum, or to both such imprisonment and such fine.

(5) The Lord Advocate, in solemn proceedings, and the prosecutor, in summary proceedings, may appeal to the High Court against any decision by a court to refuse an application under subsection (1) above; and on any such appeal the High Court may make such order as it considers appropriate.

(6) The person against whom a non-harassment order is made, or the prosecutor at whose instance the order is made, may apply to the court which made the order for its revocation or variation and, in relation to any such application the court concerned may, if it is satisfied on a balance of probabilities that it is appropriate to do so, revoke the order or vary it in such manner as it thinks fit, but not so as to increase the period for which the order is to run.

(7) For the purposes of this section 'harassment' shall be construed in accordance with section 8 of the Protection from Harassment Act 1997.'.

General

12 National security, etc

(1) If the Secretary of State certifies that in his opinion anything done by a specified person on a specified occasion related to –

(a)   national security,
(b)   the economic well-being of the United Kingdom, or
(c)   the prevention or detection of serious crime,

and was done on behalf of the Crown, the certificate is conclusive evidence that this Act does not apply to any conduct of that person on that occasion.

(2) In subsection (1), 'specified' means specified in the certificate in question.

(3) A document purporting to be a certificate under subsection (1) is to be received in evidence and, unless the contrary is proved, be treated as being such a certificate.

13 Corresponding provision for Northern Ireland

An Order in Council made under paragraph 1(1)(b) of Schedule 1 to the Northern Ireland Act 1974 which contains a statement that it is made only for purposes corresponding to those of sections 1 to 7 and 12 of this Act –

(a)   shall not be subject to sub-paragraphs (4) and (5) of paragraph 1 of that Schedule (affirmative resolution of both Houses of Parliament), but
(b)   shall be subject to annulment in pursuance of a resolution of either House of Parliament.

14 Extent

(1) Sections 1 to 7 extend to England and Wales only.

(2) Sections 8 to 11 extend to Scotland only.

(3) This Act (except section 13) does not extend to Northern Ireland.

15 Commencement

(1) Sections 1, 2, 4, 5 and 7 to 12 are to come into force on such day as the Secretary of State may by order made by statutory instrument appoint.

(2) Sections 3 and 6 are to come into force on such day as the Lord Chancellor may by order made by statutory instrument appoint.

(3) Different days may be appointed under this section for different purposes.

16 Short title

This Act may be cited as the Protection from Harassment Act 1997.

INDEX

References are to paragraph numbers.